LESSONS AND LEGACIES XII

New Directions in Holocaust Research and Education

Edited and with an introduction
by Wendy Lower and Lauren Faulkner Rossi

NORTHWESTERN UNIVERSITY PRESS   EVANSTON, ILLINOIS

Northwestern University Press
www.nupress.northwestern.edu

Holocaust Educational Foundation
of Northwestern University
Founded by Theodore Zev and Alice R. Weiss

Printed in the United States of America

10 9 8 7 6 5 4 3 2 1

ISBN 978-0-8101-3449-2 (cloth)
ISBN 978-0-8101-3448-5 (paper)
ISBN 978-0-8101-3450-8 (e-book)

Library of Congress Cataloging-in-Publication Data are available from the Library of Congress.

∞ The paper used in this publication meets the minimum requirements of the American National Standard for Information Sciences—Permanence of Paper for Printed Library Materials, ANSI Z39.48–1992.

LESSONS AND LEGACIES XII

Dedicated to my grandchildren: Tamar, David, Matthew, Benjamin, Jacob, and Zoey, with the fervent hope that they can grow up in a world where all humanity will live without fear, without prejudice—a peaceful world.
(Theodore Zev Weiss)

Contents

Theodore Zev Weiss

Foreword

THIS VOLUME PRESENTS SELECTED SCHOLARLY PAPERS FROM THE twelfth Lessons and Legacies Conference on the Holocaust, held at Northwestern University in Evanston, Illinois, in November 2012. I am extremely grateful to Wendy Lower from Claremont McKenna College and Alan Berger from Florida Atlantic University, who chaired the conference, for their hard work and devotion to ensure its success. Also, many thanks to Professors Wendy Lower and Lauren Faulkner Rossi for editing this volume.

These biennial conferences sponsored by the Holocaust Educational Foundation have become an extremely important and integral part of teaching the Holocaust in our colleges and universities, as well as for training graduate students who will be joining the ranks of those teaching the Holocaust to future generations. We are also particularly glad that many scholars have attended from outside the United States.

Lessons and Legacies conferences are only one facet of the work of the Holocaust Educational Foundation. We sponsor the Summer Institute on the Holocaust and Jewish Civilization. We provide research grants to young scholars who want to make Holocaust studies their area of concentration. And our primary work lies in assisting, supporting, and encouraging scholars in the field to ensure that Holocaust education is included in as many colleges and universities as possible throughout the United States and overseas for many years to come. As the years go on and we get further and further from the event, our work becomes an imperative.

The success of the foundation would not have been possible without the support of our board and donors and, most importantly, the multitude of scholars who share our commitment to the study and the teaching of the Holocaust. To them, I am most appreciative and eternally grateful.

Finally, I want to thank my wife, Alice; my children Deborah and Danny; their spouses; and my grandchildren for all their help and support throughout the years.

Wendy Lower and Lauren Faulkner Rossi

Introduction

IN A PREVIOUS VOLUME IN THIS SERIES, DISTINGUISHED HISTORIAN Omer Bartov confronted the challenge of how to teach the Holocaust in an era that is increasingly consumed with the broader study of genocide. He asserted that the two fields of study need not be incompatible, that studying the Holocaust should not inhibit a deeper understanding of genocide in general, and that genocide studies do not inhibit the specific reconstruction of the mass murder of Jews. But his most forceful point was his insistence on the centrality of the victims: "One must 'listen' to the voices of the protagonists . . . Listening to the voices of victims, *Jewish or not*, is crucial to the kind of empathy that brings with it a modicum of understanding."[1] While scholars may continue to argue the merits of using the Holocaust as a standard to which other genocides are compared, their reliance on testimony, and especially victim testimony, shows no signs of abating. If anything, this trend in methodology is gaining wider recognition and affecting classroom teaching globally. The contributions to this volume bear testament to this vital component of contemporary Holocaust studies.

The Holocaust Educational Foundation's twelfth international gathering of leading Holocaust scholars explored new directions in research and teaching. Out of more than seventy presentations, eighteen were selected and constitute this volume, which we, the editors, believe represent the state of the field of Holocaust studies. Collectively, they provide a survey of cutting-edge research that our contributors have published recently or will soon publish. Holocaust studies has and continues to play a leading role intellectually in the development of cultural studies, perpetrator history, and comparative genocide studies. It remains relevant today, particularly in controversies around accusations of collaboration, calls for reparations from state and private concerns, and the ethical dilemmas in artistic representations. Featured in this volume are some of the diverse methods and topics shaping Holocaust studies, from a variety of disciplines: forensics, environmental history, cultural studies, religious studies, labor history, film studies, the history of medicine, sociology, pedagogy, and public history.

Though each of the eighteen contributors has pursued a specific line of inquiry in Holocaust historiography, three themes stand out and bind the volume together. First is the aforementioned importance of *testimony*, which features explicitly in every essay and is central to most. In Holocaust studies, the centrality of testimony is not new, but our contributors underscore two aspects of the ongoing discussion about its use: its value, and the increasing availability of recorded eyewitness testimony, especially in video archives such as that of the USC Shoah Foundation Visual History Archive. More than one contributor cites Omer Bartov's observation that listening to individual testimony is of paramount importance when working in a period in which most of the witnesses were systematically murdered. Moreover, the majority of essays in this volume cite specifically *video* testimony, indicating a shift in the kind of testimony that scholars have at their disposal, as well as their willingness to use it and its digital accessibility. This usage points to an emerging methodological issue: is the use of video testimony now a matter of course in this field? Is its presence taken for granted, barely more than two decades after the USC Shoah Foundation Institute for Visual History and Education was originally founded as the Survivors of the Shoah Visual History Foundation? What are the pros and cons of the digital databases that serve as finding aids?

The second prominent theme is *complicity*. Many of the essays that engage with this theme ask us to reconceptualize the term and, in some cases, push for its redefinition. From the role of nuns to that of soldiers in the German army, from Ukrainian police personnel to the women who worked in clerical capacities for the *Reichssicherheitshauptamt* (Reich Security Main Office or RSHA), the nature of complicity is probed in different contexts, merging with questions about gender, religion, and careerism. Like the theme of testimony, complicity is not a new idea in Holocaust studies. Raul Hilberg, a doyen of Holocaust studies, made complicity a central aspect of his pioneering study of the Holocaust when he controversially spoke of it in the context of the *Judenräte* (Jewish councils) in Eastern Europe. He identified broad categories of perpetrator, victim, and bystander that have endured for decades, though increasingly their rigid boundaries have been challenged. Is it now time to consider these categories themselves historical? Or does the work of our contributors suggest, rather, a careful revision of the concept of complicity, in particular with regard to the category of bystander? The question implicit in their essays is, was this term ever neutral? While some contributors' historical judgments may be harsh, they are also persuasive. In any case, we are reminded that historians should reflect consciously on the moral categories they employ to make sense of individuals' roles in the perpetration of the Holocaust.

Finally, the third theme accentuates the postwar treatment of victims and survivors and considers the impact of reparations. The keynote essays by internationally respected scholars Jan T. Gross and Dagmar Herzog make the powerful argument that Jews were robbed twice: first of their possessions, including their property and their families, during the years of persecution and murder, and then of their minds, not only during the Holocaust but also for years after.

Gross and Herzog offer groundbreaking studies of the legal, social, and psychological ramifications of material, emotional, and mental theft. While they explore different subjects, they share a concern for the postwar reception of Holocaust victims and their stories, for the difficulties around reparations, and for the roles, often damaging, that civilians and professionals played in the aftermath of the war and genocide. Both Gross and Herzog address plunder in new ways—the material plunder of Polish Jews by their neighbors in Gross's essay; the psychological plunder of Jewish survivors by the German government and medical professionals in Herzog's piece. These essays underscore that 1945 was by no means the end of suffering for many victims. The emphasis is instead on continuity, on the persistent injustice that Jewish survivors faced and the perpetuation of antisemitism. Taken together, Gross and Herzog verify that, so long as attitudes such as greed, hatred, righteousness, and indignation were entrenched in the societies to which they returned, survivors and their families could not even begin the process of true healing.

The essays in the volume are grouped in five distinct subsections that reflect current issues in Holocaust scholarship: new cultural approaches to the Holocaust; contemporary controversies and their historical origins; themes of recovery and loss; Holocaust history viewed through the lens of gender and the family; and reconsiderations of Holocaust perpetrators.

NEW CULTURAL APPROACHES TO THE HOLOCAUST

In "Rumors in the Ghettos: A Case Study of Cultural History," Amos Goldberg (Hebrew University of Jerusalem) argues that not enough attention has been paid to the culture of the victims of the Holocaust. Goldberg finds that cultural history offers methodological tools to portray the transformative processes that the victim underwent and was powerless to resist. It is no wonder that rumors played a dramatic role in Jewish societies during the war, and especially in the ghettos. Rumors circulated daily and wildly, and they are constantly mentioned and dealt with in the writings of the time. Citing Jewish ghetto diarists who wrote about rumors, Goldberg concludes that, however illusionary and detached from reality the rumors were, they were essential for survival. In "I Am (Not) to Blame: Intent and Agency in Personal Accounts of the Holocaust," Doris L. Bergen (University of Toronto) looks closely at perpetrator intention and the agency of victims. Bergen compares the actions of several infamous camp commandants, such as Franz Stangl, Rudolf Höss, and *Aktion Reinhard* (Operation Reinhard) deputy manager Hermann Höfle, and analyzes the power of Jewish testimonies. She raises ethical and moral conundrums and offers suggestions about how scholars should approach their sources. Steven Alan Carr (Indiana University—Purdue University Fort Wayne), in "'To Encompass the Unseeable': Foreign Film, Taste Culture, and the American Encounter with the Postwar Holocaust Film," examines the first fictional feature films depicting the events of the Holocaust to be released in the United States. In particular, he looks at Bosley Crowther's reviews of *The Last Stage*, which helped to mold the expectations of American audiences in viewing films about Nazi atrocities. In "A World without Jews: Nazi Imagination from Persecution to Genocide," Alon Confino (University of Virginia, Charlottesville and Ben-Gurion University, Beer Sheva, Israel) explores Nazi cultural attacks against Jews; in particular he asks: Why did the Nazis burn the Hebrew Bible? The scholarship on *Kristallnacht* and the Holocaust, as well as general accounts of the Third Reich, have not emphasized this part of the story, Confino argues. While his essay focuses on new research about the events of *Kristallnacht* as a pogrom against Jewish culture, Confino places this event in the broader history of anti-Judaism and antisemitism in the Third Reich. He finds that time was a key feature in Nazi notions of the Jew, as a possessor of origins—of the present, past, and future; of modernity, the nation, and ultimately humanity. It was the basis for the genocidal fantasies that made the persecution and extermination of the Jews possible.

CONTEMPORARY CONTROVERSIES AND THEIR HISTORICAL ORIGINS

John-Paul Himka (University of Alberta, Edmonton), author of *Former Ukrainian Policemen in the Ukrainian National Insurgency: Continuing the Holocaust outside German Service*, analyzes Ukrainian nationalists' role in the Holocaust in the region of Volhynia (straddling modern Poland, Ukraine, and Belarus). First, he traces their placement and training with the German *Schutzstaffel* (SS); then he follows them as they deserted their posts and joined the resistance movement in the Ukrainian Insurgent Army. Himka describes how they embarked on a resistance campaign against the German occupiers and a brutal ethnic cleansing of the Polish population of Volhynia. They also continued to kill Jews whom they uncovered in hiding. Himka's analysis is based on an impressive archival base of Jewish, Ukrainian, and German testimonies and documents. In "The SNCF Affair: Cheminots in the Divided Memories of Vichy France," Ludivine Broch (University of Westminster, London) charts the complications of memory revealed in what is now called the SNCF (Société nationale des chemins de fer français or French National Railway) Affair. She focuses on the contested discourses of resistance, rescue, and collaboration involving the *cheminots*, or railway workers, who were responsible for running French trains during World War II. She explores important questions about personal and corporate responsibility as well as the national, transnational, and economic repercussions of their wartime activities. Mark Joel Webber (York University, Toronto, Canada) probes contemporary discussions of ethical questions arising from the Holocaust in "Keep Your Distance: 'Ethical Duplicity' and the Holocaust," emphasizing the importance of acknowledging the victims' dignity and agency, and of empathizing with them without appropriating their identity and voice. Webber situates the ethical challenge of finding humanity in "perpetrator fiction," specifically in an analysis of German and French novels, including Jonathan Littell's controversial *The Kindly Ones*.

RECOVERY AND LOSS

In "Khurbn Yiddish: An Absent Absence," Perla Sneh (Universidad Nacional de Tres de Febrero, Buenos Aires, Argentina) focuses on Yiddish as the lens for viewing the ideological, political, and cultural core of Judaism at the time. Sneh argues that the disappearance of Yiddish after the war tells a particularly tragic and persistent story. She believes that languages are important not as relics, but as ethical questions. The ways that we address languages are not just a methodological detail; they are at the center of what we call memory. Sneh traces how victims and survivors used Yiddish words to articulate the experience of the Holocaust as one of resistance and survival, and with a precision and rawness that is absent in much of the historiography.

Elizabeth Anthony (United States Holocaust Memorial Museum, Mandel Center for Advanced Holocaust Studies) offers a pathbreaking study in "The First Returnees: Holocaust Survivors in Vienna in the Immediate Postwar Period." She concentrates on the experiences of Austrian Jews who survived the Holocaust in Vienna and were the first to begin reconstructing the Jewish community in May 1945. She recounts how they managed to survive, and the challenges they faced in the immediate postwar period in the face of Red Army and Soviet occupiers, their Austrian neighbors, and in the deprivations in the physical ruins of the city. In "The Dispersal and Oblivion of the Ashes and Bones of Babi Yar," Karel C. Berkhoff (NIOD Institute for War, Holocaust, and Genocide Studies, Royal Netherlands Academy of Arts and Scientists, Amsterdam) scrutinizes one of the bleakest episodes of the Holocaust—the destruction and dispersal of human remains at Babi Yar, the site of a one-week massacre of more than 33,000 Jews. He investigates the scattering of the remains of the victims and the reasons for the obfuscation of the site's history.

THE HOLOCAUST AND SOCIAL HISTORY: GENDER AND THE FAMILY

The essay by Martina Cucchiara (Bluffton University, Bluffton, Ohio) illuminates the intersections of religion, gender, youth, and complicity. In "Jewish Girls in Catholic Schools in Nazi Germany, 1933–1938," she shows how the German Catholic Church fought the Reich to maintain private schools in an effort to preserve Catholic education and culture. The article examines the experiences of Jewish and Christian girls in Catholic schools prior to 1938 to determine whether the nuns who ran them succeeded in maintaining distinct and separate Catholic spheres under the Nazi regime. Cucchiara argues that nuns' efforts to incorporate only those aspects of National Socialism that they could easily reconcile with Catholic teachings about community and sacrifice actually facilitated the integration of Catholic students into the Nazi state. Taking another category of analysis, Natalia Aleksiun (Touro College, New York) looks at the history of Jewish families in hiding. In "Daily Survival: Social History of Jews in Family Bunkers in Eastern Galicia," she marshals the diverse sources of memoirs, diaries, and oral testimonies in four languages. Aleksiun offers an investigation of the social processes and dynamics of Jewish groups hiding together in rural "family" bunkers in what is today western Ukraine. What emerges is a provocative portrait of Jewish daily life during a time of war and genocide.

Women's history of perpetration is studied in Rachel Century's (Royal Holloway, University of London) "Secretaries, Secrets, and Genocide: Evidence from the Postwar Investigations of the Female Secretaries of the RSHA." Century's new research on German secretaries in Heinrich Himmler's offices offers an important case for exploring interpretations of complicity and its gendered roles. Working in a variety of departments, the many secretaries and female administrators of the *Reichssicherheitshauptamt* (Reich Security Main Office or RSHA) had access to different sources and quantities of information about the Holocaust and the crimes that their supervisors were perpetrating. Who were these women, and what prompted them to work within the Nazi apparatus? Were the secretaries of the RSHA ideologically dedicated to the tasks they carried out? To answer these questions, Century's article draws on postwar testimony given by secretaries who had formerly worked at the RSHA.

RECONSIDERING PERPETRATORS

New work on male and female perpetrators has explored various divergent issues: (1) comparative genocide phenomena; (2) forms of perpetration; and (3) representations in public discourse and education. In "Hitler's 'Ostkrieg' and the Indian Wars: Comparing Military Strategies of Conquest and Annihilation," Edward B. Westermann (Texas A&M University–San Antonio) summarizes the recent trend in the historiography of Germany, *Transfergeschichte (transfer history)*, which involves the transnational comparisons of Germany's experience as reflected in or influenced by historical, philosophical, or political forces. Westermann finds that the philosophical and ideological underpinnings of the westward march of the American empire and the displacement of Native Americans provide parallels with the Nazi conquest of the East and the conduct of a racial war of extermination against the Slavic and Jewish populations of Eastern Europe and western Russia. His essay examines the validity of this comparison with respect to military strategy and operations. In "Intrigues and Conflicts of Interest as to the Exploitation of Jewish Labor in Radom, 1942–1943," Idit Gil (Open University) examines the utilization of Jewish labor in the city of Radom, Poland, from August 1942 (when the Nazis liquidated the city's two ghettos) to November 1943 (when they destroyed the workers' ghetto, a separate site for Jews employed in the war effort). Gil's essay assesses how labor was integrated into Nazi anti-Jewish policies, and the role of the SS in exploiting Jewish labor. Although Jewish labor had no role in the Nazi economic plan (*Wirtschaftsplan*), it was used to both persecute the Jews and gain economic benefits. Throughout the war years, Nazi Jewish labor policy was not consistent because it was influenced by a circumstantial combination of racial views and practical considerations. The essay is based on extensive research in Polish, German, Israeli, and U.S. archives. Lukas Meissel (University of Vienna) presents "Not 'How Was It Possible,' but 'Who Made It Possible': The Topic of Perpetrators in Holocaust Education in Austria." Meissel's essay focuses on the topic of public history and current representations of perpetrators in Austria, and questions of guilt and responsibility. The problems and challenges of contemporary approaches to teaching the history of Nazi crimes are illustrated utilizing examples taken from practical work in the field and from public debates on the subject of perpetrators. This essay's case study, Austria, has received little scholarly attention but much criticism for failing to deal with its Nazi past. Meissel's presentation is based on a survey of projects of the Austrian nongovernmental Holocaust commemorative organization *Gedenkdienst* (Memorial Service) and his own experience as a guide at the Mauthausen Memorial at the site of the Mauthausen concentration camp near Linz, Austria. He finds that Holocaust education in Austria has allowed for a discourse about the plight of victims, but not about the responsibility of the Austrian perpetrators and ordinary Austrians.

Readers familiar with prior volumes may notice that, in this edition, scholars place new cultural and social approaches at the center of the research agenda in an unprecedented way. Culture is not treated as a creative product and commodity, nor as the fascist aesthetic of the Nazi regime. Rather, it is analyzed as a way of expression in myriad, dynamic forms of language, rumor, fantasy, ideology, and behavior. Representations do not appear in nebulous forms but as constituted by perpetrators, victims, bystanders, and a nuanced range of complicit participants. Notions of agency are problematized in new ways, and the settings and sites of action extend into bunkers, orphanages, mass graves, restitution applications, and synagogues on *Kristallnacht,* a wave of violence against Jews in November 1938. There are new faces in this book, that of German female secretaries, postwar Polish plunderers, French railway operators, and postwar social workers and psychoanalysts. Within victim categories, specific groups appear, such as Jewish girls in Nazi Germany and survivors in postwar Vienna. Comparative analysis more broadly of perpetrators as a category spanning genocides reveals how Holocaust history informs other cases of genocide. In short, this volume manifests notable strides in various disciplinary facets and conceptual angles, and attests to the continued innovative growth of the field of Holocaust studies. In many ways, these essays respond to issues taken up in previous volumes in the Lessons and Legacies series. Historian Omer Bartov affirmed the multidisciplinary trajectory of Holocaust studies while cautioning that comparative approaches might decenter the Holocaust or obfuscate the fact that its history is critical to understanding other genocides. This volume demonstrates that Holocaust research continues to drive genocide studies into new directions even as we discover more about the Holocaust.

NOTE

1. Omer Bartov, "Genocide and the Holocaust: Arguments over History and Politics," in Hilary Earl and Karl A. Schleunes, eds., *Lessons and Legacies Volume XI, Expanding Perspectives on the Holocaust in a Changing World* (Evanston, Ill.: Northwestern University Press, 2014), 20.

LESSONS AND LEGACIES XII

Jan T. Gross

Opportunistic Killings and Plunder of Jews by Their Neighbors—a Norm or an Exception in German-Occupied Europe?

I WOULD LIKE TO SHED LIGHT IN THIS ESSAY ON THE PHENOMENON OF killings and plunder of Jews by local people in German-occupied Poland—crimes that occurred on the periphery of the Holocaust. The number of Jewish victims was only a small fraction of the total killed by the Nazis and their collaborators. The loot that remained in local hands (primarily housing)—though *not* equally insignificant—was similarly only a tiny part of the Jewish wealth plundered during World War II. But as mysteries pertaining to the Holocaust abound, these marginal phenomena—adversarial interactions between Jews and their fellow citizens in occupied countries—have been catapulted decades later into the center of preoccupation for national historiographies. These local disputes have attracted extraordinary public interest both in Eastern and Western Europe. So a marginal issue in the historiography of the Shoah turned into a "sticky" one, judging by public and professional attention, not easily let go of as far as European societies under occupation are concerned.

To address this subject, one needs to contend with yet another sort of marginality, namely, that information provided by Jews about the fate they suffered during the war has often been viewed with incredulity. What I refer to, in the first place, was a perverse consequence of "unbelievable" radicalism of anti-Jewish policies pursued by the Nazis. Geoffrey Hartman, a renowned literary scholar who as a child emigrated from Germany, writes:

> Disbelief touched the survivors themselves . . . Two phrases stand out in their testimony: "I was there" and "I could not believe what

> my eyes had seen." The second phrase is not purely rhetorical. [Aharon] Appelfeld writes: "Everything that happened was so gigantic, so inconceivable, that the witness even seemed like a fabricator to himself."[1]

I can testify to this bafflement with the outsized scale of Holocaust events as reported by witnesses, from personal experience: It took me four years and a pure, lucky coincidence to realize that the testimony of Szmul Wasersztajn (Shmuel Wasserstein), who described the crime in Jedwabne—the subject of my book *Neighbors: The Destruction of the Jewish Community in Jedwabne, Poland*—was not an exaggeration but a faithful description of what had happened.[2]

Another reason for doubting information about the unfolding catastrophe of European Jews was a long-lasting memory of an Allied propaganda hoax dating back to World War I. At the time, tales of German atrocities allegedly committed against the civilian population (especially in Belgium) were grossly exaggerated. Consequently, journalists and government officials in England and the United States still viewed with caution reports of mass murder coming out of occupied Europe twenty years later. When we add to this a generally demeaning stereotype of Jews in Christian cultural tradition, we can appreciate why Jewish sources were *a priori* treated with deep ambivalence.

The French-Israeli historian Renée Poznanski describes, for example, a "generalized skepticism of high functionaries of the Foreign Office." She reports, using their own words, the state of mind in British government circles: "As a general principle, Jews have a tendency to exaggerate the severity of persecution to which they are subjected."[3] This point of view had enormous weight when held by those who controlled the most important medium of propaganda broadcasting into occupied Europe—the British Broadcasting Corporation (BBC). To ensure the effectiveness of war propaganda, the BBC took care not to exaggerate any claims, and *especially* those pertaining to the persecution of Jews, the latter to not give plausibility to a German argument that the war was being waged by the Allies on behalf, and in the interest, of the Jews. From east to west, from the Gaullist *France Libre* (Free France) broadcasts to radio programs authorized by General Władysław Sikorski's Polish government in exile (both Sikorski and Charles de Gaulle were self-exiled at the time in England), those trying to beef up anti-Nazi resistance in their home countries were anxious not to emphasize the victimization of the Jews, lest they render plausible the Nazi arguments that Jews were pulling the strings in London and in America.

It mattered, also, that the predominant mood of public opinion in countries under occupation was antisemitic. There should not be any "privileged" victims in France, and discretion in Jewish matters was advised, General de Gaulle's *France Libre* (Free France) movement was warned by its rapporteurs from across the English Channel. The Polish prime minister, General Sikorski, was bluntly told by his underground commanders that he should cut expressions of sympathy for the Jews from radio broadcasts because they made a bad impression in Poland.

As far as the Anglo-Saxon study of the war is concerned, the original direct culprit for such idiosyncratic views of the British Foreign Office, or reasons why the plight of the Jews was de-emphasized in European countries under occupation, may have been none other than Raul Hilberg, the doyen of Holocaust historiography. We are all indebted to him and will forever stand on his shoulders, but he dismissed victims' personal narratives as unreliable and, from his point of view, irrelevant.

Hilberg was interested, as was his right, in the German machinery of mass murder, and he did show indeed how its functioning can be pieced together from documentation generated by institutional participants in the process. Once the subject opened up, historians, for some time, were primarily interested in the perpetrators—naturally, a story to be dug up in the German archives rather than in the memoirs of surviving Jews.

WHAT CAN HISTORIANS DO WITH INDIVIDUAL TESTIMONIES?

Other things being equal (even though they never are), the problem of availing ourselves of "testimony," of "eyewitness" accounts about the Holocaust, derives, it seems to me, from processing the evidence according to ordinary procedures and linguistic usage of categories employed. When we take in hand an "eyewitness" account of a Holocaust victim, we place it mentally in a familiar context: we read it as a statement from an injured party. There is a victim and a victimizer in the scenario, and we hear in the narrative the victim's side of the story; presumably this is only one side of the story. And where there are "sides"—or, if you will, parties to a conflict—then we expect to hear from one party only partial truth.

It takes a moment, and a *prise de conscience*, to realize that the vocabulary we employ—"victim," "testimony," or "witness"—puts a deceptive frame on our thinking. The "semantic heredity" of such concepts leads us astray, because there is no advocacy in the narratives of Holocaust victims.[4] I know that we should not naively accept an author's stated intentions as the one and only guide to the reading of a text, but they should not be discarded out of hand, either. We must remember, therefore, that Jews deliberately wrote their testimonies about the Shoah to provide an exact account of the catastrophe. This is evidenced in numerous memoirs and journals kept by Jews at the time. The same intention informed collective efforts such as the *Oyneg Shabes* Archive kept by Emanuel Ringelblum in the Warsaw ghetto; the daunting work of the archivists from the ghetto in Kovno, Lithuania; or Herman Kruk's diaries and records compiled in the Vilna (Vilnius or Wilno) ghetto, also in Lithuania. Since it appeared impossible to save the mass of Jewish people methodically annihilated in the Nazi-organized killing process, a sense of obligation grew among the Jewish recordkeepers (they say so explicitly and repeatedly) to at least preserve the evidence of the destruction.

Thus revealed, future readers cannot dismiss the authors' intentions lightly. Clearly their aim was to produce an account of what happened, not to embellish the story. If anything, the recordkeepers' difficulty was the reverse—the reality surrounding them was such an exaggeration of everything people were accustomed to in everyday life that their concern was whether posterity would believe what had really happened—believe the record, as it were.[5]

In virtually all Holocaust-era diaries—detailed, unique, specific to the place, and reflecting the vagaries of each author's individual destiny—one finds a common theme, a recurring line: "Whatever we may have foreseen, and written about many times, it is all hardly a fraction of the actual situation."[6] One cannot grapple with the surrounding reality, all diarists seem to be saying; it cannot be communicated fully.

Holocaust memoirists labored against enormous odds, most strikingly against their own incredulity at what was happening around them. Their predicament was bewildering: nobody will believe us if we say it how it was, and yet we can, at best, tell only a fraction of what actually happened. Did they have any need or inducement to exaggerate or embellish their narratives? I think not. Rather, their one and only ultimate satisfaction—a hopeless task, we know—would come from being able to say to themselves as readers of what they have left us: "Yes, that's exactly what happened." They left carefully crafted, deliberately assembled, meaningful documents of the epoch, which deserve to be treated as such. And to make sense of our century's dark times, we should read their testimony as it was conceived—one line at a time.[7]

Personal testimonies may have finally entered the mainstream of Holocaust historiography with the most recent grand synthesis, Saul Friedländer's *The Years of Extermination*,[8] in which the author draws on such material abundantly. Christopher Browning published a similarly grounded study of a forced labor camp in Starachowice, Poland;[9] and Omer Bartov is completing his book on "communal genocide" in Buczacz (now Buchach, Ukraine). With giants in the field drawing freely on personal testimonies of Holocaust victims and survivors, historiographical standards have shifted.

But so far, it has been a struggle to fend off criticisms that easily dismiss writing on the basis of personal documents as not properly grounded and providing merely anecdotal evidence. In the meantime, for an entire spectrum of interesting subjects (the fate of Jews hiding on the so-called "Aryan" side, or resistance in provincial ghettos, for example), almost no other empirical evidence is available. The task before us, then, is to obtain a reliable understanding of a general phenomenon (in my case: killings and plunder of Polish Jews by their fellow citizens) on the basis of personal statements, which, by their very nature, offer only episodic and discrete information.

Ever since the story of the murder in Jedwabne was debated in Poland in 2000, historians have begun to study court cases prosecuted on the basis of the August 31, 1944, decree of the provisional Polish government, customarily referred to now as the "August cases."[10] The decree provided for criminalization of providing aid and assistance, broadly conceived, that furthered the German occupiers' goals to the detriment of the Polish society. Occasionally, the murder of Jews was prosecuted under this law as well. Some two decades after the war, all the August cases from court districts around the country were conveniently assembled in one archival collection under the custody of the

Main Commission for Investigation of Hitlerite Crimes.[11] Today, they are in the holdings of Poland's Institute of National Remembrance.

I shall draw here on a useful contribution of two historians who examined all the August cases in the Kielce district containing evidence about murders of Jews by the Poles in the countryside of that region. Altogether, about 250 people were brought to justice there for alleged involvement in the murder of several hundred Jews. The authors, Alina Skibińska and Jakub Petelewicz, complemented their knowledge acquired from archival readings with interviews conducted in the area.

A historian of the Holocaust would know right away that this source reveals only a "tip of the iceberg" of the phenomenon under study—partly due to a reluctance of prosecutorial authorities after the war to bring such cases to court.[12] But, most importantly, this is a body of evidence from which Jewish voices are (almost) entirely absent. These were not cases brought by Jews. The Jews who appear in these depositions were killed. And there were no Jewish witnesses left to testify about the killings, either.

On the other hand, this material—even though affording us only a partial insight—represents the entire collection of a certain kind of evidence bearing on the issue. So, with respect to it, we cannot be accused of a sample bias. By itself, this evidence does not necessarily allow us to obtain a reliable general portrait of what happened—one would still have to know about the ecology of the crime to make sure that all murder episodes did not cluster in some small subregion of the area, for example, or to determine if the entire region can be considered "typical" with respect to this kind of crime and similar to the rest of Poland. To allay doubts on this last point, let me mention a recent study of *Rzeszowszczyzna*, another Polish voivodeship (province), where murders of Jews by local Poles are documented in at least 110 locations.[13] In any case, with these caveats in mind, taking all of the evidence of a particular kind under consideration is always a good practice.

We need to focus now on what is at stake and what kind of question we are bringing to the evidence at our disposal. Essentially, we want to adjudicate between two interpretations of the phenomenon of murder and plunder of Jews by their fellow Polish citizens during the war. One interpretation would simply claim that "stuff happens": people get killed during war; there was violence all around, and so it got privatized at times; banditry was rampant; people lost their moral bearings; there is always "scum" in a society; and anyway, one should not generalize on the basis of isolated cases. In short, this was deviant behavior. Or else, it was not. To find out, I suggest that we must read the content of the cases to learn what actually happened and make sense of it.

I am now going to quote extensively from Skibińska and Petelewicz's article describing numerous murders by the Polish population of Jews hiding in the Kielce countryside. I splice together fragments of text scattered over several pages, in a continuous narrative:

> Killings by shooting . . . , with an ax, or using a wooden pole . . . were accompanied by acts of physical and psychological cruelty toward Jews who had been caught: women were raped, people were beaten, pushed around, cursed at and verbally humiliated. The accused [that is, the alleged perpetrators of crimes against the Jews] . . . were peasants, so-called, dark-blue policemen [Polish state police] from outposts closest to the site of murder, members of various guerrilla organizations, who frequently were the very peasants living during the day in their villages, rather than staying in forest detachments. In very many cases (*w bardzo wielu sprawach*) the accused held some position or function in the local officialdom: village heads, deputy village heads, district heads, employees of district office, members and commanders of local fire brigades, members of village guard . . . They were, without exception, of Roman Catholic denomination, grown-up men, in general without a prior criminal record . . . They had stable family life, wives, and children. Some of them were members of the Communist Party (PPR), or worked in the People's Militia (the police force) after the war . . . By virtue of their functions at least a part of them belonged to the local elite in the countryside . . .
>
> Women had often witnessed and observed what had happened. They belonged to passive crowds, which carried out the killings with the hands of a few of their most active participants . . . One could even venture a proposition, based on depositions from witnesses and the accused, that there were many active participants and observers in almost each of these crimes . . . As far as murders perpetrated in villages we can even speak about an aggressive, criminal crowd, where a few people play an initiating and leading role, while everybody else, by witnessing their crime, provides at the same time a background, and a "moral" alibi for the crime committed.
>
> In a certain sense the entire village takes part in it, with a

different degree of involvement or witnessing, and after the war the entire village keeps in its collective unconscious and memory events, which then took place with its participation. This anonymous crowd constitutes an extremely important element for the analysis of this phenomenon. Its presence allows responsibility for the crimes committed to be diffused and in a certain sense, silently gives permission to do what had been done to the Jews.

[In numerous files] we read detailed descriptions of the crimes, during which victims and perpetrators talked to each other. Jews defended themselves, begged and appealed to the conscience and pity of the killers: "After this man was killed this little boy stood up and said to everybody present: Poles, spare my life, I am not guilty of anything, it is my misfortune that I am a Jew." They tried to bribe the perpetrators with what they still had and thus save their lives: "We were playing cards when somebody dropped in and said that a Jew had been caught . . . I went out doors. In front of the house stood a group of people and Moshek begged to be let go. He was with his little son, and they cried . . . This little Jew said: "Give them boots, Daddy, maybe they'll let us go." Crimes were perpetrated against individuals known, often by name, against neighbors, against local folks.

A special category of perpetrators were the functionaries of the dark-blue police [Polish state police] . . . , in their majority prewar employees of the state police. Policemen implicated in crimes against the Jews were heads of families, typically with several children at home. Their material status was usually rather good . . . In their actions against the Jewish population one can notice a large element of freedom and independence from superior German authority . . . In the cases at hand there was not a single instance in which apprehended Jews were escorted back to a ghetto or to a police station—which would also mean death for them. They are usually killed right away or in a neighboring forest, and local peasants are ordered to bury the corpses.

The direct motive to commit the majority of murders and denunciations of Jews hiding in the countryside was the desire to plunder them, to take over their belongings, which were imagined to be considerable. This was a pernicious consequence of a stereotype about Jewish wealth . . . Peasants imagined that by killing these people, they will get hold of their riches. One should suppose that, in a psychological sense, the fact that hiding Jews were paying for shelter and food, and often very high prices by local

> standards, reinforced the belief that they have lots of money, which can be taken from them with impunity. Indirectly, the same motive underlay murders of Jews who no longer could pay off those giving them shelter . . . People were getting rid of them, just as they were getting rid of Jews who had witnessed crimes committed earlier.
>
> In over a dozen closely researched cases, there is mention of characteristic and telling facts which accompanied the crime. After having finished, peasants gathered in the apartment of one of the participants to drink vodka, as if to celebrate with a meal their joint deed, to divide the spoils, and probably also to decompress.

This summary does not represent my reading of the evidence from the files of "August cases" tried in the Kielce district court. Two young Polish historians provided it. It offers a composite image, and all the enumerated elements certainly could not be found in every episode they took under scrutiny. But it is, nevertheless, abundantly clear that any concept of deviance would have to be stretched beyond capacity to encompass the kind of behavior that Skibińska and Petelewicz have described.

Instead, we can note multiple ways in which killings of Jews by peasants in the Kielce countryside were socially sanctioned. Regular members of the community took part in them, not miscreants or "marginal" people. Indeed, the local elite's participation bestowed upon these crimes a kind of official imprimatur. Killings were carried out openly, often publicly, drawing crowds of onlookers.

The direct perpetrators of these crimes, the most active participants, as far as one can tell, remained members in good standing of their local communities. Some joined the Communist Party and the People's Militia after the war. In almost every file, there are group affidavits signed by inhabitants of the village where murder took place, "vouching for the good and honorable character of the accused." "This is proof," Skibińska and Petelewicz observe, "that the village was in solidarity with the accused and that in the consciousness of its inhabitants there was no need to prosecute or to expiate in any way for the crime."[14] In the conclusion of their article, the authors finally draw on interviews they conducted in the region sixty years after the events. They note an "almost total lack of interest in the fate of murdered Jews" and that "if any emotion could be found [in conversations] it was a disapproval directed toward the victims." Given the deep religiosity of the peasants, Skibińska and Petelewicz wonder why the principles of Christian ethics about how to treat other human beings were never invoked.[15]

A close reading of Skibińska and Petelewicz's study makes us wonder whether the question of how many Jews had been killed by the local population in Poland is the right one to ask to find a proper measure of this most tragic aspect of Polish-Jewish relations during the war. Should we not ask instead, how many murderers of Jews and their accomplices there were among the Poles? To quote an American legal scholar, "Open criminality implicates all who know of the conduct and fail to act."[16] One Jew killed by one direct perpetrator—but in a public manner, with approval and encouragement of a crowd of onlookers—represents a collective deed implicating all those present, a group experience of ultimate transgression marking forever the community where it took place, if only because local people had to live from then on side by side with murderers.

A CLOSE-UP OF A MURDER SCENE, OR, WHAT A DIFFERENCE A PERSONAL TESTIMONY CAN MAKE

I propose now to visit a murder scene, in the village of Gniewczyn, in another part of Poland—a large village of 5,000 inhabitants. In May of 1942, a group of local notables, including two village heads, a commander of the voluntary fire brigade, and half a dozen other associates, ferreted out several Jewish families hiding in the vicinity.[17] The villagers brought men, women, and children, sixteen persons altogether, to the house of the Trinczer family, centrally situated in the village, not far from the church. They held the captured Jews there for several days in two rooms separated by a small kitchen. One of the rooms was turned into a torture chamber. The captors raped women there and subjected men to water torture to make them reveal the whereabouts of goods left with friendly peasants, goods on which the Jews drew to pay for food and shelter while in hiding. Once the torturers obtained the desired information, their emissaries visited peasant households demanding the surrender of "Jewish rags," lest the Gestapo be informed.

The word got around Gniewczyn that the Jews were being forced to give up what remained of their belongings. One of the Jewish women managed to run away from the torture house but was caught by her pursuer, an acquaintance with whom she went to school, who dragged her by the hair back across the village. Her mother, who earlier avoided the dragnet, showed up the next morning kneeling on the steps of the church, begging the priest for the lives of her daughter and grandchildren. But he declined to help.

After a few days, when the torturers concluded that they had obtained all the Jewish property to be had, they called the gendarmes. The Germans came to the village, where the townsfolk treated them to a good meal. Then the Germans took the Jews into the courtyard, ordered them one by one to lie facedown on the ground, and shot everybody, beginning with the small children, to death.

We owe this detailed description to an eyewitness, a boy fourteen years old at the time, who wrote up the story after all the main protagonists had died. But for this narrative, which appeared in the April 2008 issue of the Catholic monthly *Znak*, a historian's inquiry revealed only one trace of this mass murder in printed sources: a note in the registry of German crimes kept by the Main Commission for Investigation of Hitlerite Crimes, stating that sixteen Jews were murdered in 1942 in the house of Leib Trinczer by gendarmes from a nearby town. That local Poles were responsible for the crime, a well-known fact in the entire community, would have not been revealed to outside observers except for one man's personal testimony.[18]

The close-up of the Gniewczyn murder scene foregrounds two phenomena, of which one is well-known and the other is speculation. Memory of wartime atrocities against the Jews is well-preserved (and passed on from generation to generation) in the Polish countryside. Journalists and scholars stumble upon it nearly every time they make an inquiry. Reporters who went to Jedwabne before the town became the site of a national scandal persuaded local people to speak unself-consciously about the crimes. Ethnographic studies conducted in the countryside on other, related subjects—by Alina Cała in the 1980s, or Joanna Tokarska-Bakir in 2006, for example—also almost inadvertently revealed the same.[19] The reason, I believe, is that these occurrences were common, and therefore quasi "normal" (and simultaneously also rare events with "significance" that took place in these communities), and remained a subject of conversations for years to come at local gatherings.

The second significant aspect of the murders revealed in this close-up is the role that torture played in the Gniewczyn crime. Torture, it seems, was common in encounters between peasants and Jews. Numerous depositions describe brutalization of Jewish victims, including the rape of women. Peasant violence, killings, and rapes in the Kielce countryside, as we discussed, are documented in court cases prosecuted after the war. But the story of Polish-Jewish relations is hardly different when told by one who has many good friends among the peasants, an ethnomusicologist who, for dozens of years, has collected peasant folklore and is enamored of village life and its culture. The ethnomusicologist, Professor Andrzej Bieńkowski, stated in a 2008 interview:

> The most painful thing for me is the attitude in the countryside toward Jews, and a universal sense of triumph because they are no longer there. Universal. And one more thing, which I rarely wrote about, and which weighs terribly on my conscience: the killings of Jews who were hiding in forests by the peasants. The number of these crimes and incidents that I know about . . . it is a terrible burden. In the book I tell one horrifying story how the father of singer S. brutally killed two small Jewish girls, and how with his band he later raped and killed a Jewish woman hiding in a forest. And I also know a story, one of many, which I have not recounted, of how a beautiful young Jewess with two small children escaped from a transport near Białobrzegi. They knew her, everybody stressed this. She went into a forest and a bunch of young men her age, with wooden poles, followed her. She could have been twenty-three years old, the children were three and four. And some twenty youths beat them to death with those poles, just for pleasure, nobody got anything out of it.[20]

Historians, as a rule, have not paid much attention to such details, focusing on the fact of the murder instead. But it stands to reason that, when time and circumstances permitted, local people applied themselves to forcing the Jews to reveal where their mythical "gold" had been hidden:

> A certain Marian Haba sought shelter in Cholerzyn (a village not far away from today's Kraków international airport in Balice). He remained in hiding, in the village, until the locals heard a rumor that Haba had gold stashed in the area. A Polish policeman, summoned a while later by the peasants, said: "When I arrived in the village, I saw not a human being but a shapeless form. People told me they had killed the Jew because he was said to have buried five kilograms of gold."[21]

We are slowly beginning to understand a disturbing feature that surfaces occasionally in the way Jews collectively remember this period: a recurring observation that the "locals" (Ukrainians, Lithuanians, or Poles, as the case may be) were "worse than the Germans." After all, it is well-known—and Jews know this better than anybody else—that the Holocaust was a German invention, which the Nazis carried around Europe as they conquered the continent. One disturbing theme in Jewish narratives of the wartime points out that death administered by people well-known to the victims evoked a special kind of suffering, one infused with deep feelings of betrayal.[22] But we now realize that death at the hands of neighbors must have been, also, literally, very painful.

HUMAN AGENCY

What renders the study of the Holocaust so frustrating is its facelessness: the scandalous anonymity of victims unrecognized in their individuality at the moment of death, which every society marks with a solemn ritual, even for the lowliest and poorest. If I may paraphrase a well-known saying, to invoke a million people gassed at Auschwitz is tantamount to just quoting a number. But such is the nature of the subject and the evidence at our disposal that, in writing Holocaust history, references to staggering numbers of victims cannot be avoided. Nonetheless, we yearn to pierce the oblivion to which this relegates individual victims, if only because violent death, which had been inflicted upon them, is by nature an intimate and personal experience. Confined to abstractions, we would not understand what had happened, and our account of the Holocaust would not be truthful. At the risk of saying the obvious, actual people were killed in this man-made calamity, and actual people did the killings. And it is at the periphery of the Holocaust that we come across the most abundant evidence personalizing what happened—when killings of Jews were carried out by their Christian neighbors.

In his study *Eichmann's Men*, historian Hans Safrian called his protagonists not bureaucrats but "pathfinders."[23] In fact, this observation applies to all Nazi perpetrators of the Holocaust in positions of authority over the Jews—there was no ready blueprint or bureaucratic routine to latch on to, and everything in their enterprise was fluid. A felicitous phrase coined by Ian Kershaw to characterize the overall functioning of the Nazi system—that by following cues emanating from the top of the hierarchy, rather than strict instructions, functionaries of the regime were "working towards the Führer"—fits admirably as a description of the mechanism of the "Final Solution."[24] No matter how large or small the domain over which they presided—a work detail, barrack, ghetto, or camp—the men in charge of solving the "Jewish question" were improvisers. Notwithstanding Raul Hilberg's painstaking reconstruction of the bureaucratic coordination required to mobilize the resources of a modern state to kill millions of Jews—very much the key aspect of what happened—at the core of the process lay improvisation. It is a point, incidentally, that Hilberg explicitly acknowledges in Claude Lanzmann's film *Shoah*.[25]

Of course, bureaucratic capacity, as well as the technology of a modern state, was necessary to carry out in a timely fashion the mass murder of widely dispersed millions of people. But bureaucratic apparatuses and routines are devised with specific goals in mind. To apply them to different tasks requires adaptation, such as special initiative. To put it in the simplest terms: trains carrying Jews to death camps—again, so instructively discussed by Hilberg in *Shoah*—did not operate according to a regular schedule. These were specially chartered trains, and somebody had to request them and steer them through the maze of regular traffic. They could have been ordered, or not; there could have been more or fewer of them; they could have moved faster or slower. And so it goes for virtually every aspect of the killing process.

At every stage of the Holocaust, decisions had to be made. It is a phenomenon filled with individual initiatives of the perpetrators, who were not simply cogs in a machine operating according to preordained rules. Far from it. Agency in the Shoah, to a degree we perhaps have not yet adequately recognized when thinking and writing about it, rests with a multitude of individuals.

Many people pushed the process along on their own initiative, and there were, ipso facto, many chokepoints where the process could have been slowed, derailed, or even temporarily halted. And throwing up obstacles was a significant and viable alternative, because, from a certain point, it became clear that the Nazis would lose the war.

To say, therefore, that nothing could have been done once the Nazi policy of killing all the Jews had been set in motion is incorrect. Many people could have done something, or not done something, with the result that hundreds of thousands of Jewish lives would have been saved.

THE SIGNIFICANCE OF "THICK DESCRIPTION"

Much of the evidence about killings or denunciations of Jews by peasants in the Polish countryside consists of uncorroborated personal testimony from survivors, their relatives, or acquaintances. Typically, the account is brief and notes the facts without many details. Much of it is secondhand information, for example, knowledge sought out and acquired after the fact by a concerned family member. Thus, the body of evidence is not "systematic" in any sense of the word, and it has not been part of any "record." So, strictly speaking, we should abstain from generalizing observations on the basis solely of what we can find about the frequency and distribution of these crimes.

To be sure, we can seek a general understanding of these events only because frequency is sufficiently high and distribution sufficiently broad to preclude an easy refutation that these were isolated episodes in strictly confined areas. But the heart of the argument has to be made, not by asking what percentage of Polish peasants hunted down local Jews (we will never be able to provide reliable statistics on this), but, rather, by reconstructing how these murders were conducted. Because a number of detailed narratives exhibit concurring characteristics, we can make a leap toward a general understanding of the phenomenon.

A society with a common past and shared customs and institutions has a degree of internal coherence. One should view it as analogous to a text, or a system, rather than a quilt stitched together from randomly assembled pieces. As a result, practices and attitudes engaging fundamental values (those concerning life and death, for example) must be intelligible beyond the confines of any local community. This is why, even in the absence of firm knowledge about the distribution and frequency of peasant murders of Jews, we can still tell whether they were an accepted social practice from close analysis of a discrete number of episodes. Given the character of these murders—that they were open, well attended, and widely discussed public events—and given the identity of people involved—that these were regular folks, including leading members of the community—a "thick description" of localized events yields knowledge about behavior in society at large.

CHANGE IN SOCIAL NORMS CONCERNING JEWISH PROPERTY

Let me now move to the question of plunder, which, as we already know, is intimately related to the killings of Jews by their neighbors. We must be aware, of course, that we are operating at the very end of a long food chain here. Real, massive plunder took place as a result of state action in Germany proper and throughout Western Europe, where many Jews were solidly middle class and had substantial wealth. The Nazis took over Jewish property through a long process of Aryanization, forced emigration, outright confiscation, and also deportation and killings. "Throughout the twelve years of the Third Reich," writes Saul Friedländer, "looting of Jewish property was of the essence. It was the most easily understood and most widely adhered-to aspect of the anti-Jewish campaign, rationalized, if necessary, by the simplest ideological tenets."[26] The Third Reich benefited most from the plunder of Jewish wealth. But Vichy France, for example, tried to get its cut as well. So this is not a uniquely East European story, although the "hands on" aspect of it may be.

Mass killings in the Podlasie region, of which the murder in Jedwabne was but one episode, were accompanied by widespread and thorough plunder of Jewish property. It would be more difficult to name townspeople who did *not* plunder Jewish houses than those who did while the former inhabitants were incinerated in a barn on the outskirts of Radziłow, an eyewitness told a journalist sixty years later. The French Catholic priest Father Patrick Desbois, while searching for mass graves of Jews in the Ukrainian countryside and talking to local witnesses, heard from one of his interlocutors: "One day we woke up in the village and we were all wearing Jews' clothes."[27] I am sure the same occurred in numerous localities east of the River Elbe. Things were not much different in southeastern Europe, either. When the Nazis deported Jews from the ancient Greek Jewish community of Salonica (now Thessaloniki) in 1943, "as soon as they were marched away, people rushed into their houses, tore up floorboards and battered down walls and ceilings, hoping to find hidden valuables . . . There was a 'complete breakdown of order' wrote an official at the time, and the secondhand shops of the city began to fill up with stolen goods."[28]

But again, whether we quote evidence from three or from thirty-three incidents, we are confronted with a discrete number of episodes, and we remain, epistemologically, on the ground of "anecdotal" (as opposed to "systematic") evidence. To overcome the inherently incomplete character of data, we need ask how things were done to get a general understanding of what happened. We can reach such understanding by analyzing in detail the character of the crimes committed, as well as by reading people's minds, so to speak, wherever a record of conversations has been preserved.

Let me offer a few examples. In her memoirs, Chaja Finkelsztajn reports how, as the mass killings were unfolding in her native Radziłow, Poland, someone suggested that she turn over whatever she still had, since together with her family she would certainly be killed. It was only right, Chaja's interlocutor argued without malice, for the good people who knew the Finkelsztajns to get their possessions, or else the killers would be rewarded.[29] To a Jewish man trying to find a hiding place with a peasant acquaintance near Węgrów, the latter's son-in-law said matter-of-factly: "Since you are going to die anyway, why should someone else get your boots? Why not give them to me so I will remember you?"[30] Miriam Rosenkranz had a moment of déjà vu during the pogrom in Kielce

> when the horror of the ghetto came back to me and this scene when I worked with sorting down [feathers] and we were about to go back to the ghetto, and they were saying that that's the end, that they were deporting us for sure, and then this [Polish] woman acquaintance looked at my feet, [and the following exchange took place] "Really, you could leave me your boots Missy." "But Mrs. Joseph, I am still alive." "Well, I wasn't saying anything, only that those are nice boots"—replied Mrs. Joseph.[31]

What we are eavesdropping on, by listening to these exchanges, are truly out-of-the-ordinary ideas. These snippets of conversations are built on an inversion of important principles regulating people's lives in common. The message, addressed to a Jewish interlocutor with the expectation of a voluntary surrender of property to a Polish person, reflects a revised understanding of private property rights, as well as the nullification of the norm of goodwill binding people who live close to one another.

Until these conversations took place, we could safely assume that local people respected the right to private property. The only occasion when they felt it might be suspended, when claims could be made legitimately to surrender what people rightfully owned, would be to relieve extreme hardship that befell other members of the community—in case of fire, flood, or earthquake—an act of goodwill, sustaining reciprocity for times when extreme hardship would in turn fall on themselves.

What does it mean that three different people, on three different occasions (and one could, of course, quote many more similar exchanges, as they caught the attention of Jewish interlocutors and were recorded), express exactly the same unusual thought about matters of fundamental importance in the life of a community?[32] I find it implausible that such a convergence of ideas inverting the meaning of private property and neighborly obligation, as far as the Jews were concerned, was purely coincidental. Again, I allude here to the assumption that practices and important beliefs in society are interconnected and must be congruent. In other words, what is accepted as a matter of fact in one segment of society could not be directly negated in another, or else people would experience cognitive dissonance. Thus, to my mind, this anecdotal evidence (and it would remain "anecdotal" even if we quoted ten or fifteen such episodes) is an indication of a shift in shared norms concerning acceptable behavior toward the Jews. In the eyes of their Polish neighbors, Jews ceased to be human beings and were perceived instead, to use the expression coined by Emanuel Ringelblum, as "deceased on holidays."

I may seem to grasp at straws here, but it is important to develop ways of argumentation portraying the plunder of Jews for what it was—namely, a social practice, rather than a "criminal" or a deviant behavior of some rogue individuals. That plunder was widespread and sanctioned by norms is revealed precisely by the form of references to it captured in language.

We find an echo of this shift in normative expectations not only among individuals speaking about interpersonal relations but also in "institutional" evaluations concerning relationships between groups, such as an early report of the underground sent to the London government in exile. The report indicated that Jews were nonresponsive to Polish (that is, Catholic) fellow citizens' approaches to take their goods, even though it was clear that otherwise everything would only end up in German hands.[33] Evidently, by not consenting to be despoiled by their neighbors, Jews were somehow favoring Germans over Poles. And so the stakes rise: a recalcitrant Jew, unwilling to surrender his or her boots to a Polish acquaintance, is not only unfriendly, but, implicitly, also unpatriotic.

Conversely, when German decrees ordered retail Jewish commercial property and real estate into Aryan trusteeship—an opportunity for enrichment, which was taken up with eagerness by Polish lawyers, for example—the decrees were also defended by suggestions that members of the Aryan corporation were rescuing this wealth from German hands. The main underground publication, *Biuletyn Informacyjny (Information bulletin)*, refused to buy that line, warning the legal profession in an article of July 19, 1940, that such behavior was objectionable. But *Biuletyn Informacyjny* was also an exceptional publication, because it published not a single line with antisemitic overtones throughout the Occupation.[34] And since the practice of "Aryanization" was continent-wide, Poland was not the only place where similar arguments had been advanced.

A certain Jozef Gorski, a well-to-do landowner from central Poland, writes the following about the Holocaust in his memoirs:

> As a Christian I could not not feel compassion with my fellow human beings . . . but as a Pole I looked at what was happening differently . . . I considered Jews to be an internal enemy . . . so I could not help feeling glad that we are getting rid of this enemy and, what's more, not with our own hands but thanks to the deeds of another, external, enemy . . . I could not hide satisfaction when I rode through our little towns, and saw that there were no more Jews . . . Asked by Thurm [a local German official who accompanied him on this occasion]: *Sehen die Polen die Befreiung vom den Juden als ein Segnen an?* [Do Poles perceive being liberated from the Jews as a blessing?] I replied *Gewiss* [Of course], being sure that I am expressing the opinion of the overwhelming majority of my fellow nationals.[35]

Gorski was reading the minds of his fellow nationals correctly. Some variation of the sentiment expressed in "We'll have to put up a monument to Hitler for having gotten rid of the Jews" was overheard in private conversations all over Poland. We have testimony to this effect not only from Jews who successfully "passed" as Aryans and later recounted what they saw and heard, but also from numerous Polish witnesses as well.

Given such widespread consensus, it is no wonder that, with

the war's end approaching, highly placed functionaries of the Polish Underground State advised the government in exile in London about a looming—what else?—"Jewish problem." The official position of the government had been that all changes resulting from decisions taken by the occupier(s) with respect to geographical boundaries, citizenship rights and status, and property confiscations—all purported legal changes, in other words—were null and void. But London was warned, repeatedly, from the home country that the matter was not as simple as it may have seemed. Roman Knoll, head of the Foreign Affairs Commission in the Government Delegate (the underground civilian administration in occupied Poland), reported that a return to the status quo ante and resumption by Jews of their economic role from before the war was an impossibility. The non-Jewish population had taken over Jewish positions in the social structure, he wrote in 1943, and this change was final and

> permanent in character . . . Should Jews attempt to return en masse [rumors and exaggerated estimates circulated about the numbers of Jews who had managed to escape into the Soviet interior and were expected to return to Poland after the war] people would not perceive this as a restoration but as an invasion, which they would resist even by physical means.[36]

In July 1945, another distinguished politician of the London-affiliated underground, Jerzy Braun, conveyed his observations about the growing antisemitism in Poland:

> Today there is no place for a Jew in small towns and villages. During the past six years (finally!) a Polish third estate has emerged which did not exist before. It completely took over trade, supplies, mediation, and local crafts in the provinces . . . Those young peasant sons and former urban proletarians, who once worked for the Jews, are determined, persistent, greedy, deprived of all moral scruples in trade, and superior to Jews in courage, initiative, and flexibility. Those masses . . . Will not relinquish what they have conquered. There is no force which could remove them.

It was understandable that Jews who survived the onslaught but could not return to their hometowns "leave ruined and broken telling the rest of the world that Poles are antisemites." But what they take for antisemitism, Braun concludes, "is only an economic law, which cannot be helped."[37]

Truth be told, the majority of Polish peasants came into possession of Jewish property because Jews all over Europe, and ipso facto in Poland, had been killed by the Germans. Some peasants helped their luck, and most liked what happened. But their involvement in these crimes was opportunistic. All that I am arguing for is recognition that when the opportunity arose, they were not shy to take it.

A NORM, NOT AN EXCEPTION

The photograph accompanying this essay is a familiar image people have seen in countless variations: peasants at harvesttime after work well done, resting contentedly with their tools, behind a pile of crops. Some people may have taken a snapshot of this kind on a summer vacation in the countryside; others carry it as a souvenir from a scouting expedition helping farmers in the backcountry bring in their crops. Every summer, similar images were regularly splashed across the front pages of newspapers half the world over, in Communist countries, in celebration of yet another bountiful harvest provided by collectivized agriculture. Visitors in art galleries and museums came upon more or less artistically refined renditions of the same picture.

Yet despite belonging to a bucolic genre (people at ease, surrounded by nature, talking to one another, who in a moment might burst into song), this particular photograph is disquieting—and not just because it is fuzzy. If there were palms protruding from behind the assembled group rather than coniferous trees, one could speculate that it was taken in a desert. Something feels off-kilter with the landscape, which cannot be pegged easily to a geographical location; the image strikes the viewer as familiar and strange at the same time. When one finally notices the "crop" scattered in front of the group—skulls and bones, no less—the mystery deepens. Where are we? Who are the people in the photograph, and what are they doing?

We are in the middle of Europe, just after World War II has ended. And we see in the photograph a group of peasants standing atop a mountain of ashes. These are the human ashes of more than 800,000 Jews gassed and cremated in the Treblinka extermination camp in Poland between July 1942 and October 1943. The Europeans in the photograph have been digging through the remains of Holocaust victims, hoping to find gold and precious stones that Nazi executioners may have overlooked despite carefully checking the body cavities of murdered Jews.[38]

One of the earliest mentions of this phenomenon (together with a few photographs of Treblinka's eerie landscape) came from two men who visited the site of the Treblinka extermination camp on September 12, 1945. The entire area, they reported, was scarred with holes several meters deep, with human bones scattered all around. People sifting through the mounds of human ashes did not bother to answer when asked what they were doing. The area was large, the scale of excavations enormous. Thousands had to have worked to produce this lunar landscape. "Mutual relationships in the Treblinka area are simply incredible," the authors of the report wrote. "People who enriched themselves with gold dug up from the graves, by night plunder their own neighbors. We were terrified because in a peasant hut some dozen meters from the house where we spent the night, a woman was tortured with live fire to reveal the place where she was hiding gold and valuables."[39] While the scale of the Treblinka excavations was unique, the practice of digging up Jewish remains from the sites of mass murder to strip them of valuables was common.

But the plunder of Jewish wealth—the main story illustrated in the photograph—was a continent-wide affair. It took place from the

Atlantic Ocean in the west to the Volga River in the east, the entire expanse of Nazi-dominated Europe wherever the Holocaust reached. The plunder was accompanied by the opportunistic behavior of the local population (despite the locals also being subjected to exploitation by Nazi conquerors). In Salonika, "Jewish tombstones were to be found in urinals and driveways, and had been used to make-up [*sic*] the dance floor of a taverna built over a corner of the former cemetery itself. Because graves had been ransacked for the treasure that had been supposedly hidden there 'many Jewish skulls and bones are visible.'"[40] Evidently, peasants from Eastern Europe were not the only ones to act in this manner.

In 1943, in anticipation of German defeat, various associations formed in occupied France to protect the interests of those Frenchmen who had acquired the so-called "Aryanized" Jewish property. Such associations continued to operate, albeit under new names, after the liberation. They defended their constituencies fiercely against the restitution of Jewish businesses or apartments to their rightful owners. "Those who bought Jewish property protected French interests," the association argued. "By buying property that the Germans threatened to liquidate, the purchasers 'preserved a precious inheritance for the national economy.'" Thus framed, stripping the Jews of their assets was cast as responsible and patriotic behavior. Little wonder that in April 1945, hundreds of demonstrators went to the streets of Paris crying, "Death to the Jews" and "France for the French."[41] The few Jews returning to their hometowns after the war, from Salonika to Warsaw to Paris, were made unwelcome by former neighbors already comfortably ensconced in their old apartments and jobs.

The story of the plunder of Jewish assets occasionally reaches the large-circulation press when Swiss banks are challenged to produce lists of dormant accounts or national museums are forced to return stolen Jewish paintings acquired through bona fide art dealers. However, its significance lies not in becoming a momentary focus of journalistic zeal but in the very fabric of what Saul Friedländer identifies as the broad consent to the Nazi-organized Holocaust by institutions and people in occupied Europe:

> Not one social group, not one religious community, not one scholarly institution or professional association in Germany and

> throughout Europe declared its solidarity with the Jews (some of the Christian churches declared that converted Jews were part of the flock, up to a point); to the contrary, many social constituencies, many power groups were directly involved in the expropriation of the Jews and eager, be it out of greed, for their wholesale disappearance. Thus, Nazi and related anti-Jewish policies could unfold to their most extreme levels without the interference of any major countervailing interests.[42]

Many across the European continent benefited from the Nazi policies stripping Jews of civic and property rights, and eliminating them from public life—or, rather, as it soon transpired, stripping the Jews of life altogether. A question and answer to frame this twentieth-century European cover story, so dramatically illustrated with the picture accompanying this essay, could run like this: What do a Swiss banker and a Polish peasant have in common? The answer to this question, only a slight exaggeration, would be: a golden tooth extracted from the jaws of a Jewish corpse.

NOTES

This essay originally appeared in *Years of Persecution, Years of Extermination: Saul Friedlander and the Future of Holocaust Studies*, edited by Christian Wiese and Paul Betts (New York: Continuum Publishing, 2010), 289–310. Used by kind permission of Bloomsbury Publishing PLC.

1. Geoffrey H. Hartman, "The Book of Destruction," in Saul Friedlander, ed., *Probing the Limits of Representation: Nazism and the "Final Solution"* (Cambridge, Mass.: Harvard University Press, 1992), 326–27.

2. Jan T. Gross, *Neighbors: The Destruction of the Jewish Community in Jedwabne, Poland* (Princeton, N.J.: Princeton University Press, 2001), which created quite a stir after it was published in Poland, took off from the deposition of Szmul Wasersztajn (Shmuel Wasserstein), who witnessed the crime committed against Jedwabne Jews by their Polish neighbors. Wasersztajn's testimony was preserved in the archives of the Jewish Historical Institute in Warsaw. I quote it in extenso on pages 16 through 20 of the Princeton edition.

3. Renée Poznanski, *Propagandes et persécutions. La Résistance et le "problème juif" 1940–1944* [Propaganda and persecution: The Resistance and the "Jewish problem" 1940–1944] (Paris: Fayard, 2008), 144.

4. Or, perhaps, they do but in a fundamental sense, so that what was to be expunged from the face of the earth—the victim, the crime, and the memory of the crime—gets saved from oblivion.

5. "However the war may end," an SS man scornfully warned, "we have won the war against you; none of you will be left to bear witness, but even if someone were to survive, the world will not believe him . . . even if some proof should remain and some of you survive, people will say that the events you describe are too monstrous to be believed." Primo Levi, *The Drowned and the Saved, trans. Raymond Rosenthal* (New York: Random House, 1989), 12. Many a Jewish memoirist knew this without an SS man's reminder.

6. Herman Kruk's diary, October 28, 1942.

7. Jan Gross, "One Line at a Time," *Poetics Today* 27, 2 (Summer 2006): 425–29.

8. Saul Friedländer, *The Years of Extermination: Nazi Germany and the Jews, 1939–1945* (New York: Harper Collins, 2007).

9. Christopher R. Browning, *Remembering Survival: Inside a Nazi Slave-Labor Camp* (New York: Norton, 2011).

10. For excellent examples of such studies, see Pawel Machcewicz and Krzysztof Persak, eds., *Wokół Jedwabnego* [Around Jedwabne] (Warsaw, Poland: Instytut Pamięci Narodowej [Institute of National Remembrance], 2002), and four issues of the yearly *Zaglada* Żydów. *Studia i materialy* [Destruction of the Jews: Studies and materials], a publication put out since 2005 by the Polish Center for Holocaust Research at the Institute of Philosophy and Sociology of the Polish Academy of Science, in Warsaw.

11. With the exception, probably due to oversight, of such cases tried in the Kraków district courts, which remain in local archives.

12. For a discussion of the rationale for adopting such a stance by Communist judiciary, see the interview with Professor Andrzej Rzepliński in *Gazeta Wyborcza* [Electoral newspaper] of July 19, 2002, and also Andrej Rzepliński, "Ten jest z ojczyzny mojej? Sprawy karne oskarżonych o wymordowanie Żydów w Jedwabnem w świetle zasady rzetelnego procesu [This one is from my homeland? Criminal defendants of the murder of Jews in Jedwabne in the light of the principle of a fair trial]" in Machcewicz and Persak, *Wokół Jedwabnego*, vol. 1, 353–459. See also Jan T. Gross, *Fear: Anti-Semitism in Poland after Auschwitz—an Essay in Historical Interpretation* (New York: Random House, 2006), 52–57.

13. Dariusz Libionka, "Zagłada domu Trinczerów—refleksje historyka [Destruction at the house of Trinczer—reflections of a historian]," *Znak* 4 (2008): 150.

14. Anna Skibińska and Jakub Petelewicz, "The Participation of the Poles in Crimes against Jews in the Swietokrzyskie Region," *Yad Vashem Studies* 35, 1 (2007): 128.

15. Ibid., 142. One should note, parenthetically, that the Catholic Church maintained its institutional presence in the Polish countryside throughout the German occupation. A local priest was then, and remains

to this day, a spiritual guide and moral beacon for inhabitants of the countryside. A full account of the phenomenon of the murders of Jews committed by Polish peasants must involve, therefore, a query about how the Catholic Church as an institution acquitted itself of its responsibilities.

16. Scott Horton, "Justice after Bush: Prosecuting an Outlaw Administration," *Harper's*, December 20, 2008: 51.

17. Tadeusz Markiel, "Zagłada domu Trinczerów [Destruction at the house of Trinczer]," *Znak* 4 (2008): 119–46.

18. Libionka, "Zagłada domu Trinczerów—refleksje historyka," 148. The Głowna Komisja Badania Zbrodni Hitlerowskich (GKBZH, or Main Commission for Investigation of Hitlerite Crimes) communiqué provides fourteen names of the victims, listing also their ages, including two one-year-old babies, as well as three- and ten-year-old children.

19. Alina Cała, *The Image of the Jew in Polish Folk Culture* (Jerusalem: Magnes Press, Hebrew University, 1995); Joanna Tokarska-Bakir, *Legendy o krwi. Antropologia przesądu* [Legends of blood: The anthropology of prejudice] (Warsaw: WAB, 2008).

20. "Nikt mi nie przybył, z profesorem Andrzejem Bieńkowskim rozmawiają Małgorzata Borczak i Ewa Sławińska-Dahlig [No one came: Małgorzata Borczak and Ewa Sławińska-Dahlig in conversation with Professor Andrzej Bieńkowski]," *Nowe Ksiazki* 3 (2008): 9. Bieńkowski, an eminent painter and professor at the Academy of Fine Arts in Warsaw, is also an ethnomusicologist and author of *Ostatni wiejscy muzykanci* [*Last village musicians*] (Warsaw: Prószyński, 2001) and *Sprzedana muzyka* [*Sold music*] (Warsaw: Wydawn, 2007).

21. Jan Grabowski, *Rescue for Money: Paid Helpers in Poland, 1939–1945* (Jerusalem: Yad Vashem Lectures and Papers Series, 2008), 38.

22. In another context, writer Gustaw Herling-Grudziński, drawing on his experience in the Gulag, stated what is also at stake in our case: "There was something inhuman in this, something mercilessly breaking the only bond which seemed to naturally bind the prisoners: solidarity vis-à-vis the oppressors": Gustaw Herling-Grudziński, *Inny świat. Zapiski sowieckie* (Warsaw: Czytelnik, 1991), 56. Published in English as Gustav Herling, *A World Apart*, trans. Joseph Marek[Andrzej Ciozkosz] (London: Heinemann, 1951).

23. Hans Safrian, "Perpetrators and Agency: The Case of Eichmann and His Men," paper presented at Workshop on Hitler's Europe: New Perspectives on Occupation, Wirtschafts Universitat, Vienna, November 9–10, 2009.

24. Ian Kershaw, "Working towards the Führer," chap. 13 in Ian Kershaw, *Hitler, 1889–1936: Hubris* (New York: Norton, 2000).

25. *Shoah*, film directed by Claude Lanzmann, produced by Les Films Aleph, 1985.

26. Friedländer, *The Years of Extermination*, 497.

27. Father Patrick Desbois, *The Holocaust by Bullets* (New York: Palgrave Macmillan, 2008), 97.

28. Mark Mazower, *Salonica, City of Ghosts: Christians, Muslims and Jews 1430–1950* (London: HarperCollins, 2004), 443, 444.

29. Extensive excerpts of Chaja Finkelsztajn's memoirs are translated into Polish and printed in Machcewicz and Persak, *Wokół Jedwabnego*, vol. 2, 263–317. This episode is recounted on page 305.

30. Shraga Feivel Bielawski, *The Last Jew from Wegrow* (New York: Praeger, 1991), 72.

31. David Shtokfish, ed., *About Our House Which Was Devastated* [Sefer Kielce] (Tel Aviv: Kielce Societies in Israel and in the Diaspora, 1981), 200.

32. See, for example, Grabowski, *Rescue for Money*, 20–21.

33. "Frequently Jews prefer to have their goods confiscated by the Germans rather than to give them to Poles for use for some time"—from an underground situation report for the period of October 15 through November 20 sent from occupied Poland to the government in exile in London, quoted by Dariusz Libionka, "'Kwestia żydowska' w Polsce w ocenie Delegatury Rzadu RP i KG ZWZ-AK w latach 1942–1944 [The "Jewish question" in Poland, in the opinion of the delegation of the government of the Republic of Poland and KG UAS-AK in 1942–1944]," paper presented at conference Les Juifs et la Pologne, 1939–2004, Bibliothèque Nationale de France, Paris, January 13–15, 2005.

34. For the best analysis of this phenomenon, see Jan Grabowski, "Polscy zarządcy powierniczy majątku żydowskiego. Zarys problematyki {Polish trust managers of Jewish property: An outline of the issues]," *Zaglada* Żydów 3 (2007): 253–60. For the reference to the article in *Biuletyn Informacyjny,* see 259.

35. Jozef Gorski, "Na przelomie dziejow [At the turn of history]," *Zaglada* Żydów 2 (2006): 288–91.

36. Libionka, "'Kwestia żydowska' w Polsce."

37. Ibid.

38. A special table where gassed victims were checked for valuables hidden in their bodies and their golden tooth crowns were extracted before being shoved into crematorium ovens is on display in the well-preserved Majdanek extermination camp, now the Majdanek State Museum, near Lublin, Poland.

39. Jan T. Gross, *Fear*, 41.

40. Mazower, *Salonica*, 450.

41. Maud S. Mandel, *In the Aftermath of Genocide: Armenians and Jews in Twentieth-Century France* (Durham, N.C.: Duke University Press, 2003), 58–59; see also Renée Poznanski, *Jews in France during World War*

II, trans. Nathan Bracher (Hanover, N.H.: Brandeis University Press, 2001), 464–67.

42. Friedländer, *The Years of Extermination*, xxi. Mark Mazower advances a more general proposition on the overall character of European responses to Nazi policies of occupation: "For much of the war . . . Europeans fell into line and contributed what [the Germans] demanded anyway. After 1945, this was conveniently forgotten." Mark Mazower, *Hitler's Empire: How the Nazis Ruled Europe* (New York: Penguin, 2008), 6 and following pages.

Dagmar Herzog

The Obscenity of Objectivity: Post-Holocaust Antisemitism and the Invention of Post-Traumatic Stress Disorder

> *Perhaps objectivity on the subject is not possible.*
>
> *—Flossenbürg survivor and psychoanalyst Jack Terry, 1984*

> *The problem is neither narrowly scientific nor blatantly ideological: one cannot define exactly what is wrong with a certain representation of the events, but . . . one senses when some interpretation or representation is wrong.*
>
> *—Holocaust historian Saul Friedländer, 1992*

THE CONCEPT OF PTSD (POST-TRAUMATIC STRESS DISORDER) ENTERED the *Diagnostic and Statistical Manual of Mental Disorders* (DSM) in 1980. This essay concerns the fraught prehistory of the category—one involving both invention and discovery.[1] Most scholarly accounts of the evolution of the PTSD concept go back to railroad and industrial accidents at the turn from the nineteenth to the twentieth centuries and to the "shell shock" experienced by soldiers in World War I. What most accounts—oddly—skip over or only mention in passing is the aftermath of the Holocaust.[2] But in fact *the* catalyst for changing the science of trauma, including the particular ways that we now, in the early twenty-first century, understand PTSD (for example, delayed reaction onset, numbness of affect, intrusive memories, and hyperarousal), was a grotesque debacle fought out during the 1950s and 1960s over financial compensation for mental health damages among Jewish survivors of the ghettos and concentration and death camps.[3] The battle was ugly because the psychiatrists appointed by the West German government to evaluate survivors regularly rejected their claims. The psychiatrists argued that whatever debilitating insomnia, nightmares, chronic melancholia, fears, fixations, disabling psychosomatic pains, difficulty concentrating, or crippling apathy survivors displayed must have their source either in the survivors' *pre*-camp lives—perhaps even in their characters from the time of birth, or in very early life experiences in their families—or in their difficulties adjusting to *post*-camp life. *Anything* but the persecutions or the camps themselves.

In other words, to understand what it took to bring the science of trauma into view and into medical and legal legitimacy, we have to understand how utterly saturated the scientific battles over reparations were by politics and emotions. It was *against* the doctors who regularly rejected survivors' claims for health damages (many, though not all, gentile Germans, though there were occasionally Jews among the "rejecters" as well) that survivors sought out second, or third, or fourth opinions from more sympathetic doctors (often, as it happens, German and Austrian Jewish refugee psychoanalytically inclined psychiatrists living in the United States, in various Western European nations, or in Israel, although it is noteworthy that there were some important gentile German sympathizer psychiatrists also). And it was up to these more sympathetic doctors to make the case that the origins of the patients' problems lay *in* the persecutions and imprisonments.

Very quickly battle lines were established and two opposing sides emerged—arguing their positions in the pages of medical journals as well as directly in the patients' case records. The records were then submitted to the reparations offices and subsequently, in the tens of thousands of cases that were appealed after initial rejections, to courts established in West Germany to adjudicate reparations claims. There was no simple explanation internal to the history of medicine for how doctors could end up on one side or the other, for most had experienced the same medical training in pre-Nazi Germany. What both the medical journal articles and the case records reveal, instead, is that the doctors' expert judgments about the survivors they encountered were deeply shaped by their own (inevitably personal as well as professional) reactions to the patients.

This essay will explore three major topics, all of which have to do with the problem of objectivity. The first is the toxic postwar climate filled with resentment against the survivors in which the (at once medical, legal, and moral) battle over mental health damages was fought and in which, in general, truth was up for grabs. The second involves the arguments of anti-reparations doctors and their attacks on the more sympathetic doctors for being—supposedly—unobjective and unscientific. The third involves the passionate counterarguments developed by the sympathizing doctors that gradually helped bring into view and coherence the multi-symptom phenomenon that was first called "survivor syndrome" and "massive psychic trauma." Eventually, by historical contingency but also by engaged activism—as doctors working with and on behalf of survivors of Nazi persecutions and camps joined forces with physicians pressing for attention to the emotional difficulties experienced by many veterans of the Vietnam War—that phenomenon came to be called PTSD.

One purpose of this essay, then, is to revisit and provide a closer analysis of the medical texts on both sides and in so doing also to reintegrate the history of post-Holocaust trauma into the history of PTSD. Doing so is valuable not least because this episode turned out to be one of the most important learning experiences for the psychiatric profession in the United States, indeed one which ultimately had global repercussions. But what is no less fascinating to ponder are the predicaments of bias and the intricacy of ideological conflict on display here. How does one attempt to put forward a scientific argument when one is oneself accused of lack of objectivity—in a situation in which it is transparently obvious to those impugned that their accusers are being just as unobjective, if not more so, and yet that the other side has greater power and authority? What, then, did it ultimately take—what combination of creativity and persistence, but also unexpected coincidence, pressure, and leverage—to bring a new version of medical, legal, and moral truth into view and, eventually, into cultural dominance? Over the first dozen or so years of the dispute, the rejecters set the terms of debate. No one, in those years, could have predicted which side would emerge vindicated.

It has been argued that the rejecting doctors were simply caught in the traditional medical orthodoxy.[4] According to the inherited doctrine, individuals with a previously normal constitution were by definition robust and should recover rapidly from stress; if mental problems continued, there were only two possible explanations. Either there must be a somatic, physiological explanation. Or the individual must have been emotionally unstable before the trauma. Certainly, psychiatrists used these traditionalist arguments to deny effective care not only to concentration camp survivors but also to disturbed German soldiers returning from Soviet prisoner of war camps.[5] Revisiting the medical disputes over concentration camp survival, however, reveals that, on this subject, the rejecters were no innocent traditionalists. The minute the topic of mental health damages to camp survivors blew up in the medical journals—by 1957 or 1958—the rejecters knew full well what they were doing and self-consciously used every rhetorical strategy at their disposal to refute their critics and justify their decisions.

Yet the sympathizing physicians were not easy heroes, but rather often maddeningly imperfect. They were caught not only in the binds created by their opponents but also in their own assumptions about human nature and the therapeutic process. Eventually, however, first incrementally and then with ever greater success, their efforts helped to generate a paradigm shift with momentous consequences. That those consequences have since, in turn, had numerous, more ambiguous ramifications is the ever-evolving next chapter of the story within which we still live. For finally, as it turned out, the achievement of the sympathizers remained an ambivalent one, fraught with unanticipated complexities.

IF THE JEWS WANT MONEY . . .

The story begins not with the Holocaust itself, but rather in its aftermath. A law triggered the debate over the status of trauma. It was passed in West Germany in 1956 as part of a broader set of negotiations underway since the end of the war between the West German government; the Western Allies, especially the Americans; and international Jewish organizations (such as the Conference on Jewish Material Claims against Germany and the United Restitution Organization), as well as the young state of Israel. The law provided for small pensions (and in some cases also therapy) for survivors whose capacity to be economically self-supporting had been damaged by at least 25 percent due to persecution and violence experienced in the Third Reich in flight and hiding, in ghettos, or in camps.

Jews who had lost property under Nazism could seek restitution under an earlier law. The law allowing survivors to seek compensation for damages to their health was, to put it bluntly, the law for the little people, the ones who had no property to reclaim—often poorer Jews and those from Eastern European territories, including parts of Poland, that had been part of the German Reich as of 1937. The only property they had, as it were, was their labor power. Hence the need to prove the 25 percent or more diminishment of the ability to be self-supporting—in whatever new land had become their refuge.

But in case after case, as noted, the initially evaluating doctors said that whatever survivors had experienced in hiding or in the camps was something from which someone with a previously healthy disposition *should* have been able to recover. Anybody having trouble afterward must have been troubled before. Maybe their parents' marriage had not been happy; maybe they were just oversensitive.[6] Or, alternatively—these rejecting doctors averred—perhaps the prospect of receiving a pension caused these survivors to display symptoms of psychological dysfunction; perhaps they were, like lazy workers or malingering soldiers had been imagined before them, best understood as "pension neurotics" (*Rentenneurotiker*)—that was indeed the term used, whether they were producing their (suddenly financially convenient) symptoms consciously or unconsciously.[7] Over and over, the rejecting doctors denied a causal link between symptoms and experience.

All of this happened in a cultural context in post-Nazi West Germany of intense public hostility—shared also by leading politicians—toward the very idea of reparations or restitution. As West German Chancellor Konrad Adenauer's close associate, the Christian Social Union's Fritz Schäffer—a conservative Catholic and the second most powerful man in the postwar government—put it with striking lack of inhibition: "If the Jews want money, they should raise it themselves by arranging for a foreign loan."[8] Schäffer was from 1949 to 1957 the head of the Ministry of Finance, and his main assistant, Ernst Féaux de la Croix, was a man given to remarking on his annoyance about the "terrible drama of Israeli-Jewish demands" and how protests in Israel "swearing revenge" provided the "background music" to the always-delicate diplomatic negotiations over reparations. In his history of the reparations process, Féaux noted that, while it might sound "distinctly antisemitic" and "strongly exaggerated" to say that reparations were "the price that American Jewry exacted of its president for allowing him to take the Federal Republic as a partner into the community of Western nations," it could "nonetheless not be denied that there was a kernel of truth" in such assertions. His account was liberally sprinkled with complaints about "world Jewry," "supervision from Jerusalem," and how "Jewry just would not let go." (By contrast, Féaux was indignant that "the Jewish press" mentioned the Nazi past of one of the bankers involved in the negotiations, deeming the exposure of this backstory the "most aggressive," "undignified personal defamation.")[9] Schäffer openly stoked public anger against survivors by provocatively prophesying that reparations would so strain the West German financial system that they would "inevitably lead to a devaluation of the Deutschmark."[10] As though—not much more than a dozen years previously—non-Jewish Germans had not been enthusiastically supportive of a criminal regime and had not benefited directly—with career opportunities and with property—from "Aryanization," Jewish flight, deportations, and murder.[11]

These two—Schäffer and Féaux—were in charge of managing the entire reparations apparatus. (In the vast majority of instances, the claimants were Jews—there were a tiny number of Roma and political resisters who put forward health claims as well.) Schäffer also liked to complain that no one was willing to break the taboo against criticizing the reparations project for fear of being accused of antisemitism.[12] But of course the taboo was broken all the time. Invoking the idea of taboo was precisely what facilitated the talk. Chancellor Adenauer himself is said to have remarked in a high-level meeting: "The Jews cheat us anyway."[13]

In the wider public and in the media, there was far blunter rhetoric around reparations. Hendrik G. van Dam, the head of the Jewish community in Germany, received hate mail with messages such as: "You get yourself out of Germany as fast as you can! Every second Jew has made false claims and enriched himself . . . The reparations must end."[14] A letter written by a pastor in Berlin to the newsmagazine *Der Spiegel* declared—commenting on a much-discussed case in 1957 in which a schoolteacher had told a survivor "in my opinion far too few Jews were gassed"—that this kind of unfortunate slip was understandable in a situation of unequal rights: "Once Jews had fewer rights than Aryans. Nowadays a problematic reparations practice has turned the legal situation into the exact opposite."[15] Or as another letter writer opined in 1958—again defending the schoolteacher's remarks: "Once again, the 'Chosen People' are, each and every one, dancing around the 'golden calf.'"[16]

Yes, various counterarguments—clever, pained, or both—were

also published. "The name of the Law for the Compensation of Victims of Nazism might better be changed into 'Law for the Reawakening and Promotion of Antisemitism,'" one letter writer observed.[17] Another noted sarcastically, "Many of our contemporaries now like to reproach the Jews for the fact that so many of them are entitled to compensation. After all, back then it was obviously due to their self-interested profit-seeking that these mercenary Semites pushed their way so eagerly into the concentration camps!"[18] And yet another reminded readers of "the grotesque deeds of the Nazis, who with ice-cold hearts turned to oppressing entire groups of peoples whose nose did not appeal to them, in order to make fertilizer out of them."[19] But one sees from the terms of debate how much dislike of Jews permeated the discourse, and how greatly on the defensive the anti-antisemites were.[20]

Every small scandal—and there were scandals—in which a claimant made a false claim or a lawyer appeared to have a conflict of interest or to profit too much from representing survivors provided a further chance to link Jews in general with greed, corruption, and unseemly self-interest. Jewish organizations were obliged to remind all potential claimants of the danger that antisemitism could be restoked. They urgently warned all involved to avoid even the appearance of malfeasance.[21]

Promptly, three actually separate matters became entangled: what a post-fascist government owes the victims of its predecessor (morally and legally); whether reparations in principle were a just concept, but the demands of "world Jewry" were unreasonable and excessive; and whether a few bad apples could be construed as representing an entire group. In this climate, avid opponents of reparations—like the Christian Democratic Union politician Jakob Diel—could frame their objections in coded but easily understood ways: "What . . . simply cannot be accepted," Diel argued, "is the shameless abuse of the good will of the Federal Republic."[22] In a long-running campaign to encourage his party, then the governing party, to turn against the entire project, Diel was given to asking rhetorical questions such as: "Can it truly be just that in countless cases individuals covered by the reparations law are better off financially now than if they had never been persecuted?"[23]

It may bear mentioning here that, while there is always a battle over the truth, this battle is especially acute in the aftermath of great horror. It is especially acute, in short, in a post-fascist environment, when people's investments in rewriting reality—massaging, spinning, and reinterpreting the facts—are particularly strong. To feel only morally indignant is to miss just how much the idea that *Jews were a problem* was part of the commonsense texture of public discussion in the aftermath of a mass-murdering dictatorship. Moreover, the blatancy of the *hypocrisy around money* is noteworthy. This was also a climate, after all, in which pensions were available not only for concentration camp guards as well as their widows but also for entire organizations of gentiles dedicated to clamoring that they had been "victims of denazification" (*Entnazifizierungsgeschädigte*), "victims of reparations" (*Restitutionsgeschädigte*), or both. The "victims of reparations" included people who were distressed that Jews whose property had been lost to "Aryanization" had come back to reclaim it.[24] A journal launched in 1953 was dedicated to expressing vituperative distress over reparations: *Die Anklage* (The Accusation)—the subtitle was "Organ for the Disenfranchised Victims Damaged by the Postwar Situation."[25]

In addition, it is important to keep in mind just how intricate were *the enmeshments of the experts* in the project of denying the recent past. What is notable about post-1945 West Germany is that the majority of professionals who were authorities during the Third Reich continued to be authoritative, respected professionals in their fields in the aftermath.

As of the end of 1966, a decade into the process, rejections amounted to more than a third of the cases, and indeed on the initial round, before a case went to the courts on the basis of more sympathetic evaluations, the rejection rate had been more than half.[26] The justifications took a multitude of forms. One evaluator in 1960, for example, found a woman who had spent three years in Auschwitz to have "a psychopathic personality with a tendency toward abnormal processing of experience and an inability to deal with life." The expert consensus, the evaluator declared—and here we see the gesture to medical orthodoxy—was that a "normal person" would have recovered six months after liberation at the latest.[27] Other victims were described variously as having "hypochondriacal attitudes"—in regard to a man who had been in one ghetto and three concentration camps, had been thrown from a truck, and had his mother, sister, wife, and four children killed—or of displaying a "hysterical faulty attitude" and a "hysterical demonstration of helplessness"—in response to a woman who made strange inarticulate sounds when being questioned about her experiences. Her experiences included not only eight to ten hours of heavy camp labor every day—this an evaluator interpreted as providing her with access to somewhat better rations—but also the murder of two children, six siblings, and two grandchildren, who had been torn from her arms.[28] Or, in another case, involving a mother who had lost several of her children in concentration camps and had difficulty sleeping, the evaluating physician declared that "many people are sensitive and have sleep disturbances. This is not a serious disability."[29] There were thousands of cases like this; a significant number of the claimants were written off as suffering from a congenital or endogenous (*anlagebedingte*) "anxiety neurosis."[30]

There was also the case of a Polish Jewish man known as Z., born in 1913,who had lost his wife, child, parents, and several siblings. He survived the Warsaw ghetto and the Falenti labor camp, where he was violently abused and from which he then escaped. He hid with a farmer in a pigsty in a coffin-size pit covered with pig dung in which he could neither move nor turn around and where he had to urinate and defecate. He was only fed every few days. He became too weak to sit up unassisted; he lay there for eighteen months, frequently in terror of the SS contingent coming through with trained police dogs. Only the pig dung piled over his pit kept the dogs from sniffing him out. Years later, he had constant pain in his joints, dizzy spells during the day, difficulty concentrating, and nightmares from which he woke screaming at night. "I should rather have died" was the survivor's own self-assessment; "congenital idiocy" was the doctor's diagnosis.[31]

Meanwhile, and in addition, the doctors intent on rejecting not only specific individuals' claims but also the basic premise on which claims were based started recurrently to impute a lack of objectivity to those physicians who began to insist that it was definitively the persecution and camp experiences that caused psychological damages. The rejecting doctors accused the other doctors of "a really very extensive application of subjective interpretations" and suggested that sympathetic assessments were more the result of the predilection of the assessor than of the facts of any particular case. For example, singling out the work of the Walther von Baeyer psychiatric clinic in Heidelberg (these were careful, cautious sympathizers), one of the nonsympathetic physicians, Hermann Witter, sneered that the evaluations of survivors produced in Heidelberg had a "downright artistic design" but that "quite often we find the evidence for the reality-content of the proffered portrait entirely lacking."[32] Or as another rejecter, Helmuth Lotz, phrased it, sympathetic doctors were indiscriminately handing out a welter of pension-securing diagnoses "without convincing evidence."[33] Over and over, the sympathetic doctors were dismissed as having "remarkably little" insight or an "empirical basis" that was "really rather thin,"[34] or they were derided for having a "naive psychological approach."[35] It was "unfortunate" that sympathetic doctors let "affective attitudes" intrude on their judgment; this made a "scientific discussion of the issues almost impossible."[36]

Most fundamentally, the very idea of granting a pension for any "neurosis" was declared by *the* lead researcher on neuroses in West Germany, Ernst Kretschmer, to be "scientifically insupportable [*wissenschaftlich unhaltbar*]." It was precisely the possibility of a pension that prevented people from recovering their health, Kretschmer averred, citing studies on shell shock from the 1920s. The official government publication to orient physicians on reparations for the victims of National Socialism, Hermann Ammermüller and Hans Wilden's *Gesundheitliche Schäden in der Wiedergutmachung* (Health damages in reparation), expressly promoted the Kretschmer position. If any pensions were granted, it would mean "breeding neuroses in a grand style, rather than healing them," Kretschmer declared, and the government publication reiterated. The whole dynamic driving most neuroses, Kretschmer commented, had nothing to do with past experiences but rather with future hopes (for money) or with a "hypochondriacal" inability to master one's present. Neuroses *could* emerge either from "familial conflicts or inner problems of character" but *not* from later external events.[37] Another official government publication by Gustav Bodechtel and three coauthors in 1960 declared, "Only on the ground of a particular psychic and somatic personality structure can damaging experiences lead to manifest illnesses. *The actual experience, as dramatic as it may seem, can thus not be considered to have any causational importance.*" In fact, to the extent that "experience" could be considered relevant at all, the authors felt that the "emotional climate" in the first year of life—even if no longer accessible to the claimant's conscious memory—should be included for consideration.[38]

The rejecters also repeatedly demanded evidence of what they called "bridge symptoms."[39] The time lag notable between liberation from the camps and the emergence of psychological distress was seen as suspicious—read as yet another sign that the survivors were motivated by the hope of financial gain. (Nowadays, a latency period between experience and symptoms is seen as one of the typical signs of post-traumatic stress; at the time, however, sympathetic experts were repeatedly put on the defensive to explain the phenomenon.)

Finally, there was the peculiar way in which Freudian psychoanalysis appeared and disappeared in rejecters' texts. Sometimes the reference was coded, as when a rejecter text simply flatly announced that "classical psychoanalysis" also had no answers when it came to the question of the relationships between external experiences and emotional damage.[40] Sometimes the slap was more explicit—and it is important to note here that the Nazis had continually both denigrated Sigmund Freud in antisemitic terms *and* simultaneously appropriated many of his ideas as their own.[41] This double move of both denigrating and (mis-)appropriating Freud continued into the postwar era and showed up particularly in debates over whether the simulation of symptoms was "conscious" or "unconscious" (here many rejecters, like Bodechtel and his coauthors, proposed that perhaps survivors were not aware that they were motivated by pensions, that the display of symptoms might "frequently" be the result of "largely unconsciously unfolding processes").[42] The double move showed up even more clearly in disputes over whether childhood experiences were more significant for character development than whatever persecutions and imprisonments had occurred later.[43]

Summarizing and protesting this state of affairs, the Israeli analyst Hillel Klein in 1983 commented in anguish on the contradictory and punitive uses of Freudianism to reject survivors:

> I am ashamed to read the evaluations by my psychiatric colleagues in Germany. They use psychoanalysis to conclude in one case: "This child was only two years old; how could he experience persecution!" while in another case maintaining, "The boy was already thirteen years old and had lived with his parents, so he had experienced the so-called warmth of the family nest." These paradoxes in the name of Freud and psychoanalysis are still perpetrated by reputable professors in Germany. I speak in anger, because I believe that many of my colleagues, with their obsessive tendencies, unconsciously identify with the aggressor.[44]

The battle between the two sides got personal, and "objectivity"—especially the relationship between evidence and explanation—became the key point of contention. Rejecters saw to it that doctors considered too sympathetic were denied the right to evaluate survivors. And sympathetic doctors in the United States, West Germany, and Israel censored themselves and deliberately approved fewer claims for pensions than they thought were medically warranted, so as to retain the right to produce evaluations at all.[45] How did the tables finally turn?

THE MURDER OF HOW MANY OF ONE'S CHILDREN?

Already in the 1940s, during and after the war, a number of survivor-professionals and soon thereafter a number of other physicians in numerous countries (including notably France, Poland, the Netherlands, and Norway) had begun to publish on the topic of psychological damage due to experiences of persecution and imprisonment. International conferences of medical specialists working on health damages from persecution and internment were held in Paris and Copenhagen in 1954 and in Brussels in 1955. But it was not until the 1956 law went into effect and claims began to be denied that physicians who were convinced of the reality of post-camp psychological damage needed not just to counter the contentions of the rejecters but also to make fuller sense of their own findings.

Among the issues sympathizers grappled with was the purported comparability between death camp experiences and those of prisoners of war or victims of bombings or expulsions. Thus an argument about the uniqueness of what we now call the Holocaust began to take shape. Hans Strauss, an émigré psychiatrist who was initially a sympathizer and later became predominantly a rejecter (making him a favorite with German authorities and reviled by some U.S. peers), emphasized already in 1957 "the singularity" (*das Eigenartige*) in the chronic depressions displayed by the victims of Nazi persecution and rejected the comparisons with victims of industrial accidents and wars. He subsequently referred to the concentration and death camps as "a psychiatric mass experiment, the like of which should never have been made and will, we hope, never be made again."[46] The widely respected Munich-based psychiatrist Kurt Kolle, one of the most remarkable German sympathizing doctors, opened his 1958 essay on the subject with the words: "The topic is new, there is no precedent." He went on to observe that "the fate of the Jews of Central Europe can in no way be compared with accidents that happen to people . . .

[or] to injuries sustained in military service." Even those who were politically or religiously persecuted at least had the opportunity and choice to change their views and adapt to the regime, he noted. Those who were racially persecuted had not the slightest chance. Moreover, he continued, "The Jewish people knew, or suspected, when they were deported and imprisoned, that they were slated for liquidation." After examining over 200 survivors, 155 of them Jews (the others were political prisoners or Roma), Kolle found a predominance of "chronic depressive conditions" and "nervous disturbances" that "substantively diminish the ability to be self-supporting." He endorsed the concept of "concentration camp syndrome" that had begun to be developed in other nations and that, he suggested, was especially notable in individuals who were the sole survivors in once-large families.[47] Another sympathizer, the Mainz-based psychiatrist Ernst Kluge, emphasized key elements of the concentration and death camp experience: the utter guiltlessness of Jews (as opposed to political prisoners who had chosen to resist), the complete powerlessness and continual vulnerability to the most primitive cruelty and sadism, the arbitrariness, the inversion of values in the camps, and the "diabolization" of the community caused by privileging some prisoners over others and making them co-responsible for the suffering of their fellows.[48] Others emphasized the shattering loss of loved ones and the guilt of surviving not just while others died but also at the cost of constant humiliation and degradation.[49] In addition, sympathizers took on directly the prevalent rejecter argument that if someone could not recover, they must have had preexisting problems. "Can one really expect of every person who becomes a victim of racial insanity that he gets over it with equanimity?" Kolle asked rhetorically.[50]

Sympathizing doctors also grappled with the complexity of the evidence they encountered. There was a bewildering variety of syndromes and symptoms, and every attempt to systematize (for example, by age at onset of persecution, or by the particularities of the camp, or by the kinds of violence encountered) only confused things more. Certainly the type of person one had been before *did* shape how one managed the camp experiences. And indisputably the conditions of post-camp life mattered as well. Was there a spouse, were there family members with whom to reunite, or was there a new love? Was there meaningful work and social respect? Some survivors had trouble adjusting in a country (whether Palestine/Israel, the United States, or any number of other nations) where they did not initially speak the language or were unable to gain a foothold. Meanwhile, how indeed could the (manifestly common) time lag in the emergence of symptoms be explained? (Was the interlude in the displaced persons camps an ongoing difficult phase, and that explained why survivors kept their agonies repressed, only to have them surface later, when things seemed to have gotten better? Or had survivors actually been "spoiled" in the DP camps—as one doctor suggested—and this, not the death camps, was the source of their later difficulties in mastering the ordinary challenges of daily life?)[51] Why did some survivors—maybe as many as three-quarters all told—seem able to build up some kind of post-camp life, sometimes even a quite successful one, and show no particular signs of debilitating psychological damage, while others were completely crushed?[52] Because sympathizing doctors were acutely aware that mainstream medical teaching in Germany, since before Nazism, had emphasized that lasting, as opposed to short-term and reparable, psychological damage after a traumatic experience could only be explained by organic somatic damage, such as a blow to the head or long-term malnutrition, some of them deliberately stressed whatever somatic findings they could uncover.[53] Indeed, they themselves had trained in this framework and were thus themselves at times hard put to explain how psychological problems could last even if there were no somatic findings. This, in turn, made them even more vulnerable to being accused by the rejecters of exaggeration, speculation, and inconsistency.[54]

There were courageous sympathizers on both sides of the Atlantic. In addition to Kurt Kolle, one of the most important German defenders of the survivors was the young physician Ulrich Venzlaff, who had been mentored by Gottfried Ewald, the sole psychiatrist in the Third Reich to openly oppose the murder of people with disabilities. Venzlaff developed the concept of "experience-reactive personality change" (*erlebnisreaktiver Persönlichkeitswandel*) to capture the causal link in the diagnostic category. In an early and much-cited sympathetic evaluation, he cleverly and strategically praised aspects of the rejecters' doctrine, only then to go on to undermine it. His focus was to try to find language that conveyed the "permanent deformation" (*Dauerverbiegung*) of the psyche caused by intense trauma.[55] A signally relevant figure in the United States was the New York-based psychoanalyst William G. Niederland, who worked tirelessly, in hundreds of sympathetic evaluations and in dozens of scholarly essays and media interviews, to achieve reversals of rejections. Among his many contributions were the development and explication of the concept of survivor guilt—a profoundly contested but, as it would turn out, a strategically important topic—and the idea of hypermnesia—heightened powers of memory, especially vivid intrusive memories, typically under abnormal conditions, such as trauma.[56] But one of the biggest contributions he made was to call attention to the point that life in hiding, often under sub-animal conditions and in constant terror of discovery, could be *as* damaging to mental health as life in the concentration and death camps. Also important was his insistence that the earlier experiences of persecution in one's hometown—perhaps especially for children being mocked, beaten, and excluded from their former circle of peers—needed to be taken into account as well.

Notably, moral outrage was not the main tack taken by the most successful sympathizers. Instead, the far more effective strategy was to combine fulsome praise for some small aspect of a prominent rejecter's insight—Niederland and Venzlaff both, for instance, praised Ernst Kretschmer on minor points—only then to go on to declare that, alas, the rejecters were sadly behind the times. They were simply not up to speed on the latest scientific findings.[57]

Perhaps the most searingly articulate critique of the rejecters, however, came from Kurt Eissler, an émigré psychoanalyst in New York who later became director of the Freud Archives. At that time, Eissler was often sought out, like Niederland, as a sympathizer who could provide a second (or third or fourth) opinion in disputed cases. Eissler dismantled the rejecters' strategies piece by piece in two essays, the first in German in 1963 (with the provocative title summing up his scathing critique of the rejecter position: "The murder of how many of one's children must one be able to survive asymptomatically to be deemed to have a normal constitution?") and a subsequent essay published in English in 1967 in the *American Journal of Psychiatry* and titled simply "Perverted Psychiatry?" Among other things, he forcefully accused the *rejecters* of lack of objectivity. In other words, he used their own weapons against them.

The emotional distance toward the patient that rejecters demanded, Eissler said, was not true objectivity in this unprecedented situation. The incapacity to feel one's way into the novelty and grotesquerie of what the Nazis had done demonstrated, in Eissler's view, a "defect" of objectivity. "I am here arguing that an adequate reaction when one is listening [to descriptions of the camp experiences] is to have the reaction: This is unbearable." Eissler was not asking doctors or judges to feel pity. Rather, he reflected on how any one of those professional men would *himself* react if he were arrested, put into prisoners' garb, forced to do heavy labor in miserable weather and on a near-starvation diet, had his children murdered, been hunted by dogs, threatened with being shot, kicked in the head, and abused so badly that his face carried permanently disfiguring scars—after three years of this, would he really be so stoic and able to resume his daily life? As Eissler concluded with deadpan fury in 1963: "It remains a mystery how such a profound malfunction of the ability to identify can emerge among educated intellectuals." It was the rejecters, he said, who had an "emotional conflict" when they were conducting evaluations. The idea that a psyche, a soul, is not autonomous and impervious, that it can in fact be damaged, indeed damaged forever, by external experiences: *This* realization, Eissler proposed, must awaken strong fears.[58] In short, Eissler began to theorize the issue of bias within countertransference—what the evaluators were bringing to their encounters with survivors.[59] Critical self-reflection, in his view, was essential to objectivity. But he was also unapologetically insisting that traumatic events could in fact cause lasting damage to the mind; there need not be measurable damage to the body.

Eissler had his own theories about the regression to primitive, pre-civilized "archaic" emotions of contempt for the weak and suffering that Nazism had encouraged and that he found persisted after 1945. Striving to sort out what about the crushed survivors of this particular catastrophe seemed to destabilize the evaluators, Eissler noted that contempt for the weak had complex roots and appeared connected, he submitted, "with the whole problem of sadomasochism." A tragic hero, no matter how narcissistic or criminal, was held in awe, and his punishment seemed reasonable. By contrast, the survivor, broken and not vengeful, with no crime to expiate, was denied "the top of that hierarchical pyramid to which Christ has elevated the humiliated and the suffering." Eissler went on to imagine that the hostile evaluators were actually deeply afraid, seeing a survivor, that they themselves, had they been in the camps, might well have reacted to their oppressors with weakness and groveling. By no means granting himself greater virtue, Eissler also reflected that the discomfiture in the face of humiliated people was "something of a universal reaction still very much alive in almost all of us." Nonetheless, his point was that anyone not critically self-aware and able to "control this archaic feeling" should recuse himself, or simply be excluded by the authorities, from conducting evaluations.[60] Unlike some other sympathizers, whose texts were filled with defensiveness—itself an indication of the imbalance of power at that time within postwar Germany between rejecters and sympathizers, Eissler went on the offensive:

> Everyone should have only one purpose in this matter: to assist in relieving the sufferings of the victims of persecution. It thus stands to reason that if anyone's personal conviction could in any way make such relieving impossible, he should silently step aside and let those take over the function of "experts" whose convictions will at least augment the chance that that suffering will be assuaged.[61]

Although Eissler's plea for the rejecters to be excluded was not accepted—unsympathetic evaluators continued their work well through the 1970s and in some cases beyond—what did happen was that the international power balance shifted. One early result of sustained pressure from the Conference on Jewish Material Claims against Germany as well as other international organizations came with a law change in 1965 in which the concept of a "concentration camp presumption" was introduced. Thenceforth, having spent one year in a camp was considered adequate evidence that there must be a link between symptoms and experience. Although rejecters found imaginative ways to get around this as well—for example by minimizing the assessed percentage of reduction in earning capacity—the law change simplified the claims process considerably.

Just as important were the changing international terms of debate among medical professionals. Only a handful of leading psychiatrists had adapted by the late 1960s. But gradually, though in many cases too late for the survivors, the climate of medical opinion shifted. This was due not least to the ongoing international conferences on survivors' health problems held in various European cities, conferences at which the German rejecters were increasingly shamed and countered. In this changed climate, courts within West Germany also increasingly reversed the initial decisions on appeal. But one of the most important dynamics involved what can only be called the "Americanization" of the debate from the late 1960s on—inextricable from the wider rise of, and indeed a major contributing factor to, Holocaust consciousness in the United States.

Especially significant were the series of conferences in Detroit organized by Niederland together with his fellow psychiatrist Henry Krystal beginning in 1963 and with results published in 1968 and 1971. The sympathetic German physician Ulrich Venzlaff was an important presence at these conferences (and able to relay American expert trends back to Germany). Additionally, the meetings brought together psychiatrists who did not just diagnose survivors but also provided therapy to them—a hugely significant topic unto itself.[62] Notably as well, the Detroit conferences brought in Robert Jay Lifton, who was to become one of the key linking figures in the subsequent development, in the course of the 1970s, of growing cooperation between experts working with Holocaust survivors (among them Niederland and Krystal) and those working with antiwar Vietnam veterans in formulating the concept of PTSD that entered the DSM-III in 1980.[63]

Ultimately, it took Vietnam to bring the Holocaust fully into focus.[64] As manifestly different as the cases of soldiers and survivors were, the incontrovertible fact was that the growing public discussion surrounding Vietnam veterans and the pressure of antiwar groups helped greatly to push PTSD into the DSM, with absolutely crucial positive results for shifting mainstream medical opinion internationally. Especially striking, among the dozens of examples by which the linkage was established as medical and popular common sense, was an essay in the *New York Post* in 1972 carrying the banner headline "Auschwitz & Viet:—The Survivors." Niederland and Lifton were both quoted under the subhead "Both Groups Feel Guilt."[65] Vietnam was also especially important for the perpetually nagging issue of the time lag. This delay that had so stumped sympathetic physicians and had given rejecters countless opportunities for mockery of survivors and their advocates was suddenly understood to be not only pervasive but also a key characteristic feature of human response in the aftermath of encounters with severely distressing events.[66] In sum, and to put the overall point another way: Initially the battle over reparations for survivors had forced advocates for survivors to articulate an early case for the uniqueness of the Holocaust, and the utter noncomparability of racial persecutions and concentration and death camp experiences with the experiences of soldiers or even of civilians during wartime. Yet, by a twist of historical fate, it later took the catastrophic decline in the United States moral authority internationally due to the war in Vietnam and the rise of a passionate antiwar movement to bring not just soldiers' but also survivors' traumas into Americans' public consciousness and into official medical nomenclature and professional policy. In this particular crucial strategic instance—and no matter how problematic the impulse to compare would also remain—the new emphasis on comparison and not just uniqueness provided an incomparable opportunity for an advance in moral, medical, and legal thinking.

While there was substantial improvement in the handling of survivors' cases in the aftermath of the entry of PTSD into the DSM, the subsequent gradual ascent of PTSD as a globally recognized concept did not by any means resolve the problems of evidence and interpretation surrounding trauma. PTSD specifically and the notion of trauma more generally remained highly unstable and often debated—an area of medicine in which subjective opinion and political climate continue to be extraordinarily relevant, and often in contradictory ways. The idea that, in the case of survivors, objectivity might be "obscene" or "perverse" comes from Martin Leonhardt, a German psychiatrist who in 2002 wrote remarkable reflections on the double binds in which non-Jewish Germans can find themselves in trying to evaluate Holocaust survivors, including the guilt that a properly sensitized German feels (but also the resentment at that guilt). Leonhardt took it as self-evident that objectivity in the face of massive suffering could simply be obscene.[67] But another argument is worth considering, one which builds on the work of Kurt Eissler. That argument is that, of course, no one was completely objective, all the experts had countertransferential issues (including overidentification with the victims in the case of some sympathizers).[68] Yet the science moved much further toward something resembling the inevitably elusive ideal of objectivity precisely at the moment when (due to political pressure from outside and impassioned arguments inside the profession) it became a consensus that, in the face of great horror, minds can be damaged as well as bodies, and there need be neither a preexisting vulnerability nor a measurable somatic sign. There was by this time no question that the science predominating before the sympathizing doctors got involved was in many ways transparently wrong. In addition, it was hugely salutary—really an enormous breakthrough—that the bias on the rejecters' side was articulated.

Nonetheless, even as PTSD is identified in, tragically, ever more locations—among victims of genocides and ethnic cleansings, wars, and natural disasters; among victims of child abuse and sexual violence; and among our own veterans of the recent wars in Iraq and Afghanistan—the category remains unstable. Its all too frequent inflationary use, its commercial implications (due not least to the proliferation of purported pharmaceutical remedies), and its implications for international development relief and international relations still need to be vigorously debated.[69] In the cross-disciplinary and continually morphing field of trauma studies, which has boomed since the early 1990s, moreover, a recent trend has been to be more skeptical of, even cuttingly sarcastic about, trauma's growing pervasiveness as an analytic and diagnostic category. Thoughtful scholars are especially worried about the potentially patronizing if not even damaging descent of well-meaning experts as well as nonexperts armed with PTSD symptom checklists into disaster zones of all types.[70] The challenge has been to remain attuned to the very real agonies experienced by war veterans and survivors of catastrophes in a context in which the idea of trauma is daily both asserted and questioned.[71]

Meanwhile, not even all experts on Holocaust trauma welcomed the rise of PTSD. Some survivors have objected to the notion of survivor guilt in particular, disclaiming any such feeling; others find the expectation that survival needs to be processed in the register of the psychological in itself an offense and absurdity.[72] Jack Terry, a child survivor of the Flossenbürg concentration camp in Germany and later a New York-based psychoanalyst, was already in 1984 contemptuous of what he identified as the intellectual sloppiness of his therapist colleagues. "In the case of the Holocaust . . . even usually reputable psychoanalysts who have distinguished themselves in other areas of psychoanalysis have failed to be even minimally objective or 'scientific.' To be more specific, when a survivor comes for treatment, the 'syndrome' is presumed and often insisted upon." Terry—understanding full well that the reparations debacle was the cause of his colleagues' frequent insistence on exterior factors such as the experiences of persecution and imprisonment as the primary or sole cause for mental health problems—took a more classically psychoanalytic stance. His position was (as a study group of the New York Psychoanalytic Society and Institute had formulated it in 1974): "No external event could be clearly independent of prior experience in the process of producing a psychic illness." Picking up on Kurt Eissler's insight into the contempt felt by many people toward survivors, Terry took the stance that the tendency to "syndromize" survivors was itself a sign of contempt, and one that robbed each survivor of his or her individuality and the specificity of his or her experiences. Terry gave multiple examples of survivors who, in the course of psychoanalysis with him, ended up discovering that the elements of their experience singled out for traumatic value were not at all necessarily the experiences in the camps, but often earlier experiences in which, for instance, a father had been revealed to be impotent in the face of Nazi aggression. In another case, the source of a patient's trouble lay in repressed conflicts with and rage at the father over having abandoned the child in the midst of the cataclysm. In still other cases, survivors were disappointed about how they were received by the world into which they returned. Terry speculated that the eagerness to diagnose trauma in survivors should perhaps be read as a sign of the guilt of psychiatrists for themselves for having escaped Germany or Austria before the deportations began.[73] This assessment is certainly harsh, but it helps us understand why there continues to be no consensus on the meaning of the story. The issues raised by traumatic experiences remain shrouded in ambiguity and pressingly painful.

NOTES

Immense gratitude goes to the editors of this volume, as well as to Omer Bartov, Brad Prager, Julie Skurski, Gary Wilder, Mohamad Junaid, Hank Greenspan, Adam Teller, and Peggy Kahn for careful critical readings of earlier drafts—and to Lawrence Langer, Robert Krell, and Na'ama Shik for important conversations. Warm thanks to Peter Gordon for inviting me to give the first iteration of this essay at Harvard University and for choosing the title. This essay appeared in slightly longer form in *Catastrophes: A History and Theory of an Operative Concept*, edited by Nitzan Lebovic and Andreas Killen (Boston: De Gruyter, 2014), 128–55.

1. The useful coinage "invention-discovery" (to describe how a category of knowledge comes to acquire density, legitimacy, and staying power over time) comes from Bruno Latour, *We Have Never Been Modern* (Cambridge, Mass.: Harvard University Press, 1993), 5.

2. So little known is this episode in the evolution of what became PTSD outside of Holocaust studies circles that in his critique of the now-extensive trauma industry, psychiatrist-historian Derek Summerfield singles

out Holocaust survivors as *the* example of a group who recovered remarkably well without the benefit of a concept of post-traumatic stress. He sees Vietnam-era concern with returning soldiers' troubles as the beginning of the (in his view deeply problematic) dissemination of the concept. See Derek Summerfield, "A Critique of Seven Assumptions behind Psychological Trauma Programmes in War-Affected Areas," *Social Science and Medicine* 48, 10 (1999): 1449–62; and Derek Summerfield, "The Invention of Post-Traumatic Stress Disorder and the Social Usefulness of a Psychiatric Category," *British Medical Journal* 322, 7278 (January 13, 2001): 95–98.

3. On the evolution of ideas about trauma from late nineteenth-century industrial accidents and World War I shell shock to PTSD, see especially: Allan Young, *The Harmony of Illusions: Inventing Post-Traumatic Stress Disorder* (Princeton, N.J.: Princeton University Press, 1997); Paul Lerner and Mark S. Micale, eds., *Traumatic Pasts: History, Psychiatry, and Trauma in the Modern Age* (Cambridge: Cambridge University Press, 2001); Ben Shephard, *A War of Nerves: Soldiers and Psychiatrists in the Twentieth Century* (Cambridge, Mass.: Harvard University Press, 2003); Edgar Jones and Simon Wessely, *Shell Shock to PTSD: Military Psychiatry from 1900 to the Gulf War* (New York: Psychology Press, 2006); and Didier Fassin and Richard Rechtmann, *The Empire of Trauma: An Inquiry into the Condition of Victimhood* (Princeton, N.J.: Princeton University Press, 2009). For significant studies centered on Holocaust trauma and the battle over reparations for health damages, see the valuable bibliography in Robert Krell and Marc I. Sherman, *eds., Medical and Psychological Effects of Concentration Camps on Holocaust Survivors* (New Brunswick, N.J.: Transaction, 1997), as well as Ruth Leys, *From Guilt to Shame: Auschwitz and After* (Princeton, N.J.: Princeton University Press, 2007); Svenja Goltermann, *Die Gesellschaft der Überlebenden: Deutsche Kriegsheimkehrer und ihre Gewalterfahrungen im Zweiten Weltkrieg* [The society of survivors: German war returnees and their experiences of violence during the Second World War] (Munich, Ger.: Deutsche, 2009); Norbert Frei, José Brunner, and Constantin Goschler, eds., *Die Praxis der Wiedergutmachung: Geschichte, Erfahrung und Wirkung in Deutschland und Israel* [The practice of reparation: History, experience, and effect in Germany and Israel] (Göttingen, Ger.: Wallstein, 2009); and the foundational work, Christian Pross, *Paying for the Past: The Struggle over Reparations for Surviving Victims of the Nazi Terror, trans. Belinda Cooper* (Baltimore, Md.: Johns Hopkins University Press, 1998).

4. See the extremely informative overview in Goltermann, *Die Gesellschaft der Überlebenden*, especially Part II: "Die Produktion des psychiatrischen Wissens [The production of psychiatric knowledge]."

5. See Frank Biess, Homecomings: Returning POWs and the Legacies

of Defeat in Postwar Germany (Princeton, N.J.: Princeton University Press, 2006); and Goltermann, *Die Gesellschaft der Überlebenden.*

6. See the case of Herr W. in Pross, *Paying for the Past,* 124–25. As survivor, displaced persons leader, and historian Samuel Gringauz summarized the trends retrospectively: "The sufferings are [in the rejecting doctors' assessments] caused by constitutional factors, caused by fate, caused by old age, caused by environment, caused by character, caused by simulation, caused by fraudulence, caused by marital conflicts, caused by the milkman, caused-by-anything-you-want, just not caused by the inferno, just not caused by hell. As far as is possible, the human- and soul-murdering inferno of German history should be denied." Samuel Gringauz, "Psychische Schäden und Besonderheiten des Verfahrens: Brückensymptome und spätere Anmeldungen [Psychological damage and special features of the process: Bridge symptoms and later applications]," *Die Wiedergutmachung* [Reparations] 256 (July 21, 1967): 1.

7. Indeed, one West German government-sponsored guidebook for evaluating psychiatrists contended that therapy could only be helpful in cases where no pension had been given, because the granting of the pension itself prevented healing. See Gustav Bodechtel, Fred Dubitscher, Friedrich Panse, and Gustav Störring, introduction to *Die "Neurose": Ihre Versorgungs- und Sozialmedizinische Beurteilung* ["Neurosis": Its assessment in healthcare and social medicine (Bonn, Ger.: Bundesminister für Arbeit und Sozialordnung, 1960), 6.

8. Fritz Schäffer quoted in Frank Stern, *Im Anfang war Auschwitz: Antisemitismus und Philosemitismus im deutschen Nachkrieg* [In the beginning was Auschwitz: Antisemitism and philosemitism in the German postwar] (Gerlingen, Ger.: Bleicher, 1991), 336.

9. Ernst Féaux de la Croix and Helmut Rumpf, *Der Werdegang des Entschädigungsrechts unter national- und völkerrechtlichem und politologischem Aspekt* [The history of the compensation law in national and international legal and political perspective] (Munich, Ger.: Beck, 1985), 10–11, 151–52, 158–59.

10. Schäffer's pronouncement summarized in "Der neue Tatbestand [The new event]," *Der Spiegel,* January 29, 1958, 13.

11. See Frank Bajohr, "'Arisierung' in Hamburg; 'Schnäppchen aus Judenkisten' ["Aryanization" in Hamburg: "Bargains from Jews' crates"]," *Der Spiegel,* January 26, 1998, accessed August 28, 2013, http://www.spiegel.de/spiegel/print/d-7809630.html; Susanne Meinl and Jutta Zwilling, *Legalisierter Raub: Die Ausplünderung der Juden im Nationalsozialismus durch die Reichsfinanzverwaltung in Hessen* [Legalized robbery: The plundering of the Jews in Nazi Germany by the Reich Finance Administration in Hesse]

(Frankfurt am Main, Ger.: Campus, 2004); and Götz Aly, *Hitler's Beneficiaries: Plunder, Racial War, and the Nazi Welfare State* (New York: Holt, 2006).

12. See Schäffer, "Der neue Tatbestand," 13: "*Keine deutsche Stelle wage etwas dagegen zu unternehmen, aus Furcht, sie könne deswegen der Judenfeindlichkeit bezichtigt warden* [No German authority dare take action for fear that it could therefore be accused of antisemitism]."

13. Konrad Adenauer's comment reported in Kai von Jena, "Versöhnung mit Israel? Die Deutsch-Israelischen Verhandlungen bis zum Wiedergutmachungsabkommen von 1952" [Reconciliation with Israel? The German-Israeli negotiations up to the 1952 reparations agreement], *Vierteljahreshefte für Zeitgeschichte* [Quarterly Journal of Contemporary History] 34, 4 (1986): 470.

14. Letter quoted in Schäffer, "Der neue Tatbestand," 13.

15. Wolfgang See, letter to the editor of *Der Spiegel*, January 8, 1958, 9.

16. Otto Schmöger, letter to the editor of *Der Spiegel*, January 8, 1959, 9. See also another commentator: "Pressure produces counterpressure. The Jews should not imagine that the German *Volk* will pay 20 or 30 or 40 billion for damages for which Moses is responsible. [*Druck erzeugt Gegendruck. Die Juden sollen sich doch nicht einbilden, dass das deutsche Volk 20 oder 30 oder 40 Milliarden für Schäden zahlt, die Moses zu verantworten hat.*]" Wilhelm Müller, letter to the editor of *Der Spiegel*, February 12, 1958, 6.

17. Walter Armbrust, letter to the editor of *Der Spiegel*, February 12, 1958, 5 (this and a few other letters were reprinted as "pro-Jewish" in the New York-based German-language paper *Aufbau*).

18. Peter Krabiell, letter to the editor of *Der Spiegel*, February 12, 1958, 5.

19. Letter to the editor, *Der Spiegel*, January 29, 1958, 6–7.

20. For a perceptive explanation of the increase in everyday expressions of antisemitism two years after the war's end, an increase caused, however paradoxically, by Nazism's defeat (replete not just with cabaret jokes such as "The Jews are eating chocolate now. Only six million were gassed. Too bad!" but also with random streetcar conversations in which "A German woman, talking about Auschwitz with a Jewish woman, was reviled by fellow passengers: 'What do you care about that Jewish sow? What the Allies are doing to the Germans today is much worse than anything that ever happened in Auschwitz'"), see Samuel Gringauz, "Our New German Policy and the DP's," *Commentary* 6 (June 1948): 508–14. The essay includes mention of a May 1947 poll of the German population in which 61 percent of those questioned "openly avowed anti-Semitism." See, as well, the study of attitudes in the early 1950s undertaken by Friedrich Pollock and Theodor Adorno, published in German in 1955, and in English as Theodor W. Adorno, *Guilt*

and Defense: On the Legacies of National Socialism in Postwar Germany (Cambridge, Mass.: Harvard University Press, 2010).

21. There was far more opportunity for potential false claims around the category of "restriction of freedom" (*Freiheitsbeschränkung*)—especially among claims made by non-German individuals living in flight or hiding in areas of German occupation during World War II—than there were around claims for damages to health, and the scandals around overly entrepreneurial lawyers more typically involved these. For example, see Schäffer, "Der neue Tatbestand," 14–16. Between 1956 and 1965, 922,879 claims involved restriction of freedom (of which 536,251 had been settled by 1965), and 485,488 involved damages to health, of which only 186,870 had been settled (and in turn just under half of which had been approved). See Pross, *Paying for the Past*, 212–14.

22. Jakob Diel, quoted in "Ich bin der Motor [I am the engine]," *Der Spiegel*, March 5, 1958.

23. Diel memorandum to his fellow Christian Democratic Union members quoted in Schäffer, "Der neue Tatbestand," 14.

24. The attacks on Jews seeking to reclaim their own property often got viciously *personal*—as though the individual Jews asking for reclamation of their own furniture or business were greedy and outrageous. See Mark Roseman, "'It Went On for Years and Years': Der Wiedergutmachungsantrag der Marianne Ellenbogen [The compensation request of Marianne Ellenbogen]," in Frei, Brunner, and Goschler, *Die Praxis der Wiedergutmachung*; and Atina Grossmann, "Family Files: Emotions and Stories of (Non-)Restitution," *German Historical Institute London Bulletin* 34, 1 (2012): 59–78. On the wider phenomenon of resentment and antisemitism over the outcome of the war (German defeat and partial Jewish survival and refusal to accept German theft without complaint), see as well Constantin Goschler, *Schuld und Schulden* [Debt and debt] (Göttingen, Ger.: Wallstein, 2005).

25. Among other things, the paper argued that "world Zionism is pushing for World World III." See "Hier die Beweise: Weltzionismus hetzt zum dritten Weltkrieg [Here the evidence: World Zionism rushes to a third world war]," *Die Anklage* 5 (January 1957): 2.

26. See Pross, *Paying for the Past*, 79. As late as 1975, the sympathizer doctor William Niederland was summarized as declaring that the problem was *not* in the law courts, the problem was with the other doctors. See Katharina Zimmer, "Ich hätte lieber sterben sollen: Viele ehemaligen KZ-Häftlinge leiden heute an Verfolgungsangst und Schuldgefühlen [I would rather have died: Many concentration camp prisoners today suffer from fear of persecution and feelings of guilt]," *Die Zeit* 44 (October 24, 1975): 54.

27. This case is discussed in Ulrich Venzlaff, "Erlebnishintergrund und

Dynamik seelischer Verfolgungsschäden [Experience background and dynamics of mental persecution damage]" in Helmut Paul and Hans-Joachim Herberg, *Psychische Spätschäden nach politischer Verfolgung* [Psychological late damage after political persecution], 2nd rev. ed. (Basel, Switz.: Karger, 1967), 157–73, here 171.

28. One of the evaluators in this latter case expressed his regret: "It is unfortunately not possible adequately to connect this faulty attitude, which lies in the realm of the voluntaristic, with the emotional burdens of racial persecution." See the discussion of the cases in Kurt R. Eissler, "Perverted Psychiatry?" *American Journal of Psychiatry* 123, 11 (May 1967): 1354–56. In the case of the woman labeled hysterical, see also his account of her evaluators in Kurt R. Eissler, "Die Ermordung von wievielen seiner Kinder muss ein Mensch symptomfrei ertragen können, um eine normale Konstitution zu haben? [The murder of how many of one's children must one be able to survive asymptomatically to be deemed to have a normal constitution?]," *Psyche* 17, 5 (1963): 276–77.

29. Case discussed in Eissler, "Die Ermordung," 269. See in sympathizing German psychiatrist Kurt Kolle's work a related case about sleep disturbances in a Jewish woman academic dismissed as simply "neurotic" rather than the result of trauma. Kurt Kolle, "Die Opfer der nationalsozialistischen Verfolgung in psychiatrischer Sicht [The victims of Nazi persecution in a psychiatric view]," *Der Nervenarzt* 29, 4 (1958): 149.

30. *Anlagebedingt* means "caused by constitutional factors"—it can either be translated as hereditary or as referring to something to which one is predisposed—in other words, the "anxiety neurosis" was caused by a prior instability endogenous to the individual, not by the external experiences in the camps, and thus also not amenable to the granting of a pension. This particular label was freely applied to people who had seen the murder of children, who had lived in near-unendurable conditions in hiding, or who had been subjected to beatings in camps. See especially the discussion of the label in Eissler, "Perverted Psychiatry?" 1354–56.

31. Case evaluated by Niederland and discussed in Zimmer, "Ich hätte lieber sterben sollen," 54.

32. Hermann Witter, "Erlebnisbedingte Schädigung durch Verfolgung [Experience-related damage through persecution]," *Der Nervenarzt* 33 (1962): 510. For insight into the von Baeyer clinic's work, see Walter von Baeyer, *Psychiatrie der Verfolgten; psychopathologische und gutachtliche Erfahrungen an Opfern der nationalsozialistischen Verfolgung und vergleichbarer Extrembelastungen* [Psychiatry of the persecuted: Psychopathological and clinical-evaluation experiences working with victims of Nazi persecution and similar situations of extreme stress] (Bern, Switz.: Springer, 1964).

33. Helmuth Lotz, "'Psychische Spätschäden nach politischer Verfol-

gung': Eine Stellungnahme zu dem Buch von H. Paul und H. J. Herberg [Psychic late damages after political persecution: A response to the book by H. Paul and H. J. Herberg]," *Rechtsprechung zum Wiedergutmachungsrecht* [Case law on the law of reparations] 15, 8–9 (1964): 351.

34. Lotz, "'Psychische Spätschäden,'" 350–51.

35. Rainer Luthe, "'Erlebnisreaktiver Persönlichkeitswandel' als Begriff der Begutachtung im Entschädigungsrecht ["Experience-reactive personality change" as a concept of review in compensation law]," *Monatsschrift für alle Gebiete nervenärztlicher Forschung und Praxis* [Monthly magazine for all areas of neurological research and practice] 39, 10 (1968), 465. Luthe was particularly obnoxious. In his essay—which was one extended attack on Ulrich Venzlaff's term "experience-reactive personality change" and which also harped on the puzzle of "the symptom-free interval or the paradoxical intensification of symptoms" (that is, the time lag between traumatic event and manifest illness)—he went so far as to suggest that suffering might ennoble and turn survivors "wise" and "holy" in the manner sought by some Eastern religions; he also suggested that it was the challenges of post-camp life and the comedown, that is, the felt discrepancy in social status between pre- and post-camp life, that was more difficult for survivors than whatever had occurred in the camps.

36. Witter, "Erlebnisbedingte Schädigung," 509.

37. Kretschmer quotations (as well as the fact of their inclusion in Hermann Ammermüller and Hans Wilden's *Gesundheitliche Schäden in der Wiedergutmachung* [Health damages in reparations]) can be found in Richard Dyck, "Die Neurosen in der Wiedergutmachung [The neuroses in reparations]," *Aufbau* 14 (March 7, 1958), 1. See the full text of the government book, Hermann Ammermüller and Hans Wilden, *Gesundheitliche Schäden in der Wiedergutmachung* (Stuttgart: Kohlhammer, 1953), 24–25. For a sample of Kretschmer's pre-Nazi-era views on "race and genius," see Ernst Kretschmer, "Genie und Rasse [Genius and race]" in Franz Weidenreich, ed., *Rasse und Geist* [Race and spirit] (Leipzig, Ger.: Johann Ambrosius Barth, 1932).

38. Bodechtel, Dubitscher, Panse, and Störring, introduction to *Die "Neurose,"* 4–5. Emphasis in the original.

39. For example, see Lotz, "Psychische Spätschäden," 349–50; and Luthe, "'Erlebnisreaktiver Persönlichkeitswandel,'" 465.

40. Luthe, "'Erlebnisreaktiver Persönlichkeitswandel,'" 465.

41. For a fuller discussion of this phenomenon, see Dagmar Herzog, *Sex after Fascism: Memory and Morality in Twentieth-Century Germany* (Princeton, N.J.: Princeton University Press, 2005), 22 and 277.

42. Bodechtel, Dubitscher, Panse, and Störring, introduction to *Die "Neurose,"* 6. Along related lines, Ammermüller and Wilden were also pleased

to quote Kretschmer invoking Freud for support on the idea that neuroses were a "flight into illness" and that there is such a thing as a "gain from illness [*Krankheitsgewinn*]." Ammermüller and Wilden, *Gesundheitliche Schäden in der Wiedergutmachung*, 24. An excellent analysis of the rejecters' (mis-)appropriations of Freud is in Wolfgang Lederer, "Persecution and Compensation: Theoretical and Practical Implications of the 'Persecution Syndrome,'" *Archives of General Psychiatry* 12, 5 (May 1965): 467.

43. The double-edged tone is evident in Christoph Jannasch, a rejecting expert, who opined snarkily in 1973 that "early childhood is decisive for the emergence of psychoneurotic disorders, not only in the primitive Freudian view. The first six years of life lay the crucial groundwork . . . The groundwork for an anxiety-neurotic structure, with all its consequences, is laid in the early years of life." See Pross, *Paying for the Past*, 125.

44. Hillel Klein, "Wiedergutmachung—Ein Akt der Retraumatisierung [Reparations—an act of repeated trauma]" in *Die Bundesrepublik Deutschland und die Opfer des Nationalsozialismus: Tagung vom 25.–27. November 1983 in Bad Boll* [The Federal Republic of Germany and the victims of Nazism: Meeting on November 25–27, 1983, in Bad Boll] (Bad Boll: Evangelische Akademie, 1984), 51–52. On Klein, see Carl Nedelmann, "No reconciliation, but self-searching in the sense of rapprochement," *International Journal of Psychoanalysis* 86, 4 (2005): 1133–42.

45. See on these points Martin Leonhardt, "Die Begutachtung von Holocaust-Überlebenden: Ein Exkurs zu den Sollbruchstellen in der Identität des forensischen Psychiaters [The assessment of Holocaust survivors: An excursion to the breaking point in the identity of the forensic psychiatrist]," *Forensische Psychiatrie und Psychotherapie* [Forensic psychiatry and psychotherapy] 3 (2002), 67; as well as Pross, *Paying for the Past*, 76–77 and 99.

46. Hans Strauss, "Besonderheiten der nichtpsychotischen seelischen Störungen [Peculiarities of nonpsychotic mental disorders]," *Der Nervenarzt* [The neurologist] 28 (1957), 344; and Hans Strauss, "Psychiatric Disturbances in Victims of Racial Persecution," in Canadian Psychiatric Association, *Proceedings of the Third World Congress of Psychiatry* (Montreal, Canada: University of Toronto Press, 1961), 1207. For a sense of the frequency with which a sympathetic doctor like William Niederland needed explicitly to counter Strauss's initial rejecting evaluations, see the case records in the William G. Niederland Collection 1903–1989, Leo Baeck Institute, New York. For the complaints about Strauss discussed in the New York-based journal *Aufbau* and expressed by sympathetic doctors in an official petition and by distressed survivors in a letter to the West German consulate general, see Pross, *Paying for the Past*, 100–101, as well as the William G. Niederland Collection in the Library of Congress, Washington, D.C.

47. Kolle, "Die Opfer der nationalsozialistischen Verfolgung," 148 and 152–53.

48. Ernst Kluge, "Über die Folgen schwerer Haftzeiten [About the severity of periods of detention]," *Der Nervenarzt* [The Neurologist] 29 (1958): 462–65.

49. Eissler makes these points in 1963, as he also argues directly that "concentration camp trauma is something historically new." Eissler, "Die Ermordung," 286.

50. Kolle, "Die Opfer der nationalsozialistischen Verfolgung," 153–54.

51. Lotz, "'Psychische Spätschäden,'" 350.

52. The 75 percent figure comes from Strauss, "Psychiatric Disturbances"; Strauss means it positively. The fact that these good recovery rates confuse the arguments sympathizers want to make is raised both by Kluge, "Über die Folgen," 462; and by von Baeyer, *Psychiatrie der Verfolgten*, vi.

53. See Miriam Rieck and Gali Eshet, "Die Bürden der Experten: Gespräche mit deutschen und israelischen Psychiatern über ihre Rolle als Gutachter in Entschädigungsverfahren [The burdens of experts: Interviews with German and Israeli psychiatrists about their role as experts in compensation proceedings]" in Frei, Brunner, and Goschler, *Die Praxis der Wiedergutmachung*.

54. For example, see Lotz, "'Psychische Spätschäden,'" 350.

55. Ulrich Venzlaff, "Erlebnisreaktiver Persönlichkeitswandel: Fiktion oder Wirklichkeit? [Experience-reactive personality change: Fiction or reality?]," *Der Nervenarzt* 40 (1969): 539–41.

56. Wolfgang Saxon, "Dr. William G. Niederland, 88; Formulated 'Survivor Syndrome,'" *New York Times*, August 5, 1993, accessed February 1, 2013, http://www.nytimes.com/1993/08/05/obituaries/dr-william-g-niederland-88-formulated-survivor-syndrome.html.

57. See Ulrich Venzlaff, *Die psychoreaktiven Störungen nach entschädigungspflichtigen Ereignissen: Die sogenannten Unfallneurosen* [The psychoreactive disorders following compensation-related occurrences: The so-called accident neuroses] (New York: Springer, 1958); and the many case records available in the William G. Niederland Collection 1903–1989, Leo Baeck Institute, New York.

58. Eissler, "Die Ermordung," 264–65, 286, 288, 291.

59. Nobody prior to Eissler had made these points. Consider the prehistory of countertransference theorizing from Freud through Donald Winnicott, Heinrich Racker, Lucia Tower, René Spitz, and Hans Loewald. See Donald W. Winnicott, "Hate in the Counter-Transference," *International Journal of Psycho-Analysis* 30, 2 (1949): 69–74; Heinrich Racker, "A Contribution to the Problem of Counter-Transference," *International Journal*

of Psycho-Analysis 34 (1953): 313–24; Lucia E. Tower, "Countertransference," *Journal of the American Psychoanalytic Association* 4 (1956): 224–55; René Spitz, "Countertransference—Comments on Its Varying Role in the Analytic Situation," *Journal of the American Psychoanalytic Association* 4 (1956): 256–65; and Hans W. Loewald, "On the Therapeutic Action of Psycho-Analysis," *International Journal of Psycho-Analysis* 41 (1960): 16–33.

60. Eissler, "Perverted Psychiatry?" 1358.

61. Ibid., 1357–58.

62. For example, the Los Angeles-based German-heritage sympathizer psychoanalyst Klaus Hoppe, who had emigrated to the United States in the 1950s, was a key figure promoting the Eisslerian insights into contempt for the weak and the importance of attending to countertransference in all its complexities. See Klaus D. Hoppe, "Psychotherapy with Concentration Camp Survivors," in Henry Krystal, ed., *Massive Psychic Trauma* (New York: International Universities Press, 1968), 204–19. See also the subsequent conference volume: William G. Niederland and Henry Krystal, eds., *Psychic Traumatization: Aftereffects in Individuals and Communities* (New York: Little, Brown, 1971). The conference discussions make clear how deeply the sympathizers were still engaging with the arguments of rejecters; for example, they discussed the case of the woman who had a breakdown *after* she got her pension, because she felt she was being paid for the child she had let die while she survived—the example was brought up to prove the point that it could not have been the desire for a pension that caused her troubles. The discussions also reveal the sympathizers' initial difficulties in making sense of the frequent time lag between traumatic event and onset of symptoms, and the possibility that preexisting conditions might matter in how individuals coped with trauma. On the initially unacknowledged problems within therapeutic efforts, see also Yael Danieli, "Therapists' Difficulties in Treating Survivors of the Nazi Holocaust and Their Children," Ph.D. diss., New York University, 1981; and Yael Danieli, "Countertransference in the Treatment and Study of Nazi Holocaust Survivors and Their Children," *Victimology: An International Journal* 5, 2–4 (1981): 45–53.

63. Robert Jay Lifton was in Detroit to report on his work with survivors of the atomic blast at Hiroshima. But in the conversations, both formal and informal, he came to see parallels between diverse survivor experiences. Ran Zwigenberg interview with Lifton, June 9, 2011; see also Robert Jay Lifton, *Witness to an Extreme Century: A Memoir* (New York: Free Press, 2011), 184–91, 241, 395–96.

64. On this point, see also Rieck and Eshet, "Die Bürden," 459.

65. "Auschwitz & Viet:—The Survivors," *New York Post*, October 3, 1972, 26.

66. See Boyce Rensberger, "Delayed Trauma in Veterans Cited: Psychia-

trists Find Vietnam Produces Guilt and Shame," *New York Times*, May 3, 1972, 19. This was not just a matter of echoes, however, but also of concretely networking individuals. In addition to Lifton, a further essential figure in the cooperation between doctors like Niederland working with Holocaust survivors and those working with Vietnam veterans was Chaim Shatan, a psychiatrist who joined Lifton in "rap groups" of anti-Vietnam war veterans. See, for example, the gesture to "death camps" in his op-ed, "Post-Vietnam Syndrome," *New York Times*, May 6, 1972, 35. Finally, most important was Nancy Andreasen, the highly respected psychiatrist (and specialist on psychiatric complications from traumatic burn injuries) who had been charged by Robert Spitzer, the lead editor for DSM-III, to head the work group that ushered PTSD into the DSM in 1980. Andreasen was familiar with Niederland's writings and determined to include concentration and death camp survivors into a definition of post-traumatic stress that went beyond what some veterans' advocates had called "post-Vietnam syndrome." Personal communication from Nancy Andreasen, August 13, 2013. The 1976 draft memorandum by Andreasen to Robert Spitzer, Lyman Wynne, Chaim Shatan, Robert Lifton, Jack Smith, and Leonard Neff on "post-traumatic disorder" (private collection of Nancy Andreasen, University of Iowa) lists at the outset the range of traumatic experiences that could cause this disorder. They include rape, military combat trauma, natural disasters such as floods and earthquakes, accidents such as airplane crashes or large fires, and also, expressly, "mass catastrophes . . . of human origin (Hiroshima, torture, death camps)." See also Nancy C. Andreasen, "Posttraumatic Stress Disorder," in Harold I. Kaplan, Alfred M. Freedman, and Benjamin J. Sadock, eds., *Comprehensive Textbook of Psychiatry/III*, vol. 2 (Baltimore, Md.: Williams and Wilkins, 1980), 1517–25.

67. See Leonhardt, "Die Begutachtung," 66; and the invocation of Leonhardt's point in Miriam Rieck, "Medizinische und psychische Spätschäden von Holocaust-Überlebenden [Medical and psychological late damage in Holocaust survivors]" in W. E. Platz and V. Schneider, eds., *Todesurteil per Meldebogen: Ärztlicher Krankenmord im NS-Staat: Beiträge zur Aktion T4* [Death sentences by registration form: Medical euthanasia and the Nazi regime, contributions to Action T4] (Berlin: Hentrich and Hentrich, 2006), 77. Noteworthy too is that even though Leonhardt's side, the sympathizer side, has largely won, as of 2002, he still acts defensive.

68. On the risk of overidentification, see Klaus D. Hoppe, "The Emotional Reactions of Psychiatrists when Confronting Survivors of Nazi Persecutions," in John A. Linden, ed., *Psychoanalytic Forum*, vol. 3 (New York: Science House, 1969), 187–211.

69. The most recent round of debate concerns the phenomenon of traumatic brain injury (TBI)—a phenomenon that is both terrifyingly real

(because the damage done to brains by improvised explosive devices are one of the distinctive features of the new postmodern wars) and simultaneously a problematic invention that serves the double function of promoting pharmaceuticals as a solution to the physical and psychological distress caused by participation in war *and* depoliticizes those wars and their consequences by decontextualizing the damage. See Matthew C. Gutmann and Catherine Lutz, "Becoming Monsters in Iraq," *Anthropology Now* 1, 1 (July 6, 2009): 12–20, accessed February 1, 2013, http://anthronow.com/articles/becoming-monsters-in-iraq-2; and David Philipps, *Lethal Warriors: When the New Band of Brothers Came Home—Uncovering the Tragic Reality of PTSD* (New York: Palgrave Macmillan, 2010).

70. See the sensitive historicizations of the category in Fassin and Rechtmann, *The Empire of Trauma*; Ethan Watters, *Crazy Like Us: The Globalization of the American Psyche* (New York: Free Press, 2010); and Summerfield, "A Critique of Seven Assumptions." Summerfield is primarily critical of how the concept of trauma medicalizes what is often actually economic and social distress, and also of how the concept neglects resilience and (in his view not just naively but often dangerously) assumes that "talking about it" helps.

71. See especially Jennifer Terry's ongoing book project—which includes attention to new forms of trauma, including sexual trauma—in the recent U.S. wars: *Attachments to War: Violence and the Production of Biomedical Knowledge in Twenty-First Century America.*

72. Personal communication from Lawrence Langer, Waltham, Mass., October 24, 2012. Along different but related lines, Auschwitz survivor and Boston-based psychoanalyst and advocate of psychoanalytic self-psychology Anna Ornstein has declared the entire debate over survivor syndrome as well as the creation of the category of PTSD "horrible." Personal communication from Anna Ornstein, Boca Raton, Fla., November 6, 2010. Her ardent commitment has been to identify the resources for resilience and recovery within survivors—often finding them in early familial relations pre-Holocaust—and she finds the preoccupation with lasting damage among her colleagues and the public at large to be both odious and empirically unsound. Anna Ornstein, "Survival and Recovery," *Psychoanalytic Inquiry* 5, 1 (1985): 99–130; Anna Ornstein, "Survival and Recovery: Psychoanalytic Reflections," *Harvard Review of Psychiatry* 9, 1 (2001): 13–22. See also the important book by transcultural trauma expert David Becker, *Die Erfindung des Traumas: Verflochtene Geschichten* [The invention of trauma: Entangled histories] (Giessen: Psychosozial-Verlag 2014); and the discussion of it in Dagmar Herzog, *Cold War Freud: Psychoanalysis in an Age of Catastrophes* (Cambridge: Cambridge University Press, 2017).

73. Jack Terry, "The Damaging Effects of the 'Survivor Syndrome,'" in Steven A. Luel and Paul Marcus, eds., *Psychoanalytic Reflections on the*

Holocaust: Selected Essays (New York: KTAV, 1984), 135, 138–40. See also "Gespräch mit Jack Terry: 'Die Zivilisation ist ein ganz dünner Firnis über der menschlichen Natur' [Conversation with Jack Terry: "Civilization is a very thin veneer on human nature"]," *BLZ [Die Bayerische Landeszentrale or Bavarian Regulatory Authority]-Report* (April 2003), accessed January 30, 2013, http://192.68.214.70/blz/report/04_03/1.html.

I. NEW CULTURAL APPROACHES TO THE HOLOCAUST

Amos Goldberg

Rumors in the Ghettos: A Case Study of Cultural History

HOW SHOULD THE HISTORY OF THE JEWS IN THE HOLOCAUST BE written? From what perspective? How should its main object of research be defined, and what should its focal point be? Historians and scholars have asked these fundamental questions since the very beginning of the field of Holocaust studies and actually already during World War II.[1] In this short essay, I will try to address them by reflecting on the extent to which cultural history can contribute to the field of Holocaust history. In the second part of this essay, I will substantiate my view through an initial analysis of the spread of rumors in Jewish ghettos during the war.

CULTURAL HISTORY AND HOLOCAUST HISTORY

In a recently published article in *Dapim: Studies on the Holocaust*, Dan Stone argued that despite the fact that cultural history has proved both a popular and fertile paradigm within the historical discipline, it has not staked much ground for itself in the study of the Holocaust.[2] It is not that "cultural histories" were not written on the Holocaust. One can mention, for example, the writings of Alon Confino, Claudia Koonz, Dominick LaCapra, Thomas Kühne, and Dan Michman as works affiliated with cultural history.[3] However, these scholars and Stone himself mostly relate to the history of the perpetrators. But what about a cultural history of the Jews during the Holocaust?

By "cultural history," I do not mean in this context a history that portrays Jewish cultural institutions during the Holocaust. Moshe Rosman has already reminded us in the context of Jewish history that cultural history is not interested in the products of creative forces within a particular group, but in the meanings these forces and products convey.[4] Or, in other words, cultural history is not concerned with describing cultural and religious institutions or their products, but rather in the mechanism of meaning-making within a society, or in what Peter Burke sees as the common basis of all branches of cultural history: "dealing with the symbolic and its interpretation."[5]

In this field of "the history of the Jews in the Holocaust," one can say that cultural history's impact is even smaller, although not altogether absent. Alexandra Garbarini and Jacek Leociak's books on diaries written by Jews during the Holocaust are good examples. Samuel Kassow's monograph on Emanuel Ringelblum or Debórah Dwork's work on the experiences of Jewish children and youth are yet other good examples.[6] However, even these works, as well as others, do not always fully expose what I consider the radical significance of cultural history to Jewish history during the Holocaust.

I believe that the fundamental challenge of writing the history of the victims in extreme cases such as genocide is to write a history of powerlessness. This is evident in the case of the Holocaust, where the devastating experience of extreme powerlessness dominates all contemporaneous sources, such as diaries and letters, written by the victims.[7] So the questions are, how can a history of powerlessness be written, and what methods of cultural history could help us in this?

These questions are even more acute from a theoretical perspective because history usually depicts what there is, not what is missing. It tends to focus on positive nouns as its objects of research and not on negative ones with the suffix "lessness," as in our case, powerlessness—the feeling and reality of lack of power—of impotence! Not total impotence in the sense of lacking any aspect of selfhood or agency, but still, overwhelming and devastating powerlessness—a sense that one's life is completely dominated by external powerful, vicious and lethal forces, evident in almost every passage of the victims' wartime writings.

Much of Holocaust historiography, which focuses on the Jews and which gained huge achievements in reconstructing Jewish life in that time, seems to have failed in this challenge. For the most part, this historiography tends to portray the victim as an autonomous, reactive, historical, more or less full agent, while avoiding altogether this challenge of powerlessness! To put it in Walter Benjamin's words, it is a historiography that wishes to write the history of the defeated as a history of the victorious.[8] Hence, in many cases, the historical image of the victim is constructed through the stark binary opposition of "inside" and "outside." For example, in many Holocaust narratives, both academic and popular, it is assumed that the victims kept, in one way or another, their "internal" individual, psychological, and communal identity more or less intact while the Holocaust took place only on the "outside" of historical reality, which was totally dominated by the Germans. Such narratives make fundamental use of such keywords as "struggle," "response," "*amida*" (a Hebrew term that will discussed later), "voices," "dignity," "agency," and at times even "resistance," because they all assume that in the Holocaust there were two distinct historical autonomous agents—the Jews and the Germans. The latter persecuted the former, but as long as there was any option for the former to "respond," "struggle against," "utter their voices," "manipulate circumstances," or even "resist," they did that. Obviously, they managed to do so only until they were completely overpowered.

I do not contend that this historiography is simplistic and superficial. It certainly does relate incidents, communities, and ghettos that failed to execute such responses,[9] but nonetheless the focus is on "response," and this is practically its main object of research. "Response" is what historians usually look for, even when they are honest about admitting their failure to find it. The question that the historian explicitly or implicitly asks within this historiographical framework is whether and to what extent a Jewish "response" did or did not take place.

This tendency dominates large parts of the Israeli school of Holocaust research, although even Christopher Browning's *Remembering Survival*,[10] which reconstructs, on the basis of 292 postwar Jewish testimonies, the history of the Wierzbnik ghetto and Starachowice labor camp in the Radom district of Poland, fails to fully depict this immanent and eminent aspect of the victims' experience and consciousness. Indeed, it does portray many aspects of the "choiceless choices" (as he calls them, following Lawrence Langer's well-known articulation) of collaboration and internal social Darwinist style rivals for survival that are inherent in the victims' gray zone. But at the same time, it celebrates and emphasizes every moment of unexpected bravery and internal solidarity. Browning asserts, in the book's concluding remarks, that terms such as "resistance" and "*amida*" are insufficient to describe the Jewish struggle for survival. He therefore suggests alternative vocabulary of such words as "ingenuity, resourcefulness, adoptability, perseverance and endurance."[11] However, and this is most important for my argument, he does not emphasize the experience and consciousness of powerlessness itself as the object of research on which one should focus. So, even if the book's historical reconstruction is extremely accurate and illuminating in the factual sense, it lacks a fundamental analysis of the victim's traumatic experience and consciousness.

The most comprehensive conceptual summary of this historiographical approach has been formulated by Yehuda Bauer in his book *Rethinking the Holocaust*.[12] In two chapters of this work, Bauer discusses the problem of the character of the history of the Jews in this era. He considers these chapters to be his major interpretive contribution to the field of Holocaust history. The key terms of Bauer's historiography, according to his own affirmation, are "resistance," "response," "reaction," and most importantly, "*amida*."

In the original English edition of the book, Bauer claims that the concept of *amida* is difficult to translate into a foreign language. The term, he says, connotes both armed and unarmed resistance, but also the smuggling of food; cultural, religious, educational, and political activity; as well as other types of action aimed at bolstering the personal and collective capacities for survival.[13] According to him, *amida* is the focal point and object of research for historians who seek to portray the history of the Jews during the Holocaust.

This historiographical tendency to grant the victim full agency has an ethical urgency as well. It is many times rightly justified by the ethical imperative to "rehumanize" the victims and to let them regain their faces, their voices, and their identity. This is undoubtedly a right and just cause because it wishes to redeem the victims from being once again an object of the perpetrators' history. As Israel Gutman has pointed out, the Israeli school in Holocaust history sought to present the Jews in both the individual and the collective sense as having resisted Nazi persecution as long as even the most meager means were available to them to do so, including actual armed resistance. As a consequence, the concept of resistance was sweepingly expanded to include almost any organized or even private act that enabled or supported Jewish existence during this era.[14] As such, Israeli historiography constituted the Jewish historical subject—on both the collective and individual planes—as an active agent, as the owner of his or her own history, whose own interiority or whose mental, cultural, religious, communal, and ethical self continued to stand strong and invincible.[15] The Jews are therefore constructed as proud historical agents whose interiority and identity cannot be crushed or even undermined.

However, this image, whether explicitly portrayed or implicitly embedded or assumed in historical representations,[16] might be somewhat misleading because, as noble as the endeavor to "rehumanize" the victim might be, the victims in many cases were actually dehumanized. The "outside" penetrated and transformed the "inside." Take, for example, the following words of Josef Zelkowicz, a leftist-oriented Yiddish intellectual of the Łódź ghetto who wrote extensively in the ghetto and was eventually murdered in Auschwitz:

> It is not only the external form of life that has changed in the ghetto . . . It is not only the clothing that has come to look tattered and the faces to wear masks of death, but the entire Jewish trend of thought has been totally transformed under the pressure of the ghetto . . . The ghetto . . . has swiftly obliterated the boundaries between sanctity and indignity, just as it obliterated the boundaries between mine and yours, permitted and forbidden, fair and unfair.[17]

This short quotation is typical of almost all Jewish texts written during the Holocaust and in the first years thereafter. Almost all of them testify to a deep transformation of basic concepts and the collapse of fundamental and essential distinctions in individual and collective life and thought under Nazi persecution. The analysis of such a transformation is precisely what Holocaust historiography lacks. As a matter of fact, these transformations were the main object of research and observation among many of the first generation of Holocaust scholars and ethnographers—many of whom perished in the Holocaust. I am talking about such figures as Chaim Kaplan, Oskar Rosenfeld, Nachman Blumenthal, Rachel Auerbach (Rokhl Oyerbakh), Hannah Arendt, and many others. But academic historiography almost completely abandoned these aspects, which are the core of the "powerlessness experience," in the seventies and thereafter. As a matter of fact, they follow, to a large extent, a dominant trend in interwar East European Jewish writings embodied, for example, in the work of Max Weinreich, one of the founders of the YIVO Institute for Jewish Research. During the 1920s and 1930s, he immersed himself in depicting the sociopsychological outcomes of discrimination among the Jews of East Europe—examining it in larger comparative, which included also the African Americans in the Southern United States.[18]

Following these precedents, I would like to contend that cultural history can give us some methodological tools to portray these transformative processes that the victim underwent and was powerless to resist. This is because, as Lynn Hunt puts it, cultural history is more about "the deciphering of meaning, rather than the inference of causal laws,"[19] In other words, the diverse field of cultural history focuses on the processes of producing meaning and their failures.[20] Hence, cultural history could be suitable for portraying the victims' breakdown of structures and cultural mechanisms, which failed to give meaning to their radical experiences.

I will illustrate this by briefly relating to the issue of rumors, which were a fundamental and extremely commonplace phenomenon in the Jewish ghettos.[21]

ANALYZING RUMORS

That rumors were commonplace among the Jewish population during the war is of very little wonder. As students of rumor research know, rumors are a practice of communication that exists in all modern societies. No matter how enlightened, technologically advanced, and rational a society is, and how developed and modernized its systems of communication, rumors always circulate.[22] Rumors increase at times of crisis and war, when such stories tend to flourish and become a significant social and cultural phenomenon and sometimes even a dominant form of mass communication.[23] Hence, such historians as Marc Bloch[24] and Paul Fussel[25] paid much attention to the historical and cultural significance of rumors during "The Great War." And Maureen Healy's study on Vienna during World War I shows how rumors came to dominate the Viennese public sphere and how they became an eminent problem for the regime.[26] This was also true for Nazi Germany during World War II.[27] Ulrich Rauf has suggested a kind of formula that is extremely relevant to our case: rumors flourish in a community under imagined or real threat, whose inmates experience isolation, loss of normal social contacts, fear, and exhaustion. In addition, in such circumstances people typically have the feeling that information is controlled and often severely distorted by the regime. Rumors tend to dramatically increase when rational critical capacities are weakened.[28]

It is no wonder, then, that rumors played a dramatic role in Jewish societies during the war, especially in the ghettos. Rumors on various themes circulated daily and wildly, and they are constantly mentioned and dealt with in the writings of the time. The Łódź ghetto even performed a play titled *Plotkes*—"Rumors."[29]

It is obvious what circumstances created this phenomenon: the isolation of the Jews from the world at a time of great, crucial, and fatal events; the lack of reliable modern means of communication—written, oral, and visual; unreliable Nazi sources of information; unprecedented and meaningless occurrences, along with constant expectation and knowledge that things were happening or about to happen; and a constant feeling of fear and immediate threat to one's life. All of these factors created conditions for rumors to flourish dramatically.

But how should one approach this major phenomenon? What questions should a historian ask about it? How can we analyze and conceptualize it to better understand Jewish life during these horrendous times?

One way to look at it is empirically, as have, for example, Christopher Browning, Israel Gutman, and Alexandra Garbarini. Browning and Gutman analyzed reports written in the spring of 1942 by Jewish informers who worked in the service of the Nazis in the Warsaw ghetto.[30] One of the major issues depicted in these reports was the rumor that circulated in the ghetto about the fate of Jews outside the ghetto and their effect on the ghetto mood (*Stimmung*). Browning is mostly interested in the accuracy of the information and the speed of its dissemination. Thus, after comparing these documents to German documents, he concluded that the time it took rumors about the gassing of Lublin Jews in the Belzec death camp in southeastern Poland to reach the Warsaw ghetto was not longer than the time it took this information to reach German officials in Lublin and Joseph Goebbels, the Nazi minister of propaganda, in Berlin. The difference lies in the details and the level of certainty of the news, not in the speed of its spread.

Gutman, on the other hand, is interested in reconstructing the motivation of these informants to report so intensively on rumors and in assessing how destructive these reports were from the ghetto point of view. His conclusion, in the spirit of the historiographical school described earlier, was that they did not cause and did not mean to cause much harm.

Garbarini also refers extensively to the issue of rumors in her book, in which she analyzes the ways by which Jews obtained news, how they read it, and how they interpreted it in the ghetto.[31] This approach comes close to mine; however, as I mentioned earlier, I am less interested in the empirical aspects of the study of rumors than in the psychological, social, and cultural ones. I wish here to discuss rumors along methodological lines that I consider related to "cultural history" and that will expose the dimension of radical transformation in Jewish public life during the Holocaust.

The first thing we have to notice in this regard is that an extremely literate society with highly developed public institutions[32] underwent a radical transformation: in a short time, as a result of Nazi persecution, Jewish societies degenerated into oral societies. Indeed, some Jewish scholars reflected on this transformation and its ramifications. In what follows I will focus on two of them: the Hebrew diarist Chaim Kaplan of the Warsaw ghetto, who was rightfully characterized by Saul Friedländer as "usually more farsighted than any other diarist,"[33] and Emil Utitz of Theresienstadt.

Obviously there were all sorts, one might even say genres, of rumors circulating in Jewish societies during the war. A popular genre was that of catastrophe rumors, which unfortunately many times proved to be accurate. Another sort of rumor frequently mentioned in contemporary texts referred to internal Jewish life and had a specific narrative structure and character. Here I shall focus on one popular kind of rumor—fantastic redemptive ones. These were overwhelmingly popular in Jewish societies. The stories usually spoke with great certainty of Nazi defeats, which seemed to presage the imminent fall or internal collapse of Nazi Germany, and prophesied the salvation of the Jews from the Nazis. Such rumors, though they often had some grain of truth in them, were an utter exaggeration and therefore totally misleading. Their interpretative conclusions usually lacked any overall real foundation and were completely delusional. Hence, depending on the source, they transformed the very character of the Jewish public sphere and its way of communication. In the following analysis, I will not relate so much to the contents of these rumors and to their accuracy, but rather to their function, which according to the sociopsychologist Jean-Noël Kapferer, who researched rumors, is about "giving meaning to unexplained facts."[34]

CHAIM KAPLAN OF WARSAW

As early as December 5, 1939, Kaplan makes one of his first observations on the issue of rumors:

> Rumors don't cease to inform that very soon will the occupier leave us.
>
> There are signs of demoralization in the German army . . . one comes and says that some officers entered a clothing shop . . . they ordered the owner to leave the shop and come back in two hours . . . Once he was back he found everything in order . . . they left their uniform and took civil suits from the shop's stock. Another one comes and tells: "The Führer died. But they hold back this information from the army in order to avoid demoralization" . . . These are the workings of the sick imagination of a despised people, which has nothing in its world but imagination.[35]

Here Kaplan talks about two rumors: one referring to the demoralization within the German army, and the second to the death of the Führer. At least the second rumor had a strong factual base—a failed assassination attempt on Hitler had been carried out by Georg Elser on November 8 of that year. Perhaps also the first rumor reflects the tensions between the army and Hitler about the war and dissatisfaction the army expressed in this regard. Nevertheless and despite this, Kaplan concludes that baseless rumors prevail and "Healthy common sense is gone. Rationality is gone and so is the sense of realism."

Half a year later, on April 11, 1940, Kaplan again speaks about the psychology of these redemptive rumors. In this entry, he writes about the way that the Jews view the Germans' spring offensive. By that time, the Germans had already occupied Denmark and Norway. He cites the British Broadcasting Corporation (BBC) radio broadcasts that reported on the Germans' naval defeat against the shores of Norway, in which thirty-seven German battleships were destroyed. Here, again, there is more than a grain of truth. The German navy did suffer heavy losses in that battle, known as Operation Weserübung. However, it was not thirty-seven ships that were destroyed, but rather the *Blücher* heavy battle cruiser and ten smaller battleships.

Whether the rumor proved true or not, Kaplan concludes sarcastically again: "An unprecedented defeat! and even if it is imaginary it heals a bit our ragged soul."

In the same spirit, Peretz Opochinski writes in the Warsaw ghetto as late as May 1942:

> The news that Kerch [now in Russian-administered Crimea] fell to German hands made a hard impression on the ghetto. Knowledgeable people are reporting that the Germans used poison gas there. This information is confirmed—so claim the ghetto politicians although we have no reliable information sources and we live in total darkness.
>
> People also tell that street battles are taking place in Kharkov [Ukraine] and the Germans evacuated the city. They also say that the Russians concentrated a huge army there and last but not least that once Kharkov will be liberated, the German victory in Kerch will lose its significance. One thing is clear: the ghetto needs daily encouragement, some illusion—without which it would really be difficult to live even one day.[36]

Here, again, there are some grains of factual truth in these rumors. But eventually General Friedrich Paulus defeated General Semyon Timoshenko in Kharkov. Kerch itself was occupied on May 16 of that year, opening the way for the *Wehrmacht,* Germany's armed forces, to conquer the Crimean Peninsula.

But although the facts are important in understanding these rumors, they are not of crucial importance, because what seems to operate here is a consistent hermeneutic apparatus that interprets the chaotic and fearful reality, transforming it into an optimistic, meaningful, hopeful one. Illusionary and detached from reality as they may be, these rumors were essential for survival, as Opochinski asserts. But that does not mean that something radical has not changed and that there is no "price" to be paid for that—even if there is no other alternative but to consume these illusions. The normal and at least partially rational and realistic apparatus of communication—that of normal times—is replaced by another, irrational and disconnected from reality. This is a clear case of an impossible dilemma, as Kaplan again sharply indicated on September 2, 1941: "Woe to the nation which lives in illusions—and well is the nation living in illusions—without illusions to amuse him he would have been lost in his disaster." These illusionary rumors are destructive as well as essential for survival; therefore, Kaplan keeps calling the Jews of Warsaw, who are addicted to these rumors, "prisoners of hope"!

A few more points should be made in this regard.

The first is that to maintain this constant circulation of redemptive rumors, people have to develop some kind of a double consciousness—on the one hand, to believe in those rumors, but on the other hand, to know that they are actually false. This double consciousness then evolves into the logic of addiction, which is based on a kind of cyclic pleasure, as Kaplan states in the following excerpt from the entry of March 25, 1941:

> We follow every move, not only on the battlefield, but also in the field of diplomacy. And because the murderer is suspected of lies, deceptions and exaggerations, and we are fed only from his source, we have ceased to believe him even when he speaks the truth. It has become customary to whisper to one another about a Nazi defeat, even though there has been no such thing. Those prisoners of hope find a little comfort in this. Sometimes the rumormongers themselves know that this is only a fairy tale, but they nevertheless spread the rumors abroad—for the sake of an hour's comfort. What do you care if the rumor has no basis? Let our Jews enjoy a little!
>
> And it could be that some person with imagination is arranging the development of matters in his head according to his wishes, and gets up and arranges the fruits of his imagination in public, as though it were fact. Then comes the disappointment which darkens our world once more. But immediately we become accustomed to the new situation, and a new encouraging hope begins to blossom.

This entry exposes to a large degree the psychological mechanism of rumors consuming the ghetto and is worth a close reading.

Here the rumor replaces the Nazi voice, which is unreliable and manipulative and has little to do with reality. At the same time, dependence on this voice is absolute: "We are fed only from his source." (In the original Hebrew, this aspect is emphasized even more because the word is not "we are fed" but *yonkim*, which literally means "we are nursed"). But in its absence, the Jews seek an alternative voice, that of rumor.

The voice of rumor, which replaces the voice of the murderer, does not intend, argues Kaplan, to disperse the vagueness and arbitrariness of the Nazi voice. It is the voice of pure delusion, utterly false (in its relation to reality)[37] and aware of its own falsehood: "Sometimes the rumormongers themselves know that this is only a fairy tale." At the same time, it is a repetitive, compulsive voice: "But immediately we become accustomed to the new situation, and a new encouraging hope begins to blossom."[38] The voice of rumor is not meant to disperse the dimness, but rather to replace one lie (the Nazi one) with another (the Jewish one).[39] Kaplan points out that the aim of the rumor is not the truth, but the pleasure it evokes—"Let our Jews enjoy a little!"—and even stresses that the end of the process is known from the start. It seems that the resulting harm outweighs the gain of the pleasure derived from a moment's hope: "Then comes the disappointment which darkens our world once more."[40]

Psychoanalytically, we could even go so far as to say that because this mechanism repeats itself and its end is known from the start, its end is in fact its purpose. The purpose of the rumor is not only the moment of hope but also the overwhelming and thrilling moment of disappointment. All these testify that the rumor carries a destructive, unconscious, primary pleasure[41] in the most fundamental sense.[42]

This mechanism reminds us of Marc Bloch's depiction of the regression and irrationality of a society in which rumors are so dominant. Bloch asserts that, when a society undergoes such a processas in wartime, written communication loses its validity, and its place is taken by rumor. Rumor, argues Bloch, is one of the symptoms of such processes.[43] Bloch's regression argument seems to be very pertinent to the context under discussion because this primary pleasure, which is so evident in Kaplan's description, originally characterizes the infant in its earliest stages of development. Primary pleasure prefers excessive and immediate satisfaction gained in fantasy, outside the real world, over a limited satisfaction gained by hard and long effort that proceeds in an indirect way but that may attain a real desired object. In Sigmund Freud's terms, echoed by Kaplan, we may say it is a complete devastation of the reality principle in favor of the pleasure principle.[44]

Perhaps we can even say that the fantastic element of the rumor functions on two levels according to this notion. On one level, the content of the rumors about the state of the Nazis is always optimistic,[45] as Kaplan notes on September 5, 1940 (and frequently elsewhere): "You will never hear a rumor of good news for the murderers." But on another level of fantasy, the rumor lends the Jews of the ghetto the illusion that the Jewish voice can replace the silent Nazi voice, put order to the chaos, and establish a world of facts and regulation. This is reflected in the sentence "And it could be that some imaginative person is arranging the development of matters in his head according to his wishes, and gets up and arranges the fruits of his imagination in public, as though it were fact." The rumor creates the illusion of power in the hands of the rumormonger.[46]

In fact, Kaplan himself is aware, even in the early days of the Occupation, that rumor plays a role on the level of the (imaginative) power. Thus he writes on January 15, 1940: "But I regret that the Jews comfort themselves by spreading false rumors. They take revenge on their enemies in things which are not real at all." It is as though, through rumors of the fall of the Nazis, the helpless Jews could avenge their sufferings.[47]

The metaphor Kaplan uses to describe the phenomenon of comforting rumors can explain their entire tragedy. As we have already mentioned, in the diary Kaplan often calls those residents of the ghetto who became addicted to comforting rumors "prisoners of hope."[48] Perhaps this metaphor even tells us that the rumor serves the incarcerators much more than the incarcerated. This brings us to an early conceptualization of this topic by Emil Utitz.

EMIL UTITZ OF THERESIENSTADT

Despite the fact that Kaplan and Utitz shared little common cultural or ideological grounds, their observations are not very different. But whereas Kaplan did not survive the war (he was murdered in Treblinka in summer 1942), Utitz did, and in 1948 he published a short book in German under the title *Psychologie des Lebens im Konzentrationslager Theresienstadt* [A psychology of life in the Theresienstadt concentration camp].[49] Utitz, who was born in Prague in 1883, studied philosophy and psychology and specialized in aesthetics. Although he converted to Christianity at a young age, Utitz belonged to a circle of Czech Jewish intellectuals and was friendly with Max Brod, Franz Kafka, and Hugo Bergmann. Utitz taught at the University of Halle and then in Prague. In July 1942, he was sent to Theresienstadt, where he was put in charge of the library. Like Leo Baeck, he gave memorable public lectures in Theresienstadt on topics related to culture and the humanities. After liberation, he returned to Prague to teach at the university and passed away in Jena in 1956. In the course of his academic career, he wrote several important books, especially in the field of aesthetics.

Early in the book, Utitz justifies writing it (this is in 1947), in spite of the fact that, as he asserts, "so much has already been written about the concentration camps in general and about Theresienstadt in particular."[50] Nevertheless, he submits that he has a unique perspective to offer, "due to my profession as a psychologist and philosopher." And, based on his three-year experience as an inmate in Theresienstadt, he is capable of providing an account of several matters that should be of scientific interest. Utitz viewed Theresienstadt as a sort of "experiment" on human social life, which possibly had never before been conducted, and which he hoped "would never again take place." The study is therefore a kind of scientific meditation on his personal experiences, through which he seeks to understand fundamental themes of the social psychology of the ghetto's residents. The book offers observations concerning a number of issues, but here I wish to focus on the topic of rumors in the ghetto, to which he dedicates a chapter.

Rumors, Utitz explains, were the only means for transmitting information from the outside world concerning critical issues such as the war's progress, the fate of the Jews, and the expected date of liberation; these matters indeed comprised the main *content* of the rumors. However, their *meaning*—and this is a distinction he makes—for ghetto residents was utterly different. Although frequently containing a kernel of truth, the rumors were ultimately grotesque inventions and exaggerations. As such, they possessed scarcely any value as news, and everyone was aware of this fact. Yet, for the most part, the rumors fulfilled an intra-social psychological function—to strengthen the hope and belief that had become moral imperatives in the ghetto, for only hope and belief enabled people to bear the intolerable hardships of ghetto life. So rumors were not actually about information and data but much more about group psychology, and as such they constructed an ethical field. Rumors, says Utitz, staked out a battlefield between the optimists who inspired hope and the pessimists who threw a pall of gloom over things; as such, the rumors instituted a new ethics. "You who are not a believer," Utitz quotes an optimist accusing a pessimist in the summer of 1942, in regard to the latter's doubts about the rumor that the Reich's collapse was nigh and would come to pass before the winter—"you are a bad person!"[51] To believe the comforting rumors was a moral imperative in the eyes of many, whereas to doubt them was perceived as sin.

These issues lead Utitz to analyze the culture of nostalgia, illusion, and delusion that existed in Theresienstadt, its modes of expression, and the mechanisms that activated it. Such mechanisms were the product of a collective mood that sought to evade the life realities of the insufferable present in any way possible and to escape into a glowing future of imminent German defeat, or else to recollect nostalgically a lost Eden as a source of inspiration for the future. In the absence of any such past, some people simply invented one. Thus, for example, Utitz describes the common tendency among Theresienstadt inmates to upgrade their prewar profession. All of the petty shop owners became successful merchants in their stories, and a distributor for a small publishing house presented himself as a professor at the Sorbonne. This culture of fantasy transformed, according to Utitz, Kaplan, and innumerable other sources, the very character of the Jewish public sphere and its way of functioning.

CONCLUSIONS: BRIEFLY BACK TO CULTURAL HISTORY AND POWERLESSNESS

As early as December 5, 1939, Chaim Kaplan wrote: "The miserable masses are waiting for a miracle. Such Messianism finds fertile ground, because every nonsensical fact is eagerly listened to. Common sense has evaporated. Rationality and a sense of reality have evaporated." Indeed, the incipient research about the collective consciousness of illusion was begun soon after the war, and not only by Kaplan and Utitz. Nachman Blumenthal, for example, viewed this form of consciousness as a distorted, even if unavoidable, way of coping with a radical state of helplessness. In one of his early essays, he deals with what he calls "magical thinking," which in his opinion characterized Jewish consciousness in the ghettos—the idea that by either acting or imagining, the Jews believed they could influence a reality which was in fact totally controlled by the Germans.[52]

I have outlined here briefly only one possible theme—rumors—that invite the incorporation of one variant of cultural history into research concerning the processes of transformation (which assumes continuity and discontinuity) that Jews underwent under Nazi occupation and highlights the mental consequences of a state of radical powerlessness. Indeed, a comprehensive study of rumors would have to examine this issue diachronically in a number of locales, under varying conditions, and in different contexts. However, the theme itself emerges powerfully in the earliest reflective texts, which I suggest should be revisited, and eloquently illustrates the gist of my argument. These texts suggest a path for writing the Jewish history of the Holocaust that takes powerlessness seriously as one of its objects of research and in which the concept of transformation plays a central role alongside, if not instead of, other concepts. I think today we would call this "cultural history."

NOTES

1. See, for example, in Emanuel Ringelblum's writings.

2. Dan Stone, "Holocaust Historiography and Cultural History," *Dapim* 23, 1 (2009): 52–68. See also the scholarly forum in the same publication, featuring responses from Dominick LaCapra, Federico Finchelstein, Carolyn J. Dean, Dan Michman, Wendy Lower, and Amos Goldberg (ibid., 69–93). See also "Forum: Cultural History and the Holocaust," *German History* 31, 1 (2013): 61–85.

3. See Claudia Koonz, *The Nazi Conscience* (Cambridge, Mass.: Harvard University Press, 2003) and Alon Confino, *A World without Jews: The Nazi Imagination from Persecution to Genocide* (New Haven, Conn.: Yale University Press, 2014); Dominick LaCapra, *Writing History, Writing Trauma* (Baltimore, Md.: John Hopkins University Press, 2001), esp. chap. 5; and in a slightly different context, Enzo Traverso, *The Origins of Nazi Violence* (New York: New Press, 2003). See also Dan Michman, *The Emergence of the Jewish Ghettos during the Holocaust* (Cambridge: Cambridge University Press, 2011) and Thomas Kühne, *Belonging and Genocide: Hitler's Community, 1918–1945* (New Haven, Conn.: Yale University Press, 2010).

4. Moshe Rosman, *How Jewish Is Jewish History?* (Oxford, U.K.: Littman Library of Jewish Civilization, 2007), 131–32.

5. Peter Burke, *What Is Cultural History?* (Cambridge, U.K: Polity, 2004), 3. See also David Chaney, *The Cultural Turn* (London: Routledge, 1994).

6. Alexandra Garbarini, *Numbered Days: Diaries and the Holocaust* (New Haven, Conn.: Yale University Press, 2006); Jacek Leociak, *Text in the Face of Destruction: Accounts from the Warsaw Ghetto Reconsidered*, trans. Emma Harris (Warsaw: Jewish Historical Institute, 2004); Samuel D. Kassow, *Who Will Write Our History? Emanuel Ringelblum, the Warsaw Ghetto, and*

the Oyneg Shabes Archive (Bloomington: Indiana University Press, 2007); Debórah Dwork, *Children with a Star* (New Haven, Conn.: Yale University Press, 1993).

7. In my own work on diaries, I distinguished between "history of trauma" and "history of crisis." See Amos Goldberg, "If This Is a Man: The Image of Man in Autobiographical and Historical Writing during and after the Holocaust," *Yad Vashem Studies* 33 (2005): 381–429.

8. Walter Benjamin, *Illuminations*, trans. Harry Zorn (New York: Schocken, 2007), 253–65.

9. See, for example, Yehuda Bauer, *The Death of the Shtetl* (New Haven, Conn.: Yale University Press, 2009).

10. Christopher R. Browning, *Remembering Survival: Inside a Nazi Slave-Labor Camp* (New York: Norton, 2010).

11. Ibid., 297.

12. Yehuda Bauer, *Rethinking the Holocaust* (New Haven, Conn.: Yale University Press, 2001).

13. Ibid., 120.

14. See, for example, the entry "Resistance," in Israel Gutman, ed., *Encyclopedia of the Holocaust* (Jerusalem: Yad Vashem, 1990), 1265–72, which is representative of this school.

15. See, for example, Israel Gutman, *Be-Alatah uve-Maavak* [In struggle and in darkness] (Tel Aviv: Sifriyat Hapoalim, 1985), 81 [in Hebrew].

16. As Barbara Taylor reminds us, every historical representation assumes, even if implicitly, a certain concept of subjectivity. See Barbara Taylor, "Historical Subjectivity," chap. 9 in Sally Alexander and Barbara Taylor, eds., *History and Psyche: Culture, Psychoanalysis, and the Past* (Basingstoke, U.K.: Palgrave Macmillan, 2013), 195–210.

17. Josef Zelkowicz, *In Those Terrible Days: Notes from the Lodz Ghetto*, ed. Michal Unger (Jerusalem: Yad Vashem, 2002), 139–41.

18. Leila Zenderland, "Social Science as a 'Weapon of the Weak': Max Weinreich, the Yiddish Scientific Institute, and the Study of Culture, Personality, and Prejudice," *Isis* 104, 4 (December 2013): 742–72.

19. Lynn Hunt, "Introduction: History, Culture, and Text," in Lynn Hunt, ed., *The New Cultural History* (Berkeley: University of California Press, 1989), 12.

20. For a fuller account of this phenomena see Amos Goldberg, "The Rumor Culture among Warsaw Jews under Nazi Occupation: A World of Catastrophe Re-enchanted" (*Jewish Social Studies*, July 2016).

21. For the diversity of this field, see Roger Chartier, *Cultural History: Between Practices and Representations* (Ithaca, N.Y.: Polity, 1988).

22. Jean-Noël Kapferer, *Rumors: Uses, Interpretations, and Images* (New Brunswick, N.J.: Transaction, 1990).

23. Tamotsu Shibutani, *Improvised News: A Sociological Study of Rumor* (Indianapolis: Bobbs Merrill, 1966).

24. Marc Bloch, *The Historian's Craft*, trans. Peter Putnam (Manchester, U.K.: Manchester University Press, 1967), 175–90.

25. Paul Fussel, *The Great War and Modern Memory* (New York: Oxford University Press, 1975), 14–154.

26. Maureen Healy, *Vienna and the Fall of the Habsburg Empire: Total War and Everyday Life in World War I* (Cambridge: Cambridge University Press, 2004), 122–49.

27. Franz Dröge, *Der Zerredete Widerstand: Soziologie und Publizistik des Gerüchts im 2. Weltkrieg* [The worn out by words resistance: Sociology and journalism of the rumor in the Second World War] (Düsseldorf, Ger.: Bertelsmann, 1970).

28. Ulrich Rauf, "Clio in den Dünsten: Über Geschichte und Gerüche [Clio in the vapors: About history and smells]," in Bedrich Lowenstein, ed., *Geschichte und Psychologie: Annährungsversuche* [History and psychology: Overtures] (Pfaffenweiler, Ger.: Centaurus, 1992), 99–114.

29. Oskar Rosenfeld, *In the Beginning Was the Ghetto: Notebooks from Łódź* (Evanston, Ill.: Northwestern University Press, 2002), 69.

30. Christopher Browning and Israel Gutman, "The Reports of a Jewish 'Informer' in the Warsaw Ghetto: Selected Documents," *Yad Vashem Studies* 17 (1986): 247–94.

31. Garbarini, Numbered Days, esp. 22–94. See also, in regard to the Łódź ghetto, Isaiah Kuperstein, "Rumors: A Socio-Historical Phenomenon in the Ghetto of Łódź," *Polish Review* 18, no. 4 (1973): 63–83.

32. For the emergence of the modern Jewish public sphere in Warsaw, see Scott Ury, *Barricades and Banners: The Revolution of 1905 and the Transformation of Warsaw Jewry*, Stanford Studies in Jewish History and Culture (Stanford, Calif.: Stanford University Press, 2012).

33. Saul Friedländer, *The Years of Extermination: Nazi Germany and the Jews, 1939–1945* (New York: HarperCollins, 2007), 41.

34. Kapferer, *Rumors*, 8

35. Kaplan's diary was published in English as *Scroll of Agony*. But since the translation is full of mistakes distortions and omissions, I translated the quoted passage myself from the Hebrew publication Chaim Aron Kaplan, *Megilat Yisurin* (Tel Aviv: Am Oved and Yad Vashem, 1966) and from the manuscripts at the Moreshet Archive, D.2.470. In the text, I therefore relate to the date alone.

36. Peretz Opochinski, *Reshimot* (Notes) [in Hebrew, my translation] (Tel Aviv: Am Oved, 1970).

37. See Zelig Kalmanovitz in the Vilna (Vilnius or Wilno) ghetto in Lithuania on the October 25, 1942: "There are various rumors going around.

You had to write it down to see: what was the situation outside and how it emerged in the imagination of the Ghetto." Zelig Kalmanovitz, *Yoman Be'getto Vilna* [A diary in the Vilna Ghetto] [in Hebrew] (Tel Aviv: Moreshet and Sifryat Hapoalim, 1977), 83.

38. Thus, for example, Opochinski writes about the rumors: "Every day the Ghetto needs some encouragement, some illusion—without which it would really be difficult to live." Opochinski, *Diaries*, 205.

39. Jurek Becker, *Jacob the Liar* (New York: Penguin, 1999). *Jacob the Liar* is a novel based entirely on the power of the lie in the Łódź ghetto. Sidra Ezrahi claims that the lie enables one to think, even if in the imagination, of another reality, and hence to break the decisiveness and inevitability of a catastrophic, historical reality. However, such an exercise of the imagination works later on for the readers, who know the factual history to which the novel is a kind of response. This is not the case when reality is pushed aside by delusion in the consciousness of the victims at the actual time the events are occurring. See Sidra DeKoven Ezrahi, "After Such Knowledge, What Laughter?" *Yale Journal of Criticism* 14, no. 1 (2001): 287–313.

40. Kaplan says more dreadful things on August 3, 1940—"Thus we were pinned down between hope and fear. A feverish state which consumes body and soul"—and also in the March 30, 1940, entry.

41. See Kaja Silverman, *The Subject of Semiotics* (New York: Oxford University Press, 1983), 66–76: "The primary process seeks immediate gratification through hallucination, but the end result is always disillusionment and unpleasure."

42. See the case in which the writer of a diary testifies to taking care to resist the temptation of this pleasure. So Zelig Kalmanovitz writes on August 9, 1943:

> We are afraid to believe it. Fanciful rumors as usual. But the rumors repeated themselves and became more real each time. Faces lit up a little and hope was awakened. But the joy was swallowed up in the fear. We want to believe but are unable to believe that success came so close. And if it is close we are in the hands of the murderers anyway. Who knows what they will inflict on us just before the end. We cannot believe our ears.

See Kalmanovitz, *A Diary from the Ghetto in Nazi Vilna,* 59. For Jewish gallows humor or false optimism, see Adam Czerniakow, *The Warsaw Diary of Adam Czerniakow: Prelude to Doom*, ed. Raul Hilberg, Stanislaw Staron, and Josef Kermish, trans. Stanislaw Staron (New York: Stein and Day 1979), 369, June 22, 1942, entry.

43. Marc Bloch, *The Historian's Craft*, trans. Peter Putnam (Manchester, U.K.: Manchester University Press, 1967)

44. Sigmund Freud, "Beyond the Pleasure Principle," *Standard Edi-*

tion of the Complete Psychological Works of Sigmund Freud, vol. 17 (London: Hogarth, 1955), 7–23.

45. See also Peretz Opochinski, *Reshimot* (Notes) [in Hebrew], 196, entry for May10, 1942. See also Abraham Lewin, *A Cup of Tears: A Diary of the Warsaw Ghetto*, ed. Antony Polonsky, trans. Christopher Hutton (Oxford, U.K.: Blackwell, 1988), entries for April 1942.

46. Kaplan, *Megilat Yisurin*. The illusion of the acquisition of power works by negation. Kaplan writes in an entry devoted in the main to rumors, "When we pray for something, it starts off an avalanche" (July 6, 1941, entire entry omitted in English version). In this case, the Jews of the ghetto do not actually manage to bring about the desired events, but they are not entirely helpless. They have an influence, even if by negation, on reality. This is very different from the reversing of the structure of power in gallows humor. Freud gives an example of a criminal who is led to the gallows on Monday who remarks, "Well, the week's beginning nicely." Sigmund Freud, "Humour," in *Complete Psychological Works*, 161–66. Here Freud claims the criminal reverses the power structure between himself and the executioners. But this change is dependent on the double meaning of irony, which acknowledges that the power is still in the hands of the executioner. The rumor, on the other hand, makes us believe for a moment that the power is truly reversed.

47. Writing as vengeance is utterly imaginative in this context. See Salek Perechodnik. *Hatfkid Ha'atzuv shel Hate'ud* [The sad task of documentation] (Jerusalem: Keter, 1993), 238. (I refer to the Hebrew edition because the English one is totally distorted.) See David Engel, "On the Bowdlerization of a Holocaust Testimony: The Wartime Journal of Calek Perchodnik, 'Am I a Murderer? Testament of a Jewish Ghetto Policeman,'" *Polin* 12 (1999): 316–29, as well as Yizhak Arran, *Mein Kleine Tsavoe* [My little testament] (in Yiddish), Yad Vashem Archives, uncataloged, 2.

48. See, for example, the entries for February 4, 1940; February 20, 1940; March 25, 1941; and June 7, 1942, among others.

49. Emil Utitz, *Psychologie des Lebens im Konzentrationslager Theresienstadt* [A psychology of life in the Theresienstadt concentration camp] (Vienna: Continental, 1948 [1947]). I wish to thank Dr. Nitzan Lebovic for drawing my attention to this fascinating study.

50. Utitz, *Psychologie*, 5.

51. Ibid., 17.

52. Nachman Blumenthal, "Magical Thinking in the Era of Nazi Occupation," *Yad Vashem Studies* 5 (1963): 175–86.

Doris L. Bergen

I Am (Not) to Blame: Intent and Agency in Personal Accounts of the Holocaust

CONSTRUCTS OF INTENT AND AGENCY HAVE BECOME CONVENTIONS in the field of Holocaust studies. Influenced by legal frameworks, intent provides a way to home in on the most frequently asked question about the killers: why did they do it? Meanwhile, efforts to integrate Jewish sources encourage a focus on victims' agency,[1] often expressed in terms of survival strategies. Considering these conventions and examining them together draws attention to several gaps and ambiguities that are the subject of this essay.

One such gap is the mismatch between scholars and the people we study. Historians of the perpetrators emphasize intent and equate it with motive, premeditation, and the galvanizing will that transforms acts of violence into genocide. Accounts by perpetrators, in contrast, regularly plead powerlessness: "It was not my fault," they protest; "I had no choice." When speaking of victims, historians present agency as fragile power salvaged from intense vulnerability;[2] highlighting agency is meant to restore dignity and humanity to those targeted for destruction.[3] Yet survivors frame their narratives quite differently. Many people reject individual agency as a key to their own survival, insisting instead on the primacy of luck and fate. Some survivors were totally powerless or nearly so, for instance children, for whom others made crucial decisions. Still, a surprising number of accounts by survivors, and by victims who perished, make strong, even extravagant claims about agency. "I am to blame," many insist, for doing the wrong thing, for not seeing what was coming, or for making some fateful choice.[4]

Considering perpetrators and victims together in this way throws into relief a paradox: perpetrators, who wielded massive power, deny responsibility, whereas victims, who were defined by powerlessness, insist on their own agency. Of course, it is to be expected that personal sources from accused or convicted killers downplay intent. Most such documents are generated through legal processes and have therefore been constructed to place the accused in the best, or least damning, light possible. Alternately, some personal accounts by perpetrators have been prepared for, by, or with an eye to children, grandchildren, and other family members. These, too, say little about intent and instead circle around issues of guilt, rationalization, and denial.[5] But how do we explain the insistence on agency in accounts by Jewish victims? How do we interpret the disconnect between the reality of abject weakness and their narratives of responsibility and self-blame?

These questions point to the chasm between those who speak as witnesses from the past and their audience, between historical actors and "us," in our own present. The Nazi system both magnified and obscured agency, of perpetrators and also of victims, and it remains the distorting lens through which we regard the Holocaust. With the construct of intent, we try to comprehend and judge the perpetrators, but they, shielded by the impunity of power, hold back. Victims, in contrast, signal the continued urgency of their need to be heard, to connect, to communicate their pain and loss. Yet their audience is elusive, attracted and repelled by suffering and always changing, and so their narratives change too. Indeed, the context of testimonies' reception alters their content over time, from the perspective of the speaker and the listener.

Scholar and subject, perpetrator and victim, power and powerlessness, past and present—all of these binaries are marked and blurred by shame. Primo Levi's often-quoted reflections on shame offer guidance for thinking about intent, agency, and how the Holocaust is narrated. When the Red Army liberated Auschwitz, Levi recalled, the soldiers seemed weighed down:

> It was the same shame which we knew so well, which submerged us after the selections, and every time we had to witness or undergo an outrage: the shame that the Germans never knew, the shame which the just man experiences when confronted by a crime committed by another, and he feels remorse because of its existence, because of its having been irrevocably introduced into the world of existing things, and because his will has proven nonexistent or feeble and was incapable of putting up a good defense.[6]

Levi called this vast shame "the shame of the world." It was felt not by those most guilty, he wrote, but by "the just" because "they sensed that what had happened around them and in their presence, and in them, was irrevocable."[7] The particular testimonies I discuss below are distinctive in the explicit and divergent ways they engage shame, as a casualty of thoughtlessness, a partner to accusation and blame, and a means of narrating loss.

RUDOLF HÖSS: INTENT AND DENIABILITY

Rudolf Höss, the former commandant of Auschwitz, mentioned shame at the end of his memoir, written in a Polish prison in 1947, as he awaited execution. But what Höss conveyed was very different from Levi's "shame of the world," and in fact underscored Levi's point that those who committed the crimes "never knew" such shame. (Levi would later write the foreword to the English edition of Höss's autobiography.) Höss's shame was not universal and moral but personal and conventional. He had often been in mortal peril, he explained, but "on every occasion fate has intervened to save my life, so that at last I might be put to death in this shameful manner. How greatly I envy those of my comrades who died a soldier's death."[8]

Höss denied any murderous intent: "Unknowingly I was a cog in the wheel of the great extermination machine created by the Third Reich. The machine has been smashed to pieces, the engine is broken, and I, too, must now be destroyed. The world demands it." To his mind, it was not what he had done but the needs of others that resulted in his condemnation: "Let the public continue to regard me as the bloodthirsty beast, the cruel sadist, and the mass murderer; for the masses could never imagine the commandant of Auschwitz in any other light. They could never understand that he, too, had a heart and that he was not evil."[9]

Höss's self-pity is abhorrent, his claim of innocent intentions absurd. But his description of the Third Reich as an "extermination machine," read alongside Levi's observation that "the shame of the world" was felt by the just and not by the guilty, points to an important characteristic of the Nazi system of destruction: at many levels, in fact, it required minimal individual intent. Indeed, a capacity to make things happen without explicit intent was one of the sources of its power and durability. Complex links between people and institutions in a way substituted for intent and at the same time provided perpetrators with convenient screens from facing the consequences of their deeds. Hannah Arendt's analysis of thoughtlessness and evil draws attention to this asymmetry between intent (limited, even unconscious) and results (massive and murderous).[10] Raul Hilberg used the image of a train to demonstrate the momentum of bureaucratized destruction, although he never lost sight of the human driver.[11] In her study of Udo Klausa, the *Landrat* (administrator) of the Będzin ghetto in Poland, Mary Fulbrook speaks of "systemic violence."[12] All these approaches analyze how the Nazi system manipulated and transformed intent. They demonstrate that interrogating intent is only one part of grappling with how and why the killers did what they did.

HERMANN HÖFLE: CRACKS IN THE ARMOR

Perpetrators' testimonies, like the systems they were part of, are set up in such a way to obscure their intentions and their deeds. Yet even perpetrator accounts reveal some cracks in the barriers of deniability. One incident should suffice to illustrate. In November 1947, U.S. military interrogators questioned a former *Sicherheitsdienst* (SD or Security Service) official named Johannes Müller about his wartime activities in the area of Lublin. Müller was asked to report on the character and current whereabouts of the men with whom he had worked. One was his boss, Odilo Globocnik. Another was Hermann Höfle, Globocnik's deputy, *Sturmbahnführer* (a rank equivalent to major), and second in command of Operation Reinhard, the program to annihilate Jews in the General Government. Müller described the role of both men in horrific massacres of Jewish children. At a meeting, Müller reported, he had heard Globocnik tell Höfle about his three-year-old niece: "Listen, I can't even stand to look at that little one if I think about those other kids."[13]

In the spring of 1943, Höfle's infant twins, only a few months old at the time, died of diphtheria. Müller, who attended the burial, described how Höfle had a fit at the cemetery and began screaming, "This is the punishment from heaven for my sins."[14] Still, whatever guilt or shame Höfle felt, his defenses temporarily weakened no doubt by grief at the death of his children, must have dissipated fairly quickly. He may have been given a leave to rest at home in Salzburg before returning to action as one of the leaders of the Operation Harvest Festival slaughters of Jews in the Lublin area in November 1943.

Did Globocnik, Höfle, and other hands-on killers deliberately devise procedures that masked their intent by forcing victims to participate in their own destruction? Did they seek to lighten any burden on their consciences by displacing guilt onto their victims? It seems impossible to determine with certainty, although such practices can be seen as symptomatic of the Nazi system and its corruption: its evil was contagious, and as Primo Levi noted, it compromised its victims, too. And there is at least some evidence that spreading the blame was deliberate: as Franz Stangl, former commandant of the Sobibor and Treblinka killing centers, explained to Gitta Sereny in an interview, spreading the blame made it easier for the killers to do their jobs. In Stangl's words, humiliation and cruelty served "to condition those who actually had to carry out the policies . . . to make it possible for them to do what they did."[15]

Recollections of survivors echo Stangl's claim. An acquaintance in Holocaust studies told me about a woman she knows, a survivor of Auschwitz, who said Josef Mengele chose her to be his personal translator during the arrival of a transport. As reported by my acquaintance, "He told her to calmly explain to the women who should go left and who should go right and assure them they would all meet shortly after." Among the group were members of the young woman's family. "Her aunt was told to give her children over to her mother and then go to the right, while the children would go with their grandmother to the left. She protested and insisted on staying with her children." According to the survivor, Mengele then instructed her to tell her aunt that she could go to the left as well. "As she put it, why would he care if another Jewish woman died?"[16] Some years later, now living in Canada with children of her own, the survivor began to wake every night screaming, "*Links!* (left)" and "*Rechts!* (right)." As was reported, "She told her husband that she was responsible for the deaths of her relatives and all the other women that she (not Mengele) had sent to their deaths."[17] The second-hand narrative offered a positive, if not happy, ending: with the help of a psychiatrist, the survivor recognized she had been powerless in that situation. Still this account, like the description of Höfle's collapse at his children's grave, reminds us that grief and shame bled across the lines of victim and perpetrator, innocence and guilt.

KAROLINA JUS AND ANDRZEJ JUS, HENRY FRIEDMAN: AGENCY AND ACCUSATION

Personal reports from victims pose challenges very different from those associated with perpetrator accounts, but they, too, are hardly clear windows into complex issues. For one thing, there are so many firsthand descriptions by survivors, and by people who died, and they vary enormously in content, form, and style. Even a single narrative may contain multiple and often conflicting statements about agency, blame, and shame. Many people dismiss the idea of agency in their own survival, asserting instead the preeminence of luck. At the same time, these positions are by no means mutually exclusive, and even accounts that vehemently reject any explanation other than chance frequently demonstrate the resources a survivor had: "good looks," quick reflexes, particular skills, or sound instincts. Ruth Kluger credited her mother's paranoia with saving their lives in Auschwitz: "It wasn't the last time that my mother thought she was pursued, and maybe it wasn't the first time. But it took the Shoah to prove her right for once."[18] Some people who were very young at the time, even infants, nonetheless narrate their survival in terms of agency: I knew what to do, or I should have known.

It is rare, at least in published accounts or interviews intended for distribution, to find discussions of agency that amount to accusations of failure by another person. But one such case offers a striking indication of how high the stakes are around eyewitness reports of agency. Karolina Jus (née Frist), born into a Jewish family, was baptized a Roman Catholic in July 1941 and married a Polish Christian. With the help of her well-connected father-in-law in Lwów (now Lviv, Ukraine), she was entered retroactively into church records as a Catholic from birth. She and her husband, Andrzej, published their jointly authored memoir in 1991.[19] In it, they describe efforts Andrzej's father made to help Karolina's Jewish parents and sisters find refuge, but according to the account, Karolina's father declined the help. Karolina survived, but all the other members of her family were murdered, shot alongside other Jews into a pit in a forest.

The coauthors provide a loving portrait of Karolina's family, and the passage in which Andrzej relates how and what he learned about their deaths is at once unflinching and profoundly respectful. Yet implicit in the memoir, and made explicit in at least three separate passages, is the view that Karolina's Jewish father was somehow at fault. He missed opportunities and made the "wrong" choices, his daughter and son-in-law suggested, because of his optimism, faith in human nature, and confidence in German culture. Karolina recalls confiding in her Catholic fiancé's father that her own father was unlikely to agree to hide in a monastery and have his wife and daughter sheltered in a convent. She blamed "his faith in the victory of justice." In her assessment, "He believes that this is a momentary, short and tragic imbalance in moral values, and that the victory of noble human feelings is imminent." She was afraid, she said, "that this philosophy will kill him."[20] A message of Christian triumphalism resounds here: it was his stubborn adherence to Judaism, the narrative suggests, that killed Karolina Jus's father.

Much more common in survivor accounts are exaggerated claims of agency linked to self-accusation. Victims and survivors express a wrenching array of recriminations from "I should have known" to "I caused the death of people I love." The opening lines of Olga Lengyel's memoir *Five Chimneys* express such agony: "*Mea culpa*, my fault, *mea maxima culpa!*"[21] Lengyel, who arrived in Auschwitz-Birkenau from Hungary in 1944, was referring to her instructions to her adolescent son, telling him to stay with his grandmother. How was she to know that children and elderly people were sent directly to the gas?

Henry Friedman's 1999 memoir *I'm No Hero* offers another perspective on agency and self-accusation. In 1943, Friedman was fifteen years old. Together with his mother, his younger brother, and an acquaintance, the boys' schoolteacher, he hid in the loft of a barn in German-occupied eastern Poland. The Ukrainian woman sheltering them was having an extramarital affair with the chief of police, an active collaborator. Unbeknownst to Friedman and his brother, their mother was pregnant when they went into hiding, and eventually it was time for the baby to be born. By his account, the denizens of the loft took a vote regarding what to do. The results were three to one (Friedman's mother dissenting) to have her deliver the baby, the teacher would then kill it, and the Ukrainian woman would bury the body. They followed the plan. By Friedman's account, "The decision we made has haunted me ever since. I wake in the middle of the night, crying. My brother still denies that he voted."[22]

If one stops reading here, Friedman sounds like a classic case of survivor guilt. What could be more devastating than having to choose for someone else to be killed so that you could have a chance to stay alive? By emphasizing the vote—his active participation in making the decision—Friedman highlights his choice. And yet he clearly understands that he was not ultimately to blame, or at least that his role was the product of a murderous system: "When I think of that part of my life in 1943, the pain comes back to haunt me and I can never forgive the Nazis for what I was forced to be a part of at the age of fifteen—to take a life, just so I could survive. I have a problem when analyzing myself. Was I so terribly selfish then?"[23]

Friedman's account is unsettling, almost unbearable. Such narratives disrupt the image of the survivor as hero, upend clichés of the triumph of the human spirit, and replace them with sheer agony. How are we to understand these cries of shame and self-recrimination? Ignore them? Fixate on them? Write them off as "survivor guilt"? But that label, which comes so easily to hand, is not an explanation but a diagnosis.

Friedman does not end his narrative with the death of the baby in the barn. Later in the book, he describes a trip he took to India in 1984. He found himself in Delhi when Indira Gandhi was shot by her Sikh bodyguards. Violence surged, and Friedman overheard hotel management discussing how they planned to kill a Sikh man who worked as the night clerk. To Friedman, the chain of events conjured up horrible memories of the end of the war, when Poles hunted out Ukrainians as they "ethnically cleansed" the region. He stayed up all night drinking with the hotel men and succeeded in persuading them to spare the Sikh.[24] Friedman does not recount this incident as somehow redemptive or compensatory, but he does make clear that he understood he exercised a very different degree of agency as an adult, a successful businessman, and a citizen of a world power than he had as a Jewish adolescent marked for death in German-occupied Poland. Unlike Karolina and Andrzej Jus, who narrated Jewish agency as blame, Friedman represented it as an opening, however small, for introspection and change. Such divergent accounts warn against resolving the ambiguity of Holocaust testimonies with our own desires for lessons or affirmation.

CALEL PERECHODNIK AND ADINA BLADY SZWAJGER: AGENCY AND AGONY

Self-questioning is normal after loss. Who has not tormented himself or herself with bitter what-ifs? But amid the magnitude of death and destruction of the Shoah, such reliving of turning points takes on a terrifying weight. Renya Kulkielko's early memoir of the Holocaust, originally published in Hebrew in 1944, describes how she and a group of friends (most of them associated with Zionist youth groups; she refers to their shared housing as a "kibbutz") witnessed the liquidation of the Będzin ghetto in occupied Poland in May 1943. Assisted by members of the Jewish police, Germans rounded up all but a remnant of the ghetto inhabitants, killing many on the spot and transporting the rest to unknown destinations that, by then, were widely known among the Jews to be lethal. The young people had planned to fight, but in Kulkielko's words, "There was nothing at all we could do to save them from being sent away." Everyone who was left "had lost someone close and dear." One of the group's leaders, a woman called Frumka, "was tearing her hair and knocking her head against the wall. We were afraid that she would attempt suicide. She cried aloud: 'I am guilty of their death. Why did I tell them to remain in their rooms? I am their murderess, it is I who sent them to their death.' It was utterly impossible to explain to her that she was not at fault."[25] Kulkielko's account provides a valuable glimpse into the heavy burden of bearing responsibility for others in deadly circumstances. It also anticipates accusations of failure leveled after the war by Jews against Jewish leaders.

Issues around Jewish agency resonate in particular ways for the Jewish police, who exercised considerable power as long as the ghettos functioned. Calel Perechodnik was a member of the Jewish police in the Otwock ghetto near Warsaw. In August 1942, his wife and baby daughter had concealed themselves to avoid a roundup and transport. He told them to come out and assured them that they would be spared because, as a member of the police, he had been promised he could exempt his family. But that was not the case, and his wife and daughter were forced onto the train to the Treblinka killing center. "Am I a murderer, my wife's executioner?" Perechodnik demanded of his diary. [26] Immediately after that searing question, however, Perechodnik offered another possibility: "I, or that Kronenberg? And maybe the two of us are only marionettes of destiny, of the evil fate of Israel."

Bernard Kronenberg was the head of the ghetto police in Otwock. Perechodnik was killed in Warsaw during the insurrection two years later, possibly a victim of Polish gentiles, not Germans.

Many of the people who blame themselves openly are not those who might be accused of having committed actual crimes, that is, not former *kapos* (concentration camp prisoners given authority over other prisoners), so-called catchers, or members of Jewish councils or Jewish police. Even Perechodnik, who fits into these categories, focused not on his offences against Jews in general or members of his community in particular, but only on his wife and child. Of course, precisely in the case of these two people, he had no intention to harm them and could realistically blame himself at most for a mistake, a misjudgment. Indeed, in this regard, his expression of blame is typical; these are cases in which it is exaggerated, even absurd for people to blame themselves. Primo Levi affirms this perception:

> Few survivors feel guilty about having deliberately damaged, robbed, or beaten a companion. Those who did so (the *Kapos*, but not only they) block out the memory. By contrast, however, almost everybody feels guilty of having omitted to offer help. The presence at your side of a weaker—or less cunning, or older, or too young—companion, hounding you with his demands for help or with his simple presence, in itself an entreaty, is a constant in the life of the Lager [camp]. The demand for solidarity, for a human word, advice, even just a listening ear, was permanent and universal but rarely satisfied.[27]

Self-accusations and the patterns in which they appear suggest that people bring out only as much as they can bear. In 1943, Adina Blady Szwajger, a former medical student, worked in the children's ward of a hospital in the Warsaw ghetto. As the ghetto was being "cleared"—that is, when Germans came in to kill the children—she gave lethal injections of morphine to the children in her care. But it was not only, or even mostly, that deed Szwajger described in her book as a cause of guilt. She blamed herself for the death of her husband, who emerged from his hiding place to try to escape to Hungary. The scheme, now known as Hotel Poland, turned out to be a trap. Szwajger narrated it like this:

> In the morning he just waved goodbye to me and went downstairs. "Don't see me off," he said. "Take care," he shouted from down-

> stairs. And he went out into the courtyard. I ran after him. Marysia [Marysia Sawicka, member of the Polish underground] too. And we saw. We saw that it wasn't buses taking them away but prison lorries. The gendarmes were collecting people up and shouting: "*Schnell, schnell!* [Quickly, quickly!]." And the people still didn't understand and were hurrying and pushing forward to get into the lorries.[28]

Szwajger and her companion managed to get away, only to be grabbed by a blackmailer, who took them to the police station. By her account, it was their despair that saved them: "Our faces seemed so composed that the policeman didn't even check our papers. Because we were composed, composed as one can only be in the face of a disaster. Because we already knew."[29] Of the many people Szwajger could have blamed for this debacle, she singled out one, herself: "And I knew, I knew beyond doubt, that it was all over. And that I had done it to him, with my own hands. Although he had wanted it, if not for me he wouldn't even have known that this could be his escape from life. The convoy went straight to Auschwitz."[30]

Szwajger discussed the incident with the children in quite different terms. She continued to practice medicine for forty years after the war:

> But somewhere underneath I thought that I had no right to carry out my profession. After all, one does not start one's work as a doctor by leading people not to life but to death. And I have lived with this knowledge to this day. And it does not help me that I know that it was all in order to save people's lives, that it was all necessary. But along the way something was not as it should have been. Maybe it was too heavy a burden for the rest of my life?[31]

Szwajger does not speak of shame about her decision to give the children lethal injections. But she does mention being ashamed to receive one of the "life tickets" the head doctor gave to some people who worked in the hospital so they could avoid the roundup: "And that was probably the worst thing of all—all those people with 'tickets' pushing to get out and live, while all the others were left behind." To her the two incidents—giving the children morphine and her escape from the ghetto—blurred together to explain why she "was always different from everybody else. And nobody ever understood this."[32]

The pun in Szwajger's title, "I Remember Nothing More," speaks to both the incompleteness and the ineradicability of memory. She makes a comparable point about the im/possibility of narration when she recounts what she framed as her most devastating action of all, the killing of a Jewish woman in hiding:

> I didn't know that the worst was yet to come. But it came. I don't know, perhaps I should have refused. After all it wasn't a job for a doctor. Except that no one understood this. There was no other doctor among us at that time. And so I didn't have anyone to talk to, to tell that I would rather die than do this. It would have been easier to die myself than to carry out euthanasia on someone who was mentally ill.
>
> She used to run out into the street and shout in Yiddish. She posed a mortal threat for the landlords and for the half a dozen or so young people hiding in the house, among them her own daughter.
>
> But I couldn't do it! But I did it. At the request of her daughter.
>
> But I don't want to write any more. Not a sentence more. About anything.[33]

Notice the contrast to the perpetrators: Rudolf Höss could not admit what he did because he actually did it, with intent. Szwajger could admit it because she knew she had not done it, or at least knew she had no choice.

ABE PASTERNAK: NARRATING LOSS

Expressions of shame and recrimination of self and others can be interpreted in multiple ways. They can be a lament for the existence of a world of suffering, an attempt to spread the blame, a cry for understanding, or a way to keep alive the memory of the dead. They can be an effort to restore some moral order to a universe of meaningless suffering. Blaming oneself becomes an assertion of one's ability to know right from wrong, even if it was impossible to do what was right or good. In Lawrence Langer's words, "As heroic memory honors the connection between agency and fate, unheroic memory records its absence."[34]

Henry Greenspan offers another possibility, which he presents as a corrective to Langer: in a society fascinated by the notion of survivor guilt, expressions of self-recrimination can result from survivors reaching out to their audiences, not merely to give them what they want or expect to hear but also to connect, to reveal the depths of loss and grief that they experienced and their inability to express it in ways that others can comprehend. Greenspan emphasizes the interaction between the survivor and his or her audience and suggests that shame sometimes provides a common ground.

In a piece in *Lessons and Legacies Volume X: Back to the Sources: Reexamining Perpetrators, Victims, and Bystanders*, Greenspan focuses on Abe Pasternak, a Holocaust survivor from Romania.[35] Pasternak arrived in Auschwitz together with his parents and his two brothers, one older, one younger than he. In a series of exhibits, publications, and documentaries, Pasternak's comments about his younger brother have been used as a "textbook example" of survivor guilt. In a 1984 interview with Sid Bolkosky, Pasternak described how, in the selection on the ramp, he told his younger brother to go with their parents: "And like a little kid, he followed—he did. Little did I know that I sent him to the crematorium. I am . . . I feel like I killed him . . . I can't get it out of my head. It hurts me, it bothers me, and I don't know what to do."[36]

By interviewing Pasternak more than once and over an extended period, Greenspan learned that there was much more to this recollection and account than appears in the brief snippets. Over the years, Pasternak learned he got a reaction from this account of selection on the ramp. He could reach his audience in a way that trying to describe piles of corpses and feelings of desolation could not. He was able to give voice to his pain, to remember his brother, in a way that audiences, at least to some extent, could share. According to Greenspan, "In one of our conversations, Abe noted: 'They can't understand, they can't relate to, the terror, the smell, the chaos, the dead bodies all around. How can they relate to that? But *this* they can relate to. I noticed that especially at one of the conferences where I spoke. Yes, I noticed that. *This* they related to.'"[37]

The online transcript includes a sentence that does not appear in the passages quoted by Greenspan or Langer. Both of them note Pasternak's reference to his older brother, who was with him on the ramp: "I feel that I am responsible for that and my brother says to me that I am not responsible for it because he is as much responsible as I."[38] But according to the transcript Pasternak continued with a kind of verbal shrug: "But there isn't very much that . . . I guess I'll have to live with it."[39] Pasternak's words reveal the coexistence of a feeling of guilt, an understanding that it is misplaced, and recognition that he can and will "live with it." Diverging interpretations of his narrative, and of other accounts of guilt and shame, are not mutually exclusive. The perpetrators did deliberately shift blame onto their victims; exaggerated claims of agency really are or can be an assertion of the survivors' sense of right and wrong. They can also be a cry of pain, an expression of resilience and endless wounding. At the same time, victims' expressions of self-recrimination may be a means of reaching an audience that is unwilling or unable to listen without some diversion or opportunity to feel safe and perhaps superior.

SARA GINAITE: NOT A MUSEUM EXHIBIT

Examining statements about agency and blame in Holocaust testimonies suggests a number of patterns and tendencies. They seem more evident in written than oral accounts. With the help of a research assistant, I examined one hundred testimonies in the USC Shoah Foundation Visual History Archive and found no explicit statements comparable to those from Friedman, Perechodnik, and Szwajger.[40] They do exist, as Pasternak proves, though they may be infrequent, particularly in interviews long after the events. Even in the written texts, extended descriptions of shame and guilt appear more often in accounts written earlier than in those that come later, so that Friedman and Szwajger are atypical. It seems logical that victims and survivors would tend to write rather than speak such recriminations to maintain more control over their narratives. Langer articulates a similar conclusion: "Unlike the witness in video testimonies, the *writer* afflicted with the chaos attending the futile pursuits of memory has available a form of closure that invites order, if not consolation . . . Narrative structure . . . allows him to impose a perspective on the camp experience that is unavailable to the oral witness."[41]

Early claims of guilt should be contextualized in a postwar climate of uncertainty and suspicion. Perhaps they were a way to try to manage one's reputation. Upon returning to Prague, the survivor Ruth Bondy says she could see the questions reflected in the eyes of others: how had she survived? "Kapo? Prostitute?"[42] And, of course, there were formal accusations against Jews charged with betraying other Jews, in the honor courts in the displaced persons camps,[43] in hearings in Poland,[44] and in trials in Israel. It used to be said that these charges came to an end with the trial of Adolf Eichmann in 1961, but

Na'ama Shik has pointed out that they did not end then, although by the 1970s such accusations had become rare.[45] No doubt, earlier and later survivors also worried about how they would be judged by their children and grandchildren. Robert Melson, who survived living in Kraków with his parents on false papers, noted that his mother was never the same after the war. She had been unable to save her parents, and, in Melson's words, "I knew too that she blamed herself for having abandoned them in the ghetto in order to save herself and me."[46]

While writing this essay, I have thought constantly of Sara Ginaite, a Holocaust survivor from Kovno (present-day Kaunas, Lithuania) and a former resistance fighter who now lives in Toronto, Canada. Dr. Ginaite once began a lecture to my students with the observation, "I am not a museum exhibit." Only some years later am I beginning to grasp what she meant.[47] Ginaite also asked me to prepare students to talk about the ethical questions raised in her book, *Resistance and Survival: The Jewish Community in Kaunas, 1941–1944*.[48] What was she referring to, I wondered? Surely not the Koniuchy controversy, the case then being investigated by the Lithuanian state prosecutor against a group of former partisans, Ginaite among them, who were accused of massacring civilians in a village in 1944?[49]

In fact, Ginaite had something else entirely in mind. To her, the central ethical question was whether she had done the right thing in leaving the ghetto to join her husband, Misha Rubinsonas, to fight with the partisans in the Rudninkai Forest. In her words:

> I felt that I was betraying my mother, leaving her to an unknown fate. I felt that I was being unfair to my closest family and that I had no moral right to leave them. In my soul, I struggled with two conflicting feelings. One whispered that I must go and fight the enemy, the other one urged me to remain with the family—either to perish with them or survive with them.[50]

Ginaite left her mother and sister behind in the ghetto, and although she later returned and tried to find hiding places for them or in some way to help them, she was unable to do so. Her mother died in the Stutthof concentration camp, and her sister Alice Benjaminavicius (Benn) took care of her mother until the end.

Decades later, Alice's daughter recalled that her mother "harbored some resentment" against her sister, celebrated after the war as a hero of the Soviet Union and the Jewish resistance:

> She often remarked how Sara had eloped and run away from the ghetto to join the Partisans, leaving her to take on the full burden of care of their mother. My mother also believed that the Partisans did not nearly experience the same level of suffering that she did being in the concentration camp. And while she was glad that her sister was spared, at some level, she wished that they had been through this together.[51]

Ginaite would agree, publicly calling her sister the true hero and working with determination until she succeeded in having Alice recognized by the Lithuanian state for her involvement in saving Jewish children during the war.

Talking with Sara Ginaite over the years has convinced me that victims' conflicting assessments of agency, self-accusations, and admissions of failure are important and need to be included in histories of the Holocaust because they demonstrate the complexity and multidimensionality of the people involved. Even Hilberg's strange insistence that the Jewish leadership was not powerless allows them a kind of dignity, in contrast to Timothy Snyder's flat presentation of victims as powerless recipients of violence in *Bloodlands*. In this age of "tributes" to survivors, plans to fete and stage them for various purposes, it is valuable to be reminded that the Holocaust was not about superheroes but about people. Turning them into something larger than life goes against what some, at least, felt and feel. In Primo Levi's memorable words, "Coming out of the darkness, one suffered because of the reacquired consciousness of having been diminished."[52]

Ruth Kluger's observations about the use of personal accounts suggest that scholars may have our own reasons to feel ashamed, of cowardice, callousness, or superficiality:

> I used to think that after the war I would have something of interest and significance to tell. A contribution. But people didn't want to hear about it, or if they did listen, it was in a certain pose, an attitude assumed for this special occasion; it was not as partners in a conversation, but as if I had imposed on them and they were graciously indulging me. The current craze for oral history and interviewing harbors a related flaw of one-sidedness, even though the interviewer is doing the imposing: he or she contributes nothing except an implied superiority to suffering. Beware of the kind of awe which easily turns into its opposite, disgust. For we like to

> keep the objects of both emotions at arm's length in instinctive revulsion.[53]

Annette Wieviorka quotes the response of Henry Bulawko, a "former Jewish inmate in France," when historians referred to him and his counterparts as "living documents":

> I suddenly saw myself transformed into a strange animal caged in a zoo with other rare species. Historians came to examine me, told me to lie down, turned me over and over as you turn the pages of a document, and asked me questions, taking notes here and there . . . The term . . . seemed to me infinitely shocking. One can go from being a "former inmate" to a "witness," then from "witness" to "document." So then, what are we? What am I?[54]

Kluger and Bulawko turn the gaze back on scholars of the Holocaust and force us to think about what we are doing. Just as the treatment of intent and agency in accounts by perpetrators and victims reflects efforts to construct narratives people can live with, historians seek to order the past, its representations, and our own emotions. We try to control the narrative and further analysis by reducing survivors to "living documents" and victims to "voices." When we isolate perpetrators' intentions from their actions, social relations, and political contexts we risk producing simplistic histories of the bad guys. Both tendencies reflect fearfulness about facing the bottomless pain of the Holocaust and feeling ourselves implicated in the shame of the world, then and now.

NOTES

1. For discussion, see Saul Friedländer, "Prologue," in Jonathan Petropoulos, Lynn Rapaport, and John K. Roth, eds., *Lessons and Legacies Volume IX: Memory, History, and Responsibility: Reassessments of the Holocaust, Implications for the Future* (Evanston, Ill.: Northwestern University Press, 2009): 3–15, in particular on integration of what Friedländer calls "the Jewish dimension," 3.

2. A concept popularized in women's studies since the 1970s, agency connotes power, room to maneuver, and strategies of self-help rather than powerlessness and passivity. Decades later, some scholars wonder whether agency may have "lost its edge" as an analytical tool. See Lynn M. Thomas, "Agency," in the session "Losing Their Edge? A Critical Evaluation of Key

Analytic Concepts in Gender History," Berkshire Conference on the History of Women, Toronto, Canada, May 23, 2014.

3. For years, however, Lawrence Langer has been calling all such comforting categories into question. See especially Lawrence L. Langer, *Holocaust Testimonies: The Ruins of Memory* (New Haven, Conn.: Yale University Press, 1991). Witnesses, Langer writes, "remain divided between the knowledge that during their ordeal they were deprived of moral agency by their circumstances and their present need to see themselves then and now as the responsible agents of their own destiny and of those around them," 185.

4. For an earlier version of my own thinking about Jewish agency in the Holocaust, see Doris L. Bergen, "No End in Sight? The Ongoing Challenge of Producing an Integrated History of the Holocaust," in Christian Wiese and Paul Betts, eds., *Years of Persecution, Years of Extermination: Saul Friedländer and the Future of Holocaust Studies* (New York: Continuum, 2010), 289–310.

5. See Katharina von Kellenbach, *The Mark of Cain: Guilt and Denial in the Post-War Lives of Nazi Perpetrators* (Oxford: Oxford University Press, 2013), esp. chap. 6, "'Understand, My Boy, This Truth about the Mistake': Inheriting Guilt," 137–62.

6. Primo Levi, *The Drowned and the Saved*, trans. Raymond Rosenthal (New York: Vintage, 1989), 72. Levi quotes here from his earlier book, *The Reawakening*, which he describes as published in Italian in 1963 but written in 1946.

7. Levi, *The Drowned and the Saved*, 85–86.

8. Rudolf Hoess [Höss], *Commandant of Auschwitz*, trans. Constantine FitzGibbon (London: Phoenix, 1995), 181; originally published in Polish, 1951; dated Cracow (Kraków), February 1947.

9. Ibid.

10. Hannah Arendt, *Eichmann in Jerusalem: A Report on the Banality of Evil* (New York: Penguin, 1963), esp. 287–88; see also her earlier reflections in Hannah Arendt, *The Human Condition* (Chicago: University of Chicago Press, 1958), 5.

11. Raul Hilberg, "German Railroads/Jewish Souls," *Society* 14, 1 (November–December 1976): 60–74; see also Raul Hilberg, *Sonderzüge nach Auschwitz* [Special trains to Auschwitz], trans. Gisela Schleicher (Mainz, Ger.: Dumjahn, 1981).

12. Mary Fulbrook, "'Unschuldig schuldig werden'? Systemische Gewalt und die Verfolgung der Juden von Będzin [To become innocently guilty? Systemic violence and the persecution of the Jews of Będzin]," in Andrea Löw, Doris L. Bergen, and Anna Hájková, eds., *Alltag im Holocaust: Jüdisches Leben im Großdeutschen Reich 1941–1945* [Everyday life in the Holocaust: Jewish life in the Greater German Reich 1941–1945] (Munich,

Ger.: Oldenbourg, 2013), 117–36. See also Mary Fulbrook, *A Small Town near Auschwitz: Ordinary Nazis and the Holocaust* (Oxford: Oxford University Press, 2012).

13. Yad Vashem Archives (YVA) has a copy of a series of interrogations of Johannes Müller in the collection M.9 (Ludwigsburg files)/ file 688 (M.9/688). The earliest is "Fragen an Johannes Mueller, Vernehmung des Johannes Hermann Mueller, Regierungsrat am 5. November 1947 von 2 bis 3 Uhr durch Mr. Larry L Wolff und Mr. Alfred Schwarz auf Veranlassung von Mr. Schwenk, SS-Sektion [Questions to Johannes Mueller, interrogation of Johannes Hermann Mueller, government council, on November 5, 1947, from 2 to 3 A.M. by Mr. Larry L Wolff and Mr. Alfred Schwarz at the instigation of Mr. Schwenk, SS(*Schutzstaffel*)-section]." Mueller is identified as born July 30, 1895, in Gota (Gotha), Kreis Delicz (Delitsch), Germany. He worked for the police in Warsaw and in September 1941 was assigned to a senior administrative position with the commander of the *Sicherheitspolizei* (Security Police) and the *Sicherheitsdienst* (SD or Security Service) in Lublin, in German-occupied Poland. A second interrogation, dated November 24, 1947, conducted by Herbert Meyer, begins on page 37 of the same file (M.9/688). A third, Interrogation 2427 B, dated November 28, 1947, begins on file page 47. Yad Vashem lists the source of the original as the Jewish Historical Documentation Center, Linz, Austria (Simon Wiesenthal Collection). Quotations regarding Odilo Globocnik's niece and Hermann Höfle's children are in "Fragen," November 5, 1947, Yad Vashem Archives, M.9/688, 16–17 (13–14 of the "Fragen"). Mueller mentioned both incidents again on November 24, 1947, Yad Vashem Archives, M.9/688, 43.

14. Ibid.

15. Gitta Sereny, *Into that Darkness: An Examination of Conscience* (New York: Vintage, 1983), 101.

16. Personal correspondence (e-mail) from Lesley Schwartz, February 4, 2014.

17. Ibid.

18. Ruth Kluger, *Still Alive: A Holocaust Girlhood Remembered* (New York: Feminist Press at the City University of New York, 2001), 104.

19. Andrzej Jus and Karolina Jus, *Our Journey in the Valley of Tears* (Toronto, Canada: University of Toronto Press, 1991).

20. Ibid., 86. See also thoughts attributed to Karolina's father, Juliusz Frist, before Germans shot him: "He knew that his confidence in human beings was false. He knew now that these Germans of the Hitler regime had nothing in common with the culture, science, and art of the past of Germany" (154); and subsequent reference to his "full awareness that he had made a mistake that would cost them their lives" (177).

21. Olga Lengyel, *Five Chimneys: The Story of Auschwitz* (New York: Howard Fertig, 1983), 1.

22. Henry Friedman, *I'm No Hero: Journeys of a Holocaust Survivor* (Seattle: University of Washington, Press, 1999), 26–27.

23. Ibid., 27.

24. Ibid., 154–57.

25. Renya Kulkielko, *Escape from the Pit* (New York: Sharon, 1947), 102.

26. Calel Perechodnik, *Am I a Murderer? Testament of a Jewish Ghetto Policeman*, ed. and trans. Frank Fox (Boulder, Colo.: Westview, 1996), 54.

27. Levi, *The Drowned and the Saved*, 78.

28. Adina Blady Szwajger, *I Remember Nothing More: The Warsaw Children's Hospital and the Jewish Resistance*, trans. Tasja Darowska and Danusia Stok (New York: Simon and Schuster, 1990), 135.

29. Ibid., 135.

30. Ibid.

31. Ibid., 166.

32. Ibid., 58.

33. Ibid., 150.

34. Langer, *Holocaust Testimonies*, 193. See also 32–33.

35. Henry Greenspan, "Collaborative Interpretation of Survivors' Accounts: A Radical Challenge to Conventional Practice," in Sara R. Horowitz, ed., *Lessons and Legacies Volume X: Back to the Sources: Reexamining Perpetrators, Victims, and Bystanders* (Evanston, Ill.: Northwestern University Press, 2012): 91–104. On the intersection of survivor and audience expectations, see also Naomi Seidman, "Elie Wiesel and the Scandal of Jewish Rage," originally published in *Jewish Social Studies* 3, 1 (1996): 1–19 but reworked as part of chap. 5 in Naomi Seidman, *Faithful Renderings: Jewish-Christian Difference and the Politics of Translation* (Chicago: University of Chicago Press, 2006), 216–36.

36. Quoted in Greenspan, "Collaborative Interpretation," 95; also in Langer, *Holocaust Testimonies*, 185–86. Langer calls the speaker "Abraham P." and describes him as from Hungary. A transcript is available online, "Abraham Pasternak, August 13, 1984: First Day in Auschwitz," in Voice/Vision Holocaust Survivor Oral History Archive (University of Michigan–Dearborn), http://holocaust.umd.umich.edu/interview.php?D=pasternak&section=11.

37. Greenspan, "Collaborative Interpretation," 99.

38. Ibid., 95; Langer, *Holocaust Testimonies,* 185–86.

39. Pasternak, "First Day in Auschwitz."

40. My thanks to Jordan Stone, who listened to more than a hundred hours of testimonies from the USC Shoah Foundation Visual History

Archive, and to the Social Sciences and Humanities Research Council of Canada, for a grant to support this research.

41. Langer, *Holocaust Testimonies*, 187.

42. Ruth Bondy, quoted in Na'ama Shik, "Infinite Loneliness: Some Aspects of the Lives of Jewish Women in the Auschwitz Camps According to Testimonies and Autobiographies from 1945–1948," in Doris L. Bergen, ed., *Lessons and Legacies Volume VIII: From Generation to Generation* (Evanston, Ill.: Northwestern University Press, 2008), 149.

43. See Margarete Myers Feinstein, *Holocaust Survivors in Postwar Germany, 1945–1957* (Cambridge: Cambridge University Press, 2010), 238–49.

44. See Agata Tuszyńska, *Vera Gran: The Accused*, trans. Charles Ruas (New York: Knopf, 2013), 115–35. The popular Jewish singer Vera Gran was the subject of at least two rounds of investigations in Warsaw in 1945 on charges of collaboration; the charges were dropped in November (132), but she never succeeded in clearing her name.

45. Na'ama Shik, "Slovakian Jewish Women at Auschwitz Camp: Reflections on a Historical Event, Trauma and Memory," paper presented at the conference New Scholars/New Research on the Holocaust, University of Toronto, Canada, October 6–7, 2013.

46. Robert Melson, *False Papers: Deception and Survival in the Holocaust* (Urbana: University of Illinois Press, 2000), 156.

47. As Gary Weissman reminds us, seeing a survivor as emblematic makes us lose sight of the individual in any meaningful sense. Gary Weissman, *Fantasies of Witnessing: Postwar Efforts to Experience the Holocaust* (Ithaca, N.Y.: Cornell University Press, 2004).

48. Sara Ginaite-Rubinson, *Resistance and Survival: The Jewish Community in Kaunas, 1941–1944* (Oakville, Canada: Mosaic, 2005).

49. See Sara Ginaite, "'Investigating' Jewish Partisans in Lithuania," *Jewish Currents* (September 2008). Koniuchy, Lithuania, is now known as Kaniūkai.

50. Ginaite-Rubinson, *Resistance and Survival*, 122.

51. Rita Benn, "A Snapshot of Remembrance through the Eyes of a Child," in Sara Ginaite-Rubinson, *Pro Memoria* (Toronto, Canada: self-publication, 2012), 11–12.

52. Levi, *The Drowned and the Saved*, 75.

53. Kluger, *Still Alive*, 94.

54. Annette Wieviorka, *The Era of the Witness*, trans. Jared Stark (Ithaca, N.Y.: Cornell University Press, 2006), 129.

Steven Alan Carr

"To Encompass the Unseeable": Foreign Film, Taste Culture, and the American Encounter with the Postwar Holocaust Film

THIS PAPER TAKES A RECEPTION-BASED APPROACH TO CONSIDER ONE of the first fictional feature films screened in the United States to depict the Holocaust, and how these early films might have initially shaped audience expectations for subsequent cinematic depictions of genocide and Nazi atrocities. In particular, this essay examines the role of *New York Times* film critic Bosley Crowther in mediating these expectations for an audience as yet unfamiliar with the emergent conventions of these films. To do this, I consider Crowther's multiple reviews and mentions of the 1948 Polish film *The Last Stage*, originally shown under the title *The Last Stop*, and how he positioned this film both through the lens of Italian neorealism, as well as against a Hollywood that had failed to adequately "encompass the unseeable." The paper thus argues that some American audiences were at least aware of cinematic depictions of the Holocaust by the late 1940s, that Italian neorealism provided a frame of reference for these films, and that early encounters with these films were deeply embedded within a globalizing taste culture—the values of a group or class of society and the cultural forms that express these values—and that its appreciation for the foreign operated across both political and geographic borders.

AN ARCHAEOLOGY OF THE HOLOCAUST FILM

Early in the film *The Diary of Anne Frank* (20th Century-Fox, 1959), a mysterious dream sequence occurs. In a nightmarish premonition, Anne imagines her best friend Sanne Devries in a concentration camp.

Significantly, the scene is the only time that the film explicitly references a camp, and it is one of the first times that a major postwar Hollywood film depicts a camp within the context of the Holocaust. Although uncredited, but at least as significant for the erasure of its cinematic provenance, the sequence comes from *The Last Stop*,[1] a 1948 Polish film shot on location at Auschwitz and based on the personal experiences of director Wanda Jakubowska, screenwriter Gerda Schneider, and some 3,500 female extras, all of whom had survived the camp and returned to reenact its history for the camera. Even for the 2003 DVD director's commentary, neither director and associate producer George Stevens Jr. nor star Millie Perkins mentioned the unique provenance of this footage.

While the commentary remembered how much had changed since the release of the film in terms of cultural understandings of the Holocaust, the remarks continued an ongoing mystification of *The Last Stop* in which the film's actuality occurs without any historical specificity. Tobias Ebbrecht calls this process "migrating images," where the visual record of the Holocaust becomes decontextualized from its own history.[2] As a film created and performed after World War II by mostly female survivors who returned to reenact their experience on location at Auschwitz, *The Last Stop* had existed as a significant cultural phenomenon and historical document in its own right, a full ten years before *Anne Frank* reduced it to a fevered dream sequence. As Hanno Loewy has argued, *The Last Stop* ultimately created a highly influential "iconography of the camps" that reinterpreted certain details through "cinematic visual traditions." As a result, the film has become something of a "film plus": an early iteration of Holocaust film, a unique document of survivor reenactment, and as Loewy observed, an authentic documentary that other films subsequently treat as evidence.[3] Its visual and narrative strategies additionally complicated traditional tripartite distinctions between perpetrator, victim, and bystander, with survivors performing the roles of perpetrators, victims engaging in acts of resistance, and viewers implicated in the subject position of bearing witness.

The subsequent appropriation of the film's iconography, together with the mystification of its provenance, ultimately worked to enhance the film's authenticity as a mystical black-and-white document that somehow managed to emerge from the ashes of Auschwitz so that other films could show us how terrible life was in a concentration camp. Like a dream sequence itself, iconography from *The Last Stop* slips in and out of other Holocaust films, leaving the audience to imagine its footage as actuality and to wake up to subsequently less authentic and more comfortably fictionalized representations of the Holocaust. Yet if such bracketing of "migrating images" works to enhance the historical authenticity of any black-and-white source, the mystification of that source material also works to disable a "relation between spectator and images" that Ebbrecht believes provides an "ability to decode the migrating images as postmemories" and "create some analytical distance" between text and audience.[4]

If the Holocaust film arguably has become its own genre, then understanding how it came to be a genre requires a unique kind of cultural archaeology. Indeed, its archaeology deploys cultural artifacts already forgotten, misplaced, and reburied as soon as they emerge from excavation. As one of these artifacts, *The Last Stop* has received renewed attention in its own right with a 2009 DVD release (as *The Last Stage*) through Polart. Yet the film, along with others, has yet to achieve full recognition both for its innovations in style as well as its historical importance. Like *The Last Stop*, the earliest Holocaust films were foreign films, and thus for American audiences through the 1960s, a primary interpretive mode through which Americans came to understand both the Holocaust as well as later American Holocaust films. Certainly, there were other interpretive modes for popular encounters with the Holocaust, including radio, novels, the stage, newsreels, and the Hollywood social problem film. The foreign Holocaust film, however, established a particularly compelling set of expectations concerning fictionalized treatment of the Nazi's campaign of mass murder in Hollywood film. Though largely forgotten today, two foreign films notably bookended the formation of this American understanding. One was *The Last Stop*, which marked the end of this formation. The other was the 1938 Soviet film *Professor Mamlock*,[5] which marked a beginning for this framing of the American encounter with fictionalized accounts of the Holocaust. Taken together, these films helped establish the Holocaust film in the same way that Shyon Baumann claimed audiences came to take Hollywood movies seriously as art. According to Baumann's framework for tracing audience perception of film as more than just mere entertainment, the Holocaust film emerged as an "opportunity space"—that is, the genre filled an unmet demand among patrons and thus won recognition as an art form—as a set of "institutionalized resources and activities," and as discursive practice.[6]

"TO ENCOMPASS THE UNSEEABLE"

Given the amount of criticism leveled against Hollywood to adequately "encompass the unseeable," as *New York Times* film critic Bosley Crowther noted in his 1949 review of *The Last Stop*, understanding how foreign film shaped American encounters with fictionalized representations of the Holocaust thus takes on added urgency.[7] Wulf Kansteiner, in considering the influence of the Holocaust film on what he called "the recalibration of collective identities after the Cold War," concluded that the United States and Western European postwar cinema misrepresented the murderous "Final Solution" by universalizing, democratizing, and popularizing the Holocaust. Ebbrecht echoed a similar concern. Drawing from Peter Novick's *The Holocaust in American Life*, Kansteiner especially singled out *The Diary of Anne Frank* as "the first international Holocaust-related media event" to offer a powerful global consensus: "no camps, no brutality, and no Jewishness, but a distinctly generic representation of innocence and tragedy in times of crisis."[8] While Kansteiner also noted that *The Last Stop* downplayed Jewishness, he found that, as a Polish film, it offered a comparatively "honest filmic exploration of the Nazi legacy," at least until the Soviet Union tightened control over Poland and its other satellite countries.[9]

While such interpretations do not offer an erroneous version of this history, in and of themselves they offer an incomplete one. This dominant view of early Holocaust film has persisted at least since the release of *Professor Mamlock*. The notion of an inherently superior European cinematic sensibility in addressing Nazism and Auschwitz certainly is not a recent development. The week following the 1949 opening of *The Last Stop* in New York, *Times* critic Crowther already had ranked the film alongside such neorealist classics as *Open City*, *Paisan*, and *Shoe Shine*. The only Hollywood film among them was *The Search* (1948), which even then was an MGM-Praesens Film international coproduction with Austria. Crowther observed that "the only films which have yet really shown some deep and mature comprehension of the great human tragedy of our times" have been made in Europe, and that it would not be fair to expect "the people working in our studios" to have "faculties sufficiently up" to making such films.[10] Without disparaging anyone's faculties, then, the same basic critique of Hollywood and the Holocaust has not changed much in the intervening nearly seventy years: when it came to depicting the Holocaust, foreign films did it better.

The legacy of European and Eastern European cinematic treatment of the Holocaust notwithstanding, one must not mistake national cinemas for national receptions. An implicit assumption behind the alleged inferiority or even absence of the Holocaust in Hollywood film, arguable at best, was that American audiences remained sheltered from and ignorant of the record of Nazi atrocities. "I was not as aware," remembered Millie Perkins for the DVD commentary on *The Diary of Anne Frank*, "of what happened during the war."[11] At the very least, Stevens's assertion that *Anne Frank* was the first mainstream Hollywood film to address the Holocaust requires qualification. It was, in fact, one of the first Hollywood films to address the Holocaust, but it certainly was not the first to deal with either the Holocaust or antisemitism after World War II. A full year earlier, *The Young Lions* (20th Century-Fox, 1958) had tackled both antisemitism in the U.S. military as well as the liberation of Jews in concentration camps in Germany. Even before that, films such as RKO's 1945 *Cornered* and 1946 *The Stranger* dealt, however fleetingly or problematically, with Nazi atrocities.

A more complete assessment of Hollywood's treatment of the Holocaust, then, would envision films such as *Cornered, The Stranger, The Young Lions*, and *The Diary of Anne Frank* as operating in relation to foreign film. If foreign film did indeed do a superior job of depicting the Holocaust, and if, by 1949, Hollywood's inadequacy in dealing with the realities of postwar Europe was well-publicized in the pages of the *New York Times*, then perhaps Hollywood films did not need to depict these realities when foreign films could do it better. Perhaps all Hollywood films had to do was to reference what foreign films could do. Ultimately, perhaps, the point of what Hollywood was doing during this period was to show deference to the foreign film, and audiences would have seen anything more than this as horrifically insensitive and tasteless overreaching that was capitalizing on the suffering of others.

Just as the art film represented an "opportunity space" offering the possibility for aesthetic mobility outside the realm of the Hollywood film, the foreign Holocaust film presented a new context to challenge the preexisting space of Hollywood movies. Because of their attendant "discursive and organizational resources,"[12] Hollywood movies were widely perceived as incapable of forthrightly addressing Nazi antisemitism. Also similar to the emergence of the art film, the Holocaust film relied upon a complex network of "institutionalized resources and activities" where small, independent theaters exhibited these films and where audiences sought to patronize these films as a superior cultural taste alternative to "the assembly line of big studio productions." Finally, with film critics like Crowther, the foreign Holocaust film had "grounding of value and legitimacy in critical discourse." While the early Holocaust film was essentially a foreign film, it functioned as a "field" of cultural production in which its networks between cultural producers, exhibitors, critics, and consumers produced, in Pierre Bourdieu's sense, cultural capital—that is, ideas and knowledge that one could profitably use to display social status and mobility.[13]

Through its "opportunity space," its institution-based resources and practices, and the cultural capital of its discourse, the foreign Holocaust film first framed the American popular encounter with Nazi antisemitism, and then the full extent of Holocaust atrocities. That framing, beginning with films like the 1938 *Professor Mamlock* and ending with the 1949 American premiere of *The Last Stop*, spawned a whole formation of rules, conventions, and expectations for subsequent depictions of the Holocaust that both governed American films dealing with this subject and inflected these films with a set of taste politics favoring a decidedly foreign sensibility. The aesthetic consensus that emerged from this formation would suggest that the birth of the Holocaust film was indeed far more globalized and international than more conventional notions of national cinemas would suggest. The 2009 release of the film on DVD under the title *The Last Stage* offers the opportunity to reacquaint American audiences with it. However, such films as *Professor Mamlock* are completely unavailable at this time. Even with its newfound availability, *The Last Stage* targets a relatively narrow cultural niche when compared to *The Diary of Anne Frank*. Thus, the current canon of historically significant anti-Nazi and Holocaust films from this period may have more to do with the necessities of new opportunity spaces, dwindling institutional resources for public viewing, current tastes, emergent technologies, and economic necessities amid present-day flows of globalization and culture, and less to do with how actual audiences experienced films between 1938 and 1949.

PROFESSOR MAMLOCK AND THE TASTE POLITICS OF THE ANTI-NAZI FOREIGN FILM

Within the framework of the Holocaust film, two interpretive polarities marked the extent and breadth of how the foreign film shaped the initial American encounter with Nazism and the Holocaust. The first, as exemplified by *The Last Stop*, involved a neorealist sensibility, marked by extensive and pivotal use of on-location cinematography that featured nonprofessional performances and slice-of-life narratives involving everyday people. The second, and arguably less recognized polarity from this period, involved the forthright and thus politically charged representation of Nazi antisemitism and its specificity in singling out Jews. Thus, the unavailability of a film like *Professor Mamlock* today belies the film's importance in the 1930s and 1940s as a lightning rod for debates about film censorship and propaganda, debates that many at the time saw as stymying more forthright depictions of Nazi antisemitism in Hollywood film.

American audiences in 1938 would have been well-versed with *Professor Mamlock*, if not with its basic story then certainly with the controversy the Soviet film engendered. As early as 1933, the *New York Times* reported that a group called the Theatre Union would perform a version of the Friedrich Wolf play on which the film was based, titled simply *Mamlock*.[14] By 1937, the Jewish Unit of the Works Progress Administration Federal Theatre Project had produced another version of the play bearing the same name as the film.[15] The play's narrative and Wolf's biography were closely intertwined. Mamlock, like Wolf, was a doctor and veteran of World War I. After the Nazis came to power, both were persecuted, with the real-life Wolf immigrating to Moscow to write *Mamlock*. Unlike Wolf, who was active in the Communist Party, the fictional Mamlock begins the play largely assimilated, patriotic, anti-Communist, and unconcerned with the rise of Nazism. Only after the anti-Jewish Nuremberg Laws of 1935 remove Mamlock from his position as chief surgeon at a university hospital, declare him a non-German, and incite attacks against his own children does he realize the full extent of the Nazi threat, but by then it is too late.

By 1938, audiences came to recognize the film version of *Professor*

Mamlock as a specific indictment of antisemitism. In the advertisement for the premiere for the film, a man appears in a white coat resembling a straightjacket with the word JUDE (JEW) scrawled across his chest. Two brownshirt officers flank him. The tagline for the film reads "a crushing indictment of Nazi terror."[16]

In fact, reviews of both the film and the play suggested that audiences already would be familiar not only with the basic story but also with a set of taste politics measuring what the film could and could not do in comparison to Hollywood. The Russian film significantly addressed "a topic which Hollywood, with its fear of jeopardizing foreign markets, has not dared to touch."[17] In an interview with the *New York Times*, Edward G. Robinson claimed that he "would give my teeth to do an American version of *Professor Mamlock*."[18] At the same time, though, Brooks Atkinson's review of the Federal Theatre Project's production of the play observed that even by 1937 "in one way or another" the play's "fiendish story has been told . . . several times" and that "the whole subject of the Nazi persecution of the Jews needs something more penetrating."[19] Similarly, film reviewer Frank S. Nugent observed that the Soviet production said "nothing new about Nazi persecution of the Jews in Germany," and he confessed to "a feeling of resentment" over the film's conflation of Jewish and Communist suffering and "the simplification of a problem which is not limited to politics but is deeply rooted as well in religious, racial, and economic soil."[20] However much the actual film fell short in its lack of originality and its conflation of Jewish with Communist suffering, it engendered both controversy and status, becoming a cause célèbre for those advocating First Amendment protections for the film industry. By 1939, the *Columbia Law Review* noted how *Mamlock* had "received much publicity" for numerous instances where public and journalistic pressure had forced censorship boards in Ohio and Chicago to permit showing the film, reversing initial exhibition bans that cited ostensible concerns for public safety and fears of rioting.[21]

For many audiences, the potent politics of *Professor Mamlock* as a forthright indictment of Nazi antisemitism heralded the postwar wave of neorealist films coming from Italy. A political hot potato amid the 1939 German-Soviet Nonaggression Pact, screenings at the Russian Pavilion during the 1939 World's Fair in New York ceased almost immediately after the Soviets had signed this surprise agreement.[22] Within a month after the Nazi invasion of the Soviet Union in June

1941, however, the *New York Times* announced what would be one of numerous revivals of the film for the duration of the war.[23] What *Professor Mamlock* could do to indict Nazi antisemitism before the war became a bellwether for what film could do in the aftermath of World War II. Author Friedrich Wolf, who by 1946 the *Times* identified as "the white hope of the current German cinema," began to articulate a new direction desperately needed for postwar film. Quoted in an article on postwar German film and specifically credited with *Professor Mamlock*, Wolf argued that Germany should be making films about concentration camps and other "anti-fascistic themes": "The reality of yesterday and today is the most touching subject, and an artist could never have invented it in more tragic, grotesque or apocalyptic terms. This inferno really did happen. To get at the bottom of it and to shape the present truth of life—that is the theme."[24]

A month later, film reviewer Bosley Crowther reiterated Wolf's statement to help make sense of what Roberto Rossellini's *Open City* (1945, distributed by Arthur Mayer and Joseph Burstyn) was doing. Crowther noted that, as Rossellini did in setting a slice-of-life story against the backdrop of on-location shooting under still Nazi-occupied Rome, "the outlook of German film men . . . is toward a realistic interpretation of modern life. All of their observation and experience in recent years has presumably fixed their attention upon this one obsessing theme: the reality of yesterday and the present truth of life."[25] That "obsessing theme" would, in turn, become the dominant frame of reference for the American reception of *The Last Stop*.

ITALIAN NEOREALISM AND THE NEW "WORLD FILM"

As a film, *The Last Stop* confounds many assumptions scholars hold about American audiences' encounters with Holocaust films. While a casual interpretation might conclude that the banal universalism of *Anne Frank* utterly drove *The Last Stop* and its specificity of depicting camp life into obscurity, the Polish film received extensive publicity well before it opened in New York. The *New York Times* first began reporting on the film in October 1948. By the end of the year, the United Nations Film Board had issued a special commendation for *The Last Stop* "in recognition of its moral and artistic values."[26] Throughout February and March, the film figured prominently in the *Times*'s coverage of foreign films screened in the United States.

By the end of May 1949, the film was about to begin its tenth-week run. Even if the film had achieved only niche appeal with a New York audience, that appeal had longevity.

The film confounds many present-day assumptions regarding the American encounter with Holocaust film, not just because many of the *Times*'s readers would have known of the film well before Hollywood produced a Holocaust film but also because those readers would have known much about the unique conditions of production for the film. The recitation of details of this production became a framework through which an audience could understand gruesome aspects of daily life in the camp. In "Nazi Concentration Camp Reactivated for Film," William Friedberg focused on the details of the film's authenticity: forty-five crew members using obsolete and inferior equipment; twenty-seven performers; 3,500 extras who were actual prisoners of Auschwitz agreeing to relive their experiences. As if anticipating the opening of Alain Resnais's *Night and Fog* (Argos, 1955) six years before that film's release, Friedberg noted how "a field of beautiful green, billowing grass that was waist high" had grown around the camp and "had to be cut down and the original filth" restored.[27]

In addition to its emphasis upon scale and actual location, Friedberg's *Times* article helped to establish the beguiling and compelling aspects of *The Last Stop*'s authenticity. So realistic and seductive, the authenticity of the production compelled the performers to slip back into their wartime behavior and roles even when the cameras were not rolling:

> Polish actors, at first reluctant to portray the hated Nazi officials, took to playing their parts so wholeheartedly that the former prisoners began to fall into their former habits. Everything about Auschwitz was restored with such frightening accuracy that during lunch hours the prisoners would go to eat five by five. In groups of five was the way they were commanded to fall out by the Nazis. The mass scenes were so realistic that the extras hesitated to break their lines until told to do so.[28]

While this recitation of scale and overwhelming actuality was certainly not new to advance publicity for a film, with the Holocaust film, it took on added urgency. Indeed, such production history lore became part of the discursive practice for Holocaust films such as *Schindler's List* (Universal Pictures and Amblin Entertainment, 1993) and *The*

Pianist (R.P. Productions, Heritage Films, Studio Babelsberg, and others, 2002), where the "making-of" history for these films became history in its own right. Even if the historical factors concerning the making of these films remained subordinate to actual Holocaust history, in their relation to the Holocaust, such details and use of location bestowed added credibility to what might otherwise serve as an ordinary fictional account.

This emphasis on production history as a way for audiences to experience the Holocaust film before, after, and even without having seen *The Last Stop* helped activate an interpretive frame through which American audiences could understand not just images of the Holocaust but also images of postwar Europe. That frame emphasized the importance of such details as on-location shooting and the use of nonprofessional extras. Indeed, *The Last Stop*'s advertising highlights the film's ties to such postwar classics as *Open City* and Rossellini's *Paisan* (Organizzazione Film Internazionali and Foreign Film Production, 1946), actively encouraging audiences to categorize the film with those films. That advertising also emphasizes the role of New York's World Theatre as showcase for this new kind of "world film." The experience of the Holocaust film thus became mediated, not just by other foreign films but also by the very theater where foreign films were shown.

The neorealist frame of reference also helped give *The Last Stop* greater exposure. In his biography of Bosley Crowther, Frank Beaver noted that Crowther went out of his way to advocate for foreign-language pictures like *Open City*, Vittorio De Sica's *Shoeshine* (Societa Cooperativa Alfa Cinematografica, 1946); or De Sica's *The Bicycle Thief* (Produzioni De Sica, 1948). Crowther frequently compared these films to the foil of Hollywood. As Beaver observed:

> Crowther was one of the first critics to review imported films on a regular basis and he urged Americans to attend them. The best of these pictures were praised for what he considered their outstanding thematic significance and realistic presentation. Hollywood was asked to study foreign films and to seek similar achievement in its own output.[29]

Today's scholarship of Holocaust films would do well to pay attention to how Italian neorealism influenced critics like Crowther in understanding contemporaneous films like *The Last Stop*. This scholarship might first consider what Crowther deemed "the techniques of realism—and the attitudes . . . shatteringly employed" in *Open City*. Using a largely nonprofessional cast "composed of random people," these films featured settings as everyday as "regular buildings and the streets and open places around Rome." Crowther's review particularly pitted "the slickly manufactured sentiments of Hollywood's studio-made pictures" against the "sincerity and candor" of a film like *Open City* that "achieves the illusion of reportage."[30]

For generations since weaned on handheld cameras and cinema verité documentaries, such techniques might not seem novel today. But for audiences of the 1940s and 1950s, this unvarnished cinematic practice seemed the only appropriate modality to respond to the Holocaust. For Crowther, a film set in Auschwitz could only be "filmed at Auschwitz amid the barren and dreary huts and mud which still stand" as "a shameful reminder of the most infamous of Nazi 'death factories.'" Similar to *Open City* and its use of nonprofessional actors, *The Last Stop* featured many who actually "were wartime inmates of that place."

The emotional response from critics like Crowther drew upon an ethical understanding of these proto-docudrama aesthetics. "No more appropriate company could have been assembled for playing it," wrote Crowther. "If we allow that such a story as it tells should specifically be told, then we have to agree that art and conscience have been most compellingly served." A documentary-like presentation, captured by a "close, observing camera that sees and dispassionately reports" on atrocity, best achieved this artistic conscience.

Not just reportage, this juxtaposition between presentation of the visible and invocation of off-screen space suggests an important link between neorealist film and Holocaust film that is as much embedded within a mode of address as it is within the iconography of two distinct genres. Use of iconic nonprofessional actors or on-location photography become important generic signifiers for how audiences read these films. But audiences read these films in terms of what took place decidedly and ironically off-screen as well. That distinction, between iconography on the one hand and mode of address on the other, opens up new interpretive possibilities for examining not just Ebbrecht's formulation of "migrating images" but that of "migrating receptions" as well.

Consider, for example, the use of off-screen space as a form of cinematic address in both *Open City* and *The Last Stop*. Iconography alone in both films cannot explain the impact this mode, particularly in its ironic use of off-screen space, had upon audiences. In both films, off-screen slaughter through editing and diegetic sound (sound whose source is visible or implied as being in the world of the film) becomes a way to invoke brutality through ironic commentary and ellipsis. For *Open City*, a key scene involving this mode of address comes when two fascist soldiers arrive at an inn with two lambs for slaughter. For *The Last Stop*, it is when a Nazi doctor murders an infant. Together, these two scenes demonstrate not only the stylistic link between neorealism and the Holocaust film but also how a shared documentary-like modality might suggest that with "migrating images" also come "migrating receptions."

The brief sequence from *Open City* parallels literal butchering of animals with metaphorical butchery taking place as a result of Nazi collaboration. The scene opens as the Italian fascists unload two live lambs from a truck and enter the kitchen of the inn. One of the soldiers announces gruffly that they have "brought meat." The owner sees the animals and shakes his head. "I'm an innkeeper," he tells them, "not a butcher." "We'll be the butchers," one of the soldiers barks. "Yes," the innkeeper responds, "You're specialists in that." The scene progresses as two members of the Italian resistance pass the soldiers to dine with a female cabaret performer who, unknown to them, also happens to be a Nazi collaborator. As they sit at a table, an off-screen gunshot interrupts their conversation. The three get up and open a shuttered window. A reverse shot shows them looking out the window before the scene cuts to a wide point-of-view shot of the two soldiers, with one of the animals lying on the ground in a pool of blood. "Poor beasts," the performer says as she shakes her head. The solder takes a gun to the head of the second animal just before the scene cuts back to the reverse shot of the window. An off-screen gunshot is heard, and the cabaret performer turns her head away from the sight of carnage. The film's visual style thus creates a layered set of ironic and distanced meanings through which audiences understand metaphoric butchery from the point of view of a collaborator.

The Last Stop similarly plays with ironic off-screen space in a way that for Crowther "marshals its terrible evidence in frank, understated episodes" that gather "final shattering impact through the power of suggestion."[31] The film, he says:

> does not show us the Nazi doctor in the camp actually killing an infant which one of the inmates has miserably borne. It simply shows us the doctor, casually whistling a little tune and loading a hypodermic needle while the baby lies wailing on his desk. Then as the doctor approaches the baby with the needle in his hand, the camera pans away to the bottle from which the hypo has been charged, the wailing ceases slowly, the casual whistling goes on and we see the bottle in sharp focus, labeled with the tell-tale skull and bones.[32]

Indeed, in the review, Crowther explicitly acknowledges "Roberto Rossellini's brilliant films" as a way to understand what *The Last Stop* is doing to ironically convey atrocity. Not only does this "frequent and artful repetition" of restraint, a "most sound cinematic technique," help realize "the repulsiveness of . . . events" and provide unspoken commentary "on matters beyond feeble words." It also "compels imagination," in Crowther's formulation, "to encompass the unseeable."[33]

Just as this understanding of neorealism, and more generally of foreign film, could guide viewer responses to understanding *The Last Stop* as a Holocaust film, subsequent Cold War ideology as easily could justify the film's obsolescence. In reviewing a 1996 festival retrospective of Polish films, *New York Times* critic Stephen Holden noted that *The Last Stop* was "bleaker and more terrifying than *Schindler's List*," yet "one false note—and it is glaring—is the movie's portrayal of Soviet Communists as the world's shining saviors." If popular discourse could so effectively establish a neorealist frame of reference for the film in 1949, how could the film's political slant have eluded critics at the height of the Cold War? The conflation of Jewish with Communist suffering in *Professor Mamlock* became a nonissue once critical reception had established that film as an indictment of Nazi antisemitism, but the propagandistic aspects of *The Last Stop* still stirred controversy in 1996, a full five years after the fall of the Berlin Wall in 1991, and nearly fifty years after the film's initial release.

With the taste politics of the Holocaust film resolved, the Holocaust film had become an autonomous cultural practice distinct from neorealism. Bearing the mark of a foreign film without having to actually be foreign, the Holocaust film no longer recalled its profound connection to Italian neorealism, at least the kind of connection original American audiences might have imagined. An expression of political taste for agitprop could hold equal discursive weight to the taste politics of the Holocaust film. Popular criticism helped to establish audience expectations for what a Holocaust film should be through a shifting discussion of aesthetic and political norms. Once it established those expectations, that criticism could just as easily forget what the norms were and then set some new ones. Given this context, the Holocaust film did not emerge fully formed by the late 1950s. Rather, notions of what a Holocaust film should be resulted from how audiences negotiated meaning through a set of flexible aesthetic, cultural, and ideological practices. And this process involved an exchange of American and European ideas and methods, a sort of migratory reception. An American understanding of Holocaust films predated what we think of as classic Hollywood Holocaust movies, and it emerged through a globalized distribution of European films, which were widely screened and discussed among critics and moviegoers in the United States.

NOTES

Versions of this paper appear on the author's website at http://stevenalancarr.pbworks.com/w/page/24704810/The%20Last%20Stage and at http://stevenalancarr.pbworks.com/To-Encompass-the-Unseeable and were presented in 2010 at a conference on Cold War Cultures at the University of Texas at Austin; in 2012 at a conference of the Society for Cinema and Media Studies in Boston and at a conference of the Association for Jewish Studies in Chicago; and at the Lessons and Legacies Conference in Evanston, Ill.

1. *The Last Stop* was the original English-language title under which the film appeared when it was first distributed in New York in March 1949. Today, the film more frequently appears under the British release title *The Last Stage,* or its Polish-language title *Ostatni etap*. For the purpose of consistency, this paper uses the English-language title of the U.S. release as *The Last Stop*.

2. Tobias Ebbrecht, "Migrating Images: Iconic Images of the Holocaust and the Representation of War in Popular Film," *Shofar: An Interdisciplinary Journal of Jewish Studies* 28, 4 (2010): 86–103.

3. Hanna Loewy, "The Mother of All Holocaust Films? Wanda Jakubowska's Auschwitz Trilogy," *Historical Journal of Film, Radio and Television* 24, 2 (2004): 179–204.

4. Ebbrecht, "Migrating Images," 92.

5. *Professor Mamlock*, directed by Herbert Rappaport and Adolf Minkin,

produced by Amkino (1938). Like *The Last Stop*, *Professor Mamlock* appears variously as *Professor Mamlok* and occasionally with the title of *Professor* abbreviated. For the purposes of consistency, I use the title listed in the print advertisements of the film at the time of release.

6. Shyon Baumann, *Hollywood Highbrow: From Entertainment to Art*, Princeton Studies in Cultural Sociology (Princeton, N.J.: Princeton University Press, 2007), 14.

7. Bosley Crowther, "The Brutal Truth: Polish Film Dramatizes Nazi Torture Camp," *New York Times*, March 27, 1949.

8. Wulf Kansteiner, "Sold Globally—Remembered Locally: Holocaust Cinema and the Construction of Collective Identities in Europe and the US" in Stefan Berger, Linas Erikonas, and Andrew Mycock, eds., *Narrating the Nation: Representations in History, Media and the Arts* (New York: Berghahn, 2008), 153–80.

9. Ibid., 155–56.

10. Crowther, "The Brutal Truth."

11. Millie Perkins and George Stevens Jr. commentary, *The Diary of Anne Frank*, directed and produced by George Stevens Jr. (1959: 20th Century-Fox Home Entertainment, 2000), DVD.

12. Bauman, *Hollywood Highbrow*, 14. Baumann's three-part framework involving an application of Paul DiMaggio's "opportunity space," "institutionalized resources and activities," and discursive practice ultimately can explain how foreign films established the representational framework within which American Holocaust films operated.

13. Ibid., 16–17.

14. Brooks Atkinson, "The Play," *New York Times*, August 23, 1933, accessed March 20, 2011, ProQuest Historical Newspapers.

15. Brooks Atkinson, "The Play: Nazi Customs and Manners," *New York Times*, April 14, 1937, accessed March 20, 2011, ProQuest Historical Newspapers.

16. Frank S. Nugent, "*Professor Mamlock*, a Russian Appraisal of Nazi Culture, Has Its Premiere at the Cameo," *New York Times*, November 8, 1937, accessed March 20, 2011, ProQuest Historical Newspapers.

17. Ibid.

18. Bosely Crowther, "Little Caesar Waits His Chance," *New York Times*, January 22, 1939, accessed March 20, 2011, ProQuest Historical Newspapers.

19. Atkinson, "The Play: Nazi Customs and Manners."

20. Nugent, "*Professor Mamlock*."

21. Columbia Law Review Association, "Film Censorship: An Administrative Analysis," *Columbia Law Review* 39, 8 (1939): 1383–1405, accessed March 20, 2011, JSTOR, http://www.jstor.org/stable/1116646.

22. "Soviet Withdraws Anti-Nazi Movie," *New York Times*, August 30, 1939, accessed March 20, 2011, ProQuest Historical Newspapers.

23. "Of Local Origin," *New York Times*, July 5, 1941, accessed March 21, 2011, ProQuest Historical Newspapers.

24. Gladwin Hill, "Whither Go German Films?" *New York Times*, February 3, 1946, accessed March 20, 2011, ProQuest Historical Newspapers.

25. Bosley Crowther, "Open City: A Powerful New Film from Italy Points a Line of European Approach," *New York Times*, March 3, 1946, accessed March 20, 2011, ProQuest Historical Newspapers.

26. Crowther, "The Brutal Truth."

27. William Friedberg, "Nazi Concentration Camp Reactivated for Film," *New York Times*, February 20, 1949.

28. Ibid.

29. Frank Eugene Beaver, *Bosley Crowther: Social Critic of the Film, 1940–1967*, Dissertations on Film (New York: Arno, 1974), 37.

30. Crowther, "Open City."

31. Crowther, "Brutal Truth."

32. Ibid.

33. Ibid.

Alon Confino

A World without Jews: Nazi Imagination from Persecution to Genocide

I SUMMON FROM THE HISTORICAL RECORD A SCENE, AN EXPERIENCE that was as exhilarating as it was marked by an intense combination of audacity and transgression. By fire and other means, a festive, expressive destruction of the Hebrew Bible was at the center of *Kristallnacht*, the Night of Broken Glass, when on November 9, 1938, more than 1,400 synagogues were set on fire in Nazi Germany. In Berlin, Germans burned the Torah scrolls in front of the Levetzow Street synagogue, while others carried the scrolls from the Fasanen Street synagogue to Wittenberg Square and burned them there.[1] In the small town of Fritzlar in Hesse, Torah scrolls were unrolled along the Nikolaus Street as Hitler Youth rode their bicycles over them.[2] In Aachen, Nazis ripped up the Torah in front of the synagogue and put the scraps in their pockets, claiming it brought good luck.[3] In Vienna, then part of the Greater German Reich, Nazis and their supporters made Jews dress in the robe and decorations of the Ark of the Covenant, then marched and chased them through downtown streets with torn Torah scrolls tied to their backs. In Frankfurt, some people forced Jews to tear the Torah themselves and then burn it.[4] In Württemberg, a man who picked up tattered Jewish prayer books strewn on the street, presumably as an act of respect toward the holy objects, was hanged publicly from a tree on the way from Steinach to Hall. As Torah scrolls burned in a synagogue's yard in Düsseldorf, German men, some wearing the robes of the rabbis and cantors, danced around the fire.[5]

Why did the Nazis burn the Hebrew Bible?

This is a good question because, in European Christian civilization, the torching of the Hebrew Bible is bound to be significant. The act demands explanation. But the scholarship on *Kristallnacht* and the Holocaust, as well as general accounts of the Third Reich, has not made this event part of the story. This silence, too, deserves an explanation.

So is the historian fantasizing? Or should we, instead, ask not only why the Nazis burned the Hebrew Bible but also what serious doubts does this case raise about current narratives of the Holocaust? Because the sources I used to reconstruct the burning of the Bible are known. I did not find them hidden in a dusty room in an unknown archive. They are testimonies of Jews and others collected shortly after *Kristallnacht* that are available at the Wiener Library in London.[6] When I first encountered these sources, I read them with shock that such a radical event took place, with surprise that it has not been made part of Holocaust history, and with uncertainty as to how to integrate the event into that history.

Let us keep these scenes in mind as we explore this historical case.

Recent accounts of the Third Reich, however sophisticated, do not pose the question "Why did the Nazis burn the Hebrew Bible?" because they view Nazi racial ideology as the fundamental source of the motivations, beliefs, and values that led to the Holocaust. According to this view, Nazi motivations sprang from the aim to build a society based on racial and biological assumptions. There is no doubt about the importance of racial ideology in understanding Nazism, but the anti-Jewish identity the Nazis created was more complex. In burning the Bible, the Nazis directed their wrath against a religious, not a racial, symbol. Other dominant directions in Holocaust research provide little help in understanding this phenomenon, viewing the Germans' motivations as embedded in the administrative state process of extermination that culminated in Auschwitz and other death camps. This view has explored in meticulous detail the bureaucratic machinery of the German state that made the Holocaust possible, from the trains used to deport the Jews to the workings of the labor and death camps. Another important approach emphasizes the brutalization of World War II, which led the German soldiers to perpetrate mass murder. Scholarship on these topics certainly helps us capture and understand aspects of the Holocaust, but it cannot assist us in interpreting the burning of the Bible.

When we consider the Holocaust as emerging from racial ideology and a state-run administrative process during a brutal war, it becomes difficult to place *Kristallnacht* and the burning of the Bible within this framework. It does not fit, because race and religion, often viewed as separate categories, commingled in *Kristallnacht*; because by burning the Bible, Germans conveyed a preoccupation with ancient roots and moral authority that cannot make sense within an exclusively racial explanation; and because the dramatic burning of a book holy both to Christians and Jews seems hardly revealing about the extermination of Jews. The point is not that racial and other accounts of the Third Reich portray *Kristallnacht* inadequately, but that their history of the persecution and extermination of the Jews holds together much better if *Kristallnacht* is excluded. The burning of the Bible does not fit in these accounts.

A world of meaning is lost when these views of racial ideology, the brutalization of war, and the state-run process of extermination dominate our understanding of the Holocaust. The question "Why did the Nazis and other Germans burn the Hebrew Bible?" demands a historical imagination that captures the Germans' culture and sensibilities. When we change our perspective and view the burning of the Bible as part of the creation by Nazis and other Germans of a new German identity, when we acknowledge that this act involved a set of motives that cannot be ignored or separated from the Holocaust, then new possibilities that challenge our perceptions emerge to help us understand the Holocaust. Burning the Bible was an intentional act: it happened all over Germany, in public for all to see and to participate in, and both those who perpetrated the act and those who watched it perceived it as a transgression, whether they supported or opposed the burning. The act was part of a larger story that Germans told themselves during the Third Reich about who they were, where they came from, how they had arrived there, and where they were headed.

A story about a journey in time, then. I asked myself how the notion of time has been considered overall in contemporary standard approaches to the Holocaust. The interpretative holy trinity of the historiography of the Third Reich is now defined by the terms "empire," "race," and "space,"[7] and with good reason. This new framework has tremendously enriched our understanding of the Nazi period. By using colonial studies, scholars have interpreted the Nazi expansion in Europe as a colonial project, and Europe as existing fundamentally to serve the interest of Germany in the same way that the colonies served the interest of the European powers. By using comparative genocide studies, scholars have placed the Holocaust within a vast Nazi program of resettlement and extermination that included genocides not only of Jews but also of Poles, Russians, Ukrainians, and others. By exploring in depth the notion of race, scholars have illuminated the "science" of racial biology as the key ideological principle of Nazism. By thinking in terms of empires, they have located the Nazi venture to conquer Europe—and perhaps the entire world—within the context of empire building in modern history overall. Thus, by combining colonialism, race, and empire, scholars have turned space into a key category for understanding Nazi ideology, the Nazis' policy of expansion, and their projects of annihilation. There can be no doubt about the fundamental contribution of this body of work.

And yet, one element is missing from this picture: the element of time. Nazi spatial policy was revolutionary: an empire devoted to expansion—from the Atlantic Ocean in the west to the Pacific Ocean shores of Siberia in the east—and to annihilation of whole groups of people. What, then, I ask, was the revolutionary concept of time that accompanied this revolutionary policy of space? The scholarship is silent on this issue. What was the imagination of time and of history that gave meaning and legitimacy to this radical spatial policy?[8]

Things began to fall into place. Nazism's apocalyptic vision, I thought, was about crafting a new creation that by extension demanded new historical origins. For Germans in 1938, the Bible represented, among others, Jewish and Christian tradition and past; in burning the Bible, Germans expressed conceptions of historical time and origins.

The argument in my book *A World without Jews: Nazi Imagination from Persecution to Genocide* is that representations of the past—of origins, to be exact—underlie the Nazis' perception of time, building of empire, and extermination of the Jews. For the Nazis, the Jews symbolized time: their persecution and extermination was driven by a desire to control memory and history. Nazism was an act of creation of a new society, of a racial civilization to mold Germany, Europe, and ultimately the world based on the systematic persecution and extermination of groups of people considered undesirable. Precisely because Nazism saw itself as a radical, novel historical departure, it paid particular attention to the past, that protean and essential factor of life in all societies. This view fit within a broader pattern of all national and revolutionary movements in the modern world, which sought to build new life based on invented and constructed collective memories. And since the Nazi biological worldview was based on the idea that origins cannot be mutated, ideas of the past became fundamental to endow the movement with that legitimacy and authenticity that come with roots. The Jews symbolized for the Nazis origins that had to be extirpated for the new Germany to arise. The notion of the Jew as possessor of origins—of the present, past, and future; of modernity, the nation, and ultimately humanity—was the basis for what I might call "the empire of time" and for the fantasy that made possible the persecution and extermination of the Jews.

The Jews represented three registers of time that were prominent in three different stages of the Third Reich and that together made up a Nazi narrative of history. We begin in 1933. Immediately after the seizure of power, the Jews epitomized a certain kind of modernity whose un-German, alien elements had to be cleansed from German society. The adjective *jüdisch* (Jewish) was attached to every phenomenon of the modern world objectionable to the Nazis, and then some. Jews were responsible for Bolshevism, Communism, Marxism, socialism, liberalism, conservatism, pacifism, cosmopolitanism, materialism, atheism, capitalism, and democracy; for the German defeat in World War I, the 1918 November Revolution in Germany, and the Weimar Republic; for Weimar's culture of entertainment in cabaret and the club scene, as well as for sexual freedom, psychoanalysis, feminism, homosexuality, and abortions; for modernist, atonal, and jazz music; for Bauhaus architecture, and for abstract painting represented in impressionism, postimpressionism, cubism, Dadaism, and expressionism.

The persecution of the Jews in the early years of the Third Reich was thus tied up with an anti-Marxist and antiliberal vision of modernity shared by many Germans and Nazis. This vision was not antimodern: it proposed a different modernity built on the ruins of Communism, liberal democracy, and Jewish influences. The Jews represented the overall meaning of the Nazi revolution, the crushing of one modernity and the making of another, because only they represented in the minds of the Nazis, at one and the same time, different, and often opposing, enemies. They could represent Marxism and liberalism, democracy and Bolshevism, Communism and cubism (not quite the artistic style favored by social realists). Differently put, the Jews represented to the Nazis a whole that was bigger than the sum of its parts. The Nazis thus created the Jew as a symbolic manual for the evils of modern history, and ultimately for an evil history overall.

The notion of race had a central place in the Nazi idea of origins. Studies of the last two decades, as we already noted, have conclusively shown both the key place occupied by racial ideology in the Third Reich as well as the complex application of the idea. Not even the Nazis knew exactly what racial identity meant, and the use of the notion of race was a work in progress about an evolving concept rather than a clear set of ideas. One result of this detailed historiography has been to acknowledge the importance of race in the Third Reich while making the true but bland observation that "it was all much more complicated than that." Did the concept of race in the Third Reich have a common denominator that linked its complex and diverse applications, while connecting it to main identities in German society? I suggest viewing Nazi racial ideas from the perspective of the idea of origin. Racial ideas claimed that the history of humankind is a story of racial conflict and that the characteristics of racial groups were predetermined and could not be fundamentally changed. Race theories did leave some room for evolution and transformation, but the basic racial traits of groups could not be changed. The notion of race, therefore, was *the* metaphor of origins in the Third Reich. By turning race into the principal idea in Germany, the Nazis transformed the notion of origin into the fundamental aspect of their policies, mentalities, and memories.

Still, the notions of race and of the origins of modernity cannot come close to constructing a revolutionary idea of time, able to carry symbolically the expansionist and genocidal plans of the Nazis: an idea, that is, represented in the Jews that would require the destruction of a key part of German civilization, thus ushering in the making of a new one. This, I would argue, happened on November 9, 1938, when the Nazis burned the Hebrew Bible. Not one copy, but thousands, not in one place but in hundreds of communities across the Reich, and not only in metropolises such as Berlin, Stettin (now Szczecin, Poland), Vienna, Dresden, Stuttgart, and Cologne, but in small communities such as Sulzburg, a Protestant village in Baden with 1,070 inhabitants, where villagers threw the stone tablets of the Ten Commandments from the roof of the synagogue, and Nazis marched mockingly up and down the main street with Torah scrolls before destroying them.

Having in mind the dominant interpretation of racial ideology as the ultimate motivation behind Nazi antisemitism, I ask a simple question: why did the Nazis, set on constructing a racial civilization, burn during *Kristallnacht* the Bible and synagogues, which are holy, religious symbols? This, I contend, was part of the Nazi idea of the Jews as possessors of origins that threatened the Third Reich. The Nazi seizure of power in 1933 placed the Jews as the origin of a certain present that Nazism sought to replace. The burning of the Bible and the synagogues placed the Jews as the origin of a certain past that, soiling the new Germany, had to be completely erased. Burning the synagogues was not targeted at Jews as liberals or Bolsheviks, and also not as racial enemies, but instead at Jews as possessors of origins embedded in a text that was *the* symbol of the roots of European-Christian civilization.

Burning the Bible was a Nazi transgressive act against a key symbol of Germany's own culture, transgressive but also liberating: the Nazis claimed a new national identity that owed nothing to the symbolic authority the Jews might derive from the Bible, but also owed nothing to previous moral and cultural constraints about the treatment of other Europeans. It was not so much an anti-Christian project as it was a project to construct a new German Christianity that owed nothing to the Jews and to other Christian Europeans. Had the Nazis limited their aims to a narrow political change from Weimar democracy to dictatorship, then removing Jews from economic and cultural positions—as origins of modernity—would have been enough. But their aim was to found a racial civilization, a new humanity, and this demanded a new register of historic time that linked the origins embedded in the ideas of race, of Christianity, and of history.

The final evolution of Nazi time as represented by the Jews came during the war, articulated in the idea that "the Jewish question is the key to world history," as the Reich Press Office announced on February 3, 1944.[9] By that time, the vast Nazi project of treating whole groups as people without rights, of building labor and concentration camps, and of waging genocides had started to create a new version of humanity. Contemporaries perceived the Nazi version as a new history, radically different from what had been experienced up until then. The Jews stood at the center of the making of the Nazi empire: their extermination gave it meaning as being experientially unprecedented. Heinrich Himmler expressed this sentiment in his notorious address to a group of *Schutzstaffel* (SS) officers in Posen (now Poznań, Poland) in 1943: "In our history, this [the extermination of the Jews] is an unwritten and never-to-be written page of glory."[10] Oskar Rosenfeld, a Viennese Jew deported to the Łódź ghetto in November 1941 and kept a remarkable diary, wrote: "There are no heroes in this tragedy. And why tragedy? Because the pain does not touch on something human, on a strange heart, but on something incomprehensible that touches on the cosmos, an event in nature like the creation of the world. In the beginning God created the ghetto."[11]

What was the idea that undergirded the total extermination of the Jews and gave it meaning? I turned to listen to Nazis, other Germans, Jews, and other Europeans. They imagined the extermination of the Jews as an act of creation, in the sense of genesis, in which the Jewish world would be destroyed to make space for the Nazi one. As an act of creation, the extermination was perceived as producing a cosmic result, either salvation or eternal damnation; as a human experience that lacked historical precedence, as every creation is by definition; and, as such, as a transgression, in the sense that it was a violation of all past known practices. The notion of creation was the organizing metaphor used by Germans, Jews, and other Europeans to make sense of what was happening to the Jews after 1941. It allowed contemporaries to represent a radical rupture, for a genesis has no roots in the past, while at the same time it fit within the Nazi evolving imagination since 1933.

However radical the extermination was, then, it shared continuities with the German cultural imagination of the preceding years. There was an inner logic to the Nazi persecution and extermination of the Jews, for the progressive removal of Jews meant the conquering of time—of the present in 1933 through the exclusion of Jews from German society; of a moral past in 1938 through the elimination of Judaism and the Bible; and ultimately of history, and therefore of the future, in 1941, through the extermination from the face of the earth of the Jews as the source of all historical evil. The idea of genesis defined the symbolic urgency of the Nazis to kill all the Jews immediately.

And so, once again, as in 1933 and 1938, the Jews stood at the center of the making of Nazi life: it was their extermination that gave meaning to the Nazi empire.

The interpretation presented in my book should be placed alongside other accounts that emphasize political, military, or ideological history. Research on the Holocaust has become so vast that it is now a big enough tent for different interpretations that shed light on the Holocaust from varied angles. Still, the story told in these pages does differ in some key points from current interpretations of the Holocaust, and I would like to articulate these differences.

I have already pointed out that I reject the dominant position of racial ideology as the ultimate source of motivation. Nazi persecution was embedded in racial ideas, but also in Christian, religious sentiments, as well as national sentiments embodied in the idea of *Heimat* (homeland). These ideas and sentiments all contributed to the Nazi imagination of the Jews and of origins.

A fundamental problem in interpreting the Holocaust has been explaining the daunting gap between the anti-Jewish persecution of the prewar years and the almost unimaginable extermination during the war. If we look for Auschwitz in prewar Nazi culture, we assume that Auschwitz was already clearly imaginable, which was not the case. If we emphasize racial ideology, we assume a causal relation that explains too little of how the jump was made from hatred to extermination.

I attempt to show how imagination in the 1930s anticipated extermination in the 1940s by following the way Germans imagined a world without Jews. This is the leading metaphor that drives our story. Our starting point is the intentions of the Nazis and the policy of the German state starting on January 30, 1933, when Hitler rose to power: the construction of a Germany, and later a world, without Jews. This perspective captures the search in the Third Reich for a Germany without Jews while taking cognizance of the different policies (such as emigration or segregation), opinions, and sentiments of the project, as well as its complexity, probability, and uncertainty. Some Germans supported the idea, some opposed it, and some were indifferent, but it was and remained a goal of the Third Reich from the beginning, a whole larger than the sum of individual Germans' views about the Jews. As we follow the story of a Germany without Jews in the 1930s, we are not required to know the story's final destination (the extermination beginning in 1941); in fact, we ought to follow the story in much the same way that Germans did after 1933, when they did not know where their imagination would lead them. Our only firm point is January 30, 1933: a moral, historical, post-Enlightenment break was made, not by planning an eventual extermination, but by thinking that a German world without Jews could become a reality, somehow.

Placing the imagination of a Germany without Jews at the center of the history of the Holocaust means shifting the focus from a story that ends in Auschwitz to the gradual making of a culture in which a Germany, and later a world, without Jews made sense to Germans. It is jarring to speak about "making sense" of the Holocaust, but it is the right phrase and the right investigation if we wish to uncover how Germans made sense of their world in the Third Reich, however morally objectionable this world was. "Made sense" also does not mean that everybody agreed to it. Rather, it means that Germans were able to imagine it, to internalize it, to make it part of their vision of the present and future, whether they agreed, opposed, or were indifferent to it. Because, in reality, it is not Auschwitz that stands at the center of the historian's study of Nazi antisemitism, but it is the making of a German world without Jews. Imagining this world was not a consequence of the war; Auschwitz was. The idea of a Germany without Jews had been in the process of becoming realized already before the war, from 1933 onward; it would have been created with or without Auschwitz. How did it settle in Germans' imagination?

The imagination of a Germany without Jews links antisemitic actions and ideas in the prewar and war years because it describes Nazi antisemitism as a work in progress. I thus challenge the mainstream view of the Holocaust in popular and scholarly understanding that the mass murder of the Jews during the war had not been anticipated, that victims and perpetrators alike scarcely believed what was happening, that it was unimaginable and unrepresentable. Primo Levi expressed this idea in one of the twentieth century's most profound statements: "Today, at this very moment as I sit writing at the table, I myself am not convinced that these things really happened."[12] The sentiment cannot be denied. At the same time, historians know that all that happened was, in some way, somehow, imagined—perhaps not literally, not exactly—but it was put into images and words that made it possible. No historical event springs from thin air, none is unique, because this implies having no links to context, past, and present. Of course, on November 9, 1938, no one could imagine the gas chamber of Auschwitz, not even Hitler himself. But on that day, one could imagine a German world in which Jews and Judaism were terminated by fire and violence. Our aim is to seek patterns of meaning and purpose in a world of fantasies that made the extermination possible precisely because it was, somehow, imaginable and representable.

Finally, the Holocaust cannot be understood without consideration of the history of European colonialism. The Nazi notions of race and of inferior groups who had no right to live belonged in the tradition of European colonialism, which, long before 1933, provided popular, "scientific," and political legitimacy to colonial genocides around the world.[13] Similarly, the enmity against and extermination of the Jews was part of a Nazi universe of racial enemies and exterminations. The Jewish genocide was bound up with a set of racial ideas that produced other Nazi mass killings and genocides of physically and mentally ill patients, Ukrainians, and Russians, among others. The Holocaust can be understood only when placed within the comparative history of modern genocides. It belongs squarely within the genre of genocides and was not an exceptional, stand-alone historical event.

But in themselves the European traditions of modern colonialism and racial ideas cannot account for the Holocaust, and at some point I part ways with the scholarship on comparative genocides and on the Nazi empire. Some scholars question the extent to which the Holocaust is central to understanding National Socialism. In making the Nazi empire, some argue, the Holocaust was a result rather than a goal of Nazism, growing out of the specific circumstances of the war.[14] Others integrate the Holocaust into a history of totalitarian genocides committed by Adolf Hitler and Joseph Stalin in Eastern Europe, implying that the Holocaust was a result of the linked policies of the two dictators as they pushed each other to commit ever-worsening crimes.[15]

The limits of these arguments should also be made clear. If the Holocaust was a result of mass murders in Eastern Europe between Hitler and Stalin, why did the Nazis choose to exterminate the Jews of the Greek island of Corfu, and by extension those of Western Europe, who had no direct relation to this conflict? If the Holocaust was essentially only part of mass murders, such as the premeditated starvation of Ukrainian peasants by Stalin in the early 1930s, then why did the NKVD, Stalin's secret police, not seek to kill all Ukrainians in the Soviet Union or indeed the world? The Gestapo, on the other hand, searched for every single Jew in occupied Europe to be murdered and, beyond that, asked the king of Bulgaria and the sultan of Morocco to hand over "their" Jews to send them to Auschwitz (both rulers refused). The problem with the arguments that the Holocaust was not central to understanding National Socialism is that they view a close description of the circumstances of World War II—that is, of what happened—as an explanation of what people believed and imagined—that is, of why things happened. According to these views, implicitly and at times explicitly, anti-Jewish sensibilities were not of major importance in the making of the Holocaust. I wonder about that. Empire building, multiple genocides, and other wartime circumstances cannot account for Germans' culture and motivations, much as the Nazi immigration policies to push the Jews out of Germany before November 1938 cannot account for burning the Bible.

My view is different. The Holocaust should be placed within a history of Nazi war and occupation, empire building, and comparative genocide. The Holocaust was not unique. But it was *perceived* during the war as unique by Germans, Jews, and other Europeans, and if we want to understand why the Holocaust happened, we ought to explain this. The comparative approach to genocide sharpens the similarities but also the differences between the Holocaust and other genocides. On the one hand, the idea of exterminating racial groups had been building in European culture and politics for a century before the Third Reich. But on the other hand, for the Nazis, the persecution and extermination of the Jews was more urgent and historically significant than other genocides they committed. Although they set out to kill all the Jews after the invasion of the Soviet Union, they did not have a similar policy for other groups of victims. This only raises the questions: why did the Nazis view the extermination of the Jews as so urgent and fateful to their survival? During the war, why did Germans, Jews, and Europeans perceive the extermination of the Jews as unlike any other genocide perpetrated by the Nazis?

My answer has been that for the Nazis and other Germans, Jews represented time, evil historical origins that had to be eradicated for Nazi civilization to arise. That is why the Holocaust was perceived as a new creation. By giving importance to historical origins, the Nazis were an inherent part of the way Europeans conceived of national identity at the time. The Nazis' peculiarity was to view the Jews as the linchpin in their story. Because the Nazis, when they searched for the essence of their identity, ultimately found the Jews, whose history and origins seemed to define for them who they were and what they were seeking.

NOTES

Earlier versions of this essay appeared as "Why the Nazis Burned the Hebrew Bible," *Commentary* 137, no. 6 (June 1, 2014): 30–34 and as "Why Did the Nazis Burn the Hebrew Bible? Nazi Germany, Representations of the Past, and the Holocaust," *Journal of Modern History* 84, no. 2 (2012): 369–400.

1. Martin Gilbert, *Kristallnacht* (New York: Harper, 2006), 47; Ben Barkow, Raphael Gross, and Michael Lenarz, eds., *Novemberpogrom 1938: Die Augenzeugenberichte der Wiener Library, London* [November pogrom 1938: The eyewitness accounts of the Wiener Library, London] (Frankfurt am Main, Ger.: Jüdischer, 2008), 153.

2. Dagmar Lohmann and Clemens Lohmann, *Das Schicksal der jüdischen Gemeinde in Fritzlar 1933–1945. Die Pogromnacht 1938* [The fate of the Jewish community in Fritzlar 1933–1946: The pogrom in 1938] (Fritzlar, Ger.: Geschichtsverein Fritzlar, 1988), 28.

3. Barkow, Gross, and Lenarz, *Novemberpogrom 1938*, 351.

4. Ibid., 380, 782.

5. Heinz Lauber, *Judenpogrom: "Reichskristallnacht" November 1938 in Großdeutschland: Daten-Fakten-Dokumente-Quellentexte-Thesen und Bewertungen* [Jewish pogrom: "Reich *Kristallnacht*" November 1938 in Greater Germany: Dates, facts, documents, source texts, theses, and reviews] (Gerlingen, Ger.: Bleicher, 1981), 159; Wolfgang Benz, "The Relapse into Barbarism," in Walter Pehle, ed., *November 1938: From "Reichskristallnacht" to Genocide* (Providence, R.I.: Bloomsbury, 1991), 14.

6. See the excellent collection in Barkow, Gross, and Lenarz, *Novemberpogrom 1938*.

7. For an excellent overview, see Shelley Baranowski, *Nazi Empire* (New York: Cambridge University Press, 2011) and Dan Stone, "Genocide, the Holocaust, and the History of Colonialism," chap. 5 in *Histories of the Holocaust* (Oxford: Oxford University Press, 2010), 203–44.

8. Of course, the Nazi sense of historical time was not simply limited to confrontation with the Jews but was noticeable in varied areas of life as, for example, in the efforts of architect Paul Troost and later those of Albert Speer to co-opt a certain Greco-Roman style of architecture or in the cult of medievalism and the Teutonic Knights in paintings and films. The moniker

of the Third Reich itself was tied to Otto von Bismarck and Charlemagne, and served as a key theme all along. I cannot discuss this important topic here. But I am ready to raise the hypothesis that the anxiety of origins—articulated in the policies against the Jews—was linked to the regime's overall insecurity about its historical roots, unable as it was to hark back to any golden age, as Benito Mussolini's Italy could, but also unwilling to cut the link to the past altogether, as in Vladimir Lenin's Soviet Union.

See the studies on the Nazi concept of time by Lothar Kroll, *Utopie als Ideologie: Geschichtsdenken und politisches Handeln im Dritten Reich* [Utopia as an ideology: Historical thought and political action in the Third Reich], 2nd ed. (Paderborn, Ger.: Schöningh, 1999) and by Franz Janka, *Die braune Gesellschaft: Ein Volk wird formatiert* [The brown society: A people is molded] (Stuttgart, Ger.: Evangelischen Gesellschaft, 1997). See Stone, *Histories of the Holocaust*, 255–56, 263–65.

9. Jeffrey Herf, *The Jewish Enemy: Nazi Propaganda during World War II and the Holocaust* (London: Belknap, 2006), 240.

10. Yitzhak Arad, Israel Gutman, and Abraham Margaliot, eds., *Documents on the Holocaust: Selected Sources on the Destruction of the Jews of Germany and Austria, Poland, and the Soviet Union* (Jerusalem: Yad Vashem, 1981), document 161, 344.

11. Oskar Rosenfeld, *In the Beginning Was the Ghetto: Notebooks from Łódź* (Evanston, Ill.: Northwestern University Press, 2002), 105–6, 133–34.

12. Primo Levi, *Survival in Auschwitz* (New York: Touchstone, 1996), 103.

13. Donald Bloxham, "The Holocaust and European History" and A. Dirk Moses, "The Holocaust and World History: Raphael Lemkin and Comparative Methodology," in Dan Stone, ed., *The Holocaust and Historical Methodology* (New York: Berghahn, 2012), 233–54, 272–89.

14. Mark Mazower, *Hitler's Empire: Nazi Rule in Occupied Europe* (New York: Penguin, 2008).

15. Timothy Snyder, *Bloodlands: Europe between Hitler and Stalin* (New York: Basic, 2010).

II. C·O·N·T·E·M·P·O·R·A·R·Y C·O·N·T·R·O·V·E·R·S·I·E·S A·N·D T·H·E·I·R H·I·S·T·O·R·I·C·A·L O·R·I·G·I·N·S

John-Paul Himka

Former Ukrainian Policemen in the Ukrainian National Insurgency: Continuing the Holocaust outside German Service

WORLD WAR II, WITH ITS TREMENDOUS VIOLENCE AND MASSIVE SCALE, unleashed many smaller conflicts fought alongside it and within it, in Eastern Europe and elsewhere. Political movements that represented none of the principal protagonists of the war made use of the militarization and disruption of society and the diffusion of weapons to pursue their own agendas of political, territorial, and ethnic transformation. Nationalists killed Communists and vice versa far from the immediate sphere of Soviet influence, for example, in Greece, Serbia, and China. Ethnic conflict also erupted, and not just in dismantled Yugoslavia. In Volhynia—a region covering what are now parts of Belarus, Poland, and Ukraine—in 1943, the Ukrainian Insurgent Army (known by its Ukrainian initials UPA) embarked on a murderous ethnic cleansing project against the region's Polish inhabitants, and Poles fought back as members of the Home Army but also as Soviet partisans and policemen in German service. Many of these conflicts influenced the course of the Holocaust where they occurred, but I know of no other case like the one I am about to describe, in which nationalists entered German service to gain training and weapons, then defected to their own insurgent organization and independently continued the Holocaust in territory under their control, using precisely the methods that the Germans had taught them.

Although a military organization under the name UPA had existed in Volhynia under the command of the Ukrainian resistance leader Taras Bulba-Borovets prior to the spring of 1943,[1] the organization's character changed profoundly at that time. When the charismatic

Bulba-Borovets was forcibly removed from command, insurgents loyal to him were disarmed and UPA came under the leadership of a faction of the Organization of Ukrainian Nationalists (OUN) headed by Stepan Bandera, abbreviated OUN-B. The new UPA was militarily superior to Bulba's, and far more aggressive. Within its ranks were thousands of Ukrainian policemen who had deserted German service and fled to the Volhynian forests. They embarked on a resistance campaign against the German occupiers and a brutal ethnic cleansing of the Polish population of Volhynia. The mass desertion occurred in the second half of March and first half of April 1943. Altogether an estimated 4,000 to 5,000 policemen fled at this time, according to one of the most authoritative researchers of the Ukrainian national insurgency, Grzegorz Motyka.[2]

Jews who managed to survive in Volhynia into 1943 recognized many of these new Ukrainian insurgents. Aron Babouch, who was hiding in the vicinity of Volodymyr-Volynskyi, the capital of a raion (administrative unit) in Volhynia oblast (province),[3] thought that the Germans had deliberately left these policemen behind to fight the Soviets.[4] Jacob Biber was working as a tanner for a Ukrainian in Siomaky, Lutsk raion, Volhynia oblast, when the Banderite UPA was formed. He and his Ukrainian employer had different feelings about the significance of the new armed force. His employer, Zachar, returned from town and ran into the barn where Biber and his wife were staying. He excitedly told them:

> The militz [i.e. the *Schutzmannschaft* or Ukrainian police] has split from the Germans . . . Our boys have run off on orders from the nationalist underground. They grabbed a lot of ammunition from the Germans and spread throughout the village. They are preparing for a battle that will be decisive in our struggle for independence . . . We are a force under the name of Taras Bulba."[5]

Biber said that he and his wife were not sure how good that news was, but they were glad that the Germans were losing ground. Zachar was sure it was good news for the Bibers. That night, as the UPA marched through the village, Zachar told them: "From now on, you are free people." But Biber wrote in his memoirs: "We did not feel free. We had mixed emotions about the force going by. We knew how many killers there were in those lines of marching men to whom independence meant a chance to fill their own pockets."[6] One of the "Bulbas" they encountered walking on the road one day was Ivan Riszhey (Ryzhy), whom they had known since childhood. Earlier, he had volunteered for the militia under the Germans and once took a German soldier's place so that he could shoot Jews all day.[7]

Soviet investigations of war crimes confirm that Ukrainian policemen who helped the Germans exterminate Jews in Volhynia subsequently served in UPA.[8] Dozens of Ukrainian members of the German auxiliary police organization *Schutzmannschaft* Battalion 118, which committed numerous atrocities in Belarus, also joined UPA in Volhynia. The supreme commander of UPA, Roman Shukhevych, had been an officer in Schutzmannschaft Battalion 201, which had also served in Belarus. Mykola Kovtoniuk (Yakymchuk), the commandant of the Lutsk city police in 1941 and a Banderite leader in Volhynia, became first commander of the Turiv military district of UPA. Stepan Yanishevsky, deputy police commander in Vinnytsia in 1941–1943, was acting head of the Zahrava military district in 1944. Omelian Hrabets, head of the regional police in Rivne in 1941 and OUN-B leader in the Rivne region in 1941–1942, commanded UPA-South in 1943–1944.[9] Clearly, not only were there large numbers of former policemen in UPA but also they naturally occupied leadership positions. They joined the nationalist units with their own weapons, which was important for partisans, especially for the undersupplied UPA. They had some military training and much experience in killing. The value of former policemen as trained cadres in conditions of civil conflict is also demonstrated by the decision of the high command of the Soviet partisans to recruit among the auxiliary police.[10] Timothy Snyder notes that as many as 12,000 auxiliary policemen defected from German service in Belarus to the Soviet partisans in February 1943.[11]

Beginning in March 1943, the Banderite UPA launched massive attacks on Polish settlements in Volhynia, and the killing reached its greatest intensity that summer. By the end of summer, few Poles were left in scattered settlements; those who survived UPA's onslaught abandoned their homes and fled to self-defense bases in fortified localities.[12] Thousands of Jews hid in bunkers and in forest camps. As winter approached, the empty houses offered necessary shelter for many of these Jewish survivors. Meanwhile, UPA made little or no progress on the anti-Polish front, and the Red Army was rapidly approaching. In fact, the Soviets recaptured Rivne and Lutsk in early February 1944; Rivne oblast was completely reconquered in March 1944; and only parts of

Volhynia oblast held out until July 1944. During this upheaval, UPA leaders in Volhynia decided to eliminate the surviving Jews.

The winter of 1943–1944, furthermore, was a period when OUN and UPA officially declared a policy of national tolerance, hoping to become acceptable partners for the Western Allies. At the OUN's Third Extraordinary Assembly, held in August 1943, the OUN faction under Bandera proclaimed a number of democratic measures, including the toleration of national minorities. Given the intensity of UPA massacres of Poles at this time, these proclamations were likely meant for external rather than internal consumption. The revolutionary Bandera movement did not hesitate to say one thing and do another. Stepan Bandera himself put it this way: "One program should be addressed to the members and sympathizers of nationalism, and the second for external factors. The first should be the main credo for members and sympathizers. The second program should exist for external consumption. It can change according to the circumstances and external situation."[13] In addition to continuing to murder Poles while ostensibly tolerating national minorities, OUN and UPA remained largely antisemitic. Responding to Soviet interrogators, Ukrainian prisoner Volodymyr Porendovsky stated that in 1941–1942, OUN openly preached a racist ideology, called for the annihilation of the Jews, and took part in their murder. Later, he said, OUN began to be ashamed of this policy and repudiated participation in such murders, "but in reality until the very end the 'leadership' of OUN stood on antisemitic positions." He related that in 1945 Dmytro Maievsky, the director of the political section (*referentura*) of the central OUN leadership, remarked: "It was a good thing that the Germans annihilated the Jews, because in this way OUN got rid of some of its enemies." Another important figure in the OUN leadership, Yaroslav Starukh, had told Porendovsky much the same thing in fall 1946.[14] At this time, Starukh led UPA troops on Zakerzonnia, a territory of Poland where many Ukrainians lived.[15]

With this contextual background, we can look at a number of Jewish testimonies, taken at different times and places, which describe deliberate mass murders of Jewish survivors by UPA in the Volhynian forests in the winter of 1943–1944. A common thread in most of the narratives is that UPA attempted to lull the Jews' suspicions and coax them out of hiding in order to kill them.

Vera Shchetinkova recalled how she hid with about eighty-five other Jews in the general vicinity of Sarny, a raion capital in Rivne oblast, in mid-January 1944. The Banderites discovered their bunkers and decided to destroy all the Jews who lived in them. In her view, the Banderites wanted no witnesses left when the Soviets came. Their goal was to round up all the Jews, take them to the village of Stepan, in Sarny raion, and shoot them there. They surrounded the bunkers and began setting up a machine gun, but the Jews rushed out of the bunkers and ran in all directions before the Banderites finished mounting the gun. The young fled, and the Banderites ended up with only the elderly and invalids. They told the captured Jews that they should go to Stepan, where they would be given work. A few of the Jews who escaped decided to go to the village, as the Banderites had instructed. However, they met a woodcutter, a member of a Protestant group called Stundists[16] from Kuzmivka (before 1945 known as Kazimierka), in the same raion, who told them not to go there. He said that graves had already been dug for them and advised them to wait a few days until the Soviets came.[17]

Pola Jasphy hid with some other Jews in the forests near Antonivka, Volodymyrets raion, Rivne oblast (about halfway between Rafalivka and Sarny), where armed Ukrainians had murdered and driven out the Polish population. Many Jews found refuge in the houses abandoned by the Poles, while others hid in the nearby forest. Jasphy estimated that there were several hundred Jewish refugees in the vicinity in the fall of 1943. They made contact with the Banderites, who said that they would not kill Jews, so the surviving Jews of the area went to work for them. This lasted until early January 1944. On the 4th of the month, she learned that all the Jews living near the former Polish houses had been killed by the Ukrainians (she in the meantime had moved to another part of the forest). She and a few others hid in the hay in a barn. The next day, some Ukrainians came searching for them with pitchforks, but missed them by a meter. She stayed in that barn for eight days. In her opinion, the Banderites had deliberately gathered the Jews together to kill them.[18]

A similar story was recorded shortly after the war by Doba Mełamed, a Jewish woman who fled to the forest with her family from the Tuchyn ghetto (Hoshcha raion, Rivne oblast):

> In the summer of 1943 the Banderites began to kill the Poles . . . We found out that near the town of Antonivka in the village of

> Rezyca,[19] Jews were . . . living in liberty, that the Banderites had announced that they will not kill the Jews because they are fighting against a common enemy. We went to Rezyca. In fact there were two hundred Jews living at liberty, working for the peasants as tanners, tailors, cobblers, and the like.

The Jews' camp was attacked by the Germans, and the group moved to Kudrianka, which if it existed today would be in Berezne raion, Rivne oblast.

> The houses of the Poles stood empty. Then the Banderites announced that England and America, as countries with which they were allied, had forbidden them to kill Jews, that they will allow Jews to take over the homes abandoned by the Poles . . . In December 1943 the Banderites again began to register the Jews. After registration they announced that if one Jew escaped, the rest would be killed . . . In December 1943 a certain Jew knocked on our windowpane and shouted: "Run for it, the Banderites have killed the Antonivka Jews." We fled to the forest. We sent the forester to investigate. He came back with the news that the Banderites had killed all the Jews, with axes and knives.[20]

Mina Grinzajd described events that probably occurred in the beginning of 1944 in the vicinity of Radyvyliv, a raion capital far to the southwest in Rivne oblast. She was in a group of 376 Jews who reached an agreement with the Banderites to work for them as tailors, cobblers, and leatherworkers. From time to time, the Banderites said they "resettled" some of the workers in groups of twenty to thirty. In reality, they shot them. At the end of three months, the original group was reduced to thirty-four.[21]

From another locality—the forests near Ozeriany and Kupychiv, Turiisk raion, Volhynia oblast—the same pattern of events has been documented. The Banderites set up a labor camp in which seventy Jews were working. They gave Jews in nearby bunkers an equivalent of the Germans' *Kennkarte* (identity cards), which would allow the Jews to leave their bunkers for work without being harmed. In fact, though, the Banderites attacked the bunkers three times, killing seventeen of the inhabitants. All seventy Jews who worked in the labor camp were murdered.[22]

Sonyah Sherer hid in woods in the area between Beresk, Rozhyshche raion, and Khorokhoryn, Lutsk raion, both in Volhynia oblast. In her postwar testimony, she related that the Banderites put announcements on the trees in these woods, urging the Jews to come to them and assuring the Jews that no harm would befall them. "It was winter, cold—and they came to those Ukrainians, to the Banderites, who shot them all."[23]

Another Volhynian Jew, Emil Goldbarten, related that many Jews hid in woods in the vicinity of Mizoch, Zdolbuniv raion, Rivne oblast. The Germans were afraid to go into the woods because of UPA activity there. (UPA had its headquarters not far away in Derman monastery.) Although UPA kept the Germans out, they killed the Jews in the woods themselves. In January 1944, three Ukrainian partisans captured Goldbarten, took him to a house, and gave him a bed. They said, "You are an intelligent man, you are going to work for us." But this was a lie, Goldbarten said in his testimony: they killed all the Jews whom they caught. In the house where he was supposed to stay was a young girl who used to work for Goldbarten before the war. She asked one of the UPA partisans what they were going to do with him. He answered, "What are we going to do? We're going to kill him." And she said, "He was such a nice man, I used to work for him, he was so nice to me." Goldbarten overheard this conversation and managed to escape. He hid in a barn in the straw and heard the partisans searching for him, asking, "Did you see a Jew here?" The housewife said no. The partisans stuck a pitchfork into the straw. Goldbarten had not had time to dig a proper cavity in the straw and was curled up. A partisan stood above him, sticking and sticking his pitchfork into the straw, but never striking his hidden target. "What the hell," he said. "Where did he disappear to?" Two or three weeks later, Goldbarten was liberated by the Red Army.[24]

Aron Baboukh, as has been mentioned earlier, survived in villages in the vicinity of Volodymyr Volynskyi, kept alive primarily through the efforts of Ukrainian rescuers who hid him from the Banderites. In February 1944, many Banderites suddenly appeared in the village where he and a friend were hiding in a bunker, and the village became unsafe for them. One day, searching for fuel, he and his friend stumbled upon some Banderites who tried to capture them and shot at them. The Banderites found the bunker with more Jewish refugees and shot every one of them. Baboukh claimed that the Banderites killed hundreds of Jews and that he was an eyewitness to their atrocities.[25]

The memoirs of Jacob Biber resonate with many of the other testimonies. His cousin had been invited by the "Bulbas," as he called the UPA men, to set up a tannery in the Stubicki forest west of Siomaky. Biber's Ukrainian employer said: "See . . . they are not touching any Jews."[26] Biber went to visit his cousin, who told him, "The Bulbas are treating me well . . . but . . . I don't trust the Bulbas, because there are too many killers among them who do not need witnesses around with the times changing the way they are. The Soviets are winning the war and getting nearer." His cousin also told him about a Jewish girl who went to work for the Bulbas in Stubicki forest and was later found shot to death in the forest.[27] In mid-December 1943, Biber visited his cousin again. He "told us he was working with a whole crew at the Bulbas' tannery and had acquired an assistant. He advised us again to be extremely careful, as some of the Bulbas were still killing any Jews they could find."[28] Some time later, the Bibers went to stay with another Ukrainian family, the Pavluks. One morning when they were all doing chores, several Bulbas came into their house. One of them, a former Red Army soldier who had now become a leader in the movement, told Biber: "Next time I find you here, I'll kill you. Right now I don't want to smear Pavluk's floor with your dirty blood."[29] The cousin was captured by a Bulba commander in the village of Chornoplesy, just west of Siomaky, and skinned alive by him and a helper. That same commander also killed the last surviving Jewish woman in Chernoplesy. The woman begged to be spared because she had nursed the commander as a baby, but he had no mercy. The Bulbas also shot another of Biber's friends at this time.[30]

In the village of Novyny (then Nowiny Czeskie), Mlyniv raion, Rivne oblast, about twenty Jews were still alive at some point in 1943 when an UPA soldier pretending to be a Soviet partisan lured them to the forest, supposedly to join the partisans. Instead, they were murdered there.[31]

Such testimonies are not numerous, but we should not expect them to be. They recount killings of defenseless people by armed men in forests, not the kind of enterprise that produces many records. As Omer Bartov has pointed out:

> From the point of view of the historian, the single most important benefit of using testimonies is that they bring into history events that would otherwise remain completely unknown, since they are missing from more conventional documentation found in archives

> and mostly written by the perpetrators or organizers of genocide. Hence personal accounts can at times save events from oblivion.[32]

This is the case here. Considering the context, the number of testimonies that are extant is impressive and indicates that these systematic murders of Jews must have been a widespread feature of the Holocaust in Volhynia. I see no reason to doubt the essential story that these testimonies tell.

The credibility of the testimonies is reinforced by the geography of the reported incidents. They all refer to Volhynia, to the region that formed UPA-North, commanded by Dmytro Kliachkivsky (also known as Klym Savur), who was one of OUN-UPA's most steadfast proponents of ethnic cleansing.[33] Rumors and false reports would probably have encompassed a larger, less cohesive area. In this region, the division headed by Mykhailo Kolodzinsky was active, and we know from the division's own reports that it routinely murdered Jews that it encountered in November and December 1943.[34]

The mass murder of Jews in the winter of 1943–1944 was also reflected in a report dated January 21, 1944, from the headquarters of the Ukrainian Soviet partisan movement: "According to official documents of the 'SB' [Security Service] of UPA in our possession, the nationalists on direct orders from above are destroying in mass the Polish and Jewish population, and also Ukrainians who have accepted the Catholic religion or are found to have family relations with Poles." The partisan report quoted from an UPA Security Service report which it had acquired: "Previously the 'SB' issued an order—to destroy all nonspecialist Jews in a conspiratorial manner so that the Jews and even our people [that is, ethnic Ukrainians] do not know it, but put out propaganda that they went to the Bolsheviks."[35] Another Banderite Sluzhba Bezpeky (Security Service) SB-OUN order from Volhynia, dated March 11, 1944, said: "Without delay liquidate communists and Jews." Another stated: "Destroy NKVD-men [officers of the Soviet law enforcement agency], informers, Jews, and Poles."[36] A 1944 report on OUN-UPA compiled for the Ukrainian Communist Party leadership also stated that among the four major operational measures conducted by UPA was: "They carry out the hunting and killing of the Jewish population."[37]

The luring of Jews out of hiding in the winter of 1943–1944 to kill them has not been analyzed conclusively in the existing historiography on UPA and the Holocaust. The murder of Jews in Antonivka-Kudrianka seems to have been mentioned first by Betty Eisenstein-Keshev in a Yiddish-language study of Volhynian Jews during World War II.[38] It was also mentioned by Philip Friedman, Shmuel Spector, and Grzegorz Motyka.[39] Friedman felt that Eisenstein-Keshev's account was "not sufficiently documented" and "subject to question." He pointed out that UPA and its camp of Jews had been attacked by the Germans in June 1943: "Conceivably, some of the Jewish inmates were left behind, fell into the hands of the Germans, and were exterminated." The Ukrainian nationalist military historian Lev Shankovsky also argued that it was the Germans who killed the Jews, during antipartisan actions in July and August 1943. As the Red Army neared Volhynia, UPA could no longer protect the camps, so it released the Jews, who were left to fend for themselves.[40]

However, overriding Friedman's doubts and Shankovsky's defensive explanation are at least two key arguments: the testimonies generally refer to a time after the summer of 1943, when the German offensive was said to have occurred; and more testimonies of the liquidation of the labor camps and the luring of Jews from hiding have come to light, indicating a pattern of activity. We do not have testimonies, on the other hand, from Jews who survived the UPA labor camps and witnessed no attempt at liquidation; nor do we have any survivor testimonies indicating that the Germans liquidated UPA camps in the crucial period of winter 1943–1944.

The victims of the Holocaust had a difficult time identifying precisely who intended to murder them.[41] In the testimonies cited in this study, UPA, as such, is not mentioned; the usual terminology was "Banderites," which indicated adherents of a particular political tendency, or "Bulbas," which indicated the insurgent force initiated by Taras Bulba-Borovets. Therefore, it may not have been regular units of UPA who committed these murders in the woods but rather specialized security forces attached to the Banderite OUN (SB-OUN). This possibility is consistent with the opinion of the Russian historian Aleksandr Dyukov that "the main burden of the battle against the Jews and other 'undesirable elements' fell not on the UPA, but on a nominally independent structure that was subordinate to its command—the Security Service of OUN."[42] It is simply not possible to verify or disprove this supposition owing to lack of evidence. We know, as noted earlier, that a regular UPA unit, the Mykhailo Kolodzinsky Division, killed Jews routinely, but we do not know for certain that it engaged in the liquidation of labor camps.

But whatever particular units of the Ukrainian nationalist insurgency were active in the liquidations, they used tactics that they had learned in German service, during the destruction of the Volhynian Jews. In *The Reconstruction of Nations*, Timothy Snyder described the role of the Ukrainian police in the latter project and then pointed out how they used what they had learned from the Germans in their ethnic cleansing campaign against the Polish population:

> The Final Solution had taught them that the mass murder of civilian populations may be achieved by way of precise organization and the timely presence of men willing to shoot men, women, and children . . . The next spring, in March–April 1943, virtually all of these Ukrainian policemen left the German service to join the Ukrainian partisans of the UPA . . . People learn to do what they are trained to do, and are good at doing what they have done many times. Ukrainian partisans who mass-murdered Poles in 1943 followed the tactics they learned as collaborators in the Holocaust in 1942: detailed advance planning and site selection; persuasive assurances to local populations prior to actions; sudden encirclements of settlements; and then physical elimination of human beings.[43]

The tactics described by Snyder in reference to the murder of the Poles are recognizable in the incidents described in the Jewish testimonies cited earlier. The Germans directly involved Ukrainian police in operations that used the stratagem of falsely declaring that the killing of Jews had ended. For example, according to a Ukrainian woman interrogated by the Extraordinary State Committee in November 1944, Ukrainian policemen in Tuchyn rounded up Jews in fall 1942 for execution by shooting. The woman saw with her own eyes two wagonloads of corpses pass by her field two days later. A week after the shootings, the woman said, "The Germans announced that 'they will no longer shoot and kill Jews.'"[44] Thus the former policemen had learned their lessons from the masters of the practice. We can recognize German methods in the general setup, that is, the establishment of labor camps, and also in details of the operation, that is, registering the Jews, posting announcements, and issuing *Kennkarten*. Moreover, former policemen already had experience in finding Jewish hideouts and bunkers, which was a routine task assigned by the Germans.

But why did the Ukrainian nationalist insurgents kill Jews after the Ukrainians had left German service? The national insurrection that broke out in spring 1943 was directed not only against the Poles but also against the Germans, and the Germans fought UPA fiercely in the summer of 1943. Perhaps the approach of the Soviets (they took Kiev, the capital of the Ukrainian Soviet Socialist Republic, in September 1943) motivated UPA to tactical cooperation, as it did in May 1944 in Galicia; the cooperation in Galicia included an UPA agreement to liquidate "Jewish gangs."[45] But we do not, at least at present, have any documentary confirmation of the same thing occurring in Volhynia.

Of course, the nationalists had a comprehensive ethnic cleansing project, and the removal of Jews was one item on their agenda. But we have documentation that the Jews were to be left for later: the conspectus of a class taken by a Volhynian, Mykhailo Smenchak, who was undergoing political training with OUN or UPA in 1943. Lesson twelve concerned "our relations towards national minorities." About Jews, the conspectus said: "We consider them agents of Muscovite imperialism, formerly tsarist but now proletarian. Still, we have to first beat (*byty*) the Muscovites and then the surviving Jews (*zhydiv nedobytkiv*)."[46] This was a consistent line in OUN doctrine, that the Jews were enemies primarily because they were agents of Russian or Soviet imperialism; they were a second-rank enemy, while Russians constituted the first-rank enemy.[47] In spite of this doctrine, it was sometimes expedient for OUN to concentrate on the murder of Jews instead of other targets that they considered more important. OUN's deep involvement in the anti-Jewish violence of the summer of 1941 and its infiltration of the Ukrainian auxiliary police and *Schutzmannschaften* fit into this category. Moreover, the identification of Jews as agents of the Soviets, although imputing a subordinate significance to Jews as such, was still highly volatile. This was, after all, the main argument of the pogromists in summer 1941. This justification would have come into play in a serious way in winter 1943–1944 in Volhynia. For Ukrainian nationalists, the Soviet Union was the ultimate evil, the Germans a lesser evil; for the Jews, the Germans were the ultimate evil, and the Soviets either a lesser evil or, for some, a positive good. The Soviets brought life to the Jews but death to the Ukrainian nationalists. Their interests were sharply opposed. As is well-known, thousands of Jews had joined the pro-Soviet partisans, UPA's mortal enemies.[48]

Moreover, UPA functioned in an environment in which ruthless preventive murder was the norm. In 1941, for example, when the Germans attacked, the NKVD made a decision to kill all the political prisoners it could not evacuate lest they offer their services to the Germans.[49] SB-OUN units in Volhynia killed former Soviet prisoners of war who worked in households because they feared the former prisoners might join Soviet partisans.[50] With the Soviets advancing on Volhynia in the winter of 1943–1944, the nationalist partisans made a chilling calculation: the Jews in hiding could prove useful to the Soviets—whether as fighters or as skilled artisans; the partisans reasoned it would be better if the Jews were dead.

Two other factors would have come into play that directly relate to the insurgents' past in German police service. One is closely related to the calculation mentioned earlier. Jews would be able to identify former policemen and bear witness to their participation in German atrocities. Indeed, around the time of the Soviet reconquest, a Soviet partisan unit captured Velyki Mezhyrichi, Korets raion, Rivne oblast. One of the Jewish partisans identified twenty-eight Ukrainian policemen to the commander, who had them summarily executed.[51] Ukrainian nationalist insurgents and former policemen had good reason to fear that the Jews would cooperate with the Soviets to punish them after Soviet reoccupation.[52] Jewish survivors Chaim Waks and Yakov Waks joined the NKVD after the Soviets returned to "take care of the Ukrainian Nazis." Chaim was killed by UPA in 1944 in the village of Malynsk, Berezne raion, Rivne oblast.[53]

The second factor that relates to the insurgents' experience as policemen is that they had spent over a year participating in the murder of Jews. True, the Germans did most, or at least much, of the actual shooting, but Ukrainian police served as their accessories. People explain to themselves why they commit murder, why the person they are killing really does deserve to die.[54] Centuries earlier, the Roman historian Tacitus had come to an important insight that explains what fuels genocides—we hate whom we have injured,[55] a point that has more recently been developed by Jan Gross in his explanation of postwar antisemitism in Poland.[56] What would motivate the former policemen to think differently about the Jews whom they had killed, especially after they had begun also to kill Poles? Killing Jews did not pose either moral or military difficulties for the former policemen turned nationalist partisans.[57] Timothy Snyder has noted: "The Nazis trained Ukrainian policemen not only in the use of weapons, but in the hatred of Jews. From the SS young Ukrainian recruits received antisemitic indoctrination in their own language."[58] Comparative perspectives support this analysis. Former "blue police"—Polish state police—who joined the Polish underground Home Army sometimes hunted and killed Jews on their own initiative.[59] Even former policemen recruited into the Soviet partisans sometimes brought their hostility toward Jews into that movement.[60] In the Soviet environment, antisemitism would have been frowned upon, at least officially. In UPA, however, the atmosphere was already poisoned by antisemitism and xenophobia. We have the diary of a young Ukrainian from Volhynia who had been forcibly recruited to UPA, who had not served in the police, and who had not initially been antisemitic or even anti-Polish; yet he soon adopted the attitudes of his fellow combatants.[61] In short, the enmity toward Jews inculcated during police service would have continued in the milieu of the nationalist insurgency.

How many Jews did UPA or SB-OUN units kill in these operations in the winter of 1943–1944? It is difficult to estimate the order of magnitude, let alone a number. Numerical estimates provided by testimonies usually reflect perceptions rather than precise, reliable data. A Jewish survivor and resistance fighter estimated that 3,000 Jews had fled to the woods and the neighboring steppe from the Tuchyn ghetto, but only several dozen survived the war. The rest died "in partisan battles and during the attacks of fascist-bandit murderers."[62]

The testimonies consulted by Władysław Siemaszko and Ewa Siemaszko suggest that Ukrainian nationalists killed over 1,210 Jews in Volhynia from 1941 to 1945; seventy-nine of these Jews have been identified by name. Of course, these figures encompass a longer period and other killing situations that fall outside the scope of this essay. Siemaszko and Siemaszko argue, however, that many more were killed, but I do not find their arguments convincing.[63] Shmuel Spector wrote of "thousands of survivors [in Volhynia] . . . slaughtered by the Ukrainian nationalist partisans."[64] Grzegorz Motyka also estimated that UPA altogether killed 1,000 to 2,000 Jews, mainly in Volhynia.[65]

Furthermore, there is a consensus developing among scholars that Ukrainians certainly killed no more than 60,000 Poles in Volhynia in 1943–1945 and perhaps no less than 35,000. UPA bears the most responsibility for these killings. In the case of the Poles, UPA surrounded whole villages, herded the inhabitants into churches, and burned the buildings to the ground. If they only succeeded in killing tens of thousands of a population concentrated in entire settlements, it is difficult to imagine that they could have killed nearly as many Jews, who had already been greatly reduced in number and who were dispersed, hiding underground, and seeking out remote places.

An estimate in the lower thousands is far from certain, however. Consider the case of the Jews in the forests near Svirzh, Peremyshliany raion, Lviv oblast, in which 500 Jews escaped certain death at the hands of the Banderites by what amounted to a fluke: one of the Banderites warned them, and they managed to escape to a fortified village, where armed Poles and Jews protected them.[66] Jews in the woods tended to cluster together for safety. If the survivor populations were concentrated enough, it may be necessary to ascribe a larger death toll to UPA and to the SB-OUN.

With the Poles gone and the Soviets approaching, UPA made a decision to find the remaining Jewish survivors and liquidate them. As the Germans had taught them, they assured the Jews that they would not be harmed, put them to useful work in a camp-like setting, and then exterminated them. These murders took place in the same period that OUN was trying to make overtures to the Western Allies (as were the East European collaborationist regimes). Whether there was any initial sincerity in promises to the Jews that things had changed and that they would no longer be killed, or whether the nationalists were taking cynical advantage of the new situational logic, is not clear. What is clear, however, is that a systematic attempt was launched at this time to eliminate Jewish survivors in Volhynia. Only some Jews' deep suspicions of the Banderites and some overly clumsy attempts at murder have made it possible for us to find out anything at all about these massacres in relatively isolated places.

Why did the nationalist insurgency begin to systematically kill Jews? It is perhaps difficult today to reconstruct the antisemitic mind-set of that toxic time under the Nazi occupation. UPA was fighting for a Ukrainian state, which they understood to be not only an independent state but one composed of Ukrainians exclusively. A report from the "Zahrava" military district in August 1943 about the situation around the city of Kostopil, Rivne region, calmly related: "There are no national minorities in the region, with the exception of a few Jews who recently voluntarily came to work for us."[67] This was in a region that only a few years earlier had a mixed population. The Ukrainian insurgents of UPA had clear ideas about what the Ukraine they were building should be like. There was also, as mentioned, the issue of valuable human capital—tanners, artisans, doctors, propagandists, teachers—falling into the hands of the Soviets. By killing these Jews, the Ukrainians were eliminating witnesses to their previous crimes. They were men who were used to killing Jews and had internalized the rationale for their murders.

By the time UPA emerged in the spring of 1943, most of the Jews of Galicia and Volhynia were already dead. The Jews whom the Ukrainian nationalist insurgents killed in winter 1943–1944 were a small number of survivors. Perhaps the total number of Jews murdered in the systematic actions was several thousand, although the number may have been higher. In the larger scheme of things, these killing operations made only a minor contribution to the Holocaust, but they made survival for Jews that much more difficult.

NOTES

I want to thank Stephen Ejack for his research assistance.

1. The predecessor to Taras Bulba-Borovets's UPA was his Polis'ka Sich. It was deeply involved in the mistreatment and then extermination of the Jewish population of Olevsk, a raion center in Zhytomyr oblast, from July through November 1941. Jared McBride and Alexander Kruglov, "Olevsk," in Martin Dean, ed., *The United States Holocaust Memorial Museum Encyclopedia of Camps and Ghettos, 1933–1945*, vol. 2: *Ghettos in German-Occupied Eastern Europe* (Bloomington: Indiana University Press in association with the United States Holocaust Memorial Museum, 2012).

2. Grzegorz Motyka, *Ukraińska partyzantka 1942–1960: działalność Organizacji Ukraińskich Nacjonalistów i Ukraińskiej Powstańczej Armii* [Ukrainian partisan warfare, 1942–1960: The activities of the Organization of Ukrainian Nationalists (OUN) and the Ukrainian Insurgent Army (UPA)] (Warsaw: Instytut Studiów Politycznych [Institute of Political Studies] PAN; Oficyna Wydawnicza RYTM, 2006), 194–97.

3. I am using current names and territorial-administrative locations for localities in this paper.

4. Aron Baboukh, interview 26557, USC Shoah Foundation Visual History Archive.

5. Jewish survivors often referred to the Banderite UPA as Bulbas, and from the time and context it is clear that Biber is doing so here.

6. Jacob Biber, *Survivors: A Personal Story of the Holocaust*, Studies in Judaica and the Holocaust (San Bernardino, Calif.: Borgo, 1989), 135–36.

7. Ibid., 137–38.

8. For example, United States Holocaust Memorial Museum, RG-22.002M; Tsentral'nyi Gosudarstvennyi Arkhiv Oktiabr'skoi Revoliutsii [Central State Archive of the October Revolution or TsGAOR] (now Gosudarstvennyi Arkhiv Rossiiskoi Federatsii [State Archive of the Russian Federation]), 7021/71/52, "Zakliuchenie [Conclusion]," November 30, 1944, f. 37. The document lists former policemen in Klesiv, Sarny raion, Rivne oblast, who were now in "bands of 'UPA.'" This source is from the Extraordinary State Commission to Investigate German-Fascist Crimes Committed on Soviet Territory.

9. Ivan Katchanovski, "Terrorists or National Heroes? Politics of the OUN and the UPA in Ukraine," paper presented at the annual conference of the Canadian Political Science Association, Montreal, June 1–3, 2010, 7, accessed October 26, 2012, http://www.cpsa-acsp.ca/papers-2010/Katchanovski.pdf.

10. John A. Armstrong, ed., *Soviet Partisans in World War II* (Madison: University of Wisconsin Press, 1964), 228–37.

11. Timothy Snyder, *Bloodlands: Europe between Hitler and Stalin* (New York: Basic, 2010), 243.

12. The course of UPA's anti-Polish actions in Volhynia is provided in Motyka, *Ukraińska partyzantka 1942–1960*, 311–60.

13. Cited in Ivan Kazymryovych Patryliak, *Viis'kova diial'nist OUN (B) u 1940–1942 rokakh* [Military activities of OUN-B in the years 1940–1942] (Kiev, Ukraine: Kyivs'kyi natsional'nyi universytet imeni Tarasa Shevchenka Instytut istorii Ukrainy [Taras Shevchenko National University of Kiev, Institute of History of Ukraine] NAN Ukrainy, 2004), 322.

14. Haluzevyi derzhavnyi arkhiv Sluzhby bezpeky Ukrainy [State Archives of the Security Service of Ukraine (HDA SBU)], fond 13, spr. 372, vol. 2, f. 198 (February 15, 1948).

15. "Starukh, Yaroslav," in Volodymyr Kubijovyč and Danylo Husar Struk, eds., *Encyclopedia of Ukraine*, vol. 5 (Toronto, Canada: University of Toronto Press, 1993).

16. Stundists are evangelical Christians, with many beliefs similar to those of Baptists.

17. Vera Shchetinkova, interview 45238, USC Shoah Foundation Visual History Archives. The Shoah Foundation interviews were conducted in 1994–2002 in many countries.

18. Pola Jasphy, interview 37150, USC Shoah Foundation Visual History Archives.

19. I have been unable to identify this locality with certainty.

20. Archiwum Żydowskiego Instytutu Historycznego [Archive of the Jewish Historical Institute (AŻIH)], 301/397, 12–14. Most of the testimonies in this collection were taken in the first year or two after the war in Poland. Murder with axes and knives was a way that the insurgency saved on ammunition.

21. Archiwum Żydowskiego Instytutu Historycznego, 301/2888. I have relied on S. Arm's Polish translation and Franziska Bruder's German translation of this Yiddish-language testimony. Franziska Bruder, *"Den ukrainischen Staat erkämpfen oder sterben!" Die Organisation Ukrainischer Nationalisten (OUN) 1929–1948* [You will attain a Ukrainian state or die! The Organization of Ukrainian Nationalists (OUN) 1929–1948] (Berlin: Metropol, 2007), 218–19. (S. Arm's translation is unpublished.) The place name mentioned in the testimony is "Kritniv," rendered by both Arm and Bruder as Krytniw. I suspect this is Korytne in Radyvyliv raion. Mina Grinzajd says the agreement was reached with the Banderites in January 1943. This is too early for the establishment of a work camp associated with the Ukrainian nationalists; as yet there was no nationalist armed force of significance, and all the other examples we know come from much later in the year. I suspect she meant January 1944. That timing fits perfectly with the other cases. Testimonies and memoirs may not be reliable when it comes to dating events.

22. Testimony of Bajla Fefer, Archiwum Żydowskiego Instytutu Historycznego, 301/1510, 2–3.

23. Sonyah Sherer, interview 17221, USC Shoah Foundation Visual History Archives. The interview was in Hebrew, but I obtained a Ukrainian translation of her testimony courtesy of Mykhailo Tiahlyi of the Ukrainian Center for Holocaust Studies.

24. Emil Goldbarten, interview 7722, USC Shoah Foundation Visual History Archives.

25. Aron Baboukh, interview 26557, ibid.

26. Biber, *Survivors*, 137.

27. Ibid., 139.

28. Ibid., 145.

29. Ibid., 145–46.

30. Ibid., 151–52.

31. Władysław Siemaszko and Ewa Siemaszko, *Ludobójstwo dokonane przez nacjonalistów ukraińskich na ludności polskiej Wołynia, 1939–1945* [The genocide carried out by Ukrainian nationalists on the Polish population of Volhynia, 1939-1945], 2 vols. (Warsaw: Von Borowiecky, 2000), 91–92.

32. Omer Bartov, "Wartime Lies and Other Testimonies: Jewish-

Christian Relations in Buczacz, 1939–1944," *East European Politics & Societies* 25, 3 (August 2011): 487.

33. "Vytiah z protokolu dopytu chlena tsentral'noho provodu OUN M. Stepaniaka [Excerpt from the record of the interrogation of the member of the central leadership of OUN, M. Stepaniak]," in Oleksandr Ishchuk and Sergeĭ Anatol'evich Kokin, eds., *Borot'ba proty povstans'koho rukhu i natsionalistychnoho pidpillia: Protokoly dopytiv zaareshtovanykh radians'kymy orhanamy derzhavnoi bezpeky kerivnykiv OUN i UPA: 1944–1945* [The struggle against the insurgent movement and nationalist underground: Records of the interrogations of leaders of OUN and UPA arrested by Soviet organs of state security: 1944-1945], new series, 9 (Kiev, Ukraine: Litopys UPA [Chronicle of UPA], 2007), 89–93. "Vytiah iz protokolu dopytu Mykhaila Stepaniaka vid 25 serpnia 1944 r. stosovno tret'oi konferentsii OUN, shcho vidbulasia v liutomu 1943 [Excerpt from the record of the interrogation of Mykhailo Stepaniak on August 25, 1944 regarding the third conference of OUN, which took place in February 1943]," in *Pol'shcha ta Ukraina u trydsiatykh-sorokovykh rokakh XX stolittlia: Nevidomi dokumenty z arkhiviv spetsial'nykh sluzhb* [Poland and Ukraine in the 1930s and 1940s: Unknown documents from the archives of special services], vol. 4: *Poliaky i Ukraintsi mizh dvoma totalitarnymy systemamy 1942–44* [Poles and Ukrainians between two totalitarian systems 1942-44], part 1 (Warsaw: Derzhavnyi arkhiv Sluzhby bezpeky Ukrainy [State Archive of the Security Service of Ukraine] et al., 2005), 230. "Vytiah iz protokolu dopytu Iuriia Stel'mashchuka vid 28 liutoho 1945 r. [Excerpt from the record of the interrogation of Yurii Stelmashchuk on February 28, 1945]," ibid., 442. On the territorial and organizational structure of UPA, see Petro Sodol, "Orhanizatsiina struktura UPA [Organizational structure of UPA]," accessed October 27, 2012, http://forum.ottawa-litopys.org/documents/dos0301_u.htm; also Petro Mirchuk, *UPA 1942–1952*, part 3: "Orhanizatsiina struktura UPA," accessed October 30, 2012, http://lib.oun-upa.org.ua/mirczuk/r302.html.

34. United States Holocaust Memorial Museum, RG-31.017M, reel 1; Derzhavnyi Arkhiv Rivnens'koi Oblasti [State Archives of Rivne Oblast (DARO)], 30/2/89, ff. 7v, 11v. For details, see John-Paul Himka, *Ukrainians, Jews and the Holocaust: Divergent Memories* (Saskatoon, Canada: Heritage, 2009), 60n18.

35. Anatolij V. Kentij, V. S. Lozyts'kyi, I. Pavlenko, and K. Abramova, comp., *Borot'ba proty UPA i natsionalistychnoho pidpillia: informatsiini dokumenty TsK KP(b)U, obkomiv partii, NKVS-MVS, MDB-KDB 1943–1949* [The struggle against the UPA and the nationalist underground: Informational documents of the Central Committee of the Communist Party (Bolshevik) of Ukraine, party obkoms, NKVD-MVD, MGB-KGB 1943–

1949], book 1: *1943–1945*, new series, 4 (Kiev, Ukraine: Litopys UPA, 2002), 125–26. From the context, it would seem that the order to destroy the nonspecialists in a conspiratorial manner would have been issued at a time when the Soviet forces were close enough for Jews to escape to, hence the winter of 1943–1944.

36. Motyka, *Ukraińska partyzantka 1942–1960*, 293–94.

37. United States Holocaust Memorial Museum, RG-31.026, Selected records from Former Archives of the Communist Party of Ukraine, reel 16; 1/23/918, f. 37. The other three operations listed were: (1) mass murder of Poles who constituted an obstacle to creating an independent Ukraine; (2) mass murder of Soviet prisoners of war hiding in villages and forests; and (3) organizing the mass murder of Soviet activists. According to the document, the mass murders were carried out "at the order of the Germans." Although the list of UPA operations was accurate enough, it is not true that the Germans favored the destruction of the Polish population at this time. In spring 1944, UPA did coordinate anti-Jewish actions with the Germans. Frank Golczewski, "Shades of Grey: Reflections on Jewish-Ukrainian and German-Ukrainian Relations in Galicia," in Ray Brandon and Wendy Lower, eds., *The Shoah in Ukraine: History, Testimony, Memorialization* (Bloomington: Indiana University Press, 2008), 143.

38. Cited in Philip Friedman, "Ukrainian-Jewish Relations during the Nazi Occupation," in Philip Friedman, *Roads to Extinction: Essays on the Holocaust*, ed. Ada June Friedman (New York: Conference on Jewish Social Studies, Jewish Publication Society of America, 1980), 189, 196n18.

39. Ibid., 189; Shmuel Spector, *The Holocaust of Volhynian Jews 1941–1944* (Jerusalem: Yad Vashem, Federation of Volhynian Jews, 1990), 272; Motyka, *Ukraińska partyzantka 1942–1960*, 294. Franziska Bruder also referred to one of these operations. See above, n. 21.

40. Lev Shankovs'kyi, "Initsiiatyvnyi komitet dlia stvorennia Ukrains'koi holovnoi vyzvol'noi rady. Postannia i diia v 1943–1944 rr. Spohad i komentar [The initiative committee for the creation of the Ukrainian Supreme Liberation Council]," in Yevhen Shtendera and Petro J. Potichnyj, eds., *Ukrains'ka holovna vyzvol'na rada. Dokumenty, ofitsiini publikatsii, materiialy* [The Ukrainian Supreme Liberation Council: Documents, official publications, materials], book 4: *Dokumenty i spohady* [Documents and memoirs] (Toronto, Canada: Litopys UPA, 2001), 59–60n26. Shankovs'kyi's information is repeated in much the same words by Volodymyr Viatrovych, "Biitsi UPA, ievrei—hidno bylysia za nezalezhnist' Ukrainy. My—tse pam'iatiemo [UPA fighters, Jews fought worthily for the independence of Ukraine. We remember this]," *Arrata*, February 1, 2008, accessed August 27, 2013, http://www.aratta-ukraine.com/text_ua.php?id=965.

41. I have elsewhere analyzed a testimony from Archiwum Żydowskiego Instytutu Historycznego by comparing what it said about events in the Lviv pogrom of 1941 to photographic evidence of these same events. I did not find a contradiction between the testimony and the pictures and films. The testimony, I concluded, accurately described what the woman who wrote it experienced. I did note, however, that she was not able to learn much about the pogromists who attacked her. Ivan Khymka, "Dostovirnist' svidchennia: reliatsiia Ruzi Vagner pro l'vivs'kyi pohrom vlitku 1941 r. [The veracity of testimony: Róża Wagner's story of the Lviv pogrom of the summer of 1941]," *Holokost i suchasnist'* [Holocaust and modernity] 2, no. 4 (2008): 43–79. Christopher Browning also observed that survivor testimony could say little about the unit he was investigating, Reserve Police Battalion 101. "Unknown men arrived, carried out their murderous task, and left. Seldom, in fact, can the survivors even remember the peculiar green uniforms of the Order Police to identify what kind of unit was involved." Christopher R. Browning, *Ordinary Men: Reserve Police Battalion 101 and the Final Solution in Poland* (New York: HarperCollins, 1992), xviii.

42. Aleksandr Diukov, *Vtorostepennyi vrag. OUN, UPA i reshenie "evreiskogo voprosa"* [The second-rank enemy: OUN, UPA and the solution of the "Jewish question"] (Moscow: Regnum, 2008), 73.

43. Timothy Snyder, *The Reconstruction of Nations: Poland, Ukraine, Lithuania, Belarus, 1569–1999* (New Haven, Conn.: Yale University Press, 2003), 160, 162.

44. United States Holocaust Memorial Museum, RG-22.002M, reel 25; TsGAOR, 7021/71/68, f. 31.

45. Golczewski, "Shades of Grey," 143.

46. United States Holocaust Memorial Museum, RG-31.017M, reel 1; Derzhavnyi Arkhiv Rivnens'koi Oblasti (DARO), 30/2/82, ff. 36v-37. Another copy of this conspectus can be found in DARO, 30/1/9, f. 3. I am grateful to Wiesław Tokarczuk for the latter information and a copy of the relevant folio.

47. John-Paul Himka, "The Lviv Pogrom of 1941: The Germans, Ukrainian Nationalists, and the Carnival Crowd," *Canadian Slavonic Papers* 53, 2–4 (2011): 223, 240.

48. Jews who served in partisan units left testimonies recounting their battles with UPA. See, for example, YIVO Institute for Jewish Research, RG 104, Eyewitness Accounts of the Holocaust Period, Series I, Shlomo Katz: "1/1943 an exchange of fire occurred with a group of three thousand Banderites, which lasted ten minutes, the Banderites fled, fifty were taken prisoner, about 150 were killed . . . [Late in 1943 near the village of Karpiłówki] we fought with the Banderites. The battle lasted three hours.

We acquired a great deal of ammunition, uniforms, and food. On the side of the Banderites about two hundred people fell. We also got 150 horses." More such entries follow.

49. Jan T. Gross, *Revolution from Abroad: The Soviet Conquest of Poland's Western Ukraine and Western Belorussia* (Princeton, N.J.: Princeton University Press, 1988), 144–86.

50. Mykhailo Podvorniak, *Viter z Volyni. Spohady* [Wind from Volhynia: Memories] (Winnipeg, Canada: Tovarystvo "Volyn'," 1981), 186–87.

51. Samuel Honigman, interview 1222, USC Shoah Foundation Visual History Archives.

52. Bruder, *"Den ukrainischen Staat erkämpfen oder sterben!"* 239, cites examples of OUN-UPA documents referring to Jews collaborating with the organs of repression in the aftermath of the return of Soviet power.

53. Mike Walsh, interview 13213, USC Shoah Foundation Visual History Archives. This and other instances of the vengeance of Jewish partisans are dealt with in Stephen Ejack, "The Jewish Soviet Partisan as an Identity Construct," honors thesis, Department of History and Classics, University of Alberta, 2011.

54. Jacques Semelin, *Purify and Destroy: The Political Uses of Massacre and Genocide* (New York: Columbia University Press, 2007), 238–307.

55. "*Proprium humani ingenii est odisse quem laeseris* [It is human nature to hate a person whom you have injured]," Tacitus, *Agricola*, 42.

56. Jan T. Gross, *Neighbors: The Destruction of the Jewish Community in Jedwabne, Poland* (Princeton, N.J.: Princeton University Press, 2001), 97, 101; Jan T. Gross, *Fear: Anti-Semitism in Poland after Auschwitz: An Essay in Historical Interpretation* (New York: Random House, 2006), 164, 248, 256.

57. It is worth noting that in the same period hunting and killing Jews posed no moral dilemma for significant sectors of the rural Polish population. See Jan Grabowski, *Hunt for the Jews: Betrayal and Murder in German-Occupied Poland* (Bloomington: Indiana University Press, 2013), esp. 82, 121–29.

58. Snyder, *Reconstruction of Nations*, 160.

59. Jan Grabowski, "Polish 'Blue' Police and the Jews in Hiding: The Rural Areas of the Cracow District, 1942–1945," paper presented at the Twelfth Lessons and Legacies Conference on the Holocaust, Northwestern University, Evanston, Ill., November 1–4, 2012.

60. Ejack, "The Jewish Soviet Partisan," 16–17 (citing William Laiwint, interview 3754, USC Shoah Foundation Visual History Archives, and Nathan Dinerman, interview 46178, ibid.); Nechama Tec, *Defiance: The Bielski Partisans* (New York: Oxford University Press, 1993), 108.

61. John-Paul Himka, "Refleksje żołnierza Ukraińskiej Powstańczej Armii. Pamiętnik Ołeksandra Powszuka (1943–1944) [Reflections of a sol-

dier of the Ukrainian Insurgent Army: The memoirs of Oleksandr Povshuk 1943–1944]," in Bogusław Paź, ed., *Prawda historyczna a prawda polityczna w badaniach naukowych. Przykład ludobójstwa na Kresach południowo-wschodniej Polski w latach 1939–1946* [Historical truth and political truth in scholarly studies: The example of the genocide in the borderlands of south-eastern Poland in the years 1939–1946] (Wrocław, Poland: Wydawnictwo Uniwersytetu Wrocławskiego [Wrocław University Press], 2011), 179–90.

62. Testimony of Melech Bakałczuk, Archiwum Żydowskiego Instytutu Historycznego, 301/652, 5.

63. Siemaszko and Siemaszko, *Ludobójstwo*, vol. 2, 1079–80.

64. Spector, *The Holocaust of Volhynian Jews*, 256.

65. Motyka, *Ukraińska partyzantka 1942–1960*, 295–97.

66. Archiwum Żydowskiego Instytutu Historycznego, 301/808, 2-3. See also: Jerzy Węgierski, *W lwowskiej Armii Krajowej* [In the Lviv Home Army] (Warsaw: Instytut Wydawniczy PAX, 1989), 105-8.

67. Cited in Oleksandr Namozov, "Ukrains'kyi povstanets' Leiba Dobrovs'kyi? [Ukrainian insurgent Leiba Dobrovsky?]" *Viche Kostopil'shchyny* [Assembly of the Kostopil region], June 20, 2009, accessed October 26, 2009, http://www.kostopilpost.com/index.php?option=com_content&task=view&id=109&Itemid=26.

Ludivine Broch

The SNCF Affair: *Cheminots* in the Divided Memories of Vichy France

EVEN BEFORE THE ALLIES ENTERED PARIS ON AUGUST 25, 1944, THE French were already building a grand narrative of their experience of World War II and, more importantly, of the German occupation: all French people had resisted the German occupier, and the French had liberated themselves.[1] The myth of the French Resistance was captured in one of the biggest postwar blockbusters, René Clément's *La Bataille du Rail*, released in English as *The Battle of the Rails* (Coopérative Générale du Cinéma Française, 1945), and often described as the most authentic cinematic representation of the Occupation.[2] The film itself focused on the railway workers—the *cheminots*—who were simultaneously portrayed as resisters, saboteurs, heroes, and martyrs. It penetrated deep into the French national consciousness, and when an American version starring Burt Lancaster was released in the 1960s, the French resented that much of the rhetoric of the Resistance had been lost from the Hollywood film.

Things changed in the 1970s as more and more people began to explore the "dark" history of Vichy France, which often cooperated with the German occupiers. The change was not a sudden one: such scholars as Stanley Hoffman had been challenging the myth of the Resistance for a while. In the late 1960s, a series of events signaled a new era: the 1968 student riots; the release of Marcel Ophüls's *Le Chagrin et la Pitié* (released in English as *The Sorrow and the Pity*; Télévision Rencontre, Norddeutsche Rundfunk, and Télévision Suissse-Romande, 1969), a documentary that revealed French collaboration with the Nazis; and the death in 1970 of ex-president Charles de Gaulle, the leader of *France Libre* (Free France) during the war. Robert Paxton's groundbreaking study of the Franco-German collaboration was published shortly after these events, and although it took another decade for it to be translated into French, a "Paxtonian Revolution" revealing Vichy's sensitive past was already in motion.[3] As Julian Jackson has noted, the French Resistance had become "taboo."[4]

By the 1990s, it was no longer just social, political, and economic collaboration that historians were interested in: it was collaboration in the extermination of the Jews. In the 1980s, colossal works by Michael Marrus and Robert Paxton and by Serge Klarsfeld had shown the extensive collaboration of the Vichy government in arresting, interning, and deporting Jews in the summer of 1942.[5] This opened the door for extensive research on Jewish life in Vichy France,[6] and on the roles of French administrations and institutions, but also German ones, in the Holocaust.[7] All of this scholarship seriously challenged the idea that France had been a "safe haven" for Jews, an idea coined by Raul Hilberg on the basis that three-quarters of Jews in France had survived the war.[8] Of course, the zeal with which antisemitic policy was applied in Eastern Europe was not mirrored in Western Europe. Moreover, Vichy's willingness to assist the German *Judenpolitik* (Jewish policy) weakened with time, and in 1943–1944 the government took far fewer initiatives in arresting Jews than it had in 1942.[9] That said, French historians now offered a far more blurred narrative of Jews under Vichy, one where French antisemitism and xenophobia were palpable. And these narratives were very much in the public eye, as films such as Rose Bosch's *La Rafle*, released in English as *The Round Up* (Légende Films, 2010); Gilles Paquet-Brenner's *Sarah's Key* (Hugo Productions, 2010); or Brian Percival's *The Book Thief* (Fox 2000 Pictures, 2013) would suggest. As Henry Rousso has famously argued, and as Tony Judt has confirmed in his essay on post-1989 Europe, toward the late twentieth century, the French became obsessed with Vichy and the Holocaust, an obsession which would continue well into the twenty-first century.[10]

Despite a growing emphasis on French collaboration in genocide, however, a discourse of rescue and resistance reemerged. Indeed, if the Resistance myth was widely discredited by the 1990s, the glorification of the French had never fully disappeared from the national narrative. Tony Judt commented on French President Jacques Chirac's groundbreaking speech in 1995: a French head of state, for the first time, condemned the French government for its collaboration in Nazi antisemitic policies.[11] However, later in the speech, Chirac quickly returned to the well-known discourse of the French Resistance: France was there, he declared,

> one and indivisible, in the heart of these "Righteous among the Nations" who, in the darkest hours, risked their lives, as wrote Serge Klarsfeld, to save three-quarters of the Jewish community residing in France. They gave their lives for what [France] does best. Humanism, liberty, justice, tolerance, all values which form the basis of French identity, which push us into the future.[12]

Indeed, the growing emphasis on victims and survivors of the Holocaust meant that those who had helped them, especially the non-Jews, were now in the spotlight. They were nominated as Righteous among the Nations by Yad Vashem in Israel. Chirac's speech showed how the Righteous had become the counter-narrative of France's collaboration. Twelve years later, France honored the French "Righteous" throughout the capital: *les Justes*, as they are known in French, entered the Pantheon alongside Jean Moulin, the most-remembered French Resistance leader, and their names were engraved on the outside wall of the Shoah Memorial in Paris.[13]

This chapter examines a recent controversy over the role of the French National Railway Company (in French, *Société nationale des chemins de fer français*, or SNCF) in the Holocaust, and in doing so seeks to address these complicated memories of resistance, collaboration, genocide, and rescue in World War II. Indeed, in the early 1990s, a Holocaust survivor exposed the SNCF's involvement in the deportation of his parents from Toulouse to Drancy, and then from Drancy to Auschwitz. As the issue gained momentum, it became a scandal that was heavily discussed in the public arena—an "affair." The topic of World War II was so sensitive in France that a number of "affairs" had already emerged: the Touvier Affair, the Aubrac Affair, and the Papon Affair have been widely discussed by scholars,[14] and more recently public debates have erupted over the literary works of Yannick Haenel, Jonathan Littell, and Laurent Binet.[15] Now, for the first time, a state-owned company was accused of complicity in the Holocaust, and the responses to these accusations were far from straightforward.

Following a long line of World War II-related affairs, the SNCF Affair, in particular, points to the complexity of memory in the twenty-first century. First, the affair shifts discussions from individual responsibility to collective, and even corporate, responsibility. Second, it has unique transnational and economic repercussions. Finally, and perhaps most importantly, it triggers questions of how collective, national, and transnational narratives of World War II interact. Indeed, the railway workers—or *cheminots*—are a group of workers with a strong sense of shared identity and history. Their collective memory had for a long time been one of resistance to the occupier, as *La Bataille du Rail* would have us believe. The SNCF Affair shattered this historical narrative, and, as it will be seen, sent shock waves through the community. But was their reaction unanimous? Were *cheminots* rejecting Holocaust history? Were they refusing to accept discourses of collaboration and deportation? This chapter shows that their responses were, in fact, far more complicated. Indeed, the *esprit de famille*—"family spirit"—within the *cheminot* community is an important factor which the historian must consider when exploring these debates around memory. This chapter will argue that *cheminots* are not stuck in a "Resistance myth," nor are they rejecting the history of the Holocaust. Rather, *cheminots* are looking to protect a shared memory of the Occupation, one on which their postwar identity has been built.

This chapter is divided into three parts. It starts by describing the SNCF Affair through the prism of the main characters involved, including first- and second-generation Holocaust survivors; lawyers and judges; journalists and politicians; and academics and public intellectuals. The chapter then moves on to examine how the "defendant," the SNCF, reacted to the affair. When accused of complicity in genocide decades after the events, how does a company respond? The last section examines the reaction of its workers. Indeed, the *cheminots* did not necessarily support the management's official responses. Based on the author's personal interactions with the *cheminot* community, this section shows that narratives of resistance have often been transplanted by narratives of rescue. The *cheminots* are not rejecting Holocaust history and memory; they are adapting it to fit their shared working-class identities and memories.

ACTORS IN THE SNCF AFFAIR

The SNCF controversy was sparked by Kurt Werner Schaechter, a second-generation Holocaust survivor of Austrian origin whose parents were deported from France in 1942 and died in Auschwitz.[16] In the early 1990s, Schaechter began searching the local archives in Toulouse for details of their deportation and extermination. There he found and photocopied (illegally) hundreds of documents, some of which proved the financial and material involvement of the SNCF in the deportations. Schaechter leaked the information to the press, and in 1993 the SNCF was accused of deliberately hiding its shadowy past.[17]

The information leaked by Schaechter awakened new interest in the role of the SNCF during the Holocaust. Until then, the role of the railway company in the deportations had never been addressed, and the history of the SNCF was firmly interlocked with that of the French Resistance.[18] Even the winds of change in the 1970s could not dismantle the myth of the *cheminot resistant*.[19] The 1980s saw some scholars begin to associate the trains with the Holocaust, among whom were Michael Marrus and Robert Paxton, who questioned *cheminots*' lack of resistance to the deportations: why had *cheminots* sabotaged so many German transports, but never any deportation trains?[20] They were not alone in asking that question; in 1984, Annie Kriegel questioned why the *cheminots*, who were so involved in the deportation process, did not resist the deportation of 76,000 Jews.[21]

But it was Schaechter's claims against the SNCF that sparked serious questioning of the SNCF's activities in the deportations, and a series of legal claims accusing the SNCF of crimes against humanity were subsequently triggered in France by second-generation Holocaust survivors. There was the first claim by Jean-Jacques Fraenkel in 1998, then Schaechter's claim in 1999, and finally in 2006, Alain Lipietz and Hélène Lipietz brought claims in the name of their father, George Lipietz, who had been deported to Drancy in 1944.[22]

The SNCF Affair was not, however, a purely French phenomenon; in fact, the biggest anti-SNCF lobbyist group is in the United States. In 2000, led by New York-based lawyer Harriet Tamen, a group of claimants, mostly second- but also first-generation survivors, requested financial compensation for their parents' ordeal.[23] Although she had no personal ties to the Holocaust, Tamen was a member of the Jewish community who felt deeply concerned by the role of cattle cars in the process of extermination. In her eyes, the Holocaust "could not have happened without SNCF" since "the Germans didn't have the rolling stock."[24] This statement was one of the pillars of the legal campaign, which has since expanded quite significantly. For instance, the Baltimore law firm Akin Gimp Strauss Hauer & Feld mobilized attention through a website known as the Coalition for Holocaust Rail Justice. This served, and continues to serve, as a platform in which claimants express their grievances.[25]

This pressure from lawyers, survivors, and family members was not, however, successfully received in the courts. French courtrooms rejected Fraenkel's claim for lack of evidence, while Schaechter's case was thrown out for lack of jurisprudence. Indeed, one could not bring a case against a company in the penal courts. The Lipietzes' claim partially succeeded in the administrative courts in 2006, and the SNCF was fined over 30,000 euros, but a subsequent appeal saw the judgment revoked for breaching jurisdictional practices.[26] Claimants in the United States faced similar jurisdictional obstacles, and so far none of the claims have been successful. One of the biggest hurdles is the Foreign Sovereign Immunities Act of 1976, which means that the SNCF, a foreign state-owned corporation, cannot be tried in America. United States courts thus have repeatedly rejected the case since 2000.[27] This, however, has not dampened lawyers' efforts, and they have continued the battle. Most recently, Tamen commenced a class action in the state of New York and has set a new process in motion to change American laws to allow the SNCF to be sued in American courts.[28]

Money is not always the primary goal of these claims. Schaechter, for instance, asked for a symbolic sum, while Lipietz requested more significant reparations. In Tamen's case, the goal was to obtain money for her claimants. In an interview in February 2011, she described how most of her claimants—who had suffered extensively at the hands of the Nazis, the French, and the SNCF—led simple and humble lives in America. The horrors of the past could not be erased, but the SNCF should acknowledge its crucial role in the "Final Solution" and pay damages for having transported thousands in inhumane conditions. In doing so, the company would assist in the daily lives of these survivors who, having endured the camps, now struggled to make ends meet in retirement. Tamen related this with great emotion, saying that she would not stop fighting until Rosette, one of her claimants who had become a dear friend, got a bit of money for everything that she had endured.[29]

Journalists, scholars, and politicians have felt compelled to comment on the growing controversies around the SNCF trials, which seem to have divided them into two camps: those who agreed that the SNCF should be put on trial and made to pay reparations, and those who were against the trials and the demonization of the railways. French media personalities have been involved in some of the most reactionary writings. In his book *Convoys of Shame*, journalist Raphael Delpard argued that the *cheminots* did nothing to stop the deportations because of their complete indifference toward the fate of the Jews.[30] And when *La Bataille du Rail* was rescreened at the 2010 Cannes Film Festival, the editor of *Paris Match* wrote an opinion piece showing his outrage:

> Cheminots, who are at the top of the charts when it comes to patriotism, are determined to stay in their golden seat forever. That's only human . . . In contrast, 70,000 Jewish compatriots perished, and their convoys were never sabotaged by the French cheminots . . . Honestly, *la Croisette* [the Cannes theater showing *La Bataille du Rail*] is distasteful.[31]

Françoise Laborde, the former head of the national regulation authority board for television and radio (the *Conseil Supérieur de l'Audiovisuel*, or CSA), became personally involved in the affair. In a nonfiction monograph in 2008, she compared the attitudes of railway strikers at the end of the century to their behavior during the Occupation:

> The SNCF claims to be a model of social solidarity, but no one dares bring up the subject of the "trains de la mort" [trains of death] which brought Jews and resisters to the extermination camps. There weren't any strikers to stop those trains, which always arrived on time, and were well paid for by the Nazis. Without French trains, how could the deportations have happened?[32]

The reaction of some members of the *cheminot* community was vicious. Laborde and her family were threatened by mail and in person, and she was called a *salope*, or bitch.[33] Laborde later published a novel loosely based on the reactions she received.[34] There is no justification for the threats against Laborde and her family, and *cheminots*' responses to the SNCF Affair will be discussed later in greater depth. Still, journalists' attacks on the role of the SNCF and its workers in the deportations generally adopted a reductive Manichean approach that divided people neatly between good and evil. From a historical perspective, such a dualistic outlook is not justifiable. Although journalists have helped to end half a century of silence over the Holocaust, their reductive conclusions and hasty accusations have demonized the SNCF and the *cheminots* and further distorted history. A journalist recently published a book that strengthened this bipolar narrative and made a further hierarchical distinction by suggesting that the working *cheminots* were "heroes," and the SNCF directors "bastards."[35]

In the immediate aftermath of the 2006 Lipietz trial, Holocaust scholar Annette Wieviorka and railway historian Georges Ribeill protested against this demonization of the SNCF.[36] They argued that the SNCF was a "cog in the wheel" of the "Final Solution" and had taken no initiatives. Moreover, France as a nation had already paid reparations to Holocaust victims, thus making further requests redundant. Others, including Henry Rousso and Michael Marrus, share the concern that these trials distort history. In fact, Marrus recently published an article on the SNCF case and its importance in establishing more precise definitions of culpability and collaboration, and legitimate compensation claims.[37]

This does not mean, however, that scholars have been reluctant to accept the darker history of the SNCF. Jean-Marc Dreyfus and Sarah Gensburger published a book that underlined the SNCF's role in the spoliation of Jewish goods, a role that only further entwines the French company to the Holocaust.[38] Still, despite wanting to openly discuss and fully understand the role of French trains in the Holocaust, scholars remain skeptical about the aims and achievements of the SNCF trials. Nazi hunter, historian, and public intellectual Serge Klarsfeld falls into this category. Klarsfeld used the trials to pressure the SNCF into funding memorial sites and exhibitions, but simultaneously criticized the French and American claimants for their shortsightedness. The attacks against the SNCF were, according to him, "unfair."[39] His son, Arno Klarsfeld, defended the SNCF in the Lipietz trial.

The comments of these scholars fit into a broader academic criticism over the usefulness of Holocaust trials. Such court cases open up archives but produce bad history; they provide closure in some ways but not in others; and they serve a theatrical purpose rather than a legal one.[40] However, these recent trials against companies and not individuals raise some new questions.[41] The legal scholar Leora Bilsky argues that class actions in civil courts against banks and railroad companies are better suited to deal with the Holocaust. They reflect its historical distinctiveness as a mass crime committed by mass perpetrators and resulting in mass victims, but equally show that the crime was committed by institutions as much as individual perpetrators. In this sense, the civil courts are more likely to capture the reality of the Holocaust. This is not to say that class actions in the civil courts are perfect, and one could argue that the demand for financial reparation seems less relevant since the primary victims are now deceased and many reparations have already been made. Still, a new discussion about collective responsibility is being opened in the courtroom, and the SNCF trials are a key part of it.[42]

American politicians eventually got involved in the SNCF Affair. A project was started several years ago to build high-speed interstate trains in California, and the SNCF, a world leader in high-speed trains, was an obvious contender for this multimillion dollar contract. However, leading Democrats in the state of California saw real ethical risks in appointing the SNCF to construct railways in America. According to Bob Blumenfeld, to think that "there could be a train made by the very same company that took Jews to the camps is unbearable."[43] The combined pressure from Harriet Tamen's claimants and local politicians saw a law pass in California in June 2010 that definitively sidelined all companies who had deported Jews or Americans during World War II from this multimillion dollar project. Similar cases subsequently arose in Florida and Maryland, and both states passed a law to the same effect.[44]

The SNCF was the bête noire, the company that had never acknowledged that it had taken part in and profited from one of the most renowned crimes in all of history. But other companies were also affected, such as Japan's national railway, which had deported American soldiers during World War II. Ultimately, these laws have conveniently sidelined two highly competitive companies from the American markets. By claiming historical integrity, it could be argued that American lawmakers were conveniently benefiting their national economy.[45] The Senate is currently considering a bill to allow claimants to sue the SNCF in American courts.[46] One only hopes that the many ironies that fill this situation—the fact that American railroads themselves were built on slave labor; that the SNCF already operates across the United States; and that other highly successful companies such as Hugo Boss, a German fashion retailer, are known to have worked closely with the Nazi Party—are not lost on those involved in this campaign.

THE SNCF REACTS

When Schaechter began to attack the history and memory of the *cheminots* in 1992, the SNCF immediately approached academics to shed light on the issue. Christian Bachelier was recommended by Henry Rousso from the *Institut pour l'Histoire du Temps Présent* (Institute for the History of the Present Time or IHTP) to look into the SNCF archives for the war period.[47] He went to Le Mans, a large railway hub famous for its sports car races. The SNCF was centralizing its scattered archives there, and Bachelier spent four years searching them in great depth. In 1996, he released his report, *Le Rapport Bachelier*, which summarized in several thousand pages the documents that he found.[48] Among other things, he addressed both themes of deportation and resistance, and in doing so broke the long-standing precedent of ignoring the role of railways in the Holocaust. *The Bachelier Report*, despite its complicated format and density, is the founding work on the SNCF during World War II.

The SNCF also backed broader academic endeavors. In 2000, it helped to organize a large conference, presided over by Henry Rousso, which gathered established historians specializing in railway, business, and industrial history.[49] The SNCF's archival department—the *Association pour l'histoire des chemins de fer en France* (Association for the History of the Railways in France or AHICF)—published the majority of the papers in a special edition of its book series.[50] The association itself has been active in promoting the history of railways during this turbulent period of French history and has edited a number of volumes related to the history and memory of the *cheminots* during the war, published in its series La Revue d'Histoire des Chemins de Fer (Review of railway history).[51]

These academic efforts fell in step with a more public outreach program that saw the SNCF promoting the history of the railways as well as Holocaust history. From 2002 to 2004, the SNCF sponsored a temporary exhibition on Jewish children deported from France in various train stations around the country.[52] In 2005, it organized an exhibition on *Les Cheminots dans la Résistance* (Railway workers in the Resistance) at the Musée Jean Moulin in Paris, in which there was a section on the Jewish deportation trains.[53] Rather unsurprisingly, this exhibition emphasized the various ways in which *cheminots* had assisted the internees. The reasons for this are more complicated than merely upholding the Resistance myth, but I will look at this more closely later. Ultimately, after years of silence over the issue, the SNCF was talking openly about the Holocaust. Needless to say, there were limits to this discussion. First, the SNCF, backed by historians, never took responsibility for the deportation trains and saw itself in many ways as another victim of the Nazi-Vichy stronghold. Second, while the deportations were mentioned, they never became a central feature of these initial efforts. That said, the deportations were no longer sidelined and were becoming an obvious and unavoidable element of SNCF history.

Yet the absence of a public apology or acknowledgment of the SNCF's activities attracted much criticism in certain circles. Lobbyists in America felt that the company was making only halfhearted efforts to include the deportations into its official history. Despite this criticism, the SNCF did not budge. Its president at the time, Louis Gallois, refused to follow in Jacques Chirac's footsteps.[54] Indeed, in 1995, Chirac, when president of France, had apologized for the first time for the crimes of Vichy France.[55] This had been a long-awaited public admittance of France's collaborationist, racist, and violent activities during World War II. Not everyone had welcomed this speech, feeling it was self-flagellation, and that in any case France had been under the Nazi boot and had little or no real choice.[56] Academics did not abide by this view, and they fully understood the significance and importance of Chirac's speech. However, in the case of the SNCF, things were different: the SNCF in itself had had no room to maneuver in these questions. Under the double supervision of Vichy and the Nazis, the state-owned railways were given strict orders on what, when, and how to transport goods and people alike. Many historians defend the view that the SNCF was one more cog in the wheel of the "Final Solution."[57] Thus Gallois's refusal to apologize fit into a certain historical narrative.

However, the laws passed in America banning the SNCF from building high-speed interstate railways backed the SNCF management into a corner. With a new president at its head, Guillaume Pepy, the SNCF began to change its tune. In November 2010, Pepy released a statement of apology in America, reminding his audience how the Holocaust was deeply entwined with politics and economics.[58] A few months later, on January 25, 2011, he was back in France in the station at Bobigny, where he inaugurated an SNCF-funded memorial to commemorate the Jewish victims of deportation. This was a significant event, with Serge Klarsfeld and Simone Veil in attendance, and all the major papers and radio stations commenting on the day.[59] Pepy once again pronounced an apology in the name of the SNCF:

> The SNCF, a state-owned company, was requisitioned, a cog in the Nazi extermination machine. We will never forget this . . . I want to express the SNCF's deep sadness and regret for the consequences of the acts of the SNCF of that era. In its name, I am humbled before the victims, the survivors, the children of deportees, and before the suffering which lives on.[60]

Pepy's efforts, however, were not appreciated by all. Some argued that these speeches, especially the first given in America, were an attempt to manipulate the American public and get another chance at those all-important railroad contracts.[61] Pepy had, basically, sold out for money. The fiercest accusations, however, came from within the railway community itself.[62]

THE *CHEMINOTS*

This final section focuses on *cheminots*' reactions to the SNCF Affair and the responses to Pepy's speech are an excellent starting point. One former *cheminot* and trade union activist blogged the following opinion piece:

> What right, and in whose name, does he have to make such declarations? If Monsieur Pepy has qualms or feels the need to justify past actions, he can do so in his own name, but most certainly not in the name of the SNCF Company and the Cheminots who have given it life! If M. Pepy is doing his "Coming Out" or his méa culpa in French vis-à-vis the Americans, it is his problem, but he has no right to usurp, betray, and taint the memory of the Cheminots who lived through those days . . . How can one submit to this horrid and insupportable blackmail, this incessant "lobbying" from certain pressure groups who speak only in the name of their own interests?[63]

It did not matter that Pepy had followed up his apology with a comment about *cheminots*' resistance and martyrdom: "I also want us at today's gathering to honor the 2,000 railway workers shot or dead in deportation, who paid with their lives for their insubordination, their resistance to the Nazi occupier and its Vichy collaborators."[64] Many railway workers felt that he had somehow betrayed the *cheminot* community, as well as its history and memory. Indeed, Chauffier was not the only one to be outraged; Robert Guicharnaud, from the Tarne-et-Garonne, was also shocked by Pepy's intervention.[65] Nor was it only *cheminots* who were displeased with his speech. Guylain Chevrier, the son of a Jewish deportee, disapproved of the memory politics behind this speech that, in his mind, belittled the terrible historical realities.[66]

The negative reactions to Pepy's speech were not, however, so unusual. Three further examples emphasize the *esprit de famille* that has largely defined the *cheminot* community throughout the twentieth century, and in doing so reveal the ongoing tensions between the *cheminots*, their history, and the SNCF Affair. In some ways, one should not read too much into this theory of a railway *esprit de famille*—the concept is a flexible one, constantly being redefined by those whom it concerns. Age, political leanings, and individual histories mean that *cheminots*' reactions are multifaceted and their community sometimes more divided than one may wish to believe. But a sense of familial belonging, solidarity, pride, insularity, and uniqueness runs throughout the *cheminot* community nonetheless, from the lowest to the highest echelons, from Alsace-Lorraine to Paris to the Basque country.[67]

The first example is of a paper I gave in April 2010, titled "Cheminots: Between Resistance and Deportation," at the *Musée de la Résistance et de la deportation de Picardie* (Museum of Resistance and Deportation in Picardie) in Tergnier, a major railway hub in Northern France. The paper began by discussing the long history of the *cheminot* community, looking back to the nineteenth century to explore the roots of *cheminot* traditions, attitudes, and behaviors. It then moved on to examine the Vichy period and argued about the extent to which these long-standing traditions had changed or altered under the German Occupation. But the main aim of the paper addressed the Vichy period in regard to the current two dominant narratives, resistance and deportation. Here, I nuanced the Resistance myth but also challenged the current accusations made against both the SNCF and the *cheminots*. In doing so, I hoped to show that my research was dislodging historical categories and narratives, and providing opportunities for new approaches to railway history during World War II.

With over one hundred attendees, the reading was one of the biggest turnouts ever seen at the museum, and included many former *cheminots* and resisters, as well as journalists, local historians, and the mayor of Tergnier. This crowd of people gave me a hugely mixed response. On the one hand, the paper was immediately followed by an enthusiastic round of applause from the audience, as well as a "Bravo!" from one man in the crowd. I was then surrounded by people who wanted to thank and congratulate me for my work. However, there were signs that the room was, in fact, divided. Already during the official question-and-answer segment after my paper, several former *cheminots* chose a passive-aggressive route, criticizing the pronunciation of certain words or a typo in the slide show presentation. Despite positive feedback from some, an undercurrent of disapproval and anger ran through the room. No one directly confronted me, but as I stayed to talk to certain people, I could hear men and woman all around me whispering rather loudly about how I had completely misunderstood this period, this community, and this history.

Several weeks later, back in London, I received a four-page letter signed by five former *cheminots* from Tergnier who had attended the talk. They attacked the paper and accused me of bad historical practice, but most impressive by far was the list they had drawn up of all the comments I had made. Underneath each point, they had inserted their own counterarguments (in their eyes, "the truth"). The most telling part of this list was that "my" comments, which they had attempted either to paraphrase or quote, were all twisted reinterpretations of what I had actually said. Even though much of my argument defended SNCF history against demonization, the fact that I had nuanced the ideas of *esprit de famille*, political protest, and resistance was, to them, an attack on their established narrative. By inserting the history of the deportations into *cheminot* history, I had somehow implied support for those accusing the SNCF of crimes against humanity and blaming the *cheminots* for passive collaboration.

The reaction of a historic railway town, one of the biggest in France, reveals the lesser-known psyche of the *cheminots*. To understand the nature of the *cheminots*' response, its deep and sensitive roots, we must look beyond the idea that the *cheminots* are simply rejecting Holocaust history and holding on to Resistance myths. The situation is, in fact, far more complicated. First, some of the responses were positive, not least from local and specialized newspapers.[68] Second, reactions to the SNCF Affair did not necessarily mirror reactions to Holocaust history. In other words, *cheminots* can simultaneously embrace the dominant Holocaust narrative and violently reject anything related to the SNCF Affair. How is this possible, and what does it indicate about the current state of *cheminot* memory at the grass roots level?

The second example is Robert Lebrun, one of the *cheminots* from Tergnier whom I interviewed in 2008. Lebrun gave me his *Résistance-Fer* medal as a gift toward the end of our session—a medal which honored railwaymen who had actively participated in the Resistance.[69] Moments later, Lebrun then asked me to help him obtain another award: the Righteous among the Nations. Lebrun had heard of this award, and since he himself had helped a Jew, he felt entitled to it. He had already applied for it, but his application had been rejected on the grounds that his gesture did not meet certain requirements—not least that he was not aware, at the time of his act, that the man he was helping was Jewish.[70] The two incidents were, for me, inherently linked: Lebrun was letting go of one narrative to embrace another.

The only *cheminot* to have been made a Righteous among the Nations so far is Léon Bronchart, a senior train driver in the 1940s. The dictionary of *les Justes* declared that Bronchart refused to drive a train of Jewish deportees. Although it also included his other activities—smuggling and assisting a Jewish family, the Rosenbergs, as well as helping Adolphe Strkowsky, a Jewish man on the run[71]—he is known mainly for this one act of refusal. Many of those attacking the SNCF in court, not least the Lipietz family, have used Bronchart's memory to contrast it with the indifference of the SNCF management and other *cheminots*, describing him as the "exemplary cheminot."[72] Further investigation into Léon Bronchart's life reveals that, in fact, the convoy he refused to drive held political prisoners, not Jews.

Aside from Paulette Babiz-Rosenberg and her sister, whom Bronchart helped to save, his daughter Madeleine played a central part in the application process carried out through Yad Vashem.[73] Bronchart became a Righteous in 1994, eight years after he died, over twenty years after the application process was started. Having interviewed Madeleine Bronchart, I understood that the family supported the application for his award. However, when Bronchart's name was used by those attacking the SNCF, everything changed. The recent attention their father received was completely rejected: Madeleine was revolted by the way some people used her father as an example of what the SNCF and the *cheminots* did not do, but should have done. She felt offended by these attempts to use his memory against the railways and claimed that any attack against the *cheminots*' wartime attitudes was a slur against the hundreds who had been deported or killed. Madeleine Bronchart's reactions revealed the tensions that existed between memory politics and corporate historical narratives, between the SNCF Affair and the *cheminots*. But more importantly, her discourse was imbued with the corporate, family spirit of the *cheminot* community. Although neither she nor her brothers worked for the SNCF, they had inherited a deep sense of identity, solidarity, and community that stayed with them throughout their lives.

The examples of the Tergnier audience, Lebrun, and Bronchart reveal that the *cheminots*' relationship to their own history, and even toward one another, is extremely complicated. Many are ready to let go of glorified Resistance titles, awards, and memories, while others seem to cling to the actions of their fathers and uncles during the German Occupation. Others are involved in recent developments in the politics of memory, not the least of which is the growing popularity of the Righteous among the Nations in France. In many ways, the Righteous carry the same overtones of glory, honor, and righteousness as did the resisters, and *the cheminots* want to be included.

The SNCF Affair has recently come to an official close in America. In December 2014, the French government agreed to pay $60 million in reparations to Holocaust victims in America; in return, the American government assured the French that there would be no more attempts to block the SNCF from bidding for railway contracts or to bring the SNCF to trial. To what extent this will actually bring the question of SNCF culpability to a close is yet unknown, but the SNCF Affair has likely reached its peak and is now dying down in many ways. What is certain is that this drawn-out affair has had a wide reach—geographically, socially, legally, and politically. It confirms many of the postwar memory battles of the late twentieth century and early twenty-first century, but also underlines new issues regarding the effect of Vichy and World War II on transnational memory and economics, on collective (national, corporate, and social) memory, but also on individual memories.

The SNCF Affair highlights, however, the need to nuance our understanding of postwar memory. The French have not completely ignored the "dark" history of Vichy: on the contrary, the first and second sections of this chapter underline the visibility of this debate in France and the number of actors involved in rewriting this history. The final section also reminds us that when *cheminots* have shown outrage at attempts to bring the SNCF to trial, it is often to preserve a nostalgic image of their railway "family" rather than due to indifference toward the crimes of the Holocaust. With time, I believe it will be possible for the memories of Holocaust rescue and railway resistance to coexist within the SNCF, but it is important not to reduce the history of the SNCF in World War II to these memories of resistance and deportation. Beneath them lie an ocean of experiences and stories of everyday life and work in Vichy France. These have yet to be fully explored and remembered.

NOTES

1. Robert Gildea, *France since 1945* (Oxford: Oxford University Press, 1996); Lynne Taylor, "Occupied France Remembered," *Contemporary European History* 13, no. 3 (2004): 357–65; Nathan Bracher, "Remembering the French Resistance: Ethics and Poetics of the Epic," *History & Memory* 19, 1 (2007): 39–67; Olivier Wieviorka, *Divided Memories: French Recollections of World War II from the Liberation to the Present* (Stanford, Calif.: Stanford University Press, 2012).

2. See Ludivine Broch, *Ordinary Workers, Vichy and the Holocaust: French Railwaymen and the Second World War* (Cambridge University Press, 2016).

3. Moshik Temkin, "'Avec Un Certain Malaise': The Paxtonian Trauma in France, 1973–74," *Journal of Contemporary History* 38, no. 2 (2003): 291–306.

4. Julian Jackson, *France: The Dark Years, 1940–1944* (Oxford: Oxford University Press, 2001), 19.

5. Serge Klarsfeld, *Vichy-Auschwitz: Le rôle de Vichy dans la solution finale de la question juive en France* [Vichy-Auschwitz: The role of Vichy in the Final Solution of the Jewish question in France] (Paris: Fayard, 1985); Michael R. Marrus and Robert O. Paxton, *Vichy France and the Jews*, rev. ed. (Stanford, Calif.: Stanford University Press, 1995); eds. Beate and Serge Klarsfeld, *Le Mémorial de la déportation des Juifs de France* (Paris: Beate and Serge Klarsfeld, 1978), published in English as *Memorial to the Jews deported from France, 1942-1944: documentation of the deportation of the victims of the Final Solution in France* (New York: Beate Klarsfeld Foundation, c1983).

6. André Kaspi, *Les Juifs pendant l'Occupation* [The Jews during the

Occupation] (Paris: Seuil, 1991); Renée Poznanski, *Jews in France during World War II*, trans. Nathan Bracher (Hanover, N.H.: University Press of New England, 2001); Nicolas Mariot and Claire Zalc, *Face à la persécution: 991 Juifs dans la guerre* [Facing persecution: 991 Jews during the war] (Paris: Odile Jacob, 2010).

7. Marc Olivier Baruch, *Servir l'État français. l'administration en France de 1940 à 1944* [Serving the French state: The administration in France from 1940 to 1944] (Paris: Fayard, 1997); Jean-Marc Berlière and Laurent Chabrun, *Les Policiers français sous l'Occupation* [The French police under the Occupation] (Paris: Perrin, 2001); Jean-Marc Dreyfus, *Pillages sur ordonnance. Aryanisation et restitution des banques en France, 1940–1953* [Looting on orders: Aryanization and restitution of the banks in France, 1940–1953] (Paris: Fayard, 2003); Tal Bruttmann, *Au bureau des Affaires Juives: L'administration française et l'application de la législation antisémite (1940–1944)* [In the Bureau of Jewish Affairs: The French administration and enforcement of antisemitic legislation (1940–1944)] (Paris: Découverte, 2006).

8. Raul Hilberg, *The Destruction of the European Jews*, rev. ed. (New York: Holmes and Meier, 1985); Peter Longerich, *Holocaust: The Nazi Persecution and Murder of the Jews* (Oxford: Oxford University Press, 2010); Bob Moore, *Survivors: Jewish Self-Help and Rescue in Nazi-Occupied Western Europe* (Oxford: Oxford University Press, 2010).

9. A recent two-day conference touched precisely on this topic: "La radicalisation des persécutions antisémites en France à partir de novembre 1943 [The radicalization of antisemitic persecution in France from November 1943]," held in the Musée d'Acquitaine, Bordeaux, France, January 22–23, 2014.

10. Henry Rousso, *The Vichy Syndrome, History and Memory in France since 1944* (Cambridge, Mass.: Harvard University Press, 1991); Tony Judt, "The Past Is Another Country: Myth and Memory in Postwar Europe," *Daedalus* (1992): 83–118; Eric Conan and Henry Rousso, *Vichy: An Ever-Present Past* (Hanover, N.H.: University Press of New England, 1998).

11. Tony Judt, *Postwar: A History of Europe since 1945* (London: Heinemann, 2005): 819.

12. Jacques Chirac, *Discours et messages de Jacques Chirac, maire de Paris, premier ministre, président de la République, en hommage aux juifs de France victimes de la collaboration de l'Etat français de Vichy avec l'occupant allemand, en hommage au CRIF et aux justes de France et en mémoire de la Shoah* [Speeches and messages of Jacques Chirac, mayor of Paris, prime minister, president of the Republic, in homage to the Jews of France victims of the collaboration of the French State of Vichy with the German occupiers, in tribute to the CRIF (Representative Council of Jewish Institutions of France)

and the Righteous of France and in memory of the Holocaust] (Paris: Les fils et filles des déportés juifs de France, 2007).

13. "Les Justes de France honorés au Panthéon [The Righteous of France honored in the Pantheon]," *Libération*, January 18, 2007, accessed March 11, 2014, http://www.liberation.fr/societe/2007/01/18/les-justes-de-france-honores-au-pantheon_9146; Sarah Gensburger, "La sociologue et l'actualité. Retour sur 'l'Hommage de la Nation aux Justes de France' [The sociologist and current events: Return to 'The Tribute of the Nation to the Righteous of France']," *Genèses* 3 (2007): 116–31; Patrick Cabanel, *Histoire des Justes en France* [History of the Righteous in France] (Paris: Armand Colin, 2012); Sarah Gensburger, "From Jerusalem to Paris: The Institutionalization of the Category of 'Righteous of France,'" *French Politics, Culture & Society* 30, 2 (2012): 150–71.

14. See Richard J. Golsan, "Que reste-t-il de l'affaire Touvier? Mémoire, histoire et justice [What remains of the Touvier Affair? Memory, history, and justice]," *French Review* 72, 1 (1998): 102–12; Susan Rubin Suleiman, "History, Heroism and Narrative Desire: The 'Aubrac Affair' and National Memory of the French Resistance," *South Central Review* 21, 1 (2004): 54–81.

15. Jérome Dupuis and Emmanuel Hecht, "Pourquoi Lanzmann s'en est-il prit au 'Karski' de Haenel? [Why is (filmmaker Claude) Lanzmann attacking (the novel about Jan) Karski by (Yannick) Haenel?]," *L'Express*, February 1, 2010; Aurélie Barjonet and Liran Razinsky, eds., *Writing the Holocaust Today: Critical Perspectives on Jonathan Littell's "The Kindly Ones"* (Amsterdam, Neth.: Rodopi, 2012).

16. "Les Convois de déportés à travers ordres et factures de la SNCF [The convoys of deportees through orders and invoices of the SNCF (French National Railway Company)]," *Résistance Réalités* [Resistance realities] 26 (Autumn 1993).

17. French National Archives (AN): 72 AJ 2288, Procès SNCF [The SNCF trial]; Archives de l'Institut d'Histoire du Temps Présent [Archives of the Institute for the History of the Present Time or IHTP): dossier de Press SNCF [SNCF press dossier], "Déportés: La SNCF avait les factures [Deportees: the SNCF had invoices]," *Le Point* 1027 (May 23, 1992); "Les Convois de déportés à travers ordres et factures de la SNCF" [Deportee convoys through SNCF orders and invoices]; Georges Ribeill, "SNCF et Déportations [SNCF and deportations]," *Historail* 4 (January 2008). Kurt Werner Schaechter has since donated these documents to the Hoover Institution Archives at Stanford University in Stanford, California. See the Kurt Werner Schaechter Collection, accessed August 26, 2013, http://findingaids.stanford.edu/xtf/view?docId=ead/hoover/schaecht.xml;chunk.id=headerlink;brand=default.

18. Paul Durand, *La SNCF pendant la guerre, sa résistance à l'occupant* [The SNCF during the war: Its resistance to the occupier] (Paris: Presses universitaires de France, 1968); Maurice Choury, *Les cheminots dans la bataille du rail* [Railway workers in the battle of the rails] (Paris: Perrin, 1970).

19. Rousso, *The Vichy Syndrome*; Martin O'Shaughnessy, "*La Bataille du Rail*: Unconventional Form, Conventional Image?" chap. 1 in H. R. Kedward and Nancy Wood, eds., *The Liberation of France: Image and Event* (Oxford, U.K.: Berg, 1995), 15–28; Bruno Bertheuil, "De l'image souvenir à l'imaginaire social: quand des cheminots filment leur grève [From memory image to social imagery: When the railway workers filmed their strike]," *L'Homme et la Société* 127, 1–2 (1998): 15–27; Michel Ionascu, *Cheminots et cinéma. la représentation d'un groupe social dans le cinéma et l'audiovisuel français* [Railway workers and cinema: The representation of a social group in the French cinema and audiovisual media] (Paris: Harmattan, 2001); Christian Chevandier, *Cheminots en grève ou la construction d'une identité: 1848–2001* [Railway workers on strike or the construction of an identity, 1848–2001] (Paris: Maisonneuve et Larose, 2002); Cécile Hochard, "Écrire l'histoire des cheminots dans la Résistance. État actuel de l'historiographie [Writing the history of the railway workers in the Resistance: The current state of historiography]," *Revue d'histoire des chemins de fer* (Review of railway history) 34 (2006): 27–36; Sylvie Lindeperg, "Political and Narrative Ambiguities in *La Bataille Du Rail*," *Historical Reflections* 35, 2 (2009): 142–62.

20. Marrus and Paxton, *Vichy France and the Jews*, 330–31.

21. Annie Kriegel, *Réflexion sur les questions juives* [Reflection on Jewish questions] (Paris: Hachette, 1984), 47.

22. "Plainte contre la SNCF pour 'crimes contre l'humanité' [Complaints against SNCF for "crimes against humanity"]," *L'Humanité*, January 12, 1999; Ribeill, "SNCF et Déportations"; Simone Gigliotti, *The Train Journey: Transit, Captivity, and Witnessing the Holocaust* (New York: Berghahn, 2009): 53.

23. Associated Press, "Lawsuit Alleges French National Railroad Profited Serving Nazi Camps," *The Independent*, June 13, 2001, Archives de l'Institut d'Histoire du Temps Présent.

24. Ralph Blumenthal, "U.S. Suit Says French Trains Took Victims to the Nazis," *New York Times*, June 13, 2001, Archives de l'Institut d'Histoire du Temps Présent.

25. Amanda Becker, "Law Firm Takes Holocaust Case to Congress," *Washington Post*, February 14, 2011. To find out more about this class action, see the Coalition for Holocaust Rail Justice website, www.holocaustrailvictims.org. A detailed study on the composition of this group of claimants would shed considerable light on Holocaust legal procedures in the twenty-first

century, but getting direct access to these claimants is extremely difficult at the moment. Special thanks to Sarah Federman for this information.

26. Michael Marrus, "The Case of the French Railways and the Deportation of Jews in 1944," in David Bankier and Dan Michman, eds., *Holocaust and Justice: Representation & Historiography of the Holocaust in Post-War Trials* (Jerusalem: Yad Vashem, 2010), 245–64; Alain Lipietz, *La SNCF et la Shoah* (Paris: Les Petits Matins, 2011). The court proceedings regarding Lipietz et al. v. Préfet de la Haute-Garonne and SNCF can be accessed through the T. M. C. Asser Institute Centre for International & European Law, The Hague, Neth., accessed August 26, 2013, http://www.asser.nl/default.aspx?site_id=36&level1=15246&level2=15248&level3=&textid=39917.

27. See Abrams v. Société Nationale des Chemins de Fer Francais, 175 F.Supp.2d 423, 433 (E.D.N.Y.2001); Abrams v. Société Nationale des Chemins de Fer Francais, 332 F.3d 173 (2nd Cir. 2003); Abrams v. Société Nationale des Chemins de Fer Français (2nd Cir. 2004), accessed September 3, 2013, http://caselaw.findlaw.com/us-2nd-circuit/1228873.html.

28. Suzanne Pollack, "Will SNCF Victims Finally Get Their Day in Court?" *Washington Jewish Week*, April 11, 2013.

29. Author interview with Harriet Tamen, March 2009, New York City.

30. Raphael Delpard, *Les convois de la honte: enquête sur la SNCF et la déportation (1941–1945)* [Convoys of shame: Investigation of the SNCF and deportation] (Neuilly-sur-Seine, France: Michel Lafond, 2005).

31. Jean Martin-Chauffier, "Quand l'histoire déraille [When history derails]," *Paris Match*, May 9, 2010.

32. Françoise Laborde, *Ça va mieux en le disant* [Feel better by saying it] (Paris: Fayard, 2008): 95–96.

33. In French, the word *salope* has a powerful and extremely negative resonance, combining the violence and sexism of the terms "bitch" and "slut," and with an effect to belittle and diminish women.

34. Françoise Laborde, *Une histoire qui fait du bruit* [A story that makes noise] (Paris: Fayard, 2011).

35. Jean-Pierre Richardot, *SNCF, héros et salauds pendant l'Occupation* [SNCF: Heroes and bastards during the Occupation] (Paris: Cherche Midi, 2012). An interview with the author is available on the France Info website, accessed August 27, 2013, http://www.franceinfo.fr/livre/le-livre-du-jour/sncf-heros-et-salauds-pendant-l-occupation-de-jean-pierre-richardot-778929–2012–10–24.

36. Annette Wieviorka, "La Shoah, la SNCF et le juge [The Shoah, the SNCF, and the judge]," *L'Histoire*, 316 (January 2007); Ribeill, "SNCF et Déportations."

37. Marrus, "The Case of the French Railways," 245–64.

38. Jean-Marc Dreyfus and Sarah Gensburger, *Nazi Labour Camps in Paris: Austerlitz, Lévitan, Bassano, July 1943–August 1944* (New York: Berghahn, 2011).

39. "Pour Serge Klarsfeld, les attaques contre la SNCF sont 'injustes' [For Serge Klarsfeld, the attacks against the SNCF are "unjust"]," *LibéOrléans* (website of the city of Orléans), January 28, 2011.

40. For literature on the subject, see Hannah Arendt, *Eichmann in Jerusalem: A Report on the Banality of Evil* (New York: Penguin, 1979); Nancy Wood, "Crimes or Misdemeanours? Memory on Trial in Contemporary France," *French Cultural Studies* 5, 13 (1994):1–21; Michael Marrus, "The Holocaust at Nuremberg," *Yad Vashem Studies* 26 (1998): 4–45; Richard J. Golsan, ed., *The Papon Affair: Memory and Justice on Trial* (Abingdon, U.K.: Routledge, 2000); Lawrence Douglas, "The Didactic Trial: Filtering History and Memory into the Courtroom," *European Review* 14, 4 (2006): 513–22; Devin O. Pendas, "Review Article—'Seeking Justice, Finding Law: Nazi Trials in Postwar Europe,'" *Journal of Modern History* 81, 2 (2009): 347–68.

41. Richard H. Weisberg, *Vichy Law and the Holocaust in France* (New York: Routledge, 1996); Edwin Black, *IBM and the Holocaust* (New York: Dialog, 2001); Christopher Kobrak and Andrea H. Schneider, "Big Business and the Third Reich: An Appraisal of the Historical Arguments," chap. 7 in Dan Stone, *Historiography of the Holocaust* (New York: Palgrave Macmillan, 2004), 141–72; Simon Reich, "Corporate Social Responsibility and the Issue of Compensation: The Case of Ford and Nazi Germany," chap. 5 in Francis R. Nicosia and Jonathan Huener, eds., *Business and Industry in Nazi Germany* (New York: Berghahn, 2004), 104–28; Kim Coleman, *IG Farben and ICI, 1925–53* (New York: Palgrave Macmillan, 2006).

42. A conference was recently organized around the topic "Corporate Liability for Human Rights Violations," Tel Aviv University, Israel, December 16–17, 2012. Michael Marrus, who focuses on the SNCF, was one of the participants.

43. Julian Ryall and Nick Allen, "California to Force Rail Companies to Come Clean on Holocaust Role," *The Telegraph*, August 15, 2010.

44. John Fritze, "Md. Holocaust Survivors Take Rail Fight to Congress," *Baltimore Sun*, September 24, 2011, http://articles.baltimoresun.com/2011–09–24/news/bs-md-holocaust-trains-20110924_1_french-railroad-holocaust-survivors-sncf-america; U.S. Senate Committee on the Judiciary, "Holocaust-Era Claims in the 21st Century: Statement of the Honorable Samuel I. 'Sand' Rosenberg, Delegate, 41st District of Maryland," June 20, 2012, accessed August 26, 2013, http://www.judiciary.senate.gov/pdf/12–6-20RosenbergTestimony.pdf.

45. Ryall and Allen, "California to Force Rail Companies to Come Clean on Holocaust Role."

46. "Senate Considering Bill to Allow Holocaust Survivors to Sue French Railways," *Jewish Telegraphic Agency*, August 1, 2013, accessed September 3, 2013, http://www.jta.org/2013/08/01/news-opinion/politics/bill-to-allow-holocaust-survivors-to-sue-railway-reintroduced-in-senate.

47. Author interview with Henry Rousso, April 13, 2010, Paris.

48. Christian Bachelier, *La SNCF sous l'occupation allemande 1940–1944, rapport documentaire* [The SNCF under German occupation, 1940–1944: Background report], 4 vols. (Paris: IHTP-CNRS, 1996). It is most easily accessible over the Internet, accessed August 26, 2013, http://www.ahicf.com/ww2/rapport/av-propos.htm.

49. *Une entreprise pendant la guerre: La SNCF 1939*–1945 [A company during the war: The SNCF 1939–1945], Paris, Assemblée Nationale, June 21–22, 2000, accessed August 26, 2013, http://www.ahicf.com/ww2/actes.htm.

50. Association pour l'Histoire des Chemins de fer Français (AHICF), *Une entreprise pendant la guerre: La SNCF 1939–1945*, Hors Collection (Paris: Presses Universitaires de France, 2001).

51. "Les cheminots dans la Résistance. Une histoire en evolution [Railway workers in the Resistance: A Story in Evolution]," *Revue d'Histoire des Chemins de Fer* (Review of railway history) 34 (2006); "Les cheminots dans la guerre et l'Occupation, témoignages et récits [Railway workers in the war and the Occupation: Testimonials and stories]," special edition, *Revue d'Histoire des Chemins de Fe* 8 (November 2004); "Mémoires d'ingénieurs, destins ferroviaires. Autobiographies professionnelles de Frédéric Surleau (1884–1972) et Robert Lévi (1895–1981) [Memoirs of engineers, railway destinies: Professional autobiographies of Frédéric Surleau (1884–1972) and Robert Lévi (1895–1981)]," special edition, *Revue d'Histoire des Chemins de Fe* 8 (March 2007).

52. Ribeill, "SNCF et Déportations," 44.

53. *Les Cheminots dans la Résistance* [Railway workers in the Resistance], exhibition at the Musée Jean Moulin, Paris (2005).

54. "Louis Gallois: La SNCF n'est pas responsible de la déportation des Juifs [Louis Gallois: The SNCF is not responsible for the deportation of Jews]," *Le Figaro*, June 6, 2006.

55. Chirac, *Discours et messages de Jacques Chirac.*

56. The neo-Gaullist Phillipe Séguin famously rejected this spirit of "self-flagellation." See "Vel d'Hiv: Hollande n'a pas clos la controverse [Vel d'Hiv: (François) Hollande has not ended the controversy]," *Marianne*, July 27, 2012, accessed September 3, 2013, http://www.marianne.net/Vel-d-Hiv-%C2%A0-Hollande-n-a-pas-clos-la-controverse_a221033.html.

57. Wieviorka, "La Shoah, la SNCF et le juge"; Ribeill, "SNCF et Déportations."

58. Hugh Schofield, "SNCF Apologises for Role in WWII Jewish Deportations," *BBC News*, November 13, 2010, accessed August 16, 2013, http://www.bbc.co.uk/news/world-europe-11751246; Elaine Ganley, "SNCF, French Railroad, Apologizes for Holocaust Role before Florida Bid," *Huffington Post*, November 14, 2010; "Echoes of the Holocaust," *Los Angeles Times*, November 20, 2010; see the speech by Guillaume Pepy, chairman of SNCF, accessed September 3, 2013, http://www.prnewswire.com/news-releases/statement-by-guillaume-pepy-chairman-of-sncf-regarding-sncfs-role-in-world-war-ii-wwii-106716278.html.

59. Maïa de la Baume, "French Railway Formally Apologizes to Holocaust Victims," *New York Times*, January 25, 2011; "Guillaume Pepy reconnait le rôle de la SNCF dans la Shoah [Guillaume Pepy recognizes the role of the railway in the Shoah]," *Le Monde*, January 25, 2011; Manuel Vicuna, "La SNCF, 'rouage de la machine nazie' [The SNCF: Cog in the Nazi machine]," *Libération*, January 25, 2011; Marie-Amélie Lombard, "La SNCF, un 'rouage de la machine nazie,'" *Le Figaro*, January 26, 2011.

60. The original speech is available on the Internet, as is its translation into English: http://39–45.sncf.com/documents/discours_bobigny_en.pdf. See also an interview with the historian Jean-Marc Dreyfus on France-Info radio, January 25, 2011, http://www.france-info.com/france-societe-2011–01–25-la-sncf-a-ete-un-rouage-de-la-machine-nazie-d-extermination-reconnait-511314–9-12.html.

61. Ganley, "SNCF, French Railroad, Apologizes for Holocaust Role."

62. The author is not aware of Pepy's exact motivations. However, the combined pressure for a public apology and to commemorate the Holocaust, added to the tensions in America, would have been considerable factors.

63. Jean-Pierre Chauffier, "A propos de Guillaume Pepy et de ses déclarations: Cheminots 'Indignez-Vous' [About Guillaume Pepy and his statements: Railway workers "Be outraged"]," January 28, 2011 (Limoges), http://lgv.limogespoitiers.info/images/stories/Guillaume_PEPY_deportation.pdf.

64. In doing so, Guillaume Pepy actually mirrored Jacques Chirac's 1995 speech, where after apologizing for the attitudes of Vichy, Chirac was also careful to mention the French Resistance, a tribute not only to Charles de Gaulle but also a clear reminder of the powerful memory of the Resistance.

65. Author interview with Robert Guicharnaud, August 15, 2011, Montauban, France.

66. Guylain Chevrier, 'SNCF et repentance: la colère d'un petit-fils de juifs déportés de France!' [SNCF and repentance: the anger of a grandson of Jews deported from France], (27 January 2011), accessed September 3,

2013. http://www.agoravox.fr/tribune-libre/article/sncf-et-repentance-la-colere-d-un-87878.

67. The Association pour l'Histoire des Chemins de fer Français (AHICF) publishes edited volumes with precise studies on *cheminot* identity, such as "Images de cheminots. Entre représentations et identités [Images of railway workers: Between representations and identities]," *Revue d'Histoire des Chemins de Fer* 36–37 (2007). The most recent and concise work, however, would be Chevandier, *Cheminots en grève ou la construction d'une identité.*

68. "Histoire: Une Conférence sur les cheminots pendant l'Occupation diversement apprécie [History: A conference on the railway workers during the Occupation diversely evaluated]," *L'Union*, March 29, 2010, accessed August 27, 2013, http://passion-trains.over-blog.com/article-histoire-une-conference-sur-les-cheminots-pendant-l-occupation-diversement-appreciee-47628320.html; Marc Delfolie, "La Résistance cheminote à l'épreuve des faits [Resistance of the railway workers to the test of facts]," *L'Aisne Nouvelle*, April 23, 2010; "Tergnier, la SNCF et la Résistance pendant l'Occupation [Tergnier, the SNCF, and the Resistance during the Occupation]," *L'Union l'Ardennais*, April 24, 2010; "Autor du circuit: le particularisme cheminot en question [Around the circuit: The particularity of railway workers in question]," April 24, 2010, accessed August 27, 2013, http://citemodele.over-blog.com/article-autour-du-circuit-le-particularisme-cheminot-en-question-49171494.html; Marc Delfolie, "La Repentance de la SNCF à l'épreuve du vécu [The repentance of the SNCF to the test of experience]," *L'Aisner Nouvelle*, February 14, 2011, accessed August 27, 2013, http://www.aisnenouvelle.fr/article/autre-actu/la-repentance-de-la-sncf-a-lepreuve-du-vecu.

69. Orders, medals, and decorations have been a significant part of French public and political history since the Revolution of 1789, a sign of civic duty in a secular state. The postwar medals relating to actions of resistance under occupation are held in particularly high esteem, and the *Résistance-Fer* (Resistance-Rail) association, which was created to bring together former *cheminot* resisters, took part in this phenomenon. In light of this, Lebrun giving the author his *Résistance-Fer* medal was particularly significant.

70. Author interview with Robert Lebrun, February 7, 2008, Tergnier, France. For more information on the problematics around the Righteous among the Nations, see Sarah Gensburger, *Les Justes de France* [The Righteous of France] (Paris: Presses de Sciences Po, 2010); Patrick Cabanel, *Histoire des Justes de France* [History of the Righteous of France] (Paris: Armand Colin, 2012). Yad Vashem (France), Dossier 6354, Léon Bronchart, letter dated June 1963, from Paulette Babiz-Rosenberg to the Director of Yad Vashem in Jerusalem.

71. Yad Vashem (France), Dossier 6354, Léon Bronchart, letter dated June 1963, from Paulette Babiz-Rosenberg to the Director of Yad Vashem in Jerusalem.

72. http://lipietz.net/?breve259 (accessed September 3, 2013).

73. Yad Vashem Archives (France), dossier 6354, Léon Bronchart.

Mark Joel Webber

Keep Your Distance: "Ethical Duplicity" and the Holocaust

CONTEMPORARY DISCUSSIONS OF ETHICAL QUESTIONS ARISING FROM the Holocaust properly emphasize the importance of acknowledging the victims' dignity and agency, of empathizing with them without appropriating their identity and voice.[1] This means neither looking away from, nor overidentifying with, the victims. In Emmanuel Levinas's analysis, *non-indifference* to others—acknowledging them as fellow human beings—is predicated precisely on the ability to recognize *difference*—the particular identity of oneself and others as fellow strangers.[2]

Applied more broadly to scholarship on the Holocaust, this understanding of ethics enjoins us to: 1) ensure a full and accurate understanding and representation of what happened; 2) resist the urge to oversimplify complexity and homogenize particularity; and 3) refuse to misappropriate and misuse the Holocaust. These ethical principles apply in multiple settings and applications, including classrooms, sites of memory, political rhetoric, and reading and writing about the Holocaust.

This paper examines the presence and function of "ethical duplicity" in fictional works in German and French that represent Holocaust perpetrators, sometimes casting themselves from the perpetrators' perspective and speaking in their voice. I understand ethical duplicity as the rendering opaque and visible of distanced otherness that might otherwise be transparent and invisible. The oxymoron (how can duplicitous behavior be ethical?) draws on the binomial structure of metaphor that powerfully links two terms but (as will be explained later) simultaneously resists the "myth" that they are identical.

In the context of this paper, duplicity is an ethical narrative stance when it respects the suffering of those "others" victimized by the Holocaust even when writing from the fictional perspective of the perpetrator. This it does by creating a tension between the credibility and perfidiousness of a perpetrator-narrator. In this respect, ethical duplicity is related to Debarati Sanyal's concept of "ironic complicity [that] coerces the reader into solidarity with the narrator, yet simultaneously sabotages this identification through irony."[3]

The rise of "perpetrator fiction" reflects growing interest in Holocaust perpetrators in general. Shedding light on the perpetrators enhances our understanding of how the Holocaust could and did unfold.[4] In understanding and evaluating fictional evocations of Holocaust perpetrators (whether or not they bear the names of historical actors), issues of perspective, distance, and balance, along with questions of the presence and efficacy of rhetorical devices, are of central importance. In a sense, the fictional status of these works is at stake. By definition and etymology, a fiction is something not only formed or fashioned but also something feigned. Both its constructedness and its pretense (or duplicity) are inherent in its nature.[5]

This paper engages duplicity as both doubleness and deceitfulness, and especially as it is instantiated through metaphor, whose double structure (linking two terms in a bridging tension between identity and difference) incorporates and provides a model for ethical duplicity. Its main theme is the interplay of grammatical, figurative, and thematic invocations of distance and identity. Exploiting intertextual opportunities, it investigates approaches to fictionalizing Holocaust perpetrators in four texts—Peter Schneider's *Vati*, Klaus Stiller's *H. Protokoll*, Jonathan Littell's *Les Bienveillantes*, and Laurent Binet's *HHhH*.

SCHNEIDER AND STILLER: SUBJUNCTIVES OF COUNTERFACTUALITY AND DISTANCING

In 2011, German writer Peter Schneider published his essay "On Dealing with Evil in Literature: Thoughts on the Question of Narrative Distance."[6] Most of Schneider's piece concerns the genesis and reception of his story *Vati* [Daddy] (1987).[7] A fictional first-person account of a father-son relationship, *Vati* also incorporates some of Mengele's actual reported words.

When Mengele's death was announced in 1979, Schneider discovered his own intersections with the family: he had attended the same secondary school as Mengele's son and was acquainted with a Mengele daughter-in-law. These factors led Schneider to ponder: "What would have become of me, how would I have behaved, how would I have come to terms with it—if I had had to call a Josef Mengele my father."[8] Schneider is not Mengele's son, but *if he were*, this or this *might have* transpired. Starting from this counterfactual premise, Schneider composed his first-person narrative, summoning the fictional but unspecified voice of the son, Rolf Mengele.

While Schneider's manuscript was still with his publisher, he read from it publicly, with unexpected results. After a reading, Schneider wondered why some in the audience would assume that, because he wrote in the voice of a perpetrator's child conversing with that perpetrator, he must be a Nazi apologist. He concluded that he "had chosen the wrong [degree of] distance to the protagonist."[9] The solution: a "minor, so-to-speak merely grammatical correction" accomplished by replacing the first-person singular with the third-person singular and converting the protagonist's statements into "indirect discourse, so into the subjunctive."[10]

Schneider is referring here to the so-called "Subjunctive I," not the "Subjunctive II" used in his initial counterfactual question "What would have become of me?" Encountered frequently in German-language reportage, Subjunctive I provides the subtle but explicit means to distance the reporter from that which is reported. One of its main virtues is that, since it is usually distinguishable from the indicative, the subjunctive of reported speech can be sustained over extensive passages without requiring "speech introducers" such as "Hitler claimed."[11]

Stiller: Distancing through Reported Speech

In 1970, Klaus Stiller employed precisely this technique in *H. Protokoll* (H. Transcript).[12] The title of this slender volume is doubly subversive. The "H." both masks and unmasks Adolf Hitler, whose writings provide the basis of Stiller's text. The claim to be a "transcript" also invites critical interrogation, for Stiller provides anything but a verbatim account of Hitler's words. In placing Hitler's ideas and rhetoric "on the record," he also distances and falsifies them, all the while signaling that he is doing so.

By remixing and remastering Hitler, Stiller produces a new composition whose sentences and paragraphs bounce off one another in ways that Hitler's own texts did not, thus exposing and illuminating the monstrosity of Hitler's language and thought. Stiller's repertoire for deforming Hitler's words includes: (1) rearranging paragraph sequences,[13] (2) adding transitions, (3) altering punctuation, (4) transforming Hitler's indicative into the subjunctive of reported speech,[14] and (5) truncating sentences.

The final paragraph of Stiller's "transcript" turns Hitler's words against himself, breaking off in the middle of an apocalyptic passage envisioning post-cataclysmic life on earth: "There would no longer be a state. Disintegrated: the bonds of all order. In pieces: the documentation of a thousand-year development. One single great, water-and-mud-covered field of corpses—."[15] Stiller operates here on a passage some halfway through *Mein Kampf* that proclaims the importance of "race" in establishing, building up, and preserving "cultural ascendency."[16] Where Hitler concludes his sentence with a period before continuing both his paragraph and his book, Stiller inserts a dash that brings his non-transcript to an open-ended close. He thus transforms the text into a bitterly ironic retrospective prediction of the fate that Hitler will visit upon himself and Germany through a "final fact" in a "thousand-year" development.[17]

Stiller's principal and pervasive tool, however, is the subjunctive. By rendering Hitler's words as reported speech, Stiller distances himself from them but also deforms them to the point that they provoke further investigation. This is the technique with which Schneider experimented before returning to *Vati*'s original first-person perspective.

Schneider: Affiliation and Estrangement

Vati is framed as the narrator's response to a former schoolmate, who has contacted him after twenty years, probably after the announcement of his father's death.[18] A telephone reunion leads to meetings with the unnamed friend. Interestingly, the narrator does not understand his own motivation for answering the friend's questions, surmising in one passage that it was "the fidelity to a friend whom I have invented for myself."[19]

In the fictional framework, the friend actually exists; it is the friendship, with its reciprocal fiduciary obligation, that is imaginary.

Simultaneously, however, the friend is a device that provides the occasion for writing. This process seems to reflect on both author and narrator, who observes: "Even the distance that I accord myself in writing seems to me to be light years too small."[20]

It was precisely the sense of (in)sufficient distance that informed a scathing review of Schneider's book. In addition to accusing him of plagiarism, Gerda-Marie Schönfeld criticized the "undertone of mystification" regarding Mengele. Mengele, she argues, is not a suitable subject for a novella, and the attempt to use a fictional voice to "come close to a specter of horror" must result in "the appearance of cozying up to" evil.[21]

Both the story's composition and initial reception, then, raised issues of proximity and distance. Some of the negative response stemmed from the automatic but mistaken assumption that any text in which a major war criminal (fictionalized or historical) has a voice is primarily "about" that offender. Trying to get close to the evildoer, decreasing the distance that keeps the individual outside contaminating proximity, was considered dangerous and unethical, especially in Germany.

Yet as more insightful studies of the work have demonstrated, to read the story in this way is to fall into a trap.[22] As in Franz Kafka, with whose writings Schneider's text repeatedly engages, the trap is at one level something into which the reader "must run"—it is inscribed in the text as a first-order, quasi-automatic response. But in its constructedness, the text also provides countermanding clues that prompt readers to disidentify themselves with this initial response and to establish a critical distance.[23]

Vati really focuses on the son's struggle to (1) come to terms with, and emancipate himself from, his father; and (2) assert himself vis-à-vis the erstwhile friend, the reciprocal relationship with whom turns out to be imaginary. This process mirrors—at a distance—the trials of Germany's '68 generation in struggling with the "fathers" and their possible complicity in National Socialist crimes.[24]

While the narrator distances himself from his father, he also exposes the disingenuousness of his own generation in simultaneously rejecting the perpetrator generation while accepting its money. This double distancing leads him finally to accept a connection with his father, whose mortality the world is reluctant to acknowledge for what it might say about other mortals: "The world does not want to let my father die, because it cannot bear the thought that even my father belongs to the circle of humanity."[25]

The figure of the son, according to Schneider's essay, was originally meant to be "combative," "representing the generation of those 'born afterwards' in facing up to the conflict with the Nazi-father."[26] The first-person narration arose from Schneider's contrary-to-fact question to himself, which he now reprises in abbreviated form: "What would have become of me, if . . ." In the process of writing, however, Schneider recognized that the character of the son had taken on a life and voice of its own, had become a persona who was less able to confront his father directly, and so was less suited to "mastering an unresolved historical task of my generation in a representative way."[27] Ironically, in his failing to reflect his author's intentions, the son actually becomes more representative of the ambivalences of Schneider's generation than if he had confronted his perpetrator-father more directly.

SCHNEIDER AND LITTELL: MORAL DEMANDS OF MEMORY

Toward the end of his essay on narrative distance, Schneider turns to Jonathan Littell's *Les Bienveillantes* (published in English as *The Kindly Ones*), in which the first-person narrator-protagonist, Maximilien Aue, recounts his career with the Nazi *Sicherheitsdienst* (Security Service or SD).[28] In comparing *Vati* and *Les Bienveillantes*, Schneider emphasizes the differences. But there are also similarities, one of which lies in the perpetrators' attempts to situate themselves within the framework of classical myth—the *Oresteia* (for Aue) and the *Odyssey* (for Mengele).

Another emerges in an interview that Littell gave in 2008: In a way, Littell says, the starting point for the book was his asking himself how he would have behaved as a Nazi if he had been born in 1913. "So, in a way, Aue is a Nazi in the same way I would have been a Nazi—very honest, very sincere, dedicated and interested in examining the question of morality."[29] Both authors frame a counterfactual condition in the subjunctive, imagining themselves in proximity to Holocaust perpetrators. Where Schneider casts himself as a perpetrator's son, Littell projects himself into the role of the perpetrator himself. Littell's "what-if" scenario appears to be commutative, however. He is interested not just in how he "would have behaved as a Nazi" but also in how a fictional Nazi would behave if he were Littell.

In Schneider's story, the fictionalized Mengele is only the *seeming* focus. The "problem" with which the book actually contends is that of the protagonist, his generation, and post-Holocaust and post-1968 German society. In Littell's case, Aue is the *actual* focus and sole voice in an almost 900-page interior monologue.

Schneider begins his critique by conceding his admiration for the scope and daring of Littell's project, acknowledging that Littell succeeds in evoking the tone and atmosphere of his historical settings. Schneider readily acknowledges that Littell's narrator is a construction, a fiction that, as fiction, is permissible (though implausible). In Schneider's eyes, however, the narrative stance that Littell has chosen is flawed.

Schneider objects to the extensive rehearsal of cruelty and atrocity as related by a first-person narrator who is a war criminal. It must necessarily result, he argues, in desensitizing the reader. His conclusion: "Perhaps mass murderers like Dr. Aue or Dr. Dr. Mengele are capable of being the subjects of literature only when the author somehow succeeds also in making visible the perspective of the victims."[30]

Schneider's interrogation of Littell's work, which is connected to his conversation with himself about *Vati* and similar works, illuminates important questions of the aesthetics and ethics of portraying perpetrators in literary fiction.[31] Both historical and fictional writing carry expectations for the writer and reader. The "moral demands of memory," to quote the title of Jeffrey Blustein's book, arise from "respect for the truths of history" and include the "duties to remember (some of) the past accurately, to find out, preserve, and relate the truth (or certain truths) about it."[32]

As Susan Rubin Suleiman says in confirming the "tremendous amount of historical research" evident in *Les Bienveillantes*:

> This kind of documentary exactitude seems necessary if a novelist is to write responsibly about an event that carries as much collective significance as the Holocaust. Indeed, it may be the best criterion for judging the ethical quality of a novel or a fiction film that purports to deal with that (or any other) historical atrocity. If a work evokes the horrors of the Holocaust arbitrarily, as mere background for a story or only for their shock effect, or else commits gross errors in historical representation, it disqualifies itself at the start.[33]

Suleiman enjoins authors: (1) to inform themselves about what really happened, (2) to avoid misrepresenting the facts,[34] and (3) to refrain from using (or abusing) atrocity arbitrarily or for their own ends. In Levinasian terms, the Holocaust deserves to have its particularity, *dignitas*, and gravitas respected. The quality of an author's research speaks to the kind and intensity of authorial fidelity to the subject, and also affects readers' assessment of the text's (and its author's) credibility.

Binet versus Littell: Fact, Fiction, Fabrication?

The immense factual compass of *Les Bienveillantes* has been the subject of both admiration and criticism. One of the most vociferous attacks on Littell has come from the French writer Laurent Binet, whose own novel *HHhH*, which deals with the assassination of Reinhard Heydrich, the *Obergruppenführer* (Senior Group Leader) of the SS, was awarded the Prix Goncourt for best first novel in 2010, four years after Littell's book had received the highest Prix Goncourt for the best prose work, the most prestigious French literary award overall.[35]

Both works identify themselves as novels, yet the two authors' approaches to fiction could not be more different. *Les Bienveillantes* is essentially a monologue by an imaginary perpetrator-*cum*-observer encompassing almost every aspect of the German war of aggression and genocide in which the authorial voice appears almost completely absent. *HHhH* features two third-person narratives on a collision course—the biography of the perpetrator Heydrich; and the background, training, and actions of his assassins, Jozef Gabčík and Jan Kubiš. To these, Binet adds first-person, authorial references to his sources (books and films) and his own thoughts on the process of writing the book and responding to its material.

Binet's writing process includes correcting himself by "taking back" things that he has already advanced as fact. Thus, in describing the German army entering Prague, Czechoslovakia, he ends one chapter with the assertion: "At 9:00 A.M., the first German tank enters the city." But the next chapter begins: "Actually, I don't know if it was a tank that first entered Prague."[36]

The explicit gesture to separate fact from fiction, to perform the *process* of writing as well as to present its *product*, is central to Binet's post-structuralist project. It also provides both the basis and expression of his criticism of Littell. Allowing that he himself is "allergic to interior monologues, at least when we are supposedly talking about history," Binet singles out the episode in *Les Bienveillantes* in which the *Schutzstaffel* (SS) officer Paul Blobel is described as having an Opel automobile; either Littell's research is superb, Binet protests, or he has perpetrated a "bluff," suggesting as factual something that is plausible but not attested.[37]

For his part, Binet meticulously and insistently separates fact from surmise and subjective response, distancing himself from his reportorial voice and constantly reflecting on and redacting what he has written. Binet presents a mixture of narrative elements and reflections, documents and fictions, and so makes explicit that tension between factual and fictional, indicative and subjunctive, whose relationship in Littell he finds insufficiently marked and elaborated.

In discussing his book's focus, Binet admits that he thinks of it as being about Heydrich. But, he says, Heydrich is "the target, not the protagonist."[38] And he then goes on to invoke Heydrich's literariness in terms of the counterfactual "as-if," conceding that "in literary terms Heydrich is a wonderful character. It's as if a Dr. Frankenstein novelist had mixed up the greatest monsters in literature to create a new and terrifying creature. Except that Heydrich is not a paper monster."[39] Binet objects that Littell is either confused about his role as writer of fiction; or does not make his assumptions, techniques, and fictional adaptations sufficiently visible to the reader and thus the subject of a conversation between author and reader.

Littell: Misapprehensions of Genre and Critical Distance

I like Binet's book better than Littell's, in part because of this approach. But I think he is himself confused about what Littell (and Littell's book) are about. In claiming that "inventing a character to understand historical facts is like fabricating evidence," Binet implies that Littell blurs the distinction between history and fiction in a manner bordering on duplicity.[40] The forensic thrust of Binet's objection continues when he contrasts the fictional detective Sherlock Holmes with Heydrich's machinations to discredit General Werner von Fritsch through allegations of homosexuality. Like Holmes, Heydrich plays the violin and investigates alleged criminal behavior. "Except that where Holmes seeks the truth, Heydrich just makes it up."[41]

Despite this swipe, Binet never accuses Littell's book of sympathizing with Nazism. That charge is referenced, only to be rightly dismissed, in Margaret-Anne Hutton's essay on *Les Bienveillantes*. She notes that it likely arises "from a critical (in both senses of the word) misapprehension of the status of Littell's first person narrator."[42]

We will further consider the status of Littell's narrator, but with regard to Binet, it seems that his real problem is with Littell's French readership, which, as he says in an interview, ostensibly saw in it

> the greatest ever book about the Second World War.
>
> What disturbed me is that when people said that, they were including works of history as well as novels. Some people said, "If you want to understand [the Eastern Front of] the Second World War, read *The Kindly Ones*. I disagree.[43]

The question then is whether Littell, intentionally or unintentionally, confuses the reader about the nature of his book. To put it in the terms of this essay, does his text incorporate and preserve disjunctive signals that would steer the attentive reader clear of such misapprehensions, or is there a lack of sufficient and proper distance between (1) the author and his character, and (2) the generic expectations and claims of historical and fictional narrative?

Several critics, and Littell himself, have pointed to techniques of narrative distancing of the kind apparently demanded and missed by Schneider and Binet. Schneider, we remember, at one point transformed *Vati*'s first-person narration into a third-person, "subjunctive version," in the effort to create precisely this distance and thus to forestall misapprehensions.[44] In his extended "Conversation on History and the Novel" with Pierre Nora, Littell argues that first-person narration affords him greater distance than does third-person narration: "Between the narrator as a constructed figure, the 'third person' of the 'first person,' and everything that he sees and describes, there is a *gap*."[45]

Critics have also noted an inconsistency or tension ("a gap") between the two narrative modes. Hutton sees the figure of Aue as a "complex literary construct," and Peter Kuon speaks of a "peculiar interweaving of a documentary and an autobiographical" approach.[46] In Kuon's view, the voice of the "chronicler" comes close to being authorial, however: "Littell thus cancels that layer of narrative stage direction that creates critical distance. Instead, he repeatedly suggests the identity of first-person narrator and author."[47] Thus, while the constructedness (and implausibility) of Aue's character could signal and contribute to narrative distance, this need not be the case, especially when the "chronicling" mode of discourse predominates so heavily. Nevertheless, it seems clear that Aue functions primarily as a narrative device, a voice that, "a little like Forrest Gump," is allowed to recount almost every crucial step and setting in the perpetration of the Holocaust, and that comes into contact with almost every important historical actor in those crimes.[48]

Littell: Myth, Music, Metaphor

In constructing his narrative, Aue (with Littell behind him) employs a wide range of literary devices. As its title indicates, the book envisions Aue's story as a twentieth-century version of the *Oresteia* of Aeschylus, in which the *Erinyes*, the goddesses of vengeance, are sometimes euphemistically referred to as the *Eumenides*, the "Kindly Ones" (in French, *Les Bienveillantes*). The chapters of Littell's book, from the opening "Toccata" to the concluding "Gigue," invoke musical forms. Both of these structuring devices are important to the biography and inner life of the protagonist, so that one cannot see them simply as having been authorially imposed. In addition, *Les Bienveillantes* abounds in references to literature and philosophy at the level of plot, but also as allusion, both explicit and implicit. Woven into the narrative are also rich metaphorical strands of whose particular implications Aue may or may not be aware.

The German classical scholar Jonas Grethlein documents the extent to which elements of Greek tragedy infuse the novel. But he argues that "the foil of tragedy, together with other intertexts and metapoetic reflections, highlights the fictionality of *Les Bienveillantes* and ultimately provokes a critical response to Aue's presentation of the Shoah."[49] The question remains whether that critical distance, which allows the reader to deconstruct Aue's narrative, is present; and whether that distance is sufficiently, visibly, and coherently embedded in the text, so that readers both enter Aue's world, accepting its immediacy, and are provided with signs that trigger their withdrawal from this immediacy to a more distanced and critical perspective.

In exploring this question in the specific context of this paper, I want to focus on the way in which metaphor, and particularly instances of metaphors that themselves invoke metaphor, function in the novel. Of Aue's many addictions, one is metaphor: the text abounds in such comparisons, including those that involve animals and bridges, to name but two important metaphorical complexes.

Sometimes, the passage is part of the setting, as in the description of the abandoned animals in the Ukrainian countryside, "horrified" and "doomed to die" after their owners have fled.[50] But there are also instances where Jews and animals are linked in ways that appear intended to obliterate any differences between the entities compared. Aue "quotes" Adolf Eichmann, himself citing Heydrich, on natural selection and Jewish survivorship:

> [Heydrich] knew that the strongest Jews, the toughest, the cleverest, the wiliest, would escape all selections and would be the hardest to destroy. And it is precisely those who form the vital reservoir from which Jewry could spring back, *the germ cell for Jewish regeneration*, as the late Obergruppenführer said. Our struggle prolongs that of Koch and Pasteur—we have to follow it through to the end.[51]

If this is meant as metaphor at all, then it is a special and perniciously duplicitous sort of metaphor that eliminates the tension between identity and duality—what Paul Ricœur critiques as "myth" in the sense of believed metaphor that improperly eliminates the tension between the two terms of a metaphor, asserting their (false) identity.[52]

Aue himself wonders about the degree of allegiance that Eichmann feels for the metaphor: "Did Eichmann really believe in them [his words]? It was the first time I had heard him talk this way, and I had the impression that he had gotten carried away, let himself be swept along by his new role, that he liked the game so much that he ended up becoming one with it."[53] In this key reflection, Aue exercises critical distance with respect to metaphor, distinguishing between rhetorical and mythic (believed) usages. In his own metaphor of what may have happened with Eichmann, Aue suggests the possibility that critical distance can be suppressed, so that someone "becomes one" with what otherwise would have been a "game," however distasteful and pernicious.

Aue thus shows himself capable of resisting the urge to join together (conflate) that which should be kept apart by "applying a critical instance." But what of his own practices of metaphorizing, comparing, and joining together phenomena whose individuality and particularity also need to be recognized and respected?

On his way back to Auschwitz I, Aue comes across a graffito: "KATYN = AUSCHWITZ." This equation, whose mathematical form suggests it operates in both directions, gives rise to speculation about who might have written it. Perhaps surprisingly, however, it does not provoke discussion as to its meaning or import.[54] Does it assert that the Katyn massacre is as bad as Auschwitz, the Soviet equivalent of what the Germans are doing? From the perspective of Polish patriots, this would make sense, especially with regard to Auschwitz, the *Stammlager* (main camp) that is still today commemorated as the site of Polish martyrdom. But as Aue reflects, there are no longer any Poles residing in the city; this implies that the slogan may have arisen in response to the Nazi propaganda campaign following the discovery of the mass graves at Katyn. In this case, the attempt to relativize German guilt through the assertion that "they are as bad as we are" backfires precisely because of the equation's bi-directionality. For if Katyn is an outrage, a crime against humanity, then, the graffito concedes and proclaims, so is Auschwitz.

But what does "Auschwitz" mean in this context? Does its scope extend to Birkenau (Auschwitz II) and Monowitz (Auschwitz III), and does it encompass everything that we now associate with the term, which has come to be a symbol and synecdoche for the Holocaust as a whole?[55] This is likely the case for the reader, if not for Aue—but the fact that he has just visited Monowitz and discussed Birkenau suggests that these may well be linked with the *Stammlager* in his mind as well.

This reading receives support from the recurring dream that Aue has after his official visits within the Auschwitz complex. Aue's own analysis reveals to him that these "serene" dreams are figurations of "the camp," though purified of anything that would cause him distress. But then Auschwitz as a whole, and the self-regulating processes that characterize it in his dreams, take on an overriding and totalizing metaphorical function and significance: "So I came to think: Wasn't the camp itself, with all the rigidity of its organization, its absurd violence, its meticulous hierarchy, just a metaphor, a *reductio ad absurdum* of everyday life?"[56]

Aue is right that he is dealing with a *reduction*—the layered structure of difference and linkage has been reduced and flattened, if Auschwitz (itself reduced from its expanse, and its internal differentiations of genesis, prisoner population, and operation diminished to simply "the camp") is to be a metaphor for "everyday life" in general. The passage portrays metaphor as a reductio ad absurdum, something that, far from incorporating truth in its duplicity, is less than senseless. To see everyday life in terms of Auschwitz is to say something devastating about everyday life. But if Auschwitz is representative of the quotidian, then Auschwitz, even as a synecdoche for the Holocaust, is stripped of its complex and horrific distinctiveness. This is then a case not of ethical duplicity but of unethically duplicitous obliteration of difference.

Aue, we have discovered, sometimes exercises his critical capacity, resisting others' tendencies to reduce (or eradicate) difference. Yet he—or his author—also repeatedly indulges himself in what I would call "indiscriminate linking" that flattens and confuses what should remain layered and separate.[57] This contradictory trope of creating and destroying linkages receives repeated expression to the extent that it begins to function structurally, through Aue's meetings with the *Wehrmacht* (armed forces) engineer Osnabrugge.

Osnabrugge, whose very name signals his "bridging" nature ("bridge" in German is *Brücke*), feels himself called to construct bridges not only as physical structures but also as works of ideas and culture. Yet there is an unbridgeable gap between his profession and his assigned tasks: he has never actually built a bridge. Aue quotes him speaking about his passion for "bridging gaps": "A bridge is a literal and material contribution to the community; it creates new roads, new links. And also, it's a beautiful thing. Not just to look at: if only you could understand the poetry of the calculations, the tensions and forces, the arches and cables, how it's all balanced by the play of mathematics!"[58]

This rapturous evocation and invocation of the bridge as something that arises from and creates culture, both material and aesthetic, captures the way in which the structure spans two localities that would otherwise not be linked. But its arch is also a matter of "equilibrium" between opposing forces, pushing and pulling, linking and dividing, held in relation to each other by the "play of mathematics."

This could be a description of how metaphor works, without letting the "game" flatten the tension, as it had when Eichmann, as quoted earlier, let his metaphor run away with him. I attribute the passage to Littell, since Osnabrugge uses the contrary-to-fact conditional in addressing Aue: "If only you could understand . . ." At the same time, the joke is on Osnabrugge. Not only has he never built a bridge, but also his wartime work is confined to blowing them up.

Littell: Perpetration and Kinship

Arguably the most contentious and important complex of linkages and comparisons in the novel involves those between perpetrators and non-perpetrators. In Aue's key conversation with his sister and her husband, the protagonist protests that the SD makes "rational" choices; the pursuit of the Jews is grounded "objectively."[59] To this the sister replies: "By killing the Jews . . . we wanted to kill ourselves, kill the Jew within us, kill that which in us resembles the idea we [construct for ourselves] of the Jew."

She goes on to relate a series of reciprocal stereotypes between Jews and Germans, arguing that both wanted to become like the other but projected onto the other those qualities within them irreconcilable with their self-image. In doing so, each party acts under an illusion. She concludes: "For if *Jew*, these days, means anything, it means Other, and Other and an Otherwise that might be impossible, but that are necessary."[60]

Like Osnabrugge, Aue's sister Una bears a "speaking" name: "Una" ("one" in Latin) suggests the unity that Aue so destructively lacks and seeks.[61] His incestuous attraction to his "fraternal" twin, which he maintains after she has ceased to reciprocate it and put distance between herself and her brother, demonstrates his inability to face mature adulthood. In this most intimate aspect of his personality, as in attempts to make sense of (or keep at bay) his experiences and actions, Aue tries to eradicate difference. This applies both to helping murder those who seem different and to "homogenizing" that which properly deserves differentiation—such as the difference between those who murder and those who do not, between perpetrators and victims.[62]

In the passage just quoted, Una again distances herself from her brother's defensive fantasy of acting rationally and objectively. She exposes the tension between self and alterity without, however, drawing the Levinasian conclusion that an acknowledgment of the role of "difference" in constituting identity leads one precisely not to be "indifferent" to the other.[63]

Aue's sister's analysis affects him powerfully, triggering both a recollection of his earlier vision of Hitler in rabbinical trappings and another bout of dreams in which he desires his sister, who has taken on some of the attributes of a concentration camp inmate.[64] Aue relates both these instances of confusing the self and the other, but apparently without allowing himself to understand what they are telling him. This knowledge is left to the reader.

But Aue attempts to make even his readers complicit, seeing himself as one of the "others" who are not personally guilty of atrocities. Aue's opening apostrophe of his "human brothers" culminates in his insistence, at the end of the novel's first section, that "I am a man like other men, I am a man like you. I tell you I am just like you!"[65] Martin von Koppenfels has aptly termed the novel's opening a *captatio malevolentiae*, a seeking of ill will, contrasting it to the more usual *captatio benevolentiae*, the rhetorical technique with which orators try to win the goodwill of their audience, making their listeners "kindly ones" in their reception of the rhetorician's argument.[66] But the Kindly Ones, from whom the novel takes its title and with whose reappearance it closes, are anything but kindly. The euphemism itself constitutes a vain attempt to obtain a favorable hearing.[67]

The opening and closing of the novel underscore its rhetorical qualities. By protesting too much, Aue's claim that, in recounting his story, he is not attempting to convince his readers of anything in particular, provokes its own negation.[68] By causing his protagonist to impeach himself as a witness to his own intentions, Littell creates the ethical duplicity that, in Peter Kuon's analysis, constitutes the strength of the novel.[69]

At the same time, it would be too facile simply to reject Aue's (and behind him: Littell's) claim of kinship with the reader and all of humankind. If it is improper to universalize the Holocaust and its victims in such a way that their particularities are obliterated, then it is also improper to universalize perpetration, either as "collective guilt" or in the sense of relativizing the individual guilt of the perpetrators.[70] Still, drawing on her reading of Primo Levi, Susannah Radstone makes a persuasive case for an augmented sense of empathy that includes an acknowledgment of the perpetrators' humanness:

> As Levi has insisted, the necessity of remembering rather than obfuscating the *distinction* between "victims and murderers" is a burden history must never abnegate. Yet the position of witness is

> a complex one that can exceed an empathic identification with victimhood to include identifications with other positions available within any given scenario, including, especially, those of perpetration. If history is not to repeat itself, the task of witnessing and remembering the sufferings of others ought not to be separated from the difficult acknowledgement of testimonial witnessing's darker side.[71]

Her argument reminds us of the words of Schneider's protagonist in *Vati*: "The world does not want to let my father die, because it cannot bear the thought that even my father belongs to the circle of humanity."[72]

FICTION AND TRUTH

When it comes to perpetrators, one is tempted to paraphrase Mikhail Bulgakov's *Heart of a Dog* in observing that the scandal is not that those responsible for the Holocaust were animals, but that they were human.[73] Extending the "circle of humanity" to include heinous perpetrators may be part of the fidelity to self that the ethical dialectic between identity (in the sense of oneness) and alterity demands. Binet's reproach that Littell is writing about himself and the present, and not about a putative historical facticity, is no reproach at all.[74] It is a definition of the fictional engagement with history that may reveal truths about the self and humanness as a condition, but may only indirectly disclose facts about particular historical actors and actions.

In this context, the ethical obligation of writers to mark fictionality extends also to readers, who afford or refuse credibility to what and whom they read. If they flatten the layering—the tension between identity and duplicity that metaphor, and its epic extension and deepening in fiction, incorporates—they fail the ethics of reception.

Fictional works like Schneider's *Vati*, Stiller's *H. Protokoll*, Littell's *Les Bienveillantes*, and Binet's *HHhH* have no credibility unless they are true to themselves as fictions. If they are, they can, by allowing us to reflect on ethical duplicity, teach us something about ourselves and our responses to the complex atrocity that was the Holocaust. But they cannot teach us history.

NOTES

My thanks to the German Academic Exchange Service (DAAD) for a grant in support of the Mark and Gail Appel Program in Holocaust and Anti-racism Education at York University in Toronto, Canada; and the editors and anonymous reviewers of this paper for their helpful suggestions. Unless indicated, translations from German are mine.

1. Dominick LaCapra, *History and Memory after Auschwitz* (Ithaca, N.Y.: Cornell University Press, 1998), 182.

2. Emmanuel Levinas, "Without Identity," in *Humanism of the Other*, ed. Richard A. Cohen, trans. Nidra Poller (Urbana: University of Illinois Press, 2006), 66 (emphasis added).

3. Debarati Sanyal, "Reading Nazi Memory in Jonathan Littell's *The Kindly Ones*," in *Memory and Complicity: Migrations in Holocaust Remembrance* (New York: Fordham University Press, 2015), 191.

4. See, for example, Michael Wildt, *Generation des Unbedingten. Das Führungskorps des Reichssicherheitshauptamtes* (published in English as *An Uncompromising Generation: The Nazi Leadership of the Reich Security Main Office*) (Hamburg, Ger.: Hamburger Edition HIS, 2003); Bettina Stangneth, *Eichmann vor Jerusalem. Das unbehelligte Leben eines Massenmörders* [published in English as *Eichmann Before Jerusalem: The Unexamined Life of a Mass Murderer*] (Reinbek bei Hamburg, Ger.: Rowohlt, 2014).

5. "Fiction, n.," *Oxford English Dictionary* (Oxford: Oxford University Press, 1989), http://www.oed.com/view/Entry/69828.

6. Peter Schneider, "Vom Umgang mit dem Bösen in der Literatur: Gedanken zur Frage des erzählerischen Abstands [On dealing with evil in literature: Thoughts on the question of narrative distance]," in Paul Michael Lützeler and Jennifer Kapczynski, eds., *Die Ethik der Literatur. Deutsche Autoren in der Gegenwart* [The ethics of literature: Contemporary German writers] (Göttingen, Ger.: Wallstein, 2011), 145–56.

7. Peter Schneider, *Vati. Erzählung* [Daddy: A story] (Darmstadt, Ger.: Luchterhand, 1989 [1987]), 847.

8. Schneider, "Vom Umgang mit dem Bösen in der Literatur," 146.

9. Ibid., 150.

10. Ibid.

11. Abraham P. ten Cate, "Modality of Verb Forms in German Reported Speech," in Theo A. J. M. Janssen and Wim van der Wurff, eds., *Reported Speech: Forms and Functions of the Verb* (Amsterdam, Neth.: John Benjamins, 1996), 193.

12. Klaus Stiller, *H. Protokoll* [H. transcript] (Frankfurt am Main, Ger.: Fischer, 1980).

13. For example, a passage from 330 of *Mein Kampf* is flanked by passages from 417 and 455 of that work.

14. Adolf Hitler, *Mein Kampf* [My struggle] (Munich, Ger.: Zentralverlag der NSDAP [Nationalsozialistische Deutsche Arbeiterpartei or Nazi Party], Frz. Eher Nachf., G.m.b.H, 1943), http://archive.org/download/Mein-Kampf2/HitlerAdolf-MeinKampf-Band1Und2855.Auflage1943818S.pdf, 330. Stiller, *H. Protokoll*, 112.

15. Stiller, *H. Protokoll*, 124.

16. Hitler, *Mein Kampf*, 432.

17. Stiller (*H. Protokoll*, 123) plucks Hitler's reference to the "*letzte Tatsache*" (last fact) (*Mein Kampf*, 756) from its context in a discussion of foreign policy and makes it into an introduction of "the end"—of his book and National Socialist Germany.

18. Schneider, *Vati*, 18. Josef Mengele died in 1979, but it was only in 1985 that the family announced his death; see "Son Says Mengele's Dead, Tells Why He Kept Silent: Learned of Death in 1979," *Los Angeles Times*, June 11, 1985, http://articles.latimes.com/1985–06–11/news/mn-10339_1_adolf-eichmann.

19. Schneider, *Vati*, 18.

20. Ibid., 19.

21. Gerda-Marie Schönfeld, "So eine Nachbarschaft. Ist Peter Schneiders Erzählung "Vati" ein schlichtes Illustrierten-Plagiat? [What a neighborhood: Is Peter Schneider's *Vati* simple plagiarism from an illustrated magazine?]," *Der Spiegel* 11, 41 (March 9, 1987), http://www.spiegel.de/spiegel/print/d-13521967.html.

22. Other helpful readings include William Collins Donahue, "Revising '68: Bernhard Schlink's *Der Vorleser*, Peter Schneider's *Vati*, and the Question of History," *Seminar: A Journal of Germanic Studies* 40, 3 (September 2004): 293–311; Elizabeth Snyder Hook, *Family Secrets and the Contemporary German Novel: Literary Explorations in the Aftermath of the Third Reich* (Rochester, N.Y.: Camden House, 2002); Erin Heather McGlothlin, "'Under a False Name': Peter Schneider's *Vati* and the Misnomer of Genre," in *Second-Generation Holocaust Literature: Legacies of Survival and Perpetration* (Rochester, N.Y.: Camden House, 2006), 143–73; Peter Morgan, "The Sins of the Fathers: A Reappraisal of the Controversy about Peter Schneider's *Vati*," *German Life and Letters* 47, 1 (January 1994): 104–33; Colin Riordan, "The Sins of the Children: Peter Schneider, Allan Massie and the Legacy of Auschwitz," *Journal of European Studies* 27, 2 (June 1997): 161–80.

23. The allusion is to Franz Kafka's text usually called "Kleine Fabel" ("A Little Fable"); the real-but-imaginary friend is reminiscent of Kafka's story "Das Urteil" (usually translated as "The Judgment"), which features a father-son conflict. Both texts in Franz Kafka, *Die Erzählungen und andere*

ausgewählte Prosa. Originalfassung [The stories and other selected prose: Original version] (Frankfurt am Main, Ger.: Fischer, 1996), 382; 47–60.

24. Birgit A. Jensen, "Peter Schneider's *Vati*: Contesting a German Taboo," *Critique: Studies in Contemporary Fiction* 43, 1 (Fall 2001): 88.

25. Schneider, *Vati*, 82.

26. Schneider, "Vom Umgang mit dem Bösen in der Literatur," 149.

27. Ibid.

28. Jonathan Littell, *Les Bienveillantes. Roman* (Paris: Gallimard, 2006). I quote from the English translation: *The Kindly Ones: A Novel*, trans. Charlotte Mandel (Toronto, Canada: McClelland and Stewart, 2009). References to "*Bienveillantes*" and "*Kindly Ones*" designate the French original and English translation, respectively.

29. Assaf Uni, "The Executioner's Song," *Haaretz*, May 30, 2008, http://web.archive.org/web/20100115073354/http://www.haaretz.com/hasen/spages/988410.html.

30. Schneider, "Vom Umgang mit dem Bösen in der Literatur," 155–56.

31. Littell's novel has inspired many and varied responses, including two volumes of critical essays: Aurélie Barjonet and Liran Razinsky, eds., *Writing the Holocaust Today: Critical Perspectives on Jonathan Littell's "The Kindly Ones"* (Amsterdam, Neth.: Rodopi, 2012); Richard J. Golsan and Philip Watts, eds., *Literature and History: Around "Suite Française" and "Les Bienveillantes,"* Yale French Studies, Number 212 (New Haven, Conn.: Yale University Press, 2012). On the specifically German response to the novel, see Wolfgang Asholt, "A German Reading of the German Reception of *The Kindly Ones*," in Barjonet and Razinsky, *Writing the Holocaust Today*, 221–38; Klaus Theweleit, "On the German Reaction to Jonathan Littell's *Les bienveillantes*," *New German Critique* 36, 1 106 (2009): 21–34.

32. Jeffrey Blustein, *The Moral Demands of Memory* (New York: Cambridge University Press, 2008), 218.

33. Susan Rubin Suleiman, "Performing a Perpetrator as Witness: Jonathan Littell's *Les Bienveillantes*," in Jakob Lothe, Susan Rubin Suleiman, and James Phelan, eds., *After Testimony: The Ethics and Aesthetics of Holocaust Narrative for the Future* (Columbus: Ohio State University Press, 2012), 102.

34. Except, as Suleiman clarifies, when the text, as in Quentin Tarantino's *Inglourious Basterds* (Universal Pictures, Weinstein Company, 2009), signals its counterfactuality (ibid., 116n5).

35. Laurent Binet, *HHhH: Roman* (Paris: Grasset and Fasquelle, 2011). *HHhH*, trans. Sam Taylor (New York: Farrar, Straus and Giroux, 2012). I cite the original as Binet F, the translation as Binet E. Behind Binet's title is the supposed contemporary jibe: "Himmlers Hirn heißt Heydrich" (Himmler's brain is named Heydrich).

36. Binet F, 130, 131; Binet E, 94. The juxtaposition would have re-

tained its full force had the English translation reproduced the original's present tense: "In fact, I don't know if it is a tank that enters Prague first." Another example: Binet F, 146; Binet E, 100.

37. The reference is to Littell, *Bienveillantes*, 43–44; Littell, *Kindly Ones*, 39. Garth Risk Hallberg, "Exclusive: The Missing Pages of Laurent Binet's HHhH," *The Millions* (2012), http://www.themillions.com/2012/04/exclusive-the-missing-pages-of-laurent-binets-hhhh.html. In the same text, Binet objects to an error in Littell's dating of the assassination of Heydrich (*Bienveillantes*, 212; *Kindly Ones*, 225).

38. Binet F, 138; Binet E, 99. The translation suggests more directly than the original a connection between Heydrich's role in history (and the "operation" that was to give the book its title) and his role as a main character in the book.

39. Binet F, 138; Binet E, 99. In the original, the metaphor is not of mixing substances or literary characteristics, but of birth: Frankenstein-as-storyteller is *delivered of* a new creature.

40. Hallberg, "Exclusive."

41. Binet F, 81–82; Binet E, 57.

42. Margaret-Anne Hutton, "Jonathan Littell's *Les Bienveillantes*: Ethics, Aesthetics and the Subject of Judgment," *Modern & Contemporary France* 18, 1 (2010): 5.

43. Jonathan Derbyshire, "The Books Interview: Laurent Binet," *New Statesman*, May 16, 2012, http://www.newstatesman.com/culture/culture/2012/05/books-interview-laurent-binet.

44. Schneider, "Vom Umgang mit dem Bösen in der Literatur," 151.

45. Jonathan Littell and Pierre Nora, "Conversation sur l'histoire et le roman [Conversation about history and the novel]," *Le Débat* 2, 144 (2007): 29. For an analysis of Littell's explanation, see Martin von Koppenfels, "*Captatio malevolentiae*. Infame Ich-Erzähler bei Céline und Littell [*Captatio malevolentiae*: Infamous first-person narrators in (Louis-Ferdinand) Céline and Littell]," *Lendemains—Etudes comparées sur la France* [Tomorrows—comparative studies on France] 34, 134–35 (2009): 262–63.

46. Hutton, "Jonathan Littell's *Les Bienveillantes*," 5; Peter Kuon, "'Wo alle schuldig sind, ist niemand schuldig'. Zu einer Denkfigur in Hannah Arendts *Eichmann in Jerusalem*, Albert Camus' *La Chute* und Jonathan Littells *Les Bienveillantes* ["Where all are guilty, no one is guilty": On a figure of thought in Hannah Arendt's *Eichmann in Jerusalem*, Albert Camus's *La Chute*, und Jonathan Littell's *Les Bienveillantes*]," *Jahrbuch der Juristischen Zeitgeschichte* [Yearbook of legal contemporary history] 12 (December 2011): 381.

47. Ibid., 382.

48. Florent Brayard, "Littell, pas si 'bienveillant' [Littell, not so kindly]," *Libération*, November 1, 2006, http://www.liberation.fr/tribune/010165065-littell-pas-si-bienveillant.

49. Jonas Grethlein, "Myth, Morals, and Metafiction in Jonathan Littell's *Les Bienveillantes*," *PMLA* 127, 1 (2012): 89.

50. Littell, *Bienveillantes*, 110–11; *Kindly Ones*, 112–13.

51. Littell, *Bienveillantes*, 714; *Kindly Ones*, 777. This passage closely paraphrases, with "enhancements," the first paragraph on page 8 of the official record of the Wannsee Conference, the 1942 meeting of senior Nazi officials to coordinate the "Final Solution"; see Robert Gerwarth, *Hitler's Hangman: The Life of Heydrich* (New Haven, Conn.: Yale University Press, 2011), 212. See also Littell, *Bienveillantes*, 524 (*Kindly Ones*, 569).

52. Paul Ricoeur, *The Rule of Metaphor: Multi-Disciplinary Studies of the Creation of Meaning in Language*, trans. Robert Czerny, University of Toronto Romance Series, 37 (Toronto, Canada: University of Toronto Press, 1977), 251–52.

53. Littell, *Bienveillantes*, 714; *Kindly Ones*, 777.

54. Littell, *Bienveillantes*, 569–70; *Kindly Ones*, 619. For background and further analysis, see Liran Razinsky, "The Similarity of Perpetrators," in Barjonet and Razinsky, *Writing the Holocaust Today*, 54–59 (see note 31).

55. See Mark Joel Webber, "Metaphorizing the Holocaust," *Images* 8, 15–16 (2011): 27. It is possible that this equation resides at the authorial level. If the assertion is really that Auschwitz and Katyn are indistinguishable, then the graffito represents an impermissible homogenization of crimes that should remain distinguishable in their particularities.

56. Littell, *Bienveillantes*, 572; *Kindly Ones*, 622.

57. Razinsky ("The Similarity of Perpetrators," 47) sees in Aue's discourse "an attack on differentiations of any kind. Aue refuses the distinctions and categorizations that serve precisely to draw boundaries between evil and us."

58. Littell, *Bienveillantes*, 131; *Kindly Ones*, 135; see Cyril Aslanov, "Visibility and Iconicity of the German Language in *The Kindly Ones*," in Barjonet and Razinsky, *Writing the Holocaust Today*, 63 (see note 31).

59. Littell, *Bienveillantes*, 801; *Kindly Ones*, 874. The reader is reminded of another "pursuit," that of Aue's inner and outer "Erinnyes" or Furies.

60. Littell, *Bienveillantes*, 801–2; *Kindly Ones*, 874–75.

61. For a discussion of "brotherhood" in *Les Bienveillantes* and the linkage between the woman partisan and Aue's sister, see Catherine Coquio, "'Oh My Human Brothers, Let Me Tell You How It Happened.' (Who Is the Perpetrator Talking To?)," in Barjonet and Razinsky, *Writing the Holocaust Today*, 87–89 (see note 31).

62. Richard Crownshaw, "Perpetrator Fictions and Transcultural Memory," *Parallax* 17, no. 4 (2011): 75–89, http://dx.doi.org/10.1080/13534645.2011.605582.

63. Levinas, "Without Identity," 66.

64. Littell, *Bienveillantes*, 802–8 (*Kindly Ones*, 875–81); for the earlier vision, see *Bienveillantes*, 431 (*Kindly Ones*, 467).

65. Littell, *Bienveillantes*, 11, 30; *Kindly Ones*, 3, 24.

66. Koppenfels, "*Captatio malevolentiae* (see note 45). Koppenfels also points out echoes to François Villon, Charles Baudelaire, and Louis-Ferdinanc Céline.

67. "Les Bienveillantes avaient retrouvé ma trace" (*Bienveillantes*, 894); "The Kindly Ones had taken up my trail again" (*Kindly Ones*, 975 [with changes]).

68. Littell, *Bienveillantes*, 11; *Kindly Ones*, 3.

69. Kuon, "'Wo alle schuldig sind, ist niemand schuldig,'" 386. Kuon acknowledges also those aspects of the book that do not demonstrate this strength.

70. On the difference between "'Eichmann is in all of us'" and "'Anyone could be Eichmann,'" see Crownshaw, "Perpetrator Fictions and Transcultural Memory," 28. On the tension between the universal and the particular, see Michael Brown, "The Universal and the Particular: Twin Foci in Holocaust Education," *Images* 8, nos. 15–16 (2011): 31–48.

71. Susannah Radstone, "Social Bonds and Psychical Order: Testimonies," *Culture Values* 5, 1 (2001): 61. I am indebted to Crownshaw's article for the reference to Radstone.

72. Schneider, *Vati*, 82.

73. Mikhail Bulgakov, *The Heart of a Dog*, trans. Avril Pyman (Moscow: Raduga, 1990), 60.

74. Derbyshire, "The Books Interview."

III. R·E·C·O·V·E·R·Y A·N·D L·O·S·S

Perla Sneh

Khurbn Yiddish: An Absent Absence

Ibergekumene tzures iz gut tsu dertseyln. ("Troubles overcome are good to tell.")

—Yiddish proverb used by Primo Levi as an epigraph to his book The Periodic Table

LET US START WITH AN ABSENCE, THE ABSENCE OF YIDDISH IN WHAT IS called "Holocaust studies." By Yiddish I mean not just the everyday language in which most of the Jews annihilated by the Nazis lived and died, but an *ideological, political, and cultural core of Judaism at the time*. Yiddish is absent from Holocaust studies not only as a language but also as a particularly tragic story that, even though ignored, silently persists. And even that absence is absent from our considerations: Yiddish is absent as an absence since it was abandoned as a primary key for research and no one seems to miss it. The most valuable works of such scholars as Samuel Kassow, David Roskies, and Alan Rosen or, from a different perspective, Ruth Wisse, Alan Astro, and Ilan Stavans are refreshing and welcomed exceptions.[1]

Not all victims spoke Yiddish (neither did all perpetrators speak German). The destruction was not limited to the Yiddish-speaking community; it encompassed other linguistic realms, but it did focus on the Yiddish world. This reveals an emphasis missing from those approaches that leave Yiddish aside, because, even if the annihilation was not limited to the Yiddish-speaking realm (actually, it reached as far as North Africa, which adds a deeper linguistic complexity to our approach), it did focus on East European Jewish civilization, whose internal tune, whose most distinctive features, crystalized into Yiddish.[2]

Ladino, as well as Yiddish, suffered the same fate as the communities they once united; both were not only the language of the victims but also victims themselves, objects of what Cyril Aslanov calls *linguicide*: they hardly survived their speakers.[3] Nevertheless, the proximity of the victims' language—Yiddish—with the henchmen's language—German—may be the uncanniest in terms of symbolic connotations.

Still, Yiddish is not a mandatory subject in Holocaust studies; it was not an official language in any of the trials of the perpetrators; there is no institution—academic or otherwise—specifically dedicated to the study and eventual translation of the huge corpus of Yiddish writings from that time. This corpus, with its undeniable poetry *during* Auschwitz, would have given an entirely different turn to the discussion of Theodor Adorno's famous dictum regarding poetry *after* Auschwitz: "To write poetry after Auschwitz is barbaric."

The still ongoing, perhaps unavoidable, discussion about the proper name of the destruction—Holocaust, Shoah, genocide, and other terms—must be reconsidered not only in light of what is said in that debate but also in light of that which is silenced: *Khurbn*, a word actually pronounced by many of the victims themselves at the time.[4] But even so, on Yad Vashem's official website, the word is barely mentioned in the preliminary discussion on the Holocaust.[5] The argument that *Khurbn* is hard to pronounce simply cannot be taken seriously.

Words are important not only as a matter of accuracy but also because of their historical and symbolic weight. And linguistic options are never neutral. They were not then; they still are not. To say Khurbn, Holocaust, or Shoah is more than an elegant nuance in a linguistic quarrel; it is a political, even an existential, statement. The absence of Yiddish has imposed some interpretative trends that must be critically questioned. The most evident of these is in the study of Jewish resistance.[6] But there are other trends, even more blatant: no Holocaust scholar interested in linguistic approaches can ignore Viktor Klemperer's work and that of many who followed in his track. Very few, on the contrary, will be familiar with the work of Israel Kaplan (*Dos folks moyl in nazi klem* [Folk expression under Nazi occupation]) or Elie Spivak (*Di shprakh in di teg fun der Foterlendisher Milkhome* [Language in the days of the great patriotic war]).[7] Perhaps Nachman Blumenthal's work is more widely known, mostly in his own translation and regarding NS (*Nationalsozialismus*)-Deutsch, that is, the German language during the Nazi era. But few seem aware of the particular perspective that Blumenthal introduces by addressing NS-Deutsch not in the light of what Nazi discourses say, but from Roland Barthes's standpoint of what it forces other languages, especially Yiddish, to say.[8] Blumenthal said it in 1948, when there were no Holocaust studies but what he and others called *Khurbn Forschung* (destruction research), and he said it in Yiddish: *Di yidishe shprakh in kamf kegn nazi rezhim* (Yiddish in the battle against the Nazi regime).[9] As we can see, contrary to the popular belief that historical research on the Holocaust began in the early 1960s, already in the early 1940s Khurbn Forschung was on its way. As early as 1943, Jews all over Europe founded historical commissions, document centers, and documentation projects.[10] It is not by chance that most of their material and most of the names—for example, *Pakhakh*, an acronym for *Partizaner, khayolim un khalutzim* (Partisans, soldiers, and pioneers) and *Tzentrale Historische Komisye* (Central Historical Commission)—were in Yiddish.

In spite of all this, linguistic studies of the Khurbn have historically focused on the language of the perpetrators. Yiddish was scarcely even considered. This should be stressed: Yiddish was ignored for these linguistics studies even though it was—at least for Nachman Blumenthal—the language most affected by Nazism after German.[11]

To address such an important topic in an approach bounded by the cultural limits of the academic community, who favor a globalized English ("Americanish"), instead of attending to the singularities of the languages at stake, ignores the importance of the influence of actual language. What is here at stake is not a comparative linguistic approach but the suppression of a fundamental reading key, a critical device for our readings of the Khurbn. From a psychoanalytical point of view, we could call this suppression an inhibition, but then we will have to make it talk. If we listen to what the absence of Yiddish has to say, it can become a symptom, and we can do something other than simply denounce it: we can interpret it. Time has come to make some room for that true linguistic trauma in our elaborations because conceptualizations are an ethical matter; that is, they bear consequences.

A kval fun mut un pathos (A source of courage and pathos), wrote Rachel Auerbach (Rokhl Oyerbakh), about the discourses and manifestos of the Jewish fighters in the Warsaw ghetto.[12] That pathos is

Yiddish, and it must be a part of Holocaust narratives: "displaced person" is far from the violence that we can hear in *oysgevortzlte person*, a person who was violently torn away from his or her roots.

Perhaps "survivor" is closer to *lebngeblibene*, but this is not the only common expression in Yiddish writings. It is easy to find others, such as *di nisht dershtokhene, di nisht gehargete, di nisht gekoylete* (the not killed, the not slain, the not gunned down). How can we fail to hear the unspoken "yet" that lingers in those expressions? And how can we fail to hear the resonances of this "yet" in today's ongoing Holocaust denial in all its forms?

Musulmaner (in German *Muselmänner*, the slang term in concentration camps for a passive prisoner near death)—the speechless specter that Giorgio Agamben wanted to consecrate as the ideal witness[13]—is different from *klepsidre* (a water clock, from the Greek words for "to steal water"),[14] a word that introduces the notion of stealing time from a mandatory death sentence.

Contrary to the *Musulmaner*—whose silence seems to preserve our imaginary distance with him—*klepsidre* is any Jew under the Nazi regime: those in the ghettos or in the camps, but also any Jew inside or outside the Nazi realms; even those who by chance of fate or chronologies could be called the "unpunctual at the time of the slaughter." That is, any of us.

Regarding this absence of Yiddish, Naomi Seidman[15] has shown the difference between *Un di velt hot geshvign* (And the world stood silent)[16] written in Yiddish and its French version *Nuit* (*Night*), both by Elie Wiesel. Reading Seidman's work (whose conclusions merit a discussion that exceeds these pages), we can perceive two different survivors: one who is vengefully alive, saturated with anger and wrath, and anxious to break the indifference that surrounds him or her, who speaks Yiddish; the other, muted, broken, plunging into the silence of his or her association with death, a walking skeleton, a living dead person with no anger or wrath and, above all, with no uncanny words; this one speaks French.

We said before that Yiddish was not an official language in any of the trials. We can read Abraham Sutzkever's anguished words in his diary in Nuremberg: "*Yiddish, umbadingt Yiddish* . . . (Yiddish, by all means, Yiddish), "I want to speak in the very language of the people they wanted to exterminate."[17]

Sutzkever's urgent wish was not fulfilled. Yet Yiddish was not entirely absent from the trials either. When the first witness in the Adolf Eichmann trial was authorized to speak Yiddish, her testimony, in the words of Lawrence Douglas,[18] suppressed all distance between the audience—that is, not only the Israeli court and the survivors themselves but also the globalized public of the trial—and those who had been annihilated during the *Endlösung* (Final Solution). What was suppressed then was the distance created by a language that was, in itself, a death sentence, as we can read in this letter found on the way to Ponar, dated in June 1944:

> We are casting out this letter on our way to Ponar, so that good people should deliver it into Jewish hands . . . so that for the 112 of us, at least one [of our murderers] should be killed in revenge. This is the duty of every Jew to our nation. With tears in our eyes we plead—avenge us! avenge us! Therefore I write in Polish, because were someone to find a letter in Yiddish, he would burn it, but in Polish some good and decent person will read it and deliver it to the Jewish resistance.[19]

We all know the fate of Yiddish in the midst of the linguistic quarrels around the birth of the State of Israel. We also know the fate of the Yiddish culture under Soviet rule. The impact of these historical events on the survival of Yiddish cannot be ignored. But maybe the absence of Yiddish, pushed to the margins as English became dominant in Holocaust studies (as brilliantly demonstrated by Alan Rosen),[20] is also (and maybe primarily) tied to that ominous lack of distance with a horror that lingers. Maybe it is tied to an illusion that Yiddish—its very words actualizing a dreadful experience—seems to undermine: that of an abstract conceptualization of horror. And maybe that illusion is the commanding force behind the only official role given to Yiddish in the scope of Holocaust studies: a kind of ritual artifact, mostly in the form of songs. A paradigmatic example is Hirsch Glick's "Partisaner Lid (Partisan song)" with its dramatic opening words: *Zog nit keynmol az du geyst dem letztn veg* (Never say that you are walking down your last road). This ritual presence seems to be the only way to approach the agonizing sounds of a language that—with all its tenderness, its joyful ability for irony and curse, and its domestic, charming tone—had to pronounce the worst words in our darkest hour.

Languages are important not as relics, but as ethical questions. The ways that we address them are not just a methodological detail; they are the core of what we call memory.

Let us discuss two brief examples of what is lost when Yiddish is suppressed from our meditations.

NEKOME—THE CENSORED WORD

> Kritz oij zij in hartzn/ Dray verter fun blut / Nekome, nekome, nekome! *("Engrave in your heart, three words made of blood / Revenge, revenge, revenge!")*
>
> —*Szmerke Kaczerginski*[21]

If we listen to the words, so often in Yiddish, actually pronounced by the Jewish fighters, we will see that saving lives from the Nazi extermination machine was rarely a main objective, not because of a romantic or sacrificial stand, but because the fighters knew they were all doomed. Still, they had other, equally powerful, reasons to fight. One was their wish to pass on to future generations the fact of their having taken arms against the murderous enemy. Another was put simply in one Yiddish word: *nekome*, vengeance.

That wish to leave a legacy for future generations is frequently mentioned in the historiography on the subject, although with hagiographical overtones; but *nekome* is a word barely recalled. Yet, for Jews experiencing the Khurbn, *nekome* was always on the horizon as a wish, a mission, or an illusion: "The dream of my life has risen to become fact. Self-defense in the ghetto will have been a reality. Jewish armed resistance and revenge [*nekome*] are facts," wrote Mordechai Anielewicz, before his death.[22] "Remember to carry on with our vengeance . . . Fulfill our wish and your obligation," wrote Tzipora Bermann.[23] "*Toyte kenen shoyn kayn nekome nisht nemen* [The dead cannot take revenge anymore]," reasoned Smerke Kaczerginski, poet and fighter in the Vilna Ghetto, at a certain point.[24]

But not only fighters spoke about *nekome*: In the already-mentioned text by Elie Spivak, we find a complete chapter dedicated to *nekome*, a word that, according to the author, became the most powerful tool in the fight for justice and law. To demonstrate this, Spivak lists many new concepts that were born in Yiddish in those days, including *nekomenemer* (avengers), *folks-nekomenemer* (people's avengers), and synonyms such as *optzol* (payment), *oysleyzung* (to arrange), and *oprekhenen zikh* (to settle accounts).[25]

Nekome: The word lingers in the shadows of so many scenes that became archetypical. Chaim Kaplan wrote in his diary on the sight of the march of the pediatrician and educator Janusz Korczak with his children to the *Umschlagplatz*, the square in Warsaw where Jews were gathered for deportation: "When you see a scene like that your blood boils in your veins. All your muscles and nerves combine in a single effort that can be summarized with the word nekome."[26] When S. N. Grutman returned to the destroyed ghetto of Kovel (then Poland, now Ukraine), he stumbled into the farewell inscriptions that the annihilated Jews left on the walls of the synagogue:

> The Jews of Kovel were destroyed on August 19th 1942. Many of them were herded into the great Synagogue and from there were taken in groups to their deaths. It was only then that the farewell inscriptions were scrawled on the walls. I already knew their fate, but I wanted to find at least something to remember them by, perhaps a photograph or something else . . . When I approached the walls, I was filled with horror. The walls began to speak: Ida Soyfer, Zelig Friedman, Friedman with wife and children. Tserun Leyzer with his daughters and Sroul Katz died at the hands of the German murderers. Avenge them![27]

A word as frequent then as it is rare now, *nekome* was uttered by believers and nonbelievers, educated and laypeople, assimilated and pious, Zionists, Bundists, socialists, Communists, and reactionaries. Written in ink, lead, charcoal, or blood, it appears in inscriptions, graffiti, *notitzn* (notes), diaries, and letters: "Are these really the last moments of my life! Nekome!"[28]

The word unfolds a dramatic crease that brings tension to the language in an almost unbearable way; its very resonance provokes the reader or listener to put up his or her guard. So close and yet so far from soothing words like "justice" or "forgiveness"! What makes it so uncanny that it cannot even be listened to?

Maybe there are some answers in other words, also pronounced in the days when *nekome* was so frequent:

> [Pesach, 1942] My father began to recite the *Shfokh Khamoskho*, the passage in the *Haggadah* entreating God—Pour out Your wrath . . . My father's *Shfokh Khamoskho* was the most powerful

> curse I ever heard in my life. It was his rage, his hatred, [and] his belief that the enemy could be mortally wounded with his words . . . At that moment, his curse was also mine. I too was killing the enemy.[29]

This very Jewish way of experiencing language, this certainty that the words can hurt, that they can even kill, that bewildering force emanating from language is Yiddish. And here it is worthwhile to listen to the words of David Roskies, speaking about his experience as a member of the Khevrah Kedishah, an organization that prepares the dead for Jewish burial:

> When first it came my turn at *shemirah*, "to guard" the dead person on the eve of burial, I was not prepared to confront the full range of emotion expressed in this ancient anthology [the Psalms] . . . Nothing in my formal education or socialization as a Jew prepared me for the anguish and anger, and especially for the elemental cries for revenge that punctuate the Psalter with such regularity.
>
> What happened to this Jewish rage and why is it so hard to retrieve? It was buried I am now convinced, with the demise of a living Yiddish culture.
>
> The most important lesson I have learned, however, as a member of a khevra kadisha is that attending the dead is a *khesed shel emes*, the highest mitzvah of all, because there is no expectation of reward. We do what is required for its own sake, and out of the public eye. In Jewish tradition it is considered a greater act of loving kindness than delivering a eulogy or reciting the Kaddish.
>
> This, then, is the prescribed way of acknowledging the break, the irreparable loss. One must first voice the Yiddish anger that lies buried just beneath the surface. One must, above all, distinguish between past significance and present meaning, which is to say, attempt to understand modern Yiddish culture on its own terms.[30]

Perhaps this is why Franz Kafka warned us that, if we listen intently to Yiddish, we will soon become afraid, not of the language, but of ourselves.[31]

DER LETZTER—THE WORD IN SOLITUDE

> Un ikh, efsher der letzter yidisher shrayber in Eyrope. *("And I, perhaps the last Yiddish writer alive in Europe.")*
>
> —*Abraham Sutzkever*

There is a frequent expression in Yiddish texts from the Khurbn: "*Ikh bin der letzter*," I am the last one. "*Di letzte fun di letzte yidn*, the last of the last Jews," Szmerke Kaczerginski called the fighters barricaded in the Vilna ghetto.[32]

Simkha Rotem, a fighter in the Warsaw ghetto, who went to the Aryan side to search for weapons and came back the night of May 8, 1943,[33] recalled in his dialogue with Claude Lanzmann in the documentary film *Shoah* (British Broadcasting Corporation, Historia, and Les Films Aleph, 1985): "I remember a moment that I felt a kind of calmness, and I said to myself: I'm the last Jew, I'm going to wait for the morning, and I'm going to wait for the Germans."[34] Even Sutzkever, in 1946, after he had survived Nazism, wrote: "And I, perhaps the last Yiddish writer alive in Europe."[35]

Der letzter—the last one—is a notion that must be considered carefully. We must avoid the temptation to merge it with "survivor," a word that, according to today's conceptualization, is considered a synonym for "victim" and has become an identifying feature that threatens to substitute for the person's name.

The generalizing overtones that pervade these conceptualizations of the survivor seem to dilute the particularities of that "*letzter*" in a kind of "reparatory ideology." In this ideology, the words of the witness are considered merely a kind of *catharsis* that may restore a supposedly lost original justice through the possibility of an "adequate" transmission of horror. But, in this rapidly globalized name—"the survivor"—the voice of *der letzter* in its singularities becomes anonymous.

Instead, *der letzter* subverts this kind of anonymity. True, something remains uncertain: The last what? To whom is the person talking if he or she is the last one? The voice of the last one rises from an uncanny place of enunciation, a place where the words are said even if there is no one to listen. These are the words of someone who stands at the limit, at the very end of the watershed, words that are addressed to no addressee. And yet, *der letzter* is the one who insists with words even if there is no one to listen; the last one insists on speaking even if there is no more language. *Der letzter* speaks to no one but, precisely in his or her loneliness, in utmost solitude, in being alone with such an unintelligible tongue, the words call forth an "other," thereby becoming an interpellation. This solitary voice challenges us. It makes present the word of the absent or, more accurately, makes present the very absence of words. It is an absence that is not merely silence but the uncanny resonance of what has been silenced. *Der letzter*, in paradoxical persistence, summons an "other" to say what the last one has no words to transmit: what it means to be in a world with no "other."

Maybe this particular value of words is what we can read in a short poem, typed in Yiddish, in the *Oyneg Shabes* Archive kept by Emanuel Ringelblum in the Warsaw ghetto.[36] It bears no author's name, not even the name of the person who typed it. We do not know if it is an original or a translation. We do not know who decided to preserve it or why. There is nothing in the poem other than its own words. And yet, we must be careful to not take these words as anonymous:

> In friling ligt der shpur
> Fun tzaytikait der harber
> S'iz eybik der natur
> Un tzaytvaylik dos shtarbn.
>
> In spring there lies a trace
> of strong maturity
> Nature is eternal
> Dying is temporary.[37]

Yiddish experienced the Khurbn, Yiddish spoke it; Yiddish is its witness. Yes, we are scholars, but we cannot afford to be neutral unless we are willing to turn Walter Benjamin's worst nightmare into a reality: to suppress—the word here should be "repress"—the voice of the doomed.[38]

NOTES

1. The work of these researchers is too vast and important to summarize in a note. Let us just say briefly that while Ruth Wisse, Alan Astro, and Ilan Stavans study Yiddish from the standpoint of its literature, Samuel Kassow, David Roskies, and Alan Rosen have addressed topics of the Holocaust that cannot be studied in depth without Yiddish culture and language. That is the case, for instance, of Samuel D. Kassow's *Who Will Write Our His-*

tory? Emanuel Ringelblum, the Warsaw Ghetto, and the Oyneg Shabes Archive (Bloomington: Indiana University Press, 2007), the first exhaustive study published in English of the archives organized by Dr. Emanuel Ringelblum in the Warsaw ghetto. Kassow shows us how Ringelblum considered the archive as a weapon—the only one that could grant Jews a posthumous justice—and directed his efforts to collect and preserve all possible material. Fluent in the many languages in which these documents were written, Kassow gives special attention to the particular Yiddish culture in which, at the end of the nineteenth and the beginning of the twentieth century, flourished a secular Jewish culture that considered the study of Yiddish history and literature as a field in itself. That was the milieu in which Ringelblum, who was founder and part of the historians' group called *di historiker* (the historians), and other intellectuals found an existential option other than the simple choice between mere assimilation or religious observance. In it, the historian becomes a main character, and historical research becomes a social practice. As Ringelblum himself, many young intellectuals followed the path of Simon Dubnow, who saw in historical conscience the expression of a secular Judaism that rejects religious ritual as its main identity feature but also rejects assimilation. Following Dubnow, young Jewish intellectuals were ready to take their past into their own hands and write their own history in their own language. This is important not only in reference to Ringelblum's work but also in reference to the remarkable "archival impulse" that pervaded the Jews under Nazi oppression, an impulse that resulted in many collections of historical documents. The *Oyneg Shabes* Archive in the Warsaw ghetto was the biggest but by no means the only one. To consider the differences among the many archives, we must consider the differences among the places where these archives were born. Thus, for example, we must consider the particularities of the Warsaw and Łódź ghettos (both had their own archives): Jews in Warsaw lived in a binational and multilingual city, while those of Łódź, the "Manchester of Poland," did not; in Warsaw, the members of the *Judenrat* (Jewish council) were not included among the archivists, while in Łódź some of them took active part in it. The same need to attend to particularities of the place holds in the case of the archives made in the *shtetlekh* (predominantly Jewish towns in Eastern Europe), from which 20 percent of the Holocaust victims came. See Perla Sneh, *Palabras para decirlo Lenguaje y exterminio* [The words to say it: Language and extermination] (Buenos Aires, Argentina: Paradiso, 2012).

2. Jacob Glatstein, Israel Knox, Samuel Margoshes, Mordecai Bernstein, and Adah B. Fogel, eds. *Anthology of Holocaust Literature* (New York: Atheneum, 1980).

3. Cyril Aslanov, *Sociolingüística histórica de las lenguas judías* [Historical sociolinguistics of Jewish languages] (Buenos Aires, Argentina: Lilmod,

2011), 183–84. Ladino or Judeoespañol (Jewish-Spanish) was spoken in medieval Spain by Jews who, when expelled in 1492, took it with them and preserved its legacies, which flourished in a rich culture. Ladino, as well as Yiddish, found its most terrible enemy in Nazism, which decimated its speakers in a linguistic drama of its own: unlike Yiddish, genetically tied to the German language, Ladino had no ties at all with Germanic tongues, and this gave way to what Aslanov call a "mute assassination." If not all the Sephardic world was threatened by Nazism, it is important to mention that even Jewish communities in Turkey were affected. In the 1920s and 1930s, many Sephardic Jews immigrated to France (especially Paris and Marseille) where, after the Nazi invasion, they were arrested by the French collaborating police. The presence among the deportees of Jews from Greece, Turkey, and, to a lesser extent, Egypt and Palestine can be appreciated in the victims lists reconstructed by Serge Klarsfeld. As Drita Tutunovic, a Sephardic Jew from Belgrade, said: *"Mi nona disho: si mos van a matar a todos, a lo manko vamos a murir avlando muestra lingua. Es la sola koza ke mos keda i no mos la van a tomar."* [My grandmother said: if they are going to kill us all, at least we will die speaking our tongue. It is the only thing that is left us and they are not going to take it away from us.] See also Salvador Santa Puche, "Una lengua en el infierno: el judeoespañol en los campos de extermino [A language in hell: Jewish-Spanish in the extermination camps]," *Tonos Digital, Revista electrónica de Estudios Filológicos* [Digital tones: Electronic journal of language studies] 5 (April 2003); https://www.um.es/tonosdigital/znum5/estudios/J-infierno.htm.

4. Even in Yiddish, the word *khurbn* is not the only one: we can also find *der mabl* (the deluge), *di katastrofe* (the catastrophe), and *dem dritn khurbn* (the third destruction). *Der umglick* (the disgrace) was a common expression among Yiddish-speaking Jews in Argentina, and it usually was associated with the time when they stopped receiving letters from their families in Europe. See José Winiecki, *Farn mabl: bilder fun Yiddish lebn in Poyln fun far dem Khurbn* [Before the flood: Pictures of Yiddish life in Poland before the destruction] (Mexico City: Tsevi Ḳesel-farlag bay der Ḳultur-ḳomisye fun Yidishn tsentral-ḳomitet, 1951); Melekh Ravitch, *Dos amoliḳe Yidishe Ṿarshe biz der shṿel fun driṭn khurbn, 1414–1939 : in lid, balade, poeme . . . : an antologye* [The former Jewish Warsaw on the threshold of the third destruction, 1414–1939: In songs, ballads, poems . . . an anthology] (Montreal: Varsheṿer Yidn, 1966); Jacob Lestschinsky, *Di Idishe ḳatastrofe—di metodes fun ir forshung* [The Jewish catastrophe—the methods of research] (n.p.: Instituṭ far Idishe enionim funem Idishn Amerikaner un ṿelt-ḳongres, 1944); Shlomo Shapiro, *Zikhroynes fun a maran in der tḳufe fun der Natzi-ḳaṭasṭrofe* [Memories of a Marrano: In the era of the Nazi catastrophe] (Buenos Aires, Argentina: Tsentral-farband fun Poylishe Yidn, 1963).

5. See Yad Vashem, *The Holocaust: Definition and Preliminary Discussion*, http://www.yadvashem.org/yv/en/holocaust/resource_center/the_holocaust.asp, where we can read: "Various interpretations of these historical events have given rise to several other terms with different shades of meaning: destruction (used in Raul Hilberg's book), catastrophe (in use mainly in the research literature in Soviet Russia), and *khurbn* (destruction) and *gezerot tash–tashah* (the decrees of 1939–1945) (used in ultra-Orthodox communities)."

6. The biases in the study of Jewish resistance are a topic in itself. Let us just mention here, briefly, the problem of the sources. There are three main books on the story of the Khurbn that, for different reasons, insist on considering only German sources: Bruno Bettelheim's *Surviving the Holocaust* (London: Fontana, 1986), Raul Hilberg's *The Destruction of the European Jews* (New Haven, Conn.: Yale University Press, 2003), and Hannah Arendt's *Eichmann in Jerusalem: A Report on the Banality of Evil* (Barcelona, Spain: Lumen, 1999). Hilberg had a methodological reason for his choice: he wanted to track down the development of the "Final Solution" precisely as it emerges from German documents. Bettelheim, instead, did not speak any Jewish language. As for Arendt, she did know some Hebrew but did not know (and probably despised) Yiddish. Perhaps a single quotation from Arendt's book is enough to state our point, what is lost when Jewish—especially Yiddish—sources are left aside. She says (p. 44): "We know, from Nazi sources, that Jews never were 'rebels.'" If the main language of the Jewish fighters was Yiddish, how can we expect to track their history in "Nazi sources"? I would like to add here that, in their time, both Arendt and Hilberg were considered as coinciding in their characterization of the Jewish leadership. But their arguments were remarkably different: what was considered by Hilberg a tragic and catastrophic error in perception was considered by Arendt as corruption and, in fact, treason. That is, she makes a moral accusation. This topic would merit a paper on its own and exceeds the limits of this work.

7. Israel Kaplan, *Dos Folks-moyl in Natzi-klem—Reydenishn in ghetto un katzet* [Popular language under Nazi oppression—expressions in ghettos and concentration camps] (Munich: Central Historical Commission of the liberated Jews in the American Zone in Germany, 1949). Israel Kaplan, a journalist in Kovno, Poland, before the war, together with Moshe Feygenbaum, created the Central Historical Commission in Munich in 1945 (alongside the already existing Central Committee of the Liberated Jews). Kaplan published a journal in Yiddish, *Fun letztn khurbn* [On our most recent catastrophe] from 1946 to 1948 that sought to gather testimonies systematically. Declaring that even under the most extreme conditions folk creativity (*folksshafung*) could not be stopped, Kaplan collected "newly

created folklore" (including gallows humor, code words, and sayings) in the ghettos and concentration camps he had survived and published this material immediately after the war, first in the periodical he edited, and in 1949 in book form (*Dos Folks-moyl in Natsi-klem*). Elie Spivak, *Di shprakh in di teg fun der Foterlendisher Milkhome* [Language in the days of the great patriotic war] (Kiev, Ukrainian Soviet Socialist Republic: Academy of Science of Ukraine, 1946). Spivak (1890–1950) was born in Vasilkov, Ukraine, and was a Yiddish linguist and a teacher. In 1933, he became head of the philological section of the Kiev Institute for Jewish Culture and editor of its periodical *Afn shprakhfront* [On the language front]. In May 1934, during the Kiev Yiddish Language Conference, he formulated the principles of word formation in Soviet Yiddish, admitting inter alia that the majority of lexical innovations were loan words or calques from Russian. An advocate of retaining Slavisms in Yiddish, he played a central role in Soviet Yiddish language planning and summed up its achievements in his monograph *Naye vortshafung* [New word formation] (Kiev, Ukrainian Soviet Socialist Republic: Melukhe farlag far di natsionale minderhaytn in Uk.S.S.R.,1939). See Gershon Hundert, ed., *The Yivo Encyclopedia of Jews in Western Europe* (New Haven, Conn.: Yale University Press, 2008), http://www.yivoencyclopedia.org/. While much of Spivak's work is biased by Soviet ideology, circumstances require an insightful reading instead of its suppression. You may even find some surprises: in Spivak's discussion of the word "rebels," we read that the word mostly used was "*moyrdim*"—and he writes it in Hebrew, disregarding the rules of "Soviet Yiddish" that were directed to sever all ties of the Yiddish language with its Hebrew sources.

8. Language is "quite simply Fascist" not because of what it silences but because of what it forces us to say, said Roland Barthes in his inaugural lecture at his accession to the Chair of Literary Semiology at the Collège de France in 1977. Luckily, Barthes gave us some hope; he added that there is literature, a way to resist the coercive forces of language. But then, again: How can we address any study of the resistance to the "coercive forces" of Nazi language without Yiddish?

9. *Bleter far geshikhte (Fertlyor Shrift)* [Pages for history] 1, 3–4 (August–December, 1948) (Warsaw: Yiddisher Historiker Institut baym Tzentral Komitet fun Yidn in Poyln, 1948).

10. Laura Jockusch, "*Khurbn Forschung*—Jewish Historical Commissions in Europe 1943–1949," in Dan Diner and David B. Ruderman, eds., special issue, *Simon Dubnow Institute Yearbook* 6 (2007): 441–70.

11. For Ruth Wisse, Yiddish was the European language most affected by Nazi rule. See Ruth R. Wisse, *The Modern Jewish Canon: A Journey through Language and Culture* (Chicago: University of Chicago Press, 2003), 191.

12. Rachel Auerbach, *Der Yiddisher Oyfshtand, Varshe, 1943* [The Jewish uprising: Warsaw, 1943] (Warsaw: Tzentral Komitet fun di Yidn in Poyln, 1948), 10.

13. Giorgio Agamben, *Lo que queda de Auschwitz—El archivo y el testigo (Homo Sacer III)*, trans. A. G. Cuspinera (Valencia, Spain: Pretextos, 2000); published in English as *The Remnants of Auschwitz: The Witness and the Archive, Homo sacer III*, trans. Daniel Heller-Roazen (New York: Zone Books, 1999).

14. Szmerke Kaczerginski, *Ikh bin geven a partizan—di grine legend* [I was a partisan—the green legend], edited by friends of the author (Buenos Aires, Argentina: "Kultur" fun mushkat un zaslavski, 1952).

15. Naomi Seidman, "Elie Wiesel and the Scandal of Jewish Rage," *Jewish Social Studies* 3, no. 1 (1996): 1–19.

16. Eliezer Wiesel, *Un di velt hot geshvign* (*And the World Stood Silent*), Bikher Serie Dos Poylishe Yidntum (Buenos Aires, Argentina: Tzentral Farband fun Poylishe Yidn in Argentine, 1956).

17. Abraham Sutzkever, "Mayn eydes zogn farn Nirnberger tribunal [My testimony at the Nuremberg tribunal]," *Di Goldene Keyt* 54 (1966): 150–68.

18. Lawrence Douglas, *The Memory of Judgment* (New Haven, Conn.: Yale University Press, 2001).

19. Wisse, *The Modern Jewish Canon*, 191.

20. Alan Rosen, *Sounds of Defiance: The Holocaust, Multilingualism and the Problem of English* (Lincoln: University of Nebraska Press, 2005).

21. See Moshe Knaphais and Shmuel Rollanski, eds., *Antologye—Vidershtand un Oyfshtand* [Anthology—Resistance and revolt] (Buenos Aires, Argentina: Ateneo Literario en el IWO, 1970).

22. Document 145 in Yitzhak Arad, Israel Gutman, and Abraham Margaliot, eds., *Documents on the Holocaust: Selected Sources on the Destruction of the Jews of Germany and Austria, Poland, and the Soviet Union* (Jerusalem: Yad Vashem, 1981), http://www.yadvashem.org/odot_pdf/MicrosoftWord-206659.pdf.

23. Ibid.

24. Kaczerginski, *Ikh bin geven a partisan.*

25. Spivak, *Di shprakh in di teg fun der Foterlendisher Milkhome.*

26. Chaim Aron Kaplan, *Scroll of Agony: The Warsaw Diary of Chaim A. Kaplan*, trans. and ed. Abraham I. Katsh (New York: Macmillan, 1965).

27. *Voices of the Ghetto*, Museum Land van Axel, Axel, Netherlands, September 7–October 29, 2011, http://www.yadvashem.org/yv/en/education/seminars/european/graduate/pdf/dirk_roodzant.pdf.

28. Nachman Blumenthal, *Shmuesn vegn der Yidisher Literatur unter*

di Daytshe Okupatzie [Conversations on Yiddish literature under German occupation] (Buenos Aires, Argentina: Tzentral Farband fun Poylishe Idn in Argentine, 1966), 49.

29. Morris Wyszogrod, *A Brush with Death: An Artist in the Death Camps* (Albany: SUNY Press, 1999) cited in Robert Rozett, "Personal Accounts of the Holocaust—What Can We Glean from Them?" in Peter Y. Medding, ed., *Jews and Violence: Images, Ideologies, Realities*, vol. 18 of *Studies in Contemporary Jewry* (New York: Oxford University Press, 2002), 219–32.

30. David Roskies, "Yiddish in the Twentieth Century: A Literature of Anger and Homecoming," in Leonard J. Greenspoon, ed., *Yiddish Language & Culture: Then & Now*, vol. 9 of *Studies in Jewish Civilization* (Omaha: Creighton University Press, 1998), 1–16.

31. Franz Kafka, "Introductory lecture on Yiddish language" (*Rede über die Jiddische Sprache*), given on February 18, 1912, as an introduction to an evening of recitation from Yiddish literature by Yiddish actor Yitzkhak Löwy. See Richard T. Gray, ed., *A Franz Kafka Encyclopedia* (Westport, Conn.: Greenwood, 2005).

32. Kaczerginski, *Ikh bin geven a partisan*, 163.

33. On that night, the command bunker of the Jewish fighters fell to the Germans, and most of the fighters in it committed suicide to avoid capture, including Mordechai Anielewicz.

34. Claude Lanzmann, text of *Shoah* (Paris: Gallimard, 1985).

35. Sutzkever, "Mayn eydes zogn farn Nirnberger tribunal."

36. The *Oyneg Shabes* Archive, also known as the Ringelblum Archive, is one of the most impressive and unique projects initiated by the Jews during the Holocaust. This underground archive was established and run by historian and community figure Dr. Emanuel Ringelblum, with the express purpose of documenting the reality of life under Nazi occupation. Ringelblum recruited people from all points of the political, religious, and ideological spectrum of Jewish society, who documented the influence of German occupation on private life and Jewish society in Warsaw and its environs. Ringelblum and his colleagues believed their principal mission to be the creation of a documentary infrastructure that would provide a description of the fate of Jewish society on all levels. For this reason, they were careful to gather testimonies that expressed the different perspectives of Jewish life in the Warsaw ghetto. They asked educators to write essays on Jewish education in the Warsaw ghetto, but at the same time they also gathered testimonies from children to gain the child's perspective. Among the documentation, there are texts written by men and women, Orthodox Jews and free thinkers, philosophers and ordinary people, all of which reflect the diversity and vitality of Jewish society in the Warsaw ghetto. See

www.yadvashem.org; for a complete study of the archive, see the book by Samuel Kassow mentioned in note 1.

37. *Poetry in Hell: Warsaw Ghetto Poems from the Ringelblum Archives*, trans. Sara Traister Moskovitz, http://poetryinhell.org/.

38. Walter Benjamin, "Tesis de filosofía de la historia" and "Para una crítica de la violencia" (Mexico City: La nave de los locos—Premiá, 1982); published in English as "On the Concept of History" or "Theses on the Philosophy of History" and "Critique of Violence."

Elizabeth Anthony

The First Returnees: Holocaust Survivors in Vienna in the Immediate Postwar Period

RELATIVELY FEW HOLOCAUST SURVIVORS RETURNED TO VIENNA AFTER more than seven years of Nazi persecution that included the plunder, forced emigration, and mass murder of the Austrian Jewish community. Some 130,000 Austrian Jews had fled the Nazi regime,[1] which murdered more than 65,000 of their coreligionists.[2] The formal Jewish community, once more than 185,000 strong, counted fewer than 5,000 members by the end of 1945.[3] Some did return, however, and they did so in waves. Different groups with different wartime experiences came back at different times. Those who somehow endured the war in the city returned—at least figuratively—first. Camp survivors followed soon after their liberation, then politically active returnees came back from exile, and finally politically unaffiliated émigrés arrived home from abroad.

The motivations for return for members of each group centered on different concepts of home. There were three variations. In general, those who survived the war in Vienna and those who returned from concentration camps sought to go back to a "familial home," the place where they last lived with family and friends. Once there, they harbored hopes of restoring or reviving their prewar existence. Politically active Jewish returnees arrived in Vienna with a desire to reengage in their "political home." They held idealistic intentions of taking part in rebuilding *their* Austria as an autonomous, democratic nation. Others returned to a "professional home." This group included individuals who felt bound to Austria by language or by specific training, such as writers and journalists, doctors, and lawyers.

This article focuses on the first group of Austrian Jewish "returnees," those who managed to survive in the capital under differing circumstances of protection and privilege, and who began to rebuild their lives immediately after the Red Army's victorious conquest. They reemerged to live in a society from which they had been shunned or forced and immediately began to rebuild their lives after years of persecution and deprivation. They never questioned whether or not to return; they had never left their familial home. And although they resurfaced among a people and under a government that would continue to prove antisemitic, and despite the further injustices to come, they remained.

SURVIVING IN VIENNA AND REEMERGING

Statistics from the *Ältestenrat* (Jewish Council of Elders) in Vienna reveal that in December 1944, 5,799 Jews resided in Vienna, 1,053 of whom practiced Judaism.[4] Nearly all those alive in the city at that point lived to see the Nazis fall from power.[5] But they emerged from different circumstances. Some of these survivors had lived under protected statuses due to work they performed that served Nazi interests; a few had simply been overlooked in roundups and deportations; and some had physically hidden from their persecutors.[6] Others who had intermarried with non-Jews, the offspring of such mixed marriages, and the relatives of some *Ältestenrat* employees also managed to survive.

Employees of the *Ältestenrat* found official protection in Nazi Vienna. The Nazis formed the *Ältestenrat* in November 1942, following the mass deportations of Viennese Jews in October and their dissolution of the *Israelitische Kultusgemeinde Wien* (Vienna's formal Jewish community, also referred to as the IKG or the *Kultusgemeinde*). The remaining few employees of the IKG comprised this group, which the Nazis tasked with serving the remnants of the Jewish community, those of mixed ancestry still in the city, and baptized Austrians with Jewish family heritage, the so-called non-Aryan Christians.[7] *Ältestenrat* employees and some of their family members lived in Nazi Vienna under special protected statuses, and nearly 500 survived until the end of the war.[8]

Historian Doron Rabinovici has argued that the formation of the *Ältestenrat* was in part a strategy for eliminating Vienna's Jewish population without frightening or harming the "*Volksgenossen*," a National

Socialist term referring to the community of Aryan German citizens.[9] The Nazis recognized that caring for the remaining Jewish population actually served the whole population, because some non-Jewish Austrians claimed Nazi-defined Jews as family members. Thus, a Jewish cemetery hosted burials and a Jewish hospital served patients. Jews also warranted medical care, even if only to save the non-Jewish population from disease, and therefore required separate Jewish medical facilities.

Marriage to Aryan spouses also afforded many Viennese Jews protected status for the duration of the war. As they helplessly watched the deportation of relatives and friends, they endured a terrified and insecure existence, recognizing the ever-present threat of the revocation of their protected status. In addition to potential Nazi whims of policy, the death of or divorce from a non-Jewish spouse could mean deportation.[10] During the war, some enjoyed a level of tolerance in their social surroundings, but many suffered discrimination and outright persecution. Their non-Jewish spouses also experienced penalties, including the loss of civil service positions, the inability to secure certain kinds of government-regulated loans, and the requirement to pay additional taxes. Teachers and students harassed schoolchildren from mixed families, while the regime obstructed custody disputes and pressured Aryan partners to divorce their Jewish spouses.[11] Most intermarried couples, as well as many of mixed ancestry, were left to fend for themselves in Nazi Vienna. The IKG and its successor institution, the *Ältestenrat*, provided little assistance because they were unable to stretch their sparse resources to aid nonmembers.[12] Despite the challenges facing intermarried couples, 85 to 87 percent of Vienna's intermarried Jews survived the Holocaust in the capital city.[13]

Many children resulting from marriages between Jews and non-Jews managed to outlast the war in Vienna. They owed their survival to the fact that the racial specifications and qualifications of the September 15, 1935, *Reichsbürgergesetz* (Reich Citizenship Law)—one of the Nuremberg Laws put into effect on November 14, 1935, to officially define Jews, and then used as the legal basis for their persecution and exclusion from society—did not deem them *voll Juden*, or "full Jews." Those receiving the designation *voll Juden* counted three or four Jewish grandparents in their lineage and as a result lost all rights of citizenship in the German Reich.[14] As "partial Jews," so-called *Mischlinge* (literally, "mongrels") retained citizenship and the

Nazis permitted them to stay in the city, although the threat of future deportation constantly hovered.

Anticipating a potential backlash to the persecution of "partial Jews," Nazi leadership sought to minimize alienating the sizable portion of the population with relatives falling into such a categorization by classifying *Mischlinge* in degrees based on the number of Jewish grandparents. A *Mischling ersten Grades* (*Mischling* of the First Degree) descended from two Jewish grandparents, while *Mischling zweiten Grades* (*Mischling* of the Second Degree) traced his or her lineage back to only one.[15] As long as a *Mischling* was not a member of the IKG, he or she might possibly remain alive in Nazi Vienna. If a person held membership in the Jewish community, however, the Nazis termed one a *Geltungsjude* (meaning that the individual counted as a "full Jew") and doomed the person to suffer the full brunt of Nazi racial policy. Other *Mischlinge* deemed *Geltungsjuden* included those married to full Jews, children born from mixed marriages that took place after September 17, 1935, and the illegitimate children resulting from Aryans' forbidden extramarital relations with Jews after July 31, 1936.[16]

Mischlinge of both degrees served in the *Wehrmacht* (the regular German army) and in the Reich Labor Service. However, the Nazis did not permit them to hold positions of authority in either organization, to become public officials, or to own an entailed farm estate.[17] Thus, with the ability to retain German citizenship and a differentiation between "full Jews," "half Jews," and even "quarter Jews," some *Mischlinge* lived precariously in Nazi Vienna, so long as they abided all regulations and policies governing their acceptance in society and as long as their Aryan parent remained alive.[18]

U-Boote (literally, submarines), the smallest group of Jews to survive in Vienna, endured the Nazi regime in hiding or by concealing their identity with forged or falsified documents. Assimilation proved the critical factor for securing a safe refuge or the necessary papers because close contact and good relationships with non-Jews better ensured their assistance.[19] Some lived for years in concealment, protected by friends and relatives. Others had felt secure in mixed marriages or because of mixed heritage for much of the Nazi period, but took to hiding in the final chaotic days. Some experts approximate that as many as 800 Jews lived to war's end in hiding in Vienna,[20] but estimating the number of *U-Boote* in the city and accurately counting those who survived proves difficult, as scholars rely on inherently flawed sources.[21]

Living in the city under differing degrees of hardship and concealment throughout the war, survivors reemerged into society in Vienna from one moment to the next. They went from living in the midst of warfare, as the Red Army forced out the *Schutzstaffel* (SS) and the *Wehrmacht*, to being free to move about their partially destroyed and Allied-occupied city, immediately engaging in what social and economic life existed or began at that moment. They instinctively responded to an impulse to resume life in their familial home, the only one they had ever known.

The final days of World War II proved some of the most dangerous and terrifying for Jews in Vienna. The end of the war brought chaos, uncertainty, and increased antisemitic hostility. In addition to harassment, violence, and risk of arrest by the Nazi authorities, bloody fighting raged in the streets between the Red Army and the *Wehrmacht* and SS, and Allied bombers threatened the city's residents from above. Jewish and non-Jewish residents of Vienna took cover in air-raid shelters and basements around the city, but in some cases, antisemitism placed Jews in additional danger. Non-Jewish neighbors denied Trude Berger's father access to the basement shelter of their apartment house. Their Second District home stood just meters from the front lines of the war, and Berger and her non-Jewish mother—both permitted in the basement—sat wracked with fear for the safety of their father and husband each time they endured a bombing.[22]

Loud explosions shook Viennese residents on the evening of April 12, 1945, as retreating Nazi troops blew up all but one bridge spanning the Danube Canal. The following day, the Russians took total control of Vienna. Hiding in a family friend's cellar apartment not far from the canal, *Mischlinge* Ruth Mirecki heard the blasts and remembers the following day's silence. She cautiously peeked from a window to assess the activity outside and for the first time saw Russian officers patrolling the streets, and no sign of SS officers or *Wehrmacht* troops.[23] Survivors' initial reactions were mixed. Those who spoke Slavic languages tried to communicate with their Red Army occupiers. Many were surprised by the presence of Jews in Russian units. Lucia Heilman's mother was shocked when she questioned a soldier in Polish and he replied in Yiddish. He then explained that he, too, was amazed; he and his comrades never expected to find Jews left alive in Vienna.[24]

From their positions of cover, Vienna's Jews experienced their city's partial destruction and finally emerged to welcome the arrival of the Red Army and the end of the war. Once the fighting stopped and residents realized that the Soviets had taken over the city, they ventured out to survey the destruction, to find food and water, and to search for surviving friends and family members. Berger and her mother emerged from the basement to discover the Second District—and especially their street, Glockengasse—severely damaged. Despite an unexploded bomb that had dropped through the roof into their top-floor apartment, they found Berger's father at home and alive. The family cleaned and settled into their partially destroyed residence, where the roof remained unrepaired for many weeks and rain poured in through the hole made by the bomb.[25]

Having accounted for immediate family members in their vicinity, survivors sought to locate relatives in other parts of the city. With public transportation out of working order, residents moved about on foot, confronting massive destruction and the remnants of battlefields. The fifty-three Allied air raids that the city had endured had damaged 28 percent of buildings of the once-grand capital of the Habsburg Empire and killed 8,769 Viennese civilians.[26] Hoping to find her maternal grandmother alive, Berger walked with her mother from the Second to the Seventh District. They started off across a temporary bridge spanning the Danube Canal and, in doing so, traversed the former front lines.[27] In the first few moments of their trek, they passed a corpse and a decapitated head.[28] They walked among dead cavalry horses and took in the appalling devastation that surrounded them. They were relieved finally to reach the grandmother's apartment and to find her at home. Moreover, neighbors had looted a nearby shop and shared their booty, including copious amounts of wine. Berger and her mother also savored the opportunity to wash for the first time in two weeks.[29]

All of the city's residents emerged from shelter taken in the last moments of war to discover a changed and partially destroyed Vienna. Citizens navigated the rubble to begin the process of starting lives anew, struggling simply to secure basic needs. The city lacked infrastructure, resources, a skilled labor force, and energy sources. Perhaps most immediately significant was the scarcity of food. In spring and summer 1945, the urban population subsisted on a near-starvation diet of, at most, 800 calories per person per day.[30] In the first weeks, the

Russians provided dried peas in bulk, which staved off actual starvation.[31] Survivors often talk of these worm-ridden peas and how tired they became of eating them day after day.

Not all emerging survivors could reclaim or return to their apartments as Trude Berger's family did, and securing a place to live became a top priority. Somewhat surprisingly, a number of Jews easily found new homes in the first chaotic weeks of peacetime. Many homes stood completely furnished but empty, because Nazis living in Vienna had fled the approaching Red Army only days before. On May 8, 1945, Elizabeth Welt Trahan and her father returned to their former apartment on the Strudlhofgasse and found it occupied. The Nazi tenants who had lived one floor below, however, had fled, and Trahan and her father assumed residence there.[32] While some simply moved into these empty homes, the Red Army assigned such residences to others. Lucia Heilman and her mother received a former Nazi's apartment from Russian officials, and she recalls sitting there after many years of hiding in a family friend's metal workshop. "There was a table and a chair and an armoire. It was an apartment, with curtains. It was amazing to me!" She had forgotten how an apartment looked.[33]

By August 1945, however, the provisional Austrian government had taken responsibility for the assignment of property, and problems and uncertainties arose. The central office created to handle such claims annulled the decisions of the local council reached under Soviet supervision and declared them "not yet legal," thus protecting those who had exploited the benefits of Nazi Aryanization programs. Jews who had regained their former businesses suddenly feared losing them again.[34] Jews and gentiles alike sought assistance with housing arrangements at the municipal *Wohnungsamt* (housing office). As officials matched the homeless with vacant apartments, they often provided Jews with the homes of Nazis, always stipulating that they agree to relinquish the property to the "rightful" owners upon their return.[35]

Arrangements for furnishings presented a problem for many, and the municipality tasked an office with providing those in need with necessary home goods, if only temporarily. The city of Vienna "lent" Gertrude Putschin's family a Nazi's abandoned furniture with the same condition of giving it back in the event of his or her return. In Putschin's case, that person did come back and request the furniture, and her family fulfilled the obligation to return it. The irony escaped no one in her family because they realized that the furniture had originally been stolen from Jews after the *Anschluss* (annexation of Austria).[36]

Reemerging survivors confronted the challenge of becoming reaccustomed to the once-familiar activities and tasks of daily life. Suddenly, they had to interact with people they had avoided or from whom they had hidden. Those coming out of hiding relearned the use of regular speaking voices after years of whispering. Children encountered others their own age, some for the first time. Trude Berger felt a deep sense of freedom after seven years of secrecy and distrust. Although her mother scolded them, she and her father reveled in speaking their minds without the need to worry about who might overhear.[37]

Above all, survivors confronted the insecurities and skepticism they had developed toward their neighbors over the course of the Nazi regime. After Lucia Heilman and her mother left their hiding place, the older woman trusted no one and said that "99% of all Austrians [were] Nazis."[38] Lucia claimed not to have encountered much antisemitism after the war but added, "at least none to my face." Blatant or not, survivors knew that Austrian antisemitism had existed for centuries and paved the way for their neighbors' enthusiastic and thorough participation in the Nazi expropriation of Jews' property, as well as the expulsion and mass murder of their coreligionists. Surely, this prejudice did not disappear from one day to the next. This awareness, coupled with caution after the violence and murder of the previous years, guided Viennese Jews' careful maneuvering to return to life, as they reclaimed their familial home despite those memories and the new or continued obstacles that they encountered. Living in the place they felt at home was more important.

REBUILDING IN THE CONTEXT OF POSTWAR OCCUPATION

The first phase of Vienna's occupation began immediately upon the Soviet conquest of the city in April 1945. Surviving Jews reemerged into a partially destroyed city that lacked most basic supplies. The Russians worked to reconstruct an infrastructure and to provide electric power, transportation, and nourishment for residents, but soldiers' feelings of anger and revenge after a traumatizing and brutally costly war sometimes took the form of aggression and violence. The first

Russian troops had arrived after advancing from the east through Hungary, and along the way witnessed *Wehrmacht* and SS crimes firsthand. Compounded with the knowledge of atrocity and mass murder that the Germans and their allies had committed against their families and communities at home, Russian soldiers found the assumption of their roles as civil occupation troops difficult and frequently turned to revenge. Many Austrian women suffered rape by Russian soldiers, and even more recall the persistent fear of such assault. Knowledge that Nazi policy upon the invasion of the Soviet Union had included the rape and institutionalized sex slavery of Soviet women in frontline bordellos fueled soldiers' anger and revenge targeted at Austrian women.

The Red Army pillaged Austrian industry and equipment systematically, as it did in its occupation zones in Germany. As historian Vladislav M. Zubok put it, the two countries constituted "a giant shopping mall where [the Soviets] did not pay for anything."[39] In the first few months, 100,000 railcars full of "construction materials" and "household goods" reached the Soviet Union from Russian occupation zones. The loads these railway cars carried included some 60,000 pianos, 459,000 radios, 188,000 carpets, almost a million "pieces of furniture," 3.3 million pairs of shoes, and 1.2 million coats.[40]

At the same time, the Soviets worked to reestablish municipal services, to restore gas and electric power missing in the first days after the war,[41] and to feed the population suffering from food shortages. With necessities scarce, a black market flourished, and Soviet officers and soldiers took part along with Austrian civilians.

Seeking to assemble a governmental structure and support for Soviet interests, Josef Stalin's generals and representatives in Vienna took advantage of being the first of the Allies to arrive in the capital. Days after their conquest of Vienna and before the official end of the war in Europe, they set in motion the assembly of Austrian leadership most favorable for the Soviet Union. This group of Austrian politicians went on to organize a provisional government that laid the footings for both foreign and domestic policy and set in motion the formation of a postwar Austrian identity as the Nazis' first victim, a myth that would endure for decades. In fact, many Austrians welcomed the annexation of their country by Nazi Germany.

The possibility to assume the role of "first victim" resulted from the wording of the October 30, 1943, Moscow Declaration of the

United States, British, and Soviet governments. It proclaimed the *Anschluss* null and void and called for the establishment of a free Austria, specified it as "the first free country to fall a victim to Hitlerite aggression," and referred to the Allies' intention to liberate the country from "German domination."[42] All four occupation powers' eventual endorsement and acceptance of this "victim myth" guided Austrian foreign and domestic policy. Throughout the tumult of postwar reconstruction and international public knowledge of the extent and ruthlessness of the Nazi genocidal campaign, Austrian leaders made no attempt to combat antisemitism. On the contrary, the period saw little reduction in antisemitism among citizens or leaders, and new forms of anti-Jewish discrimination and persecution emerged with the new role of Austria and Austrians as "victim."

Shrewd Austrian politicians of the postwar provisional government worked diligently to sidestep culpability for Nazi war crimes by placing total blame on the Germans. They took advantage of evolving Cold War politics to pit Western powers against the Soviets for financial gain and to secure all four Allies' acceptance of the narrative of Austria as the Nazis' first victim. Ignoring both the voluntary and thoroughly nonviolent nature of the union of Austria with Germany and the frenzied, joyful welcome that Nazi troops received upon entering the country, the Soviet-appointed interim chancellor Dr. Karl Renner and his government rewrote the *Anschluss* as an aggressive military invasion and occupation of a foreign power. They upheld the view that from 1938 to 1945 Austria had ceased to exist and therefore was not responsible for Nazi crimes. Further, the German occupiers had forced Austria into an unwanted war. With this logic, Austria as a country and all Austrians as individuals were victims. The "victim myth" became official Austrian foreign policy, putting in place a decades-long discourse that also involved antisemitism, because in this narrative all Austrians were victims and no subgroup was to be singled out as special or different.[43] With this argument, politicians also made great efforts to avoid providing aid to surviving Jews, particularly those living abroad.

Renner made his first official statement on April 27, 1945, when he proclaimed Austrian independence and autonomy and declared the *Anschluss* null and void. The pronouncement listed the ways that Nazi Germany had victimized Austria, including an "occupation" forced upon the "helpless" Austrian people, the degradation of Vienna to a provincial city, and the economic and cultural plunder of Austria's priceless art objects and natural resources. The provisional government stated in no uncertain terms that Germany had forced Austria into a war that "no Austrian ever wanted,"[44] although Renner himself had loudly supported *Anschluss* with Germany until 1938.[45]

Exploiting the Allies' wording of the 1943 Moscow Declaration, the provisional government assigned blame and responsibility to the Germans as invaders and occupiers, characterizing the end of the Nazi regime in Austria as "liberation" by Austrian resistance fighters and the Red Army.[46] An August 1945 memo from the chancellery about foreign policy and international legal aspects regarding the claims of Jewish victims held Germany solely responsible for Nazi crimes. It rationalized that Austria had not existed as a state from 1938 to 1945 and that "occupied Ostmark" had been powerless to prevent German actions.[47] Therefore, the newly reconstituted Austria was not accountable for Nazi offences and not responsible for fulfilling Jews' claims for restitution.[48]

The Renner government passed an *Opferfürsorgegesetz* (Victims' Welfare Act) in July 1945 for "victims of fascism," which included assistance to those persecuted on political grounds and for resistance fighters, but it made no provision for those oppressed on the basis of race, religion, and nationality. The *KZ-Verband*, an association representing the interests of former concentration camp prisoners, also initially excluded the same groups but finally took on a representative from the IKG and made *Opferausweise* (victim identification papers) available to Jewish victims in 1946.[49]

The denial of victims' welfare benefits to Jews represents a particularly shameful episode in Austrian history. Even with the Russians' practice of appropriating property, Austria and its citizens profited immensely from the vast wealth commandeered from Austrian Jews under the Nazi regime. After the war, impoverished, physically abused, and mentally traumatized Jews comprised the most vulnerable and devastated victim group. As part of the postwar quest to cast the nation as the innocent victim of the Germans, however, Austrian law delineated victim groups in a way that included almost all citizens *except* Jews. Denied the status provided to their non-Jewish compatriots, surviving Jews in Austria received neither significant monetary support nor tax relief until 1949. The government fleeced them of what should have been their entitlement as Austrian citizens during the desperate postwar years. For the second time within a decade, the Austrian government robbed the Jews.

As it excluded Austrian Jews, the government at the same time accommodated needy "Austrian war victims," including victims of political persecution, resistance fighters, and ultimately veterans of the *Wehrmacht*. By denying Austrian Jews their rightful nationality, the postwar government validated the underlying sentiment that the Jews' prewar standing as unofficial second-class citizens had been strengthened and deepened by seven years of Nazi ideology. Rather than an attitude shift accompanying what seemed a radical change in leadership and the end of persecution and genocide, Nazi racial thought remained embedded in the Austrian national mind-set and in official policy.

In its fervent effort to portray Austria internationally as distinctly not German and to evade responsibility for misdeeds in which the nation and its citizens actively took part, the Renner government revealed its understanding of the massive crimes committed. By erasing details, it defined both the distinctly *German* Nazi crimes and Austria's innocence. The government positioned itself solidly with the Allied endorsement of its "first victim" status and began a decades-long shirking of responsibility and financial obligation to its former citizens, while also framing the development of postwar Austrian national identity.

WESTERN OCCUPATION POWERS IN VIENNA

The Allies officially delineated the four occupation zones of Austria on July 4, 1945, and at the same time established the Allied Council to govern the occupation regime.[50] However, the Russians worked alone in Vienna until the end of July 1945, when U.S. advance teams arrived to commence preparations for the Allied Council and to set the groundwork for quadripartite control.[51] Upon the urging of U.S. General Mark W. Clark, the other Western powers joined the Russians in Vienna in early fall 1945, and the first Allied Council meeting took place on September 12, 1945.[52] By early 1946, the Allies had approximately 260,000 troops in Austria.[53]

Even before the end of the war, seeds of coming Cold War tensions had spurred the British and Americans to worry about the spread of Communism. Anticipating Soviet domination in Eastern Europe, the British, the French, and the Americans set their sights on securing an autonomous Austria with a goal of neutrality, which would work toward the containment of Russian expansion.[54] Distrustful of the Soviet-appointed Renner, the Western powers finally recognized the provisional government on October 20, 1945,[55] and the start of the official four-power occupation helped launch it into a position of ruling the entire country. The Allies ultimately endorsed the "first victim" version of Austrian World War II history as detailed in their own wording of the 1943 Moscow Declaration and elaborated and propagated by the Renner and subsequent administrations. All four powers accepted the fabrication and focused on the political and economic integration of Austria in the context of increasingly tense Cold War politics.

The Western Allies' tolerance of this view of Austria under the Nazis entailed dropping interest in denazification, demilitarization, and disarmament, all to quell the perceived threat of Austrian Communist leaders and a potential Soviet takeover.[56] At the same time, the Russians felt wary of Austria becoming an "American colony" and supported Austrian neutrality.[57] Cunning Austrian politicians exploited the Western Allies' fears of Soviet expansion to gain further investment, which the United States ultimately carried out with funds of the Marshall Plan,[58] which also served to ease the economic burden created by the Red Army's exploitation of its occupation zone for de facto war reparations.[59] Austrian leaders secured the nation's postwar identity as victim and shirked moral and financial responsibility for the Austrian part in Nazi crimes.

THE FIRST AUSTRIAN ELECTIONS

Throughout the initial power struggles, antisemitism in government remained constant. In October 1945, Aaron Ehrlich, the president of the Jewish Merchants' Association of Vienna, publicly cited Austrian People's Party leader Leopold Kunschak's antisemitic speeches. Ehrlich complained that Nazis still held governmental positions and that their anti-Jewish sentiments influenced the granting of licenses, the reinstatement of citizenship, and the allocation of housing. Gaining no support from the Austrian government, Ehrlich specified that the Jewish community waited and hoped for the Allied occupation officials' intervention.[60]

The first federal elections (November 25, 1945) ushered in a coalition government of the conservative Austrian Peoples' Party and the

Socialist Party of Austria, which lasted for more than twenty years. Chancellor Leopold Figl led the government and continued Renner's foreign and domestic policies, including selling Austria as the Nazis' "first victim" to the international community to reestablish Austrian national identity as particularly anti-German.[61]

The election results proved disappointing for the Jewish community, and leaders expressed dismay that not one Jew gained elected office, although the provisional Renner government had included three.[62] To make matters worse, well-known antisemites, including Leopold Kunschak and Julius Raab,[63] attained official positions, reflecting the preferences of the electorate. The IKG feared that the results would deter Austrian Jews' repatriation and that those in Austria would become more determined to emigrate.[64] Chancellor Figl's response in defense of the appointments of Raab and Kunschak was telling. He explained that, for example, Kunschak was "not antisemitic on racial grounds, but economic grounds."[65] The Allied Control Commission actually vetoed Julius Raab's appointment but permitted him to remain a member of Parliament. Kunschak retained his position.[66]

The Austrian Communist Party had also expected to earn a greater representation in the government but received only 5 percent of the votes. After years of Nazi anti-Bolshevik propaganda, the anti-Communist sentiment that existed before the *Anschluss*, and the more recent experience with the Soviet occupiers, Austrian voters felt no warmth for or interest in voting for Communist representatives.

RESTORING THE JEWISH COMMUNITY

As returning émigrés and camp survivors slowly started to join Vienna's remaining Jews in reclaiming their homes, the reviving IKG encountered numerous obstacles in restoring its community and institutions. Allied bombs had damaged the IKG headquarters on the Seitenstettengasse and destroyed most of the official records. After the Soviet occupation, the IKG gathered the surviving property and papers and moved them by horse and cart to the community-owned building at Schottenring 25, where they reestablished a central office.[67]

The Nazi-appointed *Ältestenrat* continued its leadership of the IKG in the immediate postwar days,[68] but ultimately many wartime officials were relieved of their duties. By the end of summer 1945, survivors of concentration camps—both returning Viennese residents and Eastern European Jews in the city at war's end—made up a significant portion of the IKG's constituency. Pulling together a professional staff from this physically and psychologically traumatized pool proved challenging. Determining the best ways to serve this impoverished, malnourished, and emotionally distraught group represented the community's greatest problem. The needs of their members had been previously unimaginable and unprecedented.

MEETING THE NEEDS OF A TRAUMATIZED COMMUNITY

Before 1938, looking after the community's religious affairs and a few associated charitable activities had occupied the IKG leaders and staff. After the Holocaust, the priorities and tasks shifted dramatically.[69] In 1945, no Jewish cultural or communal life remained, and the IKG had not yet resumed offering religious education.[70] Youth group efforts, such as the reestablishment of the Hakoah Jewish athletic association in Vienna, represented the only Zionist life in the city.[71] As survivor and postwar resident of Vienna Leon Zelman wrote, "[The IKG was] confronted with tasks we can't imagine today . . . just to make basic life possible."[72]

Over the course of the first year after the war, the IKG created new departments to meet the particular needs of returnees, including a newly founded *Fürsorgeabteilung* (Welfare Department) that provided financial support, clothing, and furniture to surviving Jews. The Jewish community regained its hospital on the Malzgasse and assumed care for the residents in its nursing home and pediatric hospital. A lending library, an emergency soup kitchen, and a variety of workshops began or resumed work supporting the community.[73] A December 21, 1945, article in the German-language Jewish refugee and anti-Nazi publication *Aufbau* (Construction) depicted the U.S. high commissioner for Austria General Clark and the forces under his command as particularly helpful and supportive of Vienna's Jews and their negotiations with the Allies to reclaim property and institutions in their different zones of occupation.[74]

In addition to the dramatically altered needs of the community, the postwar IKG also attracted new segments of the population to its membership. Many of those who took active roles in rebuilding the IKG had had little or no contact with a Jewish identity or with the Jewish community before 1938,[75] but their return to a home changed by Nazi ideology, exploitation, and persecution—not to mention the wholesale slaughter of 65,000 of their relatives and friends—necessitated a new outlook. Identification with and membership in the IKG took on a different meaning after Viennese Jews' shared experiences during the Holocaust. Reclaiming a familial home also required a new approach to community and identity.

SUPPORT OF FOREIGN ORGANIZATIONS

The postwar IKG depended on the financial support of foreign—mostly American—Jewish organizations. In particular, the American Jewish Joint Distribution Committee (the "Joint," or JDC) played a crucial role in providing for survivors' urgent needs.[76] Postwar issues of the German-Jewish immigrant newspaper *Aufbau* illustrate the active interest and role of support taken by American Jewish groups and individuals. Advertisements for organizations offering to ship packages of food and supplies to Jews in Europe filled its pages.[77] Many specified their service to Vienna's Jews.

The IKG and the Joint took the firm position of utilizing their limited resources to support Jewish community members only. The pre-*Anschluss* IKG, like other religious communities in Austria, received monies from the state collected through a government-regulated tax on official members. These funds supported IKG services and institutions in the city, and contributors to the system were entitled to its benefits. Those who formally left the community for whatever reason—most for the purposes of marriage to non-Jews—had officially relinquished their membership and were no longer considered part of the community, and thus had no claim to its support or services. Before March 1938, the logic of this policy went unquestioned.

The postwar IKG, however, encountered challenges when surviving *Mischlinge* and the Nazi-persecuted spouses involved in mixed marriages sought assistance as Jews. Persecuted on the basis of Nazi race laws for more than seven years, many of these survivors felt entitled to assistance, although they were not members of the IKG nor did they seek to be.[78] Others sought membership for the first time, some of them intent on showing solidarity.[79] IKG members and leadership treated such new affiliates with suspicion, concerned that they officially joined the community to ensure the receipt of material benefits, such as Joint care packages.[80]

THE "DENAZIFICATION" OF THE IKG

As the IKG reconstructed itself, controversy arose about the continuity of leadership. In 1945, the Allies brought to trial former *Ältestenrat* leaders, Jewish community employees, and Jewish doctors of the Jewish hospital to answer for their functions during the Nazi regime. The IKG naturally found this task most difficult and awkward. Nazi policies of robbery, forced emigration, and genocide had forced community leaders to provide lists first for emigration and later for deportation. As a result, many community members viewed them as collaborators with the Nazi oppressors.[81] Others claimed that they owed the leaders their lives. Historians Herbert Rosenkranz[82] and Doron Rabinovici[83] analyzed the work of the IKG (later, *Ältestenrat*) leadership, and both acknowledged the profound complexity of their extraordinary position as victims forced to serve as functionaries under the Nazis. Both scholars focused on the considerable accomplishments of the IKG in rescuing a significant portion of its community, and underscored what they have deemed as an impossibility to pass judgment. But this restraint was not possible in the immediate aftermath of the Holocaust.

Jewish leaders who served under Nazi domination would be questioned about their activities for decades to come. Vienna-based Holocaust survivor and famous Nazi hunter Simon Wiesenthal, for example, judged any and all of them guilty of collaboration with the Nazis. In 1966, he officially called for the IKG to bar all former *kapos* (concentration camp prisoners elevated to positions of authority over other prisoners) and members of the *Jüdenrate* (Jewish ghetto leadership) from Jewish community functions.[84] Despite supportive arguments on behalf of former "Elders" and functionary Jewish prisoners, and the official exoneration of many, some remained haunted, and a number committed suicide.[85] Survivors who returned to Vienna shared a common history of persecution under the Nazis, but this remnant emerged from varied wartime experiences and roles that often created new divisions and hardships which some were unable to overcome.

As Austrian Jews reemerged from varying levels of hiding and as concentration camp survivors began to make their way home, newspapers reported to an international audience that Jews did not actually wish to remain in Austria. *Aufbau* wrote in August 1945 that returnees came only to find relatives and few wanted to stay in Vienna.[86] The *New York Times* related a January 1946 poll of Viennese Jews stating that two-thirds of them wished to emigrate from Europe as soon as possible.[87] The *Jüdisches Echo*, an Austrian Jewish cultural and political magazine founded by a Jewish university student association, characterized the immediately postwar *Kultusgemeinde* as going about its work bureaucratically and claimed it lacked heart.[88]

In fact, Austrian Jews who survived the war in Vienna "returned" to reestablish their lives, and the IKG re-formed, with its first postwar open elections in the context of the foreign and domestic policies of the Austrian government gelling under the eagerly assumed "victim myth." Accustomed to navigating varying degrees of hostility and discrimination before the *Anschluss*, Viennese Jews had deftly maneuvered pervasive antisemitism, overt and otherwise, as highly assimilated and acculturated members of society. When the Nazis were finally defeated, Jews who had survived in Vienna reemerged into life in an occupied Austria, where the Allied forces—and in particular, the Americans—helped ensure them a level of acceptance. Once again, they learned what to confront and what to ignore as they assessed the everyday realities of living among people who had never intended on their return, as well as under a government set on establishing the country and its citizens as victims. Their situation amid the continuing antisemitism of postwar Vienna presented them with difficulties ranging from securing food to finding permanent housing, and gave constant reminders and conditioning that shaped the way they came to live and interact in their homes.

Many who survived in the capital never faced an actual or even a philosophical decision about "returning home." They resurfaced into the society from which the Nazis had brutally thrust them years before and went about tending to immediate daily needs, reestablishing their lives in their familial home, the only one they had ever known. They were, after all, Austrians, and they navigated Austrian politics and society with Viennese sensibilities to coexist in an unequal and precarious situation. "Yes," Trude Berger said in an interview, "and that was 'peace,' and relatively speaking it was naturally not yet peaceful, but it was the end of the war."[89]

NOTES

1. Helga Embacher, *Neubeginn ohne Illusionen: Juden in Österreich nach 1945* [New beginning without illusions: Jews in Austria after 1945] (Vienna: Picus, 1995), 19.

2. Austrian historian Jonny Moser calculated that 65,459 Austrian Jews perished in the Holocaust. See Jonny Moser, "Der Verfolgung der Juden [The persecution of the Jews]," in Wolfgang Neugebauer, ed., *Widerstand und Verfolgung in Wien 1934–1945: eine Dokumentation* [Resistance and persecution in Vienna 1934–1945: A documentation] (Vienna: Österreichischer Bundesverlag für Unterricht, Wissenschaft und Kunst, 1975), 202.

3. Ibid.

4. The Nazis formed the *Ältestenrat* in November 1942, following the mass deportations of Viennese Jews the month before. *Ältestenrat* members had been part of the leadership of the disbanded Jewish community of Vienna, and the Nazis tasked them with administering and serving the city's remaining Jews.

5. Doron Rabinovici, *Instanzen der Ohnmacht: Wien 1938–1945, Der Weg zum Judenrat* [Instances of powerlessness: Vienna 1938–1945, the path to the Jewish Council] (Frankfurt am Main, Ger.: Jüdischer, 2000), 241. Historian Jonny Moser estimated that 5,538 Jews—those who self-identified as Jewish, as well as those defined by Nazi "racial" laws—survived in Vienna to the end of the war, while Gertrude Schneider approximated a slightly higher total of 5,600. See Jonny Moser, *Demographie der jüdischen Bevölkerung Österreichs 1938–1945* [Demography of the Jewish population of Austria 1938–1945] (Vienna: Dokumentationsarchiv des österreichischen Widerstandes [Documentation Centre of Austrian Resistance, or DÖW], 1999), 55; and Gertrude Schneider, *Exile and Destruction: The Fate of Austrian Jews, 1938–1945* (Westport, Conn.: Praeger, 1995), 157.

6. Schneider, *Exile and Destruction*, 157.

7. Rabinovici, *Instanzen der Ohnmacht*, 241.

8. Embacher, *Neubeginn ohne Illusionen*, 27. Doron Rabinovici writes that as of January 17, 1943, 318 paid employees and volunteers of the Jewish community remained in Vienna, 221 of whom were subject to persecution as "full Jews" by Nazi law. The Nazis permitted each of them to protect one person, and in this way another 170 relatives were saved. See Rabinovici, *Instanzen der Ohnmacht,* 345.

9. Rabinovici, *Instanzen der Ohnmacht*, 317.

10. Embacher, *Neubeginn ohne Illusionen*, 45.

11. Evan Burr Bukey, *Jews and Intermarriage in Nazi Austria* (New York: Cambridge University Press, 2011), 3.

12. Ibid., 13–14.

13. Ibid., 191.

14. Nationalsozialistische Deutsche Arbeiterpartei (NSDAP or Nazi Party) and Robert Ley, *Organisationsbuch der NSDAP* (Munich: Zentralverlag der NSDAP, 1940), 569–75. Tables 1–6 illustrate racial specifications and qualifications of the *Reichsbürgergesetz* and the *Gesetz zum Schutze des deutschen Blutes und der deutschen Ehre* [Law for the protection of German blood and honor], both passed on September 15, 1935, and put into effect by official act on November 14, 1935.

15. Ibid., 569–75.

16. Ibid., 573.

17. Bukey, *Jews and Intermarriage in Nazi Austria*, 15.

18. Embacher, *Neubeginn ohne Illusionen*, 45.

19. C. Gwyn Moser, "Jewish *U-Boote* in Austria, 1938–1945," in *Simon Wiesenthal Center Annual*, vol. 2 (Chappaqua, N.Y.: Rossel, 1984–1990), 58.

20. Brigitte Ungar-Klein, "Überleben im Versteck—Rückkehr in die Normalität? [Survival in hiding—return to normality?]," in Alexander Friedmann, Elvira Glück, and David Vyssoki, eds., *Überleben der Shoah—und danach* [Survival of the Shoah—and beyond] (Vienna: Picus, 1999), 35.

21. Brigitte Ungar-Klein, "Bei Freunden untergetaucht—U-Boot in Wien [Into hiding with friends—U-Boot in Vienna]," in *Der Pogrom 1938: Judenverfolgung in Österreich und Deutschland. Dokumentation eines Symposiums der Volkshochschule Brigittenau* [The 1938 pogrom: Jewish persecution in Austria and Germany, documentation of a symposium of the Volkshochschule Brigittenau] (Vienna: Picus, 1990), 87.

22. Trude Berger, interview 47865, USC Shoah Foundation Visual History Archive, accessed May 2, 2010, at the Strassler Center for Holocaust and Genocide Studies, Clark University, Worcester, Mass.

23. Ruth Merecki, interview 38836, USC Shoah Foundation Visual History Archive, accessed August 1, 2011, online at the United States Holocaust Memorial Museum, Washington, D.C.

24. Lucia Heilman, interview 30402, USC Shoah Foundation Visual History Archive, accessed August 7, 2011, online at the United States Holocaust Memorial Museum.

25. Trude Berger, interview 47865, USC Shoah Foundation Visual History Archive.

26. Walter Kleindel, *Die Chronik Österreichs* [The chronicle of Austria] (Dortmund, Ger.: Chronik, 1984), 537.

27. After the Red Army's victory, the Soviets erected a makeshift bridge spanning the Danube Canal to rejoin the two sides of Vienna.

28. Trude Berger, interview 47865, USC Shoah Foundation Visual History Archive.

29. Ibid.

30. Jill Lewis, "Dancing on a Tight Rope: The Beginning of the Marshall Plan," in Günter Bischof, Anton Pelinka, and Dieter Stiefel, eds., *The Marshall Plan in Austria* (New Brunswick, N.J.: Transaction, 2000), 142.

31. Ibid.

32. Elizabeth Welt Trahan, *Walking with Ghosts: A Jewish Childhood in Wartime Vienna* (New York: Peter Lang, 1998), 214. Trahan recalled finding the previous tenants' copy of Adolf Hitler's *Mein Kampf* in a drawer. She threw it away, fearing the Russians might find it in her possession.

33. Lucia Heilman, interview 30402, USC Shoah Foundation Visual History Archive.

34. "Confusion in Austria Makes It Difficult for Jews to Regain Their Former Dwellings," *Jewish Telegraphic Agency*, August 30, 1945.

35. Historian and Holocaust survivor Jonny Moser and his family encountered this same situation in their attempts to secure an apartment. He reported that they agreed without a second thought to the condition that they give up the apartment if the former owners returned to claim it; they simply needed a place to live. Author interview with Jonny Moser, February 9, 2011, Vienna. Also see Jonny Moser, *Wallenbergs Laufbursche: Jugenderinnerungen 1938–1945* [(Raoul) Wallenberg's errand boy: Childhood memories 1938–1945] (Vienna: Picus, 2006), 349–50.

36. Brigitte Bailer, Florian Freund, Elisabeth Klamper, Wolfgang Neugebauer, Gerhard Ungar, and Brigitte Ungar-Klein, eds., *Erzählte Geschichte: Berichte von Widerstandskämpfern und Verfolgten, Band 3: Jüdische Schicksal* [Oral history: Reports of resistance fighters and victims, volume 3: Jewish destiny] (Vienna: Österreichischer Bundesverlag, 1992), 687–88. For more information on the Aryanization of Jewish property in Austria and postwar restitution and compensation, see Clemens Jabloner, Brigitte Bailer-Galanda, Eva Blimlinger, Georg Graf, Robert Knight, Lorenz Mikoletzky, Bertrand Perz, Roman Sandgruber, Karl Stuhlpfarrer, and Alice Teichova, *Schlussbericht der Historikerkommission der Republik Österreich: Vermögensentzug während der NS-Zeit sowie Rückstellungen und Entschädigungen seit 1945 in Österreich; Zusammenfassungen und Einschätzungen* [Final report of the Historians' Commission of the Republic of Austria: Expropriation during the Nazi era and restitution and compensation since 1945 in Austria, summaries and assessments] (Vienna: Oldenbourg, 2003), as well as the many publications of the Historikerkommission der Republik Österreich available in PDF form at http://www.historikerkommission.gv.at.

37. Trude Berger, interview 47865, USC Shoah Foundation Visual History Archive.

38. Lucia Heilman, interview 30402, USC Shoah Foundation Visual History Archive.

39. Vladislav M. Zubok, *A Failed Empire: The Soviet Union in the Cold*

War from Stalin to Gorbachev (Chapel Hill: University of North Carolina Press, 2009), 9.

40. Ibid.

41. Irene Bandhauer-Schöffmann and Ela Hornung, "War and Gender Identity: The Experience of Austrian Women, 1945–1950," in David F. Good, Margarete Grandner, and Mary Jo Maynes, eds., *Austrian Women in the Nineteenth and Twentieth Centuries: Cross-Disciplinary Perspectives* (Providence, R.I.: Berghahn, 1996), 219.

42. U.S. Department of State, *A Decade of American Foreign Policy: Basic Documents, 1941–49, Prepared at the Request of the Senate Committee on Foreign Relations by the Staff of the Committee and the Department of State* (Washington, D.C.: Government Printing Office, 1950).

43. For more on the "victim myth," see Heidemarie Uhl's analysis of its origins and development in her chapter "From Victim Myth to Co-Responsibility Thesis: Nazi Rule, World War II, and the Holocaust in Austrian Memory," in Richard Ned Lebow, Wulf Kansteiner, and Claudiol Fogu, eds., *The Politics of Memory in Postwar Europe* (Durham, N.C.: Duke University Press, 2006), 40–72.

44. Bundesministerium für Unterricht (Federal Ministry for Education), *Freiheit für Österreich. Dokumente* [Freedom for Austria: Documents] (Vienna: Österreichischer Bundesverlag, 1955), 11–14.

45. David Wilsford, *Political Leaders of Contemporary Western Europe: A Biographical Dictionary* (Westport, Conn: Greenwood, 1995), 385–86.

46. Uhl, "From Victim Myth to Co-Responsibility Thesis," 66.

47. After the *Anschluss* (annexation of Austria), the Nazis named the Third Reich province comprised of former autonomous Austrian territory the "Ostmark."

48. Robert Knight, *"Ich bin dafür, die Sache in die Länge zu ziehen," Wortprotokolle der österreichischen Bundesregierung von 1945–52 über die Entschädigung der Juden* ["I am in favor of letting the matter drag on," transcripts of the Austrian government from 1945–52 on compensation for Jews] (Frankfurt am Main, Ger.: Athenäum, 1988), 105.

49. Bailer, Freund, Klamper, Neugebauer, Ungar, and Ungar-Klein, *Erzählte Geschichte*, 672.

50. Günther Bischof, "Allied Plans and Policies for the Occupation of Austria, 1938–1955," in Rolf Steininger, Günther Bischof, and Michael Gehler, eds., *Austria in the Twentieth Century* (New Brunswick, N.J.: Transaction, 2009), 172.

51. Ibid., 175.

52. Ibid.

53. Marianne Enigl and Christa Zöchling, "Die ungeliebten Befreier [The unloved liberators]," *Profil* 38 (May 5, 2012): 50–52. This number

includes 150,000 Soviet, 55,000 British, 40,000 U.S., and 15,000 French occupation troops.

54. Bischof, "Allied Plans and Policies," 168.

55. Bischof, "Between East and West," 127.

56. Günther Bischof, *Austria in the First Cold War, 1945–55: The Leverage of the Weak* (New York: St. Martin's, 1999), 3.

57. Günther Bischof, "Between East and West: The Origins of Post World War II Austrian Diplomacy during the Early Occupation Period," in Günther Bischof, Anton Pelinka, and Michael Gehler, *Austrian Foreign Policy in Historical Context* (New Brunswick, N.J.: Transaction, 2006), 130.

58. Bischof, *Austria in the First Cold War*, 5.

59. Bischof, "Allied Plans and Policies," 178.

60. "Anti-Semitism in Austria Is Now as Strong as under the Nazis, Jewish Leader Charges," *Jewish Telegraphic Agency*, October 3, 1945.

61. Bischof, "Between East and West," 127.

62. "Austrian Provisional Government Includes Three Jews; Largest Number Ever Named to Cabinet," *Jewish Telegraphic Agency*, May 3, 1945.

63. Before the *Anschluss*, Julius Raab had been a Christian Social Party representative for Lower Austria in the national parliament and was an active member of the *Heimwehr*, a right-wing, conservative paramilitary group. He had given radical speeches displaying both anti-democratic and anti-semitic fanaticism. See Oliver Rathkolb, *The Paradoxical Republic: Austria 1945–2005*, trans. Otmar Binder, Eleanor Breuning, Ian Fraser, and David Sinclair-Jones (New York: Berghahn, 2010), 101.

64. "Anti-Semites Win Seats in Austrian National Council; Jewish Leaders Fearful," *Jewish Telegraphic Agency*, December 3, 1945.

65. "Anti-Semites Named to Austrian Cabinet; Allied Council Must Approve Choices," *Jewish Telegraphic Agency*, December 10, 1945.

66. "Austrian Government Drops One Anti-Semite after Allied Protest, but Retains Another," *Jewish Telegraphic Agency*, December 18, 1945.

67. Evelyn Adunka, *Die Vierte Gemeinde: die Geschichte der Wiener Juden von 1945 bis heute* [The fourth community: The history of the Jews of Vienna from 1945 to today] (Berlin: Philo, 2000), 18.

68. *Bericht des Präsidiums der Israelitischen Kultusgemeinde Wien über die Tätigkeit in den Jahren 1945 bis 1948* [Report of the Presidium of the Jewish community of Vienna on the activities in the years 1945 to 1948] (Vienna: Israelitische Kultusgemeinde Wien, 1948), 3.

69. Ibid., 5.

70. Embacher, *Neubeginn ohne Illusionen*, 28.

71. *Aufbau*, October 18, 1946, 1. Hakoah is the Viennese Jewish community's athletic association.

72. Leon Zelman, "Wiener jüdische Gemeinde nach 1945" [Viennese

Jewish community after 1945], *Mitteilungsblatt der Aktion gegen den Antisemitismus* [Newsletter on action against antisemitism] 120 (November 1990).

73. Adunka, *Die Vierte Gemeinde*, 18.

74. "Vom Leben der Juden in Wien" [From lives of Jews in Vienna], *Aufbau*, December 21, 1945, 24.

75. Embacher, *Neubeginn ohne Illusionen*, 49.

76. Embacher posits that the rebuilding of the IKG depended entirely on American Jewish organizations. See Embacher, *Neubeginn ohne Illusionen*, 28. In their 1945–1948 report of activities, IKG leadership specifically thanked the American Jewish community and American Jewish organizations for their assistance. See *Bericht des Präsidiums der Israelitischen Kultusgemeinde Wien*, 8.

77. For more information about *Aufbau*, see Tekla Szymanski, "Der *Aufbau*—'Unser Aller Tagebuch' [The *Aufbau*—"the diary of all of us"]," in Gisela Dachs, ed., *Jüdischer Almanach des Leo Baeck Instituts—Die Jeckes* [Jewish Almanac of the Leo Baeck Institute—The Jeckes], vol. 13 (Frankfurt am Main, Ger.: Jüdischer, 2005), 108–18.

78. General letter 363 from Melvin S. Goldstein, American Joint Distribution Committee (AJDC) Paris to AJDC New York, May 11, 1946, JDC Archives, Collection AR45/54, File 119, Frame 0943.

79. Embacher, *Neubeginn ohne Illusionen*, 48.

80. Ibid., 49.

81. Ibid., 31.

82. Herbert Rosenkranz, *Verfolgung und Selbstbehauptung. Die Juden in Österreich 1938–1945* [Persecution and assertiveness: The Jews in Austria 1938–1945] (Vienna: Herold, 1978).

83. Rabinovici, *Instanzen der Ohnmacht*.

84. Tom Segev, *Simon Wiesenthal: The Life and Legends* (New York: Doubleday, 2010), 134

85. Embacher, *Neubeginn ohne Illusionen*, 32.

86. *Aufbau*, August 31, 1945, 1. *Aufbau* also reported the same later, on September 27, 1946, 4.

87. "3,028 Jews in Vienna Would Quit Austria," *New York Times*, February 14, 1946, 9.

88. Embacher, *Neubeginn ohne Illusionen*, 29.

89. Trude Berger, interview 47865, USC Shoah Foundation Visual History Archive.

Karel C. Berkhoff

The Dispersal and Oblivion of the Ashes and Bones of Babi Yar

ON SEPTEMBER 29 AND 30, 1941, ON THE WESTERN OUTSKIRTS OF KIEV, in what was then the Ukrainian Soviet Socialist Republic, at the ravine of Babi Yar (Old Women's Ravine), the largest single Nazi shooting of Jews in the Soviet Union took place. In 1943, the Nazis supervised the burning of most of the bones of the murder victims and the dispersal of the ashes. After the Red Army returned at the end of the year, the destruction of the site and the human remains in it continued for decades. This essay traces how and why the ashes and bones were dispersed and obliterated, and how the real history of the site was obfuscated, largely because of intense antisemitism within the Communist Party of Soviet Ukraine.

During World War II, the occupying German army and *Schutzstaffel* (SS) and police forces had begun planning and implementing measures against the local Jews immediately after entering Kiev on September 19, 1941. Those measures included shootings. But the occupation forces found the massive explosions set off by Soviet mines on September 24 an acceptable rationale for an unprecedented immediate eradication of the entire Jewish population. On September 28, an unsigned order to the Jews of Kiev and the surrounding area was posted. It instructed them to appear the next day before 8:00 A.M. at a certain intersection and warned them that noncompliance would be met with the death penalty. From that place, the Jews were marched to Babi Yar and shot by *Sonderkommando* (special unit) 4a, a subunit of *Einsatzgruppe* (task force) C, a mobile killing squad of the Security Police (Sipo) and Security Service (SD), and by Order Police battalions 45 and 303 of the regular German police. Also present were

Ukrainian auxiliary policemen. According to a Sipo and SD report, the German forces on hand shot 33,771 Jews. They covered at least some of the human remains with a layer of chloride of lime and then half a meter of sand and earth, leveled by Soviet prisoners of war.[1] But Jews were also shot at Babi Yar on October 1 and thereafter. Numerous non-Jews were killed and dumped at the ravine, many asphyxiated in mobile gas vans.

In the spring of 1942, the Nazis created a concentration camp at Babi Yar, which they called Syrets. The Red Army recaptured the city in November 1943. But before then, for six weeks from the middle of August 1943, the Security Police attempted to erase the crime scene: it forced hundreds of mostly Jewish prisoners to dig up corpses and incinerate them. (Details of this gruesome process are known because these laborers revolted and some therefore lived to tell about it.) The Germans put up screens camouflaged with tree branches. Truck drivers from the city brought in pieces of rail, blocks of stone, timber, and barrels of oil, but they had to exit their vehicles well before the entrance to the ravine; Security Police men got on and drove them inside. Pyres were built on pieces of gravestone removed from the nearby Jewish cemetery. One group of prisoners crushed incinerated bones that had not been fully cremated, with wooden rams on granite blocks, and passed the remainder through sieves. Another group loaded the ashes onto barrows and distributed them nearby. More excavation took place nearby, because the Nazis had dumped their victims not only in the ravine but also in defensive pits dug in 1941 by the Red Army. The secrecy was pointless, however, if only because of the sky-high smoke.[2]

The German action certainly did not find and hide all bones in Babi Yar and the surrounding area. Shimon Chervinskii, born in Kiev in 1906, returned with the Red Army on November 6, 1943, and was struck by the scene at Babi Yar and the adjacent Lukianivka Cemetery: "It was cloudy and drizzling. There were few people, only some soldiers were roaming the ash-heap. It was terribly quiet. It was a real ash-heap—the ash held broken railings of burial fences, bones of adults and children, skulls, half burned children's shoes."[3] Among the Soviet journalists taken to the ravine was the famous Ilya (Ilia) Ehrenburg, who later recalled, "Nowhere else did I experience such anguish, such orphanage, as on the sands of Babi Yar. Sometimes one saw black ashes and charred bones."[4] *Pravda*'s correspondent Boris Polevoi saw something even more shocking:

> a sharp cut of the large ravine and a slice from the slope, as some kind of geological bedding, a jumble of human corpses. A layer of about two meters. Sappers were just uncovering it. Their faces were bound with humid towels—such was the stench, in spite of the rainy day. And even we, who had already seen the ditch in Kharkiv and the heaps of shot people on Poltava's outskirts, froze, were stunned by the spectacle. Some gray, disheveled woman walked about and cried and laughed, and a girl with black hair tried to take her away.[5]

This was how he described the scene in 1969. In conversation with the Jewish Ukrainian theatrical director Aleksandr Shlaen, many years later, Polevoi recalled that actually the spur had been exposed by a diverted Soviet bomb, and the horrific sight for him surpassed anything he ever saw before and since, which included Auschwitz-Birkenau.[6]

The Soviet secret police (NKVD) organized five of its own excavations of mass graves at Babi Yar, including the former Syrets camp, and concluded that in 1943 the Nazis had attempted to burn 100,000 corpses at Babi Yar. The NKVD's analysis also correctly noted that "displaying a special hatred toward the Jewish nationality, the German-fascist bandits in the city of Kiev annihilated almost all the Jews." The death count included, in September 1941 alone, "about 70,000 Jews at Babi Yar"—a number much larger than the killers' own, and not substantiated. The information was forwarded to Josef Stalin's inner circle.[7] As for the materials found, the NKVD referred to "remainders of ovens and of burned corpses" and "other items."

The excavations lasted two days and were carried out by 160 German prisoners of war. Afterward, on November 24, 1943, forty-one of them attended a "meeting" in the city (or, more likely, still at Babi Yar) convened by the NKVD, where they publicly signed a document about the excavation, a long testimony they may have composed themselves. The signatories stated:

> *Resolution*
> On November 22 and 23, 1943, we, the 850 German prisoners of war of the gathering site in Kiev, were given an opportunity by the Soviet authorities to convince ourselves of the atrocities committed in Kiev against the Russian civilian population during the

time of the German occupation. One hundred and sixty of trusted men chosen by us have carried out excavations at five of the numerous mass graves. At two sites alone they uncovered about 150 murdered Russian civilians. At other sites they stumbled upon the remains of countless burned corpses, clothes, and remainders of bones.

Thus we establish: Here in Kiev a mass murder was carried out against the Russian civilian population of an immense scale, to which, according to eyewitness accounts, tens of thousands of men, women, and children fell victim. The perpetrators are known: They are the German occupation troops, mainly units of the SS, the SD, and the Field Gendarmerie.

With horror and revulsion we renounce the elements of our people without a conscience, who ordered and carried out these evil acts. These crimes without scruples, this systematized mass murder, this raw terror, show us the true face of the Hitler government. For it, as the supreme command, is primarily responsible for this gruesome warfare.

We, the German front soldiers, the German people, did not want these war crimes. Yet as Germans we feel we share responsibility for these crimes committed also by Germans. Therefore we have the duty to protest against this depraved warfare with all the means at our disposal and to prove to the world that the German people no longer have anything in common with the Hitler government, which is exterminating and subjecting other peoples in such a criminal way. Thus we declare an utter fight against the guilty Hitler government. We want to make sure that every individual who made himself guilty toward the Russian people shall get his just punishment. We hope to have soon the opportunity to act upon our words.

These gruesome mass shootings carried out in Kiev are not war, they are nothing but evil murder. They unleash the hatred of the Russian people against our people. They will make it much harder for our beloved homeland to receive the decent peace that we all still want to create.

The mass murder of Kiev has opened our eyes. It has turned us into bitter enemies of the guilty Hitler government. May this gruesome crime also call upon our people to remember, at last, what used to give us Germans worldwide fame and respect. Not the misanthropy without scruples of a Hitler, not the medieval barbarity of his "Weltanschauung [world view]," but true human dignity and moral purity must determine the behavior of our people again.

> Then our fatherland shall receive again the place in the community of peoples befitting it.
>
> Therefore we call upon the German armed forces, the German people, in particular the German front soldiers, to prevent these elements without a conscience from continuing to carry out the orders for murders issued by Hitler and his National Socialist government. We call upon every decent German for a joint fight for a new, honest, clean, for a free Germany!
>
> In the name of the 850 prisoners of war of the gathering site in Kiev.
>
> Kiev, November 24, 1943.[8]

The resolution was probably read aloud to Soviet-held German prisoners of war at other sites but does not appear to have been printed or broadcast.

One of the signatories was Friedrich-Wilhem Krummacher, chaplain of the 208th Infantry Division, who had been captured less than a month earlier. Half a year later, in June 1944, he spoke about Babi Yar at a plenary session of the National Committee Free Germany and on Radio Free Germany; the committee's weekly newspaper carried an abbreviated version of his lecture. Krummacher, an evangelical theologian, recalled that in Kiev, he had seen a "moral catastrophe" inflicted by his countrymen on Kiev's "Soviet Russian civilians":

> A few hundred meters from the barbed wire fence of the [Syrets] camp an enormous field with corpses [*Leichenfeld*] begins, pit after pit, thousands of dead, each pit filled with seventy, eighty corpses. We were witnesses when these pits were opened, when the corpses—older decomposed corpses and recent victims from the time shortly before the German retreat—were carried out of these large, over a man deep pits where they had been shot. Russian witnesses who had escaped from this hell at the last moment, confirmed what we saw before us: the field of corpses of Kiev's German mass murders![9]

Krummacher and the other prisoners surely had been aware of the murder of Jews before, but the shock at the sight of the corpses was real. Of interest here is that Krummacher did not say that he had himself excavated human remains but called himself and others onlookers; and that he, as in the joint resolution, did not mention Jews at all—both the victims and the witnesses were "Russian," which seemingly was considered an overarching category.

Jews arriving in Kiev from the east came to Babi Yar to mourn. They grieved there, talked among themselves and to locals, left flowers—and picked up bones. Aleksandr Burakovskii visited in the spring of 1944 with his father and never forgot the terrible feeling it gave. "The banks of the ravines were steep. It was cold. The winds howled in those ravines. My father walked and wept. Somewhere along the steep banks or at the bottoms of these deep and huge ravines were the bodies of his older brother, his brother's wife, their five daughters, his older sister and her family, and more than a dozen other relatives."[10]

The site attracted mourners and curious locals. Mr. Gutin, a medical doctor, arrived with an army hospital on April 15, 1944. Walking on his own to Babi Yar, he heard a local man tell another: "Look, a real Jew." A self-declared guide tried to make money:

> Near Babi Yar some Ukrainian stood at a booth that he made and as a true guide told the Jews surrounding him what he had seen, and for greater effect he had lit a fire on the ravine bottom, so that the ashes could be seen. He talked and extended his straw hat, demanding payment. Those surrounding him eagerly caught every word, hoping to find out anything about their relatives and dear ones.

Another young Ukrainian man told how during the massacre, a Jewish woman had thrown her child toward nearby Ukrainians, but Germans saw it and threw it into the ravine. Yet another man said he had met a woman who had pretended to be dead in the ravine, crawled out at night, and was saved by a Ukrainian woman she knew. Desperate Jews in the ravine talked to no one in particular; one woman, for instance, said she should also have died there.[11]

Sarra Tartakovskaia returned to Kiev from evacuation and on September 29, 1944, joined others and went to Babi Yar, where her parents, sister, and dear ones had been murdered:

> We gathered burnt bones, arms, legs. From the slope I pulled by the hair (which had not fully burned) the head of the girl with a dried out remnant of a shawl, two little locks of hair, two hairpins, a hole in her temple. I stood and cried—it could be my sister. A man came up to me, carefully raised my hands with the head of the perished one, and called out loudly, "People, do not forget this." He took a picture of me. Even today [in 1981] I find it difficult to write about this. We gathered a mountain of bones and we buried

> them near the rabbi's home, not far from the Yar [ravine]. All of '44 I went to Babi Yar daily, we just buried and buried bones.[12]

At various sides of the ravine, Burakovskii noted, visitors left "small bouquets of field flowers, individual chrysanthemums, sometimes red roses."[13]

Iurii Shcheglov, a Jewish man who lost brothers at Babi Yar, cautions against exaggerating the Jewish remembrance efforts. "Before Stalin's death, Babi Yar was one of Kiev's emptiest outer districts. I never saw flowers there or people with mournful faces, never heard prayers for the dead. And I was often at Babi Yar, from the spring of 1944. The rare passersby stayed briefly and did not start up conversations."[14] Although it is incorrect to say that no one placed flowers or came to mourn, such visits became increasingly risky. Not only did Stalin's regime start to persecute Jewish life but also there were hostile civilians. Sarra Kolchinskaia recalls that "every year fewer and fewer came to the ravine [on September 29]. Once I went there with my brother, an army Major but wearing civilian clothing. From somewhere there appeared a crowd of hooligans who screamed, 'The kikes have come!' It became dangerous to visit the [Lukianivka] cemetery and the Yar, there were robberies."[15] This occurred amid a generally high rate of hooliganism in the city.[16]

In the fall of 1945, a group of actors led by Solomon Mikhoels arrived from Moscow to celebrate the twenty-fifth anniversary of the founding of the Kiev Jewish Theater. Mikhoels found Babi Yar, which he evidently visited, to be "neglected, disgraceful," and "not fenced off." (Back in Moscow, it inspired him to plead to his colleagues within the presidium of the Jewish Anti-Fascist Committee that they support a "movement to create monuments to the victims of fascism.")[17] On Sunday, October 7, 1945, addressing a festive meeting in the Kiev National Theatre of Operetta attended by Ukrainians such as Maksym Rylsky and guests from Moscow, Leningrad, Minsk, Odessa, and Birobidzhan, Mikhoels concluded his presentation by presenting director Moyshe Goldblatt with a large crystal vase. Eyewitnesses have variously recalled the event. According to Shimon (Semen) Kipnis, Mikhoels said the vase contained earth gathered by him at Babi Yar, and he asked for it to be filled with flower seeds, so that a symbol of Jewish revival would arise. But Moisei Loev, one of Goldblatt's codirectors, recalled that the vase held seeds, which Mikhoels asked to be sown in Babi Yar, so that the flowers growing there would serve as a memorial.[18]

Probably in the late 1940s, the poet and translator Boris Brainin gathered human bones from the bottom of the ravine and brought them to Ilya Ehrenburg in Moscow, as a "peculiar souvenir." He said Babi Yar was in a "disgraceful neglect. Cows graze there, and bones are all over the place."[19] Likewise, a demobilized soldier named Usher Vovchik saw the place in 1945 and found that "children's boots, jaws, hair, and human bones . . . completely filled Babi Yar, which stretched for two kilometers."[20]

When "Kiev was still in ruins," thus in the late 1940s, V. Savtsov saw "marauders" (*marodery*) at Babi Yar, who, "exhausted from the hard work, pulled another victim (already not of the Hitlerites—of ourselves!) from the compressed heap of corpses with handmade hooks and efficiently began groping its arms, hoping to find wedding rings, and its ears (earrings) and jaws (golden teeth and 'bridges')."[21] Viktor Nekrasov, a writer and veteran of the Battle of Stalingrad born in 1911 and living in Kiev, also has mentioned the phenomenon.[22] He might have agreed that it was a "golden harvest," the term coined by Jan Tomasz Gross and Irena Grudzińska Gross for the postwar excavation of human remains in search of valuables at the Treblinka death camp in Poland. The term rightly emphasizes that these diggers acted outside moral contexts, considering the sites not burial grounds but "fields open to gleaners."[23]

Anatolii Kuznetsov, a writer born in 1929—who wrote a widely read book about Babi Yar that appeared in Russian in 1966—had often played at the ravine before the war. Now he and some friends found pieces of human bones there. As they walked to the beginning of the former stream, where the ravine narrowed and spread out into branches, they saw some very young gold diggers:

> In one place we saw that the sand had turned grey. Suddenly we realized that we were walking on human ashes. Nearby there had been a fall of sand, following the rains, which had exposed an angular projection of granite and a seam of coal about a foot thick. There were goats grazing on the hillside with three little boys, each about eight years old, looking after them. They were hacking away diligently at the coal with little picks and breaking it up on the granite block. We went up to them. The coal was brown and crum-

> bly, as though it was a mixture of the ashes from a railway engine and carpenter's glue. "What are you doing?" I asked. "See here!" And one of them pulled out of his pocket a handful of something which glittered where it was not covered in dirt, and spread it out on his hand. It was a collection of half-melted gold rings, earrings, and teeth. They were digging for gold. We walked around the place and found many whole bones, a skull, still not dried out, of someone recently buried, and more pieces of black ash among the grey sand.[24]

Other teenage boys were hired to do the digging. One such boy was Ilia Levitas, many years later chair of one of the two Babi Yar memorial committees in Kiev. In 1944, he spent many days digging at the ravine. Every day, a van drove up there, and the people inside, who claimed to be museum workers, paid him and other boys three rubles per bucket of things gathered at Babi Yar. Those tiny buckets included letters but no watches or things of that kind, he recalls. Suddenly, the van stopped coming.[25]

By the late 1940s, the ravine had also become an unofficial garbage gathering site. Rubbish and broken things piled up despite a tablet that banned dumping and mentioned a penalty for transgressors. This garbage fell on top of many bones.[26] A little further, students of the nearby School of Military Medicine used the site as a proving ground, dropping cartridges and conducting drills. A Jewish graduate recalled in anguish sixty years later: if only we had known that we "marched, ran, and crawled as leopards across the bodies of our grandfathers and grandmothers, mothers and sisters."[27]

Party, state, and city leaders did not regard the terrain as a site of Jewish suffering that should be memorialized. On the contrary, Ukraine's Communist Party leader Nikita Khrushchev deeply mistrusted Jews, considering them extreme individualists and inclined to state treason. When Jews such as the writer Dovid Hofstein attempted to organize a commemoration in September 1944, the authorities banned it. When Ehrenburg inquired of Khrushchev about a rumor that a marketplace would be built on the massacre site, he was told to mind his own business.[28]

But Khrushchev initially did want a memorial. On March 13, 1945, the Politiburo of the Communist Party of Ukraine decided to place a monument at Babi Yar to what it called the "140,000 citizens of the city of Kiev bestially killed here by the fascist barbarians." But at the same time, the mass grave would be leveled and turned into a park with walking paths. The press mentioned the plan and even referred to a decision to place a museum. A large sum—2.5 million rubles—was allocated, and a design competition was announced.[29]

In 1950, the city authorities, led by Oleksii Davydov (longtime chair of the Executive Committee of the city soviet) canceled the competition. By then, the rulers were preoccupied with something they felt had to precede any memorial park at Babi Yar—namely, the removal of the ravine as such. The party and state officials of the Ukrainian Soviet Socialist Republic decided, in total secrecy, to obliterate Babi Yar. Nearby brick factories would pump in muddy water. Moreover, a stadium would be built. The autocratic city administration quickly had the idea rubber-stamped, and the work began. Contrary to what a former police chief believed, there is no evidence that the authorities believed that only this approach would preclude the illegal excavations in the large area.[30] One actual reason, which appears in the archival record of that time, was that leveling the area would allow the city to grow and traffic to cross.[31]

But the main reason, unstated in any available document of that time, was that since Stalin's antisemitic "anti-cosmopolitan" campaign of the late 1940s, the authorities conceived of Babi Yar as a purely Jewish site, as if no other people had been killed there; and, above all, they tended to denigrate the Jews simply for obeying the order to show up in September 1941. People going like lambs to the slaughter, party officials told Viktor Nekrasov, did not deserve any memorial. And Anatolii Kuznetsov heard them say, "What Babi Yar are you talking about? Where they shot the kikes? And who said we had to put a memorial up to some lousy kikes?"[32] The British historian Edward Crankshaw visited Kiev in 1955 and heard something similar from the local director of the Intourist travel agency, whom he asked to show him the killing site. At first, the man pretended he had never heard of Babi Yar. But when Crankshaw insisted on going there, the response became, "Why do you want to go look at a bunch of dead Jews? If you're so interested in Jews, you'll see more than enough live ones on the streets."[33]

The about ten survivors in the city preferred to keep a low profile, rightly fearful of interaction with the authorities. (Kuznetsov believed they even had good reason to fear being *arrested* for some reason.[34])

Even though the experience of the shootings or of having to burn the corpses in 1943 haunted them for the rest of their lives, they never dared raise objections to the treatment of the mass grave. But there were others.

The Jewish writer Lev Ozerov had investigated Babi Yar for *Chernaia kniga* (Black Book), a Soviet publication of documents and testimonies on the Nazi murder of the Jews, a project soon suppressed. In the late 1950s, Ozerov proposed to the influential *Literaturnaia gazeta* (Literary newspaper) in Moscow that he write about the need for proper care of the former killing site, including a memorial. Sergei Smirnov, the editor, approved but then reneged: Ozerov was unsuitable, he told him, "for a certain reason that we can guess." Several non-Jewish Ukrainian writers were approached, but they declined. Yet the Russian Nekrasov did write about Babi Yar in 1959, on his own initiative, and the newspaper met his demand for his article "Why Isn't This Done?" to appear on October 10—Yom Kippur.[35]

This published text epitomized the anti-Jewish tendencies of the Soviet press in that it did not even mention Jews. The author was standing on the shooting site, he wrote, where a friend of his had been murdered. He added, "There is no-one in Kiev who does not have resting here (no, another word is needed) a father or son, relatives, a friend, an acquaintance." Now Nekrasov observed:

> Silence. A Wasteland. Houses are being built on the other side of the ravine. There is water at the bottom of the ravine. Where does it come from? . . . Now I have been told at the Architecture Administration that Babi Yar is to be "flooded" (which explains the water!), in other words, filled in, leveled, so as to build a park and a stadium there . . . Is that possible? Who could think of this—to fill a ravine thirty meters deep and to sport and play soccer on the site of an enormous tragedy? No, this cannot be allowed! When a person dies, he is buried and a monument is placed on his grave . . . There are memorials in Buchenwald, there will be one in Auschwitz, Lidice has been fully restored; and in the Soviet Union, there are memorials in Luhansk (at the anti-tank ditch) and Kislovodsk. Why was A.V. Vlasov's memorial design [of 1945] forgotten?[36]

Kiev's authorities responded with two letters to the same periodical, which printed them. One, by a group that included a deputy in the soviet of the city district in question, said a "park with a monument in the center" was needed, as with all "graves of the victims of the past war." But, citing city planning and foreign precedent, the writers denied a need to conserve the entire mass grave—"the ravine as it is":

> At Babi Yar a new residential district is under construction, modern multistoried residential blocks with all conveniences are being built there. This outlying district will soon be connected with the city center by trolley-bus. The territory of Babi Yar will be cared for [*blagoustroena*]; there are plans for laying out a park there, and in the park a monument will be erected to the victims of Fascism. Should the ravine be kept as it is? We, the authors of the present letter, all of us veterans of the Patriotic War, residents of Shevchenko District, have discussed the problem and have come to the firm conclusion that it should not. In Lidice the ashes and the site of the shooting have not been kept as they were after the fascists were driven out. Instead, a rose garden was planted there. We think that in Babi Yar, too, a park should be laid out with a monument in the center.[37]

The second letter, by the deputy chair of the Kiev city administration, also announced that first the district would be "completely taken care of." Only the Shevchenko district's "bad state" [*neblagoustroennost'*] explained the absence of a memorial. "This year work will begin to turn Babi Yar's slopes green, in the near future a park will be laid out there where, in the future, according to a decision of the government of the Ukrainian SSR taken in December 1959, there will be placed an obelisk and pedestal with a memorial plate in memory of the Soviet citizens tortured to death by the Hitlerites in 1941."[38] These two responses to Nekrasov's appeal disregarded that such plans entailed the destruction of most of the gravesite and the human remains in it. So it was not surprising that Nekrasov's eye-catching article did not block the plan to flood the ravine.

Neither did the well-known poem "Babi Yar" by a younger Russian writer, Yevgeny Yevtushenko (Evgenii Evtushenko), which appeared in print in August 1961, after a visit to Kiev, where the poet saw trucks dump garbage into the ravine. Yevtushenko's poem mentioned the absence of a memorial but went further than Nekrasov's article in mentioning the Jews, sympathizing with them, and referring to anti-semites. Khrushchev publicly condemned it as politically immature and historically ignorant.[39]

Human bones at Babi Yar, August 1961. Courtesy of Emanuel Diamant.

The ravine gradually became a lake as the brick factories pumped in muddy water. Each year, the dams were strengthened and raised. But as was not foreseen, the mud in the lake failed to harden. On March 13, 1961, one dam fell apart and a huge mudslide occurred: a mass of heavy dirt streamed out and pushed into the city. According to one researcher, it was fourteen meters high and moved five meters per second. Entire buildings and people were swallowed. An investigation took place, and some lower-ranking officials were punished. According to government figures, the mudslide killed 145 people and wounded 143 others; but Ukraine's Communist Party leader, Petro Shelest, wrote in his private diary that 198 people died and 250 were wounded. The disaster, entirely due to human action and neglect, became known among Kievans as the Kureniovka tragedy.[40]

According to KGB reports, many Kievan Jews said the ravine should not have been filled; it was an uprising of the dead.[41] A taxi driver said it was the revenge of the "Jewish blood" for the leveling of Babi Yar. There was antisemitic talk along the lines of "At Babi Yar the kike blood began to boil, the kikes are rising." Many talked about an old woman who apparently screamed in a streetcar that passed the site, "The Jews did this, they are avenging us!"[42]

The soil that had flushed out was either spread over the destroyed area or returned to the ravine. It is likely that the moving mass had taken along human remains. Viktor Balan, a Jew who lost relatives at Babi Yar and who decades later came there dozens of times as a member of the "People's Guard" (*narodnaia druzhina*), recalled that he had to dig after the mudslide and "held the corpses of those who perished in 1941 in my hands."[43] Other pedestrians also stumbled upon bones and sometimes took a picture. The one reproduced here was taken by Emanuel Diamant after bones were deliberately arranged on a caterpillar track.[44]

The obliteration of Babi Yar continued apace. As planned years earlier, multistoried residential blocks were built on the place of the Syrets camp; again, human bones were found. The blocks lined the new arterial Novo-Okruzhna Street, completed in 1969 and now called Olena Teliha Street. In 1964 and 1968, construction workers found mass graves—possibly the Soviet antitank ditches where Jews and others had been shot too—and the regional Communist Party committee instructed a commission to list the possible burial sites of Soviet citizens who had been shot.[45] (To date, no historian has traced this list.)

In the mid-1960s, Iurii Shcheglov went there with Nekrasov and "approached a fire. Some children were roasting the tips of long sticks, so as to easier sharpen them and hook up skulls that an unknown force had thrown to the surface. I asked them why they were doing this, and heard something horrible in reply: 'We scare the women in the evening!'"[46]

In the summer of 1971, three American students went to Babi Yar and saw human bone fragments encrusted in dirt over a level area several hundred meters long. They took many remains with them, smuggled them across the Soviet border, and brought them to Yad Vashem, which arranged to have them buried at the Nahalat Yitzhak Cemetery in Givatayim, a suburb of Tel Aviv. (As Yad Vashem's director, Katriel Katz, explained to them, Yad Vashem could not accept bones, only dust.) The following year, a little-known monument was erected over the gravesite at the Israeli cemetery and dedicated by Prime Minister Golda Meir.[47]

The absence of a memorial drew increasing ire inside and outside the Soviet Union, such as from visiting members of the United States Congress. Bowing to the pressure, the Soviet authorities decided that a memorial still had to be erected. A new design competition began in 1965, but without any publicity. The design by the architect Iosif (Iosyp) Karakis, premised on the notion that one should not walk on a mass grave, impressed many: a pathway and smaller other paths led toward a large statue topped by a woman's face. Yet no winner was declared because none of the designs fully accepted the Soviet regime's preoccupation—*resistance*.[48]

A large unofficial commemoration on the twenty-fifth anniversary of the massacre, in September 1966, forced the regime to prove that it wanted a memorial. Soon afterward, it placed a granite plaque promising the construction of a real monument. Against the rule of fair play, an architect and a sculptor who had seen the designs but had not joined the competition themselves, Anatolii Ihnashchenko and Mikhailo Lysenko, were enlisted, and they began working in total secrecy. At a late stage, for reasons unclear, the authorities wanted to make sure that their design, as seen from above, did not have the shape of a Star of David. According to Ihnashchenko, Volodymyr Shcherbytsky, the head of the Soviet Ukrainian government, intervened for this reason and then, still dissatisfied, ordered the three remaining real spurs of the ravine—600,000 square meters—to be filled in.[49]

The much-reduced Babi Yar memorial opened in July 1976. In the midst of a small, artificially shaped terrain, a large bronze sculpture commemorated the "citizens of the city of Kiev and the prisoners of war" killed in Babi Yar between 1941 and 1943. There was no mention of Jews. The monument stood in the midst of the long-planned "Park of Culture and Recreation." Jews and non-Jews alike began visiting the memorial on wedding days to take pictures and leave flowers. (Visiting war memorials on wedding days was a habit of Soviet citizens; today, most couples prefer going elsewhere.)[50]

But the memorial, and before it the plaque, drew the persistent attention of young Jewish activists. The mistreatment of the mass grave made many of them attach greater importance to their own Jewishness, and what really inflamed them was the ban on displaying anything Jewish there. The KGB persecuted them. In April 1972, for instance, a group of Jews was arrested at Babi Yar for "trampling the lawns."[51]

Thus we find that although the German occupier hastily burned most victims at Babi Yar, the ravine as such remained intact and, moreover, held not only ashes but also many bones, bone fragments, and objects, often untouched since the victims and owners were murdered there. After the NKVD carried out some excavations, marauders, often very young boys, began digging. Soon the Soviet authorities led by Khrushchev concluded that Babi Yar should be commemorated as little as possible, on a fraction of the killing and burial grounds—and certainly not as a Jewish site. This essay has argued that antisemitism in official circles best explains these policies.

Independent Ukraine declared Babi Yar the official site of a National Historical-Memorial Reservation, but those who come to see can easily overlook this. They are confused by the plethora of Jewish and non-Jewish memorials that have joined the Soviet monument since 1991. The 1976 monument remains the only one on the single spot vaguely resembling the obliterated ravine. Visitors no longer are likely to stumble upon ashes or bones, which could be considered an improvement—but they are not told where those remains might lie. The corpses of Babi Yar seem to have vanished, along with the original ravine.

NOTES

Jean-Marc Dreyfus and Elisabeth Anstett kindly invited me to join the panel "Ashes and Human Remains during and after the Holocaust," proposed for the Lessons and Legacies Conference of November 2012 and funded by the European Research Council program "Corpses of Mass Violence and Genocide." Thanks also to other colleagues, too numerous to list here. My research was enabled by a J. B. and Maurice C. Shapiro Senior Scholar-in-Residence Fellowship at the Center for Advanced Holocaust Studies, United States Holocaust Memorial Museum.

1. On lime, see I. F. Stadniuk, *Ispoved' stalinista* [Confessions of a Stalinist] (Moscow: Patriot, 1993), 65–66, 101–5, citing the survivor Iakov Steiuk.

2. One of many sources describing this process is Anatolii Kuznetsov, *Babii Iar: Roman-dokument* (Moscow: Izdatel'stvo Astrel', 2010), 412–18, published in English as A. Anatoli (Kuznetsov), *Babi Yar: A Document in the Form of a Novel*, trans. David Floyd (New York: Farrar, Straus and Giroux, 1971), 313–18. For an overview of the massacre, see Karel C. Berkhoff, "Case Study: Babi Yar," in *Online Encyclopedia of Mass Violence*, May 27, 2015, accessed June 23, 2016, http://www.sciencespo.fr/mass-violence-war-massacre-resistance/en/document/babi-yar.

3. Efrem Baukh, ed., *Babii Iar* (Izdanie Soiuza zemliachestv-vykhodtsev iz SSSR: n.p., 1981), 64–65.

4. Il'ia Erenburg, *Liudi, gody, zhizn': Vospominaniia v trekh tomakh* [People, years, life: Memoirs in three volumes], rev. and exp. ed., vol. 1 (Moscow: Izdatel'stvo "Sovetskii pisatel," 1990), 285

5. Boris Polevoi, *V kontse kontsov: Niurnbergskie dnevniki* [In the end: Nuremberg diaries] (Moscow: "Sovetskaia Rossiia," 1969), 201–2.

6. Tat'iana Evstaf'eva, "Babii Iar vo vtoroi polovine XX v. [Babi Yar in the second half of the twentieth century]," in Tat'iana Evstaf'eva and Vitalii Nakhmanovich, eds., *Babii Iar: Chelovek, vlast', istoriia. Kniga 1: Istoricheskaia topografiia. Khronologiia sobytii* [Babi Yar: Man, regime, history. Book 1: Historical topography. Chronology of events] (Kiev, Ukraine: Vneshtorgizdat Ukrainy, 2004), 187.

7. T. V. Vrons'ka and O. Ie. Lysenko, eds., *Kyïv u dni natsysts'koï navaly: Za dokumentamy radians'kykh spetssluzhb. Do 60-richchia vyzvolennia Ukraïny vid hitlerivs'kykh zaharbnykiv. Naukovo-dokumental'ne vydannia* [Kiev in the days of the Nazi invasion: According to the documents of the Soviet special services. For the 60th anniversary of the liberation of Ukraine from the Hitlerite invaders. Scholarly publication of documents] (Kiev, Ukraine: Natsional'na akademiia nauk Ukraïny; Instytut istoriï Ukraïny; Kyïvs'ka mis'ka administratsiia; Derzhavnyi arkhiv Sluzhby bezpeky Ukraïny, 2003 [2004]), 418, 421.The forwarded document is in N. K. Petrova, comp., *Znat' i pomnit': Prestupleniia fashizma v gody Velikoi Otechestvennoi voiny* [To know and remember: The crimes of fascism in the years of the Great Patriotic War] (Moscow: "Veche," 2012), 145–50.

8. Gosudarstvennyi arkhiv Rossiiskoi Federatsii, 7021/65/528/1–6, cited from a copy at United States Holocaust Memorial Museum, Archives, RG-22.002M, reel 3: "Resolution" in German and in Russian translation; Vronska and Lysenko, *Kyïv u dni natsysts'koï navaly*, 422.

9. Friedrich-Wilhelm Krummacher, *Ruf zur Entscheidung: Predigten, Ansprachen, Aufsätze 1944/1945. Dokumente aus dem Arbeitskreis für Kirchliche Fragen beim Nationalkomitee "Freies Deutschland"* [Call to decision: Sermons, speeches, essays 1944/1945. Documents from the Working Group for Church Questions of the National Committee "Free Germany"] (Berlin [East]: Union, 1965), 76–84. I could not compare this publication to the original radio transcript. The shorter version is Oberkonsitorialrat [supreme consitorial counselor] Dr. theol. Krummacher, Divisionspfarrer 208 I.D., "Die moralische Katastrophe und ihre Überwindung [The moral catastrophe and its overcoming]," *Freies Deutschland* [Free Germany], June 25, 1944, 3. On Krummacher and Babi Yar, see Gerhard Besier, "Die Rolle des MfS bei der Durchsetzung der Kirchenpolitik der SED [The role of the Ministry for State Security in the enforcement of the church policy of the Socialist Unity Party of Germany]," in Klaus-Dietmar Henke and Roger Engelmann, eds., *Aktenlage: Die Bedeutung der Unterlagen des Staatssicherheitsdienstes für die*

Zeitgeschichtsforschung [Documentary record: The significance of the documents of the State Security Service for the study of contemporary history], 2nd ed. (Berlin: Ch. Links, 1995), 102–3.

10. Aleksandr Burakovskiy, "Holocaust Remembrance in Ukraine: Memorialization of the Jewish Tragedy at Babi Yar," *Nationalities Papers* 39, 3 (May 2011): 375.

11. Baukh, *Babii Iar*, 58–59; also cited in Aleksei Makarov, "Babii Iar: pamiat' obshchestva—zabvenie gosudarstva [Babi Yar: social memory and state oblivion]," in A. E. Gerber and D. V. Prokudi, eds., *My ne mozhem molchat': Shkol'niki i studenty o Kholokoste* [We cannot remain silent: schoolchildren and students about the Holocaust], vypusk 2 (Moscow: Fond 'Kholokost' and 'Academia,' 2006), 302.

12. Baukh, *Babii Iar*, 59–60.

13. Burakovskiy, "Holocaust Remembrance in Ukraine," 375.

14. Iurii Shcheglov, "V okopakh Bab'ego Iara [In the trenches of Babi Yar]," *Kontinent* 111 (January–March 2002): 288–305.

15. Baukh, *Babii Iar*, 63.

16. Serhy Yekelchyk, "Policing Postwar Kyiv: Crime, Social Control, and a Demoralized Police," *Journal of Ukrainian Studies* 35, 36 (2010): 251–63.

17. Joshua Rubenstein, "Introduction: Night of the Murdered Poets," in Joshua Rubenstein and Vladimir P. Naumov, eds., *Stalin's Secret Pogrom: The Postwar Inquisition of the Jewish Anti-Fascist Committee*, trans. Laura Esther Wolfson, abridged ed. (New Haven, Conn.: Yale University Press, 2005), 38.

18. Semen Kipnis, "Sorok let posle Bab'ego Iara [Forty years after Babi Yar]," *Novoe russkoe slovo* [New Russian word], September 25, 1981, 3; Shimon Kipnis, "Vaza, napolnennaia zemlei Bab'ego Iara [A vase filled with the earth of Babi Yar]," in Iosif [Joseph] Vinokurov, Shimon Kipnis, and Nora Levin, eds., *Kniga pamiati posviashchena zhertvam Bab'ego Iara* [Memory book devoted to the victims of Babi Yar] (Philadelphia: Publishing House of Peace, 1983), Russian section, 38–39 (does not include the request to add seeds); Shimon Kipnis, "A Crystal Vase of Earth from Babi Yar," English section, 122–23; Moisei Loev, *Ukradennaia muza: Vospominaniia o Kievskom gosudarstvennom evreiskom teatre imeni Sholom-Aleikhema. Khar'kov-Kiev-Chernovtsy. 1925–1950* [Stolen muse: Memories of the Sholem Aleichem Kiev State Jewish Theater. Kharkiv–Kiev–Chernivtsi] (Kiev, Ukraine: Dukh i litera, 2003), 137–38.

19. Mordechai Altshuler, Yitshak Arad, and Shmuel Krakowski, eds., *Sovetskie evrei pishut Il'e Erenburgu 1943–1966* [Soviet Jews write to Ilya Ehrenburg, 1943–1966] (Jerusalem: Prisma, 1993), 294–95.

20. A. Minskii, "Eto zabyt' nel'zia [It must not be forgotten]," *Novoe russkoe slovo*, September 30, 1981, 3.

21. V. Savtsov, "Bykivnia," *Radians'ka Ukraïna* [Soviet Ukraine], April 19, 1989, 3. This witness is likely Volodymyr S. Savtsov, who published anti-Zionist Soviet books in the 1980s.

22. Viktor Nekrasov, "Posle 'Holocaust,'" [After *Holocaust*] *Iehupets'* 18 (Kiev, Ukraine: n.d.): 223.

23. Jan Tomasz Gross with Irena Grudzińska Gross, *Golden Harvest: Events at the Periphery of the Holocaust* (New York: Oxford University Press, 2012), 41. In Kiev, such diggings were not limited to sites of mass graves from the Holocaust; see Karel C. Berkhoff, "Bykivnia: How Grave Robbers, Activists, and Foreigners Ended Official Silence about Stalin's Mass Graves near Kiev," in Élisabeth Anstett and Jean-Marc Dreyfus, eds., *Human Remains and Identification: Mass Violence, Genocide and the "Forensic Turn"* (Manchester, U.K.: Manchester University Press, 2015), 59–82.

24. Kuznetsov, *Babii Iar*, 38–39; quotation from Anatoli (Kuznetsov), *Babi Yar*, 3–4.

25. Ianina Sokolovskaia, "Il'ia Levitas: Ves' Kiev stoit na kostiakh [Ilia Levitas: All of Kiev is standing on bones]," *Izvestiia*, October 1, 2004.

26. Baukh, *Babii Iar*, 60.

27. Isaak Trabskii, "Zhiznennyi podvig [Feat of life]," *Slovo/Slovo* [Word] 61 (New York, 2009), accessed April 15, 2014, http://magazines.russ.ru/slovo/2009/61/tr20.html.

28. Shimon Redlich, "Khrushchev and the Jews," *Jewish Social Studies* 34, 4 (October 1972): 343–53. On Ehrenburg, see ibid., 349. On Hofstein, see G. V. Kostyrchenko, ed., *Gosudarstvennyi antisemitizm v SSSR: Ot nachala do kul'minatsii, 1938–1953* [State antisemitism in the USSR: From the beginning to the culmination, 1938–1953] (Moscow: Mezhdunarodnyi fond 'Demokratiia,' 2005), 43.

29. "Pamiatnik pogibshim v Bab'em Iaru [A memorial for those who perished in Babi Yar]," *Pravda*, April 4, 1945, 3; Katrin Boeckh, *Stalinismus in der Ukraine. Die Rekonstruktion des sowjetischen Systems nach dem Zweiten Weltkrieg* [Stalinism in Ukraine: The reconstruction of the Soviet system after the Second World War] (Wiesbaden, Ger.: Harrassowitz, 2007), 404; Evstaf'eva, "Babii Iar vo vtoroi polovine XX v.," 191, 195–97.

30. Oleksandr Anisimov, *Kurenivs'kyi Apokalipsys: Kyivs'ka trahediia 13 bereznia 1961 roku v fotohrafiiakh, dokumentakh, spohadakh . . .* [The Kureniovka Apocalypse: Kiev's tragedy of March 13, 1961 in photographs, documents, memoirs . . .] (Kiev, Ukraine: Fakt, 2000), 19.

31. Evstaf'eva, "Babii Iar vo vtoroi polovine XX v.," 194–95.

32. Nekrasov, "Posle 'Holocaust,'" 223; Viktor Nekrasov, "Babii Iar, 45 let [Forty-five years of Babi Yar]," *Novoe russkoe slovo* September 28, 1986, 4; Kuznetsov, *Babii Iar*, 516; Anatoli (Kuznetsov), *Babi Yar*, 398.

33. Richard Sheldon, "The Transformations of Babi Yar," in Terry L.

Thompson and Richard Sheldon, eds., *Soviet Society and Culture: Essays in Honor of Vera S. Dunham* (Boulder, Co.: Westview, 1988), 150.

34. Kuznetsov, *Babii Iar*, 567 (talk on Radio Liberty, May 12, 1973).

35. Lev Ozerov, "Terpen'e—muzhskaia rabota [Perseverance is men's work]," in M. N. Parkhomov, comp., *O Viktore Nekrasove: Vospominaniia (Chelovek, voin, pisatel')* [About Viktor Nekrasov: Memoirs (The man, the fighter, the writer)] (Kiev, Ukraine: "Ukraïns'kyi pys'mennyk," 1992), 232–33; L. Lazarev, *Shestoi etakh, ili perebiraia nashi daty* [The sixth floor, or sorting out our dates] (Moscow: Izdatel'stvo "Knizhnyi sad," 1999), 185–86. Lazarev, the paper's correspondent, specifically disputes Ozerov's assertion that Nekrasov was asked for the article; see L. Lazarev, review of Iurii Vilenskii, *Viktor Nekrasov: Portret zhizni* [Viktor Nekrasov: Portrait of a life] (Kiev, Ukraine: "Informatsionnye sistemy," 2001), in *Voprosy literatury* [Issues of literature] 1 (January–February 2003): 346–47.

36. Viktor Nekrasov, "Pochemu eto ne sdelano? [Why isn't this done?]" *Literaturnaia gazeta* [Literary newspaper], October 10, 1959.

37. Benjamin Pinkus, *The Soviet Government and the Jews, 1948–1967: A Documented Study* (Cambridge: Cambridge University Press, 1984), 437–38, translation (slightly modified) of V. Iarkhunov, N. Vlasov, A. Ermakov, V. Esipov, A. Konchits, P. Kurochkin, A. Mikhailov, and V. Saraev, "Eto neobkhodimo sdelat' [That must be done]," *Literaturnaia gazeta*, December 22, 1959, 2.

38. T. Skirda, "Po sledam vystuplenii 'Literaturnoi gazety' 'Pochemu eto ne sdelano?' [After the appearance in *Literary Newspaper* of "Why isn't this done?"]" *Literaturnaia gazeta*, March 3, 1960, 2.

39. Jerry Tallmer, "'Babi Yar'—Where 33,000 Died, One Poet Stood Up," *Downtown Express*, September 22–28, 2006, accessed April 15, 2014, http://www.downtownexpress.com/de_176/babiyar.html. On Khrushchev, see Redlich, "Khrushchev and the Jews," 350.

40. Anisimov, *Kurenivs'kyi Apokalipsys*. On Petro Shelest, see V. A. Smolii, ed., *Kurenivs'ka trahediia 13 bereznia 1961 r. u Kyievi: Prychyny, obstavyny, naslidky. Dokumenty i materialy* [The Kureniovka tragedy of March 13, 1961 in Kiev: Causes, circumstances, consequences. Documents and materials] (Kiev, Ukraine: Instytut istoriï Ukraïny NAN Ukraïny, 2012), 18.

41. Smolii, *Kurenivs'ka trahediia*, 48, 94.

42. Baukh, *Babii Iar*, 59–60 (on blood), 61, 62–63.

43. Kuznetsov, *Babii Iar*, 520; Anatoli (Kuznetsov), *Babi Yar*, 401; Viktor Balan, "Tuman nad Bab'im Iarom [Fog over Babi Yar]," accessed April 15, 2014, http://berkovich-zametki.com/Nomer22/Balan1.htm.

44. Emmanuil (Amik) Diamant, "Babii Iar, ili Pamiat' o tom, kak v narod prevrashchalos' stroptivoe plemia [Babi Yar, or the Memory of how the obstinate tribe became a nation]," *My zdes'!* [We are here !] 328, October

27–November 2, 2011, accessed April 15, 2014, http://newswe.com/index.php?go=Pages&in=view&id=4056, also at http://www.kby.kiev.ua/komitet/ru/history/art00065.html.

45. Il'ia Levitas, ed., *Pamiat' Bab'ego Iara: Vospominaniia. Dokumenty* [The memory of Babi Yar: Memoirs. Documents] (Kiev, Ukraine: Evreiskii sovet Ukrainy, Fond "Pamiat' Bab'ego Iara," 2001), 22–23; Evstaf'eva, "Babii Iar vo vtoroi polovine XX v.," 193.

46. In the original, "Da pugaem babok po vecheram!" Shcheglov, "V okopakh Bab'ego Iara," 304.

47. Philip Shapiro (Centreville, Va.), e-mail to Traci Rucker, Center for Advanced Holocaust Studies, United States Holocaust Memorial Museum, February 7, 2011, forwarded to Karel Berkhoff; "Bones of Jews Killed in Babi Yar, Riga Reburied in Israel," *JTA Daily Bulletin* 54, 164 (August 26, 1971): 1, accessed April 11, 2014, http://www.jta.org/1971/08/26/archive/bones-of-jews-killed-in-babi-yar-riga-reburied-in-israel.

48. Evgenii Zhovnerovskii [Zhovnirovskii], "Konkurs na pamiatnik [Competition for a memorial]," in Baukh, *Babii Iar*, 105–7. Images of Iosif Karakis's designs, accessed April 15, 2014, are at http://karakys.narod.ru/Virtual/60/Kiev_Babinjar/Kiev_Babinjar.htm.

49. Anatolii Ignashchenko and Timur Litovchenko, interviewed by Ilia Levitas, probably in 1996, in "Babii Iar: pamiat' pokolenii [Babi Yar: the memory of generations]," a text (accessed September 24, 2013) that was at http://www.babiyar-diskus.narod.ru/BY-Memorial.html but now is at: http://tim-lit.narod.ru/Baby-Yar.html; Anatolii Ignashchenko, interviewed by Vladimir Platonov in "Babii Iar: Tragediia o tragedii [Babi Yar: The tragedy of the tragedy]," *Zerkalo nedeli* [Mirror of the week], September 27, 1997, accessed April 15, 2014, http://gazeta.zn.ua/SOCIETY/babiy_yar_tragediya_o_tragedii.html. On the Star of David, see also Zhovnerovskii, "Konkurs na pamiatnik," 106.

50. "Novye svadebnye mesta stolitsy [New wedding sites of the capital]," *Segodnia* [Today] (Kiev), September 30, 2007, accessed April 15, 2014, http://kiev.segodnya.ua/kpower/novye-cvadebnye-mecta-ctolitsy.html.

51. Diamant, "Babii Iar." On 1972, see Shimon Kipnis, "Tsvety i slezy [Flowers and tears]," in Vinokurov, Kipnis, and Levin, *Kniga pamiati posviashchena zhertvam Bab'ego Iara*, 34–37. See also Mikhail Mitsel', "Zapret na uvekovechenie pamiati kak sposob zamalchivaniia Kholokosta: praktika KPU v otnoshenii Bab'ego Iara [The ban on the immortalization of memory as a way of imposing silence on the Holocaust: the practice of the Communist Party of Ukraine toward Babi Yar]," *Holokost i suchasnist'* [Holocaust and modernity] 1, 2 (2007): 9–30.

IV. THE HOLOCAUST AND SOCIAL HISTORY: GENDER AND THE FAMILY

Martina Cucchiara

Jewish Girls in Catholic Schools in Nazi Germany, 1933–1938

IN NAZI GERMANY, ANTISEMITISM IN PUBLIC SCHOOLS WAS OFTEN vicious. Martha Padawer was ten years old in 1934, and she attended a public secondary school in Dortmund, Germany. She recalled that "the trauma started then . . . [On] the first day of school I was called out by the teacher in front of the class . . . The teacher said, 'This is a dirty Jew and you are not allowed to associate with her . . . and she has to sit by herself.' None of the children broke the taboo . . . It was horrible . . . It was so horrible I don't know how I got through it."[1]

Sixteen-year-old Margaret Cohen-Tuteur suffered similarly in 1933 from the cruel treatment at the hands of teachers and students in her public school in Kaiserslautern, Germany. Margaret told her mother, "If you don't take me out of that school, I don't want to go on living."[2] Both she and Martha soon left public school and enrolled in private Catholic convent schools for girls, where they found a temporary refuge in the care of nuns.

That nuns acted benevolently toward Jewish children is, of course, not a new revelation. Holocaust scholars have identified religious women throughout occupied Europe who hid persecuted Jewish children in their convents in the 1940s.[3] But this emphasis on Catholic cloisters as separate spaces, ideal for hiding, where nuns lived medieval lives at odds with the modern world has only reinforced the women's otherwise marginal place in historical inquiries. Suzanne Vromen, who researched Belgian nuns' efforts to rescue Jews in the 1940s, wrote that the women's "activities during the war should have remedied their omission in the historiography, but this did not occur."[4] Nuns' invisibility is especially striking in the vast scholarship that examines the complex history of the Catholic Church in prewar Nazi Germany. Most historians continue to focus on the male hierarchy, whose response to National Socialism remains contested.[5]

On the rare occasions when scholars have examined nuns in Adolf Hitler's Germany, they have tended to cast the women as passive victims who depended on the protection of the clergy.[6] The theme of the male hierarchy as the protectors of nuns is especially prevalent in debates about the 1933 concordat between the Vatican and Germany, in which the Catholic Church agreed not to oppose the Nazi Party politically in exchange for a guarantee that it could manage its own affairs. For instance, Michael Kißener concluded in his assessment of the concordat that the hierarchy paid a high price to secure religious orders and Catholic schools in Nazi Germany, namely the complete depoliticization of the church.[7] Defenders of the concordat argue that the agreement proved an important defensive measure, a contractual form of noncompliance that in spite of its many imperfections protected the church's pastoral mission in Germany.[8]

If Nazi Germany had honored its agreement, the concordat should have secured convents and convent schools. The very language some scholars use in defending the concordat, such as "barrier," "contractual noncompliance," and "securing pastoral care," at least implies that Catholic institutions covered by the concordat were able to maintain distinct Catholic spheres beyond the influence of Nazism. Few scholars have challenged this view of nuns in Nazi Germany as apolitical outsiders.[9]

But the encounters of Jewish German girls and nuns in private Catholic convent schools from 1933 to 1938 reveal a more complex and ambiguous history of nuns and their institutions in prewar Nazi Germany. The postwar testimonies of Jewish women who attended private Catholic convent schools in the 1930s collected by the USC Shoah Foundation Institute for Visual History and Education do emphasize that nuns succeeded in preserving distinct free spaces under Nazism. In often extraordinary vignettes, the women tell of the efforts some nuns made to include Jewish girls in their classrooms; these nuns refused to practice the pernicious antisemitism so prevalent in public schools.

It does not follow, however, that nuns' institutions remained outside of the National Socialist state or that the women shielded most of their students from the influence of Nazism. In fact, the opposite appears true. In illuminating the interactions between nuns and Jewish and Catholic girls in private Catholic convent schools in prewar Germany, this article challenges the simplistic image of the isolated Catholic cloister and the victimized nun, and even that of the "Catholic ghetto" in Nazi Germany. Rather, Nazism permeated even convent schools, and nuns displayed considerable agency as they negotiated the often fluid boundaries between the Catholic faith community and Hitler's *Volksgemeinschaft* (people's community)—which the Nazis envisioned as a racially unified community where the interests of the state reigned supreme. The women made deliberate choices as to which tenets of National Socialism they incorporated into their curriculum, and nuns' efforts to limit the influence of Nazism in their schools benefited some Jewish girls. At the same time, these very efforts also facilitated Catholic girls' integration into the Third Reich by reconciling Catholicism and Nazism in the children's eyes. This was no accident, because the concordat freed Catholics, including nuns, to participate more fully in the state. Nuns wished to integrate their schools and their students into the new state, secure their place in it, and, of course, safeguard their Catholic identity. For Jewish students, this meant that even in private Catholic convent schools, they could never truly escape Nazism.

CONFESSIONAL SCHOOLS, NUNS, AND JEWISH CHILDREN IN IMPERIAL AND WEIMAR GERMANY

A word about the central roles of religion and the church in education in the German Empire and Weimar Germany is in order. In Prussia and Bavaria, most public *Volksschulen*,[10] compulsory schools for grades one through eight, were separated by confession—that is, by religious groups united by a particular confession of faith—as well as by gender. Each child was meant to attend the local confessional school of his or her faith. In confessional schools, religion permeated and shaped the school day.

In 1930s Bavaria, nuns still taught alongside lay teachers in public confessional schools for girls. This was the case because, in the nineteenth century, German states lacked the funds to open the needed number of compulsory schools and often relied on nuns to maintain public schools for girls, particularly in rural areas.[11] During the *Kulturkampf* (culture wars), a conflict between the Catholic Church and the German government over control of education and religious appointments, the Prussian government expelled nuns from its public confessional schools. Thereafter, nuns taught only in their own private *Volksschulen*.[12] Other German states followed suit, and only in Bavaria did nuns retain their prominent place in both public and private education well into the twentieth century.[13]

Because Jewish confessional *Volksschulen* were rare, most Jewish children attended Christian confessional *Volksschulen*.[14] Claire Heymann's situation was typical. In 1930, the six-year-old girl started elementary school. As one of only two Jewish families in the village of Grossheubach in Bavaria, her parents had no choice but to send her to the local public Catholic school, where Claire was taught by nuns.[15] Of the over 33,000 public *Volksschulen* in Prussia in 1933, only 95 were Jewish. Only two others could be found outside of Prussia, in Baden.[16] Larger Jewish communities sometimes opened their own private *Volksschulen*, but there were few of them.

Jewish middle or higher schools were even rarer than *Volksschulen*. Especially in rural areas, Jewish girls wishing to go beyond the compulsory *Volksschule*, usually after completing the first four years of elementary education, sometimes had few options outside of private Catholic convent schools. Emma Golding, the daughter of observant Orthodox Jewish parents, wished to attend a secondary school in the 1920s. Emma lived in the rural town of Kommern, near Cologne, and she enrolled in a higher private Catholic convent school in nearby Euskirchen. The school had an outstanding reputation and, according to Emma, "There was no other choice."[17] This lack of choice for girls can in part be explained by the fact that German states had traditionally viewed the secondary schooling of boys as a matter of state, but not that of girls.[18]

In the nineteenth century, nuns responded to this dearth of basic and higher educational opportunities for girls with enthusiasm. The notion that these modern nuns had little agency and lived removed from the world is a myth. Starting in the nineteenth century, when women had few options outside of marriage, nuns could combine a life of faith with the practice of a profession in the public sphere. Many newly established women religious congregations became free from male supervision and no longer practiced the strict seclusion of nuns known as cloister. As a consequence, female religious orders underwent a dramatic revival in Europe. In Germany, the number of nuns exceeded 100,000 by 1937.[19] Individual women religious congregations such as the School Sisters of Notre Dame, an order devoted to education, grew from 13 sisters in 1833 to nearly 10,000 members in Europe and the United States by the 1930s.[20] Because of their large organizations and public mission, nuns became astute businesswomen and human resources managers who maintained close ties to the state.

A not-always-easy relationship of mutual dependence developed between the German state and female religious congregations. The state came to rely on nuns for vital, low-cost social services. The women, in turn, relied on the state for much of their income in the form of salaries, subsidies, tax exemptions, and, in the case of nursing orders, health insurance reimbursements. But in their service to the state, nuns were uncompromising in their insistence on a distinct Catholic mission. For instance, Mother Theresia Gerhardinger, the founder of the School Sisters of Notre Dame, stressed in 1841 that a school without religion that restricted itself to merely academic lessons was like a grave; no matter how prettily adorned, it "brought forth only corpses that soon poison the air around them with their foul breath of decay."[21] The women's often strict practice and teaching of Catholicism invited scorn and admiration in equal measure from both government officials and citizens.

In particular, members of the bourgeoisie often feared the influence of nuns over young German girls. In the nineteenth and twentieth centuries, so-called convent atrocity stories featuring depraved nuns and ferocious mothers superior who imprisoned young, innocent girls and forced them to take the veil regularly made the rounds.[22] Nuns, in turn, became adept in dealing with adversity, a skill they believed would serve them well in Nazi Germany. Women religious congregations also worked hard to excel in their respective professions, which, over time, muted but did not entirely erase the suspicions of most Germans.

Before long, many private Catholic convent schools for girls in Germany acquired a reputation for excellence. This was one more reason why, even before 1933, Jewish parents sometimes sent their daughters to private Catholic convent schools. Six-year-old Lisa Japha from Bingen attended a private Catholic elementary school in 1927. She remembered that "going to public school, the *Volksschule* was not the done thing" because it did not promise the excellent education her parents desired, and they deemed Catholic convent school as "the right place to send a nice Jewish girl."[23] Ruth Frankel, born in 1916, grew up in an Orthodox Jewish home in Frankfurt am Main. Her parents, who could have chosen from among a variety of public schools, sent their daughter to the Marienschule an der Lahn (Saint Mary's school on the Lahn River), a private Catholic higher school for girls, where Ruth was taught by nuns from the congregation of the Poor Servants of Jesus Christ.[24] It is important to note that, for a city girl, Ruth's school choice was unusual.

The available evidence suggests that Jewish parents in urban areas preferred to send their children to public schools. Historian Hildegard Feidel-Mertz found that in larger cities, most assimilated middle-class Jewish families enrolled their children in public schools and eschewed even private Jewish secondary schools.[25] Although statistics are not available and further research is needed, the oral histories utilized for this article support this assertion.[26] It may, therefore, be reasonable to infer that the majority of the approximately 117,000 Jewish schoolchildren who were enrolled in elementary, compulsory, and higher schools in 1932–1933 lived in urban areas and attended public institutions.[27] Immediately following the Nazis' rise, many became the target of vicious antisemitism from their fellow students and their teachers.

JEWISH GIRLS IN PRIVATE CATHOLIC CONVENT SCHOOLS IN NAZI GERMANY

The day after Hitler's ascension to power in January 1933, nine-year-old Vera Hirtz found herself excluded from her school community. Her girlfriend told her that morning that "I can't be friends with you anymore because you are Jewish and I hope you will die."[28] She and her Jewish friend Ilse were outsiders until she left the school in 1934.[29] Margaret Cohen-Tuteur from Kaiserslautern, who found herself abandoned even by her half-Jewish friend, summed up her situation as follows: "I felt I had a contagious disease. I had a feeling that I was in a huge hospital for nervous diseases [and] that there were a lot of unwell, sick, psychotic and psychopathic people around us."[30] Even before the first formal attack on Jewish children in April 1933 with the Law against the Overcrowding of German Schools and Universities, which set quotas for non-Aryan students, life had become impossible for Jewish children in public schools, and some parents began to agonize over where else to send their daughters.[31]

For the reasons outlined here, Jewish schools were not an option for most children. Already few in number, Jewish schools dwindled further, from approximately 150 to only 70 in 1933, when the new Nazi government closed most one-room Jewish *Volksschulen*.[32] The newly founded *Reichsvertretung der deutschen Juden* (National Representation of German Jews) could only open ten new *Volksschulen* by Easter 1934.[33] But, even if a Jewish school was nearby, parents did not always send their daughters there. An important reason why Jewish parents chose private Catholic convent schools after 1933 was because it enabled them to keep their children in higher schools with excellent academic reputations.

As a teenager, Elsbeth Schmidt lived with her family in comfortable upper-middle-class surroundings in the large Jewish community of Worms. When she was asked to leave her nondenominational private school in the 1930s,[34] her mother decided against sending Elsbeth to the newly opened Jewish *Volksschule* in Worms. Instead, she chose a private Catholic convent school.[35] Frau Schmidt believed the Catholic school to be excellent, and although Elsbeth did not specify the name of the school or the order of nuns who ran it, it was a higher school for girls where she "learned everything from homemaking to French to English to history."[36] In comparison, the new Jewish school in Worms was just a basic *Volksschule* without advanced courses or foreign languages. Sending Elsbeth to the Jewish school would have meant giving up on a higher education altogether.

Jewish students who transferred to private Catholic convent schools in Nazi Germany provide compelling evidence that the atmosphere in these institutions often differed markedly from the pernicious climate prevailing in public schools. In their testimonies, women highlighted the efforts individual nuns made to welcome Jewish students to their schools. These sisters treated Jewish girls with great kindness and attempted to use their authority to set a more inclusive tone in their classrooms. After Margaret Cohen-Tuteur confessed in 1933 that she contemplated suicide, her mother enrolled her in the school of the Sisters of Saint Francis of Assisi in Kaiserslautern. Margaret remembered that the sisters took her in and "They were extremely kind and considerate and antisemitism as such did not exist . . . This time in the convent was a good time, a peaceful time."[37] Nowhere else did Margaret feel as safe as in the sisters' school, not even at home.

Many interviewees emphasized this sense of safety in their new

Catholic school. Anne Goodwin from Berlin was eleven in 1934 when her parents sent her to a private Catholic convent school. She remembered:

> That was fortunate, because it was staffed by nuns and lay [teachers] and they were all very good to the Jewish children. I really didn't suffer at all from antisemitism in that school . . . So I really had a very happy childhood in Germany and suffered as little as anybody could from the Nazis. Berlin was by far the best city to be under the Nazis and then going through this Catholic school, I was really very well protected.[38]

According to Anne, some of her Jewish girlfriends transferred to the school as well.[39]

Jo Ann Glickman's testimony highlights the central role of individual nuns in welcoming Jewish girls to their schools. Jo Ann started attending a private Catholic convent school in 1934 in Augsburg at the age of six, and she recalled the remarkable efforts her teacher Sister Anastasia made to include her in the classroom:

> My parents went to this Catholic institution, it was a convent . . . and my parents asked if they would enroll me and they were most gracious about it . . . I know they were absolutely wonderful to me . . . School starts in the spring, right around Easter time and at every desk, on the first day of school, there was a little green straw basket with a little chocolate bunny and jelly beans and on my desk, since it was also Passover, she [the nun] had gone out and bought a kosher candy bar, so I had something I could eat.[40]

Some readers may find the facts of this story hard to credit. But whether or not Sister Anastasia bought a kosher candy bar, what clearly stands out in Jo Ann Glickman's memory is the kindness with which she was treated.

The anecdote also highlights the centrality of religion in the classroom. Christian rituals and observances in Catholic school potentially served as a constant reminder to Jewish girls of their otherness. For some Jewish parents, placing their daughters into this intense Catholic environment was not an easy choice. Martha Padawer, who came from an observant Orthodox Jewish family in Dortmund, entered a private Catholic convent school in the 1930s. Nonetheless, her father did not want his child "subjected to a Catholic education," and Martha did not participate in religious instruction.[41] During Mass, she cleaned the chemistry lab, which she enjoyed. The evolving relationship between Martha and the nuns at her school was not without tensions, however. At a time when Christian teachings and attitudes were laced with antisemitism, Martha did indeed find it difficult at times to maintain her religious integrity; she recalled that some older nuns tried to convert her.[42]

Jewish women only rarely touched on the issue of conversion in their testimonies. It seems that most nuns respected their charges' religious beliefs. This may have been due to the fact that, since the nineteenth century, nuns had routinely admitted Protestant and Jewish girls to their schools. In 1876, Theresia Gerhardinger, mother superior of the School Sisters of Notre Dame, instructed her sisters to never press Jewish and Protestant children to participate in Catholic rituals and prayer, but to ask only that "they conduct themselves quietly and respectfully during prayer time."[43] Some Jewish women recalled that nuns resisted their wish to convert. Margit Korge, who in 1937 at the age of seven entered a Catholic boarding school in the Charlottenburg section of Berlin, remembered "tormenting" the nuns to allow her to make her confession and take Communion along with her classmates. The women refused, but they invited Margit to scatter flowers during religious processions.[44] Margit relished this shared religious experience as a sign of acceptance.

Even Martha Padawer, who resented nuns' efforts to convert her, viewed the women's religiosity as something they shared. Overall, she had "a very fond recollection of the nuns who supported us because in a way they respected our being religious in our own way."[45] Anne Goodwin believed that "most of the teachers [in Catholic school] were very sympathetic because the Roman Catholics were also persecuted to some degree by Hitler [and] that is probably why they were different."[46] Like Anne, a number of Jewish girls identified with nuns as fellow outsiders. Trudy Coppel, who attended a private Catholic convent school in Gleiwitz until 1938, stated that "it was even forced on the nuns to say 'Heil Hitler.' . . . Now we skipped 'Heil Hitler' and just greeted them with 'Good day.'"[47] Margaret Cohen-Tuteur agreed that "when they [the nuns] came into [the classroom] in the mornings, they made the sign of the cross . . . and then they had to raise their hands and say 'Heil Hitler,' and they suffered quite badly from that because as far as they were concerned, God came first still."[48] In the memories of these Jewish women, nuns were in some ways like them, and they believed that neither group could belong to the "people's community." This perhaps explains why the Nazi salute performed by nuns lost some of its sinister meaning in the eyes of these Jewish students.

CATHOLIC GIRLS IN PRIVATE CATHOLIC CONVENT SCHOOLS IN NAZI GERMANY

Stopping the analysis here would leave readers with a positive but incomplete picture of private Catholic convent schools and nuns in Hitler's Germany. It would also reinforce the prevailing view in the historiography that usually depicts nuns as benevolent, apolitical outsiders and describes cloisters as cut off from the world. In a 2012 review, John Conway was critical of this problem of selective or partial analyses in Catholic historiography that highlight the faithful's disagreements with the Nazis but too often omit discussions of the "widespread support for the new regime by most Catholics."[49] The same is true here. Nuns did not cultivate positions as outsiders in Hitler's Germany. Rather, they wished to integrate their schools and congregations into the new state, albeit on their terms.

The conclusion of the concordat in July 1933 between the Vatican and Germany freed Catholics to fully participate in the Nazi state. The concordat protected Catholic cloisters and schools, and nuns were confident that they could continue to serve the state as they had done in the past. In fact, many Catholics became enthusiastic about the new era. This enthusiasm for the nascent Nazi state is evident in the preface of the 1933 *Bredebrief* [Brede letter], the school newspaper of the School Sisters of Notre Dame's higher school for girls in Brakel, Westphalia. It reads in part:

> A winter full of anguish is behind us, a spring of sudden beginnings, a summer and autumn of joyful, dedicated work of rebuilding our fatherland are ahead of us. The German nation once again begins to value community. How familiar this word sounds to our own community . . . "These profound changes . . . present Catholic womanhood with meaningful tasks in the family and the world at large." So said the bishops of Fulda about women's new mission in our new age. We will dedicate ourselves to the program of our new age. Community can only be built through the love of sacrifice, [and] for us, the eternal and unceasing source of this love is our communion . . . with Christ and his holy church.[50]

It was nuns' engagement with the Nazi state, and their deliberate and selective incorporation of Nazi ideology and rituals into their classrooms, that enabled their schools to offer temporary shelter to some Jewish girls. It also meant that, even in private Catholic convent schools, Jewish students could not escape Nazism.

In their Catholic schools, Jewish children actually had to endure more than just nuns' unconvincing Nazi salutes. Following Hitler's ascension to power, Catholic and National Socialist rituals were performed alongside one another in private Catholic convent schools. Records from the archive of the School Sisters of Notre Dame in Westphalia show that the new school year in the sisters' higher school for girls in Arnsberg began on May 1, 1933, "with a festive Mass," and afterward students gathered in the gymnasium to listen to a radio broadcast from Berlin with speeches by Chancellor Hitler and President Paul von Hindenburg.[51] Throughout the school year 1933–1934 in the sisters' school in Arnsberg, students participated in nineteen events that incorporated aspects of both Nazism and Catholicism.[52]

Jewish students participated in these events. Susan Fleischman remembered attending a rally in Augsburg along with her Catholic school class on the occasion of a visit by Adolf Hitler: "I remember Hitler was in Augsburg and all the classes went and we had to stand there and seeing him in his open car. I assume I did the 'Heil Hitler,' just not to stand out. We were told in school that we had to do it."[53] Susan's parents were horrified when they found out that their daughter had participated in the rally, but Susan herself soon forgot about the incident. She felt safe in a community that downplayed the most vicious aspects of Nazism.

In their classrooms, Catholic sisters emphasized those National Socialist themes that they could best reconcile with their faith and aspirations. The School Sisters of Notre Dame stressed the topics of community, sacrifice, nationalism, and heroism in their curriculum and downplayed the topics of race, antisemitism, and anti-Communism. In 1934, Sister Norberta S., principal of the School Sisters' higher school for girls in in Arnsberg, Westphalia, refused to institute separate examinations on race and eugenics.[54] An analysis of essay topics in German for the school year 1933–1934 in the nuns' school in Arnsberg showed that, of a total of 105 essay choices, only 10 were topics directly pertaining to National Socialism, and none dealt with race or antisemitism.[55] Students wrote about "true patriotism" or why they participated in the Nazis' winter charity (*Winterhilfswerk*).[56]

Nonetheless, the sisters' curriculum may not have been free from antisemitism. For instance, in 1934 in Brakel, Sister Elizabeth S. led an extracurricular study group of fourteen girls that focused on Hans Grimm's novel *Volk ohne Raum* (A People without Space). Reading it, students learned about the supposed "lack of living space of the German people with all its dangers and sorrows that it caused the individual."[57] This entry in the nuns' official annual report is intriguing. The Nazis pushed the sale of Grimm's tedious 1,353-page tome, and, undoubtedly, the nuns would have been aware of the book's antisemitic themes that cast Jews as the alien "bearers of soulless materialistic culture," a characterization that matched the Catholic Church's own prejudices at the time.[58]

According to Kevin Spicer, Catholic leaders preached the toleration of religious Jews but conflated "secular" Jews with bolshevism and liberalism, denouncing them as a destructive force in German society.[59] Nuns rarely wrote about Jews and antisemitism, but the scant evidence does suggest that at least some women subscribed to the pervasive antisemitic stereotypes of the "secular" Jew as profit-driven, dishonest, and Communist.[60] It is impossible to say whether the women used Grimm to perpetuate shared antisemitic stereotypes in their schools, but the possibility must not be discounted. On the other hand, the evidence also reveals a spiritual community immersed in Catholic rituals, celebrations, and clubs as well as a continual focus on a rigorous academic curriculum.[61]

In their testimonies, Jewish women often focused on this rigorous academic environment in their private Catholic convent school. Margaret Federlin, the daughter of a Jewish butcher in Speyer, transferred to Catholic school after 1933. Margaret remembered that her parents felt Catholic school "was safer than anywhere else," and the nuns "saw to it that you got a good education and they cared for you whether you were Jewish or not."[62] Jo Ann Glickman remembered Sister Anastasia's strict attention to good grades and the scolding she received when she fell short in her studies.[63] Jewish women emphasized those aspects of their time in Catholic school that helped them keep Nazism at bay, such as the kindness of nuns, the excellent education, and Catholic rituals. But even the most benevolent nun could not shield Jewish girls from the derision of their Catholic classmates.

The distinct Catholic setting of their school appears to have shielded Jewish girls from the most pernicious aspects of Nazism, but, at the same time, seems to have functioned as a model for Catholic students on how to reconcile National Socialism and Catholicism. They could be both members of the Catholic community and the "people's community" without having to dwell too much on difficult issues such as race and eugenics, for instance. The writings of Catholic students reveal to what extent some girls reconciled Catholicism and National Socialism. In their student newspaper, the *Bredebrief*, students of the School Sisters of Notre Dame's higher school for girls in Brakel wrote about their stay in a Catholic youth hostel. There, lessons on Nazi ideology and the reading of the Nazi newspaper *Völkischer Beobachter* (People's observer) and Hitler's *Mein Kampf* were as much a part of their day as Catholic Mass and prayer.[64] In essays describing their experience at the youth hostel, the girls emphasized how much they appreciated and to what extent they could relate to Nazism's emphasis on community and sacrifice, which had long been leading principles of Catholicism.[65] In 1936, the graduating class of the School Sisters' institute in Brakel visited a labor service camp for men in nearby Driburg, which "awoke in all graduates . . . a great fervor for the idea of mandatory labor service."[66] Back in school, other students sewed a swastika flag for their building.[67]

The enthusiasm with which some girls wrote about certain aspects of National Socialism is striking. One student wrote in 1934 in the *Bredebrief*: "How we love to hear about the German farmer and about our Führer Adolf Hitler . . . and when it is the swastika's turn, we are all on fire."[68] In 1934, a student by the name of Wolfhilde Umenhof wrote an essay for the *Bredebrief* titled "A Visit with the Führer." That summer, Wolfhilde and four of her classmates spent time in a Catholic youth hostel near Hitler's mountain retreat Obersalzberg, near Berchtesgaden in Bavaria. The girls hiked to Hitler's home, and Wolfhilde wrote:

> For four hours we waited in the sun and rain for the Führer. We did not mind; we wanted to see Adolf Hitler. To chase away our boredom, we sung the Horst Wessel song [the anthem of the Nazi Party] and "Deutschland, Deutschland über alles! ["Germany, Germany above everything," the national anthem]" . . . Hitler and his staff appeared exactly at 3 o'clock. Such a crowd of people, such jostling, such cheering! Slowly Adolf Hitler came to us as far

> as the gate . . . The worst was: I could not utter one sound . . . The beautiful moment passed too quickly.[69]

This kind of excitement for Hitler and National Socialism speaks to many Catholics' enthusiasm for the regime, in particular in the early years, but it contrasts sharply with how most Catholics portrayed themselves after 1945.

In postwar memoirs, Catholics often insist on their distance from National Socialism. Elisabeth Charlotte Halder's memoir is typical. Elisabeth grew up in a Catholic family in Durmersheim, near Karlsruhe, in the 1930s. Although she admits that she became the leader of her local League of German Girls (*Bund Deutscher Mädel* or BDM), in her memoir she asserts her ignorance of and complete disinterest in Nazism; in her BDM group, she claims, she sang folk songs and made crafts. She also barely noticed the three Jewish students in her Catholic school who simply "disappeared" one day.[70] In sharp contrast, when, in the 1980s, Christel Beilmann reread her diary of her time as a student in a private Catholic convent school in the 1930s, she was shocked to discover "how we were part of it all and yet we were not . . . I remembered something different, a stronger rejection of National Socialism."[71] It was only in retrospect that Christel imposed a separation between her identities as a Catholic and as a citizen of Nazi Germany.

The eagerness of many Catholic students to be part of Hitler's "people's community" often impacted Jewish girls in private Catholic convent schools negatively. Irma Mathes attended the private school of the School Sisters of Notre Dame in Forchheim in Bavaria in 1933. She testified that "the nuns had a special part in my life. They were very good to me, but the other part of the story is the children in the classroom . . . they knew I was a Jewish girl and that was very difficult."[72] Before 1933, Irma Hannes had many gentile friends in her private Catholic convent school in Miltenberg, Bavaria. But after Hitler's ascension to power, she recalled that "it started to be less and less . . . really. I would say, 1934, or so, they started to join the Hitler Youth and they wouldn't look at me anymore; I was finished because I was Jewish."[73] Even Jo Ann Glickman, who so fondly remembered the gift of a kosher candy bar from Sister Anastasia, was quite alone in her school. She recalled that "I don't remember playing with anyone."[74] She believed that part of her isolation was due to Christian parents' fear to allow a Jewish girl into their home.

Although most Jewish women testified to the absence of antisemitism in private Catholic convent schools, they also found themselves shunned by their Catholic classmates. It appears that, whereas nuns successfully used their authority to keep the most vicious expressions of hatred toward Jews at bay in their classrooms, Jewish girls were still the victims of antisemitism in private Catholic convent schools. Even girls who had already decided to enter the convent and take religious vows were not immune to the seductions of Nazism and antisemitism. Herta Adler was a young Jewish girl in 1935, whose parents enrolled her in a private Catholic convent school. The nuns asked her to stay home on the first day of school, and she found out later that they wanted to spare her the humiliation of rejection because none of the Catholic children wanted to sit next to a Jewish girl. The nuns finally forced a candidate for sisterhood to share her desk; the girl submitted in tears.[75] In some ways Herta Adler was fortunate, because nuns did not always interfere to stop hateful behavior toward their Jewish charges.

Vera Hirtz experienced the full brunt of antisemitism in her private Catholic convent school in Hannover. She and her Jewish friend Susan transferred to a Catholic school in 1934, but for them Catholic school provided little refuge from relentless antisemitism. It was common for both lay teachers and nuns to teach in private Catholic convent school, and Vera's math teacher was an antisemite who tortured both Jewish girls in his class. He demanded that Vera and Susan sit in the back of the room, and "every once in a while he took a piece of chalk and threw it at me and called 'Hey, Jew girl, do you know the answer?'"[76] Outside of class, it was no better. When Vera and her friend left the playground, the Catholic students clapped.[77] Vera suffered a breakdown, but there was no place else for her to go and she remained in the school.

Vera's parents complained to the principal, a nun, who refused to interfere. In her interview, Vera Hirtz speculated that "she [the principal] was totally powerless over the lay teachers, because they [the nuns] were persecuted themselves . . . She had lost her power. But she was wonderful with us, as were all the nuns."[78] Starting in 1933, despite the conclusion of the concordat between Germany and the Vatican, the Nazis placed nuns and their institutions under increasing pressure, mostly in the form of financial penalties meant to erode the economic viability of Catholic institutions. Convinced that women members of religious orders competed with the National Socialist ideal of womanhood, Nazi officials believed that nuns posed a danger to the state and worked toward closing all private Catholic convent schools.[79]

That a number of Jewish girls found some respite in Catholic schools in the 1930s also did not escape Nazi officials. On May 11, 1937, the *Gauleiter* (regional party leader) for Westphalia North wrote to the *Oberpräsident* (senior president) of the state:

> The Higher School for Daughters in Warburg belongs to the School Sisters of Notre Dame. That this school is not being conducted in the National Socialist spirit becomes evident from the following: The *Untertertia* [fourth grade of secondary school] . . . comprises 12 students, two of whom are Jewish. These Jewish students are seated next to Aryan students although there are 14 benches in the classroom.[80]

Women religious congregations started to choose their battles with the regime carefully, and most were not willing to take any risks for their Jewish students, no matter how fond individual nuns were of the girls.

Instead, in response to the looming threat to their institutions, nuns worked tirelessly to convince the state of their reliability. As already mentioned, the women were no strangers to controversy and enmity, and they attempted to use the strategies that, in the past, had usually worked to win over skeptics: namely professional excellence and compliance. This meant that women religious congregations would only go so far in welcoming and protecting Jewish girls. In the effort to maintain their institutions and religious communities, nuns never openly defied state directives, however unjust. For this reason, private Catholic convent schools provided a refuge for only a small number of Jewish girls because nuns complied with the Law against the Overcrowding of German Schools and Universities, which usually limited the proportion of Jewish students to 1.5 percent.[81]

Following the pogrom in November 1938, most women religious congregations also conformed to the state's demand to expel all Jewish students from their schools. Irma Mathes attended a private *Volksschule* run by the School Sisters of Notre Dame in Forchheim, Bavaria, in 1938. Although she testified that the nuns "pampered" her, they still asked her to leave the school on November 10, 1938.[82] At this point, Irma had no options aside from attending a Jewish *Volksschule*, and she transferred to the private Jewish school Internat Hirsch in Coburg. Susan Fleischman's experience was particularly traumatic. On the morning after the November pogrom in Augsburg, two Gestapo agents came to her home and arrested her father. To maintain as much normalcy as possible, Susan's mother insisted that she attend school that morning. Susan recalled: "I got to school and . . . they [the nuns] took me aside, and they said they were very sorry but I cannot stay; they were told that I cannot go to school anymore . . . I went back home. Then I felt very rejected."[83] After her father's release from Dachau concentration camp, the family fled first to England and then to the United States.

Other Jewish students lost their place because the Nazis closed their private Catholic convent schools.[84] This happened to fifteen-year-old Eva Schuster from Berlin in 1938. Eva was one of only a few women who testified that they maintained close friendships with Catholic girls until the very end. She recalled that "the nuns were very sympathetic to us."[85] Eva added that when her principal telephoned her mother to tell her of the imminent school closure, "My mother cried really hard, and they [the nuns] especially worried about us."[86] Eva Schuster's statement highlights a common thread that runs through most testimonies, namely the kindness with which individual nuns often treated Jewish girls in their care in prewar Nazi Germany. As institutions, however, Catholic religious congregations took few risks for their Jewish charges.

The testimonies of Jewish women who attended private Catholic convent schools in prewar Nazi Germany challenge the traditional depictions of nuns in the extant historiography as passive, apolitical women whose cloisters and institutions formed barriers to Nazism. The nuns, in fact, maintained close ties to the state. The women attempted to reconcile their Catholic mission with the demands of the new Nazi state, and they incorporated Nazi rituals and ideology into their curriculum and extracurricular events. Many Catholics were also not immune to the general enthusiasm for Hitler's government in 1933.

But nuns did not blindly capitulate to Nazism, and one can even detect cautious noncompliance in some of their actions. The women attempted to stay true to their Catholic mission and were selective about which aspects of Nazi ideology they emphasized in their institutions. They downplayed the most violent aspects of National Socialism, including antisemitism. Individual nuns used their authority in their classrooms to welcome Jewish girls who could no longer attend public school. These nuns created spaces that offered a temporary respite to Jewish girls in their care.

At the same time, the experiences of Jewish girls in private Catholic convent schools highlight how deeply antisemitism had penetrated prewar German society. Whereas most Jewish girls did not suffer the hateful attacks Jewish children had to endure in most public schools, they often experienced subtler forms of antisemitism at the hands of their Christian classmates, such as shunning. The evidence suggests that, despite maintaining the distinctly Catholic character of their congregations and schools, religious congregations did not create bulwarks against Nazism. On the contrary, nuns emphasized those aspects of Nazism that they could best reconcile with Catholic teachings, which created an environment that actually facilitated Catholic students' integration into the much-touted "people's community."

Nuns' acts of kindness toward Jewish students, though sincere, also went only so far. By 1938, Catholic religious congregations were themselves under enormous pressure from the regime, and nuns' first priority was the preservation of their own religious communities. The women attempted to demonstrate their reliability to the regime through careful compliance with state directives. When the regime demanded the expulsion of all Jewish children from German schools in November 1938, most women religious congregations complied without resistance.

Only in rare cases did religious communities decide to defy the Nazi regime and keep their Jewish students. The congregation of the Sisters of Our Dear Lady in the Charlottenburg section of Berlin, where Margit Korge had lived since 1937, was one such community. The nuns hid Margit until 1942.[87] Margit's experience reveals once more that the situation of German nuns differed sharply from that of their sisters in the occupied territories during World War II. Under National Socialism, the German Catholic convent became an increasingly public space that made for precarious and short-lived sanctuaries for Jewish girls, no matter how well-intentioned its nuns. In 1942, Margit Korge was forced to leave the convent in Charlottenburg on account of repeated Gestapo searches. The cloister was no longer safe, and she was forced to go into hiding with relatives until the end of the war.[88]

NOTES

This article was made possible through a Charles H. Revson Foundation Fellowship at the Center for Advanced Holocaust Studies, United States Holocaust Memorial Museum.

1. Martha Padawer, interview 28094, USC Shoah Foundation Visual History Archive.

2. Margaret Cohen-Tuteur, interview 12235, USC Shoah Foundation Visual History Archive.

3. See, for instance, Suzanne Vromen, *Hidden Children of the Holocaust: Belgian Nuns and Their Daring Rescue of Young Jews from the Nazis* (Oxford: Oxford University Press, 2008); Martin Gilbert, *The Righteous: The Unsung Heroes of the Holocaust* (New York: Holt, 2003); Ewa Kurek, *Your Life Is Worth Mine: How Polish Nuns in World War II Saved Hundreds of Jewish Lives in German-Occupied Poland, 1939–1945* (New York: Hippocrene, 1997); and Michael Phayer and Eva Fleischner, *Cries in the Night: Women Who Challenged the Holocaust* (Kansas City, Mo.: Sheed and Ward, 1997).

4. Vromen, *Hidden Children of the Holocaust*, 77.

5. Two recent edited volumes on the Catholic Church in Nazi Germany, for instance, did not devote a single chapter to the history of women religious congregations in the Third Reich. They are Karl-Joseph Hummel and Michael Kißener, eds., *Die Katholiken und das Dritte Reich: Kontroversen und Debatten* [Catholics and the Third Reich: Controversies and debates] (Paderborn, Ger.: Schöningh, 2010) and Christoph Kösters and Mark E. Ruff, eds., *Die katholische Kirche im Dritten Reich. Eine Einführung* [The Catholic Church in the Third Reich: An introduction] (Freiburg, Ger.: Herder, 2011).

6. See, for instance, Thomas Mengel, *Das Schicksal der schlesischen Frauenklöster während des Dritten Reiches und 1945/46* [The fate of the Silesian convents during the Third Reich and 1945/46] (Cologne, Ger.: Böhlau, 1986) or Annette Mertens, *Himmler's Klostersturm. Der Angriff auf katholische Einrichtungen im Zweiten Weltkrieg und die Wiedergutmachung nach 1945* [(Heinrich) Himmler's Assault on Monasteries: The attack on Catholic institutions in the Second World War and restitution after 1945] (Paderborn, Ger.: Schöningh, 2006).

7. Michael Kißener, "Katholiken im Dritten Reich [Catholics in the Third Reich]," in Hummel and Kißener, *Die Katholiken und das Dritte Reich*, 20.

8. For recent research on the concordat between the Vatican and Ger-

many, see Frank J. Coppa, "Pope Pius XII: From Diplomacy of Impartiality to the Silence of the Holocaust," *Journal of Church and State* 55, 2 (2013): 286–306; Hubert Wolf, "Reichskonkordat für Ermächtigungsgesetz? Zur Historisierung der Scholder-Repgen-Kontroverse über das Verhältnis des Vatikans zum Nationalsozialismus [Reich Concordat for enabling act? To the historicizing of the (Klaus) Scholder-(Konrad) Repgen controversy about the relationship of the Vatican to National Socialism]," *Vierteljahrshefte für Zeitgeschichte* [Quarterly journal of contemporary history] 60, 2 (2012): 169–200; Matthias Stickler, "Kollaboration oder weltanschauliche Distanz? Katholische Kirche und NS-Staat [Collaboration or ideological distance? Catholic Church and National Socialist state]," in Hummel and Kißener, *Die Katholiken und das Dritte Reich*, 83–100; and Thomas Brechenmacher, *Das Reichskonkordat 1933: Forschungsstand, Kontroversen, Dokumente* [The Reich Concordat 1933: State of research, controversies, documents] (Paderborn, Ger.: Schöningh, 2007).

9. Karl-Joseph Hummel and Christoph Kösters, eds., *Zwangsarbeit und Katholische Kirche 1939–1945: Geschichte und Erinnerung, Entschädigung und Versöhnung* [Forced labor and the Catholic Church 1939–1945: History and memory, compensation and reconciliation] (Paderborn, Ger.: Schöningh, 2008); Winfried Süß, "Antagonistische Kooperation. Katholische Kirche und nationalsozialistisches Gesundheitswesen in den Kriegsjahren 1939–1945 [Antagonistic cooperation: The Catholic Church and National Socialist health care in the war years 1939–1945]," in Karl-Joseph Hummel and Christoph Kösters, *Kirchen im Krieg, Europa 1939–1945* [Churches in the war, Europe 1939–1945] (Paderborn, Ger.: Schöningh, 2007).

10. All children attended the first four years of the *Volksschule*, the elementary school, before deciding to stay in the *Volksschule* or transfer to a secondary school.

11. Martina Cucchiara, "Bitter Times: The Poor School Sisters of Notre Dame in Hitler's Germany, 1933–1945" (PhD diss., University of Notre Dame, South Bend, Ind., 2011), 50–53.

12. In the 1870s, Prussia closed 296 Catholic religious houses and expelled approximately 4,000 female and male members of religious orders. "Der 'Kulturkampf' [The "culture struggle"]," Deutsches Historisches Museum, accessed January 28, 2014, http://www.dhm.de/lemo/html/kaiserreich/innenpolitik/kulturkampf/.

13. In 1932, there were 16,929 private Catholic *Volksschulen* in Germany, but available statistics do not reveal how many of these schools were owned or staffed by nuns. Statistisches Reichsamt, *Statistisches Jahrbuch für das Deutsche Reich* [Statistical yearbook of the German Empire], vol. 53: 1934 (Berlin: Reimar Hobbing, 1934), 424.

14. Ibid. In 1933, of the 499,682 Germans of Jewish faith, 361,826 lived in Prussia and 41,939 in Bavaria.

15. Claire's name at birth was Klara Ullmann, but I am using interviewees' current legal names throughout this article. Claire Heymann, interview 7976, USC Shoah Foundation Visual History Archive.

16. Both the Catholic and Protestant churches exercised an inordinate influence over German schools. Of the 52,959 public *Volksschulen* in existence in 1931–1932 in Germany, 29,050 were Protestant, 15,256 were Catholic, and 97 were Jewish confessional schools; 8,291 were mixed confessional community schools; and only 295 were completely secular schools. Statistisches Reichsamt, 14, 421.

17. Emmy Golding, interview 20188, USC Shoah Foundation Visual History Archive.

18. According to James C. Albisetti, "In the 1890s, when 272 of 568 secondary schools for boys were wholly or partly supported by the Prussian state, only four of 128 girls' schools were [funded by the state]." James C. Albisetti, *Secondary School Reform in Imperial Germany* (Princeton, N.J.: Princeton University Press, 1997), 113.

19. This number compares to about 22,000 priests. Amtliche Zentralstelle für kirchliche Statistik des katholischen Deutschlands Köln [Official central office of church statistics of Catholic Germany Cologne], *Kirchliches Handbuch* [Church handbook], vol. 20, Band 1937–1938 (Cologne, Ger.: J. P. Bachem), 238.

20. *Ordensschematismus, der Armen Schulschwestern v. U. L. Frau* [Statistics of the Order of the Poor School Sisters of Notre Dame], January 1, 1929, Archiv Kloster Brede.

21. Theresia Gerhardinger to Königliches Bayerisches Landgericht und Königliche Distriktsschulinspektion [Royal Bavarian district court and royal district school inspection], July 29, 1841, in Maria Theresia von Jesu Gerhardinger, *Briefe* [Letters], vol. 2, (Munich: Ger.: Provinzialet der Armen Schulschwestern von U. L. Frau, 1979), 87–89.

22. Michael Gross, *The War against Catholicism: Liberalism and the Anti-Catholic Imagination in Nineteenth-Century Germany* (Ann Arbor: University of Michigan Press, 2004), 128–84.

23. Lisa Japha, interview 16406, USC Shoah Foundation Visual History Archive.

24. Ruth Frankel, interview 11775, USC Shoah Foundation Visual History Archive.

25. Hildegard Feidel-Mertz, "Schicksale jüdischer Lehrer und Schüler/innen in Bayern (Fates of Jewish teachers and schoolchildren in Bavaria)," in Max Liedtke, ed., *Handbuch der Geschichte des Bayerischen Bildungswesens*

[Manual of the history of the Bavarian education (system)], vol. 2, *Geschichte der Schule in Bayern von 1918 bis 1990* [History of the school in Bavaria from 1918 to 1990] (Bad Heilbronn, Ger.: Klinkhardt, 1997), 441.

26. All but two interviewees who attended private Catholic convent schools prior to 1933 lived in rural areas.

27. Scholem Adler-Rudel, *Jüdische Selbsthilfe unter dem Naziregime 1933–1939* [Jewish self-help under the Nazi regime 1933–1939] (Tübingen, Ger.: Mohr [Paul Siebeck], 1974), 20.

28. Vera Hirtz, interview 39168, USC Shoah Foundation Visual History Archive.

29. Ibid.

30. Margaret Cohen-Tuteur, interview 12235, USC Shoah Foundation Visual History Archive.

31. The law limited Jewish children's enrollment in secondary schools to 1.5 percent. In areas with large Jewish populations, the quota was 5 percent. Marion Kaplan, *Between Dignity and Despair: Jewish Life in Nazi Germany* (New York: Oxford University Press, 1998), 94.

32. Adler-Rudel, *Jüdische Selbsthilfe unter dem Naziregime*, 22.

33. The National Representation of German Jews was founded on September 17, 1933. Ibid.

34. Although Elsbeth did not name the school, she most likely referred to the private nondenominational Eleonoren-Gymnasium, which was established as a higher school for girls in 1874.

35. Elsbeth testified that she began attending private Catholic school in 1933, but it may have been as late as 1935 because the Jewish community in Worms did not establish a school until May 1935. Elsbeth Schmidt, interview 19528, USC Shoah Foundation Visual History Archive; Michael Brodhaecker, "Die jüdischen Bezirksschulen in Mainz und Worms—Normalität in schwerer Zeit [The Jewish district schools in Mainz and Worms—Normalcy in difficult times]," in *Wiesbaden und Rheinhessen in der Zeit des Nationalsozialismus* [Wiesbaden and Rheinhessen in the era of National Socialism] (Mainz, Ger.: Verein für Sozialgeschichte, 2000), 71.

36. Ibid.

37. Margaret Cohen-Tuteur, interview 12235, USC Shoah Foundation Visual History Archive.

38. Anne Goodwin, interview 44737, USC Shoah Foundation Visual History Archive.

39. Ibid.

40. Jo Ann Glickman, interview 26531, USC Shoah Foundation Visual History Archive.

41. Martha Padawer, interview 28094, USC Shoah Foundation Visual History Archive.

42. Ibid.

43. Theresia Gerhardinger to Sister Ignatia, December 3, 1876, in Maria Theresia von Jesu Gerhardinger, *Briefe*, vol. 13 (Munich, Ger.: Provinzialat der Armen Schulschwestern von U. L. Frau, 1979), 64.

44. Margit Korge, "Kindheit [Childhood] in Berlin Charlottenburg Ahornallee 33," Leo Baeck Institute, New York, ME 1252.

45. Ibid.

46. Anne Goodwin, interview 44737, USC Shoah Foundation Visual History Archive.

47. Trudy Coppel used the greeting *Grüß Gott*, literally "Greet God," which is still common in southern Germany. Trudy Coppel, interview 9906, USC Shoah Foundation Visual History Archive.

48. Margaret Cohen-Tuteur, interview 12235, USC Shoah Foundation Visual History Archive.

49. John Conway, "Review," *Catholic Historical Review* 98 (2012): 601.

50. "Zum Geleit [Introduction]," *Bredebrief* [Brede letter], 1933, Archiv Kloster Brede.

51. *Bericht über das Schuljahr 1933, Priv. kath. Oberlyzeum der Armen Schulschwestern v. U. L. Frau Arnsberg in Westf* [Report on the school year 1933: Private Catholic high school of the Poor School Sisters of Notre Dame in Arnsberg, Westphalia]," Archiv Kloster Brede, Arnsberg-Schule.

52. Ibid.

53. Susan Fleischman, interview 29858, USC Shoah Foundation Visual History Archive.

54. *Konferenz-Niederschriften* [Conference transcripts] 1933–1938, February 5, 1934, Archiv Kloster Brede, Schule-Arnsberg.

55. This number was significantly lower, 10 percent versus over 20 percent, than in the Prussian public schools analyzed by historian Wolfgang Schmitz. Wolfgang Schmitz, "Der Alltag des gymnasialen Deutschunterrichts im Dritten Reich—Eine empirische Auswertung der Aufsatzthemen in den Jahresberichten der höheren Lehranstalten Preußens [The daily routine in German class in secondary school in the Third Reich—an empirical analysis of essay topics in the annual reports of Prussian institutions of higher education]," in Reinhard Dithmar and Wolfgang Schmitz, eds., *Schule und Unterricht im Dritten Reich* [Schools and instruction in the Third Reich] (Ludwigsfelde, Ger.: Ludwigsfelder, 2001), 98.

56. Other topics unrelated to National Socialism included "Wir sind jung und das ist schön" (We are young and that is nice) (for the lower grades), "Mein Eindrücke von Shakespeares Drama 'Hamlet'" (My impressions of

Shakespeare's drama 'Hamlet'), and Rafaels 'Sixtinische Madonna'" (Rafael's 'Sistine Madonna.'), "English Students Read Works by Shakespeare, H. G. Wells, and Oscar Wilde," *Bericht über das Schuljahr 1933*, Archiv Kloster Brede, Arnsberg-Schule.

57. "Teilnahme am Freiwilligen Unterricht [Participation in voluntary lessons]," *Bredebrief* 1934, Archiv Kloster Brede.

58. Woodruff Smith, "The Colonial Novel as Political Propaganda: Hans Grimm's *Volk Ohne Raum*," *German Studies Review* 6, 2 (1983): 226.

59. Kevin P. Spicer, *Resisting the Third Reich: The Catholic Clergy in Hitler's Berlin* (DeKalb: University of Northern Illinois Press, 2004), 120, 121.

60. For instance, in an undated memorandum from 1934, Mother M. (Maria) Almeda Schricker of the Poor School Sisters of Notre Dame in Munich warned sisters about a dishonest salesman who "according to our information is a representative of a Jewish business. Let the sisters be warned!" The sisters were well-versed in antisemitic stereotypes and understood the meaning of the communiqué. M. Almeda Schricker, memorandum, 1934, OAASM, *Drittes Reich*.

61. *Bredebrief* 1933, Archiv Kloster Brede.

62. Margaret Federlin, interview 48024, USC Shoah Foundation Visual History Archive.

63. Jo Ann Glickman, interview 26531, USC Shoah Foundation Visual History Archive.

64. "Bericht über den Schulungs-Lehrgang und das Gemeinschaftsleben der Abiturientinnen im Landheim [Report on the training course and the community life of the high school graduates at a country retreat]," *Bredebrief* 1934, Archiv Kloster Brede.

65. Ibid.

66. "Nationalsozialistische Schulung durch Besuch eines männlichen Arbeitsdienstlagers in Driburg ([National Socialist training by visiting a male labor camp in Driburg]," *Bredebrief* 1936, Archiv Kloster Brede.

67. Ibid.

68. "Der schöne Samstag [The beautiful Saturday]," *Bredebrief* 1934, Archiv Kloster Brede.

69. "Ein Besuch beim Führer [A visit to the Führer]," *Bredebrief* 1934, Archiv Kloster Brede.

70. Elisabeth Charlotte-Halder, "Mädchenjahre unter Kreuz und Hakenkreuz [A girlhood under cross and swastika]," Deutsches Tagebucharchiv [German Diary Archive], Signatur 13.2

71. Christel Beilmann, *Eine katholische Jugend in Gottes und dem Dritten Reich* [A Catholic youth in God's and the Third Reich] (Wuppertal, Ger.: Peter Hammer, 1989), 9.

72. Irma Mathes, interview 45616, USC Shoah Foundation Visual History Archive.

73. Irma Hannes, interview 31361, ibid.

74. Jo Ann Glickman, interview 26531, ibid.

75. Herta Adler, interview 27454, ibid.

76. Vera Hirtz, interview 39168, ibid.

77. Ibid.

78. Ibid.

79. See, for instance, Maria Luthner, undated, "Denkschrift über das klösterl. Bildungswesen in München-Oberbayern in den Monaten Juni–September 1935 [Memorandum on the Catholic congregational education system in Munich-Upper Bavaria in the months June–September 1935]," OAAS M, *Drittes Reich*.

80. Gauleiter der NSDAP Westfalen Nord to Oberpräsidenten [regional party leader of the National Socialist Workers' Party (Nazi Party) North Westphalia to the senior president], May 11, 1937, Staatsarchiv Detmold, M 1 II B 6034.

81. Kaplan, *Between Dignity and Despair*, 94.

82. Irma Mathes, interview 45616, USC Shoah Foundation Visual History Archive.

83. Susan Fleischman, interview 29858, USC Shoah Foundation Visual History Archive.

84. Bavarian state officials took the lead in the closure of private confessional schools. In 1937 in Bavaria, 64 women religious communities owned a total of 126 secondary schools for girls, along with 58 boarding schools. On December 29, 1937, all 64 institutes received notices from the state of the immediate or planned closure of most of their congregational schools. On October 2, 1939, Bernhard Rust, Reich minister of science, education and national culture, ordered the closure of all confessional secondary schools by Easter 1940. The shutdown process was never fully completed, but the state nonetheless succeeded in closing the vast majority of confessional secondary schools by 1945. Cucchiara, "Bitter Times," 237, 288.

85. Eva Schuster, interview 27218, USC Shoah Foundation Visual History Archive.

86. Ibid.

87. Korge, "Kindheit in Berlin Charlottenburg Ahornallee 33."

88. Ibid.

Natalia Aleksiun

Daily Survival: Social History of Jews in Family Bunkers in Eastern Galicia

IN MARCH 1944, SHORTLY BEFORE HE WAS LIBERATED TOGETHER WITH his brother-in-law, Baruch Milch summed up his experiences of hiding from the Nazis, writing in his diary: "I've been here nine months already . . . During this time I have killed about a thousand lice, filled about 500 bottles of urine, sweated ten liters, wept two liters of tears, and lost three of my teeth. I have written with a liter of blood . . . and I still don't see the end."[1] Milch, who survived in a village near Czortków (Chortkiv), Eastern Galicia—then in Nazi-occupied Poland, now in Ukraine—received his medical diploma prior to the war, hence his frequent use of medical and physiological terminology. His unsettling account of misery, anger, fear, and hunger not only offers us an insight into the mind-set of a grieving father and husband but also points to physical aspects of his desperate attempts to escape death. Between the summer of 1942 and the spring of 1943, Milch and several members of his family struggled to survive by hiding in villages and forests in the vicinity of Tłuste. When the Nazis carried out mass exterminations in the region, such bunkers, attics, cellars, and larger "family camps" served as sites of temporary refuge for Jewish men, women, and children who had fled from nearby towns in Eastern Galicia.

Confined in overcrowded hideouts, Jewish men, women, and children who had escaped deportations and executions spent weeks, months, and, in some cases, years together. They faced terror and grief, prepared and rationed food, talked, read, and argued. As Marion Kaplan pointed out, "A history of daily life shows how mundane issues matter—and often dominate—even in extreme situations . . . A history of daily life also illuminates how and why the victims—and also the aggressors—adapted to their roles by showing how abuse, insidiously and incrementally, became 'normal' to some and familiar to all."[2] For Jews in hiding, otherwise routine aspects of daily life—such as sanitation, access to food and water, personal hygiene, and passing the time—became enormous challenges, both physically and emotionally. They endured ever-present danger, as the hostility of the surrounding peasant population and local partisans, as well as the occupying Germans, always threatened their existence. Still, Jews seeking shelter in Eastern Galicia confronted defining moments in their lives that could not be put on hold for the duration of their internment. Some fell in love; many fell ill; women got pregnant and gave birth; and people died.

Drawing on archival sources, oral testimonies, diaries, and memoirs in Polish, Yiddish, Hebrew, and English, this essay reconstructs several aspects of the daily experiences of Jews in hiding in what is today western Ukraine. Prior to the Nazi occupation, the region was part of Poland known as Eastern Galicia (Wschodnia Małopolska). This essay tackles Jewish experiences in the Holocaust by focusing on groups who hid together, groups that encompassed immediate and extended families, acquaintances, and many who began this traumatic period as complete strangers. Jewish fugitives, who found themselves "buried alive," struggled to organize their lives in bunkers. What did it entail "to live as though entombed"[3] in the towns, villages, and forests?[4] A close reading of testimonies reveals the daily, intimate, seemingly mundane aspects of everyday life that intersected with death and the devastating realization of its genocidal magnitude.[5] This research explores the social processes and the group dynamics among Jews in hiding, as well as their interethnic relations with local Poles and Ukrainians. In particular, it focuses on familial networks and relationships, including those that formed within the hideouts, among Jews of all ages and from a variety of social backgrounds. It analyzes the impact of fear, distress, and oppressive conditions on daily life in the bunkers.[6]

A vast and growing scholarly literature examines the social history of Jews in Eastern Europe under Nazi occupation, with many works concentrating on individual ghettos or regions,[7] and other notable studies focusing on the activities of organizations and individuals who assisted the Jews.[8] We still lack, however, a thorough understanding of the modes and means by which most Jews in hiding organized their daily existence in local and regional contexts, and especially for

Eastern Galicia.[9] When scholars from a variety of disciplines began tackling the struggles and dilemmas faced by Jews in hiding, they tended to concentrate on urban settings, both in Western and Eastern Europe, rather than on the countryside. A close analysis of the situation in Galicia offers a unique perspective on the efforts of Jews struggling to survive not only in contrast to the studies of Warsaw but also compared to studies of the other regions of Nazi-occupied Poland.[10] In Eastern Galicia, the majority of city dwellers were Polish and Jewish, while the rural population was, for the most part, Ukrainian. In the summer of 1941, Jews in Eastern Galicia found themselves under German occupation. A wave of anti-Jewish violence followed the German invasion of the region, which had been occupied by the Soviet Union since September 1939. The Germans assaulted, brutalized, and murdered them; and their property and personal possessions were plundered with the active participation of their Christian neighbors—Ukrainians and Poles.[11]

By studying the history of hiding in Eastern Galicia, this essay places the experiences of the victims at the center of the historical narrative.[12] Borrowing Saul Friedländer's metaphor, the study of the daily lives of the Jews in Eastern Galicia may be compared to "lightning flashes that illuminate parts of a landscape."[13] Unlike in other parts of Poland during World War II, the Jewish experience in Eastern Galicia was shaped by the German anti-Jewish policies in the territories occupied in the summer and fall of 1941 and by the multiethnic dynamic between Poles, Ukrainians, and Jews. Based on the flashes of light that reveal the past from the extant sources, my study provides a detailed account of how the hidden Jews of Eastern Galicia passed time together, cared for one another, worked out survival strategies, and divided resources and labor during their concealment.[14]

FROM TEMPORARY HIDEOUTS TO SEARCH FOR BUNKERS

Already before the summer of 1942, Jews faced with the murderous German campaign against them sought rescue by hiding locally or posing as non-Jews in large cities. In a testimony recorded in 1960, Aron Ringel described the situation in his native Janów Lwowski (Ivano-Frankove in today's western Ukraine): "People sought ways to leave Janów, assuming that [the situation] was better in other towns . . . Their dream was to reach Cracow [Kraków] or Warsaw, where the danger of being recognized by gentile acquaintances was small."[15] Józef Lippman of Borysław (now Borislav, Ukraine) remembers one cousin being equipped with false papers and sent to Lwów (Lviv in contemporary Ukraine)—never to be heard from again.[16] Others considered escaping across the borders. While living in Tłuste (Tovste) with his wife, son, mother-in-law, and brother-in-law, Baruch Milch constantly evaluated and reevaluated his family's options. He concluded that crossing the Romanian or Hungarian borders had become too risky.[17] Indeed, only a small minority of the small-town Jews of Eastern Galicia seem to have attempted that strategy.

The meaning of "going into hiding" changed over time as Jews in Eastern Galicia grasped the scope of the German murderous campaign against them. In their diaries and postwar testimonies, Jews described the widespread phenomenon of digging bunkers, preparing hideouts, and making arrangements with gentile acquaintances.[18] In Korolówka (Korolivka), Jews began to prepare hiding places upon hearing reports about roundups in the vicinity of their town. Esther Stermer's family initially hid in bunkers they had used during the Soviet occupation when they feared nationalization of property and arrest.[19] As conditions worsened, they

> began to dig our bunkers and dugouts deeper and in less accessible places than before. Those who did not have barns and other farm buildings beneath which to dig such hiding places dug under their bedrooms. Each of these holes in the ground was enlarged to take in the entire family. The hole was then covered with flooring and otherwise masked so that the Germans might not be able to locate it.[20]

In anticipation of the roundups in the fall of 1942, Esther Stermer and her family established six hiding places in their home, including a walled-off space in the attic.[21] Her husband decided against hiding in dugouts and went into the home of a friendly peasant. Similarly, her two sons crossed the river into the nearby fields and then reached a village where a peasant who had served in the army with the older son, Nissen, lived.[22]

In personal documents, Jews use various terms to describe different types of hideouts: "bunkers"—applied most often to hiding places in forests, as in the case of Aron Ringel, who built a bunker for himself and his immediate family near Janów Lwowski.[23] In other diaries and testimonies, shelters in cellars, barns, and attics in and outside of the ghettos have also been described as "bunkers."[24] Gerszon Taffet, who survived hiding in a forest near Gródek Jagielloński (Horodok) remembered that better-equipped hideouts (*schrony*) were called "bunkers."[25] Pepa Braun from Brody testified that she hid together with her parents and two brothers, as well as a rabbi and his wife, in a "hole" prepared in a peasant's stable, then in a forest, in a cave of a quarry, and finally in the stable again.[26] Some testimonies referred to places in which larger groups of Jews hid together in forests as "camps."[27] Marcel Drimer remembers referring to the hiding place shared with his sister on the outskirts of Drohobycz (Drohobych) as "*kuczumunia*"—a term used in the region for a clandestine shelter.[28]

Following the mass executions and deportations in the summer of 1942, many surviving Jews in Eastern Galicia struggled to come up with rescue plans for their families. Esther Stermer remembered her own anguished single-mindedness following the roundup in Korolówka and learning about the order that all the remaining Jews move to the ghetto in nearby Borszczów (Borshchiv): "All our thoughts were on how to save our lives. We considered going into the forest, as others had done, and dig a cave there. Anything rather than go like sheep to slaughter."[29] Numerous testimonies suggest that the concept of building or finding bunkers and hideouts (*bunkry i schrony*) emerged after the traumatic experiences of the first wave of *Aktionen*, operations involving the gathering, deportation, and murder of Jews. When the designated Jewish area of Buczacz was first surrounded by the Germans in November 1942, "whoever was only able to escape, ran away to villages. Nobody knew at this point about bunkers or hideouts. I also managed to flee to the fields."[30] In February 1943, shortly before the second *Aktion*, some Jews prepared bunkers in their own homes. Giza Ferber entered a bunker through a toilet and hid there with fifteen other Jews.[31] Eventually, she and her husband left Buczacz and survived hiding in the forests and with gentile peasants. After mass executions at the Jewish cemetery in May 1943, Milch and the remaining members of his family "decided that it was time to vanish, and we were not the only ones."[32] The decision taken by Milch involved finding a more permanent hiding place outside the ghetto. At the same time, Dr. Eli Kindler in Sokal made a fateful decision to flee the ghetto to join Moshe and Shmelke Maltz rather than try to hide in his well-prepared shelter inside the ghetto.[33] Thus, he decided that his family's chances for survival would be better hiding at the home of a gentile woman rather than inside the ghetto.

PERMANENT BUNKERS AND FAMILY SOLIDARITY

To "vanish," Jewish men and women organized shelters for themselves and members of their immediate family. Milch and his wife's family considered all possible strategies: "There were various suggestions: that we barricade ourselves in the caves, hide in the forest, or organize partisan units."[34] He decided against all three of these plans, which he considered impractical. He was equally critical about the prospect of hiding on a farm "because of the threat of discovery or eventual disclosure by the peasants."[35] For lack of other options, his family concluded that they would "bunker themselves somewhere else (*gdzieś się zabunkrować*)."[36] Together with his brother-in-law, Milch built a shelter at a house of a Ukrainian peasant near Tłuste.[37]

In the majority of cases, Jews approached their former Polish and Ukrainian acquaintances, school friends, employees, or business partners for help. Jack Green (Jankiel Grünschlag) from Bolechów (today Bolechiv) recalled weeks of negotiations and "comparative shopping" carried out by his father in search of a hiding place for himself and his two surviving teenage sons.[38] Brothers Sam and Arie Halpern, who were born and raised in the town of Chorostków (today Chorostkiv), managed to escape from Kamionka camp, and both safely reached the house of Jan Górniak—a business partner and friend of their father's. Górniak hid them in an attic of his barn in Iwanówka (Ivanovka) for eight months until their liberation on March 22, 1944.[39] Marcel Drimer hid with a family who had known his mother. Klara Brottman from Zbaraż (Zbarazh) relied on a network of former clients of her late husband's grain business.[40] Gertrud Podhorcer from Mikulince near Tarnopol (Ternopil) spent almost a year in the attic of the barn of her brother's Ukrainian nanny.[41] Aside from hiding with gentile acquaintances, prewar friendships proved valuable and useful for helping to find the safest and most suitable locations for bunkers. Large groups of Jews, including Esther Stermer's relatives, found caves in the fall of 1942 in which they hid with the help of gentile acquaintances: the manager of an estate in Bilcze Złote (Bilche Zolote) and a friendly Polish forester named Munko.[42] At Munko's suggestion, the second cave was located "in the fields belonging to the parish priest not far from there."[43] Realizing they were running out of time, some Jews accepted offers of shelter from people they hardly knew or trusted, among them individuals known for their antisemitism.[44] Indeed, as historian Omer Bartov pointed out in his research on Buczacz, "The distinction between rescue and denunciation was often blurred and at times nonexistent."[45] While both men and women contacted Polish and Ukrainian acquaintances, planning and construction of temporary and permanent bunkers appears to have been carried out predominantly by Jewish men.[46]

As their testimonies and diaries suggest, Jews sought to survive together, struggling to keep families intact. In Sokal, Moshe Maltz rejected his friend's suggestion "that he and I get permits to travel from village to village as rag peddlers. In this way the two of us could leave Sokal and go underground in some village as soon as we hear that an *Aktion* is imminent. But then what happens to my family."[47] But faced with recurring brutal roundups and executions, they explored various approaches, including staying together and deliberately dispersing. Hiding separately seemed to increase chances for survival of at least some members of the family. Before the deportation of Jews from Sokal in mid-September 1942 and the establishment of the ghetto for the remaining Jews a month later, Maltz opposed his friend's idea: "My plan is that our family should not hide together in one place but should be scattered, so that our whole family will not be wiped out at one blow. At least some of us must remain as living witnesses to the tragedy that befell our people."[48] Esther Stermer and her relatives hid in various bunkers in Korolówka: "Each member of our family hid in his own bunker so as not to be together; if some of us were to be taken, at least others might survive."[49] Milch preferred hiding with his wife instead of joining a larger group. He knew that "there was more chance for the two of us alone to find a hiding place than for a group of adults with a small child, all the more since our son, little Lunek, was no longer with us . . . I gave in to my wife, forwent a hiding place that had been offered to the two of us, and started to look for one that would contain us all."[50]

Parents desperately tried to secure shelter for their children. When Jews from Korolówka received the order to move to the Borszczów ghetto, Shapsy Stermer asked a friendly peasant to hide their youngest child, Shlomo. The peasant agreed to take the boy to his sister. In exchange, Stermer loaded the peasant's wagon with furniture and other movable possessions, such as new clothing and shoes. "You can imagine how happy we were in the hope that possibly our child would live through the war. As for ourselves, we were certain that we were doomed . . . When all was packed up on the wagon, we told the man to make sure that at all costs Shlomo should survive. His full reward would come after the war."[51] While adult relatives negotiated with gentile acquaintances in arranging hideouts, small children proved an obstacle and a liability. Polish and Ukrainian caretakers were reluctant to take in young children because their presence required additional provisions and, more importantly, could be easily detected. In Żółkiew (Zhovkva), the Becks, who had agreed to shelter a group of Jewish teenagers, refused to take in their toddler cousins.[52] Milch evaluated the situation of his family in Tłuste and decided against hiding in a bunker with his three-year-old son, Lunek: "Even though the poor boy was well trained and knew that he must not speak aloud or go into the street, a child could endanger everybody."[53] Sometime in the spring of 1942, in a desperate attempt to find a place for himself and his immediate family, Milch consulted his former patients, only to discover that his three-year-old son was a liability.[54] Similarly, his brother-in-law was unable to secure a hiding place for his own three-year-old son, Eliasz.[55] There were groups, however, that took in small children. Such was the case of thirty-eight Jews hiding in the cave near Bilcze Złote.[56]

A sense of responsibility in close-knit families led, in some cases, to running the risk of bringing relatives into hideouts shared with other Jews. Shimon Kitner, who hid in the cave together with Esther Stermer's family, brought in his sister Freda; a brother, Leib; and his son Sunia. His father and his married sisters had already been killed.[57] In many accounts, relatives forced to live together in hiding strove to share resources, help one another, and console one another. Seeking a rational account of the survival of her children and grandchildren, Esther Stermer declared in her memoir: "Our family in particular would not let the Germans have their way easily. We had vigor, ingenuity, and determination to survive. Above all, our family would stand together. When one of us was in danger, the others could not cover to escape. They proved their personal strength and character, time and again."[58]

Hiding over an extended period proved testing as fear and hunger affected family relations. Tension became palpable, especially with regard to those who were seen as a liability: children and the sick. Milch described candidly how three-year-old toddler Eliasz—his brother-in-law's son—brought everybody to the edge trying to move around the shelter: "His behavior drove us crazy and he became alien and repulsive to us."[59] In Milch's bitter account, his brother-in-law made their life together in a shelter they shared after the death of their wives and children increasingly testing:

> Now the true nature of my former brother-in-law, the man who is here with me and has shared all the difficulties, is emerging. How can it be, after all we've gone through together that instead of comforting each other we're making each other's lives miserable? I don't know whether it's from frayed nerves or a question of character. We probe the past, settle scores, and vainly blame each other for our loved ones' death.[60]

Despite solidarity and self-sacrifice, the constant fright and scarcity of food, water, and space also led to bitter conflicts among family members and strangers.[61]

CHALLENGES OF HIDING: ACCESS TO FOOD AND WATER

By and large, Jewish fugitives who were able to find or prepare a shelter had to procure their own food and water and faced the constant terror of being discovered and betrayed. They had to maintain hygiene to prevent illnesses and secure money to pay locals for supplies. In most hiding places, food was meager and consisted of barley, potatoes, or boiled grains and little else. Whether or not Jews sought rescue in villages or away from human domiciles, they still relied on a degree of continuous communication with rescuers and caretakers. In some arrangements, Jewish families received provisions directly at the bunkers. Such was the case of Aron Ringel: he and his family received assistance from a local Ukrainian ranger, who helped to prepare the hideout and provided its occupants with their meager food supplies.[62] Pepa Braun and her family relied on the assistance of a Ukrainian peasant—Łućko—located by her father.[63] Following months of food deprivation, Milch marveled at the quality of goods he and his brother-in-law were given by their caretakers in a village near Czortków. They even began to gain weight.[64] A contrasting case was two sisters from Buczacz who hid for fifteen months in a primitive shelter in Haje Dubieńskie with a small son. Their provisions lasted only for the initial weeks. Later, the sisters had to steal food at night from the fields. They became so emaciated that, "For a long time they stopped talking with each other and communicated only with their eyes and body language. They did not have strength left to speak."[65]

Some Jews who built clandestine shelters away from towns and villages tried to secure their necessities by buying or stealing them from peasants. In most cases, designated individuals—primarily men—left their hiding places to purchase or steal food in villages or to exchange items with gentiles.[66] They secured flour, barley, potatoes, kerosene, detergents, matches, and other essential supplies.[67] Due to the imminent danger inherent in securing these essentials "from the outside," and the physical challenge to people increasingly frail, these expeditions were kept to the minimum.[68] Inevitably, those in hiding became vulnerable to exploitation and threats by the peasants who sold them food and delivered provisions.[69] When it became difficult to secure flour from peasants, a group hiding in the cave near Bilcze Złote set up a mill to grind flour with two stones.[70] From forest hideouts, men ventured to nearby villages at night to procure food or barter for necessities: "The potatoes were beginning to grow in the fields, so our men would go out at night to steal some."[71] In the fall, Esther Stermer's family stocked up on provisions of corn and potatoes, hoping to survive through the winter.[72]

Families would ration food, with priority given to the young. Shapse and Esther Stermer gave up better food that their sons were occasionally able to procure or steal from peasants for the younger people. "We did not work as hard as they did, so we would content ourselves with a little soup; then we would go and lie down again . . . I ate only enough to keep alive. We had to consider every bite because food had become so difficult to procure."[73] Mendel Ruder placed his six-year-old son, Dalek, with a peasant named Muskaluk in Woroniaki, near Złoczów. The boy, who hid with several other Jews, remembered that "people who were with me in the stable washed me and gave me food."[74] A source of fresh water rendered some hiding places particularly suitable.[75] Otherwise, the supply of drinking water tended to be limited and had to be rationed. At times, melting snow improved the situation. Clara Kramer remembered the cautious use of water in her bunker in Żółkiew: "Water was as precious as food or money. Water was our lifeline. We used it to cook the potatoes into a soup and the water we washed our hair in was reused to soak our clothes. Not a drop was wasted. Ever."[76]

Esther Stermer and the group hidden in the cave took turns cooking on a tripod they had brought in. "I also had a large copper pan which held about a pail of water. In normal times we used it for making jams and desserts . . . No sooner were we through than the others took their turn to cook."[77] Whenever possible, cooking had to be limited to the bare minimum because it caused problems with ventilation or generated unbearable heat.[78] Jews in hiding also had to be very careful with smoke because of ventilation or the danger of smoke betraying the presence of their bunker. Cooking was therefore usually done only at night.[79] Without fire, Jews hiding in forests could not prepare food and were exposed to the elements. In the early spring of 1944, Yacov Perlmuter and his comrades hiding in the vicinity of Skalat "suffered because we had no fire and therefore we were freezing. By this time, we also had nothing to eat and were on the verge of starvation. We managed to stay alive by eating snow and frozen sugar beets left behind by the murdered Jews."[80]

HOUSEHOLD GOODS AND CLOTHING

Many Jews who went into hiding had to remain motionless for days on end. Rosa Schorman hid in Tarnopol, together with her husband, Otto; brother Dawid; and a young Jewish couple known as the Blejzes. During the day, they stood behind a false wall.[81] In most cases, there was no possibility of taking furniture or household items into these shelters. Only in some hideouts could families set up separate spaces for living quarters, cooking, and washing. Esther Stermer's group took some furniture to the caves.[82] Among the most important possessions were quilts and pillows.[83] In the large bunker prepared in Drohobycz, there were plank beds, cooking facilities, canisters for collecting water, and even a stove.[84] Among objects taken to the bunkers, the subject of clothing appears prominently in diaries. Esther Stermer observed that, while hiding in the cave "we had worn our shoes to bits and the children walked about barefoot."[85] A few Jews in hiding could rely on items or resources left by their gentile acquaintances.[86] Maltz marveled at the generosity of the Polish caretaker who "has given us four pairs of warm boots" during their first winter in her pigsty.[87]

Access to clothes increased chances of surviving, not only during the cold winter but also through improved sanitary conditions. In numerous Jewish testimonies, the subject of hygiene is closely linked with futile attempts to battle lice. Milch bemoaned the miserable condition of his clothes, especially his underwear, because he slept in his clothes after going underground.[88] Pepa Braun mentioned a weekly routine of the Jews in her hideout of washing themselves.[89] For Esther Stermer, setting up a washing area in the cave transformed their hiding place into a home and gave them a fighting chance to stay healthy, since they

> warmed water for washing ourselves. We would wash out our clothes and then boil them in hot water. We would then rinse them again in some nearby water. Drying our clothes was much more difficult. We learned to wring them well and then spread them out behind our sleeping places. After a short time they would dry out somewhat.[90]

Most lacked toilet facilities, other than buckets. In the attic over the pigsty, where Moshe Maltz hid, the Jews "screened off part of our hayloft with a cotton sheet. This is our private toilet."[91] A few more sophisticated bunkers included latrines resembling toilets aboveground.[92]

PRAYING, READING, AND BREADWINNING

In most hiding places, activities such as cooking, eating, talking, and walking were limited to nighttime, if possible at all. Those in hiding "changed night into day."[93] Little talking was allowed in bunkers built inside houses, and only at night.[94] "We blessed God for creating the miracle of night, and we often wished that it would continue forever. We hated to wake up to the martyrdom of daybreak," wrote Dr. Otto Schorman in his memoir.[95]

Because speaking aloud was in most settings too dangerous, reading offered many "entombed" Jews a chance to divert their thoughts from fear and grief and to pass the time. Few brought reading material with them. Instead, they asked for, and received, books from their caregivers. When Baruch Milch was first hiding with his family near Tłuste, he, his wife, and his brother-in-law read "anything we lay hands on. My brother-in-law brought cards and we played solitaire."[96] Later,

Milch and his father-in-law received books and news from his new caretakers near Czortków. He noted in his diary: "I read and sometimes reread various books. Mrs. Zielinski, a devout woman, gives me books about the lives of the saints. I have read the principles of the Christian faith and both the Old and the New Testaments."[97] Despite the danger of raising neighbors' suspicions over a newly found interest in newspapers, Jews in hiding—often in complete isolation from the outside world—asked their caretakers to provide them with reading material to follow the developments on the war front.[98] In the case of Milch and his brother-in-law, they begged Polish women, who assisted them by providing maps. Having obtained school atlases created by Eugeniusz Romer, a well-known Polish cartographer, they followed wartime events and movements of the front lines.[99] Maltz received Polish and German daily papers from his caretaker:

> When Mrs. Halamajowa is finished with the papers, she brings them up to us. But we have to wait until the next morning to read them, for by the time we receive them it is dark outside and there is no more light in the hayloft. In the morning I put on my winter wraps, including warm gloves, so I can stand close to a crack in the wall through which a sliver of winter daylight enters the hideout along with the icy December blasts. That's where I read the newspaper from the preceding day.[100]

Writing played an important role in helping to cope with loneliness, fill the time, and bring relief from the monotony and fear. Thus, whenever conditions allowed taking notes, young and old, prewar merchants and members of Jewish intelligentsia, wrote.[101] For young Clara Schwarz keeping a diary "was something . . . to do every day, something with purpose. It was a way to fight back."[102] In the fall of 1943, Milch referred to his diary as both a physical challenge and a form of therapy: "I am shivering with the cold and find it difficult to lift my hand from under the blanket to write. But my heart is so heavy since Mrs. P. left that I have to vent all the pain onto paper."[103] The change of seasons could also provide some relief. Esther Stermer recalled, "Winter and its snows were of some advantage to us. We felt safer, for people were less likely to stray our way."[104]

Rare moments of shared celebrations contrasted with the monotony of fear, grief, and physical discomfort. Religious traditions provided meaning and emotional relief, connecting those in bunkers with the memory of family and community life before the war. At times, the contrast painfully reminded them of loss. In the spring of 1942, shortly before finding a second cave, when Esther Stermer was hiding in an attic, her husband and son Nissen "would return at night and bring us some food. It was the Passover week but perforce we ate *chametz* [leavened foods forbidden during Passover]. There were two peasants' huts not far from our barn. Through the cracks in our walls we could see the women and their children cleaning and whitewashing their houses, readying for the Easter festival."[105] On the High Holidays in September 1943, those living in a bunker in Żółkiew noted, "We knew that chances were this might be our last Yom Kippur. And our last chance to pray for atonement in this lifetime."[106] In the cave, the group followed the calendar and observed Jewish holidays. "We also had a prayer book for the high holy days. On . . . Yom Ki[p]pur day we fasted and prayed the entire day." Her son-in-law led the services.[107] Numerous other Jewish accounts mention communal observances of Yom Kippur on October 8–9, 1943, as an emotional and heartrending experience since those in hiding were often painfully aware of the death of their families. The group hiding in Sokal asked Franciszka Halamajowa not to bring them any food because they intended to fast.[108] Yakov Perlmutter described a group of Jews in the Malinik forest near Skałat: "As it was the eve of Yom Kippur, we preceded the fast with roasted potatoes, and Moishe Leib Hecht recited the Kol-Nidre prayer from memory. The next morning, Tune Schwartz prayed and we joined in the sorrowful chants."[109] The group spent free time praying together, telling stories, singing "*yidishe folkslider*" (popular Yiddish songs) and "*hazonishe nigunim*" (cantorial tunes), as well as reading newspapers.[110]

Shared activities brought a degree of consolation and hope for a future after liberation. During a period of relative respite in the summer of 1943, Milch also kept himself occupied playing chess with his brother-in-law.[111] In the cave in which Esther Stermer and many of her relatives hid together, her granddaughter Sima-Pearl, four years old at the time, entertained everyone by reciting songs and poems she had learned from her older sister Sonia.[112] For some Jews, festive occasions were also related to Christian holidays. In the Żółkiew bunker, the children received gifts on Christmas.[113] For Milch and his brother-in-law, their benefactors organized birthday celebrations, complete with a cake and pastry.[114]

There were bunkers in which Jews continued to work to support themselves or to assist or work for their caretakers. In the first cave, near Bilcze Złote, the dental technician "arranged a sort of a workshop in the cave. His son-in-law the dentist, who remained in town, would accept orders and take the measurements and Mr. Frank would make the plates."[115] Helping with household chores or knitting seems to have been common among Jewish women given shelter. Esther Stermer's daughter Chana found shelter with a gentile woman who "was weak and Chana did all her hard work for her, besides knitting sweaters for the whole family. Chana had become an unpaid servant for them."[116]

HYGIENE AND PHYSICAL AILMENTS

In various hideouts, catching and killing lice became part of a daily routine. In the hayloft where the Maltzs and the Kindlers hid: "Each one of us has a little cup of water. When we wake up in the morning, we pick the fleas from our blankets, clothes and bodies and dunk them in the water until they drown."[117] Milch and his brother-in-law "kept ourselves busy by squeezing the lice that multiplied in our clothes which we never took off."[118] Trying to avoid diseases, Milch and his brother-in-law washed themselves and their underwear as often as possible. They also competed in catching lice and introduced an almost daily ritual of hunting for insects that Milch compared to a prayer.[119] Gertrud Podhorcer and her parents likened the routine hunt for lice to a "manicure."[120] In this way, Jews in hiding strove to present their struggle against insects—the affliction that was a cause of considerable suffering—in familiar terms and turn it into a pastime.

Many Jews hiding in the forest developed skin diseases, with open sores and infections, additionally infested with lice. Seventeen Jews, including Giza Ferber and her husband, hid in a bunker in Buczacz awaiting the return of the Red Army. Ferber recalled that they were "all covered with ulcers and scabies like lepers."[121] In the hayloft of Franciszka Halamajowa, the Maltzs and the Kinders cared for Chaye Dvora, who had become gravely ill.[122] In the spring of 1944, shortly before liberation, Jews hiding in the forests near Skalat were all described as "living corpses: barefoot, in tatters, swollen, and sick."[123] In their testimonies, survivors bring up physical ailments as a matter of fact, without dwelling on their symptoms, which at times lasted after liberation.[124]

Hiding took a heavy psychological and physical toll. Milch and his brother-in-law began complaining about various pains and diseases, headaches, and losing teeth.[125] Milch also was an acute observer of symptoms resulting from living under constant stress: "My nerves are so tight that I often get a kind of nervous tic or an uncontrollable trembling in a hand or a foot. The slightest irritation causes my whole body to shake or my legs refuse to sustain my weight."[126] Some Jews hiding together in forests died as a result of starvation and exposure, even after they were evacuated by the Soviets.[127]

TRAUMA, DEATH, AND MOURNING

The constant threat of death tormented men, women, and children in hiding. Rather than face discovery and deportation, some may have committed suicide, while others were driven close to taking their own lives.[128] Under constant stress, behavioral and psychological problems arose. Some found themselves unable to sleep.[129] Shulim Stermer suffered from a nervous shock when his family's hiding place in the first cave was discovered. He was paralyzed and unable to talk or eat.[130] In bunkers and shelters where young children hid, the issue of their uncurbed behavior led to discussions about their fate. In the case of Moshe Maltz's niece, the family decided to administer poison to the child because she would not stop crying.[131] Milch describes in detail the death of his brother-in-law's three-year-old son. Pressured by the peasant, who insisted the Jews should dispose of the child, Milch's relations debated the most humanitarian solutions. In June of 1943, following futile attempts at finding a shelter for the boy and in a moment of emotional frenzy, the child's father suffocated him in the presence of his relatives.[132] Living under constant pressure and in unbearable conditions led some Jews to a complete breakdown and to contemplate suicide.[133] It was considered the last resort for those who concluded they had been caught and who had access to poison.[134] Proper burial, of course, was not an option because that would place those still alive in mortal danger by betraying their presence to the local population.

Likewise, there was no possibility to mourn the dead because those in hiding had to remain vigilant.[135] Nevertheless, various sights and sounds continued to bring painful, unbearable memories to those in hiding as they were constantly confronted with the memory of lost family members. Some came up with strategies to help them lessen the pain. Following the death of his sister, Chaye Dvore, Maltz noted: "Our mother never looks out through the crack in the hayloft anymore because she can't bear to see the apple tree beneath which her youngest daughter is buried."[136] Milch described in his diary not only episodes of emotional numbness but also mental breakdowns from grief. He noted, "Hiding for so long is difficult. It drives you crazy. The long dark evenings and sleepless nights are worst of all, as your head bursts with images that race past your eyes. Past and present gave you no rest and I could not envision the future at all."[137] For the most part, however, sadness and grief were repressed and concealed. "No more moaning, no more crying. I have just seen my youngest sister die," noted Moshe Maltz in September 1943, with wry straightforwardness.[138]

The physical and psychological toll of hiding was compounded by the grief and a sense of guilt Jews felt about surviving after their families had been deported or killed in the vicinity. Could they have done more for their loved ones?[139] The anguish intensified with the news about others whose bunkers had been discovered. Many of these victims were relatives, neighbors, and friends.[140] Esther Stermer's sons returned deeply upset following their excursions outside the cave. They confided to their mother that "the police and their helpers had boasted that they had discovered a bunker in the forest and had killed very many Jews. Among these were our best friends . . . There had been twenty-four people in the bunker, among them Mendel Geller with four children, two boys and two girls. These children had all been friends of my children."[141] Edzia Szpeicher managed to survive together with her sister in the labor camp in Borysław and in hiding. In flight, the two women encountered the bunker that had belonged to the Sternbach family: "In front of the bunker lie tens of corpses. It made a horrible impression on us. We did not wish to struggle anymore. We decided to go to the garrison so that we would be deported to Płaszów in order to die with everybody."[142] On their way, Edzia and her sister encountered a friendly Pole and eventually found the strength to continue their struggle for survival.

Jews in Eastern Galicia sought rescue by going into hiding. Few survived; the Nazis or their helpers murdered more than 90 percent of the 500,000 Jews residing there in 1941. The Jews were either deported to the extermination camp of Bełżec (some to Sobibor) or killed in plain view in forests or cemeteries. For the majority of the Jews who tried to find shelter or build bunkers in the forests, their survival depended on their familiarity with the area and their ability to identify gentiles willing to provide assistance. Living conditions in hiding were, in most cases, extremely difficult. Moreover, the victims were often completely at the mercy of their rescuers. As such, they were in constant danger of denunciation by neighbors, sometimes by family members of the caretakers. Jews in hiding made every effort to avoid undermining the resolve of those sheltering them. Days, weeks, months, and years spent in hiding became monotonous and seemingly uneventful. But Jewish accounts speak of the daily effort in the face of various challenges, both physical and psychological: developing and cultivating relationships with Polish and Ukrainian benefactors; procuring food and clothes; and overcoming hunger, illnesses, and mental breakdowns while living with constant fear.

This research relates experiences of the Jewish victims and their accounts of imprisonment and deprivation, widening the symbolic geography of the Holocaust typically placed around ghettos and camps.[143] The research case study of Eastern Galicia points to rich resources of material describing Jewish struggles to survive in a rural area and in the social landscape of small towns. Looking at daily lives in hiding shows the dynamic of Jewish responses to persecution and genocide, and underlines individual and group efforts to adapt to, and grasp, German policies. Issues such as family decisions to stay together or hide separately, preparing hideouts, procuring supplies, and adapting daily routines to harsh conditions shed light on the extent of the Jews' agency, their ability to control their own lives, and the variety of Jewish strategies.

This essay finds that Jews in rural settings in Eastern Galicia tended to hide together in small groups, which they saw as offering them the best chances of survival. While relying on familial relationships and acquaintances, they developed resourceful strategies. Such groups utilized and shared their social capital, the collective value of social ties and the support they provide for beneficial cooperation, especially local networks and intimate knowledge of the area. The experiences of these Jews in hiding in Eastern Galicia shows that too often the question is posed in hindsight about Jewish resistance, overlooking complex dilemmas and the intense thought, planning, and strategizing by Jewish men and women who strove to survive in hiding.

NOTES

1. Baruch Milch, *Can Heaven Be Void?* (Jerusalem: Yad Vashem, 2003), 220.

2. Marion Kaplan, *Between Dignity and Despair: Jewish Life in Nazi Germany* (New York: Oxford University Press, 1998), 6.

3. Milch, *Can Heaven Be Void?* 184.

4. Several Jewish accounts compare life in hiding with being buried alive; see Esther Stermer's comment: "Here we were in the grotto, underground, buried alive. We had to arrange our lives somehow and adapt ourselves for possible survival." Esther Stermer, *We Fight to Survive* (Montreal: Jewish Institute of Higher Research, 1975), 31. Also see Bernard Mayer, *Entombed: My True Story: How Forty-Five Jews Lived Underground and Survived the Holocaust* (Ojus, Fla.: Aleric, 1994).

5. See Omer Bartov, "Communal Genocide: Personal Accounts of the Destruction of Buczacz, Eastern Galicia, 1941–1944," chap. 21 in Omer Bartov and Eric D. Weitz, eds., *Shatterzone of Empires: Coexistence and Violence in the German, Habsburg, Russian, and Ottoman Borderlands* (Bloomington: Indiana University Press, 2013), 400. My research is based primarily on testimonies of survivors, both published and unpublished. While some of these accounts were written during the war, the vast majority have been recorded after liberation by the Central Jewish Historical Commission (later the Jewish Historical Institute) in Poland and Yad Vashem in Jerusalem. Although the earliest testimonies are generally believed more credible, in the case of many aspects of daily lives, such as food preparation or personal hygiene, detailed accounts might appear only in the later testimonies and oral interviews; see, for example, Shimon Redlich, *Together and Apart in Brzezany: Poles, Jews and Ukrainians, 1919–1945* (Bloomington: Indiana University Press, 2002). See also Bartov, "Communal Genocide," 400–403.

6. This is part of a wider study of bunker life in Eastern Galicia, partially carried out as a Pearl Resnick Postdoctoral Fellow at the United States Holocaust Memorial Museum in Washington, D.C.

7. Israel Gutman, *The Jews of Warsaw, 1939–1943: Ghetto, Underground, Revolt* (Bloomington: Indiana University Press, 1982); Tikva Fatal-Knaani, *Zo lo otah Grodnoh: Kehilat Grodnoh u-sevivatah ba-milhamah uva-sho'ah, 1939–1943* [Grodno is not the same: The community of Grodno in war and the Shoah, 1939–1943] (Jerusalem: Yad Vashem, 2001); Andrea Löw, *Juden im Getto Litzmannstadt: Lebensbedingungen, Selbstwahrnehmung, Verhalten* [Jews in the Łódź ghetto: Living conditions, self-perception, behavior] (Göttingen, Ger.: Wallstein, 2006); Yehuda Bauer, *The Death of the Shtetl* (New Haven, Conn.: Yale University Press, 2009); Sara Bender, *The Jews of Białystok during World War II and the Holocaust* (Waltham, Mass.:

Brandeis University Press, 2008); Sara Bender, "*Be-eretz oyev": Yehude Keltseh veha-sevivah, 1939–1949* ["In the enemy's territory": The Jews of Kielce and vicinity, 1939–1949] (Jerusalem: Yad Vashem, 2012).

8. Teresa Prekerowa, *Konspiracyjna rada pomocy Żydom w Warszawie 1942–1945* [Underground council to aid Jews in Warsaw 1942–1945] (Warsaw: Państwowy Instytut Wydawniczy, 1982); Nechama Tec, *When Light Pierced the Darkness: Christian Rescue of Jews in Nazi-Occupied Poland* (New York: Oxford University Press, 1986); Ewa Kurek, *Your Life Is Worth Mine: How Polish Nuns Saved Hundreds of Jewish Children in German-Occupied Poland, 1939–1945* (New York: Hippocrene, 1997); Beate Kosmala, *Verbotene Hilfe: Rettung für Juden in Deutschland 1941–1945* [Forbidden help: Rescue of Jews in Germany 1941–1945] (Bonn, Ger.: Friedrich-Ebert Stiftung, 2004); Władysław Bartoszewski and Zofia Lewinówna, eds., *Ten jest z ojczyzny mojej: Polacy z pomocą Żydom 1939–1945* [This one is from my homeland: Poles to the aid of Jews 1939–1945] (Warsaw: Stowarzyszenie Żydowski Instytut Historyczny w Polsce [Association of the Jewish Historical Institute in Poland], Świat Książki, 2007); Beate Meyer, "The Inevitable Dilemma: The Reich Association (Reichsvereinigung) of Jews in Germany, the Deportations, and the Jews who went Underground," in *On Germans and Jews under the Nazi Regime. Essays by Three Generations of Historians. A Festschrift in honor of Otto Dov Kulka*, ed. Moshe Zimmermann (Jerusalem: The Richard Koebner Minerva Center for German History, Hebrew University of Jerusalem, Hebrew University Magnes Press, 2006), 297–312.

9. The few notable works that focus on Jewish daily life include Dalia Ofer and Naftali Greenwood, "Everyday Life of Jews under Nazi Occupation: Methodological Issues," *Holocaust and Genocide Studies* 9, 1 (1995); Dalia Ofer, "Cohesion and Rupture: The Jewish Family in East European Ghettos during the Holocaust," *Studies in Contemporary Jewry* 14 (1998): 143–65; and Kaplan, *Between Dignity and Despair*.

10. Gunnar S. Paulsson, *Secret City: The Hidden Jews of Warsaw, 1940–1945* (New Haven, Conn.: Yale University Press, 2002); Joanna Nalewajko-Kulikow, *Strategie przetrwania: Żydzi po aryjskiej stronie Warszawy* [Survival strategies: Jews on the Aryan side of Warsaw] (Warsaw: Neriton/IPHAN, 2004); Grzegorz Kołacz, *Czasami trudno się bronić: uwarunkowania postaw Żydów podczas okupacji hitlerowskiej w Polsce* [Sometimes it's hard to defend yourself: Determinants of the attitudes of Jews during the Nazi occupation in Poland] (Warsaw: Wydawnictwa Akademickie i Profesjonalne, 2008). For the recent studies that tackle the situation of the countryside, see Barbara Engelking, Jacek Leociak, and Dariusz Libionka, eds., *Prowincja noc: życie i Zagłada Żydów w dystrykcie warszawskim* [Province of the night: The life and murder of Jews in the Warsaw district] (Warsaw: IFiS, 2007); Barbara

Engelking, *Jest taki piękny słoneczny dzień . . . Losy Żydów szukających ratunku na wsi polskiej 1942–1945* [It is such a beautiful sunny day . . . the fate of Jews seeking refuge in the Polish countryside 1942–1945] (Warsaw: Stowarzyszenie Centrum Badań nad Zagładą Żydów, 2011); Marta Cobel-Tokarska, *Bezludna wyspa, nora, grób; wojenne kryjówki Żydów w okupowanej Polsce* [The uninhabited island, den, grave: The war hiding place of Jews in occupied Poland] (Warsaw: IPN, 2012); Jan Grabowski, *Hunt for the Jews: Betrayal and Murder in German-Occupied Poland* (Bloomington: Indiana University Press, 2013).

11. See Dieter Pohl, *Nationalsozialistische Judenverfolgung in Ostgalizien 1941–1944: Organisation und Durchführung eines staatlichen Massenverbrechens* [National Socialist persecution of the Jews in Eastern Galicia 1941–1944: Organization and implementation of a state mass crime] (Munich, Ger.: De Gruyter, 1997).

12. See, for example, the introduction to Christopher R. Browning, *Remembering Survival: Inside a Nazi Slave-Labor Camp* (New York: Norton, 2010). See also Alexandra Garbarini, "Diaries, Testimonies, and Jewish Histories of the Holocaust," chap. 5 in Norman J. W. Goda, ed., *Jewish Histories of the Holocaust: New Transnational Approaches* (New York: Berghahn, 2014), 91. For the recent publications on the region of Eastern Galicia, see Ray Brandon and Wendy Lower, eds., *The Shoah in Ukraine: History, Testimony, Memorialization* (Bloomington: Indiana University Press, 2010); Omer Bartov, "Wartime Lies and Other Testimonies: Jewish-Christian Relations in Buczacz, 1939–1944," *East European Politics & Societies* 25, 3 (2011): 486–511. See also Robert Kuwałek, "The Rescuers, the Rescued, the Denouncers, the Denounced: A Preliminary Study of Relations between Jews, Poles and Ukrainians under the German Occupation in Eastern Galicia," in Aleksandra Zinczuk, ed., *Pojednanie przez trudną pamięć. Wołyń 1943* [Reconciliation through a difficult memory: Volhynia 1943] (Lublin, Poland: Stowarzyszenie Panorama Kultur, 2013), 355–62.

13. Saul Friedländer, *The Years of Extermination: Nazi Germany and the Jews, 1939–1945* (New York: HarperCollins, 2007), xxv.

14. Scholars closely studied family camps and groups in the area of Belarus with the focus on resistance, as in the case of the Bielski brothers, partisans who rescued Jews from extermination. For the general discussion of the phenomenon, see Yitzhak Arad, "Family Camps in the Forests," in Israel Gutman, ed., *Encyclopedia of the Holocaust*, vol. 2 (Jerusalem: Yad Vashem, 1990), 467–69; Yitzhak Arad, "Family Camps in the Forests," in Israel Gutman, ed., *Nisyonot u-fe'ulot hatsalah be-teḳufat ha-Sho'ah : hartsa'ot ve-diyunim ba-kinus ha-benle'umi ha-sheni shel ḥoḳre ha-Sho'ah* [Survival Attempts and Activities during the Holocaust], Yerushalayim. Nisan 5734–April 1974 (Jerusalem: Yad Vashem, 1974), 276–94. See Nechama

Tec, *Defiance: The Bielski Partisans* (New York: Oxford University Press, 1993); Leonid Smilovitsky, *Jewish Family Camps and Groups in Belarus, 1941–1944*, trans. Anya Karasik (Tel Aviv: Diaspora Research Center of Tel Aviv University), http://www.jewishgen.org/yizkor/belarus/bel119.html.

15. Yad Vashem Archives, 0.3, folder 1637, 5.

16. Author interview with Józef Lippman, October 2012, Wrocław, Poland.

17. Milch, *Can Heaven Be Void?* 110–11.

18. At the end of August 1942, Moshe Maltz notes that in Sokal, "The Jews are looking for places to hide when the Aktion comes. Some are digging bunkers." Moshe Maltz, *Years of Horror, Glimpse of Hope: The Diary of a Family in Hiding*, trans. Gertrude Hirschler (New York: Shengold, 1993), 34.

19. Stermer, *We Fight to Survive*, 13.

20. Ibid., 21.

21. Ibid., 21, 26–27.

22. Ibid., 22–23.

23. Yad Vashem Archives, 0.3, folder 1637. Testimony recorded in 1960.

24. In September 1942, Maltz notes in his diary that "a bunker has been built under the ground floor of Shmuel Letzter's house. The entrance to this bunker is through my parents' room and is covered by several boards." Maltz, *Years of Horror*, 39. In October 1942, Maltz repeated his observation of the remaining Jews confined to a ghetto in Sokal: "The Jews in the ghetto are in the state of panic each night because they don't know when the next *Aktion* will come. People are preparing bunkers and other hideouts beneath the ground floors and in the attics of their homes in the ghetto." Ibid., 51.

25. Gerszon Taffet, *Zagłada Żydów żółkiewskich* [The extermination of the Jews of Żółkiew (Zhovkva)] (Łódź, Poland: Central Jewish Historical Commission, 1946), 42.

26. Archiwum Żydowskiego Instytutu Historycznego (Archives of the Jewish Historical Institute, AŻIH), 301/2281. Testimony written down in Katowice on April 4, 1947.

27. Jack Green referred to two groups of eleven and twenty-six Jews hiding in the same forest near Bolechów as "camps." Leonard Regnier, *Forest Days: How Father, Jack and Bumek Survived the Holocaust*, 1995, 57–58. I am grateful to the Holocaust Center of Northern California, San Francisco for making this account available to me.

28. Author interview with Marcel Drimer, July 26, 2012, Washington, D.C.

29. Stermer, *We Fight to Survive*, 28.

30. Testimony of Giza Ferber, Archiwum Żydowskiego Instytutu Historycznego, 301/2528, 1. Giza Ferber, de domo Ehensztajn, was born in

Buczacz on November 6, 1903. Her Polish testimony was recorded in Bytom, Poland, July 12, 1947.

31. Ibid., 2.

32. Milch, *Can Heaven Be Void?* 134.

33. See Maltz, *Years of Horror*, 93.

34. Ibid., 134.

35. Ibid., 134–35.

36. See the Polish edition of the diary, Baruch Milch, *Testament* (Warsaw: Ośrodek Karta, 2001), 171.

37. Milch, *Can Heaven Be Void?* 138.

38. Regnier, *Forest Days*, 47. According to Jack Green, "Father knew many people and negotiated with quite a few, but he was suspicious, fussy, and stubborn. Others were less discerning and grabbed the first opportunity."

39. Sam Halpern, *Darkness and Hope* (New York: Shengold, 1996), 118–20. See also Samuel Halpern, interview 45091, USC Shoah Foundation Visual History Archive, January 8, 1997.

40. Author interview with Paul Brottman, telephone, July 6, 2012.

41. Author interview with Gertrud Podhorcer, telephone, August 27, 2012.

42. Stermer, *We Fight to Survive*, 29–30.

43. Ibid., 63.

44. This was the case of Clara Schwarz's father, who had built a bunker at Valentin, and Julia Beck's father in Żółkiew. Before the war, the Schwarzs had employed them to wash sheets and beat rugs. Under the German occupation, they signed *Volksliste* (Deutsche Volkslist (DVL), which classified the German residents of German-occupied territories into categories based on their ethnicity). See Clara Kramer and Stephen Glantz, *Clara's War: A Young Girl's True Story of Miraculous Survival under the Nazis* (North Sydney, Australia: Ebury, 2008), 65–66.

45. Bartov, "Communal Genocide," 403.

46. For the discussion of the gender aspect, see Natalia Aleksiun, "Gender and the Daily Lives of Jews in Hiding in Eastern Galicia," *Nashim* 27, 1 (2014): 38–61. See Milch, *Can Heaven Be Void?* 134–35. In September 1942, Maltz noted: "I worry what will happen if there is an Aktion this evening, while I'm still locked up. Since I am in the Judenrat building, the Germans will probably get me at once, and how will my wife find a hiding place for herself and the children if I'm not there? I break into a cold sweat." Maltz's brother Shmelke "has prepared the cellar of the home of Ivanich, a gentile acquaintance, on New Street, as a shelter for our sisters, Leah and Yitte, and Leah's little daughter Feyge Chashe." Maltz, *Years of Horror*, 35, 36.

47. Maltz, *Years of Horror*, 34. On the other hand, Esther Stermer's son Nissen and husband, Shapsy, carried permits as junk collectors and used

their ability to stay in the area to provision the family hiding in the cave. See Stermer, *We Fight to Survive*, 32, 59.

On October 20, 1942, Maltz wrote: "People in the ghetto don't want families with little children to hide out in their bunkers during an *Aktion* because the crying of the children would give the hideout away to the Germans. Dr. Babad, a physician who was my classmate at cheder [Jewish elementary school], tells me that women are asking him for sleeping pills to give their children to keep them quiet. But some of the children who take the pills never wake up again." Maltz, *Years of Horror*, 51.

48. Maltz, *Years of Horror*, 36.

49. Stermer, *We Fight to Survive*, 21.

50. Milch, *Can Heaven Be Void?* 134.

51. Stermer, *We Fight to Survive*, 27. The boy felt suspicious and decided to leave the peasant's house. He eventually survived hiding with his mother and older siblings.

52. See Kramer and Glantz, *Clara's War*, 53–54.

53. Milch, *Can Heaven Be Void?* 117.

54. Ibid., 111.

55. Ibid., 138–48.

56. Stermer, *We Fight to Survive*, 66.

57. Ibid., 71.

58. Ibid., 61–62.

59. Milch, *Can Heaven Be Void?* 143.

60. Ibid., 180.

61. For conflicts concerning space and food, see Kramer and Glantz, *Clara's War*, 211–12. In Jack Green's account, the conflict in the bunker he joined together with his father and brother was linked with prewar class tensions. Regnier, *Forest Days*, 65. At times, a sense of resentment lingered long after the liberation. Esther Stermer noted in her memoir:

> My son-in-law Fishel had to provide two of his cousins as well as his own family with the necessary provisions. They used to give him money and he procured for them what they needed. They were older than Fishel. They did not leave the grotto even once. To this day I am troubled by this. They survived and I am very happy for them, wherever they may be. But they never once went outside, and it was my son-in-law who had to risk his life for them. Thus this should have been so isn't clear to me even now (Stermer, *We Fight to Survive*, 82).

62. Yad Vashem Archives, 0.3, folder 1637.

63. Archiwum Żydowskiego Instytutu Historycznego, 301/2281. Testimony written down in Katowice, Poland, on April 4, 1947.

64. Milch, *Can Heaven Be Void?* 169. See also ibid., 187: "Yesterday . . . on my brother-in-law's birthday, they brought a cake, made a festive lunch

with vodka, and everybody came to wish him a better future." In Maltz's diary, he described celebrating the Catholic holiday of Saint Nicholas's Day: "On December 6, Saint Nicholas's Day, Mrs. Halamajowa's daughter Hela comes to visit, with toys and candy she has bought especially for Chaim [Maltz's son]. Hela actually treats us like human beings; she seems to have a special feeling for children." Maltz, *Years of Horror*, 77–78.

65. Testimony of Tonia Szwarc-Ajzenberg, Archiwum Żydowskiego Instytutu Historycznego, 301/902. Tonia Szwarc-Ajzenberg was born in 1920 in Brody, Ukraine. Her son was born in December 1938.

66. In September 1942, Maltz noted in his diary, "On the way to Mrs. Halamajowa's house we saw a number of Jews hurrying past us along the streets near the river. They were probably looking for hiding places. Some were carrying packages; perhaps they were taking their belongings to the homes of gentile friends for safekeeping." Maltz, *Years of Horror*, 37.

67. Stermer, *We Fight to Survive*, 69.

68. See Yakov Perlmuter's testimony cited in Abraham Weissbrod, *Es shtarbt a shtetl: megiles Skalat* (published in English as *Death of a Shtetl*) (Munich, Ger.: Central Historical Commission of the Central Committee of Liberated Jews in the U.S. Zone of Germany, 1948), 153.

69. "The wheat which the peasants sold us turned out to be of the worst type. The grains were black and after milling it, the flour looked like ash." Stermer, *We Fight to Survive*, 76, 73.

70. Ibid., 73.

71. Ibid., 75.

72. Ibid., 78–79. See Regnier, *Forest Days*, 64.

73. Stermer, *We Fight to Survive*, 78.

74. Archiwum Żydowskiego Instytutu Historycznego, 301/88, 1. The undated testimony was recorded in Polish and Yiddish.

75. Stermer, *We Fight to Survive*, 65.

76. Kramer and Glantz, *Clara's War*, 226. See also Stermer, *We Fight to Survive*, 31, 34. See also Yacov Perlmuter's testimony in Weissbrod, *Es shtarbt a shtetl*, 150.

77. Stermer, *We Fight to Survive*, 68.

78. See Bernard Mayer, *Entombed: My True Story: How Forty-Five Jews Lived Underground and Survived the Holocaust* (Ojus, Fla.: Aleric, 1994), 111–12.

79. Stermer, *We Fight to Survive*, 40. See also ibid., 33–34.

80. Weissbrod, *Es shtarbt a shtetl*, 153. For the English translation, accessed September 1, 2014, see http://www.jewishgen.org/yizkor/Skalat1/ska054.html#page65.

81. Otto Schorman, "The Brown Terror," Archiwum Żydowskiego Instytutu Historycznego, Pamiętniki, 302/295, 63.

82. Esther Stermer noted in her memoir: "We had taken all our possessions into the grotto. Those who came from Rumania and the doctor's family didn't have very much. But we, Hersch, Barad and Chisdis and my sister had very many valuable objects . . . When the police saw our valuable things in the grotto they didn't leave the place, but sent for horses and wagons and began to carry away their loot." Stermer, *We Fight to Survive*, 57. See ibid., 65–66.

83. Stermer, *We Fight to Survive*, 65.

84. See Mayer, *Entombed: My True Story*, 85–91.

85. Stermer, *We Fight to Survive*, 75.

86. Such was the case of Dr. Kindler and his family in Sokal. In November 1943, he was provided winter blankets and warm clothes with the money he had left with a gentile nurse. Maltz, *Years of Horror*, 107.

87. Maltz, *Years of Horror*, 79.

88. Milch, *Can Heaven Be Void?* 206.

89. See testimony of Pepa Braun, Archiwum Żydowskiego Instytutu Historycznego, 301/2281. Pepa Braun also notes that the only bed available in the hiding place was occupied by a rabbi and his wife, while Pepa's parents and siblings slept on the floor.

90. Stermer, *We Fight to Survive*, 69.

91. Maltz, *Years of Horror*, 77.

92. Bernard Mayer marveled at the arrangements in the large bunker in Drohobycz (Drohobych). See Mayer, *Entombed*, 111.

93. Stermer, *We Fight to Survive*, 67.

94. Kramer and Glantz, *Clara's War*, 79.

95. Otto Schorman, *The Brown Terror*, Archiwum Żydowskiego Instytutu Historycznego, Pamiętniki, 302/295, 63.

96. Milch, *Can Heaven Be Void?* 145.

97. Ibid., 179–80, 172.

98. See Halpern, *Darkness and Hope*, 127.

99. Milch, *Can Heaven Be Void?* 190.

100. Maltz, *Years of Horror*, 79. "When Mrs. Halamajowa brings us the German newspaper, the first thing I look for is the Wehrmacht communiqué, which is always on the front page," 81. Clara Kramer described men reading newspapers together provided by Valentin Beck in their bunker. Kramer and Glantz, *Clara's War*, 76. See also the account of Dr. Emil Rozenzweig of Czortków, Archiwum Żydowskiego Instytutu Historycznego, 301/3206, 13, testimony recorded in Cracow (Kraków) on March 27, 1947.

101. See the introduction to Milch's diary, dated July 15, 1943; Milch, *Testament*, 8.

102. Kramer and Glantz, *Clara's War*, 77.

103. Milch, *Can Heaven Be Void?* 193–94.

104. Stermer, *We Fight to Survive*, 32.

105. Ibid., 61.

106. Kramer and Glantz, *Clara's War*, 188.

107. Stermer, *We Fight to Survive*, 81.

108. Maltz, *Years of Horror*, 106.

109. Weissbrod, *Es shtarbt a shtetl*, 150. For the English translation, see http://www.jewishgen.org/yizkor/Skalat1/ska054.html#page65.

110. Weissbrod, *Es shtarbt a shtetl*, 151–52.

111. Milch, *Can Heaven Be Void?* 188.

112. Stermer, *We Fight to Survive*, 34.

113. Kramer and Glantz, *Clara's War*, 90.

114. Milch, *Can Heaven Be Void?* 169. See also note 64.

115. Stermer, *We Fight to Survive*, 32.

116. Ibid., 80.

117. Maltz, *Years of Horror*, 100.

118. Milch, *Can Heaven Be Void?* 145.

119. Ibid., 165, 186.

120. Author interview with Gertrud Podhorcer, telephone, August 27, 2012.

121. Testimony of Giza Ferber, Archiwum Żydowskiego Instytutu Historycznego, 301/2528, 3. Yetta Dodyk implored her husband to find a sick boy hiding alone in the forest and to bring him to their hiding place in a cave near Bilcze Złote. Ulo Barad was the only member of her family still alive. When Mendel brought the boy to the cave, the boy suffered "from skin diseases and looked terrible . . . We had to set up a separate sleeping place for him so that we would not become infected ourselves from him." Stermer, *We Fight to Survive*, 71. The boy's aunt nursed him, making sure he received food and cleaning and dressing his sores. Ibid., 72.

122. Maltz, *Years of Horror*, 102–4.

123. "The Passover Seder in Camp," chap. 23 in Weissbrod, *Es shtarbt a shtetl*, http://www.jewishgen.org/yizkor/Skalat1/ska054.html#page70.

124. See testimony of Anna Mass, Archiwum Żydowskiego Instytutu Historycznego, 301/117. Mass's testimony, recorded May 10, 1945, describes hiding for eleven months with a forester near Przemyśl, Poland.

125. Milch, *Can Heaven Be Void?* 206.

126. Ibid., 197.

127. Weissbrod, *Es shtarbt a shtetl*, 154.

128. Kaplan, *Between Dignity and Despair*, 211.

129. Weissbrod, *Es shtarbt a shtetl*, 152.

130. Stermer's mother nursed him back to health, while Dr. Teibels gave him a series of some thirty injections. Stermer, *We Fight to Survive*, 53.

131. The poison did not work, and the family decided to do everything

in its power to give the child a chance to survive. Maltz, *Years of Horror*, 98–100.

132. See ibid., 144. For the discussion of infanticides by family members during the Holocaust, see Sara R. Horowitz, "'If He Knows to Make a Child . . .': Memories of Birth and Baby-Killing in Deferred Jewish Testimony Narratives," chap. 7 in Goda, *Jewish Histories of the Holocaust*, 135–51.

133. "I cried for the first time [since the discovery that both his wife and his sister-in-law were murdered]. He [Milch's brother-in-law] cried, too, and at that awful moment he tried to blame me for our not having taken the women with us. I tried to persuade him that we should kill ourselves but he . . . rejected the idea. We could always commit suicide, he counseled, but right now we had to live." Milch, *Can Heaven Be Void?* 161.

134. Author interview with Balka Eisenscher, July 20, 2013, Raanana, Israel.

135. Milch could only begin to mourn the loss of his family while in hiding with his former patient in the village of Czerwonogród. See Milch, *Can Heaven Be Void?* 148, 169.

136. Maltz, *Years of Horror*, 105.

137. Milch, *Can Heaven Be Void?* 173.

138. Maltz, *Years of Horror*, 104.

139. Kaplan, *Between Dignity and Despair*, 212.

140. For example, Milch and his brother-in-law heard about atrocities against the Jews of Kołomyja (Kolomyla) and Horodenka, both now in Ukraine, and Warsaw. Milch, *Can Heaven Be Void?* 172. They also listened to accounts of Jewish bunkers that had been found or betrayed. Ibid., 199–200. See also Maltz, *Years of Horror*, 102.

141. Stermer, *We Fight to Survive*, 77. After the war, it turned out that the youngest girl, Freidele Geller, survived.

142. Archiwum Żydowskiego Instytutu Historycznego, 301/3359, 5.

143. See Sidra DeKoven Ezrahi, "Representing Auschwitz," *History and Memory* 7, no. 2 (1996), 121–54.

Rachel Century

Secretaries, Secrets, and Genocide: Evidence from the Postwar Investigations of the Female Secretaries of the RSHA

THE WOMEN OF NAZI GERMANY HAVE BEEN THE SUBJECT OF NUMEROUS studies, partly as the result of growing interest in questions of coercion and consent. My new research on German secretaries in Heinrich Himmler's offices suggests an important case for exploring new interpretations of complicity and its gendered roles. Working in a variety of departments, the many female secretaries and administrators of the Reich Security Main Office (*Reichssicherheitshauptamt* or RSHA) had access to different sources and quantities of information about the Holocaust and the crimes that their supervisors were perpetrating. Who were these women, and what prompted them to work within the Nazi apparatus? Were the secretaries of the RSHA ideologically dedicated to the tasks they carried out? Were the women who typed up and distributed the Nazi regime's policies of persecution and extermination themselves antisemites?

To answer these questions, this article will use postwar testimony given by secretaries who had worked at the RSHA. The testimony of these women allows for a detailed insight into their working lives. Their postwar statements demonstrate that the majority of women—where they had a choice—did not seek a position within the Nazi apparatus *because* of the nature of the work they would be required to undertake. Yet, through their workloads, almost all these women became aware to some extent of Nazi anti-Jewish policy.

There has been great debate among feminist historians of Nazi Germany as to the extent to which German women in the Third Reich were perpetrators or victims. Claudia Koonz has shown that many

German women were fully supportive of the Nazi regime, either by committing crimes alongside men or by ensuring that their menfolk were made to feel accepted and nurtured.[1] Koonz sees women as perpetrators within the role of caring housewife and mother, which society allotted to them. Gisela Bock disagrees, accusing Koonz, as Herkommer notes, of "investigating [the] past with one eye on its usefulness in the present."[2] Bock's more recent research emphasizes the multiplicity of the positions of women under the National Socialist system of government.[3] This article will seek to place the secretaries of the RSHA within this debate, arguing that they contributed to the environment which supported the men in their genocidal actions.

There is limited literature about the women who administrated for the men of the *Schutzstaffel* (SS), the paramilitary wing of the Nazi Party, which ran the concentration camps and carried out the killing of Jews. However, female perpetrators, while not receiving the same degree of attention as their male equivalents, have been the subject of many studies, including Wendy Lower's recent examination of thirteen women who went to Nazi-occupied Eastern Europe, several of whom were secretaries. Lower explains how these women became witnesses, accomplices, and even, in some cases, killers. She attributes a variety of motivations to their actions, noting that the women, akin to their male counterparts, pursued the opportunities available to them.[4] The fascination with female perpetrators of the Holocaust extends beyond the realm of academia, entering both popular fiction[5] and film.[6] These women require further examination as both scholars and non-scholars grapple with the concept that daughters, mothers, and wives were capable of perpetrating the most atrocious crimes. Indeed, as Susannah Heschel noted in her article "Does Atrocity Have a Gender?" the fact that "almost no women guards were prosecuted after the war arose from disbelief among the Allies that women could have committed atrocities."[7] While there is not one universal definition of "perpetrator" within the context of the Nazi regime, a reflection of the multiple roles that were all necessary for the Holocaust to be carried out,[8] the women acting as concentration camp guards can be considered perpetrators, in roles that enabled them to exercise power over Nazi victims.[9] The circumstances that led these German women to become perpetrators within the regime were unique. They were, alongside almost all German women, immersed in Nazism, through constant propaganda and through the movements that existed for every age group.[10] Many German women contributed to the German war effort; not all were perpetrators.

Women who acted as concentration camp guards have been studied in significant depth,[11] while their counterparts in administrative roles have not been examined to the same extent.[12] Although there have been studies of high-profile, individual secretaries, women who worked as secretaries for the Nazis have received relatively little scholarly attention as a collective. Historian Gudrun Schwarz, in her book on the wives of *Schutzstaffel* (SS) men,[13] the wing of the Nazi Party that operated the concentration camps and carried out the killing of Jews, mentions secretaries of SS men who become their *Zweitfrau*—second (and illegitimate) wife—yet in her analysis it is incidental that these women are secretaries. Their professional caste is neither questioned nor analyzed. Both Yaacov Lozowick and Hans Safrian refer, in passing, to secretaries who were aware of their nature of their bosses' work,[14] yet neither probes deeper to determine exactly how the women knew of their bosses' involvement in the persecution of the Jews, whether they took action, and what became of the women. Such books often present a general overview of women, and either have one small section on the secretaries or mention only one or two examples of women of this type.

The Gestapo, the secret police of Nazi Germany, employed female administrators from its inception in April 1934. Notorious for imprisoning opponents of the Third Reich without any judicial proceedings, the Gestapo had offices across Germany and later throughout occupied Europe.[15] In 1939, Heinrich Himmler merged the Gestapo with the regular criminal police under one administrative structure, known as the *Reichssicherheitshauptamt* (Reich Main Security Office or RSHA); around 50,000 people were employed across seven different departments.[16] The female administrators of the RSHA, tasked with general duties such as dictation and letter writing, either belonged to departmental typing pools or were attached to specific male superiors. In common with the headquarters of most Nazi operations, the RSHA offices were based in several locations in Berlin. Toward the end of the war, several sites were bombed and then evacuated. Some women found themselves transferred several times, working at various locations in Berlin, southern Germany, and even as far away as Prague, Czechoslovakia,[17] because it was considered, according to one female administrator, "relatively bombproof."[18]

Even prior to the end of the war, war crimes investigators active on behalf of the Allies created lists of those who had committed "major war crimes."[19] As their knowledge of war crimes, and those perpetrating them, increased, further categories were added to the list, including the SS leadership, and Gestapo and *Sicherheitsdienst* (Security Police or SD) officers. The International Military Tribunal (IMT) in Nuremberg decided, at the suggestion of the prosecution, not to prosecute "persons employed by the Gestapo for purely clerical, stenographic, janitorial or similar unofficial routine tasks."[20] The tribunal decided that the Allies would not pursue or prosecute secretaries. Despite the ruling, some of these women had proceedings drawn up against them, as investigators realized that their contribution was not innocuously clerical. Some women were questioned, others were interned, and still others were imprisoned for a few months to five years or more. These women were pursued and imprisoned in their native Germany by the occupying forces, the Americans, Soviets, French, and British. Some women were imprisoned in the countries to which they had been sent to work, such as Czechoslovakia, Denmark, and Romania. Other women were questioned but not detained. There was no universal procedure for dealing with these women; it depended heavily on which Allied-occupied zone they resided in after the war.

In 1949, with the establishment of the Federal German Republic (East Germany) and the German Democratic Republic (West Germany), the Allies passed on their responsibilities for the process of denazification. As Germans regained sovereignty in 1949, they also took over responsibility for the prosecution of Nazi war criminals. Facing mounting criticism for a lack of rigor and zeal prosecuting alleged Nazi criminals, the West Germans established the Central Office of the Judicial Authorities for the Investigation of National Socialist Crimes (*Zentrale Stelle der Landesjustizverwaltungen zur Aufklärung nationalsozialistischer Verbrechen*) to assist with the prosecution of former Nazis.[21] This Central Office took up the most extensive investigation of the RSHA and collected the most voluminous testimonies of female secretaries, as a means of inquiry into their male superiors. These testimonies greatly informed my research.

In March 1963, the chief prosecutor's office in West Berlin, led by Hans Guenther, instigated proceedings against some of the staff of the RSHA for their involvement in killing and murder.[22] The accusation was that, as desktop murderers (*Schreibtischtäter*), they had issued the orders for murder from Berlin.[23] Although the secretaries and other female administrators could not be tried, they performed a vital role in the preparations, and hundreds of former employees of the RSHA were questioned. Women who had been questioned by the Allies previously found themselves interrogated again, this time by compatriots. The prosecution team, consisting of six prosecutors from Berlin and six from other West German federal states, located the former administrators of the RSHA throughout Germany and traveled to each destination to question the women in their own neighborhoods. In some instances, women were examined in the comfort of their own home; other women had to visit the local police station for their interviews. The statements collected by the prosecution typically carried the same format. Each witness began her testimony with a declaration that she had been informed of the line of questioning and that she was prepared to make statements about herself and her activities at the RSHA. The interrogations were a vital part of the preparations for trials, although, as stated earlier, the prosecutors did not intend to indict the women and the women were aware of that, perhaps freeing them to speak candidly about their tasks. Some of the women referred to previous instances when they had been questioned, allowing an insight into their immediate postwar experiences.[24]

The chief prosecutor's investigations resulted in the naming of 900 former employees of the RSHA as defendants. The conviction rate was negligible, indicative of the broader judicial climate at the time. A series of amnesties, applicable both to those born after 1914[25] and to those who had neither acted "out of cruelty, dishonorable sentiments, or greed" nor committed a crime of deliberate misdemeanor within the past three years,[26] reduced both the number of perpetrators to prosecute and the length of their potential sentences. A reform of the criminal code, which had come into effect in October 1968,[27] made it necessary to demonstrate that perpetrators had base motives or intentions, resulting in "an appreciable restriction on the possibility of judicial punishment of Nazi murder."[28] As a result, accomplices to murder falling within this categorization now fell outside the statute of limitations. A planned trial of almost 300 former RSHA staff members, due to begin just months later, was unable to go ahead because of this change in the law.[29] Ultimately, of all the attempted prosecutions of RSHA staff, it was possible in only four separate cases to indict and try a defendant.[30] Nonetheless, the intensive preparations for the trials that did not occur are still of use, shedding light on the secretaries, their work, and their relationship with their bosses.

The historian must tread carefully here: the investigators employed a specific line of questioning, which limits the usefulness of the sources. Christopher Browning warns that "some men deliberately lied, for they feared the judicial consequences of telling the truth as they remembered it"[31]; similarly, some women may have lied. While some of the questioning took place immediately after the war, other interviews were carried out in the late 1970s, by which time some women may have had trouble recalling events that occurred forty years before. Their memories would have been shaped by their experiences since the war, and the German collective memory may have influenced the way they recalled their own involvement within the Nazi regime. Nevertheless, despite the intrinsic limitations of testimonies,[32] they help to build up a profile of the women who were employed at the RSHA.[33]

Getting a job at the RSHA did not follow a standard procedure. The women came from a variety of backgrounds and had diverse experiences prior to their employment. Many women were conscripted into the RSHA. Three days after the outbreak of war, the Nazis introduced a requirement for any women between the ages of seventeen and twenty-five "not in paid employment, not in full-time education or undergoing vocational training, and who are not indispensable to the running of a family agricultural business" to enlist for *Reichsarbeitsdienst* (Reich Labor Service) duties.[34] In 1943, female conscription was formally introduced, compelling unmarried young women between the ages of seventeen and forty-five to work.[35] Conscription procedures were not smooth and did not follow one coherent policy. There were opportunities to avoid the call-up: loopholes were frequently exploited, and conscription was not enforced wholeheartedly.[36] The long work hours and low pay caused many women to seek excuses to avoid employment, arranging to "work" in the homes of acquaintances, pretending illness, and even, in some cases, conceiving a child to avoid registration.[37] It was therefore possible for some of the women who were sent to the RSHA to evade being drafted. However, in their postwar testimony, the majority of women emphasized a lack of choice: these women felt that they had to follow the conscription orders. Yet, many of the women later left their positions of employment voluntarily, without suffering any consequences.

Large numbers of women were conscripted into the RSHA by

their local state employment offices. Helga Beer was conscripted in 1943; she was sent by the employment office to the Gestapo, where she worked as a typist and as a clerk in its lending library.[38] Berta Rauber was conscripted to the RSHA, possibly because she had completed *Osteinsatz* (Eastern assignment)—that is, duty in Nazi-occupied Eastern Europe—which was described as "an elitist undertaking restricted to students whose National Socialist integrity was firmly established."[39] Rauber had taken care of repatriates, ethnic Germans resettled in German territories. Prior to this, she had begun to train as a schoolteacher.[40] Maria Winterstein stated in her testimony that, as a childless married woman, she could "not escape being conscripted."[41]

Whether out of need or ambition, financial motives drove many women to work for the RSHA. In some cases, these motives were borne out by the stringencies imposed by war itself. Gertrud Flickert had worked in her father's restaurant, but the onset of war decreased the restaurant's revenue, and her father could no longer support her. As a divorced mother of two children, she needed a job and was directed to the RSHA by the employment office.[42] Unsatisfied with her earnings at a private firm, Margarete Hartung applied to several authorities for a higher-paid job, resulting in her employment in the police department in Berlin as a typist.[43] When her divorce and husband's subsequent refusal to pay child support forced Elisabeth Marks to find a job, she took one at the RSHA.[44]

Family influence and contacts provided another route into the RSHA. Relations and acquaintances sometimes assisted their family members or friends in securing a job. Irmgard Martin's father obtained a job for his daughter in April 1941; he was already employed at the RSHA at the time.[45] Irene Erbe was given her job at the RSHA by Herr Koschate, with whom she had completed her *Pflichtjahr* (mandatory year), a compulsory year of service for young women.[46] Lieselotte Zimmerman's mother's friends, working in the Ministry for the East, were looking for administrators in Ukraine. She signed up on their recommendations.[47]

Many considered employment at the RSHA preferable to the alternatives. After attending commercial college, Gerda Gerner was expected to serve her *Pflichtjahr*. To avoid doing so, Gerner applied to the SS employment office but was informed that the SS had a surplus of workers. Instead, she applied to the RSHA, where she ultimately worked for several different departments, including counterintelligence and the Department for Polish Affairs.[48] Erika Hesselbarth's daughter took a job at the RSHA to avoid her obligation to the *Reichsarbeitsdienst*.[49] A female acquaintance recommended to Elsa Heine that she take a job at the RSHA to avoid being conscripted by the employment office.[50] Helga Duchstein was also keen to avoid being placed by the Labor Service; she learned shorthand and typing and applied for several posts, including positions within the air force and the army high command. The Gestapo was the first to respond to her application, so Duchstein took the job.[51] Her indifference seemingly overrode any concerns over the agency's fearsome reputation. Ottilie Bläsius completed a course in speech and writing and was poised to be conscripted by the head of the Nazi Women's League, Gertrud Scholtz-Klink. Since the work environment did not appeal to her, Bläsius approached a friend working at the RSHA, who negotiated a position for her.[52] Evidently, personal referrals and individual inclinations were common routes to employment in the RSHA.

The RSHA was not solely an alternative to less preferable working environments; some women actively sought employment there. Frida Paul had been working as a stenographer in the Reich office for wool and other animal hair, but she wished to "expand the knowledge" that she had acquired in her career to date and so she entered employment at the *Rasse- und Siedlungshauptamt* (Race and Settlement Main Office or RuSHA), the office responsible for the "racial purity" of SS men and their wives.[53] Emma Rückerl took a job as a secretary for an officer working at the *Lebensborn* (literally "spring of life") program, which aimed to increase the Aryan birth rate, because that position allowed her to keep her child with her.[54] In a letter to the RuSHA supporting a job application, Ruth Ihlow, a Nazi Party member who, in her spare time, acted as a stenographer for her local Nazi Party branch, asserted in March 1941 that her greatest wish was to be employed as a stenographer in the occupied Eastern territories.[55]

The wide variety of routes leading women to work at the RSHA reflect the multiple interests and needs of these women, supporting Bock's view that there was a multiplicity of narratives among women in Nazi Germany. Yet, regardless of their routes into employment, these women now had access to information that was not available to their peers.

For many women working at the RSHA, it was impossible during the war to deny that something grave was happening to the Jews.

There were a number of information channels through which the secretaries and female employees of the RSHA became aware of the atrocities against the Jews. Although frequently unreliable, there were many rumors, both within and outside of the workplace, that provided information for female employees. Some of these women were able to corroborate the rumors through their own work: they were the ones typing the deportation lists or registering the deaths in the concentration camps. Some women's work took them outside the offices of the Gestapo, where they directly witnessed deportations; others visited holding camps and concentration camps. Some secretaries recalled the remarks of Jews who worked in their offices and told about their mistreatment firsthand.

Knowledge gleaned through work was augmented by disclosures, rumors, gossip, and overheard conversations. These sources were not universally reliable. Nevertheless, many female employees became convinced—and admitted so after the war—that there were kernels of truth in what they heard. Helga Beer was aware from hearsay that Jews were taken from their homes without legal cause. She thought that they were taken to a work camp and would have a difficult time of it, but she testified that she had no reason to assume they would be killed.[56] Margarete Hartung heard rumors about what was happening to the Jewish citizens because the Department for Jewish Affairs was on the floor below her office. Her husband confirmed these rumors, because he had been, in a case of mistaken identity, arrested along with Jews.[57] Working in the Department for Jewish Affairs, Elisabeth Marks was informed by an SS-officer that he had been commanded by the RSHA to drive a gas truck. He described the suffocation by gas of Jewish men, women, and children trapped in the cargo area of the truck. This seemingly chance encounter was the first time that Marks was made aware of the extermination policies directed at the Jews.[58] For some women, the rumors they heard formed the basis of their knowledge and awareness of persecution, particularly if they themselves did not hold individual responsibilities directly pertaining to the mass murder.

For some of the secretaries, there was no denying that the rumors were true. Typing deportation lists or registering deaths in concentration camps, they knew firsthand that Jews were being deported and were dying, even if they could later claim to be unaware that the victims were being murdered. Trained as a bookkeeper, Luise Hering was conscripted to the Department for Jewish Affairs as a registrar. She initially recorded Jewish property, later registering death reports from concentration camps, including Auschwitz, the only camp she mentioned by name in her postwar testimony. The reports listed the name of the victim, date, time, and cause of death. Hering recalled gastroenteritis, pneumonia, and heart failure as some of the causes of death, noting that the range of stated causes of death was relatively narrow. Dealing with these death reports on a daily basis, Hering came to the conclusion that terrible events took place in concentration camps, including the killing of Jews, although she claimed no knowledge of the method of murder in her postwar testimony.[59] Similarly, Marie Knispel maintained that it was only through the death notices that she processed that she realized her department dealt exclusively with Jewish affairs. She handled reports from Auschwitz, Mauthausen, Dachau, Sachsenhausen, and Theresienstadt, many of which stated the same causes of death, predominantly heart failure and circulatory failure. Knispel, too, eventually became convinced that the Jews were being killed by "bad treatment," although her statements do not reveal the true murderous intentions of the Nazis.[60]

On one occasion, Adolf Eichmann, the head of the Department for Jewish Affairs, left his keys in his office. One of the secretaries, Elisabeth Marks, was asked to return them to him at the deportation he was supervising. She was moved to tears as she witnessed Jewish men, women, and children "being herded like cattle into trucks" and taken away. Although she had already been informed that Jews were being killed in gas trucks, she chose to believe that this deportation was a singular event. At the time, she assumed that the Jews were being resettled, albeit inhumanely.[61]

Some women worked directly with persecution policies, or in locations where the crimes were carried out. Holding camps and deportation sites required administrative staff. To facilitate the deportations of Jews from Berlin, holding camps were established in former Jewish buildings, including synagogues, a cemetery, a home for the elderly, schools, and hospitals. After the SS assembled the Jews for a transport, they transferred the Jews to a railway station. Johanna Heym was employed at one of these holding camps, in Groß Hamburger Straße, Berlin, in a Jewish home for the elderly and a Jewish school for boys.[62] Walter Dobberke, an SS *Hauptsturmführer* (a rank equivalent to captain), dictated a report to Heym after each transport, approximately once a month.[63] Heym's main task at the camp was to write reports of the interrogations of Jews. One purpose of these interrogations was to determine whether the interviewee was a "privileged" Jew—one married to an Aryan—and thus worthy of special dispensation. Heym also took the minutes of the interrogations of Jews discovered in hiding. Dobberke promised these Jews that they would be sent to Theresienstadt if they provided useful information about other hidden Jews.[64] Heym does not know whether Dobberke kept his word, although she wanted to believe that he did, indicating that she thought Theresienstadt less dangerous than other destinations.

Through the nature of their work, some secretaries gained insight, some to a greater—or clearer—extent than others, into the administrative inner workings of the persecution policies of the National Socialists. Other secretaries became eyewitnesses to the persecution. On one occasion, Erika Albrecht accompanied her boss, SS *Hauptsturmführer* Ernst Möhs, also spelled Moes, to Bergen-Belsen. Despite requesting permission to be allowed into the camp, she was instructed to remain in the commandant's building, just outside. Möhs told Albrecht that his job involved listening to complaints about the mistreatment of Jews in the camp.[65]

Many secretaries heard that their supervisors physically hit Jews; some witnessed the violence of their bosses. The technical director of the RSHA in-house Jewish work detail, Pinkus, complained repeatedly to Elisabeth Marks, about her boss, Otto Hunsche. Pinkus told Marks that Hunsche was feared and despised because he so often harassed the work detail, frequently yelling at and beating Jewish workers. Marks had no doubts about the credibility of Pinkus's accusations because she herself had witnessed Hunsche hit a member of the Jewish work detail in the face.[66] Margarete Schindler was taken to a holding camp in Berlin with one of her bosses, Schwöbel, to record an interrogation. Schwöbel possessed a reputation for brutal treatment of Jewish prisoners. While in the camp, Schindler watched as her boss beat a Jewish girl until she lost consciousness.[67] Johanna Heym was aware that in both the Groß Hamburger Straße and the Schulstraße holding camps, imprisoned Jews were beaten on occasion. She was an eyewitness to this once, when Dobberke hit a Jewish woman in her face, in the Schulstraße holding camp. The Jew, a young girl, had insulted Dobberke; Heym believed that she called him an SS pig. As a consequence, the girl was sent to Ravensbrück concentration camp, although Heym doubted that this was at Dobberke's instigation. He "cursed and raged, but left it at that."[68]

The postwar testimony of these women reveals that many of them had at least rudimentary knowledge of the atrocities committed against the Jews and other groups. The women heard rumors, witnessed persecution and physical violence, and typed orders condemning people to death. Once she was armed with the information, each secretary had an uncomfortable choice to make: to continue with her job and accept or ignore what was taking place; or to take action, however limited.

Some women did display resistance, in various forms. Conscripted in early 1943, Johanna Heym was sent to work at a holding camp for Jewish deportees in Berlin. Until that point, she was unaware that such a camp existed. The idea of working there "caused me discomfort"—suggesting some prior knowledge of what a holding camp might entail—and so she refused to go. Nevertheless, she later claimed, she was required to go anyway.[69] When Johanna Quandt was conscripted to the Department for Jewish Affairs in the summer of 1940, she knew that Jews were being persecuted and found the idea of working in this department "sinister." She reported her concerns to the employment office but was informed that she had to go where she was conscripted.[70] Neither woman was punished for her attempt to avoid assignment to a particular job.

Quandt once witnessed a woman ask an SS man in her office to call a doctor for her lodger, who was terminally ill. The SS man asked the woman if the tenant was a Jew. The woman said yes, to which the SS man replied, "Let him die." Once the woman had gone, Quandt turned to the SS man in outrage, asking how he could say such a thing; the tenant was a human. The SS man turned to Quandt and said, "Frau Quandt, I am warning you." She heard that phrase at least three times during her career at the RSHA but suffered no further repercussions.[71]

Although disturbed by the rumors they had heard and the incidents they had seen, many secretaries were reluctant to take action lest they suffer the consequences. Johanna Martha Greifendorf, working in the Department for Jewish Affairs, harbored apprehensions about the fate of the Jews and suspected that some of her colleagues felt the same, but she did not discuss her feelings, or the remarks she heard, with anybody for fear of the repercussions.[72] While working for the *Umwandererzentralstelle* (Central Emigration Office) in Łódź, Poland, Rosemarie von Godlewski had heard rumors of large numbers of Jews being murdered but was unable to gain concrete facts, or did not bother to dig too deeply, "because you risked possibly your head and your neck."[73]

Secretaries who recalled such apprehension expressed particular anxiety about the possibility of being sent to a concentration camp as punishment. Elisabeth Marks, who worked in the Department for Jewish Affairs, did not divulge what she knew about the suffocation of Jews in gas trucks to anyone outside of her workplace, not even to her fiancé, a soldier in the *Wehrmacht*, Germany's armed forces, because she feared the consequences, "such as concentration camps and the like."[74] Brunhilde Schreck, an administrator in the Department for Polish Affairs, felt that "no employee of the RSHA could refuse to do the work assigned to them." During her time working for the RSHA, circulars passed around to every staff member stated that, in the case of insubordination or arbitrary work stoppage, there was the threat of detention in a concentration camp.[75] Marie Knispel, who processed death certificates in the Department for Jewish Affairs, did not dare talk about what she knew; she had been told by her superiors that she would end up in a concentration camp if she did not remain silent.[76] Eva Nöthling, who worked as a secretary in a variety of departments in the RSHA, recalled in her testimony an incident in which a clerk of Himmler's made a suggestion that did not accord with Himmler's views. This "caused considerable excitement" as colleagues discussed, and feared, that the person responsible could be punished, and "there was even talk of an introduction to a concentration camp." This fate was averted, however, when Reinhard Heydrich, the head of the RSHA, arrived and took responsibility for the clerk.[77]

The women of the RSHA legitimately feared punishment. The threat of the concentration camp reverberated throughout those working for the Nazis: concentration camp guards were themselves warned that they would be interned if they did not adhere to the rules. Anna Fest, who became a guard at Ravensbrück women's concentration camp, was warned not to complain about the treatment of the prisoners, unless she wanted "to be on the inside too,"[78] and she was informed that many others had rebelled and had been made prisoners themselves.[79] In late January 1945, Adolf Eichmann called to his office in Kurfürstenstraße all the remaining secretaries in the Department for Jewish Affairs and told them they would be evacuated to Prague, Czechoslovakia. He specified that if any of them did not want to go, they could instead go straight to a concentration camp. One of the secretaries present, Ruth Tilgner, testified that Eichmann mentioned the camp Sachsenhausen. The implication was clear: they had little choice.[80] While the women at the RSHA may not have been able to determine whether these warnings were empty threats, concentration camps featured in the German press,[81] serving as a further deterrent to anyone who might consider taking action against the state.

Some women feigned illness to avoid their work and obtained doctors' letters testifying that they were no longer fit for service. A number of women claimed that they took this measure as an act of ideological resistance, although it could have arisen from the increased strain of managing households and full-time jobs.[82] Dealing with death reports on a daily basis, Luise Hering developed a deep aversion to her work. She came to the conclusion that terrible events took place in concentration camps, including the killing of Jews. She took sick leave and, as she related after the war, the stress caused her hair to prematurely gray.[83] After nine months in a third department proved no less palatable than her previous two posts to Waleska Bambowsky, who described them as "cruel" and "terrible" assignments, she succeeded in securing the services of an SS doctor. He certified her as not being healthy enough to work, and she was able to return to Berlin.[84] Johanna Quandt was successful in her attempts to ascertain the truth: she came to realize that the Jews would not leave the concentration camps and ghettos alive. When this realization set in, Quandt was heavily burdened and suffered a mental breakdown. She testified that she did everything in her means to leave the department. A prior medical condition, a weak heart, combined with her nervous breakdown, was enough to persuade a doctor to sign her permanently off work.[85] Whether the women imparted the true reasons for their ill health to the doctors is not clear; it is unlikely that they would have wanted to put the doctors—or themselves—at risk.

On rare occasions, secretaries took more drastic action. Having witnessed a deportation, Elisabeth Marks was curious, and determined, to find out if it was just a onetime occurrence. She exploited any opportunity she could find to browse through files, including highly confidential documentation. On one occasion, she waited until one colleague, Martin, was absent, and asked another colleague to act as a lookout. However, Martin had been conscientious and locked his safe containing the files on the secret operations, and so, despite Marks in her words, "sniffing and snooping," she was unable to uncover any of the secret documents.[86] Through her investigations and through rumors, Marks eventually determined that the Jews were being exterminated. Although she subsequently remained at her job, she refused clothing which she and her children were entitled to under Nazi distribution policies following Allied bombing because she realized that the clothes belonged to murdered Jews.

Handling correspondence which indicated that certain Jews sent to concentration camps should not be killed, Erika Albrecht began to question whether this policy was followed. Her frequent requests for explanations prompted Möhs, her boss, to brusquely tell her to stop asking him questions, but she was not punished.[87] Once she became aware that her work concerned the extermination of the Jews, she was reluctant to continue and instead attempted to disrupt her own work. However, she was asked by a half-Jewish friend, Günter Heilbrunn, to remain as long as possible in the department in his interest; he was hopeful that she would be in a position to help him or his fellow Jews. For his sake, she remained at her job but often came to work late and deliberately did not perform to the best of her ability. Heilbrunn had contacts within the tobacco industry and was able to obtain tobacco products, which he supplied to Albrecht for her to bribe Möhs and keep him in a good mood. She thereby appeased Möhs when he was annoyed with her critical attitude and her carelessness with her work.[88] Albrecht's efforts may have had negligible impact on the wider Nazi apparatus, but through her small acts of resistance, she was able to express her opposition to the regime.

Johanna Heym was also able to question her boss without adverse consequences. On one occasion, Dobberke informed Heym that between ten and twelve Jews had been mistakenly taken to Auschwitz despite not meeting the necessary requirements. The SS sent these Jews back from Auschwitz to Berlin. To Heym's surprise, they were not immediately released, nor were they brought back to the camp in Groß Hamburger Straße; instead they were taken to a work camp in the Wuhlheide district of Berlin. Following a conversation with Dobberke, Heym deduced that this was because the Jews had seen Auschwitz, and they had to be prevented from reporting what they had witnessed. Heym herself did not know what they had seen but assumed that the situation for Jews in Auschwitz was unpleasant.

She later claimed that, during the war, she had no idea there were gas chambers in Auschwitz.[89]

Those women prepared to question their bosses were taking a small, but nonetheless brave, step. They had been warned that any deviation from strict adherence to the rules might result in punishment. Nevertheless, the testimony suggests that the women who did probe their bosses, or who claimed to be unwell, did not suffer any serious repercussions.

Some of the female RSHA administrators were imprisoned after the war. Indicting the women who had acted as secretaries and administrators was not a priority for the Allies in these years, yet some of those employed by the RSHA were questioned, including the women featured here. The interrogations demonstrated they were of some interest, if not because of their own actions, then because they could provide information on their bosses' wartime activities. Despite the ruling of the International Military Tribunal, the women were subject to extensive scrutiny because they had been employed by the Nazis, and their work was considered integral to the administration of war crimes and crimes against humanity.

That some of the women who typed and administered for the RSHA were arrested and interned implies a degree of guilt, but of what were these women guilty? This article has demonstrated that German secretaries were not direct victims of the Nazi regime, at the mercy of their male bosses. Many of them chose employment at the RSHA, and most who were conscripted did not challenge their conscription orders. Yet, neither were they perpetrators in the classic definition of having physically committed a crime. However, Thomas Kühne would argue that their mere presence was enough to make these women complicit,[90] and Melissa Müller stated that the fact Traudl Junge, one of Adolf Hitler's secretaries, took no part in the murders "does not excuse her, but it should be borne in mind if we want to understand what happened."[91] Wendy Lower analyzes secretaries who, by the very nature of their work, become accomplices, some of whom played vital roles in the Nazi murder machinery, and some of whom benefited "from their proximity to power plundering in depraved ways."[92] The role and behavior of women draw attention to the fact that there is not a simple "black-and-white ideological pattern of those who see the situation as polarized between Nazi villains and anti-Fascist heroes."[93]

Rather, most of these women fall into a gray area, to borrow Primo Levi's term, a "sphere of ambiguity and compromise."[94]

Ultimately, this article strongly supports the conclusions of Gisela Bock and Claudia Koonz: the women examined here did create an environment that enabled men to perpetrate mass murder. The women who administrated for the Nazis were, however, more complicit than simply fostering an environment that allowed the men to do wrong. In addition to willingly supporting the regime, they made an active contribution to it. The tasks the women performed, such as filing interrogation reports and keeping track of deportations, were all crucial for the wars the Nazis were fighting: the war against the Jews, and the war against the Allies.

Secretaries employed at the RSHA were privy to knowledge of the Holocaust, gained through their workload; through rumors heard both within the workplace and within their personal sphere; and through incidents witnessed. Fearing the consequences and armed with limited information, many of these women chose not to discuss what they knew and took no action. A few women did strive to find out more, questioning their bosses and searching for secret files. In the most extreme cases, some women left their jobs—or attempted to—because they did not wish to be cogs in the machines of Nazi persecution. Their questioning, delving for more information, and attempts at leaving their jobs did not, however, impact on that machine; with 50,000 members of staff, there were always others who could type the orders, and the majority of secretaries at the RSHA did so willingly. It is clear from their collective postwar testimony that these secretaries had some awareness of the Holocaust, and most chose to do nothing.

Many of these women claimed to have been conscripted or forced into their position. These women were nevertheless part of the perpetrator apparatus, and, importantly, could choose to not perform their work, an option that some took. The International Military Tribunal for the Trial of German Major War Criminals issued its judgment in 1946 that the RSHA "played a leading part in the 'final solution' of the Jewish question by the extermination of the Jews."[95] The female administrators employed by the RSHA typed deportation lists, registered death notices, and took the minutes of interrogations of Jews: their contribution to the RSHA's role is undeniable.

NOTES

1. Claudia Koonz, *Mothers in the Fatherland* (London: Jonathan Cape, 1987).

2. Christina Herkommer, "Women under National Socialism: Women's Scope for Action and the Issue of Gender," in Olaf Jensen and Claus-Christian W. Szejnmann, eds., *Ordinary People as Mass Murderers*, trans. Richard Littlejohn (Basingstoke, U.K.: Palgrave Macmillan, 2008), 108.

3. Gisela Bock, "Ordinary Women in Nazi Germany: Perpetrators, Victims, Followers, and Bystanders," in Dalia Ofer and Lenore J. Weitzman, eds., *Women in the Holocaust* (New Haven, Conn.: Yale University Press, 1998), 95. See also Susannah Heschel, "Does Atrocity Have a Gender? Feminist Interpretations of Women in the SS," in Jeffry M. Diefendorf, ed., *Lessons and Legacies Volume VI: New Currents in Holocaust Research* (Evanston, Ill.: Northwestern University Press, 2004), 314.

4. Wendy Lower, *Hitler's Furies: German Women in the Nazi Killing Fields* (London: Chatto and Windus, 2013), 166.

5. See, for example, Pam Jenoff, *The Kommandant's Girl* (New York: Mira, 2007) and Bernhard Schlink, *Der Vorleser* (Zurich, Switz.: Diogenes, 1995), published in English as *The Reader*, trans. Carol Brown Janeway (New York: Vintage, 1997).

6. Films depicting female perpetrators include Andrzej Munk's *Passenger* (Zespol Filmowy "Kamera," 1963), Lina Wertmüller's *Seven Beauties* (Medusa Distribuzione, 1975), Don Edmond's *Ilsa, She Wolf of the SS* (Aeteas, 1975), Daniel Mann and Joseph Sargent's *Playing for Time* (Szygzy, 1980), Joseph Sargent's *Out of the Ashes* (Ardent, Contenders Only, Cypress Point, and Lietuvos, 2003) and *The Reader* (Mirage and Neunte Babelsberg, 2008), an Oscar-winning adaptation of Bernhard Schlink's *Der Vorleser*. For a detailed discussion of the phenomena of films featuring Nazi female perpetrators, see Adam Brown, "Screening Women's Complicity in the Holocaust: The Problems of Judgement and Representation," *Holocaust Studies* 17, 2–3 (Summer–Autumn 2012): 95–127.

7. Heschel, "Does Atrocity Have a Gender?" 318.

8. See, for example, Dan Stone, *Histories of the Holocaust* (Oxford: Oxford University Press, 2010), for a discussion of recent work on *Täterforschung* (perpetrator research).

9. For a discussion of the definition of "perpetrators," see, for example, Rebecca Wittmann, *Beyond Justice: The Auschwitz Trial* (Cambridge, Mass.: Harvard University Press, 2005), 40–41.

10. The extent to which Nazi propaganda was successful is discussed by David Welch, *The Third Reich: Politics and Propaganda* (London: Routledge, 2002), and Jeffrey Herf, *The Jewish Enemy: Nazi Propaganda during*

World War II and the Holocaust (Cambridge, Mass.: Harvard University Press, 2006), for example.

11. See, for example, Daniel Patrick Brown, *The Camp Women: The Female Auxiliaries Who Assisted the SS in Running the Nazi Concentration Camp System* (Atglen, Pa.: Schiffer, 2002); Ulrike Weckel and Edgar Wolfrum, eds., *"Bestien" und "Befehlsempfänger": Frauen und Männer in NS-Prozessen nach 1945* ["Beasts" and "subordinates": Women and men in Nazi trials after 1945] (Göttingen, Ger.: Vandenhoeck and Ruprecht, 2003); and Jensen and Szejnmann, *Ordinary People as Mass Murderers.*

12. Other groups of women in Nazi Germany have been the subject of some research. See, for example, Jill Stephenson, *Women in Nazi Germany* (Harlow, U.K.: Pearson Education, 2001); Jill Stephenson, *The Nazi Organisation of Women* (Oxford, U.K.: Taylor and Francis, 1981); Elizabeth Harvey, *Women and the Nazi East: Agents and Witnesses of Germanization* (New Haven, Conn.: Yale University Press, 2003); Elizabeth D. Heineman, *What Difference Does a Husband Make?* (Berkeley: University of California Press, 1999), 38; and Jane Caplan, "Gender and the Concentration Camps" in Jane Caplan and Nikolaus Wachsmann, eds., *Concentration Camps in Nazi Germany: The New Histories* (Oxford, U.K.: Routledge, 2010).

13. Gudrun Schwarz, *Eine Frau an seiner Seite* [A woman at his side] (Hamburg, Ger.: Hamburger, 1997).

14. Yaacov Lozowick, *Hitler's Bureaucrats: The Nazi Security Police and the Banality of Evil*, trans. Haim Watzman (London: Continuum, 2002); Hans Safrian, *Eichmann's Men*, trans. Ute Stargardt (New York: Cambridge University Press, in association with the United States Holocaust Memorial Museum, 2010).

15. Heinz Höhne, *Der Orden unter dem Totenkopf* [The order of the death's head] (Munich, Ger.: Bertelsmann, 1976).

16. Klaus Hesse and Andreas Sander, *Topography of Terror: Gestapo, SS and Reich Security Main Office on Wilhelm- and Prinz-Albrecht-Strasse, a Documentation*, trans. Karen Margolis and Pamela Selwyn (Berlin: Stiftung Topographie des Terrors, 2010), 127.

17. See, for example, the postwar testimony given by Ingeborg Schoenemann and Ursula Rogge, both in Bundesarchiv Berlin B162 4173.

18. "Relative bombensichere Prag [Relatively bombproof Prague]," testimony of Hildegard Topel, October 17, 1967, Bundesarchiv Berlin 162/4174 (Ludwigsburg).

19. The term "major war crimes" was developed later, at the Nuremberg Trials, and was based on a definition in the London Agreement of the International Military Tribunal, published on August 8, 1945, http://avalon.law.yale.edu/imt/imtchart.asp.

20. Miscellaneous No.12 (1946), Judgment of the International Mili-

tary Tribunal for the Trial of German Major War Criminals; P.P. 1946–1947 Cmd.6964 XXV.511. The Nuremberg Trials, which took place between November 1945 and October 1946, were aimed at prosecuting the most significant of those who had been captured by the Allies. For more information on the Nuremberg Trials, see, for example, H. R. Reginbogen and C. J. M. Safferling, eds., *Nuremberg Trials: International Criminal Law since 1945* (Munich, Ger.: K. G. Saur, 2006); Telford Taylor, *The Anatomy of the Nuremberg Trials: A Personal Memoir* (London: Bloomsbury, 1993); and Michael D. Biddiss, ed., *Ethos, the Nuremberg Trial and the Third Reich* (Harlow, U.K.: Longman, 1992).

21. Landesarchiv Berlin [Berlin State Archive or LAB] Rep. 057–01 Findbuch.

22. Ibid.

23. Landesarchiv Berlin Rep. 057–01 327 and Landesarchiv Berlin Rep. 057–01 329.

24. Michael Wildt, *An Uncompromising Generation: The Nazi Leadership of the Reich Security Main Office*, trans. Tom Lampert (Madison: University of Wisconsin Press, 2009), 410–18, and see also the testimony given by the women as cited in this article.

25. Traudl Junge, *Until the Final Hour*, ed. Melissa Müller, trans. Anthea Bell (London: Weidenfeld and Nicolson, 2003), 234–35.

26. Norbert Frei, *Adenauer's Germany and the Nazi Past*, trans. Joel Golb (New York: Columbia University Press, 2002), 14–19.

27. Hesse and Sander, *Topography of Terror*, 127.

28. In German, a "spürbaren Einschränkung der Möglichkeiten einer gerichtlichen Ahndung nationalsozialistischer Mordtaten": Adalbert Rückerl, *NS-Verbrechen von Gericht* [Nazi crimes in court] (Heidelberg, Ger.: Müller, 1982), 190.

29. Hesse and Sander, *Topography of Terror*, 127.

30. Landesarchiv Berlin Rep. 057–01 Findbuch.

31. Christopher R. Browning, *Ordinary Men: Reserve Police Battalion 101 and the Final Solution* (New York: HarperCollins, 1992), xvi.

32. See, for example, Dick de Mildt, *In the Name of the People: Perpetrators of Genocide in the Reflection of Their Post-War Prosecution in West Germany: The "Euthanasia" and "Aktion Reinhard" Trial Cases* (The Hague, Neth.: Martinus Nijhoff, 1996).

33. Elisabeth Kohlhaas, "Gertrud Slottke—Angestellte im niederländischen Judenreferat der Sicherheitspolizei [Gertrud Slottke—employee in the Dutch Jewish section of the security police]," in Klaus-Michael Mallmann and Gerhard Paul, eds., *Karrieren der Gewalt, Nationalsozialistische Täterbiographien* [Careers of violence: National Socialist perpetrators' biographies] (Darmstadt, Ger.: Wissenschaftliche, 2004), for example.

34. Ute Frevert, *Women in German History*, trans. Stuart McKinnon-Evans, Barbara Norden, and Terry Bond (Oxford, U.K.: Berg, 1997), 227.

35. Stephenson, *Women in Nazi Germany*, 55.

36. Stephenson, *The Nazi Organisation of Women*, 181; see also Heinz Boberach, ed., *Meldungen aus dem Reich, Auswahl den geheimen Lageberichten des Sicherheitsdienstes der SS 1939–1944* [Reports from the Reich: Selection from the secret location reports of the SS 1939–1949] (Munich, Ger.: Deutscher, 1968), 294–95, 384, 405; and Heineman, *What Difference Does a Husband Make?* 63.

37. Meldungen aus dem Reich [Reports from the Reich or MadR], in the Bundesarchiv Koblenz: MadR, no. 120, September 2, 1940, BA, R 58/154 and MadR, no. 356, February 4, 1943, BA, R 58/180; Leila Rupp, "I don't call that *Volksgemeinschaft*," in Carol R. Berkin and Clara M. Lovett, eds., *Women, War, and Revolution* (Teaneck, N.J.: Holmes and Meier, 1979), 42–43.

38. Testimony of Helga Beer, November 28, 1967, Topography of Terror Archive (TOTA), Landgericht [district court] Berlin 3P Ks 1/71 gegen Otto Bovensiepen und andere [against Otto Bovensiepen and others], Bd. XXXIV, 168–71.

39. Jacques R. Pauwels, *Women, Nazis, and Universities* (London: Greenwood, 1984), 122.

40. Testimony of Berta Rauber, January 1, 1965, Landesarchiv Berlin, Rep 057.01 2590.

41. In German, "der Dienstverpflichtung nicht entziehen," testimony of Maria Winterstein, November 26, 1968, Bundesarchiv Berlin 162/4560 (Ludwigsburg).

42. Testimony of Gertrud Flickert, March 9, 1965, Bundesarchiv Berlin 162/4555 (Ludwigsburg).

43. Testimony of Margarete Hartung, November 10, 1965, Topography of Terror Archive, Landgericht Berlin, 3P Ks 1/71 gegen Otto Bovensiepen und andere, Bd. XII, 119–24.

44. Testimony of Elisabeth Marks, September 8, 1966, Bundesarchiv Berlin 162/4170 (Ludwigsburg).

45. Testimony of Irmgard Martin, August 19, 1966, Landgericht Berlin, 3P Ks 1/71 gegen Otto Bovensiepen und andere Bd. XXII, 88–92.

46. Testimony of Irene Erbe, August 7, 1968, Bundesarchiv Berlin 162/4555 (Ludwigsburg).

47. Author interview with Lieselotte Zimmerman, July 27, 2011, Hannover, Germany.

48. Testimony of Gerda Gerner, August 9, 1966, Bundesarchiv Berlin 162/4556 (Ludwigsburg).

49. Testimony of Erika Hesselbarth, April 23, 1965, Bundesarchiv Berlin 162/4556 (Ludwigsburg).

50. Testimony of Elsa Heine, June 21, 1966, Bundesarchiv Berlin 162/4168 (Ludwigsburg).

51. Testimony of Helga Duchstein, October 12, 1966, Bundesarchiv Berlin 162/4555 (Ludwigsburg).

52. Testimony of Ottilie Bläsius, June 26, 1966, Bundesarchiv Berlin 162/4553 (Ludwigsburg).

53. In German, "erworbenen Kenntnisse zu erweitern," curriculum vitae of Frida Paul, undated, Bundesarchiv SF B0015.

54. Literally "spring of life," the *Lebensborn* program provided assistance to the wives of SS men and unmarried mothers. Curriculum vitae of Emma Rückerl, undated, Bundesarchiv SF B0024.

55. Letter to the *Rasse- und Siedlungshauptamt* [Race and Settlement Main Office], March 31, 1941, Bundesarchiv SF A0037.

56. Testimony of Helga Beer, November 28, 1967, Topography of Terror Archive, Landgericht Berlin 3P Ks 1/71 gegen Otto Bovensiepen und andere, Bd. XXXIV, 168–71.

57. Testimony of Margarete Hartung, November 10, 1965, Topography of Terror Archive, Landgericht Berlin, 3P Ks 1/71 gegen Otto Bovensiepen und andere, Bd. XII, 119–24.

58. Testimony of Elisabeth Marks, January 25, 1971, and September 3, 1970, Topography of Terror Archive, Landgericht Berlin, 3P Ks 1/71 gegen Otto Bovensiepen und andere, Sonderband II, 64–71g.

59. Testimony of Luise Hering, June 7, 1967, Topography of Terror Archive, Landgericht Berlin, 3P Ks 1/71 gegen Otto Bovensiepen und andere, Bd. XXXIII, 53–58.

60. Testimony of Marie Knispel, April 23, 1970, Topography of Terror Archive, Landgericht Berlin, 3P Ks 1/71 gegen Otto Bovensiepen und andere, Bd. 80, 131–35.

61. In German, "die unter Gebrüll wie Vieh auf Lastwagen gepfercht wurden," testimony of Elisabeth Marks, January 25, 1971, and September 3, 1970, Topography of Terror Archive, Landgericht Berlin, 3P Ks 1/71 gegen Otto Bovensiepen und andere, Sonderband II, 64–71g.

62. Ulrich Eckhardt and Andreas Nachama, eds., *Jüdische Orte in Berlin* [Jewish places in Berlin] (Berlin: Nicolai, 2005), 20–21.

63. Testimony of Johanna Heym, June 14, 1966, Topography of Terror Archive, Landgericht Berlin, 3P Ks 1/71 gegen Otto Bovensiepen und andere, Bd. XIX, 125–48; see also Peter Wyden, *Stella* (New York: Simon and Shuster, 1992), 152.

64. Ibid.

65. Testimony of Erika Albrecht, Landgericht Berlin, October 24, 1967, Topography of Terror Archive, 3P Ks 1/71 gegen Otto Bovensiepen und andere, Bd. XXXVIII, 127–48. See also http://www.bergenbelsen.co.uk/pages/Staff/Staff.asp?CampStaffID=283.

66. Ibid.

67. Testimony of Margarete Schindler, June 8, 1967, Landgericht Berlin, 3P Ks 1/71 gegen Otto Bovensiepen und andere, Bd. XXXII, 45–49.

68. In German, "schimpfte und tobte zwar, liess es aber dabei bewenden," testimony of Johanna Heym, June 14, 1966, Landgericht Berlin, 3P Ks 1/71 gegen Otto Bovensiepen und andere, Bd. XIX, 125–48.

69. In German, "bereitete mir Unbehagen," testimony of Johanna Heym, June 14, 1966, Landgericht Berlin, 3P Ks 1/71 gegen Otto Bovensiepen und andere, Bd. XIX, 125–48.

70. In German, "unheimlich," testimony of Johanna Quandt, January 4, 1968, Landgericht Berlin, 3P Ks 1/71 gegen Otto Bovensiepen und andere, Bd. XXXIV, 227–35.

71. In German, "Frau Quandt, ich warne Sie," testimony of Johanna Quandt, January 4, 1968, Topography of Terror Archive, Landgericht Berlin, 3P Ks 1/71 gegen Otto Bovensiepen und andere, Bd. XXXIV, 227–35.

72. Testimony of Johanna Martha Greifendorf, June 7, 1967, Topography of Terror Archive, Landgericht Berlin, 3P Ks 1/71 gegen Otto Bovensiepen und andere, Bd. XXXII, 153–59.

73. In German, "weil man möglicherweise selbst Kopf und Kragen riskierte," testimony of Rosemarie von Godlewski, June 12, 1967, Landgericht Berlin, 3P Ks 1/71 gegen Otto Bovensiepen und andere, Bd. XXXIII, 297–304.

74. In German, "wie KZ und dergleichen," testimony of Elisabeth Marks, January 25, 1971 and September 3, 1970, Landgericht Berlin, 3P Ks 1/71 gegen Otto Bovensiepen und andere, Sonderband II, 64–71g.

75. In German, "kein Angehöriger des RSHA sich weigern konnte, die ihm aufgetragenen Arbeiten zu erledigen," testimony of Brunhilde Schreck, July 3, 1968, Bundesarchiv Berlin 162/4559 (Ludwigsburg).

76. Testimony of Marie Knispel, November 3, 1967, Bundesarchiv Berlin 162/4169 (Ludwigsburg).

77. In German, "herrschte erhebliche Aufregung," "es wurde sogar von der Einweisung in ein KL gesprochen," testimony of Eva Nöthling, September 25, 1969, Bundesarchiv Berlin 162/4557 (Ludwigsburg).

78. Interview with Alison Owings; Alison Owings, *Frauen: German Women Recall the Third Reich* (New Brunswick, N.J.: Rutgers University Press, 1994), 317–18.

79. For an example of a guard who was put inside a camp, see Rudolf

Höss, *Death Dealer: The Memoirs of the SS Kommandant at Auschwitz*, ed. Steven Paskuly, trans. Andrew Pollinger (New York: Da Capo, 1996), 149.

80. Testimony of Ruth Tilgner, October 15, 1965, Bundesarchiv Berlin 162/4174 (Ludwigsburg).

81. Robert Gellately, "Concentration Camps and Media Reports," chap. 3 in *Backing Hitler: Consent and Coercion in Nazi Germany* (Oxford: Oxford University Press, 2001), 51–69.

82. For statistics on the numbers of women in employment and their marital status, see Heineman, *What Difference Does a Husband Make?* 38–42.

83. In German, "die Ursache meiner weißen Haare," testimony of Luise Hering, June 7, 1967, Landgericht Berlin, 3P Ks 1/71 gegen Otto Bovensiepen und andere, Bd. XXXIII, 53–58.

84. In German, "grausam," "furchtbar," testimony of Waleska Bambowsky, March 5, 1965, Bundesarchiv Berlin 162/4553 (Ludwigsburg).

85. Testimony of Johanna Quandt, January 4, 1968, Landgericht Berlin, 3P Ks 1/71 gegen Otto Bovensiepen und andere, Bd. XXXIV, 227–35.

86. In German, "schnüffeln und zu schmökern," testimony of Elisabeth Marks, January 25, 1971 and September 3, 1970, Topography of Terror Archive, Landgericht Berlin, 3P Ks 1/71 gegen Otto Bovensiepen und andere, Sonderband II, 64–71g.

87. Testimony of Erika Miethling (married name Albrecht), June 20, 1967, Topography of Terror Archive, Landgericht Berlin, 3P Ks 1/71 gegen Otto Bovensiepen und andere, Bd. XXXII, 204–11.

88. Testimony of Erika Albrecht, Landgericht Berlin, October 24, 1967, Topography of Terror Archive, 3P Ks 1/71 gegen Otto Bovensiepen und andere, Bd. XXXVIII, 127–48.

89. Testimony of Johanna Heym, June 14, 1966, Landgericht Berlin, 3P Ks 1/71 gegen Otto Bovensiepen und andere, Bd. XIX, 125–48.

90. Thomas Kühne, *Belonging and Genocide: Hitler's Community, 1918–1945* (New Haven, Conn.: Yale University Press, 2010), 1, 137–38.

91. Melissa Müller, "Confronting Guilt," in Junge, *Until the Final Hour*, 216.

92. Lower, *Hitler's Furies*, 113.

93. Ibid.

94. Primo Levi, *The Drowned and the Saved*, trans. Raymond Rosenthal (New York: Vintage, 1989), 67. For a detailed exploration of this, see Jonathan Petropoulos and John K. Roth, *Gray Zones: Ambiguity and Compromise in the Holocaust and Its Aftermath* (New York: Berghahn, 2005). Even with respect to this gray zone, there is still debate as to whether ordinary people bore any responsibility. Claudia Koonz argued that women were perpetrators within their role of caring housewife or mother because they created a society

that accepted and nurtured the men who committed atrocities and waged war (Koonz, *Mothers in the Fatherland*, 418–19). It therefore follows that this classification would stretch to include the female administrators; they, too, provided the necessary surroundings that allowed the men to commit their crimes, and Koonz would classify them, also, as perpetrators. However, to demonstrate that Koonz's statement is a sweeping generalization, Gisela Bock and Christina Herkommer both emphasize the multiplicity and variety of roles of women under the Nazis (Herkommer, "Women under National Socialism," 110).

95. Miscellaneous No. 12 (1946), Judgment of the International Military Tribunal for the Trial of German Major War Criminals; P.P, 1946–47 Cmd. 6964 XXV.511.

V. R·E·C·O·N·S·I·D·E·R·I·N·G P·E·R·P·E·T·R·A·T·O·R·S

Edward B. Westermann

Hitler's *Ostkrieg* and the Indian Wars: Comparing Military Strategies of Conquest and Annihilation

A RECENT TREND IN THE HISTORIOGRAPHY OF GERMANY INVOLVES the transnational comparison of Germany's experience as reflected in or influenced by historical, philosophical, or political forces in the United States. For example, Jens-Uwe Guettel's analysis of the *longue durée* (long duration) of U.S.-German relations reveals the ways by which the United States and the concept of "American exceptionalism" became both a model for framing Imperial Germany's views and policies on the issues of race and space, and a foil for the Third Reich's views and policies on the same issues.[1] In another example, Dirk Bönker's *Militarism in a Global Age* examines "the pursuit of maritime force by two dynamic industrial nation-states [Germany and the United States] that moved along strikingly similar, and parallel, national trajectories in the new global age."[2] In a similar way, this essay provides a transnational comparison between the military strategies that framed conquest of the American West between 1850 and 1890 and the Nazi occupation of areas of Eastern Europe during World War II.[3]

As Adolf Hitler prepared for and waged his war of annihilation on the Eastern Front, he repeatedly drew parallels between the Nazi quest for *Lebensraum* or "living space" in the East and the concept of Manifest Destiny and the treatment of Native Americans during the United States expansion into the West. In a conversation in October 1941, Hitler offered his vision of a "German East" populated by former soldiers settled on millions of homesteads and remarked, "Our Mississippi must be the Volga."[4] The philosophical and ideological underpinnings of the westward march of the American empire and the displacement of Native Americans provide parallels with the Nazi conquest of the East and the conduct of a racial war of extermination against the Slavic and Jewish populations of Eastern Europe and western Russia. This essay examines the validity of this comparison with respect to military strategy and operations.

Nazi conquest in the East, regardless of the ultimate racial and economic motives, was based on a series of preplanned and organized military campaigns involving massed troop formations conducting operations against the conventional armies of an opposing nation-state. In the invasion of the Soviet Union alone, over 3 million German and Axis allies combined for the opening assault along the borders of the Soviet Union in June 1941. For their part, *Wehrmacht* (German armed forces) senior military leaders envisioned large-scale battles using superior maneuvers to encircle the opposing military forces and better firepower to annihilate them. In fact, the concept of the *Kesselschlacht* (literally "cauldron battle") had formed the ideal for Prussian military leaders since the reign of Frederick the Great in the 1700s. Robert Citino described this "German way of war" as the quest for "a way to fight short, sharp wars that ended rapidly in a decisive battlefield victory, a front-loaded conflict that left the enemy too weak or frightened to consider a second round."[5] The destruction of enemy forces on the battlefield not only borrowed from elements of the traditional Prussian and German operational strategy of envelopment and annihilation but also proved fully in consonance with the racial imperatives of the National Socialist regime and its depiction of Slavs as subhumans (*Untermenschen*).

In short, military strategy in the East was based on the premise that German military forces could, in fact, achieve the ideal of *Blitzkrieg* or "lightning war" by quickly overpowering their adversary in a series of rapid military campaigns. The six-week campaign in Poland in 1939, the rapid defeat of French forces in the West in 1940, and the swift conquest of Yugoslavia and Greece in 1941 seemed to provide both the template and the validation for this concept. In the case of the East, military conquest was to be followed by military and civil administration designed to exploit these areas and to prepare them for future German settlement.

In contrast to *Wehrmacht* conventional operations in the East, the U.S. Army in the American West faced an opponent adept at irregular and guerrilla operations and a diverse collection of tribes operating in a variety of climates from the deserts of the Southwest, to the Great

Plains, the forests of the Pacific Northwest, and the mountain ranges of the Continental Divide. The Indian tribes refused to engage in the set-piece Napoleonic battles taught to future army officers at West Point and the types of battles that typified the American Civil War. Indian tactics emphasized the use of relatively small groups of warriors conducting raids against isolated targets of opportunity, such as homesteads, wagon trains, mining settlements, and herds of livestock. The objective of U.S. Army strategy, especially during the reservation period, focused on operations to "pursue and punish" Indian bands who had abandoned the reservation. The purpose of these operations centered on the capture or killing of Indians accused of raiding and "depredations."

Throughout U.S. history, army strategies for dealing with the tribes contained both elements of annihilation and attrition. One military historian argued, "If the conduct of the Civil War had prepared the United States Army to employ a strategy of annihilation, sometimes with frightful literalness, in its wars against the Indians, the strategy was much in harmony with post-Civil War policy."[6] Certainly, both Generals William T. Sherman and Philip Sheridan learned lessons during the Civil War and brought these lessons—and the military experience gained in the war—with them to the West. One such lesson involved the use of "punishment" against an opponent. In his memoirs, Sherman discussed his objective with respect to the Confederate Army and wrote, "My aim then was to whip the rebels, to humble their pride, to follow them to their inmost recesses, and make them fear and dread us. 'Fear of the Lord is the beginning of wisdom.'"[7]

Although Sherman's words evoked the image of biblical retribution, the use of brutal punishment operations against Indian bands by military forces and people on the frontier clearly predated the Civil War. Soldiers and settlers destroyed Indian encampments and crops, killed women and children, took captives, and assassinated Indian leaders.[8] Whether or not the Civil War inured military leaders to mass slaughter and created a strategy of annihilation, Major General John Sullivan led a punishment campaign against the Iroquois in 1779 with the object of a "feed fight" aimed at "the deliberate destruction of crops and villages."[9] Similarly, the campaigns against the Seminoles in Florida in the first half of the nineteenth century provide evidence of operations designed to impoverish the tribes and to destroy their means of subsistence. In fact, campaigns against various Indian tribes prior to the Civil War, despite individual acts of atrocity and mass killing, incorporated punishment and not complete physical extermination as their primary military objective, a goal that faced the tribes with the bitter choice of "starvation or submission."[10]

Addressing the brutality of the Indian Wars, General William T. Sherman highlighted the conflicting demands placed on the army by white settlers and Eastern reformers in dealing with the various Indian tribes: "There are two classes of people, one demanding the utter extinction of the Indians, and the other full of love for their conversion to civilization." He continued, "Unfortunately, the army stands between them and gets the cuff from both sides."[11] In many instances, it was not Regular Army forces who proved most willing to engage in mass slaughter, but rather state or territorial volunteers, militia members, law enforcement groups such as the Texas Rangers, and groups of citizen vigilantes. Indeed, the precedent for atrocity and mass murder by nonmilitary forces was established as early as the sixteenth century in the actions of frontier settlers against Indian noncombatants, a practice that continued into the nineteenth century.[12]

U.S. ARMY POLICY IN THE WEST

In his annual report of 1857, Secretary of War John B. Floyd argued that the existing strength of the army at 15,764 men was inadequate for guarding and controlling a frontier of 11,000 miles and an area of 3 million square miles. The area of his main concern included the western frontier bordering the Indian territories. Along with a plea for an increase in the size of the army, Floyd proposed a new military strategy involving the creation of a dual line of frontier posts along the western and eastern borders of Indian Territory with an additional band of forts along the lines of communication between the Mississippi River and the Pacific Ocean.[13] Floyd justified his request by stating that "scarcely a week elapses without bringing to us intelligence of some Indian massacre, or outrage more shocking than death." He continued, "It most frequently happens that these acts go unpunished altogether either from the want of troops for pursuit, or from their remoteness from the scenes of slaughter, which renders pursuit useless."[14] Floyd argued that a double line of forts placed near the "Indians usual habitations" would serve as a deterrent for raids against the white settlements and would allow for "prompt retaliation" upon the Indian communities in the event that deterrence failed.

Floyd's report raised several issues related to army strategy against the tribes in the West. First, the report demonstrated the War Department's belief that it was being asked to do too much with too little. Second, it created the perception that, as a result of this manpower shortage, the army was not in a position to deal with Indian raids or attacks against settlers. Third, it displayed a sense of exasperation in dealing with a foe whose "only strength lies in a capacity to elude pursuit."[15] The failure of the army to develop a formal doctrine in dealing with the Indians' unique style of warfare reflected either an inability or an unwillingness to foresee the need for this capability. According to one historian, "The Indian troubles that occupied the army year after year called forth a body of essentially orthodox strategies only slightly modified by the special conditions of the police function."[16] In the end, army strategy reflected a reliance on a general punishment strategy aimed at deterring or, when necessary, responding to real or perceived Indian outrages.

The increasing settlement of the West presented the U.S. Army with a dilemma. On the one hand, the army in the West existed to protect white settlers from the Indians, but, on the other hand, the army also was charged with protecting the Indians from the depredations and encroachment of white settlers, speculators, and traders. The influx of white settlers into Indian Territory and along the overland trails increased the probability of interaction and conflict between the two groups. By 1865, one army general, Alexander McCook, envisioned only three possible alternatives for dealing with the situation. The first involved the creation of a permanent Indian territory from Kansas to California restricted to the Indian tribes alone. The second called for the creation of Indian reservations in the West with the army serving as both guardians and wardens of the tribes placed within the reservations. McCook's final alternative involved the extermination of the Indian tribes. For his part, McCook discounted the first alternative based on the economic realities and resources present in the western territories. He likewise rejected the third option of annihilation as "so cruel and inhumane that the idea of it cannot be entertained."[17]

McCook's statement raises an important point with respect to army policy. Many historians have pointed to the words and statements of senior military leaders, including Ulysses S. Grant, William T. Sherman, and Philip Sheridan, that advocated acts of extermination or annihilation against the tribes.[18] To be sure, these officers and others used the rhetoric of annihilation on numerous occasions in their personal and official correspondence. However, it is equally clear that physical extermination of the Indians as an ethnic group never became a goal of army strategy. For example, while still the commanding general of the army in 1868, Grant vowed to protect emigrant routes in the West "even if the extermination of every Indian tribe was necessary to secure such a result."[19] A year later, in his inaugural address to Congress, then-President Grant stated, "A system which looks towards the extinction of a race is too horrible for a nation to adopt without entailing upon itself the wrath of all Christendom, and without engendering in the citizen a disregard for human life." Grant continued, "I see no substitute for such a system except in placing all the Indians on large reservations, as rapidly as it can be done, and giving them absolute protections there."[20] Grant's volte-face may be explained in part by the president's decision to introduce his "Peace Policy" and a renewed effort to promote the existing reservation system and to extend this system to all the Indian tribes.

Perhaps no other army leader became more associated with the concept of extermination than General Philip H. Sheridan, a man purported to have said, "The only good Indians I ever saw were dead."[21] As commanding general for the Military Division of the Missouri, Sheridan became the senior military leader responsible for overseeing army operations against the Indian tribes in the West. Sheridan certainly used exterminationist vocabulary in some orders and directives to his field commanders. For example, in orders to Colonel Ranald Mackenzie in a campaign against the Kickapoo on the Mexican border in 1873, Sheridan wrote, "I want you to be bold, enterprising, and at all times full of energy, when you begin, let it be a campaign of annihilation, obliteration, and complete destruction."[22] The resulting operation against the Kickapoo resulted in the killing of an estimated twenty and the capture of approximately fifty, mostly women and children.[23] Even in this case, orders for "a campaign of annihilation" and "complete destruction" did not translate into total physical extermination.

Sheridan, like many army officers, felt that persuasion was ineffective and that punishment was a necessary part of army policy. In 1869, he ordered a subordinate commander to hang any Indians found guilty of murder and to imprison those found guilty of robbery. He remarked, "The trouble heretofore with Indians has been caused by the absence of all punishment for crimes committed against the settlements. No people, especially those in a wild state, can be expected to behave themselves where there are no laws providing punishment for crime."[24]

THE RED RIVER WAR

In the winter of 1874, the tribes of the southern plains occupied Sheridan's attention. As a result of the government's failure to deliver promised rations—combined with the decimation of the southern buffalo herds by white hunters—frustration, starvation, and desperation among the tribes boiled over into open conflict in the spring of 1874.[25] The uprising seemed to come at a particularly auspicious moment based on the prophecies of a Kwahada (Comanche) medicine man, Isatai. Isatai declared that the performance of the Sun Dance held the power to achieve the annihilation of the whites and the rebirth of the buffalo herds.[26] Up against seemingly inevitable decline in the face of federal power and fueled by Isatai's visions, groups of Comanche, Cheyenne, and Kiowa launched raids aimed at the white hunters who were decimating the bison herd, as well as a series of attacks against white settlers in Texas, sparking a large-scale military response.

The Indian attacks led the federal government to revoke the prohibition of conducting army operations on the reservations.[27] The initial plan reflected the army's penchant for traditional operations. Sheridan's strategy for the campaign focused on five converging columns against an estimated 4,800 Indians camped along the headwaters of the Washita River. In his instructions, he ordered that "all captured Indians must be treated as prisoners of war and all captured stock regarded as government property." He continued, "All surrenders must be total and absolute and arms of every description delivered also."[28]

The resulting Red River War demonstrated the ability of the army to pursue the tribes even if it largely failed in bringing them to battle. The battle at Palo Duro Canyon on September 28, 1874, provides one example of army strategy in these campaigns. In this engagement, U.S. Army forces surprised a large group of Comanche, Kiowa, and Cheyenne encamped on the floor of the canyon. The ensuing battle led to the deaths of three Indians, but the major significance in the engagement involved the soldiers' destruction of over 200 tepees and hundreds of blankets and robes, the capture of 1,400 horses, and the burning of vast stores of food. In the words of one historian, the engagement at Palo Duro Canyon symbolized the "collapse" of the Comanche empire due more to economic factors than the military superiority of the U.S. Army.[29] In fact, the army's pursuit of the tribes during the winter had its intended effect by weakening the Comanche and their allies to the point of surrender, a case in which exhaustion and not annihilation proved the decisive factor.

Reflecting on the campaign, Robert Utley offered the following summary: "There were few clashes and little bloodshed, but gradually the exhaustion of the chase, the discomforts of weather and hunger, and, above all, the constant gnawing fear of soldiers storming into their camps at dawn wore them down."[30] By the spring of 1875, all of the tribes had returned to their reservations. A military commission was established, consisting of five officers with directions to try all Indians suspected of murder, stealing animals, or having killed army personnel.[31] Upon their arrival at Fort Sill, the army disarmed the captured warriors, took away their horses, and imprisoned the men in a windowless and roofless ice house, while their women and children were sent to separate camps.[32] Eventually, seventy-four of those designated as "ringleaders" were sent by rail to an old Spanish fortress on the coast of Florida. The end of the conflict signaled the end of war on the southern plains and an end to Comanche, Kiowa, Cheyenne, and Arapaho raids into Kansas and Texas.[33]

The Red River War proved an important watershed in army operational strategy. First, army leaders recognized the value of winter campaigns as an effective means to harass and weaken Indian resistance at a time of year when food was scarce and adequate lodging most critical. Second, it signaled the demise of the "Peace Policy" but also demonstrated the limits of army objectives. The designation of captured Indians as prisoners of war and the subsequent imprisonment of so-called ringleaders provided a caveat to existing "exterminationist rhetoric." The army's response, in fact, represented a continuation of the existing policy of punishment and coercion in contrast to annihilation. The absence of a premeditated strategy of annihilation does not, however, imply that the army and other military, paramilitary, and vigilante groups did not commit acts of atrocity and reprisal against specific tribes.

A STRATEGY OF INDIRECT ANNIHILATION?

The use of winter campaigning during the Red River War points to a critical issue in the Indian tribes' way of life. Although some tribes pursued agrarian activities, the Plains Indians operated in a hunter-gatherer society and depended primarily on the buffalo herds for their existence. They relied on the spring and summer hunts to supply not only dried meat for the coming winter but also hides to be used in the construction of lodgings and the making of outer garments. The encroachment of increasing numbers of white settlers with their livestock into the West threatened not only the buffalo herds but also the supply of game in general and became a key point of white settler and Indian conflict between 1830 and 1860. One member of the Southern Cheyenne complained to an army officer in 1845 that "the whites have been amongst us, and destroyed our buffalo, antelope, and deer, and have cut down our timber."[34] The loss of game had a significant impact on the tribes, particularly those confined to the reservations, especially during the winter, when hunger became a perennial fact of Indian life. In fact, the Comanche phrase for the period between February and March literally translates as the time "when babies cry for food."[35]

In 1855, one Indian agent reported that the disappearance of the buffalo had forced the southern Plains Indians to slaughter their own horses and mules for meat.[36] The competition for the buffalo herds had two major implications for the Plains Indians and other tribes who relied on this resource. First, the loss of the herds provided a justification for raids on white settlers and emigrant trains to steal horses and cattle.[37] These raids became a key element of settler and Indian antagonism throughout the period of westward expansion, and minor raids and acts of reprisal often planted the seeds for larger conflicts. Second, the 1870s witnessed an increased demand for buffalo hides that resulted in a dramatic influx of white hunters seeking to make their fortunes. Like the competition for beaver pelts in the previous century, European and American fashion trends created a market that was exploited by whites and Indians alike. This issue became more acute after the buffalo herds of the plains began to decline as early as the 1840s from "drought, habitat destruction, competition from exotic species, and introduced diseases."[38] Furthermore, the later organized and systematic slaughter of the buffalo was not solely a function of white hunters but also partially attributable to the "prodigious hunting" efforts of the Indians and the continuing impact of disease on the herds.[39]

The loss of the bison herds had enormous implications for the Plains Indians in particular. The loss of the buffalo not only "cut the heart from the Plains Indian economy" but also had a profound impact on the "cosmology" of Indian life.[40] The destruction of the bison also had critical consequences on the ability of the tribes to fight and organize for warfare, a fact recognized by senior army officers. For example, Sheridan addressed the Texas Legislature in 1875, stating his opposition to a bill designed to protect the vanishing buffalo herds. He contended, "These men [the buffalo hunters] have done in the last two years, and will do more in the next years, to settle the vexed Indian question, than the entire Regular Army has done in the last thirty years . . . [by] destroying the Indian's commissary; and it is a well-known fact that an army losing its base of supplies is placed at a great disadvantage."[41] Six years later, Sheridan repeated this argument in calling for the destruction of the northern herd by stating, "The destruction of this herd would do more to keep the Indians quiet than anything else that could happen."[42]

Sheridan's comments reflected a belief in the military utility of separating an opposing army from its source of provisions, a strategy pursued throughout the course of human conflict. This strategy certainly had major implications not only for the ability of Indian warriors to conduct war but also on the Indian populations themselves. This strategy, however, was aimed primarily at impoverishment rather than annihilation and reflected the belief that the absence of available sustenance on the plains would tie the Indians to the reservations, prevent their ability to conduct mobile operations, and force them to adopt farming as the only available alternative. Although the army may have supported a "scorched earth" campaign against the buffalo, commercial and economic interests drove the demise of the buffalo with the unintended, if not unwelcome, consequences expressed by Sheridan for the Indians.

WEHRMACHT POLICY IN THE EAST

For many *Wehrmacht* officers and senior leaders, the campaign against Poland was not a war of conquest, but a *Reconquista* (reconquest) aimed at the defeat of an "eternal enemy" and the reacquisition of

German lands unjustly lost in the "shameful peace of Versailles."[43] If the acquisition of *Lebensraum* in Eastern Europe formed a keystone of Hitler's worldview, then the recovery of German lands in Poland was a "critical priority of all German military leaders after 1919 . . . and the major line of thinking and planning was directed toward that end."[44]

From an operational perspective, the centerpiece of the campaign into Poland involved the use of highly mobile panzer (tank) divisions designed to encircle enemy forces in the quest for the decisive battle of annihilation, or *Kesselschlacht*, the Holy Grail of German operational warfare since the Wars of German Unification in the 1860s.[45] During initial planning for the invasion in April 1939, army strategists emphasized the need for surprise coupled with "sudden, heavy blows" to quickly destroy Poland's military strength.[46] In fact, the key planning consideration of the Army High Command (*Oberkommando des Heeres* or OKH) for the attack against Poland involved the need to defeat Polish forces as quickly as possible to shift German forces back to the western border with France.[47]

THE INVASION OF POLAND: A FIRST STEP TO GENOCIDE

Facing an opponent suffering from technological and geographical disadvantages, five German armies poured into Poland on September 1, 1939, in a series of concentric drives designed to trap and destroy Polish forces. By the third day of the offensive, German forces had captured 15,000 Polish prisoners of war, as the *Wehrmacht* and the Western press heralded the birth of *Blitzkrieg*, or "lightning war." By September 19, the combined German onslaught using tanks, motorized vehicles, artillery, infantry, and airpower had overwhelmed Polish resistance, with the exception of Warsaw.[48] The forces in the Polish capital surrendered eight days later after enduring a hellish artillery and aerial bombardment that claimed the lives of thousands, if not tens of thousands, of civilians.[49] The massive loss of civilian life became one of the defining characteristics of modern industrial warfare, in which the consequences of war would be borne by combatant and noncombatant alike.

The major distinguishing feature of Germany's "Campaign of Eighteen Days" in Poland was not the speed of the German victory or the use of combined arms, but rather the introduction of a style of warfare based on racial and ideological precepts. In his examination of the German invasion of Poland, Alexander Rossino argued, "Perhaps the most decisive change that occurred in the German method of waging war was the morally corrosive influence of National Socialism." He continued, "This influence manifested itself in the deadly racial-political policies that the SS [*Schutzstaffel*], police, and German army implemented against Poland's civilian population, both Christian and Jewish."[50] This statement raises two fundamental issues for investigation. First, it is necessary to analyze how the campaign and the resulting occupation of Poland were conducted. Second, and equally important, it is necessary to examine the array of actors involved with the enforcement of racial policy and, by extension, acts of atrocity and mass murder.

As German military units entered Poland, followed by SS and police forces, their mission included not only the defeat of the enemy forces but also the support and enforcement of Nazi racial policies. But the *Wehrmacht* was not the only force involved in the war in the East because the invasion of Poland "not only initiated a campaign of atrocity and mass murder in Germany's war of conquest, but . . . also tested relationships and forged partnerships between organizations that constituted a deadly triad in the East: the SS and police, the *Wehrmacht*, and indigenous auxiliaries."[51] In fact, one of the unique aspects of the war in the East involved the interaction and complicity of each of these groups in the conduct of mass murder and genocide.

Despite orders from *Reichsführer-SS* Heinrich Himmler on September 7 that *police units were responsible* for executions and not the army, *Wehrmacht* forces continued to play an active role in the killings.[52] In fact, one of the army's largest victim groups was Polish prisoners of war (POWs). In one example, after a firefight that resulted in the death of a German army captain and fourteen soldiers, the colonel in charge of the unit ordered the 300 captured Polish soldiers to remove their uniforms and then had them shot as insurgents.[53] The POWs at most risk were the Jews. Jewish prisoners were separated from other Polish POWs and routinely subjected to physical abuse and starvation.[54] Required to perform forced labor and living in separate "ghetto POW camps," an estimated 25,000 Jewish prisoners, some 50 percent of the total captured, perished by early 1940.[55]

In summary, German forces pursued two complementary objectives aimed at the destruction of the Polish state. First, the *Wehrmacht* forces sought to destroy the Polish military in a series of battles of annihilation. Second, five *Einsatzgruppen*, or special mission units, composed of SS and police forces subordinate to Himmler but with instructions "to maintain close working relationships with all local military commanders," followed *Wehrmacht* forces with orders to combat "enemies of the German people and state in the rear areas behind the fighting troops."[56] In practice, these orders translated into the elimination of the putative racial and political enemies of the Third Reich, including Polish nationalists, members of the Catholic clergy, nobility, intellectuals, and Jews.[57] By the beginning of December 1939, the number of victims stood at 50,000, including some 7,000 Polish Jews.[58] If the attack on Poland had been a "dress rehearsal" for annihilation, the war in Russia would provide the stage for a sanguinary bravura performance.

OPERATION BARBAROSSA: WAR AND GENOCIDE

The planning for the invasion of the Soviet Union far exceeded in scale and resources all earlier *Wehrmacht* campaigns of conquest. Prior to the invasion, Hitler repeatedly stated to *Wehrmacht* leaders that this was to be a "war of annihilation," and the army leadership planned accordingly. The army's planning directive described the operational strategy: "During the initial phase the bulk of the Russian Army stationed in western Russia is to be destroyed in a series of daring operations spearheaded by armored thrusts."[59] In short, the armored forces would serve as iron wedges to rapidly penetrate Soviet forward defenses and thrust deep into their rear to cut off, encircle, and then destroy the Russian armies.[60] Army planners envisioned a campaign that incorporated the speed and mobility embodied in *Blitzkrieg* combined with the maneuvering and firepower of *Kesselschlacht* to annihilate Russian forces.

The success of the initial operations by all three army groups appeared to vindicate Hitler's prediction of a rapid campaign and to justify the army's plan of attack. On July 3, General Franz Halder, the chief of staff of the army, gloated, "It is thus probably no overstatement to say that the Russian campaign has been won in the space of two weeks."[61] Halder's celebration may have been premature, but it was not based on wishful thinking. All along the thousand-mile front, German armored forces advanced at an astounding pace. The tanks in Army Group Center (*Heeresgruppe Mitte*) advanced 270 miles toward

Moscow in the first week of the invasion, and the German army successfully completed a series of large-scale encirclements that inflicted "appalling" losses on Soviet forces and netted almost 2 million prisoners by the end of August.[62]

Despite the tremendous losses suffered by Soviet forces, the Red Army continued to throw troops and matériel against the German advance, and by mid-August the Army High Command's certainty of a rapid victory began to evaporate. In a journal entry of August 11, Halder worriedly wrote, "The whole situation makes it increasingly plain that we have underestimated the Russian colossus."[63] In point of fact, German military intelligence had severely underestimated the size of the Red Army, the ability of the Soviet state to mobilize reserves, and the technological capability of Soviet weapons, especially tanks.[64] In addition to the challenge posed by Soviet forces, Hitler's army, like Napoleon's *Grand Armée* in 1812, began to experience the challenges imposed by distance and poor transportation networks. For every kilometer they advanced, German forces lengthened their lines of resupply and increased the difficulties associated with transporting fuel, food, and ammunition to the forward lines.[65] In contrast, each German thrust forward shortened the Soviet lines of supply and movement.

Between August and September 1941, even as German forces moved toward Leningrad and Moscow in the Union of Soviet Socialist Republics (U.S.S.R.) and Kiev in what was then the Ukrainian Soviet Socialist Republic, the Army High Command searched for a knockout blow as Hitler shuttled his armored forces from one group to the next. Despite the diversion of forces away from the advance on Moscow, the German army in the south scored a major victory near Kiev in mid-September by capturing 665,000 prisoners of war, over 3,000 artillery pieces and antitank guns, and almost 900 tanks.[66] At the same time, Army Group North closed a vise around the city of Leningrad, starting a 900-day siege that would eventually claim the lives of as many as 2 million Soviet civilians and combatants.[67] By the end of September, the forces of Army Group Center prepared for what Hitler and his army planners expected to be the climactic attack on Moscow. On the eve of the offensive, the Führer addressed the army in the East in a radio broadcast with the following exhortation: "In these 3 ½ months, my soldiers, the conditions have finally been created for the last colossal stroke, which still, before the onset of winter, should crush this enemy . . . Today is the beginning of the last great battle of decision in this year."[68] The initial success made by the German army in the first two weeks of October seemed to justify Hitler's optimism as the *Wehrmacht* captured or killed an estimated 1 million Soviet soldiers while suffering 277,000 casualties of its own; however, these losses, combined with overstretched supply lines and fierce Soviet resistance, caused the offensive to stall literally within sight of the Kremlin's famous "onion domes" by the start of December.[69] With the arrival of "General Winter"—the winter climate of Russia that contributed to the military failure of several invasions—and a seemingly inexhaustible supply of Soviet manpower, German forces had reached the end of their advance, and a pending Soviet counteroffensive seemed to imperil their entire position.

THE GERMAN GENERALS TALK

In planning for the invasion of Russia, General Walther von Brauchitsch, the commander in chief of the army, informed his subordinate commanders that "this struggle [the attack on Russia] is being waged by one race against another, and [must] proceed with the necessary harshness."[70] In May 1941, General Erich Hoepner, the commander of Armored Group 4, echoed these sentiments with his order that "every combat action, in its conception and conduct, must be governed by the iron will to pitiless and complete annihilation of the enemy. In particular there is no mercy for the carriers of the current Russian-Bolshevik system."[71] These orders, originating at the highest levels of the German army, set the tone for a "war without mercy" founded on the regime's own racial proclamations. Furthermore, the support by senior military leaders for the regime's racial and ideological objectives found repeated expression in the fall of 1941 in the infamous orders of senior *Wehrmacht* commanders such as Field Marshal Walther von Reichenau and General Hermann Hoth. As German forces began their assault on Moscow, the former called for "the extermination of the Asiatic [that is, Jewish-Bolshevik] influence in the sphere of European culture" and the conduct of "tasks which go beyond the conventional purely military ones."[72] Similarly Hoth asserted, "This battle can only end with the annihilation of one side or the other . . . Resistance or any other type of intrigue by Jewish-Bolshevist rabble-rousers is to be immediately and mercilessly exterminated."[73] The widespread dissemination of such orders, combined with the criminal directives that preceded the attack into Russia, clearly framed the conflict in the East as an apocalyptic battle between two antithetical ideologies. Seen in whole, these polices served to radicalize the conduct of the war and not only promoted but also justified widespread acts of premeditated murder and cold-blooded atrocity in the East.

ASSESSING A WAR OF ANNIHILATION

In assessing the scale of slaughter in the East, one might be reminded of the battles of annihilation fought in World War I some three decades earlier. For example, German casualties in the Battles of Verdun (1915) and the Somme (1916) alone totaled almost 800,000, while Russia suffered 1.8 million dead and 3.9 million wounded during the war.[74] What distinguished the *Wehrmacht*'s strategy and conduct of the war in Russia, then, was not the number of killed and wounded, but rather the objectives and conduct of operations. The horrific casualties of World War I occurred, in part, from the mass introduction of lethal technologies, including the machine gun, artillery, and poison gas. They also arose from a bankrupt tactical and operational imagination that repeatedly led commanders to send thousands of men "over the top" into the face of the murderously efficient weapons of modern warfare. In contrast to the incompetence and a lack of imagination displayed by military commanders in World War I, which led to mass slaughter, German military and political leaders planned and conducted a premeditated campaign focused on the annihilation of the putative military, political, and racial enemies of the Nazi regime.

The *Wehrmacht*'s complicity in the regime's exterminatory objectives can be seen in a number of areas, including the army's cooperation with the *Einsatzgruppen* ("task forces," death squads responsible for mass killings), the mass murder of Soviet prisoners of war, the army's role in the "anti-partisan" campaign, the economic exploitation of the East and the use of slave labor, and, finally, the genocide of the Jews, Sinti, and Roma. In his study of the *Wehrmacht* on the Eastern Front, Dieter Pohl estimates that frontline German forces participated, directly or indirectly, in the deaths of approximately 2 million persons, including Jews, other civilians, and prisoners of war in "the most brutal occupation regime . . . in history."[75] Furthermore, the Army High Command and especially the General Quartermaster

Corps played a hitherto under-recognized role in the formulation, planning, and conduct of the war. In the case of the former, Pohl argues, "The importance of the Army High Command has been largely underappreciated with respect to the war of annihilation in the case of mass crimes and the atrocious treatment of the civilians in the East."[76]

COMPARING THE AMERICAN WEST AND THE NAZI EAST

The preceding discussion of U.S. Army strategy in the American West and German military strategy in Eastern Europe reveals some points of similarity with respect to the use of rhetoric and in the conduct of operations at the tactical level. Army generals such as Sherman and Sheridan, like German generals in the East, made extensive use of annihilatory rhetoric; however, it is equally apparent that the implementation of such orders proved fundamentally different in execution. Without doubt, Sheridan and Sherman, like many of their contemporaries, viewed and described Indians as "savages" and felt them capable of treachery and cruelty. Despite these feelings, other military officers, such as George Crook and Nelson Miles, proved ready to use force to punish or coerce but displayed a deep respect and admiration for their adversaries and the Indians' culture. The ultimate goal of military and political policy in the period involved the assimilation of the Indian tribes under the guise of civilizing and Christianizing these "savage" and wayward children of a lesser God, even if this policy entailed the "cultural annihilation" of the Indians.

In general, military force was used to enforce specific behaviors or to control the actions of the tribes. Likewise, the U.S. Army often found itself trapped between conflicting demands. On the one hand, the army's mission included the charter to prevent white encroachment upon the reservations and to protect Indian rights and property. On the other hand, the army was responsible for "pursuing and punishing" tribes or bands of Indians who left the reservation or became involved in hostilities with white settlers. The *Wehrmacht* had no such obligation to the native peoples of the East. In fact, the racial and ideological imperatives that drove the war in the East explicitly freed soldiers, SS, and police forces from any legal responsibilities or restraints with respect to Slavs and Jews, who were seen as essentially subhuman. In the East, assimilation only applied to a select few who displayed supposedly Aryan characteristics. The remaining Slavs, the vast majority of the population, were to be expelled, exploited through slave labor, starved, and exterminated when deemed appropriate.

One of the fundamental differences between the two cases involved the role of political leaders in the process of establishing the acceptable goals and limits related to military strategy. In the case of the American West, the army found its scope of action significantly circumscribed by the Bureau of Indian Affairs and its policies. Likewise, the authority of the president and Congress set limits on military objectives and the parameters of acceptable action.

If U.S. political officials could and did choose on occasion to moderate military responses to the Indian tribes, such was clearly not the case for the Nazi Eastern Empire. Adolf Hitler once remarked that the conquest of the American West had been attained "after the white man had shot down the millions of redskins to a few hundred thousand."[77] In this sense, the importance of Hitler's declaration is not related to the accuracy or inaccuracy of the Führer's assessment, but rather to *his own belief* in the historical truth of this statement. Indeed, if Hitler envisioned the conquest of the American West as a process that included the murder of millions, then he also could imagine the subjugation of German *Lebensraum* in the East through a process of mass annihilation. Hitler's boasts of creating a new frontier in the East to rival that of the American West in the previous century not only demonstrated the Führer's limited understanding of U.S. history but also exposed the genocidal impulse that underpinned his conception of conquest and exploitation in Eastern Europe.

NOTES

1. Jens-Uwe Guettel, *German Expansionism, Imperial Liberalism, and the United States, 1776–1945* (Cambridge: Cambridge University Press, 2012).

2. Dirk Bönker, *Militarism in a Global Age: Naval Ambitions in Germany and the United States before World War I* (Ithaca, N.Y.: Cornell University Press, 2012), 4.

3. Two monographs that reach significantly different conclusions related to this topic are Edward B. Westermann, *Hitler's Ostkrieg and the Indian Wars: Comparing Conquest and Genocide* (Norman: University of Oklahoma Press, 2016) and Carroll P. Kakel, *The American West and the Nazi East: A Comparative and Interpretive Perspective* (New York: Palgrave Macmillan,

2011). In addition, for an insightful review essay on the current scholarship related to this trend, see Thomas Kühne, "Colonialism and the Holocaust: Continuities, Causations, and Complexities," *Journal of Genocide Research* 15, 3 (2013): 339–62.

4. Ian Kershaw, *Hitler: 1936–1945 Nemesis* (New York: Norton, 2000), 434.

5. Robert M. Citino, *The German Way of War: From the Thirty Years' War to the Third Reich* (Lawrence: University Press of Kansas, 2005), xiii.

6. Russell Weigley, *The American Way of War: A History of United States Military Strategy and Policy* (Bloomington: Indiana University Press, 1973), 153.

7. William T. Sherman, *The Memoirs of General W. T. Sherman*, Project Gutenberg e-book 4361 (2006), http://www.gutenberg.org/files/4361/4361-h/4361-h.htm.

8. John Grenier, *The First Way of War: American War Making on the Frontier, 1607–1814* (New York: Cambridge University Press, 2005), 5. Scholarship from the field of genocide studies dealing with this topic includes Jürgen Zimmerer, "Colonialism and the Holocaust: Towards an Archeology of Genocide," in A. Dirk Moses, ed., *Genocide and Settler Society: Frontier Violence and Stolen Indigenous Children in Australian History* (New York: Berghahn, 2004), 49–76; Patrick Wolfe, "Settler Colonialism and the Elimination of the Native," *Journal of Genocide Research* 8, 4 (December 2006): 387–409; and A. Dirk Moses, "Genocide and Settler Society in Australian History," in Moses, *Genocide and Settler Society*, 3–48.

9. Wayne E. Lee, *Barbarians and Brothers: Anglo-American Warfare, 1500–1865* (New York: Oxford University Press, 2011), 222. Major General John Sullivan and his regular forces set out looking for a set-piece battle to destroy Iroquois military power. However, as in the American West, the Indians refused to engage in direct battle and chose simply to harass the Continentals before melting away into the forests.

10. David S. Heidler and Jeanne T. Heidler, *Old Hickory's War: Andrew Jackson and the Quest for Empire* (Mechanicsburg, Pa.: Stackpole, 1996), 226.

11. Allan R. Millett and Peter Maslowski, *For the Common Defense: A Military History of the United States of America* (New York: Free Press, 1984), 237.

12. Grenier, *First Way of War*, 11.

13. War Department Annual Report for 1857, M997, Reel 11, United States National Archives and Records Administration.

14. Ibid.

15. Ibid. This comment referred explicitly to the seemingly interminable campaign against the Seminole Indians in Florida but reflected a general frustration in bringing the Indians to battle.

16. Robert M. Utley, *Frontier Regulars: The United States Army and the Indian, 1866–1890* (New York: Macmillan, 1973), 47.

17. Sherry L. Smith, *The View from Officers' Row: Army Perceptions of Western Indians* (Tucson: University of Arizona Press, 1990), 92.

18. For examples, see Weigley, *American Way of War*, 153–63, and David Stannard, *The American Holocaust: Columbus and the Conquest of the New World* (New York: Oxford University Press, 1992).

19. Weigley, *American Way of War*, 159.

20. Ulysses S. Grant Papers, reel 4, Library of Congress. Wording denotes changes made by Grant to the original draft of the text.

21. Stuart Banner, *How the Indians Lost Their Land: Law and Power on the Frontier* (Cambridge, Mass.: Harvard University Press, 2005), 228–29.

22. Clarence Clendenen, *Blood on the Border: The United States Army and the Mexican Irregulars* (New York: Macmillan, 1969), 66.

23. Ibid., 68.

24. Sherry, *View from Officer's Row*, 99–100.

25. Pekka Hämäläinen, *The Comanche Empire* (New Haven, Conn.: Yale University Press, 2008), 336–37.

26. Ibid., 337.

27. Robert M. Utley, *The Indian Frontier of the American West, 1846–1890* (Albuquerque: University of New Mexico Press, 1984), 174–75.

28. Papers of General Philip H. Sheridan, reel 6, letter dated October 1874, Library of Congress.

29. Hämäläinen, *Comanche Empire*, 339.

30. Utley, *Indian Frontier*, 176.

31. Papers of General Philip H. Sheridan, reel 6, letter dated November 20, 1874, Library of Congress.

32. Hämäläinen, *Comanche Empire*, 341.

33. Utley, *Indian Frontier*, 177–78.

34. Elliott West, *The Contested Plains: Indians, Goldseekers, and the Rush to Colorado* (Lawrence: University Press of Kansas, 1998), 90.

35. Ernest Wallace and E. Adamson Hoebel, *The Comanches: Lords of the South Plains* (Norman: University of Oklahoma Press, 1952), 70.

36. Wallace and Hoebel, *The Comanches*, 64.

37. West, *The Contested Plains*, 92.

38. Richard White, *"It's Your Misfortune and None of My Own": A New History of the American West* (Norman: University of Oklahoma Press, 1991), 216.

39. West, *The Contested Plains*, 90.

40. White, *"It's Your Misfortune,"* 219.

41. Henry E. Davies, *Ten Days on the Plains*, ed. Paul Andrew Hutton (Dallas, Tex.: Southern Methodist University Press, 1985), 14.

42. Davies, *Ten Days*, 16.

43. Geoffrey P. Megargee, *Inside Hitler's High Command* (Lawrence: University Press of Kansas, 2000), 68.

44. Gerhard L. Weinberg, *Germany, Hitler and World War II: Essays in Modern German and World History* (Cambridge: Cambridge University Press, 1995), 130.

45. Citino, *German Way of War*, 254.

46. Jeremy Noakes and Geoffrey Pridham, eds., *Nazism, 1919–1945*, vol. 3, *Foreign Policy, War and Racial Extermination* (Exeter, U.K.: University of Exeter Press, 1988), 735–36.

47. Megargee, *Inside Hitler's High Command*, 68.

48. Citino, *German Way of War*, 256–64.

49. Michael Burleigh, *Moral Combat: Good and Evil in World War II* (New York: HarperCollins, 2011), 120.

50. Alexander B. Rossino, *Hitler Strikes Poland: Blitzkrieg, Ideology, and Atrocity* (Lawrence: University Press of Kansas, 2003), xiii.

51. Edward B. Westermann, "Partners in Genocide: The German Police and the Wehrmacht in the Soviet Union," *Journal of Strategic Studies* 31, 5 (October 2008): 773.

52. Klaus-Michael Mallmann, "'Mißgeburten,' die nicht auf diese Welt gehören: Die deutsche Ordnungspolizei in Polen 1939–1941 ["Monstrosities," which do not belong to this world: The German police order in Poland 1939–1941]," in Klaus-Michael Mallmann and Bogdan Musial, eds., *Genesis des Genozids, Polen 1939–1941* [Genesis of genocide: Poland 1939–1941] (Darmstadt, Ger.: Wissenschaftliche, 2004), 73.

53. Burleigh, *Moral Combat*, 121.

54. Jochen Böhler, "'Tragische Verstrickung,' oder Auftakt zum Vernichtungskrieg? Die Wehrmacht in Polen 1939 ["Tragic entanglement," or a prelude to the war of extinction: The Wehrmacht in Poland 1939]," in Mallmann and Musial, *Genesis des Genozids*, 49–50.

55. Burleigh, *Moral Combat*, 121.

56. Rossino, *Hitler Strikes Poland*, 13, and Helmut Krausnick and Hans-Heinrich Wilhelm, *Die Truppen des Weltanschauungskrieges: Die Einsatzgruppen der Sicherheitspolizei und des SD, 1938–1942* [The troops of the ideological war: The Einsatzgruppen of the Security Police and the SD, 1938–1942] (Stuttgart, Ger.: Deutsche, 1981), 29.

57. Włodzimierz Borodziej, *Terror und Politik: Die Deutsche Polizei und die Polnische Widerstandsbewegung im Generalgouvernement, 1939–1944* [Terror and politics: The German police and the Polish resistance movement in the General Government, 1939–1944] (Mainz, Ger.: Philipp von Zabern, 1999), 26.

58. Rossino, *Hitler Strikes Poland*, 1, 14, 234.

59. Quoted in Citino, *German Way of War*, 292.

60. Geoffrey P. Megargee, *War of Annihilation: Combat and Genocide on the Eastern Front, 1941* (Lanham, Md.: Rowman and Littlefield, 2006), 25.

61. Quoted in Kershaw, *Nemesis*, 391.

62. Citino, *German Way of War*, 293–94.

63. Quoted in Kershaw, *Nemesis*, 391.

64. Citino, *German Way of War*, 295–96, and Megargee, *War of Annihilation*, 26–28.

65. David Stahel, *Operation Typhoon: Hitler's March on Moscow, October 1941* (Cambridge: Cambridge University Press, 2013), 92.

66. Megargee, *War of Annihilation*, 83.

67. Stephen G. Fritz, *Ostkrieg: Hitler's War of Extermination in the East* (Lexington: University Press of Kentucky, 2011), 385.

68. Quoted in Megargee, *War of Annihilation*, 99.

69. Ibid., 99–115.

70. Ibid., 33.

71. Ibid., 38.

72. Quoted in Noakes and Pridham, *Nazism, 1919–1945*, 1096. Walther von Reichenau was the commander of the Sixth Army.

73. Reinhard Rürup, *Der Krieg gegen die Sowjetunion, 1941–1945* [The war against the Soviet Union, 1941–1945] (Berlin: Argon, 1991), 63. Hermann Hoth was the commander of the Seventeenth Army.

74. Hew Strachan, ed., *The Oxford Illustrated History of the First World War* (Oxford: Oxford University Press, 1998), 182–87, 197.

75. Dieter Pohl, *Die Herrschaft der Wehrmacht: Deutsche Militärbesatzung und einheimische Bevölkerung in der Sowjetunion 1941–1944* [The rule of the *Wehrmacht*: German military occupation and indigenous peoples in the Soviet Union 1941–1944] (Frankfurt am Main, Ger.: Fischer, 2011), 337.

76. Pohl, *Herrschaft der Wehrmacht*, 96.

77. Quoted in Ian Kershaw, *Fateful Choices: Ten Decisions That Changed the World, 1940–1941* (New York: Penguin, 2007), 387.

Idit Gil

Intrigues and Conflicts of Interest as to the Exploitation of Jewish Labor in Radom, 1942–1943

ON THE NIGHT OF AUGUST 4–5, 1942, THE NAZIS LIQUIDATED THE GLINice ghetto in Radom, Poland, and sent about 6,000 Radom inhabitants to Treblinka. That day, *Oberquartiermeister* (head quartermaster) Albert Forster, the officer in charge of army supply in the General Government, sent an angry telegram to the military command in Kraków. The General Government was a territorial unit covering the central third of occupied Poland, which the Nazis used as a colony, which provided agricultural products to the Reich. Forster protested that a large group of Jews was taken during the night without previous notification to the military authorities. He claimed: "As a result, less than half of the Jewish workers of the *Armee Verpflegungslager* (military supply depot) in Radom, A.V.L showed up for work that day, and it was impossible to seize other Jewish workers." The workers were needed to load 600 cattle for a transport scheduled to arrive at the battlefront the next day. In the coming days, vital shipments of cattle and flour would be disrupted because of the withdrawal of the workers. Furthermore, Forster complained, "The 52 wagons that were prepared to transport the cattle were used for other purposes. Thus, the lack of proper replacement for the Jewish workers was deemed to harm the war efforts." He requested that "a solution be found."[1]

A solution was found. On August 8, the head of the *Sicherheitsdienst* (Security Police or SD) in the General Government, Dr. Karl Schöngarth, and armaments inspection officers agreed that all armaments employers in the General Government would be notified in advance.[2] Thus, on the eve of the city's large ghetto liquidation in mid-August, all the Jewish workers of the A.V.L were asked not to return to the ghetto but to remain in their workplaces. For the time being, the military was able to preserve its workers, but it became dependent on the *Schutzstaffel* (SS), the paramilitary wing of the Nazi Party that was responsible for the implementation of the Nazi racial policies. In Radom, as in the whole of the General Government following Operation Reinhard, the Nazi program to exterminate Polish Jews, the SS became the dominant factor in controlling Jewish labor, replacing the labor departments of the civil administration.

This article examines the utilization of Jewish labor in the city of Radom from August 1942 (when the SS liquidated the city's two nonworkers' ghettos) to November 1943 (when the workers' ghetto, which replaced the nonworkers' ghettos, was liquidated). It assesses how labor was integrated into Nazi anti-Jewish policies and the role of the SS within those policies. Although Jewish labor had no role in the Nazi economic plan (*Wirtschaftsplan*), the Nazis exploited Jewish workers both to persecute the Jews and to gain economic benefits. Throughout the war years, Nazi Jewish labor policy was not consistent, influenced by a circumstantial combination of racial views and practical considerations. This policy evolved at an interesting conjuncture during 1942 and 1943, when, on the one hand, Operation Reinhard *was* in full force, and, on the other hand, the Germans experienced a severe shortage of laborers. The war on the Eastern Front transformed from a *Blitzkrieg* ("lightning war") into a protracted total war, requiring a huge number of slave laborers to supply the increased demand for armaments. Yet millions of Soviet prisoners of war, who could have served as laborers, were killed or continued to die in German captivity.

The year 1942 also turned out to be significant for the SS as it became greatly involved in economic activities. The SS sought to expand its commercial operations; however, it achieved its main economic power through control of labor, which it rented to private and state businesses. In April 1942, the SS integrated the concentration camps into its Economic and Administrative Main Office (*Wirtschafts- und Verwaltungshauptamt* or WVHA), changing the character of the camps by making them reservoirs of labor for construction and industrial production.[3]

The years 1942 and 1943 were crucial for Jewish labor as the Nazis disputed the use of Jewish workers as a tactical measure. Albert Speer, the minister of armaments and munitions, often disagreed with *Reichs-*

führer-SS Heinrich Himmler, the commander of the *Schutzstaffel*, the wing of the Nazi Party that ran the concentration camps and carried out the murders of Jews. The contradiction between the Nazis' aims to implement the "Final Solution" and their exigent needs for labor during the spring and summer of 1942 generated conflicts over the prospects of Polish workers replacing Jewish forced laborers in the General Government. These conflicts peaked in the fall, as can be seen in statements, agreements, and directives by Himmler, Speer, and their subordinates in the General Government. While the SS emphasized the temporary nature of Jewish labor, the military command in the General Government stressed the pressing necessity of their work for the war economy. In September 1942, Hitler and Speer agreed that Jewish armaments workers could remain in the General Government and would not be deported. Himmler agreed, on the condition that these Jews would be in separate camps under SS control. He repeated his July 19 statement that only Jews who contributed to the war effort could stay. Yet there were important regional variations in how this directive was followed. In November 1943, during the Harvest Festival Massacre, the Nazis killed most of the Jews of Lublin, Poland, and the SS manufacturing firms there collapsed. In the Radom district, the Germans killed only a few laboring Jews and their families at that time, and so SS firms were affected less than in other places.[4]

Despite the unique and important economic power of the SS in Radom during those years, there are no comprehensive studies of the SS economy in Radom. The excellent studies on Jewish labor in Radom have focused on specific workplaces or have discussed Jewish labor as part of the whole Nazi policy in the district.[5] The historiography on Nazi labor policies in the General Government and the specific studies on the SS's economic power have focused on the SS in Lublin under the influence of its head, Odilo Globocnik, whose policies demonstrated the dominance of ideological views over economic considerations. Historians have mainly considered the SS in Radom in the shadow of the powerful SS in the neighboring district of Lublin, and thus they have underappreciated its role in the distinctive fate of Radom Jewish laborers.[6]

This article studies the SS process of gaining control over Jewish labor in the city of Radom by examining two of its main practices: selections and transports to armaments factories. In addition, it focuses on the nature of the projects commissioned directly by the SS as a way to see how Himmler's directives were implemented. These features are discussed in three chronological stages: the summer of 1942, the spring of 1943, and the fall of 1943. The article contends that local SS policy to strengthen the armaments industry and to establish workshops in armaments factory camps may explain how the majority of Radom Jewish workers were spared from the massacres of most working Jews in the General Government in the summer and fall of 1943. In addition, the greed of the Radom SS and its efforts to gain power within the SS system and to wring financial profits from its operations determined how it exploited Radom Jews.

The city of Radom in central Poland was the headquarters of the Radom district, one of the five districts comprising the General Government. The district was known for its wood, leather, metal, enamel, bricks, and weaponry industries. It was one of the three most important industrial areas in prewar Poland and therefore was also significant for the Nazi war economy.[7] The city stood at the intersection of railroads, and thus, when the war expanded eastward in the summer of 1941, it acquired further important economic and strategic value: the German occupiers established airstrips and transit bases for soldiers, transferred supplies to the front, and brought wounded soldiers to the local hospital.

The war on the Eastern Front affected the work patterns and the "opportunities" of Radom Jews, who were cramped into two ghettos as of April 1941: Wallowa, a large ghetto in the city center; and Glinice, in a suburb next to the light industry area. Unlike many other ghetto dwellers, most Radom Jews worked outside their confined living area. They worked for various authorities: the civil administration, the military, the SS, or small private industries, which were mostly owned by Polish or German trustees producing goods for the war effort (for example, tanneries, foundries, and factories manufacturing armaments, shoes, porcelain, furniture, and brick). In addition, tradesmen and merchants who served the German population in town kept their businesses and continued working in the private market outside or inside the ghetto.[8]

In the summer of 1942, throughout the General Government, the SS became the main player controlling Jewish labor. Radom was no exception. Officially, on June 25, the SS replaced the labor departments, becoming responsible for the transfers of workers between regions and to the armaments industry.[9] Practically, the SS used this prerogative to expand its control over all Jewish labor during the selections—the choice of victims for the gas chambers—that coincided with the liquidations of the ghettos.

The SS used the selections to manipulate the intricate relations between economic needs and ideological views when labor became the only justification for Jews to live. Having a valid worker's identification or labor assignment was a necessary condition for survival, but not sufficient to prevent being deported. The SS made the selections in two stages. First, it separated the summoned Jews into those with labor cards and those without. The latter were promptly sent to the trains. The former had to stand in line and then pass by an SS examiner. The selector determined the person's fate according to several criteria: the type of his or her workplace, stature, age, family connections, and the number of "vacancies" in the railway cars. The place of work was a crucial factor only during the Glinice deportation, when all workers were subject to the selection.[10] Two workplaces were considered indispensable: the SS facilities and the local armaments factory Steyr-Daimler-Puch. The workers of these places could remain in Radom. The additional criteria were mostly applied against Jews working in other places. In some lines, the selectors did not even look at the cards. They directed the muscular and the young to wait in the Gelka leather factory yard and tore up the cards of the others. Furthermore, the SS deported those under fifteen years of age, even if they had work experience and an essential workplace. Family members (siblings, fathers and sons, or husbands and wives) who stood next to each other were often separated, and the weakest were expelled.[11] These criteria, then, gave men an advantage over women. According to a testimony, only nineteen women passed the selection made on August 5.[12]

Palpably, the selections gave the SS the power to determine the size and character of the Jewish labor force. Between 500 and 1,000 Glinice ghetto residents were spared from deportation.[13] Between 2,000 and 3,000 Wallowa ghetto residents passed the selections there. Although the SS could not intervene with the workers kept in the military and the civil administration facilities, it demonstrated its dominance in some exceptional cases. SS men, armed with lists, arrived at these facilities and took out workers under the age of fifteen. An SS commander prevented the head of the agricultural department from allowing a Jewish woman to return to the department offices.[14] Thus, out of about 32,000 Jews living in Radom at the beginning of

August 1942, by the end of the month, only 5,000 Jews remained. Many had to change their living quarters. In accordance with Himmler's directives, 2,000 Radom Jews lived in camps in or near their workplaces, and 3,000 slave laborers crowded into the main ghetto, which had shrunk into four streets and was officially named *Jüdisches Zwangsarbeitslager Radom*, Jewish Forced Labor Camp Radom. In the subsequent months, the number of ghetto residents grew as hundreds of Jews fleeing liquidations and deportations from nearby labor camps and ghettos sought refuge in the ghettos of Radom.[15]

The selections also gave the SS the power to allocate the labor force according to its priorities, and in this way to control the workplaces. The few Jews who operated a business without a trustee could not do it anymore.[16] Jews could now work only for German and not for Polish employers. However, not all Germans could keep their Jewish laborers. The SS determined which Germans kept their workforce and how many slave workers they could have. As a result, some businesses lost their workers, while others gained. The main losers were private enterprises, which, although classified as highly contributing to the war economy (*Betriebe A* or "A establishments"), were deprived of most or all of their Jews. Only some metal foundries; a brickworks; factories producing candles, shoes, and furniture; and the Kromolowski leather factory were allowed to keep a small number of Jewish slave laborers. The Brago iron foundry lost two of its three managers, the Pulka shoe factory retained only between 60 and 100 shoemakers out of several hundreds, and the Bata shoe factory was left with 120 Jewish laborers.[17]

The main beneficiary from the selections was the SS, which directly utilized most Jews in three main departments: *SS-Truppenwirtschaftslager* (Economic Base for the SS Troops or T.W.L.); the *Bauleitung* (Building Directorate); and the tradesmen's workshops. The Jews worked to sustain SS interests (provision and maintenance) as they previously had (although without wages). They fulfilled private SS interests; were engaged in the byproducts of the "Final Solution" by collecting, sorting, repairing and preparing the confiscated Jewish property for delivery; and took part in SS commercial entrepreneurship.

Before August 1942, the SS employed fewer Jews than the civil administration or the military. Jews toiled in various departments such as the T.W.L, the *Bauleitung*, the *SS-Veterinär-Ersatzabteilung* (SS Veterinary Reinforcement Division) at Koscinski Street, and the *SS-*

Standortverwaltung (SS Garrison Administration) at 11 Planty Street.[18] Such assignments needed the approval of the civil labor department. For example, every month the SS had to file an employment form for Bruno Wrobelski, a talented automobile mechanic, who fixed the SS leaders' official cars. After the deportations, such approval was not needed. Wrobelski worked directly for the SS within the *Bauleitung*, which expanded.[19]

Before the ghetto liquidations, T.W.L was the largest SS department to employ Jews. Sixty Jewish male workers loaded and unloaded mainly coal and sacks of flour and sugar for the SS personnel in the district. Occasionally, they unloaded sardines, sausages, cheese, and wine.[20] The work was arduous, and although they were harshly treated, at least they were safe from the gas chambers. They continued to work at T.W.L after the deportations, with an additional twenty to thirty laborers. Several women, relatives of the veteran workers, were brought in to cook in the kitchen for the workers. After the deportations, Jewish workers could not leave the base at 18 Kolejowa Street. Most new workers toiled in a carpentry, preparing boxes intended for shipping stolen Jewish property.[21]

The *Bauleitung*, the second SS department at 27 Slowacki Street, included three commands: Margules, Korona, and the builders. The Margules firm for scrap and rags (Jammelstelle für Alteisen und Textilabfälle) was taken over by a Polish trustee on June 4, 1941, during the ghetto period.[22] However, its 100 Jewish workers continued to collect much-needed glass, cloth, and scrap iron for foundries. They had special green armbands, allowing them to move independently in town. Most of the existing workers were deported, but after the deportations the SS brought more workers and their number grew. Several hundred workers labored for several months to collect the abandoned property and material left behind by the deported Jews. It was brought to the firm's yard for sorting.[23] The SS then sold furniture and household goods to the Poles. This constituted the main share of 20,927,203.25 złotys, which was deposited in the SS bank in Lublin at the end of the year.[24]

On the second floor of the former Korona leather factory, sixty women sorted the clothing and linen of the deported Jews from the entire district, which was sent to Germany to the *Nationalsozialistische Volkswohlfahrt* (National Socialist People's Welfare Association or NSV), and also used to supply foreign workers. On the first floor, two watchmakers and a goldsmith repaired watches and made rings and bracelets out of gold teeth. Korona operated until November 1943.[25]

The third command in this *Bauleitung* was the construction unit, formed two days after the second deportation, in the SS and police headquarters. Two hundred builders and tradesmen worked on public and private building projects. Their first job was to adapt two buildings into workshops, and then to build a bowling alley. Occasionally, they were taken to fulfill urgent needs, such as cleaning a bloodstained apartment following a shooting or rebuilding some Luftwaffe barracks, which were burned in Wolanów in November 1942. But their main official task was to retrieve bricks from dilapidated houses and use them for constructing new housing for SS personnel, in an effort to relieve the severe housing shortage in the city.[26]

Nevertheless, the builders often worked within the SS "neighborhood" to fulfill individual needs of the SS. Non-skilled workers served as personal butlers, nannies, or cleaners in private and public buildings (such as the public swimming pool). Heads and vice heads of SS departments (and their female secretaries, wives, and lovers) exploited Jewish labor on a regular basis to clean their homes, wash and iron their laundry, and feed their pets. The best Radom craftsmen worked to provide and maintain household goods, often luxury items. Moszek Zylberberg and Alec Zylberberg, two expert builders of brick and ceramic ovens, and their apprentice, Chaskiel Zagdanski, constructed and maintained decorative fireplaces. Wolf Mandelman, a well-known carpenter, fixed ornamental furniture, and Moshe Perl and his four helpers hung drapes. Perl, a trained artist, wrote SS member Wilhelm Blum's Reich address on wooden crates that the unit carpenters made, in oil paint.[27]

Other leading artisans toiled in the workshops, *Werkstätten SS*, the third SS department to directly exploit Jewish labor. The workshops were formed after the Glinice deportation by several tradesmen, who hoped to save themselves and their families. The *Judenrat* (Jewish council) helped them organize the workshops in Rynek Street numbers 6, 7, 8, 9, and 10. Two thousand men and women registered as tradesmen.[28] As in the case of the builders, Herbert Böttcher, the SS and police leader—*SS- und Polizeiführer*, commander of large units of the SS and the regular German police—in Radom, was personally involved in the operation. After the Wallowa deportation, Böttcher

Clocks made in Osti Radom. Photograph courtesy of Yad Vashem.

nominated Gerhard Günnewig, an *Untersturmführer* (a rank similar to second lieutenant), to manage the workshops. He also brought in out-of-town tradesmen whose products satisfied him.[29]

Tradesmen with their machines and raw materials toiled in two large buildings connected by a passage at the edge of the workers' ghetto. One entrance was on Rathausplatz, on the Aryan side, and the back entrance was on the side of the ghetto. Between 600 and 1,000 Jews worked in a tailoring workshop for men, women, and children (the largest workshop); in workshops for hats, mittens, clocks, brushes, mattresses, goldsmiths, shoemakers, and women's underwear; in a carpentry for furniture; and in a small carpentry (five to six workers) for children's toys.[30]

The workshops served Radom's German population, consisting of the civil administration, the military, the SS, *Reichsbahn* (German Railway) personnel, business managers, and their families.[31] The shops operated from 7 A.M. to 7 P.M. The workers' lunch, usually soup, was brought to the site from the ghetto's kitchen. Workers arrived from the ghetto side, while the clients entered from the Aryan side. The building was modified to allow only limited contact between Jews and Germans. All meetings took place on the entrance floor. The client entered an office, where a Jewish clerk would discuss the order with him or her, making sure the client brought the needed material and that the appropriate artisan would be summoned. Five or six children, who functioned as runners, were responsible for bringing the needed artisan or notifying the clerks that a repair or a new order was ready. Several fitting rooms were nearby. Moszek Birenbaum testified that, on an average day, he tailored stolen clothing into suits for six to eight people. Others revealed that before holidays, hats, boots, shirts, and sweaters for families in the Reich were in high demand and orders increased. Some satisfied returning clients brought food to the tradesmen as a token of appreciation. The customers paid a nominal fee to the SS headquarters. At the trial of Wilhelm Blum, the deputy SS and police leader in Radom, his wife, Pinny, testified that in Radom she obtained her wardrobe at the workshops and even ordered bedroom furniture for her Düsseldorf home, which was destroyed in the Allied bombings.[32]

Working for the Germans was a fragile safe haven, which would last for only four months. After finishing work on the abandoned Jewish property in town, the subtle balance between ideological views and economic needs tipped again toward the ideological. The SS deported more than 1,500 Jews in three sweeps. The first sweep sent several hundreds to the "Restored Ghetto" in Szydłowiec, Poland, on December 5, 1942. It was one of four "Restored Ghettos" established in the Radom district after the liquidation of the ghettos to amass hiding Jews. Most of its 5,000 Jewish inhabitants were transported to the death camp at Treblinka on January 13, 1943. On that day in the "Palestina Deportation," more than 1,000 Radom Jews, who registered as having relatives in Palestine, were also transported to Treblinka. The third sweep on March 23, 1943, became known as the "Intelligence Massacre." The Germans registered all Jews with a university diploma, and murdered about 100 of them in Szydłowiec cemetery.[33] Except for those who worked to fulfill the individual needs of the SS and the armaments factory workers, all other Jewish workers were subjected to selections. On these occasions, the work of Jews in the civil administration and in most of *Betriebe A*, the small private factories, ceased completely.[34] Once again, the SS used the selections to determine the size of the Jewish labor force and to control the workplaces.

Individual SS men benefited financially from the selections. Before the ghetto liquidations, the civil administration clerks in the ghetto's Jewish labor office accepted bribes to find jobs for desperate Jews who hoped to survive by obtaining a working card. Afterward, the SS personnel received the payments. While some Jews paid to remain in their diminishing workplace, others paid to be transferred to a new job after their workplace shut down. After the war, Maria Friedman described the process in the Kromolowski leather factory:

The Jewish slave laborers who toiled in the SS *Heereskraftfahrpark* (Army Vehicles Maintenance) garage. Photograph courtesy of Leon Wynryb.

> The SS had the list of all workers, composed of some skilled and many non-skilled workers. The merchants paid a lot of money to be registered as skilled workers. During selections, the non-skilled ones were taken. Thus, selections always harmed the poor. Rich people bribed the overseers and the SS. One day on December 1942, I was warned about my approaching expulsion. I gave bribe. I handed over a beautiful crystal. I succeeded. I was not expelled.[35]

The Margules firm for scrap and rags operated until January 1943. When it shut down, many of its workers paid large sums of money to be assigned to other places. Some, including women, paid substantial amounts to become part of the crew of mechanics in the *Heereskraft-fahrpark* (Army Vehicles Maintenance or H.K.P.), a garage for broken trucks brought from the East, managed by the SS.[36]

The SS completed the process of gaining control over the entire Radom Jewish labor force in May 1943. All military camps were transferred to the SS, and the last two private firms in *Betriebe A* in the city, Bata and Kromolowski, lost all their Jewish slave laborers. The withdrawal of the workers from the last two private firms did not make economic sense because both firms were producing for the war effort. According to a business report issued by the Radom governor in January 1940, Kromolowski was the leading commercial business in the district. The factory produced saddles, belts, and pouches for the Polish military and then for the German armed forces. During the war, it was the second most significant Radom factory producing for the military, after the Steyr-Daimler-Puch armaments factory.[37]

The gradual elimination of the Bata Jewish labor force illuminates the SS methods and policies. Bata Radom, *Bata Schuh- und Lederwerke A. G. Zweigfabrik* (Bata shoe and leatherworks company branch factory), was the biggest shoe factory in the General Government. It produced various types of footwear, including work and military shoes manufactured according to the needs of the *Ostbahn* (Eastern railway), the post office, the police, the *Waffen-SS* (the armed wing of the SS), and some important factories in the General Government and the *Wehrmacht*, Germany's armed forces.[38] The character of the Jewish labor force can be studied through the 841 personnel files of Bata Jewish workers, which contain dates of employment and reasons for ending the employment.[39] In the spring of 1942, Bata employed 1,200 workers, of whom 30 percent were Jews.[40] According to the head of the human resources department, only Jews who had an approval certificate from the labor department could be employed.[41] Thus, 364 Jewish shoemakers and cobblers worked in the production departments. The average age of Jewish workers was 31.6 years.

The removal of Bata Jews was done in several ways.[42] During the Glinice liquidation, the SS took 133 Bata Jewish workers. Their cards showed that they were fired on August 15 because they had failed to show up for work since August 8, after the evacuation of the ghetto.[43] The rush to find German workplaces brought 116 new Jewish workers, who officially started work on August 10. Most did not work for more than a week, even though prior to the Wallowa liquidation the factory manager wrote a letter to the head of the industrial department in the civil administration notifying him that the evacuation of the Jewish laborers would severely impair production for the military.[44] Nevertheless, during the Wallowa ghetto's liquidation, 196 Bata workers did not pass the selection.[45] The SS took several dozen more to work at the Steyr-Daimler-Puch armaments factory.[46] In August 1942, Bata lost two-thirds of its Jewish workforce. Those who remained could not work in most production departments but only in maintenance and in the wooden shoes department, ostensibly manufacturing clogs for prisoners in the SS camps.[47]

In September, following a factory request to the SS, the number of Jews working in Bata increased to 265. Yet, a month later, in accordance with the SS directives on October 16, 1942, to take renounceable Jewish laborers out of *Betriebe A* firms,[48] most Bata Jewish workers were taken away. By December, only 52 Jews remained to toil in the factory. The deportations of December 1942 and January 1943 reduced their number again. The last 32 Jews labored in the factory for the final period in April 1943.[49] In late 1942, Bata also lost 200 Polish workers, taken for construction service. The labor department in the civil administration enabled the 58 skilled workers among them to return.[50]

Having all of Radom's Jews working only for the SS and for the armaments factory corresponded to Himmler's distinction between armaments workers, who manufactured equipment such as uniforms and shoes, and "real" armaments workers, who produced weapons and ammunition. The *Betriebe A* slave laborers, manufacturing equipment, had to be put in concentration camps. The weapons producers remained in factory camps. This rigid policy not only harmed crucial equipment factories but also impaired the armaments industry.[51] In the spring of 1943, Steyr-Daimler-Puch doubled its demands for gas. However, the municipal gas company could not supply it because of a shortage of workers to unload coal wagons. The gas company repeatedly asked the labor department for sixteen workers, suggesting that prisoners of war could do the work. It warned the head of the labor department that not getting the needed sixteen workers would force the company to be turned over to the person in charge in the district for war affairs. During this time, Jewish workers were taken from works, but no one suggested assigning them for assistance.[52]

By the summer of 1943, most Jews working for the SS were employed in the SS firm *Ostindustrie GmbH* (East Industry Limited), known as Osti. In March 1943, the SS Economic and Administrative Main Office established Osti as part of its efforts to gain economic power. Osti's main activities were in the Lublin district, where the organizational skills and influence of its SS and police leader, Odilo Globocnik, played an important role in the establishment of the firm.[53]

Nevertheless, Osti encountered difficulties in transferring a brush factory from the Warsaw ghetto and in taking over the enterprises in Radom district. Not until July 1 were Radom plants transferred to Osti management.[54]

It is not known why Osti Radom, Osti IV, started to operate so late, because preparations had been made in advance and the SS had agreed in principle. One can assume that the SS in Radom postponed the transfer to gain as many local advantages as it could. Indeed, it received financial profits and became the owner of all Jewish workers not employed in armaments. Essentially, Osti provided the SS and police leader in Radom the opportunity to extend SS influence to all Jewish workers in the district. According to an unwritten agreement, Osti had to pay the SS and police leaders in Radom and Lublin 1.60 złotys per Jew per day. Profits permitting, they had to be given an additional 3.40 złotys for male Jews and 2.40 złotys for female Jews. Later, it was agreed that the SS and police leader in Radom would receive a fixed rate of 3.70 złotys per Jew per day. During its eight months of operation, Osti paid the SS and police leader there a total of 1,635,764.29 złotys.[55]

Osti Radom employed 6,000 Jews in four enterprises: (1) the workshops on the Rathausplatz; (2) a newly established peat project, to supply much-needed fuel, which employed 700 Jews drawn from the *Bauleitung* and private industries; (3) a printing shop at 10 Stare Miasto (Old Town) Square, based on machines and 120 printers arriving in May from the Warsaw ghetto; and (4) workshops in Bliżyn, which enslaved 4,000 Jews.[56]

Osti aimed to exploit Jewish labor and property in the General Government and make commercial profits. Its business manager, Max Horn, was unsure how to combine the two. In a meeting in Berlin regarding the establishment of Osti, Horn asked Oswald Pohl, the head of the SS Economic and Administrative Main Office:

> Must this mandate be regarded primarily from a political-police or from an economic point of view? If it is primarily of a political-police nature, political considerations (concentration of the Jews) have to rank foremost, economic considerations have to remain in the background. If it is to be primarily of an economic nature, economic considerations must, however, predominate in the matter of the concentration of the Jews, as ordered.[57]

Following the example of the Radom SS, Osti Radom was able to achieve the first aim—exploiting Jewish labor and property. The question was how to make a profit, given that the workshops were operating on a made-to-measure basis for the welfare of the local German population and not for mass production, that the peat was only for local use, and the printshop machines, such as paper rolls for cigarettes and envelopes, often broke down.[58]

Osti Radom's most lucrative enterprises were the workshops in Bliżyn, twenty-six miles from Radom. Bliżyn, a former estate of a Polish nobleman and then a Soviet prisoner of war camp, was based on machines and Jews transferred from the tailoring and shoemakers' workshops in the military supply depot and tanneries in Radom, the workshops in Piotrków, the workshops and brush factory in Tomaszów Mazowiecki, workshops in the Białystok ghetto, and laborers from Częstochowa, Kielce, Ostrowiec, and Pionki.[59] In addition to laboring in a stone quarry, the workers toiled in various workshops, which supplied equipment for the military, concentration camps, and the local casino.[60] As in other Osti firms, the products were based mostly on repairs and refurbishing. Shoemakers fixed torn shoes; knitters cut and knitted torn and bloodstained socks; launderers washed soldiers' backpacks, torn and soiled with blood and dirt, and then brought them to the tannery for new leather trimmings; tailors and seamstresses mended holes in military jackets, coats, and underwear; and carpenters fixed ammunition crates. In addition, tailors prepared jackets for the winter in which one side was green and the other white, and shoemakers made wooden clogs for concentration camp inmates.[61]

The venture was cheap to operate, yielding modest profits. Osti Radom brought the machines from other camps and gave severe punishments to workers who engaged in sabotage or who accidentally broke needles.[62] Many workers hand-sewed with needles, and there was no need to invest heavily in raw material. The success led to an expansion of the workshop for repairing shell baskets for the safe transport of explosive shells.

Osti Radom combined SS discipline with commercial incentives to achieve its political and economic goals. According to Alter Lipszyc, Osti's Jewish accountant, Oswald Pohl, Odilo Globocnik, and Max Horn sent regular instructions on how to increase production. Osti Radom's business manager was Hans Seifert, who was responsible for Osti earnings and the turnover of millions of złotys. Five SS men worked with him; Paul Nell was notorious among them.[63] Osti management set high quotas in Bliżyn's plants and the peat project and punished workers who failed to make the quota. The shops in Bliżyn operated in three shifts of eight hours each, and tradesmen were occasionally tested for their skills.[64]

As noted, the SS also reinforced Jewish work in armaments factories within the Radom district. It was an effective policy. In a 1941 military report, five of the eight most important military factories in the General Government operated in the district.[65] The SS in Radom took full advantage of it. Since the summer of 1942, the armaments factories in the district started to staff their production departments with Jews. This policy contributed to the war effort and to the SS treasury. According to the Radom *Kriegstagbuch* (daily war book), Steyr-Daimler-Puch saw a steep increase in its production of Mauser guns and Vis pistols during 1942 and 1943.[66] The SS profited by demanding higher daily wage rates—taking in 5 złotys for every male worker and 4 złotys for every woman per day. In June 1943, 18,414 Jews worked in armaments factories in the district, 1,008 of them in the city of Radom.[67] This proved most profitable. Between the summer of 1942 and November 1943, the SS sent hundreds of transports of Jews to the armaments factories within the Radom district. Wilhelm Blum, the deputy SS and police leader, was personally involved in the transports. Occasionally, he sent transports of Jews to the armaments factories on his own initiative, not at the request of the factories.[68] The workers were taken after selections from ghettos and camps that were closing.

Steyr-Daimler-Puch started to employ Jews earlier than the other armaments factories in the district. In the summer of 1941, the first Jewish workers started in maintenance jobs. By the spring of 1942, the first group of carpenters and strong men began to work in production. Following the liquidation of the Glinice ghetto, 100 Jews were brought to the factory.[69] The SS sent several hundred there after the Wallowa liquidation. Two hundred more were assigned in November, and another large group on January 1943. About two-thirds of the Jewish laborers in the factory came from the city. The SS transferred several hundred others from liquidated ghettos and forced labor camps. The transports, comprised of 50 to 150 laborers each, arrived between the summer of 1942 and the summer of 1943 from Białobrzegi (three transports), Sandomierz (three), Staszów, Wollanow, Piotrków, and Zwoleń.[70]

In September 1943, Albert Speer was granted jurisdiction over all armaments workers. As a result, the SS Economic and Administrative Main Office leadership decided to transform ten camps in the General Government into concentration camps. Radom was one of them.[71] In October, the SS headquarters in Radom started preparations. The peat mine was closed, and the workshops were reduced in size. About thirty workers were sent to expand the Szkolna camp, which served as sleeping quarters for the Jewish workers of the Steyr-Daimler-Puch armaments factory and also housed Osti administrative offices and a truck repair shop. The SS transferred other workers to Majdanek and the armaments factory camps in Pionki, Starachowice, and Ostrowiec.[72] It was the first time that workers from Radom were sent to armaments factories outside the city. Apparently, financial considerations drove this policy. By transforming the Radom armaments factory camp into a concentration camp, the Steyr-Daimler-Puch payments for each prisoner would go to the SS Economic and Administrative Main Office in Berlin rather than the SS in Radom. To get as many payments as possible, the SS in Radom sent a few hundred workers to other armaments factories in the district.

In the fall of 1943, the shortage of workers diminished.[73] On November 3 and 4, the SS murdered some 42,000 Lublin Jews, including most Osti workers.[74] Only laborers who worked in armaments in Budzyń and Majdanek and those who worked personally for the SS were spared. On November 8, the SS liquidated the Radom ghetto. One hundred fifty workers did not pass the selection. The others, together with the workshops' machines, were transferred to Szkolna. Two hundred fifty started work in the armaments factory, and several hundred continued to operate the curtailed workshops. Several dozen builders, who worked for the *Bauleitung*, continued their work, having to walk a longer distance every day to the SS private houses. In January 1944, Szkolna and Bliżyn became the Radom concentration camp, a sub-camp of Majdanek.[75]

Before the summer of 1942, Nazi labor policy toward the Jews was a single component among many, within the overall policy vis-à-vis the Jews in the General Government. Following Operation Reinhard, labor policies toward the Jews became the policy per se. The SS tried to seize complete control over and profit from the significant and essential economic resources in the district by taking control of Jewish labor through selections and transports. With the liquidation of the two Radom ghettos, the SS began to exploit Radom's' Jews, who were assigned to work directly for SS units and enterprises, or for the armaments factories in the district that increasingly came under SS control. After the August 1942 deportations, a limited number of Jews worked for the civil administration, at military camps, and in private factories, producing equipment for the armed forces. Gradually, until November 1943, all those Jews were killed, transferred to armaments factories, or transferred to work directly for the SS. In the fall of 1943, while the number of those working under the SS decreased, the number of those employed to produce weapons grew, from which the SS profited.

This policy was a flexible interpretation of Heinrich Himmler's call to spare only the Jews who contributed to the war effort. Serving the individual interests of the SS seemed to be an indispensable contribution. Such conduct was probably not unique. (A memorandum on Osti shops taken over by *Deutsche Ausrüstungswerke* [German Equipment Works or DAW] stipulated that "community shops" serving families of SS and police should employ no more than fifty to one hundred workers).[76]

Nevertheless, the SS in Radom also strengthened and expanded the armaments production in the district, in part by setting up workshops as part of a factory camp system. Szkolna served as a labor camp both for Jewish prisoners of Osti in Radom as well as for Steyr-Daimler-Puch. Osti enterprises in Bliżyn and Radom, despite their geographical distance, continued to have mutual command and management. Thus, it can be argued that because of this particular SS policy, in November 1943, Radom Jewish workers were among the most fortunate to survive among the Jewish workers in the General Government.

NOTES

The research on which this article is based benefited from support by the 2010–2011 Phyllis Greenbuerg Heideman and Richard D. Heiderman Fellowship at the Center for Advanced Holocaust Studies of the United States Holocaust Memorial Museum, and a grant by the Israeli Science Foundation.

1. International Tracing Service (ITS) Digital Collection, 1.2.7.3, United States Holocaust Memorial Museum, 82181297, 82181298, Mili-

tärbefehlshaber im Generalgouvernement, Kriegstagebuch [Military commander in the General Government, daily war book], Oberquartiermeister [head quartermaster] entries of August 5, 1942, no. 172, 173.

2. International Tracing Service Digital Collection, 1.2.7.3, United States Holocaust Memorial Museum, 82181301, Militärbefehlshaber im Generalgouvernement, Kriegstagebuch, Oberquartiermeister entry of August 9, 1942, no. 185.

3. Nikolaus Wachsmann, "The Dynamics of Destruction: The Development of the Concentration Camps 1933–1945" in Jane Caplan and Nikolaus Wachsman, eds., *Concentration Camps in Nazi Germany: The New Histories* (New York: Routledge, 2010), 29–30.

4. On the conflicts between the SS and the military, see Christopher R. Browning, *Nazi Policy, Jewish Workers, German Killers* (Cambridge: Cambridge University Press, 2000), 75–79; Dieter Pohl, "Die großen Zwangsarbeitslager der SS-und Polizeiführer für Juden im Generalgouvernement 1942–1945 [The great forced labor camps of the SS and police leader for Jews in the General Government 1942–1945]," in Ulrich Herbert, Karin Orth, and Christoph Dieckmann, eds., *Die nationalsozialistischen Konzentrationslager: Entwicklung und Struktur* [The Nazi concentration camp: Development and structure] (Göttingen, Ger.: Wallstein, 1998), 419–20; Felicja Karay, "Ha-immut bein Ha-rashuiot Ha-Germaniyot sviv Machanot Avota Liyhudim ba-General Goubernemen" [The conflict among German authorities over Jewish slave labor camps in the general government,] *Yalkut Moreshet* 2 (2004): 226–29.

5. Sara Bender, "Ha-machanot le-avodat kfiya shel Yehudim bemachoz Radom (1939–1945)—Mabat Clali" [Slave labor camps for Jews in the Radom District (1939–1945)—a general view], in Shmuel Almog, David Bankier, Daniel Blatman, and Dalia Ofer, eds., *Ha-Shoa—Historia Ve-zikaron: Ma'amrim lichvod Israel Gutman* [The Holocaust, history and memory: Essays presented in honor of Israel Gutman] (Jerusalem: Yad Vashem, 2001), 105–32; Christopher R. Browning, *Remembering Survival: Inside a Nazi Slave-Labor Camp* (New York: Norton, 2010); Felicja Karay, *Death Comes in Yellow: Skarżysko-Kamienna Slave Labor Camp* (Amsterdam, Neth.: OPA, 1996); Jacek Andrzej Młynarczyk, *Judenmord in Zentralpolen. Der Distrikt Radom im Generalgouvernement 1939–1945* [Jewish murder in central Poland: The Radom district of the General Government 1939–1945] (Darmstadt, Ger.: WBG, 2007); Pohl, "Die großen Zwangsarbeitslager," 415–38.

6. Michael Thad Allen, *The Business of Genocide: The SS, Slave Labor, and the Concentration Camps* (Chapel Hill: University of North Carolina Press, 2002); Wolf Gruner, *Jewish Forced Labor under the Nazis: Economic*

Needs and Racial Aims, 1938–1944 (Cambridge: Cambridge University Press, 2006).

7. Robert Seidel, *Deutsche Besatzungspolitik in Polen: der District Radom 1939–1945* [German occupation policy in Poland: The Radom district 1939–1945] (Paderborn, Ger.: Schöningh, 2006), 88.

8. United States Holocaust Memorial Museum, HE9278.R33 A47 1942, Amtliches Fernsprechbuch für den Distrikt Radom [Official telephone book for the Radom district], 1942 Deutsche Post Osten, 12, 15, 154; Nathan Gottlieb, Yad Vashem Archives O.3/12865; author interview with Sarna Weinryb, May 7, 2010, Toronto, Canada.

9. International Tracing Service Digital Collection, 1.2.7.4, United States Holocaust Memorial Museum, 82184489, Militärbefehlshaber im Generalgouvernement (letter on June 25, 1942, from Dr. Max Frauendorfer, head of the labor department in the General Government to all managers of the labor departments in the General Government).

10. During the liquidation of the Wallowa ghetto, the workers for all SS and military facilities, the armaments factory, some large private factories such as the Kromolowski leather factory, a furniture factory, and some of the civil administration departments were kept in their workplaces during the selections.

11. Pinkus Karafiol, Yad Vashem Archives, M1E/1181; Henry Zagdanski, *It Must Never Happen Again* (Toronto, Canada: Colombo, 1998), 42. On separating family members, see, for example, Reuven Adler, Yad Vashem Archives, O.3/13084; Victor Cuiker, interview 40787, USC Shoah Foundation Visual History Archive; Harry Kirshenblat, interview 31506, ibid.

12. Lejzor Fischman, Yad Vashem Archives, M49E/2559.

13. Młynarczyk, *Judenmord in Zentralpolen*, 265.

14. Author interview with Yehuda Rosenberg, February 10, 2009, Herzliya, Israel; author interview with Eliezer Ayalon, June 6, 2010, Jerusalem; author interview with Michael Gotfryd, July 30, 2009, New York.

15. Emil Karp, Yad Vashem Archives, M49E/58; Rosana Kozuchowicz Meiches, *Nos Campos da Memória: A História de Kiwa Kozuchowicz Prisioneiro B513—Sobrevivente do Holocausto* [In the fields of memory: The story of Kiwa Kozuchowicz, prisoner B513—survivor of the Holocaust] (São Paulo, Brazil: Humanitas, 2012), 97.

16. Author interview with Bernard Gotfried, August 1, 2009, New York; author interview with Haim Gil, May 5, 2010, Tel Aviv.

17. Nathan Gotlieb, Yad Vashem Archives, O.3/12865; Jchiel Lencz, ibid., M49E/56; Josek Tauber, ibid., O.53.73, the Herbert Böttcher Trial; Tzvi Tartako, United States Holocaust Memorial Museum, RG50.120.0155; Itzchak Shtein, ed., *Sefer Radom* [The book of Radom] (Tel Aviv: Irgun

yots'e Radom, 1961), 247, 249; published in English as Alfred Lipson, ed. and comp., *The Book of Radom* (New York: United Radomer Relief, 1963).

18. Trial of the Major War Criminals before the International Military Tribunal, Blue Series, vol. 36, 955-D (Mojzes Goldberg's statement); Herman Borenkrant, Mordka Birenbaum, and Mojzes Goldberg, United States Holocaust Memorial Museum, RG15.155M.49/903/BD 4680, Karl Grabau trial.

19. See, for example, United States Holocaust Memorial Museum, RG15.134M.2.147, Records of the Governor of Radom District (Kroschel, SS-Oberscarführer und Verwaltungsführer to Personalamt [Kroschel, SS senior squad leader and administrative leader, to personnel office], Radom, March 5, 1942); ibid., RG15.134M.2.168 (report, Der Gouverneur des Distrikts Radom Abteilung Finanzen [The Governor of Radom district finance department], March 27, 1942); ibid., RG15.134M.2.136 (report, Abteilung Finanzen, April 10, 1942).

20. Henry Starkman, interview 19233, USC Shoah Foundation Visual History Archive; Sam Epstein, interview 22503, ibid.

21. Hyman Gutman, *What I Remember as a Survivor* (River Forest, Ill.: Concordia University Chair in Canadian Jewish Studies, 2001), vol. 15b; Jacob Gutman, *A Survivor's Memoir* (River Forest, Ill.: Concordia University Chair in Canadian Jewish Studies, 1999), vol. 4; Peter Mora, interview 51239, USC Shoah Foundation Visual History Archive.

22. United States Holocaust Memorial Museum, RG15.114.M. 12.1122/1140, Der Ober-Ältestenrat der Judischen Bevölkerung des Districts Radom in Radom [High council of elders of the Jewish population of the Radom district in Radom], identity card of Pinkus Margules.

23. Author interview with Eli Gat, January 12, 2011, Herzliya, Israel; Wayne Alan, Fortunoff Archives/2295.

24. Młynarczyk, *Judenmord in Zentralpolen*, 278–79.

25. Author interview with Moshe Frydman, May 11, 2010, Toronto, Canada; author interview with Ada Givoni, April 1, 2009, Givatayim, Israel; Zagdanski, *It Must Never Happen Again*, 53; Jur Cynamon, Yad Vashem Archives, M1E/1193. According to Alter Lipszyc, Osti Radom accountant, the jewelry and watches were sent to the main office of the SS Economic and Administrative Main Office in Berlin, U.S. National Archives, RG238/58, NO-3127, Records of the International Military Tribunal (IMT) at Nuremberg.

26. Ted Back, interview 9086, USC Shoah Foundation Visual History Archive; Shlomo Krakowski, interview 11997, ibid.; Abram Laks, Yad Vashem Archives, M49E/2558; Kozuchowicz Meiches, *Nos Campos da Memória*, 101.

27. Szaja Altman, Yad Vashem Archives, M1E/1403; Zagdanski, *It Must Never Happen Again*, 51–52, 77–79; Moshe Perl, *Ha-Tofet Ve-Hanekama* [The hell and the revenge], (Tel-Aviv: Perl-Neon, 1992), 45, 54. Remembering the address, Perl and several friends went after the war to Wilhelm Blum's house in Düsseldorf, setting off his arrest and trial.

28. Lejzer Fiszman, Yad Vashem Archives, M49E/2559; Chaim Zajde, ibid., M49E/4501.

29. Herbert Böttcher testimony at his trial, Yad Vashem Archives, O.53/73; Sam Isinberg, interview 45673, USC Shoah Foundation Visual History Archive.

30. Moszyk Birenbaum, Yad Vashem Archives, O2/265; Mojszes Bojm, ibid., M49/59; Mieczyslaw Buch, ibid., M1E/959; David Wainapel, *From Death Row to Freedom* (New York: Block, 1984), 83.

31. Author interviews with Eli Gat, January 12, 2011, Herzliya, Israel; and with Mina Stashevski (Rozenbaum), July 7, 2009, Tel Aviv; Yad Vashem Archives, O.6/426, photos of products made in Osti Radom. Photo 5209 shows various types of clocks, including fancy ones.

32. Moszyk Birenbaum, Yad Vashem Archives, O2/265; Pinkus Epstein, ibid., M49E/6214; Benjamin Schpesman, interview 3171, USC Shoah Foundation Visual History Archive; written testimony of Pinny Blum in Wilhelm Blum's trial in Radom, United States Holocaust Memorial Museum, RG15.183M/4709/32.

33. Seidel, *Deutsche Besatzungspolitik*, 338; Młynarczyk, *Judenmord in Zentralpolen*, 283; Lipson, *The Book of Radom*, 59–60.

34. Rubin Adler, Yad Vashem Archives, M1E/1323; Maria Fridman, ibid., M49E/2161; Abraham Horn, ibid., TR.10 /3676/1214; the trial against Jakob Holz; Jchiel Lencz, ibid., M49E/56; Benjamin Schpesman, interview 3171, USC Shoah Foundation Visual History Archive.

35. Maria Friedman, Yad Vashem Archives, M49E/2161.

36. Author interview with Mina Stashevski (Rozenbaum), July 7, 2009, Tel Aviv; author interview with Leon Wynryb, May 7, 2010, Toronto, Canada. Among the twenty-seven garage workers seen in a picture taken in front of the garage, four were middle-aged women. My thanks to Leon Wynryb for the picture.

37. United States Holocaust Memorial Museum, RG15.134.M.1.0546, Records of the Governor of Radom District (economic report about the ten most important commercial businesses in Radom, January 27, 1940).

38. United States Holocaust Memorial Museum, RG15.134M.13.596, Records of the Governor of Radom District (letter from Bata headquarters in Kraków to the construction department in Kraków, November 27, 1942).

39. United States Holocaust Memorial Museum, RG15.135M, Ra-

domskie Zaklady Obuwia, personnel files of the Jewish workers in the Bata shoe factory in Radom.

40. Sebastian Piatowski, "Żydowscy robotnicy przymusowi w radomskiej fabryce obuwia 'Bata' (1941–1943) [Jewish forced laborers in Radom shoe factory "Bata" (1941–1943)]," *Kwartalnik Historii Zydow* [Quarterly Jewish history] 3 (2008): 329.

41. Remsak Tomasz, Yad Vashem Archives, M 49 E/7094.

42. The number of workers taken in each deportation, and those each month, are based on Piatowski, "Żydowscy robotnicy," 329–31.

43. See for example, Maurich Perec Dykshtajn, United States Holocaust Memorial Museum, RG15.135M.3.396, Radomskie Zaklady Obuwia.

44. Piatowski, "Żydowscy robotnicy," 330.

45. On their cards appeared: "Fired on August 22 1942 as he/she failed to appear for work since August 17 after the evacuation of the ghetto." See, for example, Moszek Blumsztan, RG15.135M.2.182, Radomskie Zaklady Obuwia.

46. Their cards indicated that they stopped working on August 29, 1942, by order of the SS. Their names appear among the Steyr-Daimler-Puch workers. See, for example, Jojna David Bess, RG15.135M.1.852 and Israel Cynamon, RG15.135M.3.27, Yad Vashem Archives O-51/9, the Natzweiler Records, "A" transport list.

47. Author interview with Maurice Goldman, telephone, March 21, 2011 (Goldman's father was one of the factory's managers); Remsak Tomasz, Yad Vashem Archives, M 49 E/7094.

48. Młynarczyk, *Judenmord in Zentralpolen*, 337–38.

49. The letter to the SS and the number of the workers in Piatkowski, "Żydowscy robotnicy."

50. United States Holocaust Memorial Museum, RG15.134M.13.600, Radomskie Zaklady Obuwia.

51. Trials of War Criminals before the Nuremberg Military Tribunals, Green Series, vol. 5, "The [Oswald] Pohl Case," NO-1611 (Heinrich Himmler to Oswald Pohl, Friedrich-Wilhelm Krüger, Odilo Globocnik, Reich Security Main Office [RSHA], and Karl Wolff, October 9, 1942).

52. United States Holocaust Memorial Museum, RG15134M. 8.427/437/444, Records of the Governor of Radom District (letters to the head of the labor department in Radom, July 1, 1943; September 7, 1943; and November 13, 1943).

53. Allen, *The Business of Genocide*, 245; Browning, *Nazi Policy*, 84.

54. U.S. National Archives, RG238/58, International Military Tribunal, NO-2187 (Osti 1943 business report, March 13, 1944).

55. Nuremberg Military Tribunals, NO-1271 (Osti Auditing Report, March 1943–February 29, 1944), June 21, 1944.

56. Alter Lipszyc, Yad Vashem Archives, M1E/933.

57. Nuremberg Military Tribunals, NO-1270 (queries concerning the proposed establishment of Osti Limited in the General Government).

58. Miriam Biderman, *Neurim bezel Ha-Mavet* [Youth in the Shadow of Death], (Tel Aviv: Davar, 1960), 113; Nathan Gottlieb, Yad Vashem Archives, O.3/12865.

59. Alter Lipszyc, Yad Vashem Archives, M1E/933; Seidel, *Deutsche Besatzungspolitik*, 336, 357–58. The SS and police leader in Radom used Bliżyn as a punishment camp for Poles. International Tracing Service Digital Collection, 1.2.7.7, United States Holocaust Memorial Museum, 82184601 (Herbert Böttcher to heads of labor departments, March 29, 1943).

60. International Tracing Service Digital Collection, 1.1.01, United States Holocaust Memorial Museum, 82063219, HIST Informationsordner [information folder] SS—Wirtschafts- und Verwaltungshauptamt [SS Economic and Administrative Main Office], *Deutsche Ausrüstungswerke* [German Equipment Works or DAW] Radom-Bliżyn financial report for December 31, 1944.

61. Sam Epstein, interview 22503, USC Shoah Foundation Visual History Archive; Nina Frenkiel, interview 19718, ibid.; Avraham Kapitash, interview 30715, ibid.; Zwi Ruszcki, interview 39885, ibid.; Pinkus Steinhart, interview 17912, ibid.; Roman Goldman, Yad Vashem Archives, M.49.E/5346.

62. Many of the machines came from Białystok, which was considered one of the most productive ghettos. Israel Gutman, *Ba'alata u-vama'avak* [Struggles in darkness] (Tel Aviv: Moreshet and Sifriyat Poalim, 1985), 116. According to the final Osti auditing report on June 21, 1944, Osti Radom invested 335,000 złotys for machines, machine installations, and business equipment, and 30,000 złotys for tools. Nuremberg Military Tribunals, NO-1271 (Osti Auditing Report, March 1943–February 29, 1944), June 21, 1944). On punishments, see Pola Goldfarb (Friedman), interview 33439, USC Shoah Foundation Visual History Archive.

63. Yad Vashem Archives, O.68/346, SS personal files.

64. Alter Lipszyc, Yad Vashem Archives, M1E/933; on testing workers, see Moshe Flamenboim, Yad Vashem Archives, M1E/2488; Murray Mapen, interview 5278, USC Shoah Foundation Visual History Archive; on high quotas in peat, see Joseph Freeman, *Job: The Story of a Holocaust Survivor* (St. Paul, Minn., Paragon House, 1996), 42–43; on high quotas in knitting, see Roman Goldman, Yad Vashem Archives, M.49.E/5346; on shifts, see Zwi Ruszcki, interview 39885, USC Shoah Foundation Visual History Archive.

65. International Tracing Service Digital Collection, Militärbefehlshaber im Generalgouvernement, 1.2.7.3, United States Holocaust Memorial

Museum, 82181429, military report 13 on the armaments industry in the General Government, September 24, 1941.

66. U.S. National Archives, T77/619/1807468, Radom Kriegstagbuch [daily war book], entry of March 22, 1943.

67. Karay, *Death Comes in Yellow*, 53–54.

68. Yad Vashem Archives, O.5/79a Wytwornia Broni W Radomiu, testimonies edited by Towia Friedman.

69. U.S. National Archives, T77/619/1807405, Radom Kriegstagbuch, entry of August 5, 1942.

70. The transports are based on testimonies and the laborers' transport list to Vaihingen, Germany, Yad Vashem Archives, O-51/9, the Natzweiler Records.

71. United States Holocaust Memorial Museum, RG15.174M. 4.255.162, trial against Josef Bühler (Oswald Pohl's directives to transfer labor camps to concentration camps).

72. Eugenia Gutstadt, Yad Vashem Archives, M49E/28; Jules Schelvis, *Inside the Gates: An Authentic Story of Two Years in German Concentration Camps*, trans. Senta Kushkulei-Engelstein and Gerda Baardman (Amstelveen, Neth.: Elzenhorst, 1990), 80.

73. While retreating, the German armies took slave laborers to the Reich with them. Adam Tooze, *The Wages of Destruction: The Making and Breaking of the Nazi Economy* (New York: Penguin, 2006), 518.

74. On the *Erntefest* (harvest festival) massacre, see Browning, *Nazi Policy*, 85–86.

75. International Tracing Service Digital Collection, 1.1.19, United States Holocaust Memorial Museum, 82115261–82115268, memorandum on the transfer of forced labor camps into concentration camps, January 13, 1944.

76. Ibid.

Lukas Meissel

Not "How Was It Possible," but "Who Made It Possible": The Topic of Perpetrators in Holocaust Education in Austria

> *What I do not accept . . . are the old clichés that to explain is to excuse, to understand is to forgive. Explaining is not excusing; understanding is not forgiving.*
>
> —*Christopher Browning*

THE FOLLOWING ESSAY FOCUSES ON THE TOPIC OF NAZI PERPETRATORS by questioning the roles of guilt and responsibility in Austrian Holocaust education. Contemporary approaches toward the teaching of Nazi crimes will be analyzed, drawing from firsthand experience as an educator in various contemporary history projects and as a tour guide at the Mauthausen Memorial, the museum at the site of the Mauthausen concentration camp near Linz, Austria, and from recent Austrian debates on the importance of perpetrator history. Very little has been researched and published on the topic of perpetrators in Holocaust education in Austria, although activists in the country's nongovernmental Holocaust studies organization, *Gedenkdienst* (Memorial Service), which was established in 1992, have dealt with this topic for many years.[1]

The history of perpetrators has not been adequately addressed in Austrian educational programs. Although there is a political and public acceptance of the necessity of Holocaust education, there are still major gaps in educational programs indicating that certain taboos persist in Austria's attempts to deal with its Nazi past. In short, Holocaust education in Austria has allowed for a discourse about the plight of the victims, but not about the responsibility of Austrian perpetrators and "ordinary Austrians."[2]

WHY PERPETRATORS?

Holocaust education in Austria focuses on victims and the personal stories of the persecuted. This approach has many positive aspects. For instance, it allows participants to individualize history from the perspectives of actual people and to connect faces to the numbers. This leads to the personalization of victims of the Nazi genocide and makes it possible to empathize. Furthermore, it literally rehumanizes the victims, who had been stripped of their selfhood and dignity by their persecutors. The personalization permits discussion of the (individual) consequences of antisemitism and Nazi ideology. In Austria, the public association *erinnern.at* ("remember") is working intensely on such pedagogical concepts with its emphasis on survivors' stories. One focus is the production of multimedia-based programs to develop the virtual experience of encountering a survivor when, in the near future, none will remain alive. The association's work indicates that Austrian students who participated in pedagogical programs about survivors showed interest in the personal life stories and were touched by them.[3] Werner Dreier, one of the founders of *erinnern.at*, calls his approach toward teaching individual stories of victims "reflected empathy" (in reference to the historian Dominick LaCapra), which he claims will allow an individual to engage the subject between neutral objectivity and total identification.[4]

Dealing with the other side of Nazi crimes—with the perpetrators (male and female)—has, however, not been a common subject of educational programs about Nazism and the Holocaust in Austria. There are various explanations for this absence. One reason might be to avoid a confrontation with the difficult question of guilt. Another theory argues that, especially in Germany and Austria, the focus on victims' stories and thus an identification with the victims and not the perpetrators allowed descendants of perpetrators to switch to the "morally right side." This leads to an avoidance of dealing with Nazism in the personal stories of the grandparents and parents.[5]

However, shying away from confrontation with the perpetrators is not merely an exclusion of one aspect of "the story" but rather depriving the history of the depth it deserves. In the context of pure historiography or even criminology, the idea of ignoring those responsible when talking about a crime seems unthinkable. As Raul Hilberg pointed out, there were several groups of people involved in Nazi crimes. He separated them into perpetrators, victims, and bystanders.[6] It would not be possible to tell a comprehensive history of the Holocaust without mentioning those three groups.

In Germany, on the other hand, a few initiatives focus their pedagogical work on the history of the perpetrators. The Ravensbrück Memorial Site, for example, displayed an exhibition about female *Schutzstaffel* (SS) guards.[7] The *Haus der Wannsee-Konferenz* (House of the Wannsee Conference) in Berlin, where senior Nazi officials met in 1942 to coordinate the "Final Solution";[8] the Topography of Terror, also in Berlin;[9] and the Villa ten Hompel in Münster—the former home of industrialist Rudolf ten Hompel and now a memorial site for offenses committed by the police and local government during the Nazi period[10]—all deal with Nazi crimes with a main emphasis on the perpetrators. The *Erinnerungsort Topf & Söhne* in Erfurt—the memorial site at the former factory of Topf and Sons, oven builders—has exhibitions about the profiteers who manufactured the cremation ovens for Auschwitz and other camps.[11] However, there is a tendency in Germany to distinguish between different types of memorial sites for dealing with the victims or the perpetrators.[12] In contrast to Germany, the situation in Austria is more difficult because there are no institutions at all that deal primarily with Nazi perpetrators. In fact, there is not even a Holocaust museum. In general, few or no pedagogical publications with an Austrian perspective focus primarily on the topic of perpetrators, and there are almost no concrete concepts about this subject in educational programs.

The discourse about perpetrators in educational programs is more present in Germany. Ido Abram and Matthias Heyl wrote important works about the subject in which they point out the importance of addressing the topic of perpetrators in reference to Theodor W. Adorno's text *Erziehung nach Auschwitz* (*Education after Auschwitz*).[13] Abram argues that it is important to raise a deeper understanding of the perpetrators (as Adorno had demanded), as well as comprehension of the victims and the bystanders.[14] Abram also emphasizes the use of (auto-)biographical material from perpetrators and bystanders.[15] Abram refers to Adorno's term "identification," which does not involve actually identifying with someone in the sense of approving of the person's point of view, but rather means putting oneself in another's position to imagine unfamiliar situations.[16] Matthias Heyl, head of the pedagogical department of the Ravensbrück Memorial Site, integrated Hilberg's social triangle into his educational work and expanded it to other categories: Jews, the escaped, the persecuted, the helpers of the persecuted, the spectators, the fellow travelers (*Mitläufer*), the helpers of the perpetrators, the perpetrators, and the Nazis. The idea is that these groups may overlap or merge, and that it is often difficult to put individuals in only one category—especially the non-victimized Germans and Austrians. Heyl calls this concept the "Society of the Holocaust."[17] This educational method shows the importance of understanding the social context of the Holocaust to grasp the different roles that people played—voluntarily or unwillingly, as victims, perpetrators, bystanders, and beyond. Calling for a more comprehensive history that includes all the persons involved is not only a call to understand all the roles and moral dilemmas that individuals faced but also is necessary for explaining the history of the Holocaust.

Programs based exclusively on stories of victims enable us to deal with the consequences of Nazi policy while largely disregarding debates about the origins of these crimes. However, presenting Nazi atrocities as a story without a cause or as something totally unimaginable is actually detrimental to the goal of understanding and learning from the history of the Holocaust. It is essential to regard the Nazi savagery as crimes instead of as something akin to a natural disaster; and to emphasize that, as crimes, they were, by definition, perpetrated by humans. In educational practice, it would be problematic to create the impression that Nazi crimes stand only as metaphors for pure evil, which easily creates a tendency to trivialize[18]—especially since there were concrete criminals who have to be identified and dealt with in educational programs. Pedagogical concepts that rely heavily on the victims' stories should present them as stories of people who were not born into the role of victims but rather were victimized for specific reasons. The sociopolitical context of the crimes and the events leading up to them have to be addressed to understand this process of victimization. Consequently, the history of Nazi persecution cannot be understood by only looking at victims' stories. The victimizers must also be included.

AUSTRIAN NARRATIVES AS A FRAME OF REFERENCE

The wider historical and political context of Nazi crimes is a topic of special significance in "perpetrator societies" such as Germany and Austria. The term "perpetrator society" is intended to underline that large parts of the population were directly or indirectly involved in Nazi crimes: 1.3 million Austrians were drafted into the *Wehrmacht*, Germany's unified armed forces, and around 60,000 Austrians were members of the *Waffen-SS*, the armed wing of the SS.[19] Furthermore, many groups or individuals participated in one way or another in Nazi crimes: Nazi Party members, police, bureaucrats and state servants, railway workers, doctors and nursing staff, neighbors and friends of deportees, and others.

The personal reference of Austrians and Germans to the topic of perpetrators is often connected to their family history. For instance, some participants might interpret talking about crimes committed by *Wehrmacht* soldiers and the participation in crimes by the *Wehrmacht* itself as an insult to their grandfathers. Especially members of the third generation of non-victimized Germans and Austrians tend to see their grandparents as resisters of Nazism rather than former members of criminal organizations.[20] Participants of Holocaust education projects often try to find excuses for soldiers or other people who were involved in Nazi crimes. Often, they can more readily identify with the dilemmas, questions, and choices faced by the perpetrators than with those faced by the victims.[21] Even for young Germans and Austrians who lack family backgrounds connected to Nazi crimes and, therefore, do not have a specific family history associated with the question of guilt, this, as well as the question of responsibility, is highly significant.[22] The experiences of study trips and guided tours at the Mauthausen Memorial show that young Austrians are generally interested in contemporary history. They desire to know more about the generation that was in one way or another involved in World War II, especially the perpetrators, even if these topics are not intended to be part of the program.[23]

The sociopolitical background of participants of Holocaust education programs and their references to the politics of memory are the frame of reference in educational settings. Following this assumption, the varying aspects of a group's interpretation(s) of Nazi history should be taken into consideration. Educational programs should always reflect the historical narratives that the participants of a group share. It is rarely the case that groups have no (preconceived) images, explanations, and expectations concerning Nazi history. Consequently, it is possible to integrate the discussions, debates, and conflicts that might evolve out of the participants' perspectives into the larger program. Austrian groups mainly consist of people who were socialized in a specific national context. Therein lies the necessity of dealing with Austrian references toward Nazi history. To underline the significance of this framework, it is important to look at how Austria deals with its history.

The Austrian National Socialist Party was not merely a spin-off of the German Nazi Party but a movement of its own whose history does not start with the so-called *Anschluss* (annexation) in March 1938.[24] During the 1930s, Austrian Nazis carried out various terror attacks and assassinations of Jews and political opponents in Austria. They organized an unsuccessful coup in July 1934, during which they killed Austrian Chancellor Engelbert Dollfuß.[25] Between 1933 and 1938, the Nazi Party and Nazi activities were officially forbidden in Austria. Despite this official ban, the Austro-fascist government, a fascist regime that had been established in Austria before the *Anschluss*, installed Nazis in high-ranking positions (after the Austro-German Agreement in July 1936, and in February 1938 after a meeting between Adolf Hitler and Austrian Chancellor Kurt Schuschnigg).[26] In the days of the *Anschluss*, Austrian antisemites needed no encouragement from Germans to engage in violence against Jewish Austrians.[27] Adolf Eichmann, his *Eichmann-Männer* (Eichmann's men), and their role in the Shoah have been extensively researched by historian Hans Safrian.[28] In addition, some of the leading Nazis and major criminals of the Holocaust were Austrians: Ernst Kaltenbrunner, Odilo Globocnik, Franz Stangl, Arthur Seyß-Inquart, and Adolf Hitler himself, to name just a few.

After the liberation of Europe by the Allies, the official Austrian point of view was that Austria was the first victim of Nazi aggression. This "victim myth" had significant and sometimes contradictory consequences for Austrian postwar society. Through reference to the Moscow Declaration of 1943, the official position of the Republic of Austria until the late 1980s was to portray itself as a victim of National Socialist aggression and thereby negate any and all responsibility. It emphasized and overestimated the role of the Austrian resistance, which was interpreted as representing a general anti-Nazi attitude in the Austrian population. In contrast to the official position concerning Austria's role in National Socialism, municipal, local, and federal authorities embraced a tendency to build memorials for fallen Austrian soldiers of the *Wehrmacht* and *Waffen-SS* that often celebrated them as "heroes" who died in the service for the "Fatherland." This shows the gap between the official argumentation on the political level and the social reality.[29]

A further consequence of the so-called "victim myth" was a step-by-step reintegration of Nazis into all levels of the Austrian society on the one hand, and official ignorance of the victims' experiences on the other. Although socially marginalized, "these memories [of the victims] remained unconsciously and indirectly ever present."[30] This can be seen in recurring critical confrontations and public debates about the involvement of Austrians in Nazi crimes and how to deal with these criminals. Immediately after the 1945 liberation, there were discussions about denazification policy. In the 1950s, amnesties for perpetrators led to controversy. The acquittals in trials against Nazis in the 1960s were publicly followed by supporters and opponents of the accused and criticized in Austria and abroad. In 1975, there was a debate between Simon Wiesenthal and then Chancellor Bruno Kreisky (who as a Jew and a socialist had fled from the Nazis) about former Nazis in Kreisky's government.

In 1986, there was a broad public debate about the past of Kurt Waldheim, then running for the Austrian presidency as the candidate of the conservative *Österreichische Volkspartei* (Austrian People's Party or ÖVP). Waldheim, the former secretary general of the United Nations, was confronted with his career as an officer of the *Wehrmacht* and his possible involvement in war crimes. This controversy developed into a broader debate about Waldheim's generation and its involvement in Nazi crimes and eventually led to a shift in the self-conception of the Austrian state.[31] In the context of the Waldheim debate, new critical positions appeared in the Austrian public. Nowadays, the "Waldheim affair" is often interpreted as a major impetus for a new reflective approach (on a state level) toward Austria's past. Particularly in 1988, which marked the fiftieth anniversary of the *Anschluss*, a broader public interest in the "dark chapters" of Austrian history emerged. This new interest was also a starting point for further studies about Austrian Nazi perpetrators, who up to that point had not been subjected to historical research on a broad scale.[32] In the aftermath of the Waldheim affair, then-Chancellor Franz Vranitzky of the *Sozialdemokratische Partei Österreichs* (Social Democratic Party of Austria or SPÖ) admitted that Austrians were involved in Nazi crimes, which is often seen as a turning point in the official Austrian position toward its past.[33]

However, this supposed change did not affect the lack of criminal prosecution of Nazi criminals.[34] In 2006, Efraim Zuroff, the head of the Simon Wiesenthal Center in Jerusalem, a human rights organization, stated correctly that "Austria is a paradise for Nazi criminals."[35] The new official perspective toward Austria's involvement in Nazi crimes also did not prevent the rise of revisionist and extreme right-wing political movements in Austria. The post-Waldheim years were marked by the ascent of the right-wing extremist party *Freiheitliche Partei Österreichs* (FPÖ, Freedom Party of Austria),[36] which eventually garnered 27 percent of votes in the 1999 national election and so participated in a coalition government with the ÖVP. This new government was heavily criticized on an international level, and the European Union issued sanctions against Austria.[37]

Educational programs must incorporate these combined references to Nazi history originating in national narratives and popular culture and images. The particular national narratives have to be incorporated in Austrian Holocaust education and might even be of use to contextualize both historical and contemporary conceptions of the Nazi past and the perpetrators.

EVENTS AND TABOOS

The following chapter examines two different approaches to perpetrators in Austrian Holocaust education and reflects on the impact cultural images of perpetrators have.

After the year 2000, a new trend in public historical projects emerged. Public commemoration events tried to express a general sensitivity toward Austria's past. One of the largest of these events was "A Letter to the Stars," which illustrates very well the problems that can occur when the topic of perpetrators is avoided in Holocaust education.

"A Letter to the Stars" was initiated in 2003 as a heavily subsidized school project that consciously excluded questions about the perpetrators and their ideology.[38] The project's first main event offered teenage students the possibility to research the story of individual Shoah victims from Austria. As a result of their research, on May 5, 2003, more than 15,000 students released white balloons with personal letters addressed to murdered Austrian Jews on Heldenplatz, a public square in Vienna—the same place where Adolf Hitler proclaimed the *Anschluss* in 1938.[39] The program comprised various projects in the following years that focused on inviting survivors to visit Austria.

In the course of "A Letter to the Stars," different institutions heavily criticized it, including some that had cooperated with the project earlier. The *Lagergemeinschaft Ravensbrück und Freundinnen* (Ravensbrück camp community and friends, an association representing former inmates of the women's concentration camp Ravensbrück) pointed out that the project ignored questions concerning the perpetrators.[40] The Jewish Community,[41] the Jewish Welcome Service (an Austrian organization that invites Austrian Shoah survivors and their relatives to visit Austria), and the Documentation Centre of Austrian Resistance (*Dokumentationsarchiv des Österreichischen Widerstandes* or DÖW) distanced themselves from "A Letter to the Stars" as well.[42] The main criticism concerned the project's character as a public relations event, the objectification of the survivors who participated in the project, and the lack of an educational concept, including a thematization of the perpetrators and antisemitism.[43]

"A Letter to the Stars" unintentionally generated a variety of sources that are useful in analyzing the impact of the project: the letters that the students wrote to Nazi victims were published as a book[44] and on the project's website.[45] They show that there was only superficial understanding of the history of the Shoah and made few references to responsibility for the crimes. The participants often compared the Shoah to contemporary events such as the Iraq War and expressed their wish for a peaceful world. The refrain of the "anthem" of "A Letter to the Stars" illustrates the ahistorical approach of the project:

> Letter to the Stars
> And I keep on wishing
> Letter to the Stars
> For a better living
> Letter to the Stars
> Please stop the fighting
> Letter to the Stars
> For no more crying.[46]

Sometimes students referred directly to their grandparents and seemed to unintentionally reflect family narratives, as shown by the following excerpt of a published letter of a fourteen-year-old girl, addressed to a murdered Jewish woman from Salzburg: "My grandfather fought in the war as well, although he was actually against it, but if you would have said anything against it, you would have been arrested by the Gestapo and been brought to a concentration camp."[47] Questions that went beyond the stories of the victims were obviously present but not reflected in the project.

"A Letter to the Stars" did not succeed in giving students a broader historical understanding of the Shoah and the specific circumstances of the mass murder of the Austrian Jews. Although there was an interest in the stories of individual victims, the reasons for and context of their murders were not present in the project. Consequently, many students saw the Shoah as an abstract symbol of evil and war without any historical and political depth. The project was even more problematic because it was carried out under a government with right-wing extremist members, and it failed to address any consequences of Nazism in Austria.

Initiatives such as *Gedenkdienst* have attempted to overcome the taboo of questions concerning guilt and responsibility and promote an inclusion of perpetrators in Holocaust education. *Gedenkdienst*[48]—"commemoration service" in German—is a nonprofit nongovernmental organization without state subsidies based in Vienna with the primary objective to give young Austrians the possibility to work as volunteers in institutions all over the world connected to the history of Nazi crimes.[49] This objective is designed to insist on a collective Austrian responsibility to deal with Nazi history. This volunteer work abroad includes caring for survivors of Nazi persecution, educational efforts, and a commitment to historical research as well as archival preservation of documents. Additionally, *Gedenkdienst* is active in raising awareness of Nazi history, Austrian involvement in Nazi crimes, and the aftermath of Nazism and fascism in contemporary Austria. Apart from National Socialism, *Gedenkdienst* also deals with the history of Austro-fascism. It is not possible to elaborate on the history of Austro-fascism and its connection to Nazi history as well as contemporary Austrian debates about this topic in this essay. However, the history of both right-wing Austrian regimes is of significance for pedagogical concepts about the Holocaust with a focus on Austria, especially because of the ideological and personal connections as well as the continuities between the two regimes.[50]

To achieve its goals, activists in the association organize weekly meetings that include workshops, film presentations, and discussions; they plan monthly academic lectures with the so-called *Geh Denken!* lecture program (a play on words with the German words "commemorate" and "go and think"), and organize an annual international conference. Central aspects of the work of *Gedenkdienst* are educational programs that consist of workshops with school students, apprentices, and adults, and so-called study trips (*Studienfahrten*). One of the main goals of these programs is to focus on Austrian Nazi perpetrators, the impact of the Nazi era on contemporary Austrian society, and the often-denied or downplayed involvement of Austrians in Nazi crimes. Therefore, the subject of perpetrators is highly present in various activities of *Gedenkdienst.*

The focus on perpetrators is especially true for the study trips, where many pedagogical concepts, including programs about perpetrators, have originated. The *Gedenkdienst* study trips last for several days and lead to various places across Europe. Destinations of study trips include memorial sites at the Oświęcim/Auschwitz concentration camp in Poland, the Terezín/Theresienstadt camp in what is now the Czech Republic, and in Marzabotto, the site of a mass murder of civilians by the Nazis in Italy. Study trips also go to "places with history"—such as Berlin; Trieste, Italy; Budapest, Hungary; Lublin, Poland; and Vilnius, Lithuania—which are often not directly connected to a memorial site. The idea is to "explore" the history of various places and regions in a journey that lasts several days under close didactical and historical supervision and to connect the places and topics to one another.[51] The study trips not only treat memorial sites as places of historical events but also relate to James E. Young's understanding of memorials as sites that "remember the past according to a variety of national myths, ideals, and political needs."[52] *Gedenkdienst* tours do not present memorial sites as an option to experience "authentic places"—and to therefore meet participants' common expectations of visits to former Nazi camps[53]—but as multilayered places with both historical and contemporary dimensions. Another goal of *Gedenkdienst* is to connect the destinations of study trips to Austrian history and, therefore, to connect it with the groups that are mainly from Austria (which means the participants were influenced by Austrian historical narratives). In Terezín/Theresienstadt, for instance, it is especially significant to connect the former ghetto and the development of anti-Jewish policy in Austria after 1938 with the deportation of Austrian Jews.[54] Understanding history as a development with causes and reasons—for example, by addressing the step-by-step radicalization of Nazi policy and a reflection of the production of historical knowledge itself—are central in this approach.[55]

It is important to point out that educational programs about Nazi crimes are, in a majority of cases, not the first time that young people are exposed to this topic—actively or passively.[56] Apart from exhibitions, museums, memorial sites, schools, projects, or workshops, there are media portrayals of Nazis, the Holocaust, and other Nazi crimes in movies, video games, books, theater plays, and the like. It is, therefore, significant for educators to be aware that participants of educational programs have a variety of relations to the addressed topic.[57] The participants oftentimes find themselves faced with a seemingly overwhelming number of images and stereotypes of Nazi perpetrators. Educational practice must reflect this, particularly because these images are often connected to interpretations of motivations of the perpetrators and explanations for their crimes. The impact of "Nazi images" must not be underestimated, which is illustrated by the following example.

In 2013, the German public service television broadcaster ZDF (*Zweites Deutsches Fernsehen*) and the Austrian national public service television network ORF (*Österreichischer Rundfunk*) showed the TV production *Unsere Mütter, unsere Väter* ("Our mothers, our fathers"; the English title is *Generation War*), a trilogy about young Germans and their involvement in World War II and Nazism between 1941 and 1945. Although not an Austrian production, it was shown during prime time on the same days in Germany and Austria, indicating that the audiences of both countries might share a similar interest in the miniseries. The fictional drama focuses on five friends whose story is supposed to resemble what people might have experienced during the war: two brothers are drafted into the *Wehrmacht*, a nurse volunteers in a field hospital on the Eastern Front, a singer has an affair with a Gestapo officer, and a Jewish tailor is deported but manages to escape and later joins the Polish partisans. It is important to note that the show is not based on real stories. The viewing figures in Austria and Germany were high,[58] and the rights to the show have been sold to over sixty countries so far.[59]

The broadcast of *Unsere Mütter, unsere Väter* was intended to be a historic family event, and the producers of the series encouraged a public debate about the "war generation."[60] The epilogue of the third part includes fictional birth and death dates of the main protagonists—one of the fictional characters, Wilhelm, a former *Wehrmacht* officer, is assumed to be still alive. This is intended to foster dialogue with the remaining members of "Generation *Wehrmacht*." Supposedly this hint is not intended to confront the guilt of anyone but rather to encourage discussion about the war with still-living grandparents who survived those times. This innocent approach toward the criminal history of large segments of a generation is made easy by the general conception and narrative of the TV series: the main characters are neither anti-semites nor Nazis. Although some of them do get involved in crimes, their participation is attributed to the general circumstances of the war. None of the "heroes" are political or fanatical, but "the War" changes them. The broadcast of the show subsequently led to controversies in Germany, Poland, Russia, and the United States.[61] Major discussions covered the presentation of the *Armia Krajowa* (the Polish Home Army) and the Red Army, as well as the role of Nazi ideology and the depiction of the generation of the protagonists in general. The debates illustrate the clashes of national narratives and deviant interpretations of responsibilities for Nazi crimes.

The trilogy does represent certain common German and Austrian approaches toward Nazism and the Holocaust, which are also present in study trips and other educational programs of *Gedenkdienst*. The experience of the work with groups shows that, in general, participants are interested in workshops about contemporary history. However, at the beginning of such programs, they often show little or no understanding of the reasons for Nazi crimes, and it is common that they explain involvement in crimes as the pressure of circumstances. Additionally, there is also a tendency to depoliticize (individual) Nazi history: a grandfather or grandmother might be guilty, but at least he or she was not a Nazi.

Historical guilt is often talked about or portrayed in a somewhat elusive way, making it easy to relativize. *Unsere Mütter, unsere Väter* does this in at least three ways:

1. The Poles are shown as even more antisemitic than the Germans. Furthermore, they are presented as convinced ideological antisemites, whereas the German characters are portrayed mostly as not ideological.

2. Soviet soldiers are presented in a primarily negative light. In the third part of the series, members of the Red Army are shown shooting wounded Germans in a field hospital and raping nurses without any context given to explain the situation.

3. In the series, the Americans (and not the Germans) use "former" Nazis to pursue their own interests, as illustrated at the end of the last episode, when an American officer integrates a former Gestapo officer into the newly established bureaucracy.

These are three common stereotypes sometimes brought up by participants during study trips to downplay Nazi crimes. The general argument is that everyone was guilty to some degree and was simultaneously a victim at some point—even if it was only as a "victim of the circumstances." The common assumption is that individual Germans and Austrians were not responsible for the situations in which they lived and, therefore, cannot be held responsible for what they did personally.

FUTURE CHALLENGES OF HOLOCAUST EDUCATION IN AUSTRIA

It is a difficult task to contextualize Nazi crimes properly in educational programs, especially if there is a restricted time for workshops, study trips, and similar projects. The following brief suggestions seem especially important in conveying the Nazi crimes in a complex way without trivializing or oversimplifying them, and should be understood as an encouragement to reflect on common approaches in Holocaust education, relevant for Austria but also meant as a general basis for teaching about Nazi crimes:

1. Educators must make clear what the topic is actually about: crimes committed by people against other people. The Nazi crimes must not be presented as metaphors for pure evil.

2. Active language: educators should not present Nazi crimes in passive sentences such as "was deported to Auschwitz" but rather in active sentences that describe these crimes as acts committed by humans against other humans in a specific context.[62]

3. Educators should include controversies in the historical debate about the origins and genesis of Nazi crimes. Consequently, participants of educational programs can be confronted with different interpretations of motives and reasons for the crimes to gain a deeper understanding of the complexity of the topic and the relevance of dealing with this historical subject through discussion.

4. Educational programs should feature perpetrators as historical protagonists who made decisions in their lives that in one way or another led to their role as perpetrators in these crimes. Consequently, questions of responsibility and guilt for the crimes should be addressed.

5. The historical context of the crimes should be shown without oversimplifying the complexity of the topic and without excusing or trivializing the people responsible for the crimes.

6. National narratives, the sociopolitical background of a group, and the history of the politics of memory have an influence on interpretations of Nazi history. They constitute interpretations of the motives of the perpetrators and the origins of the crimes. Holocaust education should reflect this and might include this frame of reference in its programs.

7. Educational programs are seldom the first encounter that participants have with Nazi history. Educators have to recognize the impact of the immense number of images and common explanations for Nazi history and its consequences.

8. Nazi perpetrators as a topic cannot be ignored in teaching about Nazi crimes. They are commonly selected as an important theme by the participants themselves—directly or indirectly. Therefore, concrete methods for dealing with this topic have to be created.

It is problematic to educate about crimes without examining the criminals involved. Subsequently, Nazi perpetrators have to be addressed in educational programs about Nazi crimes. Even if this subject is addressed only indirectly, questions concerning guilt and responsibility are present, especially in Austria and Germany. Therefore, a differentiated and complex approach should be employed to not trivialize Nazi crimes as a subject for educational programs.

Holocaust education in Austria should reconsider its exclusive focus on victims' stories, which can lead to problematic outcomes if the reasons and background for victimization are not addressed. An understanding of the origins of the process of persecution and facing those responsible for the crimes—especially in a "perpetrator society" such as Austria—is necessary to humanize the story of the victims. A profound educational approach toward the stories of victims should always make clear that there were people who actively victimized them. Before addressing the objects of discrimination, persecution, and murder, it must be stressed and emphasized who was responsible. Otherwise Nazi crimes will eventually stop appearing as human crimes, for they will lack the criminals.

NOTES

The chapter epigraph is taken from Donald G. Schilling, "The Dead End of Demonizing: Dealing with the Perpetrators in Teaching the Holocaust," chap. 15 in Rochelle L. Millen, ed., *New Perspectives on the Holocaust: A Guide for Teachers and Scholars* (New York: New York University Press, 1996), 199. (Quoted in Matthias Heyl and Heide Schöllhorn, "Zur Auseinandersetzung mit Täterschaft in der Arbeit der Pädagogischen Dienste der Mahn- und Gedenkstätte Ravensbrück [On the treatment of war crimes in the work of the pedagogical services of the Ravensbrück Memorial]," in Simone Erpel, Johannes Schwartz, Jeanette Toussaint, and Lavern Wulfram, eds., *Im Gefolge der SS: Aufseherinnen des Frauen-KZ Ravensbrück. Begleitband zur Ausstellung* [Following the SS: Guards of the women's concentration camp Ravensbrück, companion volume to the exhibition] (Berlin: Metropol, 2007), 349.

1. The theses and the argumentation of this essay are based in part on the following article: Lukas Meissel, "Verbrechen ohne VerbrecherInnen? Thematisierung von NS-TäterInnen in der historisch-politischen Bildungsarbeit zum Nationalsozialismus [Crime without criminals? Themes of Nazi perpetrators in the historical-political education about National Socialism]," in Till Hilmar, *Ort, Subjekt, Verbrechen. Koordinaten historisch-politischer Bildungsarbeit zum Nationalsozialismus* [Place, subject, crimes: Coordinates of the historical-political education about National Socialism] (Vienna: Czernin, 2010), 236–51.

2. Florian Wenninger, "Die Wohnung des Rottenführers D. Über Opferfokus und Täterabsenz in der zeitgeschichtlichen Vermittlungsarbeit [The apartment of Rottenführer D: About victim focus and absence of

perpetrators in contemporary educational work]," in Hilmar, *Ort, Subjekt, Verbrechen*, 64.

3. Werner Dreier, "Trauer, Scham—Verstehen, Lernen [Sadness, shame—understand, learn]" in Dokumentationsarchiv des österreichischen Widerstandes (Documentation Centre of Austrian Resistance or DÖW), *Forschungen zum Nationalsozialismus und dessen Nachwirkungen in Österreich. Festschrift für Brigitte Bailer* [Research on National Socialism and its aftermath in Austria: Commemoration of Brigitte Bailer] (Vienna: DÖW, 2012), 335–36.

4. Ibid., 338.

5. Jana Jelitzki and Mirko Wetzel, *Über Täter und Täterinnen sprechen: Nationalsozialistische Täterschaft in der pädagogischen Arbeit von KZ-Gedenkstätten* [Talking about perpetrators: National Socialist war crimes in the educational work of concentration camp memorials] (Berlin: Metropol, 2010), 128–29.

6. Raul Hilberg, *Perpetrators, Victims, Bystanders: The Jewish Catastrophe, 1933–1945* (New York: Aaron Asher, 1992).

7. For further information about this exhibition dealing with female perpetrators, see Erpel, Schwartz, Toussaint, and Wulfram, eds., *Im Gefolge der SS*.

8. Gideon Botsch and Michael Haupt, eds., *The Wannsee Conference and the Genocide of the European Jews: Catalogue of the Permanent Exhibition with DVD* (Berlin: Gedenk- und Bildungsstätte Haus der Wannsee-Konferenz [House of the Wannsee Conference, memorial and education site], 2009).

9. Klaus Hesse and Andreas Sander, *Topography of Terror. Gestapo, SS and Reichssicherheitshauptamt on the "Prinz-Albrecht-Terrain." A Documentation* (Berlin: Stiftung Topographie des Terrors, 2006).

10. See the following article, which deals with the Villa ten Hompel as a "crime scene" (*Tatort*) with a focus on perpetrators: Alfons Kenkmann, "Die Auseinandersetzung mit NS-Tätern und Mitläufern als didaktische Herausforderung. Politische Bildung am Beispiel der Münsteraner,Villa ten Hompel [The confrontation with Nazi criminals and fellow travelers as an education challenge: Political education using the example of the Villa ten Hompel in Münster," in Heidi Behrens-Cobet, ed., *Erinnern, gedenken und lernen. Erwachsenenbildung in Gedenkstätten und an Erinnerungsorten* [Remember, commemorate, and learn: Education at memorial sites and places of memory] (Essen: Klartext, 1998), 91–109.

11. See the publication of the head of the memorial site at the former factory of Topf & Söhne: Annegret Schüle, *Industrie und Holocaust. Topf & Söhne—Die Ofenbauer von Auschwitz* [Industry and the Holocaust: Topf and Sons, oven builders of Auschwitz] (Göttingen, Ger.: Wallstein, 2010).

12. Heyl and Schöllhorn, "Zur Auseinandersetzung mit Täterschaft," 347.

13. Theodor W. Adorno, *Erziehung zur Mündigkeit. Vorträge und Gespräche mit Hellmut Becker 1959–1969* [Education for maturity: Lectures and discussions with Hellmut Becker 1959–1969] (Frankfurt am Main, Ger.: Suhrkamp, 1970), 92–109.

14. Ido Abram, "Erziehung und humane Orientierung [Education and human orientation]," in Ido Abram and Matthias Heyl, *Thema Holocaust, Ein Buch für die Schule* [Topic Holocaust: A book for school] (Reinbek bei Hamburg, Ger.: Rowohlt, 1996),16.

15. Ibid., 43.

16. Ibid., 18.

17. Matthias Heyl, "'Jews Are No Metaphors' oder die Kontextualisierung des Holocaust in Deutschland ["Jews Are No Metaphors," or the contextualization of the Holocaust in Germany]," in Helmut Schreier and Matthias Heyl, eds., *"Daß Auschwitz nicht noch einmal sei . . ." zur Erziehung nach Auschwitz* ["That Auschwitz will never again be . . .": *On Education after Auschwitz*] (Hamburg, Ger.: Krämer, 1995), 53–55.

18. A contemporary example is Mark Herman's movie *The Boy in the Striped Pajamas* (Miramax, BBC Films, and Heyday Films, 2008). For a critical review, see Johannes Breit and Till Hilmar, "Filmkritik: Die starrenden blauen Augen der Unschuld [Movie review: The staring blue eyes of innocence]," *Gedenkdienst* [Memorial service] 4, 12 (September 9, 2013), http://www.gedenkdienst.at/index.php?id=796.

19. The Austrian historian Oliver Rathkolb argues that this number is significantly high compared to the Austrian population's share in the German Reich, which was 8.81 percent. However, he does not give figures of how many people volunteered for the SS and how many were actually drafted in the latter half of the war. Oliver Rathkolb, *The Paradoxical Republic: Austria, 1945–2005* (New York: Berghahn, 2010), 249.

20. The study "Opa war kein Nazi" ("Grandpa was not a Nazi") deals with transgenerational transmissions of family stories in German families: Harald Welzer, Sabine Moller, and Karoline Tschugnall, *"Opa war kein Nazi." Nationalsozialismus und Holocaust im Familiengedächtnis* ["Grandpa was not a Nazi": National Socialism and the Holocaust in the family memory] (Frankfurt am Main, Ger.: Fischer, 2002).

21. Concerning the identification of Austrian participants with perpetrators and its educational possibilities, see Wenninger, "Opferfokus und Täterabsenz."

22. Viola Georgi analyzed different identity models of young Germans with a migration background concerning the German Nazi past: Viola B.

Georgi, *Entliehene Erinnerung. Geschichtsbilder junger Migranten in Deutschland* [Borrowed memory: Historical images of young migrants in Germany] (Hamburg, Ger.: Hamburger, 2003).

23. Matthias Heyl states that in the Ravensbrück Memorial, school classes show a special interest in perpetrators, even before the establishment of a special exhibition about this topic. Heyl and Schöllhorn, "Zur Auseinandersetzung mit Täterschaft," 350.

24. Historian Christiane Rothländer wrote a profound monograph about the early years of the Viennese SS, which underlines the specific Austrian development: Christiane Rothländer, *Die Anfänge der Wiener SS* [The beginnings of the Viennese SS] (Vienna: Böhlau, 2012).

25. Historian Kurt Bauer claims in his new study that Adolf Hitler himself ordered the putsch in which Austrian Chancellor Engelbert Dollfuß was assassinated. Kurt Bauer, *Hitlers zweiter Putsch. Dollfuß, die Nazis und der 25. Juli 1934* [Hitler's second putsch: Dollfuß, the Nazis, and July 25, 1934] (St. Pölten, Austria: Residenz, 2014).

26. For the illegal Austrian Nazi Party, see Winfried R. Garscha, "Nationalsozialisten in Österreich 1933–1938 [Nazis in Austria 1933–1938]," in Emmerich Tálos and Wolfgang Neugebauer, eds., *Austrofaschismus. Politik, Ökonomie, Kultur. 1933–1938* [Austro-fascism: Politics, economy, culture 1933–1938] (Vienna: LIT, 2012), 100–120.

27. There are several documents that prove the broad involvement of the Viennese in the pogroms in 1938. See the following commented source collection: Hans Safrian and Hans Witek, *Und keiner war dabei. Dokumente des alltäglichen Antisemitismus in Wien 1938* [And no one was there: Documents of everyday antisemitism in Vienna 1938] (Vienna: Picus, 2008).

28. See the English version of Safrian's study: Hans Safrian, *Eichmann's Men*, trans. Ute Stargardt (Cambridge: Cambridge University Press, 2010).

29. Based on the theses of historian Heidemarie Uhl: Heidemarie Uhl, "Das 'erste Opfer'. Der österreichische Opfermythos und seine Transformation in der Zweiten Republik [The "first victim": The Austrian victim myth and its transformation during the Second Republic]," *Österreichische Zeitschrift für Politikwissenschaft* [Austrian Journal of Political Science] 30, 1 (2001): 20.

30. Rathkolb, *Paradoxical Republic*, 238.

31. Only the surface of this debate, on an internal and external political level in Austria, can be scratched in this article. For a multi-perspective depiction of the Kurt Waldheim affair, see Barbara Tóth and Hubertus Czernin, *1986. Das Jahr, das Österreich veränderte* [1986: The year that changed Austria] (Vienna: Czernin, 2006).

32. Hans Safrian, "Tabuisierte Täter. Staatliche Legitimationsdefizite

und blinde Flecken der Zeitgeschichte in Österreich [Taboo perpetrators: The public lack of legitimacy and blind spots of contemporary history in Austria]," in Gerhard Botz and Gerald Sprengnagel, eds., *Kontroversen um Österreichs Zeitgeschichte, Verdrängte Vergangenheit, Österreich-Identität, Waldheim und die Historiker* [Controversies surrounding Austria's contemporary history, repressed past, Austrian identity, Waldheim, and the historians] (Frankfurt am Main, Ger.: Campus, 2008), 531.

33. Rathkolb, *Paradoxical Republic*, 237.

34. The last big trial in Austria concerned Heinrich Gross, a doctor who was involved in the Nazi euthanasia program. The documentary *Meine liebe Republik* [My beloved republic] examines Gross's life from the perspective of the survivor Friedrich Zawrel: Elisabeth Scharang and Florian Klenk, *Meine liebe Republik* (Polyfilm, Austria, 2006).

35. "Zuroff: 'Österreich ein Paradies für NS-Verbrecher' ["Austria is a paradise for Nazi criminals"]," *Der Standard*, February 1, 2006, accessed August 30, 2013, http://derstandard.at/2327230?seite=2.

36. For the history of the *Freiheitliche Partei Österreichs* (Freedom Party of Austria or FPÖ) and the characterization of the party as right-wing extremist, see the following article: Brigitte Bailer and Wolfgang Neugebauer, "Die FPÖ: Vom Liberalismus zum Rechtsextremismus [The FPÖ: From liberalism to right-wing extremism]" in Stiftung Dokumentationsarchiv des österreichischen Widerstandes [Foundation of the Documentation Centre of Austrian Resistance or DÖW], *Handbuch des österreichischen Rechtsextremismus* [Handbook of Austrian right-wing extremism] (Vienna: DÖW, 1996), 357–494.

37. The European Union issued so-called sanctions against Austria out of concern over the FPÖ's involvement in the government. Rathkolb, *Paradoxical Republic*, 128–30.

38. Josef Neumayer and Andreas Kuba, who initiated the project, stated that antisemitism should not be discussed in the project. Kuba said, "We are not against something, but for something" (*Wir sind nicht gegen etwas, sondern für etwas)*. Hannah Fröhlich, "Springtime for Hitler. Gespräche über 'Letter to the stars' [Springtime for Hitler: Talks about "Letter to the Stars"]," *Context* 21, 2–3 (2003), accessed August 9, 2013, http://www.contextxxi.at/context/context/content/view/150/89/index.html.

39. "A Letter to the Stars," accessed October 15, 2012, http://www.lettertothestars.at/en/page_id_77.html.

40. Malmoe on the Web, "A Letter to the Stars," accessed September 9, 2013, http://www.malmoe.org/artikel/widersprechen/1161.

41. "Event mit 'Kirtagscharakter,'" *Der Standard*, December 20, 2007, accessed September 9, 2013, http://derstandard.at/3151625.

42. "'A Letter to the Stars' unter Beschuss [under fire]," *Der Standard*, December 11, 2007, accessed September 9, 2013, http://derstandard.at/3029175.

43. An overview of the controversies about the project can be found at the following link, accessed September 9, 2013: http://www.erinnern.at/bundeslaender/oesterreich/e_bibliothek/miscellen/kontroversen-um-letter-to-the-stars.

44. Alfred Worm, Harald Krassnitzer, and Andreas Kuba, *A letter to the stars. Schüler schreiben Geschichte. Briefe an den Himmel* [A Letter to the Stars: Students write history, letters to the sky] (Vienna: Verein Lernen aus der Zeitgeschichte, 2003).

45. "Briefe in den Himmel [Letters in the sky]," accessed September 9, 2013, http://www.lettertothestars.at/livingmemorial.php?lmshow=7.

46. The song was written by Bianca Stojka, the daughter of a Holocaust survivor, and was first performed on May 5, 2003, on Heldenplatz at the central event of the "Letter to the Stars" project. Worm, Krassnitzer, and Kuba, *A letter to the stars*, 39.

47. "Mein Opa hat im Krieg genauso gekämpft, obwohl er eigentlich dagegen war, aber wenn man etwas dagegen gesagt hat, wurde man gleich von der Gestapo gefangen genommen und selber ins KZ gebracht." See Worm, Krassnitzer, and Kuba, *A letter to the stars*, 39.

48. Anton Legerer's book includes a detailed history of the *Gedenkdienst* association: Anton Legerer, *Tatort: Versöhnung. Aktion Sühnezeichen in der BRD und in der DDR und Gedenkdienst in Österreich* [Scene of the crime: Reconciliation, project reconciliation in West Germany and East Germany and *Gedenkdienst* in Austria] (Leipzig, Ger.: Evangelische, 2011).

49. Although *Gedenkdienst* does not get subsidies, the male volunteers, whose volunteer year is accepted as an alternative to obligatory military service, get financial support from the Austrian state.

50. For the history of Austro-fascism, see Tálos and Neugebauer, *Austrofaschismus*; Ilse Reiter-Zatloukal, Christiane Rothländer, and Pia Schölnberger, eds., *Österreich 1933–1938. Interdisziplinäre Annäherungen an das Dollfuß-/Schuschnigg-Regime* [Austria 1933–1938: Interdisciplinary approaches to the Dollfuß-Schuschnigg regime] (Vienna: Böhlau, 2012); Florian Wenninger and Lucile Dreidemy, eds., *Das Dollfuß-Schuschnigg-Regime 1933–1938. Vermessung eines Forschungsfeldes* [The Dollfuß-Schuschnigg regime 1933–1938: Surveying a research field] (Vienna: Böhlau, 2013); Emmerich Tálos, *Das austrofaschistische Herrschaftssystem. Österreich 1933–1938* [The Austro-fascist system of rule: Austria 1933–1938] (Berlin: Lit, 2013).

51. Till Hilmar, "Abschied vom Erinnerungsort. Studienfahrten als Form der Auseinandersetzung mit NS und Holocaust [Farewell to the me-

morial site: Study trips as a form of confrontation with Nazism and the Holocaust]," in Hilmar, *Ort, Subjekt, Verbrechen*, 76.

52. James E. Young, *The Texture of Memory: Holocaust Memorials and Meaning* (New Haven, Conn.: Yale University Press, 1993), 1.

53. Till Hilmar, "Ausgehend vom historischen Ort, wohin? 'Diskursive' Orte der Vermittlungsarbeit zum Nationalsozialismus auf Studienfahrten [Starting from the historic site, where to? "Discursive" places the work of mediation toward National Socialism on study trips]" in Linda Erker, Klaus Kienesberger, Erich Vogl, and Fritz Hausjell, eds., *Gedächtnis-Verlust? Geschichtsvermittlung und-didaktik in der Mediengesellschaft* [Memory loss: History teaching and didactics in the media society] (Cologne, Ger.: Herbert von Halem, 2013), 73.

54. The *Wiener Modell* (Viennese model) of anti-Jewish policy, which was mainly shaped by Nazis surrounding Adolf Eichmann, became a template for other anti-Jewish measures to come and is closely connected to the Theresienstadt ghetto. Hans Safrian, *Eichmann und seine Gehilfen* [Eichmann and his assistants] (Vienna: Fischer, 1997), 46.

55. *Gedenkdienst* tries to integrate new concepts of historical learning in its programs. For an overview of new developments in Holocaust education and its aims, which are currently reflected in the work of *Gedenkdienst*, see Robert Sigel, "Holocaust Education oder historisch-politischer Unterricht zum Nationalsozialismus? Veränderte Paradigmen in der Vermittlung des Themas Holocaust [Holocaust education or historical-political education about National Socialism? Changing paradigms in the teaching of Holocaust themes]," in Michael Brenner and Maximilian Strnad, eds., *Der Holocaust in der deutschsprachigen Geschichtswissenschaft. Bilanz und Perspektiven* [The Holocaust in German-language historiography: Review and perspectives] (Göttingen, Ger.: Wallstein, 2012), 130–44, here 131.

56. Sigel, "Holocaust Education oder historisch-politischer Unterricht zum Nationalsozialismus?" 134.

57. In the Ravensbrück Memorial, for instance, the participants of educational programs have often read *The Reader* by Bernhard Schlink, which tells the story of a former female SS guard. Because the book is a work of fiction, the participants often have expectations and conceptions that do not match the historical reality. For instance, they are often astonished that the majority of the female SS guards were actually able to read and write. Heyl and Schöllhorn, "Zur Auseinandersetzung mit Täterschaft," 351.

58. See for the viewing figures in Germany, accessed September 30, 2013: http://www.quotenmeter.de/n/62717/primetime-check-montag-18-maerz-2013eg; in Austria, accessed September 30, 2013: http://derstandard.at/1363705616241/622000-zu-Gast-beim-Universum.

59. Uwe Mantel, "'Unsere Mütter, unsere Väter' wird zum Export-Hit

[*Generation War* is becoming an export hit]," *DWDL.de*, June 16, 2013, accessed August 30, 2013, http://www.dwdl.de/nachrichten/41277/unsere_muetter_unsere_vaeter_wird_zum_exporthit/.

60. "Ihre Meinung, Ihre Geschichte [Your opinion, your story]" Forum, March 7, 2013, accessed September 30, 2013, http://www.zdf.de/Unsere-M%C3%BCtter-unsere-V%C3%A4ter/Ihre-Meinung-Ihre-Geschichten-26935824.html.

61. As an example of various German articles concerning the miniseries, see an article in *Spiegel Online* about critiques in the United States, Poland, and Russia: "'Unsere Mütter, unsere Väter' in den USA: 'Fünf Stunden Selbstmitleid' [*Generation War* in the U.S.A.: "Five hours of self-pity"]," *Spiegel Online*, January 15, 2014, accessed October 24, 2014, http://www.spiegel.de/kultur/kino/vernichtende-kritiken-fuer-unsere-muetter-unsere-vaeter-in-den-usa-a-943743.html.

62. In Germany, there was a debate in the 1990s surrounding the usage of the passive form in describing Nazi crimes (especially in West Germany). Heyl and Schöllhorn, "Zur Auseinandersetzung mit Täterschaft," 348.

Notes on Contributors

NATALIA ALEKSIUN is an associate professor of modern Jewish history at Touro College, Graduate School of Jewish Studies, New York. She has published a monograph in Polish titled *Dokad dalej? Ruch syjonistyczny w Polsce 1944–1950* [Where to? The Zionist movement in Poland, 1944–1950], as well as numerous articles in *Yad Vashem Studies*, *Polish Review*, *Dapim*, *East European Jewish Affairs*, *Studies in Contemporary Jewry*, *Polin*, *Gal-Ed*, *East European Politics & Societies*, *Nashim*, and *German History*. She coedited two collections of *Polin: Studies in Polish Jewry* (vols. 20 and 29).

ELIZABETH ANTHONY is the International Tracing Service and partnerships program manager at the Jack, Joseph and Morton Mandel Center for Advanced Holocaust Studies at the United States Holocaust Memorial Museum in Washington, D.C. She received her Ph.D. in history from Clark University in Worcester, Massachusetts, in 2016 with a dissertation titled "Return Home: Holocaust Survivors Reestablishing Lives in Postwar Vienna."

DORIS L. BERGEN is the Chancellor Rose and Ray Wolfe Professor of Holocaust Studies in the Department of History at the University of Toronto. Her research and teaching focus on religion, gender, and ethnicity in the Holocaust, World War II, and other cases of extreme violence. Bergen is the author or editor of five books: *War and Genocide: A Concise History of the Holocaust*; *Twisted Cross: The German Christian Movement in the Third Reich*; *The Sword of the Lord: Military Chaplains from the First to the Twenty-First Century*; *Lessons and Legacies Volume VIII: From Generation to Generation* (Northwestern, 2008);

and *Alltag im Holocaust: Jüdisches Leben im Großdeutschen Reich 1941–1945* [Everyday life in the Holocaust: Jewish life in the Greater German Reich 1941–1945] (edited with Andrea Löw and Anna Hájková).

Karel C. Berkhoff is a senior researcher at the NIOD Institute for War, Holocaust, and Genocide Studies at the Royal Netherlands Academy of Arts and Sciences. He is the author of *Harvest of Despair: Life and Death in Ukraine under Nazi Rule* and *Motherland in Danger: Soviet Propaganda during World War II.*

Ludivine Broch is a history lecturer at the University of Westminster in London. She is the author of *Ordinary Workers, Vichy and the Holocaust: French Railwaymen and the Second World War* and coeditor of *France in an Era of Global War, 1914–1945: Occupation, Politics, Empire and Entanglements.*

Steven Alan Carr is an associate professor of communication at Indiana University–Purdue University Fort Wayne, where he directs the Institute for Holocaust and Genocide Studies. He is the author of *Hollywood and Anti-Semitism: A Cultural History up to World War II.*

Rachel Century is the Holocaust Memorial Day development manager at the Holocaust Memorial Day Trust in the United Kingdom. She received her Ph.D. in history from Royal Holloway, University of London, in 2013 with a dissertation titled “Dictating the Holocaust: Female Administrators of the Third Reich.” She is a fellow of the Imperial War Museum in Holocaust education and has taught courses on the Holocaust, National Socialism and German society, fascism in Western Europe, and the Germans and the Jews, 1871–present.

Alon Confino is a professor of history at the University of Virginia in Charlottesville and at Ben-Gurion University of the Negev in Beersheba, Israel. His recent books are *Foundational Pasts: The Holocaust as Historical Understanding* and *A World without Jews: The Nazi Imagination from Persecution to Genocide*, which won a 2011 Guggenheim Fellowship.

Martina Cucchiara is an assistant professor of history at Bluffton University in Bluffton, Ohio, where she teaches courses in European history, the Holocaust, World War II, and Nazi Germany. She has been awarded an Eli Lilly Presidential Fellowship at Notre Dame as well as a Charles H. Revson Foundation Fellowship at the United States Holocaust Memorial Museum in Washington, D.C. She has published in *European History Quarterly*.

Idit Gil is a senior lecturer in the master's program in democratic studies at the Open University of Israel. She participated in the first research group in the International Tracing Service (ITS) Archive in Bad Arolsen, Germany; was a Phyllis Greenberg Heideman and Richard D. Heideman Fellow at the Center for Advanced Holocaust Studies of the United States Holocaust Memorial Museum in Washington, D.C.; and received a grant from the Israel Science Foundation to study the wartime labor experiences of a transport of Jewish laborers from Radom, Poland. She has published several articles on Israel and the Holocaust and on Nazi labor policies toward Jews.

Amos Goldberg is a senior lecturer in Holocaust studies at the Hebrew University of Jerusalem. His major fields of research are cultural history of the Jews in the Holocaust, Holocaust historiography, and Holocaust memory in a global world. Among his publications is a book in Hebrew, *Trauma in the First Person: Diary Writing during the Holocaust*, to be published in English by Indiana University Press in 2017. Two coedited volumes appeared in 2015: the first in Hebrew with Bashir Bashir, *The Holocaust and the Nakba: Memory, National Identity, and Jewish-Arab Partnership*, and the second in English with Haim Hazan, *Marking Evil: Holocaust Memory in the Global Age*.

Jan T. Gross is a professor of history at Princeton University in New Jersey, where he teaches courses on twentieth-century Eastern Europe and totalitarianism. He is the author of *Polish Society under German Occupation*; *Revolution from Abroad: The Soviet Conquest of Poland's Western Ukraine and Western Belorussia*; *Neighbors: The Destruction of the Jewish Community in Jedwabne, Poland*; and *Fear: Anti-Semitism in Poland after Auschwitz*, among other books.

Dagmar Herzog is Distinguished Professor of History and Daniel Rose Faculty Scholar at the Graduate Center, City University of New York. She has published extensively on the history of religion, the history of the Holocaust and its aftermath, and the histories of gender and sexuality. Among her books are *Sex after Fascism: Memory and Morality in Twentieth-Century Germany* and, most recently, *Sexuality in Europe: A Twentieth-Century History*.

John-Paul Himka is an emeritus professor of history at the University of Alberta in Edmonton. He has written four books on Ukrainian history and also coauthored, edited, or coedited eight other books, among them *Bringing the Dark Past to Light: The Reception of the Holocaust in Postcommunist Europe* (coedited with Joanna Beata Michlic) and *The World to Come: Ukrainian Images of the Last Judgment* (coauthored with Liliya Berezhnaya).

Lukas Meissel is a historian at the Israelitische Kultusgemeinde Wien (Archives of the Jewish Community of Vienna). He takes part in various projects and organizations connected to the history of Nazism, including the nongovernmental organization *Gedenkdienst* (Holocaust Memorial Service) and the Mauthausen Komitee Österreich (Austrian Mauthausen Committee). His research focuses include perpetrator history, Holocaust education, antisemitism, and visual history.

Perla Sneh is an associate professor in Jewish and Jewish-Latin American studies at the M.A. Program on Cultural Diversity as well as a senior researcher at the Center for Genocide Studies at the Universidad Nacional de Tres de Febrero in Buenos Aires, Argentina. Her most recent article, "Polin down South: Among Mysteries and Silences: On Polish Jewish Literary Legacies in Argentina," was published in *Polin: Studies in Polish Jewry* in 2016. She is the author of, among others, *La Shoah en el siglo: del lenguaje del exterminio al exterminio del discurso* [The Shoah in the century: From language extermination to the extermination of discourse] and *Palabras para decirlo: lenguaje y exterminio* [Words to say it: Language and extermination], a book that focuses on three languages—German, Yiddish, and Spanish—and their relations to annihilation. This book was awarded the National Prize for Literature by the Ministry of Culture in Argentina (2009–2013).

Mark Joel Webber is an associate professor of German Studies emeritus and senior scholar at York University in Toronto, Canada. At York, he served as founding director of the Canadian Centre for German and European Studies and the Ontario-Baden-Württemberg Student Exchange Program, for which he was awarded the Officer's Cross of the Order of Merit of the German Federal Republic. With Michael Brown, he initiated and co-led the Mark and Gail Appel Program in Holocaust and Antiracism Education. His teaching and publications have focused on issues of interculturality, metaphor, and rhetoric; the representation of the Holocaust in literature and film; and foreign language pedagogy.

EDWARD B. WESTERMANN is a professor of history at Texas A&M University–San Antonio. He teaches courses on European history, the Holocaust, and war and society. He has been a Fulbright Fellow, a German Academic Exchange Service Fellow, and a Fellow at the U.S. Holocaust Memorial Museum. He is the author of numerous publications including *Hitler's Police Battalions: Enforcing Racial War in the East* and *Flak: German Anti-Aircraft Defenses, 1914–1945*. His latest book, *Hitler's Ostkrieg and the Indian Wars: Comparing Conquest and Genocide*, was published in 2016.